The Valuation Handbook

Founded in 1807, John Wiley & Sons is the oldest independent publishing company in the United States. With offices in North America, Europe, Australia, and Asia, Wiley is globally committed to developing and marketing print and electronic products and services for our customers' professional and personal knowledge and understanding.

The Wiley Finance series contains books written specifically for finance and investment professionals as well as sophisticated individual investors and their financial advisors. Book topics range from portfolio management to e-commerce, risk management, financial engineering, valuation, and financial instrument analysis, as well as much more.

For a list of available titles, please visit our Web site at www.Wiley Finance.com.

The Valuation Handbook

Valuation Techniques from Today's Top Practitioners

RAWLEY THOMAS
BENTON E. GUP

John Wiley & Sons, Inc.

Published by John Wiley & Sons, Inc., Hoboken, New Jersey.
Published simultaneously in Canada.

For general information on our other products and services or for technical support, please contact our Customer Care Department within the United States at (800) 762-2974, outside the United States at (317) 572-3993 or fax (317) 572-4002.

Wiley also publishes its books in a variety of electronic formats. Some content that appears in print may not be available in electronic books. For more information about Wiley products, visit our web site at www.wiley.com.

Library of Congress Cataloging-in-Publication Data:

Thomas, Rawley, 1946-
  The valuation handbook : valuation techniques from today's top practitioners / Rawley Thomas, Benton E. Gup.
       p.   cm.   –   (Wiley finance ; 480)
  Includes bibliographical references and index.
    ISBN 978-0-470-38579-1 (hardback)
  1. Corporations–Valuation.   2. Stocks–Prices.   I. Gup, Benton E.   II. Title.
    HG4028.V3.T48 2010
    332.63221–dc22

                                                                    2009028345

Printed in the United States of America

10 9 8 7 6 5 4 3 2 1

Contents

CHAPTER 9
The Economic Profit Approach to Securities Valuation   **226**
James L. Grant

CHAPTER 10
Valuation for Managers: Closing the Gap between
Theory and Practice   **255**
Dennis N. Aust

CHAPTER 11
The LifeCycle Returns Valuation System   **273**
Rawley Thomas and Robert J. Atra

Preface

VALUATIONS ARE IMPORTANT

Valuations are important simply because they form the basis for making decisions involving significant amounts of money or wealth transferred from one party to another.

Why do people perform valuations? What are they used for? The following is a short list, which is by no means complete. Valuations are normally done to:

- Buy or sell a stock of a publicly held firm.
- Buy or sell a privately held business.
- Determine how much estate tax is owed the government.
- Settle a divorce.
- Resolve a dispute with a minority shareholder who wants out.
- Give an accounting auditor value basis for reporting.
- Determine the amount of compensation for executives, division or business unit managers, and employee-owners.
- Determine whether to proceed with strategic initiatives and/or major investment opportunities.
- Offer fairness opinions in the purchase or sale of companies.

VALUATION CHALLENGES: WHICH TECHNIQUES TO APPLY

Broadly, valuation techniques may divide into two categories:

1. Those relying on quoted market prices of the specific security.
2. Those applying advanced professional knowledge to a set of data.

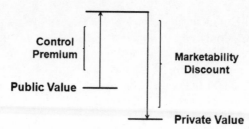

EXHIBIT P1.1 What is the Purpose of Valuation?

The second category may further divide into three subcategories:

1. Applying a set of comparable company valuations to the subject firm.
2. Labor-intensive, expert techniques, such as discounted cash flow.
3. Use of multiple regressions or expert systems.

As the chapters in this book suggest, the lines of demarcation between these categories and subcategories blur in actual application. As illustrated in Exhibit P1.1, several possible values exist. They reflect the purpose of the valuation:

- Minority interests in a nonpublic company incorporate discounts for lack of marketability.
- A sale of a business in its entirety to a strategic buyer includes a premium for control that captures a portion of the synergies or restructuring opportunities that the buyer expects.
- The usual case for minority interests in public firms incorporates neither discount nor premium.

Valuation providers are jugglers. They use all available methods—discounted cash flow, multiples, and other methods. Ultimately, they employ their experience on the proper factors to pick a valuation number or a range.

"Valuations Still Part Art" is the title of a recent article in the *Wall Street Journal*. The article began by asking, "If you invested $100 million in GMAC LLC in 2006, what would it be worth today? (A) $90 million; (B) $80 million; (C) $75 million; (D) all of the above." The correct answer is all of the above. One reason for three different values is that book value accounting was used in 2006, and fair value accounting was adopted in 2008. Another reason is that three private equity firms using fair value accounting valued the assets of GMAC differently.

Why did they derive three different values? Part of the answer is that they made different assumptions about the financial data, time horizons, and other factors. Suppose that one of the private equity firms needs five inputs to estimate an intrinsic value, and it has only five inputs from which to choose. There is only one possible answer. However, suppose the firm still needs to choose five inputs, but now has 10 possible choices. Then there are 252 possible answers. Thus, even if the three firms used the same valuation model, they might make different assumptions, so the odds are small that they would come up with the same valuation. The problem is complicated when different valuation models are used.

So how do professional experts and consulting firms value companies? In theory, valuation is a relatively simple process of discounting a firm's expected cash flows by investors' required rates of return. In practice, valuation is highly complex because there are numerous valuation models and techniques. Structures of valuation models often include many assumptions and parameters. Each valuation model and technique has its own strengths and weaknesses. Thus, they are not perfect substitutes for each other. Stated otherwise, you must choose the valuation models and techniques that are best suited for your needs.

The Valuation Handbook differs significantly from other sources of information because the contributors are practitioners representing consulting and investment firms plus academics—all of whom explain how they value companies and other assets. This book provides unique perspectives on how today's leading practitioners and academics value both publicly traded and privately held companies. Most practitioners agree that, in theory, the value of a firm is based on the present value of its expected cash flows. However, their applications of the theory vary widely. To some extent, it depends on the end use of the valuation. Valuing a large number of companies for purposes of trading stocks presents different challenges than valuing future growth opportunities within a firm, or valuing a dental practice that is for sale. Thus, the emphasis in this book is on *how* to value firms rather than the theories underlying the valuation process.

This book includes many of the best practitioners in the world on the core subject of valuation. For the first time, to our knowledge, these top practitioners have collected their thoughts in one place for you, the reader, to study. In these times of enormous economic stress, the profession needs to rethink many of its assumptions and processes involving the core topic of valuation. This *Valuation Handbook* may help that process of reevaluation.

CONTRIBUTORS

Contributors to the book include the following individuals. Their biographical information appears in "About the Contributors."

Abbott, Ashok, University of West Virginia

Atra, Robert J., Lewis University

Aust, Dennis N., CharterMast Partners

Brouwer, Arjan J., University of Amsterdam and Pricewaterhouse Coopers

Cimasi, Robert James, Health Capital Consultants

Copeland, Thomas E., Massachusetts Institute of Technology (MIT)

Dorsey, Pat, Morningstar

Grant, James L., JLG Research and University of Massachusetts Boston

Gup, Benton E., University of Alabama

Hass, William J., CTP, TeamWork Technologies, Inc.

Johnson, Roy E., dba Corporate Strategy

Madden, Bartley J., independent researcher, formerly Credit Suisse

Mahoney, William F., *Valuation Issues*

Pollock, Stanley L., Professional Practice Planners

Pryor, Shepherd G., IV, Board Resources, a Division of TeamWork Technologies, Inc.

Schostag, Randall, Minnesota Business Valuation Group

Sutherland, Andrew G., Stern Stewart

Taylor, Gary K., University of Alabama

Thomas, Rawley, LifeCycle Returns, Inc. (LCRT)

Trainer, David, New Constructs

Ubelhart, Mark C., Hewitt Associates

Williams, Jeffrey R., Carnegie-Mellon University

Yang, Dandan, LifeCycle Returns

Zavanelli, Max, ZPR Investment Research

Zigrang, Todd A., Health Capital Consultants

CHAPTER SUMMARIES

Obviously, this book is about valuation—valuation of public companies, private companies, illiquid companies, start-ups, and business units. It covers specific techniques, research processes, and organizational challenges. These insights apply to investment firms where security analysts pick stocks and managers combine those stocks into diversified portfolios. They also apply to corporations where managements try to create shareholder wealth in a highly competitive economy.

The book naturally divides into four groups:

1. Valuation, valued-based management, governance, and drivers.
2. Residual income.
3. Cash return and net cash flow valuation methods.
4. Specialized valuations, liquidity, and other topics.

Benton Gup's Chapter 1 covers "Two Frameworks for Understanding Valuation Models." On the one hand for a small number of firms, the top-down approach examines the major factors influencing the demand for a firm's products and services. Those factors include the business environment, economic activity, and industry factors, including the life cycle. These are factors over which the firm has no control, but they can make or break the firm. On the other hand, the bottom-up approach takes advantage of large databases and quantitative techniques to estimate intrinsic values.

In Chapter 2, "The Value Edge: Reap the Advantage of Disciplined Techniques," Bill Hass and Shep Pryor describe value management from both a historical and a strategic point of view. They suggest avoiding simplistic solutions and allude to many of the techniques covered in other chapters.

Bart Madden describes five critical choices that guided the development of the CFROI life-cycle valuation model in Chapter 3, "Applying a Systems Mind-Set to Stock Valuation." This approach emphasizes accuracy in the measurement of firms' track records and the assignment of a discount rate that is dependent on the procedures used to forecast firms' future cash flows.

The reader may wish to peruse together both Tom Copeland's Chapter 4 on "Comparing Valuation Models" and Bob Atra and Rawley Thomas's Chapter 5 on "Developing an Automated Discounted Cash Flow Model." Copeland focuses on the important question of how to evaluate valuation models—suggesting that the convergence of the market price to the model price is best for portfolio management, and goodness of fit is best when the objective is for the model price to be as close as possible to the market fair price. Copeland provides empirical results for a large sample of valuations using an expert system. It is similar to Atra/Thomas's automated DCF.

Given the plethora of valuation models, it is a good idea to have a consistent methodology to measure their accuracy, effectiveness, and predictive capability. The computer power available today can be applied against large fundamental databases.

Related to Chapters 4 and 5, Randall Schostag in Chapter 15, "Portfolio Valuation: Challenges and Opportunities Using Automation," covers the history of legal precedent in valuing privately held firms. Randall suggests that the new possibility of automated approaches can provide cost-effective ways to mark to model in addition to marking to market. In fact, the traditional labor-intensive method of valuation becomes simply impractical to perform over the large number of securities in portfolios to comply with FAS 157 at anything close to reasonable cost. Various discussions have proposed disclosure of both mark to market and mark to model as most relevant to investor decision making. Regulatory forbearance of equity requirements under mark to market may offer a better solution to give banks breathing room than fudging core disclosure for investor decisions.

Roy Johnson's Chapter 6, "The Essence of Value-Based Finance," covers the practical realities of employing the value drivers of the models to focus and simplify management effort. An adjustment should be greater than 5 to 10 percent in order to merit inclusion in the effort. Growth adds shareholder value only if returns exceed the cost of capital. In contrast to the traditional capital budgeting process, Roy also concludes that: "The major program (for example, an important operational or strategic initiative) is the absolute lowest level for which value-based analysis should be performed." "For what matters in any system is the performance of the whole." Forget IRR and DCF analyses on those machines. Concentrate your effort on strategic initiatives and overlays.

The second group of chapters (Chapters 7 to 9) offers three complementary perspectives on residual income. Benton Gup and Gary Taylor in Chapter 7, "Residual Income and Stock Valuation Techniques: Does It Matter Which One You Use?" conclude that all the methods are mathematically equivalent. Thus, the choice of the model is a matter of individual preference.

David Trainer in Chapter 8, "Modern Tools for Valuation," describes in detail the methodologies used at New Constructs to separate most attractive from most dangerous stocks. The methodologies employ comprehensive financial data sets to assess true economic earnings, as opposed to relying on reported accounting earnings. In addition, dynamic DCF modeling enables quantification of expectations for future cash flows that are embedded in stock prices. Full transparency and extensive use of footnotes characterize the framework.

Jim Grant's Chapter 9, "The Economic Profit Approach to Securities Valuation," provides a highly readable, detailed explanation of economic profit valuation. The chapter covers both constant and variable growth EVA® valuation models and provides several numerical examples for students and professionals to learn equity valuation concepts and calculations. Jim shows the equivalence of economic profit and free cash flow (FCF) approaches to equity analysis. Importantly, he notes that intrinsic valuations are highly sensitive to the input assumptions, such as the cost of capital and the length of the economic profit period, and he provides real-world insight on the application of economic profit valuation in practice.

Chapters 10 to 12 form the third group, cash flow return and net cash flow valuation models.

Despite widespread lip service to the concept of shareholder value, formal value management programs have all too often been rejected, ignored, or abandoned by results-oriented management teams. Dennis Aust's Chapter 10, "Valuation for Managers: Closing the Gap between Theory and Practice," attributes this to excessive focus on theoretical purity rather than practical benefits. He suggests an excellent solution to this conundrum, describing a simplified valuation model that directs management attention to a limited number of key business value drivers: cash profit, depreciating (fixed) assets, and nondepreciating assets. Combining these three drivers implicitly incorporates the balance sheet to ensure that the firm achieves returns above the cost of capital. Dennis's solution keeps any complexity of the valuation model under the hood, while retaining the accuracy necessary to drive wealth-creating behavior within the firm's culture.

The Thomas/Atra Chapter 11 describes "The LifeCycle Returns Valuation System." An appendix compares traditional CAPM costs of capital with investor market derived real discount rates.

Pat Dorsey's Chapter 12, "Morningstar's Approach to Equity Analysis and Security Valuation," covers the practical details of valuation employed at one of the premier firms in the profession. The concept of a moat deserves deep study by students of this book, because it places valuation within the strategic context of competitive industry dynamics. "Moat" compares closely to the "T" horizon concept in Stern Stewart EVA® and the "fade" rates employed by the Callard, Madden offshoots in cash returns.

Specialized valuation, liquidity, and other topics create the basis for the fourth and final group within *The Valuation Handbook*.

Chapter 13, "Valuing Real Options: Insights from Competitive Strategy," by Andrew Sutherland and Jeffrey Williams, offers a look at an increasingly important corporate finance application. This chapter outlines a number of valuation approaches designed to bring about heightened understanding of strategic capabilities and limitations of the firm in relation to its real option opportunities. By incorporating insights from competitive strategy into the valuation exercise and using a variety of approaches to triangulate on investment values, the real options management process will be better informed.

Max Zavanelli's Chapter 14, "GRAPES: A Theory of Stock Prices," describes in detail the results and methodology of a highly successful approach to stock selection and portfolio construction. GRAPES stands for Growth Rate Arbitrage Price Equilibrium System. Those interested in quantitative approaches to the market should definitely read this chapter. His new theory of stock prices, the first in 40 years, also applies to asset pricing in general and the value of private corporations and acquisitions.

Bob Cimasi and Todd Zigrang's Chapter 16, "The Valuation of Health Care Professional Practices," and Stan Pollock's Chapter 17, "Valuing Dental Practices," cover in astonishingly extensive, professional detail the valuation of privately held health care professional service firms. The contrast between these labor-intensive, law-compliance-driven, privately held valuations and publicly held firms is stark. Bridging these two schools of thought and real-world, practical applications should become a long-range goal of the profession.

Ashok Abbott's Chapter 18, "Measures of Discount for Lack of Marketability and Liquidity," relaxes the traditional academic assumption of efficient markets by measuring blockage trading discounts. With the meltdown and freeze-up of markets currently occurring worldwide, a deeper economic understanding of markets has become paramount to practitioners, regulators, and politicians.

Everyone knows the importance in today's information economy of people and intellectual property. However, recognizing its importance is far different than actually measuring the effects. Mark Ubelhart's Chapter 19, "An Economic View of the Impact of Human Capital on Firm Performance and Valuation," employs Hewitt Associates' unique proprietary database of 20 million employees in the United States. Hewitt's research confirms that increases in shareholder wealth result from the migration of pivotal employees from one firm to another. Retention of top performers, who create the intellectual property, therefore becomes a high strategic priority. Lacking the equivalent of GAAP in human capital reporting, this chapter demonstrates how firms may employ standardized metrics to address this priority for investors, management, and the board of directors as well as professional researchers who seek to advance the state of the art of valuation.

Arjan Brouwer and Benton Gup's Chapter 20, "EBITDA: Down but Not Out," examines the use of EBITDA by companies from Europe's largest capital markets, and discusses the benefits and shortcomings of this measure. This information is relevant for U.S. analysts who must be prepared for the increased reporting of alternative performance measures like EBITDA, as the International Financial Reporting Standards (IFRS) are gaining more ground in the United States.

Bill Mahoney's Chapter 21, "Optimizing the Value of Investor Relations," ties many of the chapters together into implications for the communications from firms to their investors. Most important, Bill recommends that investor relations professionals transform their role from a simple service public relation function to being the resident investment market expert. By deeply understanding investor behavior, the market, multifactor quant, and DCF intrinsic value frameworks, investor relations develops the core skills necessary to bridge between the firm's shareholder wealth-creating objectives and the investors who provide the capital.

The Thomas/Yang/Atra chapter, Chapter 22, "Lower Risk and Higher Returns: Linking Stable Paretian Distributions and Discounted Cash Flow," combines Benoit Mandelbrot's research on fat-tailed distributions with Life-Cycle's DCF. Replacing standard deviation with the stable Paretian "alpha peakedness parameter" as the primary risk measure turns the traditional conclusions upside down. Lower risk and higher returns result from purchasing undervalued stocks and short-selling overvalued stocks. Purchasing fairly valued stock actually increases risk. Consequently, combining Chapter 22's results on new risk measures with Chapter 11's discussion of market derived real discount rates creates a possible replacement for traditional CAPM cost of capital theory.

Now, as you read *The Valuation Handbook*, consider applying the authors' various insights to your own personal decisions about:

- *Your portfolio.* Do you employ a passive or an active approach? If active, do you only analyze price patterns, or do you employ discounted cash flow to measure the intrinsic valuation of each stock you own?
- *Your business.* What is it worth, if you sell? How can you make your business worth more?

June 2009   Benton Gup
                                                                             Rawley Thomas

CHAPTER 1

Two Frameworks for Understanding Valuation Models

Benton E. Gup
Chair of Banking University of Alabama

There is a saying that if you don't know what to look for, you are not going to see it. That is especially true for readers of this book who have a limited background in finance and investments. This chapter provides two concepts that will help put the valuation models and concepts presented in this book in context. The two concepts are top-down/bottom-up analysis and the life cycle.[1]

TOP-DOWN/BOTTOM-UP ANALYSIS

The traditional approach to analyzing investments is commonly called *fundamental analysis*. That approach is represented in Exhibit 1.1 as the *top-down analysis* of securities. The basic idea of top-down analysis is to start with a company, such as Microsoft, and then examine the major factors that affect the firm now and are likely to affect it in the future. This includes but is not limited to information about the economic outlook, legislation that may affect the company, industry information, demographics, and other factors that may be important when estimating a firm's growth potential. Then analyze the firm and determine its intrinsic value. *Intrinsic value* is the theoretical value of a security, and it may differ from the market price. The simplified *dividend valuation model* is one method of determining intrinsic value, and it is shown here in equation (1.1). The equation states that the price of a stock is equal to expected dividends discounted by the rate of return required by investors.

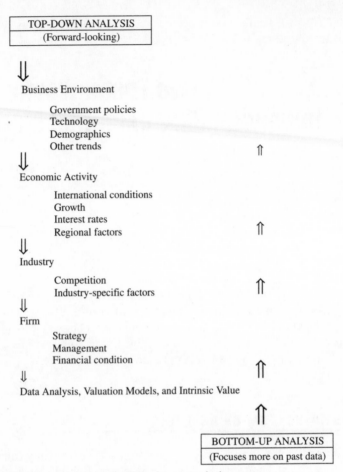

EXHIBIT 1.1   Top-Down/Bottom-Up Analysis

Because the model is simplified, it applies only to firms that pay cash dividends, and it covers only one time period. Thus, the model is shown here for purposes of illustration, and it is not known for its accuracy. Nevertheless, the model is useful in explaining fundamental analysis. For example, an increasing demand for a firm's products may lead to higher revenues and higher dividends. From the equation, it can be seen that higher dividends result in higher stock prices. Therefore, when considering the fundamental factors that are about to be discussed, think about how they affect a firm's future revenues, its dividends, and the returns required by investors.

$$P_0 = \frac{D_1}{k - g} \tag{1.1}$$

where P_0 = current price (at time 0)
   D_1 = cash dividend in time period 1
   k = the rate of return required by equity investors
   g = growth rate of cash dividends

Top-down analysis works well when analyzing a small number of firms. We examine top-down analysis first so that you understand the various factors affecting intrinsic value. Then we are going to reverse the process and do bottom-up analysis, which is more suitable for investors making extensive use of databases containing many firms' financial data.

Major Factors Affecting Firms Are Beyond Their Control

An important insight from top-down analysis is that the major factors affecting firms are beyond their control. The major factors affecting the demand for firms' products and services include but are not limited to the business environment, economic activity, industry factors, and other factors such as global warming.

Business Environment *Government policies*, such as defense spending, environmental controls, and Medicare, will benefit some firms and harm others. By way of illustration, since federal spending is a limited dollar amount, an increase in spending on submarines will help defense contractors. But what is spent on submarines cannot be spent on Medicare.

Changes in *technology*, such as the development of the Internet and wireless communications, are driving the growth of telecommunications, creating new opportunities for e-commerce and new ways to invest funds.

Think about the industries affected by changes in *demographics*—the aging population, increased immigration, and more females in the labor force. These changes affect health care, housing, retailers, and many other industries.

Economic Activity The states' domestic and international economic activity affects the demand for firms' products and subsequently their revenues. If the economy is strong and growing, firms tend to prosper. When it falters, companies fail. By way of illustration, in 2008, the high costs of fuel caused some airlines to go bankrupt.

Some products such as automobiles, clothing, and television sets that were traditionally made by U.S. firms are increasingly being imported, reflecting an increase in globalization. A related factor is that an increasing number of foreign companies are investing in U.S. firms. For example, India's Sterlite Industries bought the assets of Tucson-based copper miner Asarco; and France's Vivendi will acquire American video game maker Activision.

Changes in Federal Reserve interest rate policies have both short-run and long-run macroeconomic effects. We know from the dividend valuation model shown in equation (1.1) that in the short term an increase in interest rates will adversely affect stock prices. In the long term, it may reduce the demand for a firm's products, which would adversely affect its earnings, dividends, and stock price.

While the discussion has focused on global and macroeconomic changes, some companies are strictly regional. By way of illustration, small and medium-size banks tend to serve local markets. Thus, the floods in Iowa in June 2008 affected local banks, but not banks in California or Florida. Similarly, Hurricane Katrina adversely affected markets in New Orleans, but not markets in Chicago or New York.

Industry   It is important to understand the economic structure of industries before investing in them. One type of economic structure is *pure competition*, with many firms competing and no single firm able to influence the prices. Wheat farming is a classic example of pure competition because no one farmer can influence the price of this standardized commodity. Also consider the restaurant industry. There are more than 504,000 eating and drinking places in the United States.[2] That is about one eating and drinking place for every 558 people, so it is a very competitive market.[3] Nevertheless, some firms such as McDonald's and Starbucks are able to differentiate their products.

Imperfect competition prevails in markets where various firms try to convince you that their products are better than those of competitors. The differences can be real or imagined. The dozens of brands of beer, cereal, shampoo, and toothpaste to choose from are examples of imperfect competition.

Next, there are *oligopolies* where a few large firms dominate a market. Oligopolies tend to be capital intensive, which means that large dollar amounts are required to produce products such as cars, jet engines, and steel. The high costs of entry and the complexity of production tend to restrict the number of firms in such industries.

Finally, there are *monopolies* where one firm controls the market. Local public utilities, such a power companies, have near monopoly power. Because they are government regulated, their monopoly does not guarantee them excess profits. Also consider the pharmaceutical industry. It consists of a small number of large companies, in part because it costs so much to develop new prescription drugs. The developmental costs of a new drug may exceed $1 billion, and the process may take five years or longer. Once a drug is developed and approved by the government for general use, the pharmaceutical company holding a patent on it has a monopoly on that drug for 17 or more years. That may result in large profits, or profits may be short-lived because other companies can make competing products. Monopolies don't guarantee profits.

Bottom-Up Approaches

The top-down approach works fine when analyzing a small number of companies. However, today there are thousands of companies that can be analyzed in U.S. and foreign markets. The top-down approach is too time-consuming when dealing with large numbers of companies. Because of the availability of large databases containing financial and other corporate information, high-speed computers, and improved quantitative techniques, many analysts today begin by analyzing the financial data for a large number of companies. Then they make projections about the future prospects of selected firms. Some of these bottom-up techniques are discussed in the other chapters of this book.

Implications

Grow or Die What are the implications of the factors that we have discussed? First, *grow or die*. Everybody wants firms to grow and be more profitable. The chief executive officer of a firm wants it to make more money so that he or she can get a raise. The employees want higher salaries. The shareholders want their stock to appreciate and to receive higher dividends. The community and state where the firm is located want more tax revenue and want the firm to support community activities.

Firms must grow and respond to changes in the market or they will go out of business as competitors take over their markets. A firm can make an excellent product, be profitable in the short run, and then be driven out of business because its customers' preferences shift over time. Consider how covered wagons were replaced by cars, trains, and planes. Typewriters have been largely replaced by computers, and coin-operated telephone booths by wireless phones.

Limited Control Second, firms are limited as to what they can control. They cannot control the factors in the business environment or economic activity that were previously discussed. These are some of the most important factors driving the demand for their products and services, and subsequently their revenues.

They can control their assets (what they own) and their liabilities (what they owe), and can make management decisions (expansion, diversification, marketing, corporate structure, etc.). But such control in and of itself does not guarantee success. To paraphrase Charles Darwin, only the fittest firms will survive.

One key to survival and growth is to have a sustainable competitive advantage over other firms. A *sustainable competitive advantage* can take many different forms: Coca-Cola's and McDonald's *brand names* are a sustainable competitive advantage. Microsoft's *market power* is a sustainable competitive advantage. Wal-Mart's *size and distribution system* give it an advantage. *Patents* provide a competitive advantage.

A sustainable competitive advantage is something that is not easily copied by other firms. But it is not going to last forever. Oldsmobile was a great brand name for many years, but cars are no longer manufactured under that name. Montgomery Ward and W.T. Grant were two of the leading department stores in the United States; now they are out of business. Polaroid had a monopoly on instant photographs, but its competitive advantage ended with the development of one-hour film processing and the growth of digital photography.

The lesson to be learned is that having a well-managed, profitable firm is a necessary, but not sufficient, condition for survival. Markets are dynamic, and firms must respond effectively and evolve if they are to survive.

LIFE CYCLE

Understanding the life cycle provides unique insights into corporate growth, survival, and financial behavior. All products, firms, and industries evolve through stages of development called a *life cycle*. Exhibit 1.2 illustrates a typical industry life cycle that is divided into four phases: pioneering, expansion, stabilization, and decline.

Pioneering Phase

We begin with a single firm that has one new product line that either will be successful or it will fail. The price of the new product is high, and there are no profits in this phase of the life cycle because of low sales volume and high development and marketing costs. Because there are no profits, there are no dividends to be paid.

The risk to the firm, as measured by beta, is also high. *Beta* is a measure of systematic risk and volatility. *Systematic risk* is risk that is common to all stocks, and it cannot be eliminated by diversification. The average beta for all stocks is 1. A beta of 1.8 is considered high, and a beta of 0.5 is low. Betas tend to high during the pioneering phase and then diminish as the firms mature.

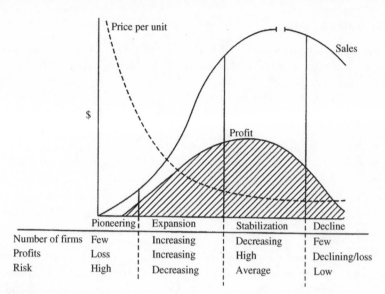

	Pioneering	Expansion	Stabilization	Decline
Number of firms	Few	Increasing	Decreasing	Few
Profits	Loss	Increasing	High	Declining/loss
Risk	High	Decreasing	Average	Low

EXHIBIT 1.2   Life Cycle

Expansion Phase

The expansion phase of the life cycle is characterized by increasing competition, declining product prices, and rising industry profits. If the product is successful, other firms enter the market and competition drives the price of the product down. For example, the first wireless telephones cost $4,200 each when they were introduced in 1984, and now they are given away when you buy telephone service contracts.[4] Similarly, handheld calculators cost $120 when they were introduced in 1970, and now they, too, are given away. The point here is that the price of a commodity-type product tends to decline as a result of competition and changes in technology.

As shown in Exhibit 1.2, sales revenues are increasing, but at a decreasing rate. Industry profits are increasing as well, and beta is high, but not as high as it was during the pioneering phase. As profits rise, the firms begin to pay cash dividends.

The expansion phase is a period of spectacular successes and spectacular failures. Only the fittest firms survive. By way of illustration, consider the automobile industry. During the expansion phase of the life cycle, there were about 1,500 automobile companies in the United States.[5] Today, only Ford, General Motors, and Chrysler remain, and several foreign-owned companies are producing cars in the United States. The prices of the mass-produced cars are relatively low in real terms. The survivors dominate the industry in terms of total revenues.

Stabilization Phase

During the stabilization phase of the life cycle, total sales continue to rise, but at a slower pace, while prices decline and industry profits in real terms, though high, begin to fall. The number of firms continues to decline, and the *dividend payout ratio* (cash dividends/earnings) increases. Beta is about 1.

The surviving firms have the following four characteristics:

1. Sufficient *capital* to finance their operations.
2. Sufficient *technology* to produce a continuous stream of new products.
3. Sufficient *scale* or size so that the products can be mass-produced at the lowest possible cost.
4. Sufficient *marketing and distribution channels* to sell, service, and finance their products.

One way for successful companies to grow is by acquiring other companies. The acquisitions usually occur during the later part of the expansion phase or in the stabilization phase. For example, Cisco Systems and General Electric have acquired large numbers of smaller, faster-growing companies. Strategic alliances are another avenue for expansion. For example, Citigroup and Nikko Cordial formed an alliance in order to create one of Japan's leading financial services groups and to enable the combined franchise to pursue important new growth opportunities.[6] Strategic alliances are sometimes used as precursors to acquisitions.

Another aspect of firms in the stabilization phase of the life cycle is that they introduce new products to extend the duration of that phase. Consider the case of McDonald's Corporation, which was the innovator of fast-food restaurants. Its first product was a hamburger. As shown in Exhibit 1.3, when the growth rate of sales of hamburgers slowed, McDonald's introduced the Big Mac. When the growth rate of Big Mac sales slowed, the company introduced Egg McMuffin, Chicken McNuggets, and other new products, and began to enter new markets such as Europe and Asia to increase revenues. The point here is that even major brands, such as McDonald's, must be reinvigorated with new products and services if they are to survive. However, not every new product is going to be a success. For example, deep-fried zucchini was a loser.

Declining Phase

The declining phase of the life cycle is similar to old age in human beings. The firm or industry is over the hill and on the way out. However, there is one significant difference between humans and firms or industries. Once humans have matured, it is unlikely that they can be rejuvenated and be young again, but *rejuvenation* is possible with industries. For example,

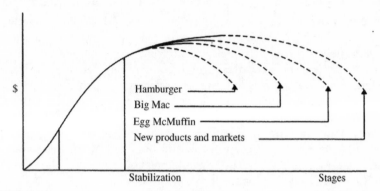

EXHIBIT 1.3 Extending the Life Cycle of McDonald's

higher energy costs have contributed to the rejuvenation of the coal industry. Similarly, ceiling fans were a common means of cooling homes before central air-conditioning became widespread. Then they went out of style. But when energy prices soared in the late 1970s and early 1980s, people sought ways to reduce their energy costs and once again turned to ceiling fans. Note that an external economic factor—higher energy prices—is the force that is driving the demand for coal and ceiling fans.

Similarly, high oil prices in 2008 increased the demand for hybrid vehicles. The use of ethanol in gasoline drove up the price of corn, and subsequently the price of food. Thus, *external factors*, such as the cost of energy, oil, and corn, have had a major impact on the demand for selected products and the companies that produce them.

FIRMS

At the firm level, we need to understand their strategies and current developments. Many firms have web sites that provide access to their annual reports, Securities and Exchange Commission (SEC) filings, press releases, news stories, and current research reports. Firms also provide financial guidance. These forward-looking statements include projections about the expected growth rates, sales forecasts, and other specified financial items. A word of caution is in order. No forward-looking statement can be guaranteed, and actual results may differ materially from those projected. Despite these limitations, such information is required reading, and is particularly useful in monitoring investments.

By way of illustration, Merck & Co., Inc. explains its strategy in its annual report, which is available online.[7] Simply stated, research and development (R&D) is the key to Merck's success. Other companies may or may not be as explicit about their strategies. Merck's strategy is to discover important new medicines through breakthrough research. Furthermore, its financial goal is to be a top-tier growth company by performing over the long term in the top quartile of leading health care companies.

We also need to understand the financial condition of the firm, with particular emphasis on profitability, financial leverage, and other factors that are beyond the scope of this chapter.

Finally, we use all of the information obtained in various valuation models that are explained in the other chapters of this book. The valuation models are used to determine the firm's intrinsic value.

CONCLUSION

Traditional security analysis begins with a particular company in mind. The top-down approach then examines the major factors influencing the demand for that firm's products and services. Those factors include the business environment, economic activity, and industry factors including the life cycle. These are factors over which the firm has no control, but they can make or break the firm. Then the firm itself is analyzed. This technique is suitable when analyzing a small number of companies. However, the bottom-up approach is better when evaluating a large number of companies. The bottom-up approach takes advantage of large databases and quantitative techniques to estimate intrinsic values.

NOTES

1. For additional information on the life cycles, see Benton E. Gup, *Investing Online* (Malden, MA: Blackwell Publishing Ltd., 2003).
2. U.S. Bureau of the Census, NAICS 722110, www.census.gov/econ/census02/data/industry/E722110.HTM. Data are for 2002.
3. Data are from the U.S. Bureau of Census, U.S. Census 2000, www.census.gov/main/www/cen2000.html.
4. Juan Enriquez, *As the Future Catches You: How Genomics & Other Forces Are Changing Your Life, Work, Health & Wealth* (New York: Crown, 2001).
5. Donald L. Kemmerer and C. Clyde Jones, *American Economic History* (New York: McGraw-Hill, 1959), 325.
6. "Citigroup and Nikko Cordial Agree on Comprehensive Strategic Alliance," Citigroup press release, March 6, 2007.
7. www.merck.com/finance/annualreport/ar2007/pipeline.html.

CHAPTER 2

The Value Edge

Reap the Advantage of Disciplined Techniques

William J. Hass
CEO TeamWork Technologies

Shepherd G. Pryor IV
Board Resources

This chapter traces the evolution of valuation techniques and provides an overview of the challenges faced by analysts and investors. It includes advances by academics and practitioners in response to the problems with accounting based on generally accepted accounting principles (GAAP). Both academics and practitioners have benefited from years of experience and the availability of better data for model testing. This chapter briefly reviews the historical development of current financial theory and practice. It exposes many of the myths and simplistic solutions that have been used to explain the link between corporate intrinsic value and stock price. A review of the literature and current practices suggest that discounted cash flow (DCF) models are near a tipping point and are overtaking the frequently used shortcuts of accounting-based multiples.

Valuation shortcuts, simplistic solutions, and rules of thumb fail to explain how value is added at the strategic business unit (SBU) level. We describe how organizations move through a value journey as they gain greater insights on value building missed by simplistic solutions and popular rules of thumb. A wave of the future is in combining insight on business fundamentals and organizational culture with the power of DCF models, calibrated with extensive databases of market information.

In the book *The Private Equity Edge: How Private Equity Players and the World's Top Companies Build Value and Wealth* (Laffer, Hass, and Pryor 2009), the authors use private equity firms as the standard for comparison, because private equity investors' goal is to manage for value. This provides a meaningful comparison with public companies, because private equity leaders understand the deficiencies of GAAP accounting, have their own proven and advanced valuation frameworks, and employ greater discipline in measuring value. Private equity investors are action oriented, and communicate more frequently with their portfolio companies. This enables them to work with management to develop better assumptions about the future cash flows than their public peers can develop. As a result, private equity leaders typically have a strong focus on both capital allocation and the cash flow generation capability of businesses in which they invest. Most sophisticated money managers and senior business people understand the basics behind discounted cash flow (DCF) models. However, far too many stick to more simplistic valuation models, which fail to describe reality. Value-disciplined investors and executives put DCF models to use better than others, and more frequently produce above-average returns.

In the following sections we provide insights on the four major steps for embarking on the value journey. We also include a series of questions that can help any investor or management team use improved valuation techniques to increase the chances of building value.

VALUATION DECISIONS ARE MADE DIFFERENTLY BY DIFFERENT PEOPLE

We all search for simple solutions in life. However, as we gain experience and examine the data, simple solutions often become too simplistic to represent reality. The growth of computerized databases has fostered academic research and learning on valuation, as well as growing use by practitioners looking for better models that describe market price levels and movements. Coming from all types of backgrounds, valuation practitioners bring their experience and biases with them. Even day traders are influenced by insights on valuation. When we talk about valuation practitioners, however, we are talking primarily about investors and corporate leaders, both of whom are more concerned with longer-term intrinsic value than with today's stock price. (See Exhibit 2.1.)

Simplistic solutions, shortcuts, personal bias, politics, poor communication, and misdirected incentives make valuations difficult and subject to wide variations. There is a fog about how corporate insiders, outside investors, and analysts value companies. Corporate leaders generally receive

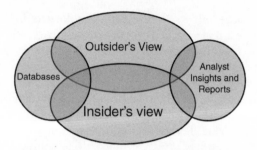

EXHIBIT 2.1 Valuation Depends on Perspective and Use
Source: Copyright © 2009, Board Resources.

incentives to build value, but the payments may be heavily weighted on weak value drivers like revenue and GAAP earnings per share (EPS). As one goes further down the organization, the links between incentive compensation and value creation are even weaker. Rarely does the head of a business unit in a public company have a sense of ownership of the performance and reporting of the unit. Many performance measures used by public companies to judge their division heads, such as quarterly sales and earnings growth, are poor replacements for real value-building metrics, such as growth of cash flow and return on invested capital (ROIC) over the long term.

Both insiders and outsiders are mining databases to make better value-building decisions. Analysts who develop a deep understanding of both the company fundamentals and how the company compares to the broader corporate universe are on the leading edge of value thinking.

How a public or private company approaches value building is of great interest to both the outside analyst and management. There is a growing body of knowledge dealing with how people influence markets with their personal biases, wishes, hopes, and not-always-rational behavior. For example, agency risk and so-called moral hazard play unfortunate roles, as managers too frequently find themselves in positions where they can benefit from taking inordinate risks, due to asymmetrical payoffs under their compensation arrangements.

Valuing a business or a stock from the outside requires mastering insight in two opposing dimensions. The fact that people participate in markets means that the right-brain creative insights and the left-brain analytic urge to quantify are often at odds. Since analysts and managers are all wired differently, it is not surprising that we all have different views on valuation and how the world actually works. People make their own decisions, and often defy the logic of the best economic model. All too frequently, the carefully computed numbers effect is completely overwhelmed by the unanticipated people effect, wreaking havoc on plans and projections, and occasionally causing bubbles. Because people make decisions in every activity, the people effect has an impact on everything from a divisional projection to overall market efficiency (Thaler and Sustein 2008).

Wise leaders have often repeated, "What gets measured gets managed!" Yet we see a wide variety of communication styles and approaches to business measurement. Regulatory authorities attempt to prescribe how public corporations communicate to their investors, with minimum standards for frequency and disclosure. For years accounting bodies in the United States have been setting standards and rules resulting in the development of GAAP. Despite their best efforts, GAAP still is an imperfect measurement system, and now with globalization it must face international challenges from the International Financial Reporting Standards (IFRS). Accounting improvements and acceptance never seem to keep pace with the creativity of new financial instruments and business models. While most managers and valuation professionals in the United States must rely on GAAP, they find it poorly suited to understanding the real economics of a business and estimating intrinsic value. GAAP provides only a starting point, and a distorted one at that.

In the growing spirit of improving transparency, many corporate leaders stick to GAAP and EPS-speak, despite its well-known weaknesses. Yet some more enlightened corporate leaders have gone beyond GAAP to disclose both non-GAAP measures and forecasts of future performance. While public companies are reluctant to give forecasts due to frequent changes in the environment, private-equity-owned businesses are required to provide forecasts and cash budgets to their owners. This more disciplined forecasting and planning requirement alone can give private equity fund managers a great advantage over their public company and mutual fund peers.

Because people are different, there will always be a wide variety of valuation techniques, from the simple to the most complex. While some analysts swear by simple multiples, sophisticated managers and private equity investors dig deeper into the drivers of future cash flow. The better ones allocate limited capital based on DCF approaches, not accounting ratios. The more sophisticated analysts, money managers, and corporate executives use more advanced versions of the basic DCF techniques. Because DCF is not a perfect valuation tool, they use it as a framework to adjust for risk, while adding a variety of refinements such as scenarios, option models, and simulations. The better corporate value builders find ways to communicate these value-building metrics and techniques. They use every opportunity to inform everyone both inside and outside the company that management has a plan and understands the path to greater value.

TECHNIQUES OF COMMUNICATING VALUE CAN DEMONSTRATE A COMMITMENT TO VALUE BUILDING

Let's look at some of the wide differences in disclosures of public companies. Anyone who reviews the annual report of a public company can get a feeling for how the company, its top management, and the people on the factory floor view the importance of value building. Analysts are likely to get important insights on management's commitment to value building from disclosures in required Securities and Exchange Commission (SEC) filings as well as the tone and facts disclosed in presentations to analysts.

According to Karen Dolan, a senior analyst and director of fund analyses at Morningstar, Inc., "The best shareholder letters are easy to understand, and provide insight into what is working and what is not working" (Jones 2009). John Deere and Best Buy are our poster children for value-based disclosures, underscoring management's commitment to drive value-based thinking to frontline employees.

For several years running, John Deere has disclosed in its annual report operating return on assets (OROA) and shareholder value added (SVA) for each of its key lines of business. These non-GAAP metrics are relatively simple to compute and disclose in the annual report, but the commitment to make the disclosures on a consistent multiyear basis is not simplistic. Disclosure of these value-based metrics says a great deal about Deere's commitment to building a value-creating culture. As we will see later, Deere management puts teeth in its annual report disclosures made to employees and investors by linking incentive compensation to some of the same key metrics.

In a similar manner, for several years running, Best Buy's annual report has disclosed return on invested capital (ROIC) on a corporate basis. In addition, Best Buy educates frontline store employees on how they can improve the ROIC for their store and department. Our quick sample of public corporations found that more companies are disclosing ROIC in their annual reports. Those that are serious about value building dedicate significant space to demonstrate how ROIC is computed, and what it means to the company. Value builders are willing to disclose more than the typical GAAP one-liners. Simply disclosing ROIC and helping all employees understand its importance is one of many reasons Best Buy has outperformed its peers.

The outside and inside analyst will both benefit from the growing number of public companies that are doing a better job of prominently disclosing value metrics and talking about intrinsic value. Just take a look at the following sample of better value-building annual reports. These companies go far beyond GAAP revenue and EPS to disclose non-GAAP metrics that are better measures and drivers of value. These companies demonstrate a concern for value, and their value-based disclosures are more than one-liners. Warren Buffett's annual letter to Berkshire Hathaway shareholders is a value-focused exposé on the volatility of the market. Buffett describes intrinsic value as a discounted cash flow stream but displays growth in net asset value. Buffett apologizes, as net asset value is a weak surrogate, since intrinsic value is likely to be estimated differently by different people.

Other examples of model value-based disclosures follow:

- Best Buy discloses ROIC in an easy-to-understand full page in the annual report.
- Corn Products discloses return on capital employed (ROCE), market capitalization, and debt to capitalization.
- Chevron discloses cash dividends, ROCE, and debt to enterprise value.
- Clorox discloses free cash flow, economic profit, and total shareholder return.
- Hewlett-Packard discloses cash flow from operations and free cash flow.
- General Electric has a great one-page scorecard that discloses total shareholder return (TSR), average total capital, and cumulative cash flow.
- Manitowoc discloses economic value added (EVA) and market value, tracked over several years with full explanations.
- Temple Inland discloses return on investment (ROI) by sector and says it has a commitment to ROI first and growth second. Temple Inland has sold major divisions to improve focus and returns.
- Whole Foods discloses EVA as a tool for major decisions and incentives for 750 senior managers.

Unfortunately, the list of public corporations with a real observable commitment to value building and better valuation is short relative to those committed to minimum GAAP disclosures. Contrast the disclosures of the list with the more limiting GAAP or EPS-speak accounting metrics found in the annual report disclosures of Hospira (a 2004 spin-off of Abbott Labs) and once-great Kodak.

What is a fair return? As disclosed in Hospira's 2007 annual report, Hospira's commitment to its shareholders is to safeguard their investment and provide a "fair return." Yet while it lists its two key strategies from day one as "investing for growth and improving margins and cash flow," these metrics are not prominently disclosed, explained in detail, or trended (Hospira 2007). The five-year corporate performance graph required in the proxy shows Hospira outperforming the S&P 500 index and S&P Health Care Index for the period 2004 to 2007, but the company missed an opportunity to tie these favorable results to performance goals.

Another EPS-speak example is Kodak. The company is having financial and competitive difficulty, so the annual report is nothing more than the 10-K. A once-great company known for visuals is now limiting disclosure to EPS-speak and minimum disclosures required by the SEC. Kodak is an example of value-based reporting and disclosure techniques lost.

ANALYSTS BEWARE: ONCE-SUCCESSFUL PUBLIC COMPANIES CAN LOSE THEIR WAY

Most private equity firms purchase businesses they believe they can improve. They seek to earn a high rate of return over a three-to-six-year horizon, and then sell. In contrast, public companies are slow to divest underperforming units. It's hard to believe that General Motors was once the model of the modern corporation. Alfred Sloan was ahead of his time when his mandate was for each operating division to earn a return above its cost of capital. As General Motors looked for ways to cut costs, it consolidated operations and it lost the clarity of its goal for each division to earn a return on capital. Eventually, divisions were shuttered, but only after multiple attempts to revive them and after years of low or negative returns.

FMC Corporation was an early leader in value-based management, but a change in management in the mid-1990s led to a switch from the 1980s focus on value building to a greater emphasis on growth. The change resulted from requests from operating managers for simpler measures. Managers at FMC found the value-based metrics too difficult to manipulate for higher bonuses. Once one of these operating people assumed a leadership position, FMC gave up the more complex value-building metrics in favor of a simplistic short-term revenue growth goal. Unfortunately, not all revenue growth builds value. FMC's experience underscores the need to balance complexity with directionality but also not to give in to simplistic metrics that do not result in long-term value building.

Don't be distracted by quarter-to-quarter noise. The more successful private equity investors are likely to separate the noise from the trend because they spend more time monitoring their investments from the ground up and are able to change management when performance falls below expectations. Quarter-to-quarter changes can occur because of a wide range of factors: timing of expense or revenue recognition, changes in short-term marketing practices, or even changes in accounting estimates and interpretations. None of these guarantee a sustainable change in EPS, yet any could produce changes in EPS that are indistinguishable from a real uptrend. Effective analysts dig deeper than EPS and seek to understand whether the EPS performance is temporary or signals long-term sustainability in cash flow. They are not usually fooled by changes in GAAP accounting results.

INCENTIVE COMPENSATION TECHNIQUES BASED ON VALUE ARE BETTER

It is simple but not simplistic to improve annual reports with value-based metrics. The annual report and proxy materials can also demonstrate a corporation's commitment to value. This commitment is important to the pockets of the company management and employees, as well as to investors.

Let's again contrast public company compensation techniques and board governance with those of private equity. Because private equity firms buy businesses with the goal of creating value and high returns over a period of three to six years, they measure management and provide incentives for creating value. In contrast, public companies rarely see the value realized from an investment in a new product or division as clearly as a private equity fund does.

The inability of public companies to measure value created in terms of a sale cannot be underestimated. In fact, it is hard for us to believe that there are still large companies with operating divisions that lack complete income statements and balance sheets. Complete financial statements are needed to track return on investment and improve capital allocation. Without these basic tools, division leaders of any company—public or private—simply cannot be measured on value creation.

Compensation discussions are tough for any board of directors, especially when performance is below expectations or market averages. The board and CEO need to establish a value-building culture. Too often the culture of the company is focused too much on products or EPS, and value is eroded. Consider the U.S. auto industry. Management had a love affair with building cars and forgot about making sure every employee in the organization understood that the company also had to produce a rate of return above the cost of capital for its shareholders.

Bob Lane's story at Deere demonstrates a case in point and highlights the challenges of the value journey. According to Lane, who became CEO of Deere in 2000, most employees at Deere had no idea of the importance of earning a reasonable return, or why the stock price moved so radically with the business cycle. Deere was considered by many investors to be a good company, but it had suffered from the strong economic cycle for farm and construction products, and from a unionized workforce. For years Lane campaigned, appealed, and repeatedly explained to all employees that they had great products, but not a great business. He set in place a culture change program designed to get every employee to understand that there was work to do to create a business as great as Deere's products.

Lane made educating employees on value and economics a top priority. The theme emblazoned on the annual report for six years, and communicated to employees, was easy for all to understand: "Growing a business as great as our products." Compensation goals were set based on producing shareholder value added (SVA). This meant earning a minimum target return on capital that was realistic and related to the business cycle. In good years of the business cycle the return goal was set at 28 percent, at midcycle 20 percent, and at the bottom of the cycle 12 percent. To put greater meaning in the goals and make them actionable, every product team at Deere must have a plan in place to achieve these goals as part of its short-term incentive program. The use of the different goals for different stages of the macroeconomic environment has allowed Deere to achieve higher levels of return at each stage of the cycle because it reflects the reality of the business.

A simple concept with major educational value was to charge each business unit and division 1 percent per month for capital employed. While simple in concept, the 12 percent per year capital charge was not simplistic. It helped everyone in the organization understand that an economic or value-producing profit would not be achieved without covering the cost of capital. According to Bob Lane in a discussion with the authors on December 18, 2007, "the concept of economic profit and how it is applied is understood by thousands of managers, not by a few financial people at the top."

Because of the problems with GAAP accounting, Lane needed to go beyond the required GAAP disclosures and explain non-GAAP metrics in Deere's annual report over several years—not just the good years. Deere discloses and educates investors and employees on OROA of its key product lines. It communicates to Wall Street analysts in its analyst presentations with value-based concepts like SVA. We see the investor relations presentations at www.JohnDeere.com as examples of what is needed in many public companies.

Absolute gains in economic profit are used as the basis for medium-term incentive bonuses. To avoid bonus boom and bust, the bonus payouts are based on a four-year moving average. This has resulted in losing bonus dollars earned over several good years due to a poor performance in one subsequent year. As part of Deere's long-term incentive program, the top 1,000 executives are required to own equity. Deere knows that its stock price does not always rise in step with creation of value. As a result, it bases its award of 50 percent stock options and 50 percent restricted stock to the top 40 executives on achieving positive SVA, not the more traditional GAAP earnings goals. Deere's compensation program clearly supports its commitment to value building more than most public companies, and mirrors some aspects of the compensation programs of the better-managed top private-equity-owned companies.

Lane considers value-based metrics like SVA to be more effective for its scoreboard, which has helped change the culture's focus toward value creation and away from product lines governed by GAAP. With value-based metrics Deere gets people to think about the importance of effective use of capital.

While time spent by directors is an important factor differentiating public and private companies, size and complexity also indicate differences in corporate governance. Despite the publicity given the huge private equity buyouts of large public companies in 2007 and 2008, most private equity investments are made in smaller middle-market companies that are easy to understand. In contrast, the recent bank bailouts related to the credit crisis demonstrate the point of complexity in the banking system. In 2009 newspapers opined that the largest banks had so many diverse businesses, an ordinary director could never master their complexity. Business headlines questioned both investors and shareholders: "Can anyone manage a company as diverse as Citibank?"

As we have seen, a simple but important technique helps analysts determine a company's commitment to value building. It requires going beyond the GAAP metrics found in today's many financial databases and requires a bit of digging into the tone of the annual report and compensation disclosures. Consider the following questions that can be asked by any outside analyst when refining his or her assumption about a company:

- Does the company have a disciplined strategy and scorecard based on value building?
  □ Is the scorecard prominently displayed?
  □ Is it oriented toward value accounting or toward GAAP accounting?
- Does the executive compensation program support the scorecard and promote value building as an overarching goal?
  □ Are the goals repeated and understood by all employees?
  □ Are the goals linked to a robust market-based valuation technique or framework?

New Valuation Techniques Build on Data and Experience

A variety of value-based information providers developed in the 1980s. They launched their products due to the GAAP accounting's problems and weak linkage to market value, and the growth of modern finance theory. Their proprietary approaches were documented in various articles, and eventually in more complete books with examples. We note some of these on the Tree of Valuation Methodologies shown in Exhibit 2.2. Most of the new approaches relied on the simultaneous growth of financial databases and personal computing power to help both the outside and inside analysts

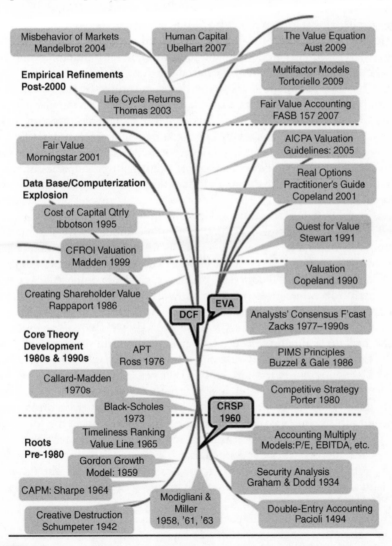

EXHIBIT 2.2   Tree of Valuation Methodologies (with Major Publication Dates)
Source: Copyright © 2009, Board Resources.

develop a view of future performance from historical accounting perform-ance. The growth in public company databases allowed comparisons to ac-tual results and helped develop more refined theories and practitioner approaches to valuation.

Let's look at some of the roots and branches that have developed over time. We focus on major publication dates rather than argue about what was in use at specific times. Please note that any effort to establish a chro-nology like this is sure to be controversial, so we beg forgiveness in advance. This is only our perception of the many methodologies and insights that have developed into modern finance and valuation techniques. Publication dates usually occur years after the initial use.

The roots of valuation are founded in accounting and the theory of the firm. Luca Pacioli, an Italian monk, was first to publish a detailed descrip-tion of double-entry accounting (his *Summa*). He collaborated on a later book (*Divine Proportion*) with Leonardo da Vinci. Pacioli described the accounting system that was in use by Venetian merchants during the Ren-aissance. Pacioli's *Summa* was the first scholarly text on accounting. Its publication in 1494 set the stage for centuries of subsequent refinements (Livio 2002).

Most modern accounting models and multiples go back to the 1920s and 1930s with frameworks like the DuPont model, which related in-come statement and balance sheet ratios to return on assets and return on equity. *Security Analysis* by Columbia University professors Benjamin Graham and David Dodd was published in 1934 and still serves as the bible for value investors such as Warren Buffett and his disciples. Graham is known for refining "a framework for making people think what those (financial) numbers really mean" (Lowe 1994). The discipline that became value investing was grounded in the analysis of facts that supported what Ben Graham called estimating an "intrinsic value" and how it compared to book and market values. Graham and later Buf-fett were known to look for low prices that allowed for a "margin of safety" if bad things happened. Interpreting the intrinsic value from accounting statements and estimating future earnings was the job of the analyst. Graham was as critical of the poor corporate accounting disclo-sures and the volatility of "Mr. Market" as investors are today. Graham looked to a corporation's ability to pay cash dividends into the future as a critical element of true measure of value of a security (Lowe 1994; Schroeder 2008).

New insights on the impact of competition and creative destruction from Schumpeter (Schumpeter 1942) made models that assumed continu-ous growth in cash dividends like the Gordon growth model (circa 1959) popular but too academic. Corporate cost accounting and capital budgeting were refined in the 1960s and stimulated analyzing the firm as a series of investment projects.

It wasn't until 1960 when the Center for Research in Security Prices (CRSP) was founded at the University of Chicago Booth School of Business that research on security prices could rely on an ever-improving clean database of stock prices. The modern concepts of finance took a leap forward with the work of Franco Modigliani and Merton Miller (Modigliani and Miller 1961) and the capital asset pricing model (CAPM) of William Sharpe (Sharpe 1964). In 1965 Value Line introduced its five-part timeliness ranking of stocks, which it based on its computer valuation models.

About the same time CRSP was developing its database of stock prices, the Profit Impact of Market Strategy (PIMS) Program, based on business strategy research at General Electric and later at Harvard University, was developing a database of nonfinancial and financial business unit data to determine the drivers of business unit profitability and value. The results of the study of over 3,200 business unit experiences was published over a decade later in book form as *The PIMS Principles* (Buzzel and Gale 1986). Michael Porter, who was a user of the PIMS database at Harvard in the early 1970s, produced his landmark book on business strategy setting forth the five forces framework: *Competitive Strategy* (Porter 1980). Porter emphasized that one of management's key strategy and value-based decisions was choosing the industries in which to compete. As the PIMS database indicated, one of the primary determinants of business unit profitability and value was a well-chosen "served market."

The lagging economy of the 1970s and the record inflation of the early 1980s caused greater attention to be paid to macroeconomic factors, as financial statements reflected inadequate information on economic return on investments (Callard and Kleinman 1985). The combination of new insights on stock prices and the growing awareness of the link between business strategy and profitability led to an explosion of value-based thinking and strategic planning in the 1980s. Business strategy and valuation became a powerful intertwined pair.

From there, two major branches of financial valuation applications developed. One was heavily based on understanding DCF and the other focused on residual income, economic margin, or EVA-related models. Practitioners developed their proprietary models that were used to analyze the value of the leveraged buyouts (LBOs) and mergers of the 1980s. Many of these proprietary valuation models found their way into major consulting firms that promised their clients value-creating strategic improvements and processes. Others found their way into the hands of analysts at money management firms. With a number of successful corporate case examples completed, the value-based practitioners eventually produced books documenting their calculation techniques and value-building successes. These books were published in the late 1980s and 1990s. The more popular ones include:

- *Creating Shareholder Value: The New Standard for Business Performance* (Rappaport 1986), which documented the problems with accounting ratios and set forth a discounted cash flow methodology as well as a reference to modeling software. Rappaport's software was heavily used at the consulting firm LEK Consulting.
- *Valuation: Measuring and Managing the Value of Companies* (Copeland, Koller, and Murrin 1994), which documented McKinsey's approach to building value with case examples and terrific graphical presentations.
- *The Quest for Value* (Stewart 1991), which set forth the Stern Stewart models for computing economic value added (EVA), a term that the firm later copyrighted. The EVA approach to valuation also became popular at a variety of consulting firms and in limited non-GAAP financial statement disclosures.
- *CFROI Valuation* (Madden 1999), which documented the systematic analysis of a firm's accounting data to uncover a real cash flow return on investment. The book was an outgrowth of Madden's work at Callard Madden Associates (CMA) and HOLT Value Associates over the prior decades. In 1985, HOLT Planning was founded as Hendricks, Olsen, Lipson, and Thomas and separated from CMA. In 1992, Boston Consulting Group (BCG) acquired HOLT Planning as BCG/HOLT to support the growing interest in value-based planning and licensed the intellectual property to HOLT Value Associates. However, in 1995 HOLT Value spun out to permit greater concentration on model development and marketing to the investment community. *Later HOLT Value* was acquired by Credit Suisse First Boston (CSFB) in early 2002 to broaden its suite of valuation methodologies available to its analysts. CFROI-based and other proprietary approaches to valuation also became available through successors of the original CMA firm at Ativo Research, LLC; CharterMast Partners, LLC; LifeCycle Returns (LCRT), LLC; and former employees of HOLT at the Applied Finance Group (1995). Lafferty Associates also provides CFROI—based valuation products, based on its association with Chuck Callard in the 1980s.

Other firms supplied data to support the need to understand cost of capital and analyst estimates. Ibbotson Associates, now part of Morningstar, began to publish the *Cost of Capital Annual* and *Cost of Capital*

Quarterly in 1995. They were key data sources for cost of capital data used in DCF valuations of the time. Alternatives to the basic CAPM model, such as arbitrage pricing theory (APT), also appeared. The APT model was developed by Stephen Ross at Yale University in 1976 to account for systematic risk in key macroeconomic factors such as interest rate spreads, yield curves, inflation, and industrial production. Zacks Investment Research began gathering and distributing analysts' estimates in 1977. However, these estimates did not gain widespread usage until the Internet explosion in the 1990s.

The refinements to valuation models continued in 2001 with publication of Morningstar's fair value estimates on approximately 500 stocks. Its models incorporate the Buffett strategic concept of an "economic or competitive moat," growth, and return on capital. The estimates further combine human analyst insights on competitive strategy with a standardized DCF framework for over 2,000 stocks. See Pat Dorsey's more complete explanation in Chapter 12 of how Morningstar looks at intrinsic value.

The Misbehavior of Markets (Mandelbrot 2004) sets forth the challenges to the basic assumptions of CAPM. The 2008 global economic crisis again proved returns are not always statistically normal.

Real Options Practitioner's Guide (Copeland and Antikarov 2001) points out that DCF has some weakness in dealing with sequential investments. However, improvements like real options have not caught on due to the complexity and assumptions required. Some practitioners believe real options will become the primary method for valuing sequential investment alternatives in the next decade. (See Chapter 13.)

Despite the apparent misbehavior of markets, quant models continue to grow. Some require analyst overrides; some do not. *Quantitative Strategies for Achieving Alpha* (Tortoriello 2009) outlines some of the advances and issues of multifactor models.

Refinements to basic models and techniques like those disclosed in this handbook will continue to be made as new data becomes available. Space does not permit displaying all new and emerging techniques and methodologies. The top portion of the Tree of Value Methodology contains a selection of these techniques in no specific order. Examples shown at the top of the tree include advances in thinking, such as Hewitt Associates' insights on human capital (Mark Ubelhart's Chapter 19), LifeCycle Returns' thinking about nonnormal distributions (Rawley Thomas's Chapter 22), and CharterMast's thinking on a simple but not simplistic Value Equation (Dennis Aust's Chapter 10).

Valuations are focused on the future, and there will be a growing variety of approaches, techniques, and refinements to valuation methodology. Users need to understand the strengths and weaknesses of the proprietary models they use. Probably the best general approach is one used in weather forecasting. The modern meteorologist looks at a variety of models and then attaches a range of values to his or her prediction. Many different models are available to today's modern analyst with the click of a mouse, at Internet speed. This has long been the case with technical analysis and is becoming true with more computer-aided DCF valuation tools. The skilled analyst looking at the fundamentals can choose the model that best reflects the best description of the situation and assure that key assumptions and value drivers make sense.

The assumptions behind any of these techniques and models will be challenged by the passage of time and actual performance under future conditions. The main challenge will always involve the inside or outside analyst choosing the right approach for the problem at hand. How the risk of unknown effects on future cash flows and the cost of capital are included in the model will be the choice of the user. Users will continue to learn which approach or combinations of approaches works best for them. Insiders will always have the edge on the best data about any company, while outsiders will have the edge on relative market performance and an outsider's assessment of management's plans and commitment to building value.

VALUATION TECHNIQUES FOR PRIVATE
COMPANIES ARE ALSO MORE DATA DRIVEN

While most of the preceding comments on advances in valuation techniques relate to public companies, there are advances in the valuation of private companies as well. Guidelines established by the American Institute of Certified Public Accountants (AICPA) and Financial Accounting Standards Board (FASB) affect the valuations of both public and private corporations. Shannon Pratt is probably the best-known widely published authority on valuation of private companies, employee stock ownership plans (ESOPs), and closely held corporations. Several of his books treat the subject of valuing privately owned businesses (Pratt 2008).

As spreadsheet valuation models became more popular, major banks sought to automate the loan approval process and financial analysis of potential borrowers. The models and databases have grown to include not only public companies but private corporate borrowers as well. These proprietary databases have replaced the books of annual financial statement benchmarks that became part of the banker's tool kit in the 1970s and 1980s. Several of these private company databases (e.g., Pratt's Stats, Mergerstat) also contain periodically updated valuation information, as well as the traditional income statement and balance sheet ratios.

Industry-specific valuation information is also advancing, as we see in the valuation of physician and dental practices later in this handbook (Chapters 16 and 17).

ESTIMATES OF VALUE MAY DIFFER DEPENDING ON DATA INTEGRITY

Ultimately, the highest bidder will win in an acquisition contest. Without full access to the cultural and financial details that affect value, assumptions about missing data can prove to be costly. AOL Time Warner's loss of $54 billion in the second quarter of 2002 is a perfect example (Klein 2003 and Hu 2005).

Note that where fraud has been involved, estimates of value can be starkly different. Refco Inc., once the largest independent U.S. futures trader, was taken public in August 2005, raising $670 million in newly issued common stock. Two months later, the value was vaporized as the company disclosed that it had discovered internal fraud. Refco's former chairman, Phillip Bennett, later pleaded guilty to fraud and conspiracy in this disaster that cost investors $2.4 billion (Glovin and Hurtado 2008).

Disciplined Techniques Work Better Than Simplistic Solutions

Boards of directors and senior management are the custodians of corporate value, but they may find themselves rudderless if they cannot agree on a way to identify and measure corporate value. Corporate leaders must find credible indicators of value. They need enough theory to enable decisions that are consistent with building corporate value. Value-oriented targets allow these leaders to move beyond trial-and-error, simplistic solutions and rules of thumb (Hass and Pryor 2006).

The difficulty of driving long-term corporate value is not an unrecognized problem. In October 2006 the National Association of Corporate Directors (NACD) devoted much of its national conference to focusing on "Driving Long-Term Value." Panel members surfaced numerous ideas to boost value through better corporate oversight, more strategic focus, and management accountability for results. At the same time, there was a pervasive unease with the difficulty of pursuing long-term goals in the face of mounting pressure to meet short-term targets. See Pryor, Hass, and Aust (2006).

For example, at the conference some corporate leaders feared that investors who are just passing through will demand radical short-term changes. While these changes might grab stockholder attention and cause a boost in price in the short term, they may only lead to wreckage in the future. By then the short-term investors may have long since dumped the company.

Unfortunately, none of these high-level panels clarified how to measure long-term value or how to differentiate between those strategies and operating programs that would contribute to value and those that would diminish it. In essence, many of the most sophisticated members of the business community who are truly concerned about corporate value and corporate governance know there is a problem, but lack the tools to solve it.

The problem will continue to rage until corporate leaders realize that they lack a functioning definition of long-term or intrinsic value. Until then, they will continue to be victimized by faddish crusades to maximize the wrong variables. Single-minded pursuit of net income, growth in earnings per share (EPS), growth in sales (at the wrong time), stock option value, and even "funds from operations" have all led to disasters in the past. (Consider Enron.) Collapses of once-great firms such as Bear Stearns, Lehman Brothers, and American International Group (AIG) can all be traced to decisions about value and risk that ignored the broad context in which such companies operate.

Corporate leaders can benefit from frameworks that distinguish between actions that build and those that destroy value. To use such frameworks, they will need to avoid many simplistic solutions that are commonly used.

First we highlight some of these simplistic solutions and approaches. The next step is to provide some guidance to help corporate leaders better understand corporate value. Finally, we provide methods that can be useful in pinpointing which business units and activities contribute to or detract from corporate value. Using this foundation, corporate leaders can begin to embed value-building approaches into their decision making.

Simplistic Solution—Accounting Accounting values provide lenders with useful information about assets and cash that can be used to retire debt. However, they are of far less use to investors and management, who need to focus on corporate value and cash flow. Simplistic solutions to clear up include the use of EPS growth, price-earnings (P/E) ratios, and multiples of earnings before interest, taxes, depreciation, and amortization (EBITDA) as proxies for value.

Unfortunately, all of these seemingly innocent variables have turned on their users from time to time. In an effort to simplify, boards have agreed on rule-of-thumb goals that could be manipulated by management teams in pursuit of higher compensation. But, beyond that, management teams acting in good faith, but in pursuit of the wrong goals, have driven value out of their companies, all while being congratulated for reaching their goals. For example, the conglomerates of the 1960s and 1970s could produce EPS growth virtually on demand by managing the pace of their acquisitions. However, the value of these companies collapsed because their method was to buy ever-poorer performers. Another example is the use of EBITDA multiples to value or benchmark businesses. Unfortunately, the multiple changes with capital intensity, nature of the business, and sustainability of the cash flow. Like a chain saw, EBITDA should have a warning label saying, "This tool can be dangerous if used improperly."

Simplistic Solution—Quarterly Performance   Media pundits constantly discuss quarterly performance measures, and the subsequent reaction of the stock market. The false implication is that the market cares only about this quarter's EPS.

Hidden under the blast of noise about the quarterly EPS is a comparison of that earnings number with performance that is expected by outside analysts. Where does this expectation come from? Rarely discussed in detail, these expectations are not just so-called whisper numbers from CFOs. For competent analysts, they have a much deeper meaning. The expectations are estimates of the long-term sustainable amounts of cash that the company is able to generate from its operations. When these expectations are not met, the implication is about the long term, not just this quarter. Further, when a company takes short-term actions to shore up its reported quarterly performance (such as cutting advertising expenses), perceptive analysts see through the move and act accordingly.

Management should never act as though short-term traders run the market. Even traders have to sell stock to other market participants to realize any gain. Unless the market is populated by "greater fools" or following false signals, the trader will not benefit by pressuring a company to focus on short-term results at the expense of sustainable long-term results.

Boards and management should be wary of pressure from any investor to take actions to produce short-term results at the expense of long-term value. The outcome could be the undermining of valuable long-term strategies, or hasty announcement of strategic initiatives that the company cannot fulfill. Either way, the market will ultimately see through the misguided actions and the market value of the company will decline.

Simplistic Solution—Sell, Sell, Sell   Sales growth is not a panacea. In fact, it can kill. When companies consistently earn above their cost of capital and grow, they create value. However, when a company consistently earns below its cost of capital and grows, it actively destroys value.

Sometimes in a growing company, directors may sense that management is "buying business" by cutting margins, but management may push back with comments about protecting market share or demonstrating that the products in question are still "profitable." However, the directors' sense that something is wrong may be on target. This can occur because accounting profit does not account for the cost of capital.

Growth is sometimes supported by increasing debt loads and leverage. The increasing size of the tax shelter provided by the debt is welcomed as an additional source of free cash. However, increasing debt raises failure risk, which the market will not ignore. Unfortunately, some managers do ignore it at their peril.

Directors should beware of what they ask for. Placing high incentives on growth in sales or using leverage to boost returns on equity may pull the plug on value.

Simplistic Solutions—The Stock Market and Value Many corporate leaders, in frustration, just assume that the market is irrational. There is plenty of media commentary to support this idea, but adopting it is perilous. The markets may be more rational than management teams.

The stock market is the mechanism that ultimately pays investors for their investments. Thus, the stock price must, over time, approximate or move around the right measure. However, the level of volatility in stock prices is convincing evidence that the stock price isn't right every day. Add to this the previous comments regarding quarterly performance measures, and you have recipe for a big misunderstanding between corporate managements and the stock market.

Exhibit 2.3 depicts the flow of information between a company and its owners: the market as the owner of a public company and, later, private equity where the company has gone private. For public companies, the overlap of information is in the published financial statements and such performance indicators as EPS. This limited slice of information is never up to the real task. Investors want to know more about strategy, operations, internal resources, and overall management capability, in order to judge the sustainability and quality of reported earnings and cash flow. The formality of communication between the CEO and the analysts creates its own problems. The CEO frequently wrongly infers from the conversations that the only important indicator of performance is the current quarter's EPS.

In addition, the investors' perspective is inherently broader than that of management, and they are perpetually asking themselves whether their investment in any particular company is justified, relative to alternative investments.

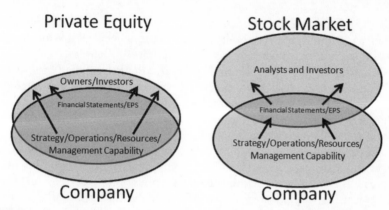

EXHIBIT 2.3 Ideal Information Flow Occurs in Private Equity, Rarely in Public Markets
Source: Copyright © 2009, Board Resources.

When private equity investors are the owners, the flow of information is not constrained by SEC rules, and investors dig beyond the financial statements and into the facts about strategy, operations, internal resources, and management capability.

A major issue is transparency. All investors want to see the underlying truth about the companies they invest in. However, managers may try to portray the results to fit what they think stockholders want, rather that presenting an underlying truth about the company. Private equity's solution to the problem is to communicate clearly to the management team and all employees and require reporting that is more focused on providing the owners' needs for value building. Public company leaders could learn a lot from private equity about improving communication with stockholders and employees as well as focusing more attention on better techniques to monitor and build long-term intrinsic value.

FINANCE THEORY AND CORPORATE VALUE

While some finance theorists can be criticized for their baffling and arcane presentations, on the whole they exhibit a great dedication to constructing objective methods of determining corporate value. Some use combinations of simplifying assumptions and logic to build their theories, and some start with empirical data and infer how markets deduce value.

Most modern theorists agree at some level that the value of a corporation arises from the cash that it will return to investors. Accounting for the timing, they estimate the value by discounting the projected cash. Empirical studies have found that the results of these various theories are linked with actual stock market values, with varying amounts of accuracy.

Much of the literature devoted to finance theory is aimed at investors and portfolio managers. In this arena, a few basis points of return can be worth millions of dollars; hence it is highly worthwhile to focus on nuanced differences among the different valuation models. As a result, the investment community has embraced many of the theories and models.

A broad range of valuation models are sufficiently accurate to be useful for corporate decision makers. Unfortunately, corporate directors and managers are likely to reject portfolio-related theories and models, finding them to be confusing, complicated, incomprehensible, or just not workable if the detail must be explained to thousands of workers in a large company. This is highly unfortunate, for there can be great value in finding a model that is directionally correct for use within a company. This standard is far less rigorous than the standard that a portfolio manager might need to apply in choosing a valuation model. *Valuation Handbook* contributor Dennis Aust sets forth this distinction with remarkable clarity in Chapter 10 as the "value equation."

Still, many senior corporate decision makers continue to sacrifice value in their pursuit of quarterly EPS targets. These targets do not satisfy the analysts and do not always guarantee value creation. What satisfies the analysts is an uptrend in long-term sustainable cash flow, not reported net income.

There is an undying difference between finance and accounting. Financial values come from expectations about the future, and reported accounting earnings are all about the past. With a forward-looking numerator and a denominator arising from the past, is it any wonder that price-earnings ratios are faulty indicators of value?

To avoid the traps of misusing P/E ratios and EBITDA, financial theorists track cash as the wellspring of corporate value. By articulating their assumptions clearly and describing their logic in mathematical terms, they set forth their findings with great clarity, to their peers. Unfortunately, few of their peers sit in corner offices as CEOs or on boards. These decision makers use tools they can understand, or those that seem sufficiently accessible. As a result, the use of EBITDA and P/E multiples continues, despite potentially inferior results. These measures do not adequately track value, and their continued use is costly. Companies that shift from performance measurement based on accounting to measurement based on value may find that a third of their prior decisions on capital allocation and value of business units were just plain wrong (Thomas and Edwards 1993).

Fundamental analysis still has an important place in valuation. In order to understand the future cash flows of any company, it is important to

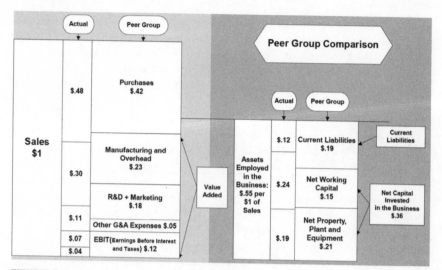

EXHIBIT 2.4 Basic Graphic to Compare Financial Fundamentals with Industry Benchmarks

Source: Copyright © 2009 Board Resources. Adapted from William J. Hass and Shepherd G. Pryor IV, *Building Value through Strategy, Risk Assessment, and Renewal* (Chicago: CCH Inc., 2006).

develop a basic understanding of the economics of key business units in relation to industry peers. Ratios too different from those in the industry may indicate a failure to adopt the best practices of the industry, or worse, the presence of fraud or creative accounting. Exhibit 2.4 graphically displays a simple (not simplistic) method for visualizing how a company's financials and business model compare with industry benchmarks. The analyst or manager can use this tool and knowledge of the business to examine the impact of deviations from industry ratios on estimates of corporate value.

THE VALUE EDGE BEGINS AT THE STRATEGIC BUSINESS UNIT LEVEL

Large companies are generally built from a number of strategic business units (SBUs). Companies have broad latitude in defining these units. Depending on the nature of the business, the units may be defined by product line, geography, or customer type. Internally, management may have clear definitions and goals for individual business units, but the performance of the units is frequently blended in some way before issuing public reports. This practice complicates the benchmarking practice discussed earlier.

Once management has chosen how to set up the SBUs, tracking and benchmarking the value of the individual units is a core management principle for building value in the overall company. If the typical board and management team can find a way to determine which units build value and which ones detract from overall corporate value, their decision making will be greatly improved.

THE WATERFALL OF VALUE IDENTIFIES VALUE CREATORS AND DESTROYERS

One analysis can be used to compare SBUs, whether they are defined by product line, geography, or customer base. The analysis uses a waterfall diagram, focusing on intrinsic value.

Exhibit 2.5 applies a value analysis to the SBUs of a hypothetical company. What jumps off the page is that some of the units are chugging along,

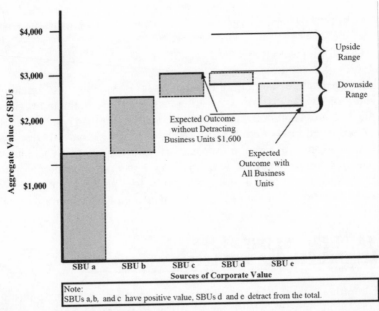

EXHIBIT 2.5 The Waterfall of SBU Values Highlights Management's Challenges
Source: Copyright © 2009 Board Resources. Adapted from William J. Hass and Shepherd G. Pryor IV, *Building Value through Strategy, Risk Assessment, and Renewal* (Chicago: CCH Inc., 2006).

producing value, while others are wasting the corporation's capital. Those that drag down the value do so by returning less than enough to support the unit's cost of capital. Unfortunately, some of these SBUs are able to report accounting profits and favorable budget variances. While the outcome of the analysis can be displayed with clarity, the underlying analysis is far from simplistic.

The waterfall of SBU values is based on the proposition that the market compiles value as a sum of the parts. A common theme is the importance of a company producing returns in excess of the cost of capital in order to build value. The implication for managers is directional. The implication for investors seeking the intrinsic value of a company is that they may have to make further assumptions regarding synergy, covariance, or other aspects of combined operations.

In the blink of an eye, the waterfall can prompt a director to ask more questions about a business unit that is reducing the company's value. When the underlying analysis is undertaken with empirically sound analytical methods, many of which are elucidated throughout this book, management and the board can rely on the waterfall to guide their decision processes. To build the waterfall, varying methods of analysis are available and can be matched with the company's level of sophistication or budget. For management, the most important aspect of the model chosen is that it be directionally correct, differentiating between the SBUs that add to value and those that subtract.

Note that the waterfall focuses on the intrinsic value of a company and its SBUs. A great deal of early research on stock prices focused on price changes. While this was mathematically satisfying to the researchers, it did not translate well into useful principles for corporate decision makers. Our emphasis on intrinsic value is parallel to newer trends in research on stock prices, which focus on price levels, not just price changes.

BETTER VALUATION FRAMEWORKS
PROVIDE DISCIPLINE

Better valuation frameworks and models promote a greater understanding of the cash flows of the business, as well as the underlying strategies that produce those cash flows. Exhibits 2.6 and 2.7 provide an example. The upper portion of Exhibit 2.6 portrays the traditional cash flow forecast included in a multiyear business plan. The typical financial forecast is driven by an understanding of the business model and outlook. The lower portion

Five Year Forecast		Year 1	Year 2	Year 3	Year 4	Year 5
Total Market		$7,407	$8,529	$9,822	$11,311	$13,026
Market Share		13.5%	13.6%	13.7%	13.8%	13.9%
Base Case Sales		$1,000	$1,160	$1,346	$ 1,561	$ 1,811
Less: Cost of Goods Sold		650	754	875	1,015	1,177
Gross Margin		350	406	471	546	634
Less: SG&A		145	168	195	226	263
Operating Earnings (EBIT)		205	238	276	320	371
Less: Taxes		72	83	97	112	130
Operating Cash Flow		133	155	179	208	241
Fixed Asset Additions		114	116	119	122	125
Change in Working Capital		12	14	17	19	22
Free Cash Flow		7	24	44	67	94
Cost of Capital		12%	12%	12%	12%	12%
PV of Cash Flows (years 1–5)	$ 153	6	19	31	43	53

Terminal Value Calculation		
EBIT in Terminal Year	$ 371.2	Assume no growth after terminal year
Tax Rate	35%	
Op Earnings After Tax in Terminal Year	241.3	
Plus Depreciation	105.0	
Less CapEx	105.0	(If Growth = 0, CapEx = Depreciation)
Less: Net Working Capital Increase	0	(If Growth = 0, W/C does not grow)
Cash Flow	$ 241.3	
Cost of Capital (Ks)	12.0%	
Value at End of Terminal Year	$ 2,010.6	= Terminal year cash flow/Ks
PVIF 15%, 5 periods	0.567	= Present value of terminal value received in 5 years
TV=Terminal Value×PVIF	1,140.8	(Note how important terminal value is to the total enterprise value)
Add PV of Cash Flows (years 1–5)	152.8	
Enterprise Value of Company	$1,293.6	= Sum of PV of cash flows and TV
Less: Debt	$ 500.0	
Other Adjustments (Net)	$ (100.0)	= +/– nonearning assets, pension liabilities, etc.
Intrinsic Value of Equity	$1,393.6	= Enterprise value less debt and adjustments

EXHIBIT 2.6 Practitioners Use Discounted Cash Flow Spreadsheet Models
Source: Copyright © 2009, Board Resources.

of the exhibit makes further assumptions about value after the plan period, and other adjustments—like an underfunded pension plan—not reflected in the cash flows. The value and cash flows can then be reduced to an estimate of enterprise value, which is the sum of obligations to debt holders and the intrinsic value of equity.

Exhibit 2.7 proposes a framework to assess the impact of changes in the market environment and competitive environment, with company actions and the potential financial results. Such a framework can be used to stress test or evaluate the impact of different scenarios or assumptions on intrinsic value.

Frameworks like this help the investor or analyst understand which customers and served markets will allow a company to earn its cost of capital. Companies want to provide value for the customers, but customers must be willing to pay enough for the products and services to allow the company a return above its cost of capital.

ENVIRONMENT	ACTION	RESULTS
Is the served market growing or declining?	Is management increasing or decreasing prices to gain market share?	What has been the impact on sales growth and profitability? (+/– 10%)
Is competition increasing or decreasing?	Is management increasing or decreasing its margins?	What has been the impact on profitability? (+/– 15%)

EXHIBIT 2.7 Simple Frameworks Help Identify Key Actions That Create Value
Source: Copyright © 2009, Board Resources.

THE VALUE JOURNEY HAS MANY STEPS ALONG THE WAY

Just as a company and its management must pursue value building through a variety of steps, the outside analyst also goes through a similar series of steps in valuing a company. For the outside analyst it is a choice between using simple multiples or more detailed, sophisticated, and robust DCF techniques. On the corporate side, a successful journey toward value requires the discipline of tracking progress and making changes along the way. Conducting an annual valuation and producing the waterfall for the board along with the annual business plan and budget is a great first step. An engaged board, guided by a well-constructed value analysis, will be in the best position to assist management in refining its strategies, tactics, and resources toward the goal of building corporate value.

There are four major steps on the journey to top value builder status. Corporate executives can use them to guide their way. Outside investors and analysts can evaluate public company management on their progress toward top value builder status. The steps are:

1. Talking and thinking about value in everything you do, constantly communicating to the workforce, and providing full disclosure to the shareholders:
   - This involves setting the right goals and priorities.
   - This involves communicating verbally and in annual and periodic reports, while changing the culture to ensure all employees understand how to build value.
2. Implementing metrics that drive cash flow such as return on invested capital, customer retention and growth, and understanding changing markets and market share:

- This includes providing incentive compensation based on value-building metrics.
- This involves going far beyond simplistic EPS-speak metrics.

3. Reporting and acting on value and value driver trends on a regular basis, not just when the trend is positive:
   - This involves reporting on value-based measures monthly at the operational level and at least quarterly to the board.
   - This involves developing action plans describing how better results will be achieved.

4. Pushing toward the goal of and achieving top value builder status with total shareholder returns of 20 percent or more.

Discounted cash flow techniques have been driven to a tipping point by more sophisticated practitioners. Private equity firms have taken advantage of the discrepancies in valuation of companies to make billions of dollars. They have a stronger focus on future cash flows and value than most analysts, investors, and corporate decision makers.

Public company decision makers can benefit from these advanced DCF techniques. With the right data at both the macroeconomic and company levels, better decisions and a better understanding of value are possible. Questions that can help corporate executives and investors build value along the value journey are listed with best practices. *They are questions used by many successful private equity players.*

- How do we determine which parts of our business build or destroy value?
  - Perform periodic valuations of key business units.
  - Manage parts of your business as a portfolio.
- How do we assess the macroeconomic environment and the signals it provides?
  - Maintain a corporate chart book.
  - Document the factors and trends that impact operations and value, such as interest rates, oil prices, and key commodity prices.
- How do we ensure management and the board are committed to long-term value?
  - Educate the board on value metrics.
  - Ensure the board has skin in the game.
- How do we effectively identify and track key value drivers?
  - Make sure each business leader has identified and tracks controllable and noncontrollable factors.
  - Adopt an intrinsic value model that uses a broad set of value drivers appropriate for each of your businesses.

- How do we insulate management from forces that might push for short-term illusory increases in accounting results rather than long-term value?
  - ☐ Adopt an intrinsic value model that uses a broad set of value drivers appropriate for each of your businesses.
  - ☐ Identify both GAAP and non-GAAP value drivers, but give more weight to non-GAAP measures.
- How can we best communicate that our goal is to improve investor returns through focus on intrinsic value?
  - ☐ Publish and trend goals on value drivers.
  - ☐ Write and talk about intrinsic value drivers at every opportunity, but especially in employee communications and quarterly and annual reports.
- How do we continue to improve our small but engaged board and ensure that they and the management team remain focused on value creation?
  - ☐ Make each director responsible for periodically presenting a complete understanding of one or more of the key business units and/or value drivers.
  - ☐ Be sure directors are also investors and have skin in the game.
- How do we value the company? How do we best communicate the value to the rank and file?
  - ☐ Use a simplistic metric like net book value but qualify it with more robust measures such as adopting use of an intrinsic value model.
  - ☐ Adopt an intrinsic value model that uses a broad set of value drivers appropriate for each of your businesses.
- How do we rank-order our business units by value, and evaluate how they contribute to our current stock price and intrinsic value?
  - ☐ Adopt an intrinsic value model that uses a broad set of value drivers appropriate for each of your businesses.
  - ☐ Prepare an annual report with a value waterfall for internal purposes and the board meetings.
- For any unit that supports another, more successful unit, should we be consolidating those units for reporting purposes?
  - ☐ Ask unit management to run scenarios.
  - ☐ Look at the intrinsic value of the combination.
- What should we do to rectify a situation where a unit is not capable of earning its cost of capital over the long term and is decreasing the value of the overall enterprise?
  - ☐ Act sooner than your competitors.
  - ☐ Spin out the unit to a buyer with a better strategic fit.

■ How can we find ways to improve our insights on value creation?
    ☐ Experiment with new concepts and valuation approaches.
    ☐ Involve others in improving the value creation process.
■ How do we install a cost of capital discipline into our organization?
    ☐ Educate all employees in basic finance concepts.
    ☐ Ensure that key people have an incentive to earn more than their cost of capital.

ACKNOWLEDGMENTS

We owe a debt of gratitude to several people who assisted in the adaptation by reviewing and providing insights, including Sean Falmer, Rawley Thomas, Robert Agnew, Duncan Borne, and many others.

REFERENCES

Callard, C., and D. Kleinman. 1985. Inflation-adjusted accounting: Does it matter? *Financial Analysts Journal* (May–June).

Copeland, T., T. Koller, and J. Murrin. 1994. *Valuation: Measuring and managing the value of companies.* 2nd ed. New York: John Wiley & Sons. (Orig. pub. 1990 by McKinsey & Co.).

Copeland, T., and V. Antikarov. 2001. *Real Options: A practitioner's guide.* New York: Monitor Group.

Glovin, D., and P. Hurtado.Ex-Refco Chief Bennett's guilty plea may help former deputies. *Bloomberg.com*, February 16, 2008. www.bloomberg.com/apps/news?pid=20601087&sid=aAKxBfxG9fhU&refer=home.

Hass, W., and S. Pryor. 2006. *Building value through strategy, risk assessment, and renewal.* Chicago: CCH Inc.

Hospira. 2007. Annual report.

Hu, J. 2005. Case accepts blame for AOL-Time Warner debacle. *CNET News.com*, published on *ZDNet News*, January 12, 2005. See also: AOL Time Warner Inc. 2002. 10-Q report, second quarter 2002 (August 14), 35: "Upon adoption of FAS 142 in the first quarter of 2002, AOL Time Warner recorded a one-time, noncash charge of approximately $54 billion to reduce the carrying value of its goodwill." See also: UC Newsroom. 2003. AOL and Time Warner executives accused of pocketing nearly $1 billion. www.universityofcalifornia.edu/news/article/5311.

Jones, S. 2009. Sears boss lets loose on a lot: Lampert's letter ranges far and wide; profit down 55%. *Chicago Tribune*, February 27, 25.

Klein, A. 2003. *Stealing time: Steve Case, Jerry Levin, and the collapse of AOL Time Warner*. New York: Simon & Schuster Paperbacks, 68–78.

Laffer, A., W. Hass, and S. Pryor. 2009. *The private equity edge: How private equity players and the world's top companies create value and wealth*. New York: McGraw-Hill.

Livio, M. 2002. *The Golden Ratio: The story of phi, the world's most astonishing number*. New York: Broadway Books/Random House, 128–137.

Lowe, J. 1994. *Benjamin Graham on value investing: Lessons from the dean of Wall Street*. Chicago: Dearborn Financial Publishing.

Madden, B. 1999. *CFROI valuation: Cash flow return on investment*. Woburn, MA: Butterworth-Heinemann. See also: Madden, B. 2007. For better corporate governance: The shareholder value review. *Journal of Applied Corporate Finance* 19, no. 1 (Winter): 102–114.

Mandelbrot, B., and R. Hudson. 2004. *The (Mis)Behavior of Markets: A fractal view of risk, ruin and reward*. New York: Basic Books.

Modigliani, F., and M. Miller. 1961. Dividend policy, growth and the valuation of shares, *Journal of Business* 34 (October): 411–433.

Porter, Michael. 1980. *Competitive strategy*. New York: Free Press/Simon & Schuster. (Porter received an MBA with high distinction in 1971 from Harvard Business School, where he was a George F. Baker Scholar, and a PhD in business economics from Harvard University in 1973, during which time he researched the PIMS data.)

Pratt, S., and A. Niculita. 2008. *Valuing a business: The analysis and appraisal of closely held companies*. 5th ed. New York: McGraw-Hill. See also: Pratt, S., R. Reilly, and R. Schweihs. 1998. *Valuing small businesses and professional practices*. 3rd ed. New York: McGraw-Hill.

Pryor, Shepherd, William Hass, and Dennis Aust. 2006. Driving long-term value: What are the next steps? Directors Monthly 30, no. 12 (December): 1.

Rappaport, A. 1986. *Creating shareholder value: The new standard for business performance*. New York: Free Press.

Schroeder, A. 2008. *The snowball: Warren Buffett and the business of life*. New York: Bantam Books. See also: Buffett, W. 1996. An owner's manual. Omaha, NE: Berkshire Hathaway. Originally produced in June 1996 and updated on www.berkshirehathaway.com.

Schumpeter, J. 1942. *Capitalism, socialism and democracy*. New York: Harper & Brothers.

Sharpe, W. 1964. Capital asset prices: A theory of market equilibrium under conditions of risk. *Journal of Finance* 19: 425–442.

Stewart, G. 1991. *The quest for value: The EVA® management guide*. New York: HarperBusiness, 40–41. See also: Colvin, G. 2008. A new way to value the market: The latest technology enables novel analysis of whether stocks are attractively priced now. (Hint: They might be.) *Fortune*, February 21. http://money.cnn.com/2008/02/15/magazines/fortune/investing/colvin_eva.fortune/index.htm.

Thaler, R., and C. Sunstein. 2008. *Nudge: Improving decisions about health, wealth, and happiness.* New Haven, CT: Yale University Press.

Thomas, R., and L. Edwards. 1993. How HOLT methods work: For good decisions, determine business value more accurately. *Corporate Cashflow* (September).

Tortoriello, R. 2009. *Quantitative Strategies for Achieving Alpha.* New York: McGraw-Hill.

CHAPTER 3

Applying a Systems Mindset
to Stock Valuation

Bartley J. Madden
Independent Researcher

Research on the life-cycle valuation model began in 1969 at Callard, Madden & Associates in order to improve stock selection and investment returns. Beginning in the mid-1980s, the model was extensively refined and commercialized by HOLT Value Associates. Today, many institutional money managers use the life-cycle valuation model, as well as relevant data from the global database of 20,000 companies in 60 countries provided by Credit Suisse HOLT.

This is a review of the five important choices that guided this 40-year research journey. A systems mindset that stressed intensive measurement and experimentation with variables was especially instrumental to the evolution of the life-cycle model. Systems thinking led to distinct departures from mainstream finance practices. For example, the life-cycle model uses a discount rate that is dependent on the procedure used to forecast a firm's long-term, net cash receipt (NCR) stream.

Based on this research experience, I offer suggestions about the potential evolution of a new research program to address additional important, practical needs.

CHOICE 1: A SYSTEMS MINDSET

Knowledge improvement generally is a product of inquiry, undertaken to better understand or solve a perceived problem (Umpleby and Dent 1999). When we are involved in inquiry, we are as much a part of the inquiry as the external environment because we have preconceptions that affect what is, literally, observed, and the conceptual interpretations of those observations (Madden 1991).

Being constructs of human thought, all theories are actually conditional statements subject to tests of their usefulness for solving a problem in its context. Users of a theory (or model) want it to reliably serve as a guide for taking action to achieve an intended goal. This is the ultimate predictability test of a model.

Researchers who have chosen a systems mindset begin with intensive observations and trial descriptions of phenomena to uncover both critically important variables and consequential relationships among them. For example, the life-cycle model uses a discount rate that is *dependent* on the procedure used to forecast a firm's long-term, net cash receipt stream. In general, a systems mindset promotes bottom-up (inductive) thinking that is crucial to discovering essential but difficult-to-quantify variables, the kind that might be observed in data as outliers and omitted as anomalies or that might be buried in error terms in the construction of econometric models.

However straightforward and commonsense systems thinking is in principle, it often times is ignored in practice. For example, many mainstream finance researchers rely heavily on top-down (deductive) theory such as market efficiency and the capital asset pricing model (CAPM). In the past, the strong pull of this dominant view slowed down experimentation with variables that could jeopardize the market efficiency and CAPM constructs. For example, note how long it took for behavioral finance to emerge.

An overemphasis on top-down theory can be harmful, as articulated by Robert Haugen (1999, 139, 140):

> Finance scholars have long embraced the notion that we advance faster and better by *first* creating theories that make predictions about the way the world works. *Next* we turn to the data to see if the numbers conform to the predictions. If we find that they do not, we either (a) "refine" the theories, by altering the assumptions upon which they are based, or (b) "refine" the empirical tests until the data speaks in a voice we can *appreciate and understand.* . . .
> But most of the major advances in the frontier of human knowledge did not follow an arrow running through the theories into the empirical tests. Rather, *most of our greatest triumphs proceeded in the opposite direction from data to theory.* The arrow goes from straightforward empirical observation to the development of theories which give us the insights *to understand what we have seen.* . . . We have two choices. We can *advance* by developing radically new theories to help us understand what we now see

in the data. Or we can *go back*, denying what is now readily apparent to most, bending the data through ever more convoluted econometric processes, *until it screams its compliance with our preconceptions.* (italics in original)

Modern finance researchers by and large have used CAPM to guide much of their work, so much so that Perold (2004) would say it dominated modern finance. An elegant explanation of a mathematically logical relationship between expected returns on stocks and risk, CAPM provides a blueprint, given its assumptions, for investors to optimize their portfolios to the highest expected return for a given level of risk. Notwithstanding CAPM's poor empirical record of predictability (Fama and French 2004) and its challengeable assumptions, it continues to exert a strong hold on mainstream finance.[1]

In the past decade or so, behavioral finance researchers have presented serious challenges to the premises and empirical underpinnings of mainstream finance theory (Thaler 2005). But proponents of the status quo seem little concerned about the weaknesses of their theory. Rather, they take the offensive, asking: Where is the better theory? Believing none has been offered yet, they have not significantly changed the core body of knowledge presented in finance textbooks and taught to finance students. Thus the dominant theory remains intact.

The intended takeaway from this quick sidetrack into the philosophy of knowing is that empirical work based on innovative formulations of questions/problems and different ways of manipulating and testing variables can: (1) reveal deeply rooted, but flawed, assumptions, (2) improve the specification of components of an existing model, and (3) lead to new conceptual advancements—that is, better theory for "insights to understand what we have seen," and for reliably guiding action to achieve a goal.

CHOICE 2: FIRMS' COMPETITIVE LIFE CYCLE

Early on in life cycle research, the accepted goal of the research program became to better understand *levels* and *changes* in company stock prices on a global basis so portfolio managers could make better investment decisions. In contrast, mainstream finance was focused on a logically consistent equilibrium model that related risk to expected return—and CAPM became the answer. CAPM was not designed to explain the level of firms' market prices, but rather the *change* in prices that drive investor returns.

A dominant academic premise has been that the market is efficient in incorporating all value-relevant information into stock prices. Consequently, finance academics gave relatively little attention to the process of forecasting firms' long-term, net cash receipt (NCR) streams. Why? Because stock prices have already incorporated these forecasts, and forecasting better than the market is ruled out by the efficiency assumption.

In contrast, the commercial research program on life cycles wanted a vehicle to deal with NCR forecasts so that both levels and changes in stock prices could be fruitfully studied (without any preconceived beliefs about market efficiency). We chose the firms' competitive life cycle construct in order to connect firms' economic performance to market valuation in a conceptual way that incorporates competition, and yet was useful for forecasting NCRs.

Exhibit 3.1 illustrates the firms' competitive life cycle in four stages captured as patterns of the four key variables that drive a firm's economic performance. The assumed role for competition over time had especially strong empirical support and was aptly stated by George Stigler (1963, 54):

> *There is no more important proposition in economic theory than that, under competition, the rate of return on investment tends toward equality in all industries. Entrepreneurs will seek to leave relatively unprofitable industries and enter relatively profitable industries.*

In the life cycle framework one can observe the effects of Joseph Schumpeter's (1942, 84) creative destruction at work—the "kind of competition which counts . . . competition from the new commodity, the new technology, the new source of supply, the new type of organizations . . . competition which commands a decisive cost or quality advantage and which strikes not at the margins of the profits and the outputs of the existing firms but at their foundations and their very lives."

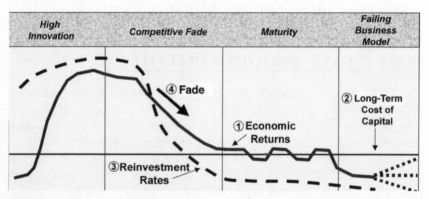

EXHIBIT 3.1 Firms' Competitive Life Cycle
Source: Madden (2005).

The radical competition Schumpeter alludes to often comes from firms in the High Innovation stage. These firms have satisfied the fundamental criterion of wealth creation, namely *economic returns* clearly in excess of the *cost of capital*. Particularly successful firms exhibit high *reinvestment rates* (i.e., growth in operating assets) in order to meet high demand for their products or services, and this creates additional wealth.

As competitors attempt to duplicate and improve on the highly demanded innovative product/service, the Competitive Fade stage (Wiggins and Ruefli 2005) follows. Due to competitive pressure, firms' economic returns fade toward the cost of capital and reinvestment rates fade to lower levels (Fama and French 2000).

Next is the Maturity life cycle stage wherein top management is typically lulled into a business-as-usual complacency. Inertia prevails, with a bias toward making perceived low-risk investments that incrementally expand businesses that were profitable in the past.

A transition to the Failing Business Model stage occurs as profitability declines, which is consistent with a shortfall, relative to competitors, in providing value to customers. At this stage, purging bureaucratic inefficiencies and downsizing/refocusing are almost always needed in order to restore profitability and avoid bankruptcy.

A critical task in the application of the life cycle concept to actual firms is to estimate economic returns (discussed later). Life cycle track records, based on firms' reported, or suitably adjusted, accounting data and stock price histories are a valuable tool for better understanding the past, and thereby for making better forecasts of the future. The life cycle track record for Kmart from 1960 to its bankruptcy in 2002 is displayed in Exhibit 3.2.

The top panel shows inflation-adjusted (real) economic returns, estimated as a cash flow return on investment (CFROI®, registered trademark of Credit Suisse Securities). The panel includes a benchmark, long-term, corporate average CFROI of 6 percent real to approximate the cost of capital.[2] The middle panel shows real asset growth rates. The bottom panel shows a cumulative index that reflects annual changes in the yearly excess (positive or negative) of the total shareholder return (dividends plus price appreciation) of the company's stock relative to the S&P 500. A positive share performance versus the S&P 500 is depicted by rising trends in the relative wealth index, and negative performance by falling trends.

Shareholder returns in excess (positive/negative) of the general market are attributed to firms' fade rates being more/less favorable than investors expected. That is, at the margin, investors were positively/negatively surprised. From 1960 to the early 1970s, Kmart's innovative concept of a discount store propelled its CFROIs from barely positive levels to above the

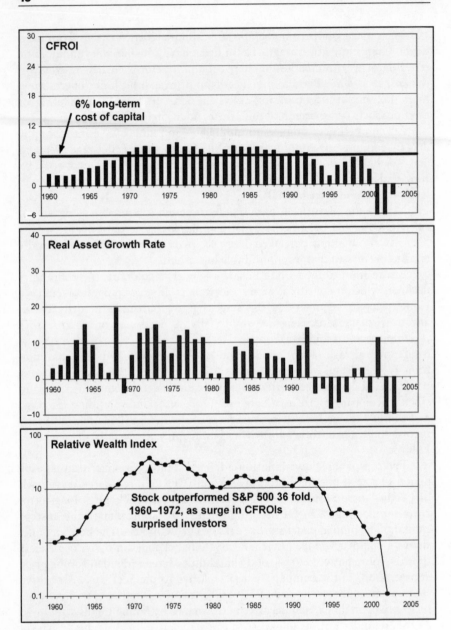

EXHIBIT 3.2 Kmart Life Cycle Performance, 1960 to 2002
Source: Credit Suisse HOLT ValueSearch global database.

cost of capital. This unanticipated upward fade of CFROIs enabled long-term shareholders to outperform the market 36-fold during this period. Then, over the next 20 years, Kmart slightly underperformed the market while CFROIs averaged around 7 percent. From the mid-1990s to bankruptcy in 2002, Kmart had four CEOs. Each failed to develop and execute a viable strategy to counteract fierce competition from Wal-Mart.

Let's turn now to some important technical issues in life cycle research.

CHOICE 3: INFLATION ADJUSTMENTS AND ECONOMIC RETURNS

In the early 1970s, it occurred to me that a project orientation would be useful for developing the CFROI metric (Larsen and Holland 2008, 119–143). An *economic return* was specified as the standard return on investment (ROI) measure of a completed project, reflecting each period's NCR over the full project life. When all outflows and inflows are expressed in monetary units of equivalent purchasing power, the calculated ROI is an inflation-adjusted, or real, economic return.

A firm was then viewed as a portfolio of ongoing projects (Larsen and Holland 2008, 159–163). The problem facing an analyst using reported financial statements is to estimate the average economic returns being achieved on the aggregate of the firm's ongoing portfolio of projects.

The balance sheet and income statement data provide gross assets, cash flow, nondepreciating assets, and life. These can be arranged as a project ROI with an initial outlay of gross assets, followed by equal cash flows over the assigned life with a release of nondepreciating assets in the final year. When the ROI calculation uses assets marked up to match the purchasing power of cash flows, the result is a real CFROI.

I chose not to use a conventional return on net assets (RONA) for three reasons. First, explicit identification of the ROI components helps resolve problems in adjusting accounting data to match business economics in order to more closely approximate economic returns. Second, the productive capacity of plant and equipment does not decline as rapidly as implied by straight-line depreciation (Thomas 2002, 2–3), which is wired into most RONA calculations.

Third, the project emphasis used to construct a CFROI is a useful tie-in to the value of existing assets. At any specific point in time, a portfolio of projects has different vintages, from the oldest to the most recent project started. The oldest projects have the shortest remaining economic lives, and typically have the least amount of cash flows remaining, whereas the opposite is true for the newest projects. A project orientation easily translates into a conceptual view of the valuation of existing assets as the winddown of cash flows as projects meet the ends of their economic lives.

This valuation perspective of the cash flow wind-down of existing assets had more plausibility compared to the conventional, and mathematically convenient, present value of existing assets as a perpetuity (current earnings divided by the cost of capital). This is particularly evident, for example, in the use of the wind-down approach when estimating the value of a firm's existing oil/gas reserves.

Keep in mind that progress with the task of connecting firms' economic performance to market valuation involves learning better ways to *approximate* important variables such as economic returns and investor expectations. For example, a time series of CFROIs can help one infer the level of economic returns being earned by the firm, and thus help in making a forecast of ROIs on future investments—a key variable driving long-term NCRs.

Arguably, a prerequisite in working with, and learning from, time series data is that key variables should have the same meaning over time (Madden 1999, 17). All of the components of the life-cycle valuation model are real variables in order to minimize the noise due to fluctuations in monetary unit values (different inflation/deflation rates). Consequently, levels of and changes in CFROIs and discount rates can be meaningfully compared across historical time periods and across national borders.

There is a large body of academic work in the accounting literature on the connection between economic returns and accounting returns (Brief 1986). But the research tends to be mathematical exercises, absent track record analyses. Also, researchers have devoted considerable energy to residual-income valuation models (Ohlson 1995; Feltham and Ohlson 1995, 1996), which ignore the divergence between true economic returns and accounting returns such as earnings on book equity. The assumption is that in forecasting a long-term earnings stream, biases will offset (e.g., a bias of too-low book equity would be offset by too-high earnings on book equity). In finessing the flaws in accounting data in this way, the residual income proponents shut off a potential learning process, a learning process that is integral to a systems mindset.

CHOICE 4: DENOMINATOR DEPENDS ON THE NUMERATOR

All conceptually sound, discounted cash flow valuation models incorporate some form of the four fundamental life cycle variables: economic returns,

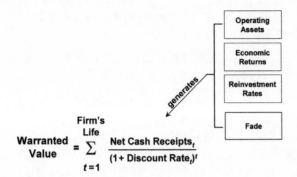

EXHIBIT 3.3 Life-Cycle Valuation Model
Source: Madden (2005).

reinvestment rates, competitive fade, and cost of capital (investors' discount rate). Exhibit 3.3 maps the role of these variables in generating net cash receipts, which are discounted to a present value (i.e., a warranted value contingent on the forecasted variables).

How one specifies operating assets influences the calculated values of economic returns and reinvestment rates. Consequently, the *observed* historical fade rates for economic returns and asset growth rates (proxy for reinvestment rates) also depend on the specification of operating assets. For example, the life cycle track record for a typical pharmaceutical company is significantly different if research and development (R&D) expenditures are capitalized and included in operating assets.

Let's go another step. Since forecasted fade rates are a key driver of NCRs (the numerator), discount rates (the denominator) depend on the analysis of historical fade rates used as the basis for forecasting future fade rates. Thus, a less obvious relationship is that the assignment of a company-specific discount rate should be logically consistent with the NCR forecasting procedure being used.

Applying systems thinking to discount rates is not an unreasonable point of view. Bond investors set market prices for bonds by applying a forward-looking discount rate—their demanded yield to maturity (YTM)—to an expected NCR stream of interest and principal payments. So, too, for common stock investors, although it is far more difficult to estimate expected NCR streams for business firms. Help in this area came from client feedback as part of the commercial research process. Portfolio managers and security analysts, with in-depth knowledge of individual companies, provided a continual stream of problems whose solutions involved new ways to better estimate economic returns. This, in turn, helped improve NCR forecasting.

Net Cash Receipt Streams, Discount Rates, and Problem Solving

First, let's specify a procedure for forecasting NCRs. Then we'll discuss how forecasted NCRs are used to calculate a company's forward-looking (market-derived) cost of capital or discount rate.

NCRs are driven by a forecast life cycle. The present value today of NCRs from investments made beyond 40 years in the future is quite small, especially when those investments are expected to earn close to cost of capital economic returns. A life cycle forecast period of 40 years (Madden 1999, 173) is one practical choice, although the selection of a longer horizon does not much impact warranted value calculations.

As today is year T, a near-term fade window from T + 1 to T + 5 begins with a normalized T + 1 CFROI, which is derived from consensus analyst earnings per share (EPS) forecasts for years T, T + 1, and T + 2. The fade of both CFROIs and reinvestment rates from T + 1 to T + 5 is primarily based on past company CFROI variability and asset growth rates (Madden 1999, 165–167). From T + 5 to T + 40, CFROIs regress to a long-term corporate average CFROI of 6 percent real. And asset growth rates regress to a mature economy growth rate at T + 40. Improved fade forecasts, in particular for the early part of firms' future life cycles, continue to be researched and implemented.

This has been the standard NCR forecast procedure used for many years. An argument to add a longer, more favorable near-term fade window for certain types of companies hinges on the strength of economic reasons and empirical data presented to support more customized forecasting procedures. Note that the forecast procedures being discussed are *standardized* procedures used to maintain a monitored database of companies.

Company-specific discount rates at points in time are calculated with a regression equation. Given the standard fade forecast for a company keyed to a normalized forecast T + 1 CFROI, the market-derived discount rate is the rate that provides a present value of the future NCR stream equal to today's known market value.[3] This forward-looking discount rate is the dependent variable.

There are two independent variables (Madden 1999, 102–104). Because CFROIs include the benefit to cash flows from tax-deductible interest payments, an offsetting risk differential for financial leverage is called for. That is, higher leverage should result in higher discount rates, all else being equal. The other independent variable is a liquidity risk differential. That is, all else being equal, less liquid companies involve higher trading costs and should result in higher demanded returns as compensation. Less liquid companies are small companies. As the economic environment becomes better/

worse for small companies, this effect will decrease/increase the measured liquidity risk differential.

In summary, the application of a market-derived process for assigning a discount rate to a particular company can be compared to estimating the average yield to maturity (YTM) for bonds with a particular credit rating. For a sample of bonds, one could assemble data for a regression equation with YTM as the dependent variable and credit rating as the independent variable. A regression line for bonds then transforms a credit rating into an expected YTM. In a similar manner, for stocks, a regression line value for a company's discount rate is contingent on its financial leverage and trading liquidity. Market-derived discount rates serve as an alternative to CAPM costs of capital.

Market-derived discount rates do not address important CAPM issues such as how investors are assumed to handle systematic or market risk in building their portfolios. Rather, market-derived discount rates represent the end result of how investors are currently pricing individual company risks in terms of financial leverage and liquidity.

An ability to assign a specific discount rate to a specific firm at a specific point in time enabled the development of a warranted value chart. This is the workhorse automated tool for identifying problems. It is a long-term plotting of both a company's annual stock price ranges and annual warranted values based on the standardized NCR forecasts using estimated company-specific discount rates. Systematic overtracking or undertracking of actual prices compared to warranted values are seen as red flags for possible problems. Other common sources of problems are when life cycle track record data for a company seems implausible compared to industry peers, and/or relative stock price performance does not make sense when compared to time series data for CFROIs and reinvestment rates.

Dealing with a problem almost always begins with skepticism about how closely accounting data matches business economics. A small sample of issues includes: capitalization of R&D expenses, operating lease capitalization, acquisition intangibles, financial subsidiaries, off-balance-sheet liabilities, special items, stock option expenses, and asset lives. A typical fix for a problem would entail finding an economically sound reason to adjust accounting data that not only improves the original company situation, but also results in similar improvements for other companies that share this economic characteristic. Improvement is gauged by closer tracking of actual versus warranted values.

The ongoing life-cycle research program leads to insightful ways to adjust accounting data to better estimate economic returns. *Improved NCR forecasts lead to improved discount rates.*

Taiwan Mystery Resolved   A recent experience with Taiwanese companies serves as an excellent example of the benefit of a systems mindset. In a systems approach, learning is a function of identifying problems and developing solutions by paying attention to interactions among variables. In a 2006 Credit Suisse HOLT report, Ng, Jhaveri, and Graziano described a major improvement for Taiwanese companies.

Let's begin with problem recognition. The aggregate market-derived discount rate for Taiwanese companies seemed implausibly high. Also, Taiwanese companies with low financial leverage had *higher* discount rates than the high-leverage companies—a negative leverage risk differential that did not make economic sense.

The root cause of these problems was identified as excessively high CFROIs for the many companies that generously dispensed shares for employee stock bonuses. From the shareholders' perspective, this outlay was clearly an economic expense, although it was ignored in computing accounting net income.[4] This artificially boosted CFROIs, which in turn boosted market-derived discount rates.

Exhibit 3.3 is helpful in understanding this point. Substitute a firm's known market value for the warranted value. The market value can be matched by either (1) discounting higher NCRs (boosted by ignoring employee stock bonuses) at a higher rate or (2) discounting lower NCRs (this is more accurate) at a lower rate.

The solution was to incorporate an appropriate charge, which lowered cash flow used in calculating CFROI. With the new lower CFROIs (better reflecting business economics), calculated market-derived discount rates declined. Interestingly, technology companies were the biggest users of employee stock bonuses, and these companies also tend to have low financial leverage. Thus, the CFROI fix also resolved the mystery of a too-high discount rate for low-leverage companies. Finally, there was an across-the-board improvement in the tracking of warranted values with actual stock prices.

CAPM Is a Problem   CAPM captured and still holds the minds (and hearts?) of finance academics with its elegant mathematics grounded in the neoclassical economic principles of equilibrium, rationality, and efficient markets.

In general, finance textbooks (Brealey, Myers, and Allen 2006 is an example) explain portfolio construction as investors striving to achieve higher expected returns and to reduce risk. CAPM is an integral part of this explanation. In this manner, CAPM becomes a foundation for thinking about stock prices.

CAPM was brought into discounted cash flow valuation of individual firms as the basis for assigning a firm's equity cost of capital. A firm's equity discount rate equals the *risk-free rate* plus the product of a stock's *beta* (i.e., volatility) times the *risk premium* of the overall equity market (i.e., expected excess return of the equity market over the risk-free rate). This is the standard method finance students are taught to use for estimating a firm's cost of equity capital.

One objection to market-derived discount rates replacing CAPM rates is the necessity for maintaining a monitored database and attending to all sorts of issues concerning accounting conventions versus business economics. Fair enough. But increased valuation accuracy through more appropriate company-specific discount rates can generate big rewards.

The other major objection is more subtle. This criticism is that the market-derived discount rate methodology can produce illogical discount rates. For example, consider a technology company and a food company that have approximately the same financial leverage and the same liquidity (company size). The previously described regression procedure for assigning discount rates would give the same discount rate to both companies. Yet, as critics point out, everyone knows that food companies have a lower cost of capital than technology companies because food companies have more stable and predictable cash flows and lower betas than technology companies.

The false perception of illogic only shows the absence of a systems mindset. The life-cycle valuation model's standard fade forecast for a typical technology company is much less favorable compared to that of a typical food company. A technology company with above-cost-of-capital, but highly variable, economic returns and/or high reinvestment rates would be assigned a faster downward fade compared to a food company, which typically has more stable economic returns and slower reinvestment rates. The life cycle approach handles the risk difference in the numerator.

There are at least two important reasons to consider for rejecting the standard CAPM equation in favor of the market-derived approach for use in valuation models. First, application of the CAPM equation requires two inputs that are notoriously difficult to judge—beta and the equity market risk premium over the risk-free rate. These are applied as forward-looking variables but they are necessarily estimated from historical data.

Estimates based on historical time periods are especially troublesome when tax legislation, such as capital gains tax rates, that affects investors' after-tax returns (and thus their demanded returns) is expected to pass or becomes law (Madden 1999, 97–99, 250–252). Market-derived discount rates immediately reflect these changes.

Depending on the past time periods selected, a stock's beta could easily range from, say, 1.2 to 1.5, and the market premium could easily range from, say, 4 percent to 7 percent. Users of CAPM have little to guide them in the selection of these two critical inputs. Combining a risk-free rate of 3 percent with a beta of 1.2 and a 4 percent market premium yields a 7.8 percent equity cost of capital. In contrast, substitution of a beta of 1.5 and a market premium of 7 percent yields a 13.5 percent equity cost of capital.

The valuation impact of using either a 7.8 percent or a 13.5 percent equity cost of capital is enormous. A similar big impact on an economic value added (EVA) calculation occurs when the equity cost of capital is estimated with the CAPM equation or alternative procedures, such as arbitrage pricing theory or the Fama-French three-factor model, which is increasingly being used by quantitative portfolio managers (Fabozzi, Focardi, and Jonas 2008).

In practice, market-derived discount rates for a sample of companies have a much smaller range. Particularly important is that these discount rates have a hand-in-glove compatibility fit with the valuation model in which the discount rate is applied.

In contrast, two analysts using radically different assumptions for forecasting long-term fade rates (read as risk adjustments) and using the same CAPM cost of capital would calculate widely different valuations. But they would not have a clue about the impact of parachuting into their valuation models a discount rate that is totally independent of how NCRs are forecasted.

Another reason for rejecting CAPM equity rates is, as noted earlier, that the systems mindset promotes intensive data analysis as part of a process to improve higher-level understanding. In valuation applications, CAPM users tend to implement theory that arrives on a plate served up by the theory developers. But theory developers don't analyze firms' track records, struggle with measurement issues, calibrate market expectations, forecast future NCR streams, and make investment decisions. These activities focus the mind on all sorts of important technical issues that have implications for higher-order model building.

In my opinion, which is echoed by many portfolio managers and analysts who actively work with life cycle data, business risk analysis is most usefully handled in the numerator and not the denominator.

CHOICE 5: INSIGHTS AND PLAUSIBILITY JUDGMENTS

Mainstream finance, as reflected in standard corporate finance textbooks, has little to say about how the users of valuation models develop their skill in making forecasts. In other words, the users' forecasting skill is viewed as being independent from the model.

Not so with the life cycle research program. The three primary research tools—life cycle track records, warranted value charts, and valuation model to translate forecast inputs (see Exhibit 3.3) to warranted values—comprise the product provided to institutional money manager clients. Client users sharpen their forecasting skills by participating in the same learning process as the research staff.

When users employ these tools to investigate a firm, they gain an opportunity to study the causes of a firm's long-term fade within the unique context of an industry and economic environment, and to build up expertise in understanding how the market makes forecasts (sets expectations) and revises these expectations as new data arrive.

The more experience users accumulate with the application of these tools, the better prepared they are to analyze a new company. There are two main analytical benefits.

First, users can quickly generate insights as to the key valuation issues for a particular firm and to the actions management should give top priority to taking in order to maximize long-term shareholder value. Second, the users' growing base of experience facilitates plausibility judgments about investor forecasts (expectations), their own forecasts, and the forecasts of others. Judging the degree of difficulty in achieving these forecasted levels of performance is greatly aided by a comparison to the type of companies that have historically achieved these same levels of life cycle performance.

As for plausibility judgments and investor expectations, an informative application of the life-cycle model was reported in a September 9, 1996, *Forbes* article, "Follow the Cash" (Samuels 1996). The article described the life-cycle framework used by HOLT Value Associates in consulting with institutional investors. *Forbes* pointed out that HOLT had rated Wal-Mart as a strong sell five years earlier before it sharply declined, whereas HOLT now considered Wal-Mart a strong buy. The main point here is not that these two recommendations produced returns consistent with the sell-buy recommendations; rather, the important point being illustrated is the judgment process for competitive fade and managerial skill at those two points in time versus investor expectations.

Although the Wal-Mart success story is well known, the magnitude of Wal-Mart's wealth creation achievement is striking when displayed in life cycle terms as seen in Exhibit 3.4. We see CFROIs rising from 12 percent to about 15 percent from 1970 to 1990 coupled with enormous real asset growth rates. That remarkable performance was continually underestimated by investors, and the stock outperformed the S&P 500 100-fold from 1970 to 1990.

In 1991, Wal-Mart's stock price implied no downward competitive fade in both CFROIs and real asset growth rates for the next five years.

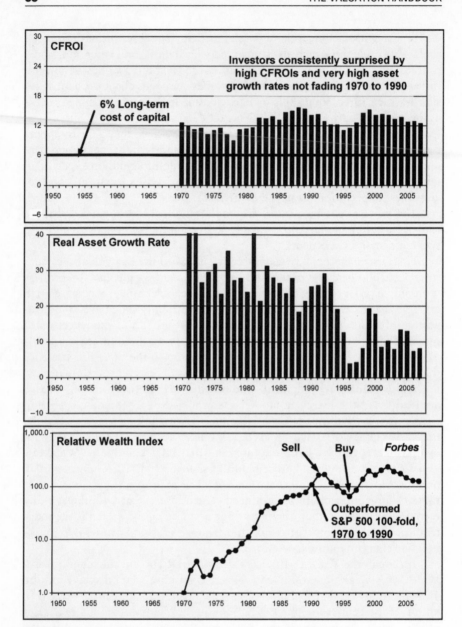

EXHIBIT 3.4   Wal-Mart Life Cycle Performance, 1970 to 2007
Source: Credit Suisse HOLT ValueSearch global database.

While possible, our experience suggested that, at its much bigger size relative to the 1970s and 1980s, Wal-Mart was unlikely to meet those extremely optimistic investor expectations. The stock subsequently underperformed the market substantially from 1991 to 1996 (see bottom panel of Exhibit 3.4) as CFROIs declined and asset growth sharply fell off.

At the time of the 1996 *Forbes* article, investor expectations were for Wal-Mart's CFROIs to rapidly fade downward over the next five years to a level close to the long-term corporate average of 6 percent CFROIs. We felt comfortable in betting against an expectation that Wal-Mart was on the verge of becoming an average firm. This time, the stock subsequently rose sharply more than the S&P 500 during the next three years as Wal-Mart handily beat the 1996 expectations.

Although it is convenient to distill investor expectations into a single best-estimate forecast, more rigorous analysis deals with warranted value as the expected value of a probability-weighted distribution of scenarios for future fade of economic returns and reinvestment rates (Alessandri, Ford, Lander, Leggio, and Taylor 2004).

To illustrate the concept of fade distribution, let's return to Exhibit 3.4 and reflect on the process that produced such extraordinary excess shareholder returns during the 1970s and 1980s. At various times during this period, I analyzed Wal-Mart and decided not to buy it because I viewed the probability as low for a scenario in which Wal-Mart would maintain high CFROIs while sustaining an extraordinarily high 25 percent per year organic asset growth rate. I was wrong. My mistake was in not sufficiently understanding Wal-Mart's business model and exceptional managerial skill, which enabled the firm to perform so spectacularly as to drive its chief competitor, Kmart, into bankruptcy.

BACK TO THE FUTURE

The life-cycle model is but one application of discounted cash flow that specifies a cause-and-effect relationship for (1) firms' economic performance, leading to a market valuation, and (2) investor expectations and the firm's subsequent economic performance, leading to excess (positive/negative) shareholder returns.

Whatever the life-cycle research program's contribution to knowledge is, it is the product of a different way of thinking and going about research as compared to mainstream practices. The life-cycle research process has always been grounded in data observations with a bottom-up, inductive path for its constructs (e.g., a market-derived discount rate, fade, etc.).

Because mainstream theory was not at the foundation of our work, the CAPM never had a top-down, deductive hold on our thinking and doing.

Believers in either CAPM or the life-cycle model can easily lose skepticism about what they think they know. The important point is that theory building often makes the most progress when problems are approached from new angles, where a healthy competition exists among alternative models, and when commitment is strong enough to actively search for situations where one's preferred model fails (Carlile and Christensen 2005). These attitudes, I submit, would serve well for the evolution of a powerful research program that could significantly improve our understanding of how firms' strategies, business processes, organizational structures, cultures, financing decisions, and the like produce the firms' long-term, net cash receipt streams—and how this gets reflected in levels and changes in stock prices over time.

Empirical testing of a large menu of different valuation models for overall usefulness would be most fruitful when applied to a broad range of environmental conditions and user circumstances. Testing valuation models with innovative research designs might produce strong-enough evidence to overcome deeply held beliefs (Atra and Thomas 2008).

In this way, theory building would increasingly become part of the process in which researchers continually loop through intensive data observations and measurement challenges coupled with ongoing deeper understanding of cause and effect. So, how to get from here to there?

Let's speculate on how finance academics, and both investment and corporate practitioners, could jointly evolve improved valuation models that better serve the practical needs of users. The foundation for just such a joint collaboration has already been laid with the Financial Management Association's recent start-up of the Practitioner Demand Driven Academic Research Initiative (PDDARI).[5]

PDDARI is coordinating an intellectual marketplace for ideas with the goal of expediting big advancements in finance theory that are of a high practical value. A major target is a new theory that integrates both risk/return and the level of firms' market valuations.

SEARCHING FOR FAILURES AND SUCCESSES

Searching for failures as well as successes can be the bridge needed for genuine collaboration among finance academics and those who work in the trenches (Heuer 1999).

As for environmental conditions and user circumstances, one classification system to consider would be the five categories briefly discussed next.

Firm Maturity

According to firm size and/or life cycle position, how much can different valuation models benefit from analyses of firms' historical financial data in order to make most likely or best-estimate forecasts of the input variables of the various models?

In addition, how capable are these models in handling risk in the numerator? That is, how does accuracy vary when historical data are used as part of a process for calculating the expected value of a probability-weighted distribution of potential scenarios for a firm's future profitability?

For example, consider a bullish scenario for an early-stage firm with a specified level of high economic returns and high reinvestment rates in the future. The historical frequency of achieving that level of economic performance for early-stage firms could be tabulated after certain milestones were delivered. A milestone could be one quarter of 25+ percent organic sales growth, or two back-to-back quarters of 25+ percent growth. This type of information could help assign a probability for a particular early-stage firm to achieve a bullish scenario. For the same early-stage firm, historical frequencies could be tabulated for a bearish scenario, giving consideration to the data on cash balances and product diversification in addition to sales growth. This perspective seems better suited for handling firms with low-probability/high-valuation impact scenarios compared to a simple, most likely estimate forecast of future profitability.

Industry

Users of models employing EVA, CFROI, or other metrics that stress economic performance accept that valuation accuracy improves after accounting data are adjusted to more closely mirror business economics. How does valuation accuracy vary across industries and across valuation models as different types of accounting adjustments are implemented? For a given industry, how does valuation model accuracy vary as the estimated proportion of intangibles in firms' economic assets changes and as asset life changes?

Model Users

Connecting firms' operating performance to market valuation is clearly important to investors, managements, boards of directors, and accounting rule makers. How well do models perform to meet the primary needs of each group? Government officials involved with wealth creation issues include managements of regulatory agencies as well as politicians and their staffs.

Policy decisions about corporate tax rates, personal tax rates, regulation, property rights, and the like impact a society's ability to create wealth. In what innovative ways can these macroeconomic policy lever variables be connected via valuation models to levels and changes in aggregate stock prices for countries over longer time periods?

Data

Value-relevant data sources include:

- *Market prices for ownership claims.* At points in time when firms could easily fall into bankruptcy, does the concurrent market price behavior of equity, debt, and options reveal fundamental weaknesses in how valuation models incorporate risk? Another question of interest is: Do the fat-tailed distributions of actual stock price changes lead to insights about the environmental (institutional) causes of firms' economic performance? At the macro level, Baumol (2002) argues convincingly that productive entrepreneurial activity is the dominant source of a society's wealth generation. Perhaps the conditions that favor more/less entrepreneurial activity set the stage for Schumpeter's creative destruction and result in an increase/decrease in the fat tails of a country's distribution of long-term shareholder returns (Fogel, Morck, and Yeung 2006).
- *Accounting data.* As intangible assets increase in importance (Corrado, Haltiwanger, and Sichel 2005), accounting rule makers and corporate executives are grappling with measuring and managing intangibles. Valuation models (including real options) could provide new empirical angles to help decide if an outlay (e.g., R&D expenditures) should be capitalized as an intangible asset and expensed (Hand and Lev 2003), and how best to do this (Healy, Myers, and Howe 2002). To handle this extremely difficult challenge, does it not make sense for academic researchers to join forces with CFOs and their staffs (those closest to the data)?
- *Human capital data.* Some intangibles are so soft and qualitative that they are not candidates for inclusion in reported accounting data. Many of the long-term benefits of human capital fit this category. For example, Toyota's efficiency seems to result not only from its lean production techniques, but also from its *culture* that promotes continuous learning and problem solving, with every layer of employees deeply involved, including top management (Liker and Hoseus 2008). Although quite difficult to measure, the effects of human capital improvements or degradations can be broadly observed in firms' long-term fade rates.

Creativity in developing new measuring sticks is needed. Hewitt Associates has taken a step in this direction by showing that a measure of firms' ability to attract and retain higher-grade (pivotal) employees correlates with *future* fade of CFROIs.[6]

Management Dynamics

At any point in time, management could be initiating improvements in strategy, core business processes, or corporate culture, yet the reported accounting data usually does not adequately reflect the value change at an early stage. For example, most valuation models have a component for the present value of future investments. But consider, for example, the potential misperception during the early stage of a firm's successful transformation to lean manufacturing. During this period, lean processes free up a great deal of capacity to enable management to pursue new opportunities without having to make the kind of capital outlays customary in its less efficient past. The resulting decrease in the asset growth rate could easily be misread as a reduction in new investment opportunities and a concomitant reduction in the warranted value of future investments. Alternatively, management could be asleep at the switch, as was the case for Kmart for many years, yet the reported accounting data did not reflect the extent of shareholder value deterioration. How do different valuation models fare in their quickness to pick up these big value changes? Given firm maturity and the type of high-priority initiatives that management has disclosed in the annual report, what signals are helpful in the early identification of the direction and magnitude of the value change?

CONCLUSION

To guide our actions so that we may achieve a goal, we develop models about how the world works. Straightforward as that may seem, any *future* knowledge-building process is made difficult by our *existing* knowledge assumptions. At any point in time, assumptions representing faulty concepts impact how we perceive the world, define problems, explore data, and generate hypotheses to test. Therefore, a significant challenge is to manage the personal biases that always exist, even if the researcher is not consciously aware of them. Leamer (1983, 36) summarized the challenge:

> *The econometric art as it is practiced at the computer terminal involves fitting many, perhaps thousands, of statistical models. One or several that the researcher finds pleasing are selected for*

reporting purposes. This searching for a model is often well intentioned, but there can be no doubt that such a specification search invalidates the traditional theories of inference. The concepts of unbiasedness, consistency, efficiency, maximum likelihood estimation, in fact, all the concepts of traditional theory, utterly lose their meaning by the time an applied researcher pulls from the bramble of computer output the one thorn of a model he likes best, the one he chooses to portray as a rose.

The new research program outlined in this chapter, keyed to searching for the failures as well as the successes of any model, holds the potential to gain knowledge by overcoming our personal biases. A better understanding of cause and effect throughout the wealth creation process will lead to better decisions for the long-term, mutual benefit of customers, employees, and shareholders.

Most especially, managements and boards of directors need better valuation tools in order to make the right long-term decisions. Their decisions may, at times, disappoint Wall Street's myopic fixation on quarterly earnings expectations. But managements should finally quit playing Wall Street's game. Managers should employ an insightful valuation model and value-relevant accounting information to make sure their decisions make economic sense (Madden 2007). Then, they need to clearly communicate to investors the rationale for their decisions.

NOTES

1. Friedman's (1953) methodology of positive economics promoted the view that the realism of assumptions is immaterial as long as the world behaves as if the assumptions were true. This gave added credibility to mathematical models such as CAPM, and deflected criticism of the use of empirically unsupported assumptions (Frankfurter and McGoun 1996).
2. For the period 1960 to 1996, aggregate U.S. industrial CFROIs approximated 6 percent real, and a market-derived real discount rate (cost of capital) also averaged approximately 6 percent real (Madden 1999, 92). For the nonfinancial sector, 1950 to 1996, Fama and French (1999) estimated the real cost of capital at 5.95 percent and the return on corporate assets, unadjusted for inflation, at 7.38 percent.
3. Especially difficult-to-forecast companies, such as biotech start-ups, should be excluded from the universe of companies used for the regression.
4. Starting in 2008, Taiwan companies are required to expense the cost of employee stock bonuses.
5. See www.fma.org/pddari/pddari.htm.
6. See www.evidence-basedmanagement.com/guests/ubelhart_jan07.html.

REFERENCES

Alessandri, Todd M., David N. Ford, Diane M. Lander, Karyl B. Leggio, and Marilyn Taylor. 2004. Managing risk and uncertainty in complex capital projects. *Quarterly Review of Economics and Finance* 44, no. 5 (December): 751–767.

Atra, Robert J., and Rawley Thomas. 2008. The fundamentals of automated DCF modeling. www.fma.org/texas/PDDARI/accepts.htm.

Baumol, William J. 2002. *The free-market innovation machine: Analyzing the growth miracle of capitalism.* Princeton, NJ: Princeton University Press.

Brealey, Richard A., Stewart C. Myers, and Franklin Allen. 2006. *Principles of corporate finance.* 8th ed. New York: McGraw-Hill Irwin.

Brief, Richard P., ed. 1986. *Estimating the economic rate of return from accounting data.* New York: Garland Publishing.

Carlile, Paul R., and Clayton Christensen. 2005. The cycles of theory building in management research, version 6.0. Harvard Business School Working Paper 05-057.

Corrado, Carol, John Haltiwanger, and Daniel Sichel. 2005. *Measuring capital in the new economy.* Chicago: University of Chicago Press.

Fabozzi, Frank J., Sergio M. Focardi, and Caroline Jonas. 2008. *Challenges in quantitative equity management.* Charlottesville, VA: Research Foundation of CFA Institute.

Fama, E. F., and K. R. French. 1999. The corporate cost of capital and the return on corporate investment. *Journal of Finance* 54, no. 6 (December): 1939–1967.

Fama, E. F., and K. R. French. 2000. Forecasting profitability and earnings. *Journal of Business* 73, no. 2 (April): 161–175.

Fama, E. F., and K. R. French. 2004. The capital asset pricing model: Theory and evidence. *Journal of Economic Perspectives* 18, no. 3 (Summer): 25–46.

Feltham, Gerald A., and James A. Ohlson. 1995. Valuation and clean surplus accounting for operating and financial activities. *Contemporary Accounting Review* 11(Spring): 689–731.

Feltham, Gerald A., and James A. Ohlson. 1996. Uncertainty resolution and the theory of depreciation measurement. *Journal of Accounting Research* 34 (Autumn): 209–234.

Fogel, Kathy, Randall Morck, and Bernard Yeung. 2006. Big business stability and economic growth: Is what's good for General Motors good for America? NBER Working Paper 12394.

Frankfurter, George M., and Elton G. McGoun. 1996. *Toward finance with meaning: The methodology of finance, what it is and what it can be.* Greenwich, CT: JAI Press.

Friedman, Milton. 1953. *Essays in positive economics.* Chicago: University of Chicago Press.

Hand, J., and B. Lev, eds. 2003. *Intangible assets: Values, measures, and risks.* London: Oxford University Press.

Haugen, Robert A. 1999. *The new finance: The case against efficient markets.* 2nd ed. Upper Saddle River, NJ: Prentice Hall.

Healy, Paul M., Stewart C. Myers, and Christopher D. Howe. 2002. R&D accounting and the tradeoff between relevance and objectivity. *Journal of Accounting Research* 40, no. 3 (June): 677–710.

Heuer, Richards J. 1999. *Psychology of intelligence analysis.* Washington, DC: Government Printing Office. Free download at www.cia.gov/library/center-for-the-study-of-intelligence/csi-publications/books-and-monographs/psychology-of-intelligence-analysis/psychofintelnew.pdf.

Larsen, Tom, and David Holland. 2008. Beyond earnings: A user's guide to excess return models and the HOLT CFROI® framework. In *Equity Valuation: Models from Leading Investment Banks,* ed. Jan Viebig, Thorsten Poddig, and Armin Varmaz.West Sussex, England: John Wiley & Sons.

Leamer, Edward E. 1983. Let's take the con out of econometrics. *American Economic Review* 73(1): 31–43.

Liker, Jeffrey K., and Michael Hoseus. 2008. *Toyota culture: The heart and soul of the Toyota way.* New York: McGraw-Hill.

Madden, Bartley J. 1991. A transactional approach to economic research. *Journal of Socio-Economics* 20(1): 57–71.

Madden, Bartley J. 1999. *CFROI valuation—A total system approach to valuing the firm.* Oxford: Butterworth-Heinemann.

Madden, Bartley J. 2005. *Maximizing shareholder value and the greater good.* Naperville, IL: LearningWhatWorks, Inc.

Madden, Bartley J. 2007. Guidepost to wealth creation: Value-relevant track records. *Journal of Applied Finance* 17, no. 2 (Fall/Winter): 102–114.

Ng, Chiew Leng, Viral Jhaveri, and Ron Graziano. 2006. HOLT Taiwan: Accounting for employee stock bonus. Credit Suisse HOLT, December 5.

Ohlson, James A. 1995. Earnings, book values, and dividends in equity valuation. *Contemporary Accounting Research* 11 (Spring): 661–687.

Perold, Andre F. 2004. The capital asset pricing model. *Journal of Economic Perspectives* 18, no. 3 (Summer): 3–24.

Samuels, Gary, 1996. "Follow the cash: HOLT Value Associates hated Wal-Mart in 1991. Its unique valuation system tells HOLT to love Wal-Mart now," *Forbes,* September 9.

Schumpeter, Joseph A. 1942. *Capitalism, socialism and democracy.* New York: Harper & Row.

Stigler, George. 1963. *Capital and rates of return in manufacturing industries.* Princeton, NJ: Princeton University Press.

Thaler, Richard H. 2005. *Advances in behavioral finance.* Vol. 2. Princeton, NJ: Princeton University Press.

Thomas, Rawley. 2002. Value management—Past, present, and future. Working paper, LifeCycle Returns. www.lcrt.com/value_management_past_present_future_3_19_02.pdf.

Umpleby, Stuart A., and Eric B. Dent. 1999. The origins and purposes of several traditions in systems theory and cybernetics. *Cybernetics and Systems: An International Journal* 30: 79–103.

Wiggins, R. R., and T. W. Ruefli. 2005. Schumpeter's ghost: Is hypercompetition making the best of times shorter? *Strategic Management Journal* 26 (10): 887–911.

CHAPTER 4

Comparing Valuation Models

Thomas E. Copeland, Ph.D.
Founder, Copeland Valuation Consultants

Herein I focus attention on a seemingly simple question: "Which valuation model is best?"[1] The marketplace, of course, determines the actual transaction prices of all types of assets in addition to companies—houses, automobiles, planes, racehorses, gems, artwork, first editions, and so forth. But the current market price can deviate from the fundamentals in the short run. Valuation models claim to provide equilibrium or intrinsic value estimates. How does one decide which valuation model is best?

A classic valuation approach has been to find a comparable asset that has traded recently and to adjust the comparable's trading price to that of the asset being valued by scaling with an alleged value driver such as earnings. Unfortunately, while one-carat flawless diamonds are close substitutes to each other, a company in the chemicals industry with $5 billion of annual sales that grows at 4 percent a year may not be even vaguely similar to another chemical company with $50 million of sales that has been growing at 12 percent, even though their current earnings might be similar. In the past 70 years or so, comparables have been replaced with various discounted cash flow (DCF) models. Are they any better than comparables? How should one decide?

The measure of the quality of a valuation model depends on its intended use. For legal purposes, such as taxation, inheritance, and division of property, one may judge the quality of a valuation by the magnitude of the difference between the model value and the market (or trading) value of a company—a measure of the *goodness of fit*. The smaller the difference, the better the model is. I will use various statistics to put this concept to use later on in the chapter.

However, for the purpose of investment, I suggest that in order to compare valuation models, it does not matter what the difference (or error term) is between the model and the market value. In fact, a perfect fit would be useless for the purpose of investment. Neither does the correlation between the two values make a difference, nor do the slope and intercept of a cross-sectional regression equation. What does make a difference is the *time series convergence* between them. In particular, does the market price move toward the model price? If it does, then the model has some economic validity; and, by the way, the market is not instantaneously efficient. The better model provides the more useful information. Said information has value only if the set of state-contingent actions that result from its acquisition result in higher payout (or utility) than the next best alternative.

After a brief review of the literature, I describe the discounted cash flow approach for valuation of a company, and introduce an expert system that I developed in order to supply valuations for sample sets of company monthly observations that are in the thousands. Its virtue is that it performs detailed DCF valuations very quickly—in less than five seconds per company. Thereafter, I test the goodness of fit and the time series convergence that are provided by various valuation approaches, including ratios, simple formulas, and the DCF model as estimated by the expert system. I find that the convergence property of the DCF valuation model is positive and statistically significant. It is the best of the models compared in this chapter, but not by a wide margin.

LITERATURE REVIEW

Very few comparisons of valuation models of companies have been published. Kaplan and Ruback (1995) used an adjusted present value (APV) model to estimate the market value of 51 highly leveraged transactions (HLTs), then compared the error rates of their APV estimates with the error rates of valuations derived from multiples of comparable companies. This goodness of fit approach concluded that the APV model valuations had error rates at least as small as valuations that used multiples. Results showed that the model explained around 70 percent of the cross-sectional variation in market price scaled by book value. Bailey (1991) used an option pricing corporate equity valuation model in a horse race with a discounted cash flow model to see which came closer to explaining the market values of rubber plantations in Malaysia and Singapore. He reasoned that the plantations resembled switching options because when the price of oil was high relative to natural rubber for the production of close substitutes such as pencil erasers, the rubber plantations would harvest natural rubber from their trees. When the price of oil was low, the rubber plantations were shut down. It was among the first papers to directly compare the traditional DCF approach with an option-pricing approach to the valuation of companies. Bailey found that the option approach had smaller error terms than the DCF approach. Copeland, Koller, and Murrin (1994) regressed analyst-generated discounted cash flow estimates (in 1988) of the values of a set of 35 large industrial companies against their market values and found an r-squared of 94 percent. The regression was repeated in 1999 for 31 survivors from the original set and the r-squared was 92 percent. This is also a type of goodness of fit comparison.

This body of evidence is based on relatively small samples, mainly due to the fact that it is a time-intensive effort to use DCF to value even a single company. For example, in an interview with a top Wall Street analyst, I was told that an experienced analyst required four to eight hours to complete a standard DCF valuation. An additional problem was that analysts within the same securities analysis group often failed to apply the same interpretation of the standard DCF methodology.

A major concern with the publications discussed earlier is that none of these comparisons reported time series (or convergence) behavior concerning the null hypothesis that the information content of the valuation model for the purpose of investment is, in fact, zero. They studied goodness of fit but not time series behavior. Later in the chapter I show that the standard DCF model exhibits biases in its goodness of fit that are associated with revenue growth and stock price volatility. Goodness of fit seems to be marginally improved when one uses option pricing parameters to adjust the DCF valuation. Convergence is also improved if the DCF model bias is corrected.

BRIEF DESCRIPTION OF THE VALUATION MODELS THAT ARE COMPARED

The time-worn and traditional approach to valuation, still used by Wall Street analysts and investment bankers, is a multiples approach that selects a value driver that is deemed appropriate to the value of a company, then ratios it to the market price of comparable companies. One common example of a multiple is the average of the comparable's market price per share divided by their earnings before interest, taxes, depreciation, and amortization (EBITDA):

$$\text{Market value}_t = (\text{EBITDA multiple}_t)[E_t(\text{EBITDA}_{t+1})] \qquad (4.1)$$

Often EBITDA_{t+1} is the expected number for the company being valued, denoted in Equation 4.1 as E(EBITDA). Other multiples are the price-earnings ratio, a market-to-book ratio, and a multiple of revenue:

$$
\begin{aligned}
\text{Market value per share}_{t+1} &= (\text{Price per share}_t/\text{Net income per share}_t) \\
&\quad \times E(\text{Net income per share}_{t+1}) \\
&= (\text{Price per share}_t/\text{Book value of equity per share}_t) \\
&\quad \times E(\text{Per share book value of equity}_{t+1}) \\
&= (\text{Price per share}_t/\text{Revenue per share}_t) \\
&\quad \times E(\text{Revenue per share}_{t+1})
\end{aligned}
$$

Sometimes the ratios are industry specific, such as the population passed by a length of cable in the telecommunications industry (called POPs). All of the aforementioned are referred to as multiples.

For a long time, before the advent of computerized spreadsheets in the 1980s, discounted cash flow models were based on simple mathematical formulas. Two examples are the cash flow perpetuity and the dividend growth model. We will use both. The perpetuity model is the present value of a constant infinite annuity. Implied in it is the assumption that the return on invested capital and the cost of capital of a company are equal to each other. Therefore, while earnings may grow, the growth adds nothing to the value of the company.

Perpetuity model:

$$
V = E(FCF)/WACC \tag{4.2}
$$

Here, we define V as the value of the entity being valued. The definition of expected free cash flows is the expectation of earnings before interest and taxes $E(EBIT)$ multiplied by 1 minus the tax rate that the firm would have if it had no debt. The weighted average cost of capital (WACC) is the weighted average of the marginal costs of the firm's debt and equity financing. To convert the entity values of equations (4.2) and (4.3) and the entity DCF value to equity values, I added excess marketable securities, and subtracted debt and other liabilities (e.g., unfunded pension plans).

A slightly more sophisticated discounted cash flow formula allows one to account for the fact that often cash flows grow and contribute to value because they earn a return on invested capital that exceeds the firm's WACC. It is called the Gordon growth model, and it provides higher estimates of value.

Growth model:

$$
V = E(FCF)(1+g)/(WACC - g), \text{ given that } WACC > g \tag{4.3}
$$

Finally, there is the discounted cash flow (DCF) model. It is only slightly more sophisticated than the perpetuity and growth models. Generally, it uses a spreadsheet model of the expected free cash flows of the firm, given an explicit forecast for five to ten years, followed by either the perpetuity or growth models that estimate the so-called continuing value (CV) of the firm, which is nothing more than the present value of cash flows from the end of the explicit forecast period to infinity. The CV as a percentage of the total value often exceeds 50 percent.

The DCF approach is more sophisticated than the others because: (1) it is founded on cash flows that are derived from both income statement and balance sheet information, (2) it appropriately accounts for the opportunity cost of capital (debt and equity), and (3) it reflects the timing of cash flows within the explicit forecast period.

AN EXPERT SYSTEM THAT DOES VALUATION

All tests of valuation models have had relatively small sample size, and have been done by hand. I wanted large sample size. In an attempt to have a tool that does a complete discounted cash flow valuation quickly, I developed an expert system. It produces the set of outputs that are illustrated in this chapter's appendix for Intel in 2008. All together there are 14 exhibits on 16 pages of output.

1. Market and DCF price history.
2. Valuation summary.
3. Value driver summary.
4. Revenue growth forecast.
5. Operating margin forecast.
6. Net property, plant, and equipment.
7. Operating working capital.
8. Weighted average cost of capital.
9–10. Income statement.
11–12. Balance sheet.
13. NOPLAT and taxes on EBIT.
14. Free cash flows and financial flows.
15. Invested capital.
16. Continuing value.

The data is read in, the calculations are performed, and then output tables are filled—all in less than five seconds per company. It is possible, therefore, to study a large sample of consistently executed DCF valuations. Later in the chapter, I attempt to assess whether the DCFs produced by the expert system are any good—a separate question.

An expert system is a process that inputs facts and uses rules to produce a solution about some particular problem domain. In this case, our system is a consistent set of decision rules that produces an estimate of the market value of a company. The system loads historical company-specific and market data, performs a historical analysis, estimates a weighted average cost of capital, forecasts short-term and long-term free cash flows based on analyst forecasts and extrapolation, and derives a continuing value estimate. The system was developed using data from 1994. Tests were run on out-of-sample data between 1995 and 2000, and separately on a sample from 2000 to 2008.

An expert system mimics human expertise at much lower cost. While true experts are scarce, expensive, and hard to duplicate, an expert system can be widely distributed and easily duplicated. An expert system can exceed human capacity in both speed and accuracy. While a living expert spends at least four hours to value a company, an expert system can produce answers with similar accuracy in a few seconds. The expert system is flexible, and one can even use a neural network to train it and solve more complicated problems.

As input to the expert system, I used historical accounting statements and credit ratings from Compustat, estimates of beta (from Compustat and Value Line), market information about the risk-free rate and credit spread (Federal Reserve Board), an estimate of the market risk premium (Ibbotson), and analyst forecasts of revenue growth, operating margin, and capital expenditures—for the current year, the second year of the forecast period, and three to five years out.

I used the DCF model that is found in *Valuation: Measuring and Managing the Value of Companies, 2nd Edition* (1994) by Copeland, Koller, and Murrin. Free cash flows to the entity are defined there as earnings before interest and cash taxes (i.e., the tax the firm would pay if it had no debt), plus depreciation, less capital expenditures and increases in operating working capital. Taxes are assessed at the marginal *cash* tax rate (i.e., the rate the firm would pay on its EBIT if it had no debt). The expected free cash flows of the firm are discounted back to the present using a weighted average cost of capital (WACC) based on the capital asset pricing model (CAPM). I used Compustat or Value Line betas. The risk-free rate was defined as the 10-year yield to maturity on U.S. Treasuries. The market risk premium was 5.5 percent in all years and based on the long-term arithmetic average market risk premium, less 2 percent survivorship bias. The continuing value formula was chosen by the expert system to be one of the following three formulas:

$$CV = NOPLAT_{11}(1 - g/ROIC)/(WACC - g) \text{ growth formula} \qquad (4.4)$$

$$CV = NOPLAT_{11}/WACC \text{ perpetuity formula} \qquad (4.5)$$

(assumes : ROIC = WACC)

$$CV = NOPLAT_{11}/ku + TB + K(NOPLAT_{11})N[(ROIC - WACC)/ \atop WACC(1 + WACC) \text{ finite supernormal growth formula}^2} \quad (4.6)$$

The perpetuity formula assumes that the firm's return on invested capital (ROIC) equals its weighted average cost of capital (WACC) every year beyond the explicit forecast period (usually 10 years). Of the three choices, it produces the lowest continuing value estimate. At the opposite extreme is the "value driver", or growth formula. It assumes that ROIC will perpetually exceed WACC by a constant spread, and that g (growth) is financed by retaining K percent of free cash flows, where $K = g/ROIC$. The intermediate alternative assumes that the spread between ROIC and WACC closes over a T-year interval. The larger the spread at the end of the explicit forecast period, the larger is the adjustment interval, T.

The expert system chooses among these three alternatives by examining return on invested capital forecasts. If the forecasted ROIC is greater than the weighted average cost of capital by the same margin as in the past, the expert system assumes that the spread is structural and proceeds to use the value driver formula. If the ROIC appears to be trending toward the WACC or to be unsustainable, the expert system uses the finite supernormal approach. Finally, if the ROIC has been and is forecasted to remain close to the WACC, the expert system uses the perpetuity formula.

Exhibit 4.1 shows a simplified flow chart for the expert system. It illustrates the inputs to the program, the logic flow, and the outputs. Although the expert system is ad hoc, it does reflect the experience of the valuation expert who built it, and it can be revised after testing to provide better goodness of fit results. There is no harm in efforts to revise the model so that it provides tighter fits to the actual market data. However, when it comes to efforts to improve the time series relationship between the model and the market, it is important to avoid a specification search. It is improper to test the model on historical data, then retest a revised model on the same data, and to do so iteratively until a successful model is finally found.

The flow of logic in the expert system is quite standard. It begins with data inputs as described earlier—for example, financial statements that go back for at least five and as long as 10 years. The program then executes a series of forecasting routines (called "forecast engines") that delve into revenue growth, operating margin, and capital expenditure forecasts whose validity is checked by comparing them with industry median forecasts of their closest industry and with long-term expectations of economic growth. Next, the weighted average cost of capital and the

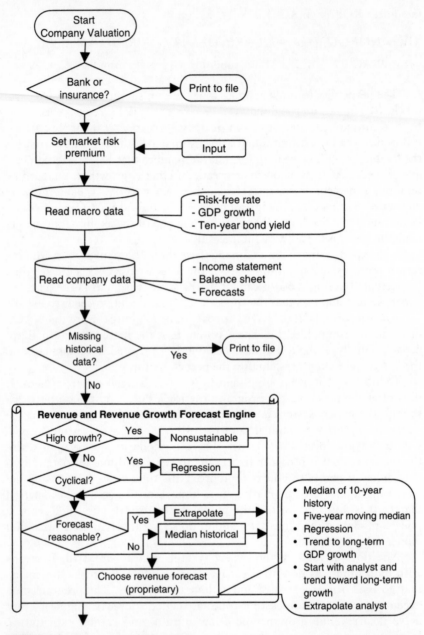

EXHIBIT 4.1 Expert System Flowchart

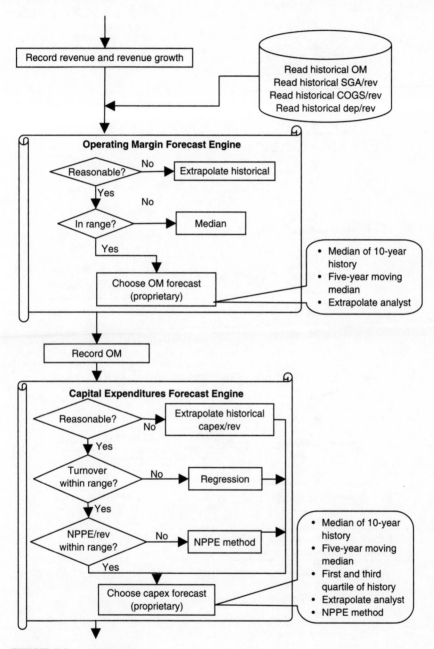

EXHIBIT 4.1 *(Continued)*

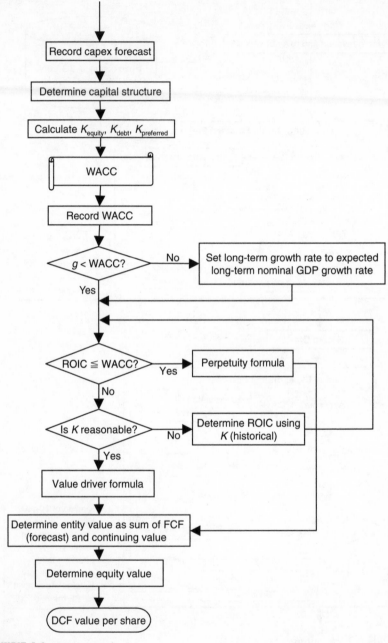

EXHIBIT 4.1 (*Continued*)

continuing value are estimated. The final step is to estimate the entity value of operations, add marketable securities, and subtract the estimated market value of debt in order to derive the final result—an estimate of the market value of the firm.

In the test results, we worked hard to search for the expert system that minimized the percentage error between the live (industry-specific) market price as of a given date and the model-estimated price on the same date. We did so before testing the portfolio performance of the stocks chosen by the model. Later, we used out-of-period (i.e., holdout) data.

GOODNESS OF FIT: INITIAL SAMPLE (1,395 VALUATIONS 1993 TO 2000)

The first of two sample universes was the Standard & Poor's 500 companies from 1993 to 2000. Exhibit 4.2 shows that companies were excluded because they were financial firms (wrong industry) or utilities (types of companies not handled by the expert system), because there was missing data, because the valuation was out of range (negative equity value), or because the book value of equity was negative. These exclusions reduced the sample size from 4,000 company observations to 1,395. Nevertheless, this sample is 26 times the largest sample published to date.

EXHIBIT 4.2   Sample Size, 1993–2000

Year	1993	1994	1995	1996	1997	1998	1999	2000	Total
Original sample	500	500	500	500	500	500	500	500	4,000
Missing data	217	212	198	193	176	139	124	121	1,380
Wrong industry	105	107	114	112	112	117	123	124	914
Out of range	31	31	30	29	21	40	48	24	254
Negative book value	10	10	8	6	7	5	7	4	57
Sample size	137	140	150	160	184	199	198	227	1,395
Percent usable	34%	28%	28%	30%	37%	40%	40%	45%	35%

Error Terms

The error terms are defined in percentages of the market price as:

$$\text{Error}_t = (\text{Model price per share}_{t+1} - \text{Market price per share}_t)/ \quad (4.7)$$
$$(\text{Market price per share}_t)$$

The distribution of error terms is provided in Exhibit 4.3. This result is encouraging. It can be said that roughly 83 percent of the companies that were valued had errors between 0 and plus or minus 50 percent of their market value.

Cross-Section Regressions

I applied several different goodness of fit criteria using cross-section data. In addition to the distribution of error terms in Exhibit 4.3, I looked at

EXHIBIT 4.3   Distribution of Error Terms, 1993–2000

Year	E≤15%	15% <E≤25%	25%< E≤50%	50% <E ≤100%	100% <E ≤200%	E>200%
1993	49	42	36	8	1	1
	36%	31%	26%	6%	1%	1%
1994	27	52	53	6	2	0
	19%	37%	38%	4%	1%	0%
1995	41	20	36	28	13	10
	28%	14%	24%	19%	9%	7%
1996	46	50	47	8	4	2
	29%	32%	30%	5%	3%	1%
1997	49	65	43	9	11	4
	27%	36%	24%	5%	6%	2%
1998	54	44	55	22	15	5
	28%	23%	28%	11%	8%	3%
1999	45	54	67	17	10	2
	23%	28%	34%	9%	5%	1%
2000	54	44	46	31	35	11
	24%	20%	21%	14%	16%	5%
Average percent	27%	28%	28%	9%	6%	3%
Cumulative percent	27%	55%	83%	92%	98%	100%

The error terms are for the absolute value of (DCF – Market)/Market.

regressions of the market value of equity divided by the book value of equity versus the DCF model value of equity divided by its book value; see equation (4.8). I also looked at the per share values; see equation (4.9).

$$(\text{Model value of equity}/\text{Book value})_t = \\ a + b(\text{Market value of equity}/\text{Book value})_t \quad (4.8)$$

$$\text{Model price}/\text{Book price} = a + b(\text{Market price}/\text{Book price}) \quad (4.9)$$

A perfect fit happens if the intercept term is not significantly different from zero, if the slope is not significantly different from 1, and if the r-squared is 1. Actual results are in Exhibit 4.4, which provides the cross-section regression results for equation (4.8).

The error terms in Exhibit 4.3 provide the absolute value of the percent error for various ranges. For example, in 1993 there were 49 observations where the percent error was between plus or minus 15 percent. This was 36 percent of the total of 137 observations that year. In the second column of Exhibit 4.3 are the 42 observations that represent errors between an absolute value of 15 and 25 percent. The third column gives all errors between −25 percent and −50 percent as well as those between 15 percent and 25 percent. The next to last row averages these percentages across the years, and the last row sums them. For example, 83 percent of the sample had errors of absolute value less than 50 percent.

In the ordinary least squares (OLS) regressions of Exhibit 4.4, all but one of the constant terms are significantly higher than zero, and three of

EXHIBIT 4.4 Goodness of Fit: S&P 500 Cross-Section Regression (OLS and Robust) for Market/Book versus DCF/Book

Year	OLS Constant	OLS T-statistic (vs. zero)	OLS Slope	OLS T-statistic (vs. 1)	OLS R-squared	Robust Constant	Robust Slope
1993	1.04	3.94	0.90	−1.65*	.60	1.50	0.65
1994	−0.31	−1.34*	1.57	9.70	.84	1.36	0.69
1995	0.96	5.05	0.85	−4.09	.78	1.56	0.56
1996	1.70	7.11	0.72	−5.74	.60	1.39	0.71
1997	1.94	6.02	0.69	−7.74	.68	1.41	0.76
1998	1.02	2.36	0.92	−1.28*	.55	0.74	0.77
1999	1.00	2.15	1.06	0.85*	.56	0.38	0.99
2000	2.12	5.89	0.52	−9.47	.32	0.90	0.50

The average r-squared is 62% and the median is 60%. An asterisk (*) indicates insignificance.

eight of the slope estimates are not statistically different from 1.0. These results are largely corroborated by the robust regressions that are discussed next. This is not good news for the DCF valuations done by the expert system. Slopes that are too low and intercepts that are too high usually imply a missing variable or an equation misspecification.

A second cross-sectional test was based on robust regression. The motivation for so doing was to accept the empirical fact that the distribution of residuals in the standard linear regressions is not normally distributed as is assumed when one employs a standard OLS regression. Robust regression makes no such distributional assumptions and produces more general results. It is accomplished by randomly selecting pairs of observations from the universe of pairs in the data sample. Next, it calculates the slope and intercept of each pair and rank-orders them. The median slope and intercept are then used as asymptotically unbiased estimates of the true intercept and slope for the cross-sectional relationship between the two variables. (See Exhibit 4.4.) In all eight years, the intercepts were positive, and the slope coefficients were less than 1.0.

TESTS OF DCF IN A HOLDOUT SAMPLE (NEW SAMPLE 2000–2008)

Now I use a second sample, a holdout sample of over 70,000 valuations done between January 2000 and July 2008. I wanted to use a holdout sample because the DCF model was developed and tested during the earlier time interval (1993–2000), and was not fit to the data in the holdout sample (2000–2008). Consequently, there is no chance of performing a specification search, where various models are tried on the same data set until a good fit turns up. Before explaining convergence, let's look at the goodness of fit for this new sample.

Exhibit 4.5 describes the data set. Starting with a universe of the S&P 900, observations were dropped because data was missing, because the company was financial (wrong industry), because the DCF was out of range (negative), or because the company had negative book value. From a possible 93,600 observations, the sample actually included 69,429.

Goodness of Fit

Exhibit 4.6 provides the first goodness of fit statistic, namely the distribution of error terms measured as the DCF value minus the market value, all divided by the market value. In this case, 51.9 percent of the error terms fell

EXHIBIT 4.5 Sample Size, 2000–2008

	2000	2001	2002	2003	2004	2005	2006	2007	2008	Total
Original sample	900	900	900	900	900	900	900	900	900	93,600
Missing data	201	176	162	151	150	151	153	150	99	16,429
Wrong industry	25	32	40	43	47	53	56	60	75	4,818
Out of range	24	20	22	19	15	16	16	18	23	1,985
Negative book value	9	10	9	15	8	5	7	10	6	939
Sample size	642	661	667	673	680	674	668	662	696	69,429
Percent usable	71%	73%	74%	75%	76%	75%	74%	74%	77%	74%

The sample size reported for each year is the average monthly sample size during that year. The total column reports the size of the entire sample in aggregate.

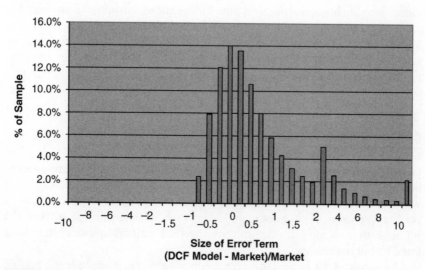

EXHIBIT 4.6 Distribution of Error Terms for DCF Valuations, 2000–2008

EXHIBIT 4.7   Goodness of Fit: S&P 900 Cross-Section Regression for DCF/Book versus Market/Book

	OLS	OLS	OLS	OLS	OLS
	Constant	T-statistic (vs. zero)	Slope	T-statistic (vs. 1)	R-squared
2000	3.07	5.59	0.83	−2.86	0.16
2001	4.26	18.74	0.90	−3.36	0.34
2002	3.03	17.44	1.18	10.31	0.63
2003	1.75	14.36	1.20	13.01	0.68
2004	1.20	12.42	1.08	5.55	0.65
2005	2.27	36.26	0.73	−32.37	0.71
2006	0.06	0.86*	1.23	23.55	0.83
2007	−0.77	−7.67	1.48	55.09	0.89
2008	1.07	7.14	1.43	23.41	0.76

An asterisk(*) indicates insignificance.

between plus or minus 50 percent of the market value. Later we compare this with the error terms of two other valuation methods, namely the market-to-book ratio and the perpetuity model.

Exhibit 4.7 shows the cross-section regression results, a second goodness of fit criterion. The dependent variable is the model price divided by the book value, and the independent variable is the market value divided by the book value. All 12 months are pooled each year. In all but one year, the intercept is significantly different from zero and the slope is significantly different from 1. It was less than 1.0 in three of nine years. These results would lead one to reject the DCF approach as a reasonable fit.

CONVERGENCE TESTS

Convergence tests are of interest because they focus on the predictive ability of signals generated by the DCF model. Basically, we are interested in whether the DCF value of the equity of a company is a leading indicator of the market value of that company. If no such relationship exists, then the message that is being transmitted by the DCF valuation model may be a good fit but is valueless.

Equation 4.10 is an OLS regression where the independent variable is the gap between the model DCF value and the actual market value in the current time period as a percentage of the market value. The dependent variable is the closure of the gap by movement in the actual market value a time period later, scaled by the market value at the start of the period.

$$(\text{Closure at } t + 1)/(\text{Market at } t) = a + b(\text{Gap at } t)/(\text{Market at } t) \quad (4.10)$$

where
$$\text{Gap at } t = \text{Model at } t - \text{Market at } t$$
$$\text{Closure at } t + 1 = \text{Market at } t + 1 - \text{Market at } t$$

We expect that if the intercept, a, is equal to zero and the slope, b, is equal to 1, the market price is adjusting toward the model price perfectly within one time period. The simple algebra is:

$$(\text{Market at } t + 1 - \text{Market at } t)/(\text{Market at } t)$$
$$= a + b(\text{Model at } t - \text{Market at } t)/(\text{Market at } t)$$

and if $a = 0$ and $b = 1$, then:

$$\text{Market at } t + 1 = \text{Model at } t$$

In other words, the market price adjusts during the period toward the model price at the beginning of the period. If the intercept a is significantly different from 0.0, there is bias in the estimated regression equation. If the coefficient of closure is between zero and one ($0 < b < 1$), then there is partial adjustment during the time period, and if the slope b is significantly greater than zero, the adjustment is statistically significant.

One often hears the comment that convergence is nothing more than a proxy for the rate of return. Nothing could be further from the truth. Return is the change in the market price (plus dividends) over a time period divided by the starting market price. If the price goes up, the return is positive; and if it goes down, the return is negative. Convergence is the adjustment in the market price toward the DCF estimate at the beginning of the period. For example, if the market price starts the period higher than the DCF estimate at the beginning of the period, then falls toward it, there is convergence, and the rate of return is also positive because downward convergence is accompanied by a short position. Thus, while convergence of the market price toward the model price is always a good thing, it is not the same thing as the realized rate of return from a long-only position.

A more extensive form of equation (4.10) uses a multiple regression with up to six closure intervals (i.e., up to six months). See Exhibit 4.8, Panel B.

Exhibit 4.8 is the summary of over 800 individual company regressions run on data spanning one, two, and up to six months, for the time interval between January 2000 and July 2008. Panel A shows the

EXHIBIT 4.8   Convergence of the DCF Model

Panel A: Regressions over a Single Time Period (1, 2, . . . , 6 Months)

Time Interval	Number of Observations	% of $b < 0$	% of $b > 0$	% of b with t-stat > 2.0	% of $a > 0$	% of a with t-stat > 2.0
One month	928	21.1%	78.9%	21.4%	58.5%	12.5%
Two months	897	29.4%	70.6%	16.0%	46.8%	6.4%
Three months	893	31.1%	68.9%	17.4%	52.7%	6.2%
Four months	890	31.3%	68.7%	14.4%	55.4%	7.3%
Five months	882	31.1%	68.9%	16.3%	55.0%	7.2%
Six months	879	30.7%	69.3%	14.4%	54.6%	7.5%

Panel B: Regressions over Multiple One-Month Time Periods

Months	Number of Observations	% of $b < 0$	% of $b > 0$	% of b with t-stat > 2.0	% of $a > 0$	% of a with t-stat > 2.0
1–2/mo. 1st mo.	897	29.4%	70.6%	16.0%	60.3%	11.8%
1–2/mo. 2nd mo.		47.3%	52.7%	6.4%		
1–3/mo. 1st mo.	893	31.1%	68.9%	17.4%	59.9%	12.9%
1–3/mo. 2nd mo.		47.3%	52.7%	6.2%		
1–3/mo. 3rd mo.		59.2%	40.8%	4.4%		
1–4/mo. 1st	890	31.1%	68.7%	14.4%	58.2%	12.7%
1–4/mo. 2nd		44.6%	55.4%	7.3%		
1–4/mo. 3rd		59.9%	40.1%	4.8%		
1–4/mo. 4th		46.0%	54.0%	9.6%		
1–5/mo. 1st	882	31.1%	68.9%	16.3%	57.4%	11.7%
1–5/mo. 2nd		45.0%	55.0%	7.2%		
1–5/mo. 3rd		58.6%	41.4%	3.6%		
1–5/mo. 4th		49.2%	50.8%	7.6%		
1–5/mo. 5th		44.7%	55.3%	8.2%		
1–6/mo. 1st	879	30.7%	69.3%	14.4%	57.0%	10.0%
1–6/mo. 2nd		45.4%	54.6%	7.5%		
1–6/mo. 3rd		59.3%	40.7%	4.5%		
1–6/mo. 4th		48.0%	52.0%	7.4%		
1–6/mo. 5th		50.5%	49.5%	6.7%		
1–6/mo. 6th		45.3%	54.7%	7.1%		

magnitude of the intercept and the slope coefficient that measures the speed of adjustment in closing the gap between the beginning of period model value and the market value. The fourth column is the percentage of the regressions with positive measures of b, the coefficient of convergence in equation (4.10). Convergence between zero and 1.0 indicates that the market price moves toward the model price over the period, but only partially. A coefficient of 1.0 indicates full adjustment, and if greater than 1.0, it indicates overadjustment. Note, however, that coefficients greater than 1.0 are rare. In Panel A, 78.9 percent of the convergence coefficients are positive during the first month and 21.4 percent of them are significantly greater than zero, where one would expect only 5 percent to be significant by chance. Note also, that the percentage of positive convergence coefficients is greatest for one month, then declines as the time interval lengthens, until for a six-month adjustment interval only 69.3 percent of the adjustment coefficients are positive, and of those 14.4 percent have t-statistics greater than 2.0. The majority (58.5 percent) of the intercept terms are positive (Panel A, column 6), and 12.5 percent are significantly greater than zero. One may conclude from the test of convergence in Exhibit 4.8, Panel A, that the market price does, in fact, adjust to the model price. Therefore, the model is not without value, and the market (before considering transaction costs) is not instantaneously efficient.

Panel B of Table 4.8 looks at the convergence differently because it is a multiple regression with a separate one-month interval of adjustment for each set of months from two to six.

First, note that the percent of positive convergence coefficients for month 1 is no less than 68.7 percent and no more than 70.6 percent, regardless of the number of adjustment terms in the multiple regression—a narrow range. Furthermore, this one-month convergence is statistically significant in no less than 14.4 percent and no more than 17.4 percent of the regressions, where by chance one would expect it to be significantly positive 5 percent of the time. Finally, the intercept terms in Panel B are positive in the multiple regressions between 57.0 percent and 60.3 percent of the time, and are significantly positive in between 10.0 percent and 12.9 percent of the regressions—again, statistically significant.

In sum, the empirical test of convergence of market prices toward the DCF estimated by an expert system indicates that convergence is statistically significant, although biased. In a world without costly information or transaction costs, this result would imply market inefficiency. I cannot make such a claim in this chapter, because I have not introduced either cost into my tests of the model.

STRAW MAN HORSE RACES (COMPARISON OF THREE MODELS)

I have no DCF model other than the standard methodology found embedded in the aforementioned expert system; therefore, I develop two straw men to illustrate how models may be compared with each other using goodness of fit and convergence as criteria. It turns out that goodness of fit and convergence are quite different among the various approaches to valuation.

Defining the Straw Men

The first straw man, and the most naive, is the value estimate that re-sults when the sector median market-price-to-book-value (M/B) ratio is multiplied by the current book value of a given company to estimate its market value.

The second straw man uses the perpetuity version of the continuing value formula from the DCF model as of the current year. There is no at-tempt to forecast cash flows during an explicit forecast period. Instead, I feed the relevant valuation parameters into the perpetuity model. Those pa-rameters are (1) earnings before interest and taxes next year times 1 minus the corporate cash tax rate and (2) the weighted average cost of capital. I do not use the value driver formula because too many observations are lost due to the requirement that the company's weighted average cost of capital must be higher than its growth rate.

Goodness of Fit

To test their goodness of fit, I produced histograms of the error rates of all three methods that are competing in the statistics horse race. See Exhibit 4.9 and Exhibit 4.10, where the results are summarized. In Exhibit 4.11, I pro-vide the results of cross-section regressions of the model/book versus the market/book.

If the distribution of errors were the only relevant criterion, then we might conclude that the market-to-book ratio is the model that has the most estimates close to the market value. It has 69.4 percent within plus or minus 50 percent of the market value, while the DCF model has only 52 per-cent and the perpetuity model has only 18.6 percent. However, if we broaden the relevant range to plus or minus 100 percent, the ranking of the three models changes. Although the market/book model still has the highest percent in range (91.5 percent), the second best is the perpetuity model

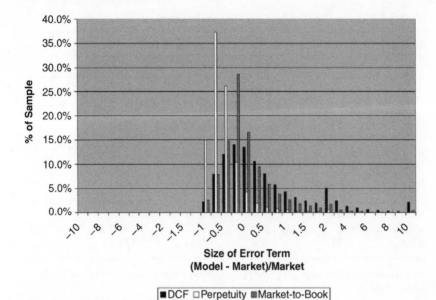

EXHIBIT 4.9 Distributions of Error Terms for Market-to-Book Valuations: Error Rate Histograms of Valuation Methods

(83 percent), and DCF is worst (79.5 percent). What drives these changes in rank? Looking at the histograms in Exhibit 4.9, we see that there is considerable skewness in the distribution of errors. It distorts the interpretation of the results. The perpetuity model is badly skewed toward undervaluation (negative errors).

Goodness of fit can also be measured by cross-section regressions of the model/book ratio against the market/book ratio. As was explained earlier, one would expect a perfect model to have an intercept of zero and a slope of 1.0. Exhibit 4.11 provides the results for the data sample covering the perpetuity and market/book models for the 2000–2008 time period. Exhibit 4.7 has the DCF results. If this were the test of the DCF valuation model, it

EXHIBIT 4.10 Summary of Error Rates for Three Models

	Multiple of Book	DCF (Expert System)	Perpetuity
% > 0	29.6	50.1	6.9
−50 < % < 50	69.4	52.0	18.6
−100 < % < 100	91.5	79.5	83.0

EXHIBIT 4.11   Goodness of Fit, Cross-Section Regressions

Panel A: Perpetuity Mode/Book. versus Market/Book 2000–2008

	OLS	OLS	OLS	OLS	OLS
	Constant	T-statistic (vs. zero)	Slope	T-statistic (vs. 1)	R-squared
2000	1.19	50.43	0.12	−351.74	0.49
2001	0.63	21.29	0.33	−173.51	0.71
2002	0.82	28.85	0.30	−244.98	0.78
2003	0.91	32.07	0.29	−196.82	0.70
2004	0.19	9.51	0.41	−195.31	0.85
2005	−1.10	−27.02	0.79	−39.32	0.86
2006	−0.01	−0.64	0.47	−173.52	0.87
2007	0.22	9.08	0.40	−283.33	0.90
2008	0.53	14.87	0.44	−121.49	0.82

Panel B: Sector Market/Book prior period versus Market/Book current period, 2000–2008

	OLS	OLS	OLS	OLS	OLS
	Constant	T-statistic (vs. zero)	Slope	T-statistic (vs. 1)	R-squared
2000	2.95	63.05	0.24	−152.98	0.49
2001	3.10	108.07	0.11	−237.90	0.34
2002	2.88	135.96	0.04	−444.41	0.23
2003	2.75	145.51	0.06	−394.29	0.27
2004	2.96	155.98	0.07	−323.99	0.28
2005	2.49	78.83	0.21	−187.44	0.49
2006	2.90	104.51	0.11	−236.37	0.31
2007	3.05	60.77	0.11	−205.72	0.28
2008	2.64	74.29	0.08	−200.19	0.26

would do better than the other two models, primarily because its slope coefficients are closer to one.

Panel A of Exhibit 4.11 shows the cross-section regressions that are a measure of goodness of fit of the perpetuity model. The slopes should average 1.0, but they are all significantly less than 1.0. Furthermore, the intercepts should be equal to 0.0, and all are significantly different.

Panel B provides the results of an OLS regression of the sector market/book versus the actual equity value divided by the book value. It has results that are even worse than the perpetuity model's results.

The DCF model results that were given in Exhibit 4.7 at least show slope coefficients that are distributed around 1.0, and are therefore less biased than either of the two straw men.

CONVERGENCE

Exhibit 4.12, Panel A, provides the convergence coefficients for all three of the competing valuation models. Referring to the bottom row in Panel A, the DCF model using the expert system has good convergence properties; 79 percent of the regressions have positive adjustment coefficients, indicating that the market price moves toward the DCF price that was calculated at the beginning of the year. The perpetuity model, however, is slightly better, having 81 percent positive convergence coefficients, and the sector market/book is third, having 76 percent of its coefficients positive.

Panel B uses as an additional comparison the percentage of slope terms that are significant compared to the percentage that one would expect by chance. For example, one would expect that roughly 15 percent of the equations would have t-tests greater than an absolute value of 1.5 just by chance. The expert system has 30.7 percent of its slope terms that are significant at this level (t-test greater than 1.5), versus 15 percent if the observations were random. This is good, but the results for the perpetuity are slightly better and the market/book model is only slightly worse with 31.9 and 26.3 percent respectively. The percentage of intercept terms that are significantly different from zero is also of interest (see Exhibit 4.12, Panel B). The expert system has roughly the same number of significant intercept terms as would have occurred by chance (13.7 percent), the perpetuity has too many significantly positive intercept terms (33.8 percent), and the Market/Book approach is roughly random (16.8 percent).

Taking the evidence on goodness of fit and on convergence together, one gets the impression that the perpetuity model tends to undervalue stocks, a fact that is apparent from the distribution of error terms in Exhibit 4.10 that indicates only 6.9 percent of the error terms are greater than zero. Consistent with this is the observation from Exhibit 4.12 that convergence is somewhat greater (i.e., slope coefficients that measure convergence are more frequent) in the $0.1 < b < 0.4$ range, while they are less frequent in the $0.0 < b < 0.1$ range. This appears to happen because the perpetuity value gap is greater than the expert system DCF value gap; therefore, the perpetuity model shows greater convergence because it has further to go. Regardless of which model wins in the statistics horse race, there appears to be strong support for convergence of the market value toward the model value.

EXHIBIT 4.12 Comparison of Convergence Coefficients and Intercepts

Panel A: Convergence Coefficients of Three Models

Coefficient Range	Expert System	Perpetuity	Market/Book
$b < -1.0$	0.00%	0.00%	0.90%
$-1.0 < b < -0.8$	0.00%	0.00%	0.00%
$-0.8 < b < -0.6$	0.11%	0.00%	0.00%
$-0.6 < b < -0.4$	0.11%	0.55%	0.00%
$-0.4 < b < -0.2$	0.33%	0.89%	1.00%
$-0.2 < b < -0.1$	0.55%	1.55%	2.50%
$-0.1 < b < 0.0$	20.31%	16.32%	19.30%
$0.0 < b < 0.1$	68.26%	44.06%	54.10%
$0.1 < b < 0.2$	5.88%	16.43%	12.90%
$0.2 < b < 0.4$	3.11%	13.54%	7.40%
$0.4 < b < 0.6$	0.44%	3.22%	0.70%
$0.6 < b < 0.8$	0.55%	1.22%	0.50%
$0.8 < b < 1.0$	0.11%	0.55%	0.10%
$b > 1.0$	0.22%	1.66%	0.70%
$b < 0$	21.42%	19.31%	23.68%
$b \geq 0$	78.58%	80.69%	76.32%

Panel B: Significance of Slope and Intercept Terms

	Expert DCF		Perpetuity		Market/Book	
	Slope	Intercept	Slope	Intercept	Slope	Intercept
$x < -2.5$	0.9%	1.7%	0.30%	0.40%	0.40%	1.70%
$-2.5 < x < -2$	0.4%	2.3%	0.60%	1.30%	0.90%	1.90%
$-2 < x < -1.5$	1.0%	5.1%	1.40%	1.60%	1.00%	5.30%
$-1.5 < x < 0$	19.1%	32.7%	17.00%	16.20%	29.30%	31.20%
$0 < x < 1.5$	47.6%	44.4%	48.80%	46.60%	50.10%	43.10%
$1.5 < x < 2$	14.4%	6.3%	12.90%	13.40%	12.70%	8.50%
$2 < x < 2.5$	9.3%	5.0%	10.00%	10.40%	7.10%	5.60%
$2.5 < x$	7.0%	2.4%	9.00%	10.00%	6.50%	2.70%
Percent > 1.5	30.7%	13.70%	31.90%	33.80%	26.30%	16.80%

CONCLUSION

This chapter has discussed two measures of valuation models: goodness of fit and convergence. The former is useful for courtroom testimony because what is desired is the minimum error. Therefore, the better valuation model is the one that produces the smallest discrepancy between the fair market price and the model price. However, for deeper questions of market efficiency and portfolio performance, the goodness of fit criterion is not helpful. A superior measure is one that measures the convergence between the price determined by the model and the market price. Specifically, the market price must converge to the model price and not vice versa.

To illustrate a comparison of valuation models, I chose three commonly used models—the DCF model, the market/book ratio, and the perpetuity model. The data were valuations done for each company, each month between January 2000 and July 2008. The final sample consisted of nearly 70,000 valuations of each type.

The goodness of fit criterion seemed to favor the DCF model for two reasons: First, its error terms were more symmetrical, and second, although it did a poor job in a cross-section regression against the market/book value, it did better than the other two measures.

The crucial convergence criterion favored the perpetuity model slightly over the DCF approach. It had more companies whose market values adjusted toward the beginning-of-period DCF value (80.7 percent) than either of the other two models, and more of these adjustment coefficients were statistically significant than could have occurred by chance. The major drawback of the perpetuity model was that the percentage of the intercept terms coefficients that were statistically significant was much higher than can be expected to occur randomly—an undesirable result.

In the final analysis, however, one must test the actual return performance of the alternative valuation models by using a back-test procedure. Goodness of fit and convergence are tools that are useful, but they do not tell the whole story.

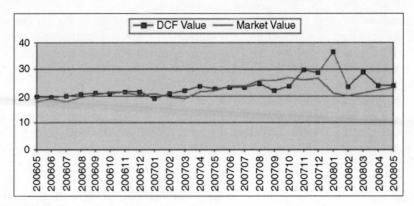

EXHIBIT 4A.1 Market and DCF Price History

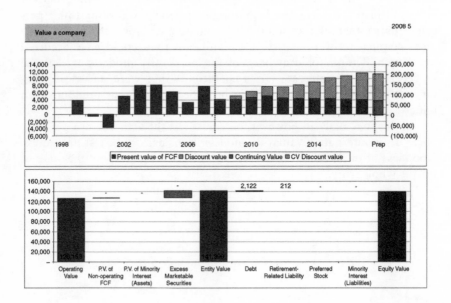

	Per Share	Per Share/Bk			Market Entry	DCF Exit
DCF Value	23.90	3.25				
				Entity	136,983	203,396
Market Price 5/2008	23.18	3.15				
				EBITDA	13,895	34,381
$\text{Value Spread} = \dfrac{DCF-M}{M}$ 3.1%				Multiple	9.9	5.9
				Shares Outstanding (MM)	5,818	

EXHIBIT 4A.2 Valuation Summary

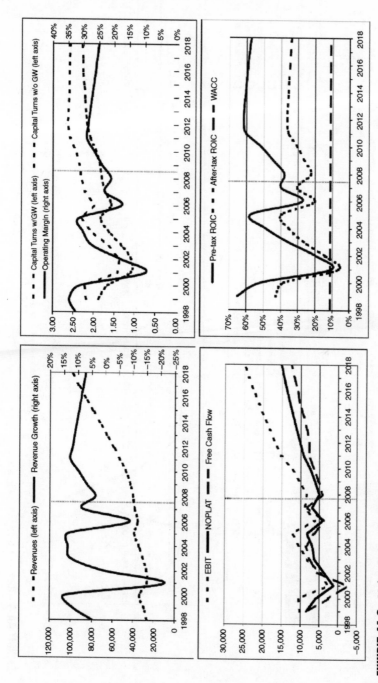

EXHIBIT 4A.3 Value Driver Summary

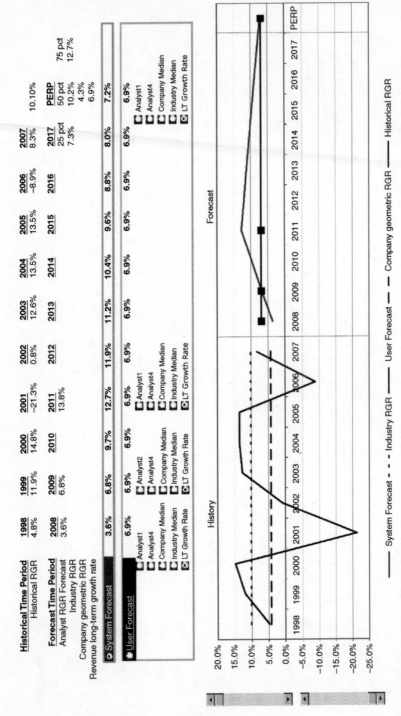

EXHIBIT 4A.4 Revenue Growth Forecast

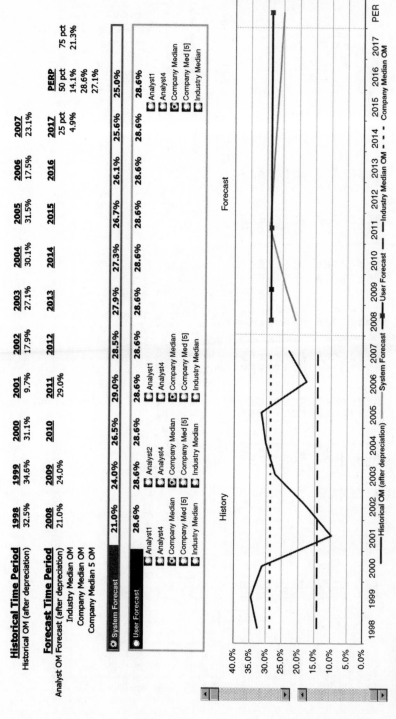

EXHIBIT 4A.5 Operating Margin Forecast

Historical year	1998	1999	2000	2001	2002	2003	2004	2005	2006	2007
GPPE [T-1]/Rev	69.0%	71.7%	69.8%	106.5%	128.4%	122.5%	113.1%	102.6%	124.7%	122.8%
CapEx/Rev[T-1]		12.5%	27.6%	27.2%	18.0%	14.1%	13.2%	17.0%	13.8%	11.6%
Less: Ret/GPPE[T-1]		-3.8%	-14.5%	-10.8%	-6.4%	-5.4%	-7.3%	-3.8%	-5.4%	-10.9%
GPPE/Rev	80.2%	80.2%	83.8%	129.5%	137.9%	128.4%	116.4%	113.7%	133.1%	120.1%
Acc Dep/GPPE	44.9%	50.3%	46.9%	47.3%	51.6%	56.9%	60.4%	61.2%	62.6%	63.3%
NPPE/(Rev)	44.2%	39.9%	44.5%	68.3%	66.7%	55.3%	46.1%	44.1%	49.7%	44.1%
(NPPE+GW)/(Rev)	62.7%	56.5%	59.0%	86.7%	84.9%	71.5%	60.3%	56.6%	53.5%	56.9%

Forecast year	2008	2009	2010	2011	2012	2013	2014	2015	2016	2017	PERP
GPPE [T-1]/Rev	116.0%	113.4%	108.0%	100.2%	95.0%	94.5%	94.9%	95.1%	94.5%	94.7%	94.9%
CapEx/Rev[T-1]	13.1%	13.1%	13.1%	14.1%	18.1%	18.1%	17.1%	15.1%	15.1%	14.1%	13.1%
Less: Ret/GPPE[T-1]	-6.4%	-6.4%	-6.4%	-6.4%	-6.4%	-6.4%	-6.4%	-6.4%	-6.4%	-6.4%	-6.4%
GPPE/Rev	121.2%	118.4%	113.0%	106.3%	105.1%	104.7%	104.3%	102.8%	102.3%	101.7%	101.0%
Acc Dep/GPPE	63.0%	62.2%	62.5%	62.2%	62.0%	61.7%	61.5%	61.2%	60.9%	60.7%	60.4%
NPPE/(Rev)	44.8%	44.1%	42.4%	40.2%	40.0%	40.1%	40.2%	39.9%	40.0%	40.0%	40.0%
(NPPE+GW)/(Rev)	57.1%	55.6%	52.9%	49.5%	48.3%	47.6%	47.0%	46.1%	45.6%	45.9%	44.9%

CAP EX
Company median 14.1%

Analyst (1 yr) 13.1% Analyst (3-5 yr) 13.1%

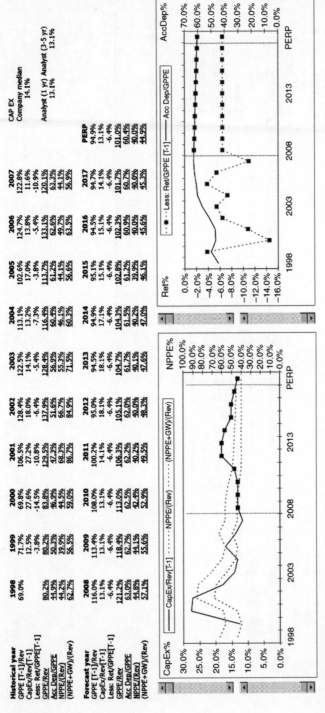

EXHIBIT 4A.6 Net Property, Plant, and Equipment

Historical year	1998	1999	2000	2001	2002	2003	2004	2005	2006	2007
Operating Cash	2.0%	2.0%	2.0%	2.0%	2.0%	2.0%	2.0%	2.0%	2.0%	2.0%
Accounts Receivable	13.4%	12.6%	12.2%	9.8%	9.6%	9.8%	8.8%	10.1%	7.7%	6.7%
Inventories	6.0%	5.0%	6.6%	8.5%	8.5%	8.4%	7.7%	8.1%	12.2%	8.8%
Other	2.8%	2.9%	2.8%	4.6%	5.6%	4.1%	3.7%	3.6%	3.5%	6.7%
Operating Current Asset	24.3%	22.5%	23.7%	24.9%	25.7%	24.3%	22.1%	23.7%	25.4%	24.2%
Accounts Payable	4.7%	4.7%	7.1%	6.7%	5.8%	5.5%	5.7%	5.8%	6.4%	6.2%
Other Liabilities and Tax	16.8%	18.7%	17.4%	16.5%	17.2%	16.5%	17.1%	17.2%	17.2%	15.8%
Non-Interest Bearing Lia	21.5%	23.4%	24.5%	23.2%	23.0%	22.1%	22.8%	23.0%	23.6%	22.0%
Working Capital	2.8%	-0.9%	-0.8%	1.7%	2.7%	2.2%	-0.7%	0.7%	1.8%	2.2%

Forecast year	2008	2009	2010	2011	2012	2013	2014	2015	2016	2017	2018
Operating Cash	2.0%	2.0%	2.0%	2.0%	2.0%	2.0%	2.0%	2.0%	2.0%	2.0%	2.0%
Accounts Receivable	7.0%	7.3%	7.6%	7.9%	8.2%	8.5%	8.8%	9.1%	9.4%	9.7%	10.0%
Inventories	8.7%	8.7%	8.6%	8.6%	8.5%	8.5%	8.4%	8.4%	8.3%	8.3%	8.2%
Other	6.5%	6.2%	6.0%	5.7%	5.5%	5.2%	5.0%	4.7%	4.5%	4.2%	4.0%
Operating Current Asset	24.2%	24.2%	24.2%	24.2%	24.2%	24.2%	24.2%	24.2%	24.2%	24.2%	24.2%
Accounts Payable	6.1%	6.1%	6.1%	6.0%	6.0%	6.0%	5.9%	5.9%	5.8%	5.8%	5.8%
Other Liabilities and Tax	15.9%	16.0%	16.1%	16.3%	16.4%	16.5%	16.6%	16.7%	16.8%	16.9%	17.0%
Non-Interest Bearing Lia	22.1%	22.1%	22.2%	22.3%	22.3%	22.4%	22.5%	22.6%	22.6%	22.7%	22.8%
Working Capital	2.2%	2.1%	2.0%	1.9%	1.9%	1.8%	1.7%	1.6%	1.6%	1.5%	1.4%

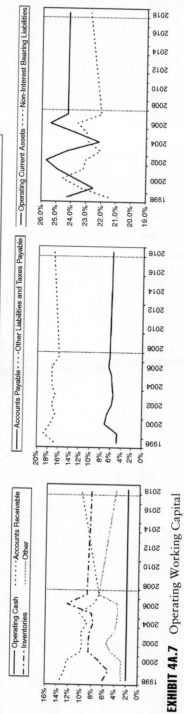

EXHIBIT 4A.7 Operating Working Capital

Capital Source	Cost (K)	Market Value (V)	Target MV Weights	Contribution
Debt	6.60%	2,122.0	1.35%	0.05%
Equity	11.23%	155,107.9	98.52%	11.06%
Preferred	8.91%	0.0	0.00%	0.00%
Retirement Liability	6.60%	212.0	0.13%	0.01%
Capitalized Leases	6.60%	0.0	0.00%	0.00%
Operating Leases	6.60%	0.0	0.00%	0.00%
Other	6.60%	0.0	0.00%	0.00%
Total	--	157,441.9	100.00%	11.12%

Note: WACC is assumed to be constant during history.

Beta	1.30
Risk-Free Rate	4.08%
Market Risk Premium	5.50%
Marginal Tax Rate	41.0%
Bond Rating*	A+
Bond Rate	6.60%

Debt Haircut? (% of book) 100.00%

*A company without a bond rating is assumed to have an A rating.

EXHIBIT 4A.8   Weighted Average Cost of Capital

Exhibit 4A.9 — Income Statement

Year	1998	1999	2000	2001	2002	2003	2004	2005	2006	2007	Forecast 2008	Forecast 2009	Forecast 2010	Forecast 2011	Forecast 2012	Forecast 2013	Forecast 2014	Forecast 2015	Forecast 2016	Forecast 2017	2018	Perpetuity
Revenue	28273	29369	33726	28539	26764	30141	34209	38826	35382	38334	39714	42415	46529	52438	58678	65250	72036	78951	85999	92771	99451	
Operating expense	(14922)	(16044)	(18415)	(17909)	(18932)	(16989)	(19057)	(22128)	(24323)	(24891)	(27226)	(27934)	(29639)	(31998)	(34844)	(39121)	(43384)	(49521)	(54371)	(59661)	(65070)	
Depreciation expense	(2807)	(3166)	(4807)	(6052)	(5042)	(4972)	(4860)	(4468)	(4852)	(4798)	(4148)	(4301)	(4562)	(5233)	(7111)	(7624)	(8386)	(8350)	(9109)	(9360)	(9518)	
Operating income	8544	10159	10504	2578	4790	8180	10292	12230	6207	8645	8340	10179	12339	15207	16723	16205	19666	21080	22420	23749	24863	
Goodwill amortization	0	0	(1558)	(1921)	(366)	(321)	(270)	0	(199)	(252)	0	0	0	0	0	0	0	0	0	0	0	
Non-operating income	199	379	1644	378	392	(277)	(24)	(30)	69	161	161	161	161	161	161	161	161	161	161	161	161	
Interest income	593	618	920	615	296	248	301	577	636	404	919	1095	1342	1675	2012	2393	2832	3345	3905	4531	5221	
Interest expense	(34)	(36)	(35)	(56)	(84)	(62)	(50)	(19)	(24)	(15)	(20)	(26)	(31)	(37)	(42)	(48)	(53)	(59)	(64)	(69)	(75)	
Special items	(155)	(362)	2108	(479)	(406)	(647)	(102)	(140)	160	(629)	0	0	0	0	0	0	0	0	0	0	0	
Earnings before taxes	9137	11228	13583	282	3838	7121	10147	12610	6859	8914	9400	11410	13802	17006	18854	20011	22605	24528	26422	28372	30169	
Income taxes	(3069)	(3916)	(4606)	(692)	(1087)	(1801)	(2901)	(3946)	(2024)	(2190)	(3854)	(4678)	(5659)	(6972)	(7730)	(8492)	(9268)	(10056)	(10833)	(11632)	(12369)	
Net income	5958	7314	8977	(630)	2751	5320	7246	8664	4845	6724	5546	6732	8143	10034	11124	12220	13337	14471	15589	16739	17800	
Net income (source)	6068	7314	10535	1291	3117	5641	7516	8664	5044	6676												

Statement of Retained Earnings

	1998	1999	2000	2001	2002	2003	2004	2005	2006	2007	2008	2009	2010	2011	2012	2013	2014	2015	2016	2017	2018
Beginning retained ea...	15984	17962	21426	28738	27182	27860	31051	32325	29910	29097	31172	34100	38214	43739	51154	59680	69262	79981	91834	104805	118927
Net income	6068	7314	8977	(630)	2751	5320	7246	8664	4845	6724	5546	6732	8143	10034	11124	12220	13337	14471	15589	16739	17800
Common dividend	(168)	(36)	(470)	(638)	(533)	(524)	(1022)	(1958)	(2320)	(2618)	(2618)	(2618)	(2618)	(2618)	(2618)	(2618)	(2618)	(2618)	(2618)	(2618)	(2618)
Adjustment to retained	(3932)	(3472)	(1197)	(386)	(1540)	(1605)	(4950)	(9121)	(3338)	(2031)											
Ending retained ear...	17952	21426	28738	27182	27860	31051	32325	29910	29097	31172	34100	38214	43739	51154	59680	69282	79981	91834	104805	118927	134109

EXHIBIT 4A.9 Income Statement

Growth rates

Revenue	4.8%	11.9%	14.8%	-21.3%	0.8%	12.0%	13.5%	13.5%	-8.0%	8.3%	3.6%	8.6%	9.7%	11.9%	11.2%	12.7%	11.9%	11.2%	10.4%	9.6%	8.8%	8.0%	7.2%
Non-op income	-16.0%	341.7%	87.0%	-128.9%	-17.5%	-29.3%	-91.3%	56.3%	-334.2%	80.9%	0.0%	0.0%	0.0%	0.0%	0.0%	0.0%	0.0%	0.0%	0.0%	0.0%	0.0%	0.0%	0.0%

Operating Ratios

Revenue/revenue	100.0%	100.0%	100.0%	100.0%	100.0%	100.0%	100.0%	100.0%	100.0%	100.0%	100.0%	100.0%	100.0%	100.0%	100.0%	100.0%	100.0%	100.0%	100.0%	100.0%	100.0%	100.0%	100.0%
Operating expense/rev	-56.6%	-54.6%	-54.6%	67.6%	-83.3%	-56.4%	-55.7%	-57.0%	-68.7%	-64.4%	-68.6%	-65.9%	-63.7%	-59.4%	-60.0%	-61.0%	-59.4%	-60.0%	-61.1%	-62.7%	-63.3%	-64.3%	-65.4%
Depreciation expense/	-10.7%	-10.9%	-14.3%	-22.8%	-18.8%	-16.5%	-14.2%	-11.5%	-13.7%	-12.5%	-10.4%	-10.1%	-9.8%	-12.1%	-12.1%	-10.0%	-12.1%	-12.1%	-11.6%	-10.6%	-10.6%	-10.1%	-9.6%
Operating income/rev	32.5%	34.8%	31.1%	9.7%	17.9%	27.1%	30.1%	31.5%	17.5%	23.1%	21.0%	24.0%	26.5%	28.5%	27.9%	29.0%	28.5%	27.9%	27.3%	26.7%	26.1%	25.6%	25.0%
Goodwill amortization/	0.0%	0.0%	-4.6%	-7.2%	-1.4%	-1.1%	-0.8%	0.0%	-0.6%	-0.7%	0.0%	0.0%	0.0%	0.0%	0.0%	0.0%	0.0%	0.0%	0.0%	0.0%	0.0%	0.0%	0.0%
Non-operating income	0.8%	3.0%	4.9%	-1.8%	-1.5%	-0.9%	-0.1%	-0.1%	0.3%	0.4%	0.4%	0.4%	0.3%	0.3%	0.2%	0.3%	0.3%	0.2%	0.2%	0.2%	0.2%	0.2%	0.2%
Interest income/cash i	7.8%	5.2%	8.7%	5.3%	2.4%	1.5%	1.8%	4.5%	6.4%	5.2%	5.2%	5.2%	5.2%	5.2%	5.2%	5.2%	5.2%	5.2%	5.2%	5.2%	5.2%	5.2%	5.2%
Interest expense/debt	-3.9%	-3.0%	-3.2%	-3.8%	-6.2%	-5.3%	-5.5%	-0.8%	-1.2%	-0.7%	-1.0%	-1.2%	-1.5%	-2.0%	-2.2%	-1.7%	-2.0%	-2.2%	-2.5%	-2.8%	-3.0%	-3.3%	-3.5%
Special items/revenue	-0.6%	-1.3%	6.3%	-1.8%	-1.5%	-2.1%	-0.3%	-0.4%	0.5%	-1.6%	0.0%	0.0%	0.0%	0.0%	0.0%	0.0%	0.0%	0.0%	0.0%	0.0%	0.0%	0.0%	0.0%
Earnings before taxes/	34.8%	38.2%	40.3%	1.0%	14.3%	23.6%	29.7%	32.5%	19.4%	23.3%	25.7%	28.4%	30.6%	32.0%	31.1%	32.8%	32.0%	31.1%	30.3%	29.4%	28.5%	27.7%	26.9%
Income taxes/revenue	-11.7%	-13.3%	-13.7%	-3.4%	-4.1%	-6.0%	-8.5%	-10.2%	-5.7%	-5.9%	-5.9%	-6.0%	-6.1%	-6.4%	-6.5%	-6.3%	-6.4%	-6.5%	-6.7%	-6.8%	-7.0%	-7.1%	-7.2%
Net income/revenue	23.1%	24.9%	26.6%	-2.4%	10.3%	17.7%	21.2%	22.3%	13.7%	17.5%	19.8%	22.4%	24.5%	25.5%	24.6%	26.5%	25.5%	24.6%	23.8%	22.8%	21.6%	20.6%	19.6%
Net income (source)/r	23.1%	24.9%	31.2%	4.9%	11.6%	18.7%	22.0%	22.3%	14.3%	16.2%	@NA	@NA	@NA	@NA	@NA	@NA	@NA	@NA	@NA	@NA	@NA	@NA	@NA

EXHIBIT 4A.9 (*Continued*)

EXHIBIT 4A.10 Balance Sheet

Year	1998	1999	2000	2001	2002	2003	2004	2005	2006	2007	Forecast 2008	Forecast 2009	Forecast 2010	Forecast 2011	Forecast 2012	Forecast 2013	Forecast 2014	Forecast 2015	Forecast 2016	Forecast 2017	Perpetuity 2018
Operating cash	525	588	675	631	535	603	684	777	708	767	794	848	931	1,049	1,174	1,305	1,441	1,579	1,718	1,856	1,989
Excess marketable security	7,101	11,200	13,148	10,919	12,052	15,561	16,488	11,995	9,294	14,596	16,772	20,074	24,713	30,914	37,258	44,400	52,636	62,300	72,847	84,654	97,682
Cash and equivalent	7,626	11,788	13,823	11,550	12,587	16,164	17,172	12,772	10,002	15,363	17,566	20,922	25,644	31,963	38,432	45,705	54,076	63,079	74,565	86,509	99,671
Accounts receivable	3,527	3,700	4,129	2,607	2,574	2,990	2,999	3,814	2,709	2,576	2,787	3,103	3,543	4,149	4,818	5,552	6,344	7,189	8,078	9,000	9,945
Inventory	1,582	1,478	2,241	2,253	2,276	2,519	2,621	3,126	4,314	3,370	3,470	3,683	4,016	4,468	5,002	5,527	6,064	6,604	7,139	7,561	8,159
Other current asset	740	853	957	1,223	1,488	1,239	1,266	1,382	1,256	2,576	2,571	2,640	2,782	3,065	3,218	3,417	3,594	3,744	3,861	3,940	3,978
Total current asset	13,475	17,819	21,150	17,633	18,925	22,882	24,058	21,194	18,280	23,885	26,384	30,349	35,984	43,645	51,469	60,202	70,078	81,415	93,842	107,111	121,753
Total current asset (source)	13,475	17,819	21,150	17,633	18,925	22,882	24,058	21,194	18,280	23,885											
Gross PP&E	21,068	23,557	28,253	34,356	36,912	38,692	39,833	44,132	47,084	46,052	48,119	50,234	52,567	56,756	61,671	68,337	75,112	81,173	87,089	94,365	100,468
Accumulated depr	(9,459)	(11,842)	(13,240)	(16,235)	(19,065)	(22,031)	(24,065)	(27,021)	(29,482)	(29,134)	(30,317)	(31,519)	(32,847)	(34,660)	(38,217)	(42,170)	(46,157)	(49,671)	(53,553)	(57,255)	(60,697)
Net PP&E	11,609	11,715	15,013	18,121	17,847	16,661	15,768	17,111	17,602	16,918	17,802	18,714	19,720	21,060	23,455	26,167	28,955	31,502	34,336	37,110	39,770
Goodwill and intangible		4,322	5,941	5,127	5,164	4,364	4,396	4,527	4,848	4,876	4,876	4,876	4,876	4,876	4,876	4,876	4,876	4,876	4,876	4,876	4,876
Other operating asset	1,022	2,082	2,129	2,040	232	159	195	249	484	677	677	653	629	606	581	557	533	509	485	461	437
Investment and advance	5,365	7,811	3,712	1,474	2,056	3,077	3,729	5,233	7,154	9,295	9,295	9,295	9,295	9,295	9,295	9,295	9,295	9,295	9,295	9,295	9,295
Total asset	31,471	43,849	47,945	44,395	44,224	47,143	48,143	48,314	48,368	55,651	59,044	63,888	70,504	79,482	89,676	101,096	113,738	127,597	142,634	158,853	176,132
Short-term debt	159	230	378	409	436	224	201	313	180	142	142	142	142	142	142	142	142	142	142	142	142
Accounts payable*	1,244	1,370	2,387	1,769	1,543	1,060	1,943	2,249	2,256	2,381	2,432	2,583	2,817	3,157	3,513	3,883	4,262	4,644	5,023	5,393	5,747
Other current liab and tax	4,401	5,499	5,885	4,392	4,616	4,995	5,862	6,672	6,078	6,048	6,329	6,804	7,514	8,524	9,601	10,746	11,939	13,170	14,420	15,872	16,907
Total current liability	5,804	7,099	8,650	6,570	6,595	6,879	8,006	9,234	8,514	8,571	8,903	9,529	10,473	11,823	13,255	14,771	16,344	17,956	19,585	21,208	22,796
New long-term debt																					
Long-term debt	702	965	707	1,050	929	936	703	2,106	1,848	1,980	1,960	1,960	1,960	1,960	1,960	1,980	1,960	1,960	1,980	1,980	1,980
Deferred income tax	1,387	3,130	1,266	945	1,232	1,482	855	703	265	411	519	654	827	1,055	1,319	1,620	1,957	2,331	2,738	3,175	3,637
Other operating liability					(85)	(107)	(134)	(69)													
Retirement-related liab									786	1,715	1,715	1,654	1,593	1,533	1,472	1,411	1,350	1,289	1,229	1,168	1,107
Minority interest payments					85	107	134	158	203	212	212	212	212	212	212	212	212	212	212	212	212
Total liability	7,893	11,184	10,623	8,565	8,756	9,297	9,564	12,132	11,616	12,889	13,329	14,030	15,086	16,603	18,238	19,993	21,643	23,768	25,744	27,742	29,732

Exhibit 4A.10 — financial model continuation (values in thousands unless percentages)

Item																					
Total liability (source)	7,893	11,184	10,623	8,565	8,756	9,297	9,564	12,132	11,616	12,889	11,653	11,653	11,653	11,653	11,653	11,653	11,653	11,653	11,653	11,653	11,653
Common stock outstanding (ex treasury stock)	4,822	7,316	8,389	8,859	7,578	6,734	6,139	6,246	7,825												
Preferred stock	201	130																			
Retained earning	17,952	21,428	28,738	27,182	27,860	31,051	32,325	29,910	29,097	31,172	34,100	36,214	43,739	51,154	59,680	69,282	79,981	91,834	104,806	118,927	134,109
Cumulative foreign exchange and other	603	3,791	195	(7)	30	81	115	27	(170)	(63)	(63)	(63)	(63)	(63)	(63)	(63)	(63)	(63)	(63)	(63)	(63)
Total equity	23,578	32,665	37,322	35,830	35,468	37,848	38,579	38,182	36,752	42,762	45,690	49,804	55,329	62,744	71,250	80,852	91,571	103,424	118,395	130,517	145,699
Total equity (source)	23,578	32,665	37,322	35,830	35,468	37,848	38,579	38,182	36,752	42,762											
Total liability and equity	31,471	43,849	47,945	44,395	44,224	47,143	48,143	48,314	48,368	55,651	59,019	63,833	70,414	79,247	89,488	100,846	113,415	127,193	142,139	158,259	175,430
Balance											25	54	89	134	188	251	323	405	495	595	701
ST debt/equity ratio	1%	1%	1%	1%	1%	1%	1%		0%	0%	0%	0%	0%	0%	0%	0%	0%	0%	0%	0%	0%
LT debt/equity ratio	3%	2%	3%	3%	3%	2%	2%		5%	5%	5%	5%	5%	5%	5%	5%	5%	5%	5%	5%	5%
Deferred income tax/revenue	5%	-11%	4%	4%	5%	5%	2%	2%	1%	1%	1%	2%	2%	2%	2%	2%	3%	3%	3%	3%	4%
Other Oth Ast Growth	104%	104%	2%	-4%	-89%	-31%	23%	25%	94%	40%											
Other Oth Liab Growth	#DIV/0!	#DIV/0!	#DIV/0!	#DIV/0!	#DIV/0!	28%	25%	-49%	-1239%	118%											
Net Other Ast Growth	104%	2%	-4%	-84%	-16%	-3%	24%	-196%	244%	0%	-4%	-4%	-4%	-4%	-4%	-4%	-5%	-5%	-5%	-5%	-5%
Other Oth Ast/Rev	2%	6%	8%	1%	1%	1%	1%	2%	2%	2%	1%	1%	1%	1%	1%	1%	1%	1%	1%	0%	0%
Other Oth Liab/Rev	0%	0%	0%	0%	0%	0%	0%	0%	0%	4%	4%	3%	3%	3%	2%	2%	2%	1%	1%	1%	1%
Net Oth Ast / Rev	6%	6%	8%	8%	1%	1%	1%	-1%	-1%	-3%	-3%	-2%	-2%	-2%	-2%	-1%	-1%	-1%	-1%	-1%	-1%
Inventory / Rev	7%	7%	8%	6%	6%	8%	8%	12%	12%	9%	9%	9%	9%	8%	8%	8%	8%	8%	8%	8%	8%
*Accounts Payable Breakdown																					
Acct pay/Rev	5%	7%	5%	7%	6%	6%	6%	6%	6%	6%	6%	6%	6%	6%	6%	6%	6%	6%	6%	6%	6%
LT acct pay/Rev	0%	0%	0%	0%	0%	0%	0%	0%	0%	0%	0%	0%	0%	0%	0%	0%	0%	0%	0%	0%	0%
Cur acct pay/Rev	5%	7%	5%	7%	6%	6%	6%	6%	6%	6%	6%	6%	6%	6%	6%	6%	6%	6%	6%	6%	6%
LT acct payable																					
Cur acct pay	1,244	1,370	2,387	1,769	1,543	1,680	1,943	2,249	2,256	2,361	2,432	2,583	2,817	3,157	3,513	3,883	4,282	4,644	5,023	5,393	5,747
INVADV / Revenue	20%	27%	11%	6%	8%	10%	11%	13%	20%	24%	23%	22%	21%	20%	19%	18%	17%	16%	14%	13%	12%

EXHIBIT 4A.10 (Continued)

NOPLAT Statement

	1998	1999	2000	2001	History 2002	2003	2004	2005	2006	2007	2008	2009	2010	2011	Forecast 2012	2013	2014	2015	2016	2017	2018
Revenue	28,273	29,389	33,728	28,539	26,784	30,141	34,209	38,828	35,382	38,334	39,714	42,415	46,529	52,438	58,678	65,250	72,039	78,951	85,899	92,771	99,451
Operating expense	(14,922)	(16,044)	(18,415)	(17,909)	(16,932)	(16,989)	(19,057)	(22,128)	(24,323)	(24,691)	(27,226)	(27,934)	(29,636)	(31,998)	(34,844)	(39,121)	(43,984)	(49,521)	(54,371)	(59,661)	(65,070)
Depreciation expense	(2,807)	(3,186)	(4,807)	(6,052)	(5,042)	(4,972)	(4,860)	(4,468)	(4,852)	(4,798)	(4,148)	(4,301)	(4,562)	(5,233)	(7,111)	(7,924)	(8,388)	(8,350)	(9,109)	(9,360)	(9,518)
EBIT	8,544	10,159	10,504	2,578	4,790	8,180	10,292	12,230	6,207	8,845	8,340	10,179	12,330	15,207	16,723	18,205	19,666	21,080	22,420	23,749	24,863
Taxes on EBIT	(2,826)	(3,476)	(2,705)	(1,054)	(1,327)	(2,104)	(2,650)	(3,790)	(1,671)	(2,058)	(3,419)	(4,174)	(5,055)	(6,235)	(6,857)	(7,464)	(8,083)	(8,643)	(9,192)	(9,737)	(10,194)
Change in deferred ta	311	1,743	(1,864)	(321)	287	250	(827)	(152)	(438)	146	108	135	173	228	263	301	338	373	407	437	462
NOPLAT	6,029	8,426	5,935	1,203	3,750	6,328	6,815	8,288	4,098	6,933	5,029	6,141	7,448	9,200	10,130	11,042	11,941	12,811	13,635	14,449	15,131

Taxes on EBIT

	1998	1999	2000	2001	History 2002	2003	2004	2005	2006	2007	2008	2009	2010	2011	Forecast 2012	2013	2014	2015	2016	2017	2018
Provision for income t	3,069	3,914	4,806	892	1,087	1,801	2,901	3,948	2,024	2,190	3,854	4,678	5,659	6,972	7,730	8,492	9,288	10,098	10,833	11,832	12,369
Tax shield on interest	14	15	14	23	34	25	20	8	10	6	11	11	13	15	17	20	22	24	26	28	31
Tax on interest incom	(243)	(253)	(377)	(252)	(122)	(102)	(123)	(237)	(261)	(330)	(377)	(449)	(550)	(687)	(825)	(981)	(1,161)	(1,372)	(1,601)	(1,858)	(2,141)
Tax on non-operating	(14)	(200)	(1,538)	391	328	379	52	73	(102)	192	(66)	(66)	(66)	(66)	(66)	(66)	(66)	(66)	(66)	(66)	(66)
Less: Tax from un																					
Taxes on EBIT	2,826	3,476	2,705	1,054	1,327	2,104	2,650	3,790	1,671	2,058	3,419	4,174	5,055	6,235	6,857	7,464	8,083	8,643	9,192	9,737	10,194

EXHIBIT 4A.11 NOPLAT and Taxes on EBIT

Free Cash Flows Statement

	1998	1999	2000	2001	2002	2003	2004	2005	2006	2007	2008	2009	2010	2011	2012	2013	2014	2015	2016	2017	2018
					History										Forecast						
EBIT		10,159	10,504	2,578	4,790	8,180	10,292	12,230	6,207	6,845	8,340	10,779	12,330	15,207	16,723	18,205	19,666	21,090	22,420	23,749	24,863
Taxes on EBIT		(3,476)	(2,705)	(1,054)	(1,327)	(2,104)	(2,850)	(3,790)	(1,871)	(2,058)	(3,419)	(4,174)	(5,055)	(6,235)	(6,857)	(7,464)	(8,063)	(8,643)	(9,192)	(9,797)	(10,194)
Change in Def Taxes		1,743	(1,864)	(321)	287	250	(627)	(152)	(436)	146	108	135	173	226	283	301	336	373	407	437	462
NOPLAT		8,426	5,935	1,203	3,750	6,326	6,815	8,288	4,098	4,798	5,029	6,141	7,448	9,200	10,130	11,042	11,941	12,811	13,635	14,449	15,131
Depreciation		3,186	4,807	6,052	5,042	4,972	4,860	4,468	4,852	4,798	4,148	4,301	4,562	5,233	7,111	7,924	8,386	8,350	9,109	9,360	9,518
Gross Cash Flow		11,612	10,742	7,255	8,792	11,298	11,675	12,756	8,950	11,731	9,177	10,441	12,010	14,433	17,241	18,995	20,327	21,181	22,243	23,810	24,649
Increase in Working Capital		(680)	(20)	723	282	(46)	(901)	512	374	208	(24)	(2)	16	36	24	12	(4)	(21)	(40)	(60)	(80)
Capital Expenditures		3,292	8,105	9,160	4,768	3,786	3,967	5,811	5,343	4,114	5,032	5,213	5,568	6,573	9,605	10,636	11,175	10,897	11,943	12,135	12,178
Incr in Other Assets Net of Other		1,050	47	(69)	(1,723)	(51)	63	(11)	(620)	(736)	-	37	37	37	37	37	37	37	37	37	37
Gross Investment		3,372	8,132	9,794	3,307	3,687	3,129	6,312	5,097	3,586	5,008	5,248	5,621	6,645	9,586	10,686	11,208	10,912	11,940	12,112	12,134
Free cash flow		8,240	2,610	2,539	5,485	7,612	8,546	6,443	3,853	8,145	4,169	5,193	6,389	7,788	7,675	8,281	9,119	10,248	10,804	11,698	12,515
Less: Investment in Goodwill		(4,322)	(3,177)	(1,107)	(403)	479	(302)	(131)	(520)	(280)	-	-	-	-	-	-	-	-	-	-	0
Free cash flow after goodwill		3,918	(567)	(3,646)	5,082	8,091	8,244	6,312	3,333	7,865	4,169	5,193	6,389	7,788	7,675	8,281	9,119	10,248	10,804	11,698	12,515
Non-operating Cash Flow		(2,269)	6,413	1,876	(1,054)	(1,566)	(723)	(1,612)	(1,774)	(2,417)	95	95	95	95	95	95	95	95	95	95	95
Foreign exchange and other		3,198	(3,596)	(202)	37	31	54	(88)	(197)	107											
Cash Flow Available to Investors		4,847	2,250	(2,173)	4,065	6,556	7,575	4,612	1,362	5,554	4,264	5,288	6,484	7,883	7,770	8,376	9,214	10,343	10,899	11,793	12,610

Financing Flows Statement

	1998	1999	2000	2001	2002	2003	2004	2005	2006	2007	2008	2009	2010	2011	2012	2013	2014	2015	2016	2017	2018
					History										Forecast						
After-tax interest income		(385)	(543)	(363)	(176)	(346)	(178)	(340)	(375)	(474)	(542)	(646)	(792)	(988)	(1,187)	(1,412)	(1,671)	(1,974)	(2,304)	(2,673)	(3,060)
Decrease/(increase) in debt		(324)	100	(374)	94	205	256	(1,515)	391	(94)	-										
Decrease/(increase) retirement-re		-	-	-	(85)	(22)	(27)	(24)	(45)	(9)	-										
Total Sources of Funds		(689)	(443)	(737)	(167)	(163)	51	(1,879)	(29)	(577)	(542)	(646)	(792)	(988)	(1,187)	(1,412)	(1,671)	(1,974)	(2,304)	(2,673)	(3,060)
Minority interest																					
Increase/(decrease) in excess mk		4,100	1,946	(2,129)	1,033	3,509	927	(4,492)	(2,701)	5,302	2,176	3,302	4,639	6,231	6,314	7,142	8,235	9,665	10,547	11,807	13,028
After-tax interest expense		21	21	33	50	37	29	11	14	9	12	16	18	22	25	28	31	35	38	41	44
Total Uses of Funds		4,121	1,999	(2,096)	1,082	3,546	956	(4,481)	(2,687)	5,311	2,188	3,317	4,658	6,253	6,339	7,070	8,266	9,699	10,585	11,848	13,072
Preferred dividends		71	130																		
(Increase)/decrease in preferred		366	470	536	533	524	1,022	1,958	2,320	2,618	2,618	2,618	2,618	2,618	2,618	2,618	2,618	2,618	2,618	2,618	2,618
Common dividends		(2,694)	(1,073)	(296)	1,077	844	595	(106)	(1,540)	(3,629)											
(Increase)/decrease in common s		3,472	1,197	388	1,540	1,605	4,950	9,121	3,338	2,031											
Misc. adj. to retained earnings		1,415	724	660	3,150	2,972	6,567	10,973	4,075	821											
Total Shareholder Flows		1,415	724	660	3,150	2,972	6,567	10,973	4,075	821	2,618	2,618	2,618	2,618	2,618	2,618	2,618	2,618	2,618	2,618	2,618
Financing Flows Total		4,847	2,250	(2,173)	4,065	6,556	7,575	4,612	1,362	5,554	4,263	5,286	6,484	7,863	7,770	8,376	9,214	10,343	10,889	11,793	12,610

EXHIBIT 4A.12 Invested Capital

Invested Capital Statement

	1998	1999	2000	2001	2002	2003	2004	2005	2006	2007	2008	2009	2010	2011	2012	2013	2014	2015	2016	2017	2018
					History										Forecast						
Operating current assets	6,374	6,619	8,002	6,614	6,873	7,321	7,570	9,199	8,986	9,280	9,602	10,233	11,201	12,597	14,065	15,606	17,192	16,801	20,410	21,995	23,526
Non-Interest Bearing	5,645	6,869	8,272	6,161	6,159	6,655	7,805	8,921	8,334	8,429	8,767	9,399	10,351	11,711	13,155	14,685	16,274	17,904	19,554	21,198	22,810
Working Capital	729	(250)	(270)	453	714	666	(235)	278	652	850	836	834	850	886	910	922	918	897	857	797	717
GPPE	21,068	23,557	28,253	34,356	36,912	38,692	39,833	44,132	47,084	46,052	48,119	50,234	52,567	55,756	61,671	68,337	75,112	81,173	87,889	94,365	100,468
Accumulated depreciation	(9,459)	(11,842)	(13,240)	(16,235)	(19,065)	(22,031)	(24,065)	(27,021)	(29,482)	(29,134)	30,317	31,519	32,847	34,696	38,217	42,170	46,157	49,671	53,553	57,255	60,697
NPPE	11,609	11,715	15,013	18,121	17,847	16,661	15,768	17,111	17,602	16,918	17,802	18,714	19,720	21,060	23,455	26,167	28,955	31,502	34,336	37,110	39,770
NPPE (source)																					
Other operating asset	1,022	2,082	2,129	2,040	232	159	195	249	484	677	677	653	629	605	581	557	533	509	485	461	437
Other operating liability					(85)	(107)	(134)	(69)	786	1,715	1,715	1,654	1,593	1,533	1,472	1,411	1,350	1,289	1,229	1,168	1,107
Other asset net of other	1,022	2,082	2,129	2,040	317	266	329	318	(302)	(1,038)	(1,038)	(1,001)	(964)	(928)	(891)	(854)	(817)	(780)	(744)	(707)	(670)
Excess Marketable Securities	7,101	11,200	13,148	11,019	12,052	15,561	16,488	11,995	9,294	14,596	18,772	20,074	24,713	30,944	37,258	44,400	52,636	62,300	72,847	84,654	97,682
Goodwill		4,322	5,941	5,127	5,164	4,364	4,396	4,527	4,846	4,876	4,876	4,876	4,876	4,876	4,876	4,876	4,876	4,876	4,876	4,876	4,876
Investments & Advances	5,365	7,911	3,712	1,474	2,056	3,077	3,726	5,233	7,154	9,295	9,295	9,295	9,295	9,295	9,295	9,295	9,295	9,295	9,295	9,295	9,295
Total investor funds	25,826	36,990	39,673	38,234	38,150	40,595	40,472	39,462	39,248	45,507	46,543	52,792	58,490	66,134	74,903	84,806	95,862	108,089	121,467	136,025	151,670
Reconciliation																					
Equity	23,578	32,665	37,322	35,830	35,468	37,846	38,579	36,182	36,752	42,762	45,690	49,804	55,329	62,744	71,250	80,852	91,571	103,424	116,395	130,517	145,699
Deferred Income Taxes	1,387	3,130	1,266	945	1,232	1,482	855	703	265	411	519	654	827	1,055	1,319	1,620	1,957	2,331	2,738	3,175	3,637
Adjusted Equity	24,965	35,795	38,588	36,775	36,700	39,328	39,434	36,885	37,017	43,173	46,209	50,458	56,156	63,800	72,569	82,472	93,528	105,755	119,133	133,691	149,336
Interest Bearing Debt	861	1,185	1,065	1,459	1,365	1,160	904	2,419	2,026	2,122	2,122	2,122	2,122	2,122	2,122	2,122	2,122	2,122	2,122	2,122	2,122
Retirement Rel Liab					85	107	134	158	203	212	212	212	212	212	212	212	212	212	212	212	212
Total investor funds	25,826	36,990	39,673	38,234	38,150	40,595	40,472	39,462	39,248	45,507	46,543	52,792	58,490	66,134	74,903	84,806	95,862	106,089	121,467	136,025	151,670

EXHIBIT 4A.13 Free Cash Flows and Financial Flows

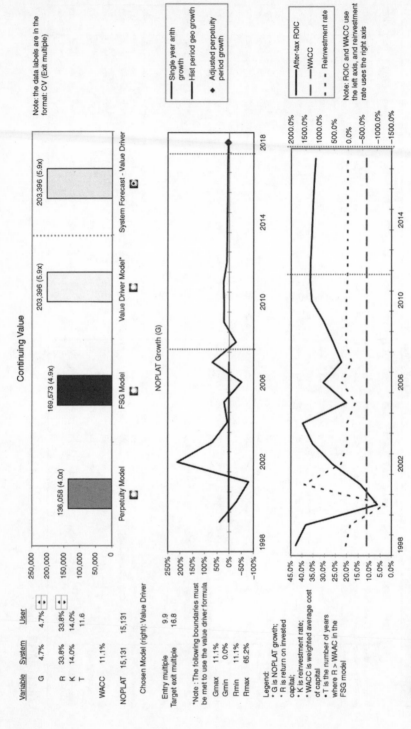

EXHIBIT 4A.14 Continuing Value

NOTES

1. I would like to thank Chris Cha for programming assistance.
2. This uses a linear approximation of the growth term in the finite supernormal growth formula. The approximation holds as long as g is reasonably close to WACC and N is small.

REFERENCES

Bailey, W. 1991. Valuing agricultural firms: An examination of the contingent claims approach to pricing real options. *Journal of Economic Dynamics and Control* 15: 771–791.

Copeland, T., T. Koller, and J. Murrin. 1994. *Valuation: Measuring and managing the value of companies.* 2nd ed. New York: John Wiley & Sons.

Kaplan, S., and R. Ruback. 1995. The valuation of cash flow forecasts: An empirical analysis. *Journal of Finance* 50 (4): 1059–1093.

CHAPTER 5

Developing an Automated Discounted Cash Flow Model

Robert J. Atra
Chair of the Finance Department, Lewis University

Rawley Thomas
President, LifeCycle Returns, Inc.

Intrinsic value is the investment concept on which our views of security analysis are founded. Without some defined standards of value for judging whether securities are over- or underpriced in the marketplace, the analyst is a potential victim of the tides of pessimism and euphoria which sweep the security markets.
—Cottle, Murray, and Block (*Graham and Dodd's Security Analysis, 5th Edition*, 1988)

Discounted cash flow (DCF) forms the core of finance. While its basic structure has existed for many years, DCF valuation now takes many forms, from the simplistic, such as the Gordon model, to the extraordinarily sophisticated, such as proprietary free cash flow models. Though professionals may employ other methods of valuation, such as relative valuation and the contingent claims approach, DCF forms the basis for all other valuation (Damodaran 2002).

Underscoring the importance of DCF valuation is the fact that it provides a linchpin to link various fields of finance. Security analysts should value stocks in much the same manner as corporate managers value projects. In the case of a project, managers estimate cash flows and discount them back to the present. They then net the present value of those cash flows against the cost of the project and decide whether to accept or reject the project. Since, conceptually, an investor can view any firm as simply a bundle of projects, security valuation should be similar to project valuation.

This chapter will examine how best to develop a subset of valuation models, namely those related to equity valuation. Analysts typically refer to the results of such models as "intrinsic values" of the equity, which they can compare to actual market prices to determine to what extent current stock prices are under- or overvalued. That information provides the basis for buy/sell recommendations.

Models producing intrinsic values are of value not only to security analysts and portfolio managers but to corporate managers as well. As firms compensate managers based on stock performance to eliminate agency problems, intrinsic valuation provides a valuable tool to judge their performance (Madden 2007). Of course, market prices provide a metric to judge managerial skill, but factors not under the control of managers often influence market prices. Furthermore, market noise obfuscates the ability to tell whether a movement in market price is genuinely due to managerial decisions. Consequently, even principles of finance textbooks are now emphasizing the need for managers to maximize intrinsic value as opposed to current market price (Brigham and Houston 2007).

Despite the historical importance of DCF valuation, security analysis and portfolio management research seems to be trending away from DCF and toward statistical methods such as multifactor analysis.[1] We find this trend unfortunate, since DCF may provide insights that are simply not available with pure statistical approaches to security selection. The DCF approach models price *level* as opposed to price *change*, and thus can help explain the price formation process of how market participants actually determine market prices. Understanding *how* the market values securities is critical to both external valuation professionals as well as managers.

For example, once an analyst has developed an accurate valuation model, the model can provide valuable information to the managers on how to increase the intrinsic value (and ultimately the market price) of their stock. Finding the economic value drivers is an essential result of developing a DCF model. Note that determining value drivers is *not* a benefit from other types of security valuation and portfolio management techniques such as multifactor models. For instance, if research determines that low price-to-book ratios predict future returns, of what value is that relationship to a corporate manager's decision-making process?

A common—and certainly justified—criticism of discounted cash flow valuation is that it is often performed on a case-by-case basis, with little empirical support for the results—especially the structure of the terminal value. Kaplan and Ruback (1995) emphasize this point: "Most economists readily accept the concept of estimating market value by calculating the discounted value of the relevant cash flows. However, little empirical evidence exists to show that discounted cash flows provide a reliable estimate of market value." One possible explanation for this conclusion is that researchers view DCF models as rather ad hoc, primarily driven by *subjective inputs* by analysts. (See Thomas Copeland's Chapter 4 and Randy Schostag's Chapter 15 for related material.) This subjectivity in the traditional analyst's process apparently makes a widespread evaluation of models difficult to examine. We disagree. We assert that valuation professionals can develop and test DCF models through a rigorous, formal process, improving both the understanding of valuation *and* the enhancement of investment performance.

Specifically, this chapter focuses on providing guidance in developing *automated* DCF models with no analyst intervention. An automated DCF model defined *a priori* yields many benefits. An automated model can cover a much larger universe of stocks than one that requires analysts' judgment and input. In fact, the automated model can value literally thousands of stocks, increasing the scope of possible investments when an investor wishes to both diversify broadly and still engage in a fundamental analysis strategy.[2] Models with good dispersion across industries promise better diversification than ones concentrated in particular industries. The large number of stocks covered by an automated model allows the model to be *empirically validated* in that the developer can quantitatively analyze and statistically test the model. Automated models should be free from anecdotal evidence and perform well over a substantial portion of the investable universe.

Covering such a large universe may be critical, for example, if portfolio managers seek to develop an index portfolio based not on market values but on company fundamentals. Arnott, Hsu, and Moore (2005) contend that portfolio managers should not weight index portfolios by market values since noise will result in overvalued stocks being overweighted and undervalued stocks being underweighted. Instead of market weights, they recommend fundamentally weighting an index by the "economic footprint" of the company. An intrinsic value is the model's determination of the economic footprint of a company's stock and, therefore, becomes the appropriate weight in a fundamentally indexed portfolio.

An automated system may also diminish the influence of emotion and herd behaviors in determining intrinsic prices and hence buy/sell recommendations. If widely used, an accurate automated DCF model should be able to detect systematic over- or undervaluation of stocks and provide a natural tether on current security prices, thus avoiding pricing bubbles. Finally, once built, automated DCF models should achieve substantial economies of scale, since the cost of the model is spread over perhaps thousands of securities. In contrast, security analysts may be able to cover only 15 to 20 securities.

Despite the advantages, automated DCF models do not preclude analyst input. In fact, developers may create models flexible enough to allow for analysts' input when expert analysis adds value. In such a case, the automated DCF model does most of the heavy lifting by quantifying how value is determined, and the analyst fine-tunes the model by changing particular inputs. For example, an analyst who has superior insight regarding the return on equity of a firm can override the normal automated process of estimating return on equity, and the model can determine an adjusted intrinsic value based on the analyst's insight. Naturally, this process allows an effective way to judge an analyst's recommendations, as the onus is now on the analyst to show that overriding the model has added value. The model's intrinsic values thus become a benchmark to monitor and evaluate analysts' opinions. This process should also point analysts to areas where their information advantage is the greatest, such as adjusting recent accounting information or forecasting near-term events, and make off limits areas where analyst intervention may simply add noise, such as changing distant terminal values.[3]

Ultimately, researchers should develop and evaluate an automated DCF model based on the following measurement principles:

- *Robustness.* What area of the universe of possible investments can the model reasonably value?
- *Accuracy.* Does the model's intrinsic values yield results that are close to actual prices?
- *Unbiasedness.* Does the model avoid systematically under- or overvaluing the securities in its scope and against its economic drivers?
- *Predictability.* Does the model actually forecast stock returns as opposed to simply estimating current prices?

A fundamentally sound automated DCF model does not use these as isolated features of the model, but rather as part of an integrated model building process. We present evidence that shows the most robust, accurate, and unbiased models are also the most predictive. Some valuation practitioners' primary interest lies in establishing an accurate value for a firm, while others focus on valuation in order to make investment recommendations. This range of professionals should find solace in knowing that a well-developed automated DCF model can achieve both objectives.

MODELS EXAMINED

In order to demonstrate the model development process, we examine several versions of dividend discount models (DDMs). DDMs have several advantages over other models. First, they are commonly accepted and examined in both academic and practitioner literature. Second, they represent actual cash flows received by investors and do not depend on the calculation of a hypothetical dividend that may be a source of controversy and error. Finally, DDMs represent an excellent choice to demonstrate model development since they need only a small number of inputs. The tractable number of inputs enables us to examine the model-building process without overshadowing the process with the sheer number of inputs used, parameters estimated, or complex theory expounded on in building the valuation model.

Using DDMs possesses disadvantages as well. They are not nearly as robust as other models, as they can only apply to dividend-paying firms. Models with strict assumptions, such as the Gordon model, are even less robust given that they assume a constant growth rate. Furthermore, some DDMs, such as the ROPE[4] model discussed later, require that companies have positive earnings in order to estimate future dividends. We examine the importance of this issue in the section on robustness.

Additionally, DDMs that allow for a fading of the dividend still depend on a terminal value. Intrinsic values produced by the DDM may exhibit extreme sensitivity to the terminal value, which can represent a large portion of the total present value and can be difficult to estimate. Finally, some research concludes that DDMs produce biased estimators of actual stock values (Bethke and Boyd 1983) and are, therefore, inherently inaccurate. Later, we address the issues of accuracy and bias as well as how best to handle those two issues in the process of building a DCF model.

Because this chapter primarily focuses on building an *automated* DCF model, our process does not rely on analysts' estimates, but simply extrapolates historical data to compute intrinsic values. We therefore avoid look-ahead bias—such as when analysts may infer future terminal values from current prices—in our automated process.

We demonstrate our process using three particular DDMs: (1) the constant growth or Gordon model, (2) a DDM based on the fading growth rate of the dividend, termed the GROW[5] model, and (3) a DDM based on a fading return on equity and an increasing payout ratio, termed the ROPE model.[6]

The Gordon model (Gordon 1962) assumes a constant growth rate and takes on the following form:

$$P_0 = \frac{D_1}{K - G} \tag{5.1}$$

where D_1 is the dividend received one year from the point of the present value calculation, K is the equity discount rate, and G is the growth rate in the dividend, which is assumed to be constant. As applied in our work, we estimate the parameters and the resulting P_0 becomes the model's estimate for the intrinsic value of the stock price. We refer to the Gordon model as a "one-phase model" in that it assumes a constant growth rate and, therefore, assumes the company is in the last phase of its life cycle (i.e., the company is mature).

We refer to the GROW and ROPE models as "multistage" or "multi-phase" DDMs. Both models usually assume an initial stage when dividends grow at a high rate (phase 1), a fade period or regression toward the mean where the dividend growth rate declines (phase 2), and a terminal period in which the dividend growth rate becomes constant (phase 3). The models' flexibility stems from the fact that the model builder can adjust the three stages based on experience, judgment, and empirical evidence. Both the GROW and ROPE models discount all cash flows at a constant discount rate.

The primary difference between the GROW and ROPE models relates to the way the growth rate of the dividend fades. In the GROW formulation, the growth rate simply fades linearly to the terminal growth rate according to the following formula:[7]

$$\Delta G = \frac{G_t - G_1}{N_2} \tag{5.2}$$

where ΔG represents the annual change in the growth rate, G_t represents the growth rate in phase 3 (terminal growth rate), G_1 represents the initial growth rate in phase 1, and N_2 is the number of years in phase 2. Analysts must estimate both the growth rates and the phase lengths. Once phase 2 ends, the Gordon model can compute the terminal value for the GROW model where G_t would serve as the constant growth rate.

The ROPE model does not assume that the growth rate fades in such a simple fashion, but instead uses the sustainable growth framework to construct the fade. In the sustainable growth framework, the dividend equals the product of the initial book value for the period, the return on equity (ROE) for the period, and 1 minus the retention rate (RR). As the ROE and RR fade, the dividend changes (not necessarily decreases) and the result implies a growth rate in the dividend. In the ROPE model, we assume the ROE and RR fade in the same linear manner as the growth rate in dividends in the GROW model and, therefore, compute the change as:

$$\Delta ROE = \frac{ROE_t - ROE_1}{N_2} \tag{5.3}$$

$$\Delta RR = \frac{RR_t - RR_1}{N_2} \tag{5.4}$$

where we define the time subscripts as in equation (5.2). As with the GROW model, once phase 2 ends, the terminal value for the ROPE model computes according to equation (5.1).

Depending on the relative fade rates of the ROE and RR, the dividend growth rate may actually *increase* during the fade period due to the dominant effect of a fading RR. The previous research of Rozeff (1990) and our own experience suggest this increase in dividend growth rates may be a more accurate representation of the dividend pattern of maturing companies.

DATA AND INITIAL PARAMETERIZATION

The data for our example are from Ipreo and, in all, include over 5,000 companies from January 1, 1996, through the second quarter of 2007, which results in over 48,000 company years of data. We chose not to limit the span of sectors examined but rather to truly stress test the models by examining how they perform over the entire universe.

To compare our models, we must choose some initial parameters. In selecting those parameters for the three models, we recognize the fact that previous research has indicated a consistent bias in DDMs to tend to underestimate intrinsic values. We therefore choose initial parameters that tend to increase the intrinsic values, though we will adjust those later in an attempt to improve the model. For each firm, we begin by estimating a capital asset pricing model (CAPM) discount rate, using the long-term Treasury bond rate, the firm's median industry beta, and an equity risk premium of 3 percent. Though the estimate of the risk premium may seem low compared to historical risk premiums, that premium represents just an initial parameterization that yields generally unbiased estimates of intrinsic values relative to stock prices according to DDMs.[8] We estimate 5 percent terminal growth rates for the three models.[9] Finally, we assume the simplest fade model, one that immediately starts fading the growth rate, which, in essence, turns the GROW and ROPE into two-phase models. Note that we chose these as the *initial* inputs, which serve as a *first step* in the model-building process. After testing the models based on the initial parameterization, we propose ways to improve them.

MEASUREMENT PRINCIPLES

All valuation models are estimations of the actual underlying valuation process.[10] Mathematical constructions of the models will limit the allowable inputs and, therefore, restrict the model from valuing all possible investments. For example, the Gordon model with its constant growth assumption can value only firms where the expected growth rate of the dividend is less than the discount rate—a very strict limitation indeed. However, even those DDMs that incorporate a fading growth rate have limitations. The GROW model can value only firms where $D > 0$ since it relies on a base dividend to determine the next period's dividend. In contrast, the ROPE model does not rely on a base dividend since it allows for an initial RR of 1. As the RR fades from 1, dividends commence and the model becomes able to value the stock. Despite the advantage of not relying on a base dividend, the ROPE model cannot value every stock. Since the ROPE model uses sustainable growth, it does require positive earnings to generate a meaningful retention rate.

Robustness

Robustness is our term for how many of the stocks in the universe the model is able to value. We measure robustness as the number of company years where a model produces meaningful values for stocks in the universe as a percentage of the total number of company years in the data set. Exhibit 5.1 gives results for the entire period, which has a maximum of 48,299 company years.

As indicated in the table, the Gordon model is the least robust, and the ROPE model performs the best in terms of robustness, covering almost 50 percent of the universe. The robustness information indicates that of the two models with a fading growth rate, the ROPE model covers almost twice the number of stocks that the GROW model covers. Clearly, the ROPE model offers analysts the most opportunity in terms of the number of securities that they can value via an automated valuation model.

Naturally, models exist that cover a greater percentage of the universe than those presented here. The preceding analysis does point out, however, that the model builder must present robustness as a critical feature of any valuation model. Even models with very similar characteristics—both the GROW and the ROPE are dividend models incorporating fading growth rates—possess very different degrees of robustness.

EXHIBIT 5.1 1996–2007 Results

Period	Gordon		GROW		ROPE	
	Stocks	% of Total	Stocks	% of Total	Stocks	% of Total
1996–2007	5,004	10.4%	12,104	25.1%	23,999	49.7%

Accuracy

An intuitively attractive feature of any valuation model is whether it produces results consistent with actual market prices. While nobody expects a model to be perfectly accurate, models that produce intrinsic values far from actual prices are suspect. In general, analysts can measure the accuracy of a model by examining a pricing error, computed as:

$$\text{Error} = \frac{IV_{it} - P_{it}}{P_{it}} \qquad (5.5)$$

where P_{it} is the market price of security i at time t and IV_{it} is the intrinsic value produced by the respective model for security i at time t. The smaller the pricing errors produced by the model, the more accurate the model. One can consider errors in absolute value if one is only concerned about accuracy or, as defined earlier, if one is primarily concerned about systematic bias (overall under- or overvaluation of the securities).

Our definition of pricing error has intuitive appeal for later use in predicting returns. Since we view intrinsic value as the true price, we would expect the market price to migrate toward the intrinsic value.[11] In such a case, our definition of pricing error produces the return from purchasing the stock and having the price move to the intrinsic value. Furthermore, the definition in equation (5.5) gives the correct ordering of stock values—the most undervalued would exhibit the largest positive errors, while the most overvalued would have the largest negative errors.

Because the pricing errors are not likely to be normally distributed, the mean pricing error likely misleads. For example, consider the intrinsic values produced by the Gordon model. The model produces values from near zero (for stocks with small dividends, small growth rates, and large discount rates) to values tending toward infinity (for stocks where the growth rate approaches the discount rate). Clearly, the model will lead to skewed pricing errors. Thus, the median pricing error in these cases may yield a better measure of central tendency, which we present later.

Exhibit 5.2 presents the absolute values of percentage pricing errors for the 40th, 50th (median), and 60th percentiles for the Gordon, GROW, and ROPE models. The errors are extremely large, indicating that the models overall are not very accurate, though the Gordon and ROPE perform much better than the GROW model, exhibiting not only a smaller median but a much smaller range between the 40th and 60th percentiles. The large errors may indicate a poorly specified model—one where the analyst could more accurately estimate the discount rate or growth rates. A large part of our work will demonstrate how to improve the accuracy of the model.

While the percentiles contain valuable information, we believe that examining the entire distribution of pricing errors is the easiest way to

EXHIBIT 5.2 Absolute Percentage Pricing Errors of Three DDMs

Percentile	Gordon	GROW	ROPE
40th	54.205	110.031	76.641
50th	67.079	208.961	120.732
60th	78.617	321.304	238.906

evaluate the accuracy of a model. The plot of the cumulative distribution function (CDF) of the absolute errors provides a convenient way to instantly assess accuracy. Tracking of the model's accuracy by the CDF also allows the model builder to visualize accuracy *across* models. We present a hypothetical example of a CDF for accuracy in Exhibit 5.3. The more accurate model's sharply steep curve on the left side of the CDF horizontal scale implies lower errors and a tighter distribution of errors. The less accurate model has a flatter CDF. The flatter CDF in the figure reveals that the model's errors have more variability and are of greater magnitude. The most accurate models, therefore, will plot up and to the left.

Combining Accuracy and Robustness

Examining only accuracy or robustness may misrepresent a model's true value. For example, examine the percentage errors in Exhibit 5.2. The table clearly demonstrates that the Gordon model and ROPE model exhibit superior accuracy when compared to the GROW model, but are close in

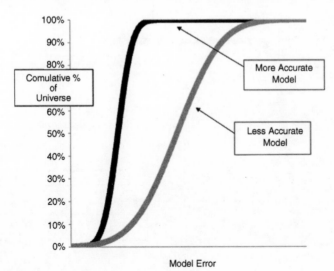

EXHIBIT 5.3 Comparing the Accuracy of Models

accuracy when compared to each other. Which one, therefore, should analysts considered superior? The problem is that we are not comparing the models on an equal basis. Recall from Exhibit 5.1 that the ROPE model, despite similar accuracy to the Gordon model, values over *five times* the number of securities! The Gordon model handles only mature companies, which may be considerably easier to value, whereas the ROPE model's scope encompasses all firms with positive earnings, making the model a much more fruitful candidate for refinement.

One way to visualize the value of a model in terms of *both* robustness and accuracy is to use a CDF-type diagram, but adjust the vertical scale by the percentage of stocks of the entire universe that the model can value. Exhibit 5.4 represents a diagram that compares three hypothetical models on the principles of robustness and accuracy. The first model not only exhibits accuracy as evidenced by its steep slope but it also rises high on the vertical axis. The height of the curve demonstrates its robustness, as it is able to cover over 80 percent of the universe. The second model in our diagram demonstrates accuracy—it has a steep slope toward the left of the horizontal scale—but scores low on robustness, covering less than 20 percent of the universe. The final hypothetical model displays neither accuracy nor robustness. The line is relatively flat, indicating errors are substantial and varied. Furthermore, the model only covers between 15 percent and 20 percent of the stocks in the universe. With one diagram, an investment manager can

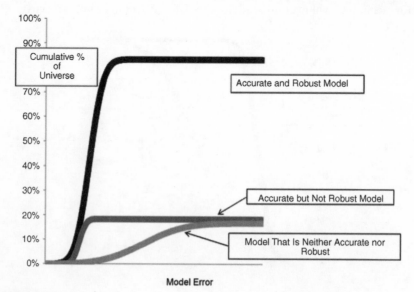

EXHIBIT 5.4   Comparing the Accuracy and Robustness of Models

directly compare several models on two fundamental principles of valuation—accuracy and robustness.

Exhibit 5.4 also yields great practical insight as to what direction a firm should take when it comes to allocating its resources. Take, for example, the accurate and robust model in the diagram. Clearly, the model provides accurate valuations on a large number of securities. Analyst input regarding stocks covered by that model is likely to have only incremental benefits. Instead, firms should direct resources and analyst skill toward the approximate 20 percent of the universe that the model does not cover. For the model that displays accuracy but not robustness, firms should invest more resources in model improvement to allow for a greater breadth of coverage.

Now let us examine the combined accuracy and robustness of DDMs. As discussed earlier, the diagram plots the percentage of the universe that the model covers on the vertical axis and the absolute value of errors on the horizontal axis. The scale on the vertical axis is set to log base 2 for easier visualization. Exhibit 5.5 shows that the Gordon model performs relatively poorly, particularly in terms of robustness, as it covers only a small portion of the universe. Exhibit 5.6 includes the GROW model, which although not very accurate, does display increased robustness resulting in a vertical increase over the Gordon model. Finally, Exhibit 5.7 includes all three models. Clearly, the ROPE model performs much better than the Gordon or GROW models, rising more quickly and to a greater vertical distance than the other models.

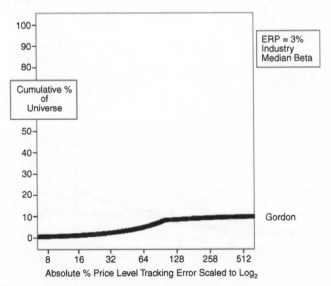

EXHIBIT 5.5   Accuracy and Robustness of Gordon Model

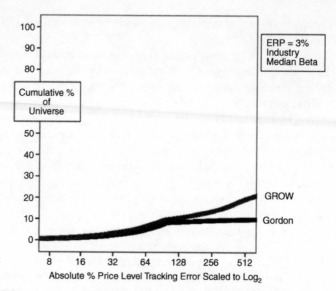

EXHIBIT 5.6   Accuracy and Robustness of Gordon and GROW Models

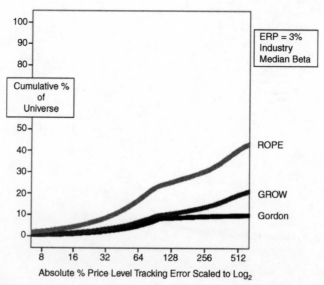

EXHIBIT 5.7   Accuracy and Robustness of Gordon, GROW and ROPE Models

EXHIBIT 5.8   Signed Percentage Pricing Errors of Three DDMs

Percentile	Gordon	GROW	ROPE
30th	−58.495	−37.551	−26.664
40th	−45.364	−20.805	−12.052
50th	−29.521	−1.528	3.222
60th	−11.676	19.627	19.210
70th	14.119	43.783	37.996

Unbiasedness

Bias, as we use the term, refers to the tendency of a model to systematically over- or undervalue securities. We view an unbiased model as one where 50 percent of securities are overvalued and 50 percent are undervalued against intrinsic values.[12] Clearly, a relationship should exist between bias and accuracy—a model that systematically places too low or too high intrinsic values on securities becomes unlikely to produce accurate estimates. Unbiasedness, therefore, represents a most desirable feature of a model. Valuation practitioners will not find models that consistently recommend all buy or all sell signals very beneficial.

As evidence of the connection between unbiasedness and accuracy, we examine the *signed* errors for the models under consideration. Exhibit 5.8 presents the signed errors for the three models for the 30th through 70th percentiles. The data indicate that the GROW and ROPE exhibit the least bias, with the Gordon model biased toward overvaluation. While neither is perfectly unbiased, each demonstrates a change from overvaluing to undervaluing securities within one decile of the median. In contrast, the Gordon model tends to overvalue securities, as evidenced by the negative errors that do not turn positive until above the 60th percentile.

A second type of bias not commonly researched in the valuation literature relates to the bias caused by a particular parameter. Examining this type of bias becomes particularly useful in improving a model's performance. A subsequent section covers in detail reducing parameter model bias to improve model performance.

Predictive Capability

Ultimately, the value of the measurement principles of robustness, accuracy, and unbiasedness to practitioners lies in their ability to produce superior investment decisions. Unlike much of the previous academic work, which has tended to focus on whether models are replicating the true underlying valuation process, we intend to show that the most robust, accurate, and unbiased models also become the most predictive. We will concentrate on an intermodel comparison and not attempt to show that any of the DDMs beat the market. Our experience with both these simplistic models and in the development of the LifeCycle Returns proprietary models (Chapter 11) finds that models with the best opportunity to earn superior returns also perform well on the measurement principles of accuracy, robustness, and unbiasedness.

Some people may find it ironic that an accurate model—one that computes intrinsic values close to actual market prices—becomes best suited to earn excess returns. Indeed, a perfectly accurate model makes no recommendations as to which securities are under- or overvalued. Our view posits that market prices represent errors around intrinsic values.[13] Thus, the under- or overvaluation indicated by the model predicts the direction of future stock prices. The migration of prices *toward* intrinsic values produces the return from the under- or overvaluation. In that migration sense, we agree with Lee (2001), who makes the analogy that the market is moving toward efficiency like "the ocean is constantly trying to become flat." The market may not be instantaneously efficient, but it is trying to correct pricing errors. Inaccurate models do not produce theoretically correct intrinsic values and, therefore, provide inaccurate *signals* on the future movements of stock prices.

To test whether models that perform well on the previously discussed measurement principles demonstrate more predictive capability, we divide each model's intrinsic values into deciles at the beginning of the year, ranking intrinsic values from the most overvalued to most undervalued. Since annual accounting information is not available at the beginning of the year, we allow for a disclosure lag by subsequently tracking the performance of the decile portfolios over the following 3 to 15 months. In addition, we oversample the tails, tracking the performance of the top and bottom 1 percent and 5 percent of the over- and undervaluations. Oversampling the tails is a convenient way to test the extreme results of the model. We repeat our portfolio procedure for the entire period from 1996 to 2007 and compute average returns. For models that perform well on our predictive capability criterion, the most overvalued portfolios should perform the worst, while the most undervalued portfolios should perform the best.

Empirical results for our models' portfolios sorted on over- and undervaluations appear in Exhibit 5.9. For clarity, we present the empirical results for only the ROPE model in Exhibit 5.10. As the reader may see, the models do not perform exceptionally well. However, with the exception of the bottom 30 percent of more overvalued securities, the ROPE does exhibit some predictive ability by producing increasing returns in the range

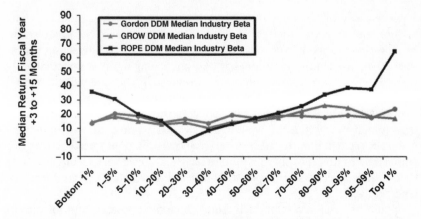

EXHIBIT 5.9 Median Returns for Dividend Discount Models

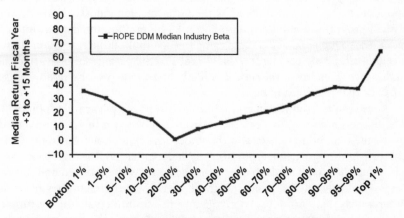

EXHIBIT 5.10 Median Returns for ROPE Model

between the 30th and 100th percentiles. Of course, we obtained these results with a first pass of the model-building process. Since this chapter
focuses on model *development*, not just model selection, we need to demonstrate how to improve the models.

Parameter Bias and Model Improvement

Thus far, we have presented limited information that more robust, accurate,
and unbiased models are also the most predictive. Model builders need,

however, a systematic way to *improve* the accuracy of their models, which should lead to better predictive ability. To detect where the greatest improvements are likely to occur, we use a parameter bias-detecting procedure. This procedure determines if any particular input is systematically related to the under- or overvaluations produced by the model. If so, removing the bias will increase the accuracy of the model.

To demonstrate our procedure, we concentrate on the discount rate as determined by the CAPM. Recall that we first estimated our models by using the median industry beta to determine the discount rate. There are, of course, alternatives. Numerous studies have employed various discount rate specifications such as firm-specific betas, industry betas, and uniform discount rates.

Since we have several models from which to choose, we opt to concentrate on the one with the most promise, the ROPE model. Because the errors are not likely to be normally distributed, we test for parameter bias by running a regression of the fractional ranks of the over-/undervaluation errors produced by the ROPE model against the fractional ranks of the corresponding firms' betas (estimated by the firms' median industry betas).[14] Statistical programs compute fractional ranks by ranking the data of interest from low to high and assigning a value to each rank. If the regression shows a relationship between the fractional ranks of the parameter values and the under-/overvaluations, the model is likely to be improved by removing the effect of that relationship bias.

Our results from the fractional rank regression appear in Exhibit 5.11. The figure shows a clear negative relationship between the fractional rank of the median industry beta and the under-/overvaluations. Since the vertical scale in the figure runs from over- to undervaluation, the regression indicates that the model tends to overvalue securities with high median industry betas, while it tends to undervalue those with low median industry betas. In other words, beta produces too large an impact on the valuation estimate. Beta drives down the intrinsic values of the high-beta securities to the point where the securities become overvalued. Conversely, the undervaluation results from the too-low discount rate associated with low-beta securities.

To remove the bias associated with the beta, we simply set the beta to 1 for all securities, resulting in a uniform discount rate. Better valuation results with uniform discount rates are not uncommon in academic literature. See Kaplan and Ruback (1995) and Sougiannis and Yaekura (2001) for examples of uniform discount rates.

After removing the bias due to the discount rate, we retest the model using our fundamental measurement principles. Using the scaled CDF graph, we see the improvements in the accuracy of the model in Exhibit 5.12. The slope of the ROPE model with a beta of 1 rises more rapidly compared to

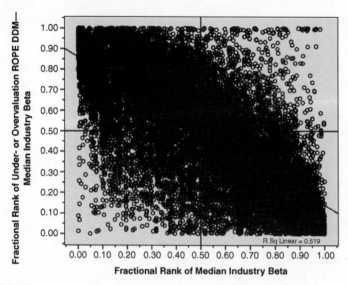

EXHIBIT 5.11 Relationship Between Under (over) Valuation and Beta

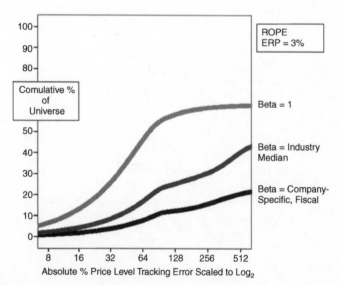

EXHIBIT 5.12 Accuracy and Robustness with Different Beta Specifications

the ROPE model with the median industry beta. For comparison, we also include the scaled CDF of the ROPE model incorporating a firm-specific (fiscal year) beta, which demonstrates poorer performance than the other two ROPE specifications. Our results not only agree with Kaplan and Ruback (1995) and Sougiannis and Yaekura (2001), but are also in the same spirit as Fama and French (1992)—*beta, as computed here, is not useful in valuing the securities in our sample.*

What effect does the increase in accuracy have on the predictive capability? To examine that issue, we revisit the diagram from our decile analysis, but now with a comparison between various specifications of the beta for the ROPE model. As Exhibit 5.13 illustrates, the ROPE model with the beta bias removed performs substantially better. Unlike the returns for the ROPE formulation with firm-specific or median industry betas, the ROPE model with a beta of 1 shows a steady increase from the bottom 1 percent (most overvalued) to the top 1 percent (most undervalued). Though the returns were generally positive for the market during this period, the spread between the top and bottom 1 percent is extraordinarily large for the improved ROPE model. The other model specifications seem to have much more difficulty with securities in the tails, showing very large returns for *overvalued* securities as defined by the model.

As a check, we also revisit the Gordon and GROW models' performance with a beta equal to 1 to determine if they outperform the ROPE. Comparing across models in Exhibit 5.14, we see that the most promising model, the ROPE, exhibits superior performance, while the other two models fail to demonstrate the consistency of the ROPE model across the deciles.

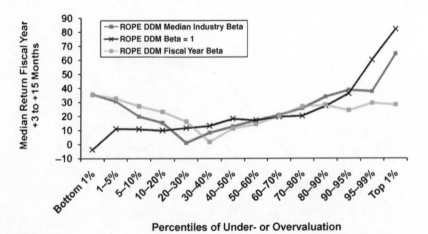

Percentiles of Under- or Overvaluation

EXHIBIT 5.13 Median Returns for ROPE Model with Different Beta Specfications

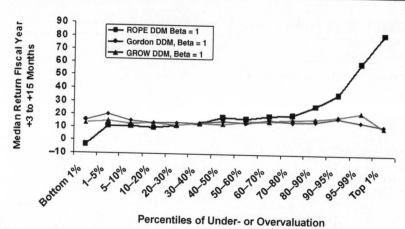

EXHIBIT 5.14   Median Returns for Three Dividend Models, Beta = 1

We provide additional support for the hypothesis that removing the bias improves the model's peformance by constructing portfolios with the under- and overvalued securities as indicated by the three models in Exhibit 5.14. Since analysts focus primarily on the most under- or overvalued securities, we construct four portfolios: (1) a portfolio consisting of the 20 percent most undervalued securities, (2) a portfolio consisting of the 10 percent most undervalued securities, (3) a long/short portfolio that invests long in the 20 percent most undervalued and shorts the 20 percent most overvalued securities, and (4) a long/short portfolio that invests long in the 10 percent most undervalued and shorts the 10 percent most overvalued securities.

Results for our portfolios appear in Exhibit 5.15. Since the market was generally up, the long-only portfolios perform much better, but in all cases the adjusted ROPE—the ROPE with a beta equal to 1—outperforms the other ROPE models. The removal of the bias results in increased performance for the adjusted ROPE model above the initial ROPE specifications for all of the portfolio constructions. The increase in portfolio returns due to the removal of the bias ranges from about 6 percent for the 20/20 long/short portfolio to about 10 percent for the other portfolios.

PROPRIETARY MODELS

Dividend discount models represent relatively simple and straightforward valuation models. Their simplicity, however, limits the model builder. More sophisticated models, such as those that estimate a firm's free cash

EXHIBIT 5.15 Portfolio Results for Three ROPE Model Specifications

Portfolio	Portfolio Percentage Return
Long Only (Top 20% Undervalued)	
ROPE DDM Beta = 1	38.88
ROPE DDM Median industry beta	29.89
ROPE DDM Fiscal year beta	27.35
Long Only (Top 10% Undervalued)	
ROPE DDM Beta = 1	50.45
ROPE DDM Median industry beta	40.83
ROPE DDM Fiscal year beta	26.73
Long/Short (20% Undervalued/20% Overvalued)	
ROPE DDM Beta = 1	14.52
ROPE DDM Median industry beta	8.35
ROPE DDM Fiscal year beta	0.25
Long/Short (10% Undervalued/10% Overvalued)	
ROPE DDM Beta = 1	20.30
ROPE DDM Median industry beta	10.08
ROPE DDM Fiscal year beta	(0.06)

flow, contain more levers the analyst can pull in order to create a model that performs better as measured by robustness, accuracy, unbiasedness, and predictive capability. How does a more sophisticated model compare to a simpler construction? We answer that question by presenting results from the LifeCycle models.[15]

Recall from our earlier discussion that both the Gordon and GROW models were restricted to performing valuations on stocks that pay dividends. Furthermore, the Gordon model was only able to value firms whose expected growth rate was less than the discount rate. Consequently, valuation models that estimate future cash flows independent of dividends may obtain a significant advantage in terms of robustness. The ROPE model, in contrast, did not assume an initial dividend, but estimated a dividend based on earnings and retention rates. However, what if earnings are not positive? Once again, a model able to handle the difficulty of firms with negative earnings will obtain a large advantage over simpler models in terms of robustness.

More sophisticated models should also possess greater accuracy due to the additional amount of information they pull into the valuation process. For instance, dividend models generally do not incorporate the balance sheet in establishing firm value. The ROPE model does include return on equity in its computation, but does not specifically include any analysis of the lives of the assets producing that return on equity. Proprietary models dig deeper into the drivers of the cash flows by examining both the income statement and the balance sheet. Accounting information, however, is not necessarily reflective of the economics of the firm. Analysts must adjust the information to cure any distortions caused by generally accepted accounting principles (GAAP) accounting—and those adjustments should lead to increased model accuracy.

Using the LifeCycle model as an example, we demonstrate an increase in accuracy and robustness over the best dividend discount model. Our S-curve diagram for the LifeCycle model and the ROPE model appears in Exhibit 5.16. The height of the curve demonstrates that the LifeCycle model is more robust—it can value securities the ROPE model simply cannot, despite the ROPE model being the most robust of the DDMs. The LifeCycle model values approximately 50 percent more securities than are covered by the ROPE.

We contend that the increase in firms covered by a model does not necessarily come at a cost of accuracy. Indeed, Exhibit 5.16 provides evidence of that as well. The steeper slope represents the increase in accuracy of the proprietary model, as the adjustments made in the model better reflect the true underlying cash flows of the firm, and, hence, provide more

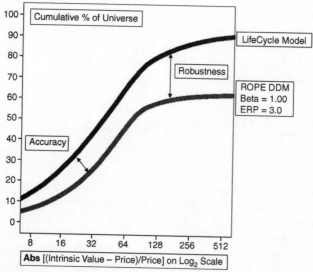

EXHIBIT 5.16 Accuracy and Robustness of LifeCycle Model Compared to Gordon Model

accurate valuations. Despite covering much more difficult firms to value—those with negative earnings, such as start-ups—the LifeCycle model does so with more accuracy. While a complete analysis of proprietary models versus commonly accepted models, such as the DDMs, is beyond the scope of this chapter, the evidence in Exhibit 5.16 should console analysts that trade-offs between the number of securities covered and accuracy are not a foregone conclusion. Developers may, indeed, build superior models on both accuracy and robustness!

CONCLUSION

Using dividend discount models as examples, we have demonstrated how to evaluate and improve automated discounted cash flow models. Our results from this sample suggest that the fundamental measurement principles of robustness, accuracy, unbiasedness, and predictive capability are not separate concepts but part of an integrated model-building process. Furthermore, we showed in our sample how to improve the model with respect to accuracy and predictive capability once we remove the bias influence from a particular parameter.

Despite the simplistic models used, the results are consistent with our basic premise that models can achieve superior robustness, accuracy, unbiasedness, and predictive capability. Moreover, builders can improve even the best of a subset of models in some systematic fashion. Our initial results should encourage model builders that choosing between models does not necessarily involve trade-offs between the measurement principles. Following our process, they may indeed develop dominant proprietary models, leading to improved investment decisions and portfolio performance.

APPENDIX: ACADEMIC LITERATURE

There exists a substantial and growing body of literature investigating the performance of valuation models. In the academic literature, researchers are primarily concerned about the ability of valuation models to provide accurate and unbiased estimates of market prices. Rozeff produced one of the earlier works on the topic (1990), where he analyzes the performance of two different three-phase dividend discount models—one that fades the dividend growth rate and another that fades the return on equity and retention rate in a linear fashion. Our chapter revisited those two models as an example of our model-building process. Central to Rozeff's evaluation of the dividend discount models is the analysis of pricing errors, defined as

$(V_{it} - P_{it})/P_{it}$, where V_{it} is the value predicted by the model for stock i at time t and P_{it} is the corresponding market price. Researchers consider models that lead to lower pricing errors superior in terms of estimating how the market sets prices.

Numerous other studies have utilized a similar criterion for evaluating and comparing valuation models. Francis, Olsson, and Oswald (2001) use a pricing error definition as in Rozeff to compare the accuracy of dividend, free cash flow, and abnormal earnings models and later to compare mechanical earnings and residual income models. Penman and Sougiannis (1998) define a valuation error as $(P_{it} - V_{it})/P_{it}$ to compare dividend, free cash flow, and earnings models; and Sougiannis and Yaekura (2001) use the same definition of valuation error to compute the accuracy of analysts' earnings forecasts. More recently, Bakshi and Chen (2005) define a valuation error similarly in evaluating the accuracy of a stochastic valuation model.

Downs (1991) employs an "overvalue ratio" as P_{it}/V_{it} to evaluate an asset-based valuation model. Alternatively, Frankel and Lee (1998) use the inverse of Downs's overvalue ratio to research an analyst-based valuation model, and Kaplan and Ruback (1995) use the natural log of V_{it}/P_{it} to determine if DCF models accurately value highly leveraged transactions. Courteau, Kao, O'Keefe, and Richardson (2003) compute mean squared pricing errors and interpercentile ranges in their comparison of direct valuation and multiplier approaches.

In addition to accuracy, most studies also examine the issue of their models' biases. Rozeff explicitly factors bias in his models by adjusting the models so that the pricing errors average out to zero, thus making the models unbiased by that definition. Others such as Francis, Olsson, and Oswald (2000) examine the sign of the median pricing errors. Kaplan and Ruback (1995), Sougiannis and Yaekura (2001), and Courteau, Kao, and Richardson (2001) use linear regression to test for bias by regressing some form of prices on model values. If model values are unbiased, the regression should yield an intercept of zero and slope of one. The regression analysis simultaneously tests for accuracy since models that produce values close to their actual prices will result in regressions with a high r-squared.

In addition, some previous research has investigated another type of bias that relates pricing errors to various subsets of the data or systematic factors. Francis, Olsson, and Oswald (2000), for instance, test whether model accuracy is different between high and low accrual firms or between firms with varying degrees of research and development spending. Bakshi and Chen (2005), based on their observation that pricing errors are contemporaneously correlated across stocks, test whether factors such as default spreads, term spreads, size premiums, and value premiums can explain pricing errors.

In examining accuracy and bias, many studies also investigate the distribution of pricing or valuation errors. Bakshi and Chen, for example, examine standard deviation of the pricing errors, while Rozeff presents quartiles of the pricing errors. Kaplan and Ruback display the actual distribution of pricing errors for their DCF models. The consensus of previous work concludes that researchers should employ both the *central tendency* and the *dispersion* of pricing errors in evaluating models.

Compared to the issues of accuracy and bias, fewer studies have examined whether accurate models are more predictive. Rozeff alludes to the issue by stating that a more accurate model is more likely to be successful. Courteau, Kao, and Richardson (2001) recommend that future research move beyond an assumption of market efficiency and test whether different models have varying predictive capability. Frankel and Lee (1998) test the concept of predictive capability and find the V_{it}/P_{it} ratio produced by their residual income model to be correlated with long-term future returns. Similarly, Francis et al. find the V_{it}/P_{it} ratio to be predictive of returns in excess of those relative to CAPM but not relative to a three-factor model.

With increasing frequency, academic researchers are investigating the measurement principles of accuracy, bias, predictive capability, and, to a lesser extent, robustness. Previous academic literature, however, primarily has presented the principles as evaluation techniques rather than *tools* to systematically improve models. We believe our chapter help fills that gap of systematic model improvement in the literature.

NOTES

1. For example, DCF and valuation research primarily appears in accounting journals as opposed to journals strictly related to finance.
2. A recent study by Domian, Louton, and Racine (2007) suggests that the number of stocks needed to adequately diversify is well in excess of 100.
3. It is possible that analysts will have insight regarding terminal values. In such a case, that insight should become part of the normal model-building process to ensure the terminal value adjustments are empirically validated.
4. Rozeff never specifies precisely what the "ROPE" acronym means. Atra and Thomas guess from its context and calculations that "ROPE" may mean "Return on Payout and Return on Equity."
5. Rozeff never specifies precisely what the "GROW" acronym means. From its context and calculations, "GROW" may mean the specified, multi-stage "growth" model.
6. These terms are found in academic literature such as Rozeff (1990).
7. In our description, we assume the fade is linear. Other fade patterns are possible as well. For instance, the model may employ an exponential fade pattern as in

Bernstein, Kirschner, and Lui (2002). Numerical examples of the fading patterns appear in Rozeff.

8. Both theoretical literature (Cornell 1999) and some practitioner literature (Lawson 2002) suggest a lower equity risk premium than historically observed.

9. Since the ROPE model requires estimates of both ROE and RR, we estimate these to be 8.33 percent and 60 percent, respectively, to achieve the same 5 percent growth rate.

10. We present a review of the academic literature related to the measurement principles in the chapter's appendix.

11. The authors acknowledge a discussion with Tom Copeland in 2004 regarding this point.

12. There may be a theoretical reason for an overall under- or overvaluation of securities. For example, an accurate macroeconomic model may suggest at a given point in time that the entire market is over- or undervalued, and that model may therefore be useful in asset allocation. Since the models of concern in this chapter primarily concentrate on practitioner security selection, we leave the issue of integrating a macroeconomic model with a security selection model for future research.

13. Our view, therefore, contrasts with the traditional view of market efficiency, which assumes that intrinsic values represent errors around the (true) market price.

14. Our (unreported) tests of normality of the errors confirm that they are not normal but instead fat-tailed.

15. Chapter 11 provides details of the computations in the LifeCycle models.

REFERENCES

Arnott, R., J. Hsu, and P. Moore. 2005. Fundamental indexation. *Financial Analysts Journal* 61 (March/April): 83–99.

Bakshi, G., and Z. Chen. 2005. Stock valuation in dynamic economies. *Journal of Financial Markets* 8 (May): 111–151.

Bernstein, R., L. Kirschner, and K. Lui. 2002. Quantitative primer: A guide to concepts, models, and techniques. *Merrill Lynch Global Securities Research and Economics Group* (September).

Bethke, W., and S. Boyd. 1983. Should dividend discount models be yield-tilted? *Journal of Portfolio Management* 9 (Spring): 23–27.

Brigham, E., and J. Houston. 2007. *Fundamentals of financial management.* 11th ed. Mason, OH: Thomson-Southwestern, 8–11.

Cornell, B. 1999. *The equity risk premium.* New York: John Wiley & Sons, 126–157.

Cottle, S., R. Murray, and F. Block. 1988. *Graham and Dodd's Security Analysis.* 5th ed. New York: McGraw-Hill, 41.

Courteau, L., J. Kao, T. O'Keefe, and G. Richardson. 2003. Gains to valuation accuracy of direct valuation over industry multiplier approaches. (April 4) Available at SSRN: http://ssrn.com/abstract=393120.

Courteau, L., J. Kao, and G. Richardson. 2001. Equity valuation employing the ideal versus ad hoc terminal value expressions. *Contemporary Accounting Research* 18 (Winter): 625–661.

Damodaran, A. 2002. *Investment valuation: Tools and techniques for determining the value of any asset.* 2nd ed. New York: John Wiley & Sons, 11–25.

Domian, D., D. Louton, and M. Racine. 2007. Diversification in portfolios of individual stocks: 100 stocks are not enough. *Financial Review* 42 (November): 557–570.

Downs, T. 1991. An alternative approach to fundamental analysis: The asset side of the equation. *Journal of Portfolio Management* (Winter): 6–16.

Fama, E., and K. French. 1992. The cross-section of expected returns. *Journal of Finance* 43: 153–194.

Francis, J., P. Olsson, and D. Oswald. 2000. Comparing the accuracy and explainability of dividend, free cash flow, and abnormal earnings equity value estimates. *Journal of Accounting Research* 38 (Spring): 45–69.

Francis, J., P. Olsson, and D. Oswald. 2001. Using mechanical earnings and residual income forecasts in equity valuation. Working paper (April): 1–36.

Frankel, R., and C. Lee. 1998. Accounting valuation, market expectation, and cross-sectional stock returns. *Journal of Accounting and Economics* 25: 283–319.

Gordon, M. 1962. *The investment, financing and valuation of the corporation.* Homewood, IL: Irwin.

Kaplan, S., and R. Ruback. 1995. The valuation of cash flow forecasts: An empirical analysis. *Journal of Finance* 50 (September): 1059–1093.

Lawson, S. 2002. The equity risk premium: It's lower than you think. *Goldman Sachs CEO Confidential* 14 (November).

Lee, C. 2001. Market efficiency and accounting research. *Journal of Accounting and Economics* 31: 233–253.

Madden, B. 2007. For better corporate governance, the shareholder value review. *Journal of Applied Corporate Finance* 19(1): 102–114.

Penman, S., and T. Sougiannis. 1998. A comparison of dividend, cash flow, and earnings approaches to equity valuation. *Contemporary Accounting Research* 15 (Fall): 343–383.

Rozeff, M. 1990. The three-phase dividend discount model and the ROPE model. *Journal of Portfolio Management* (Winter): 36–42.

Sougiannis, T., and T. Yaekura. 2001. The accuracy and bias of equity values inferred from analysts' earnings forecasts. *Journal of Accounting, Auditing, and Finance* 16: 331–362.

CHAPTER 6

The Essence of Value-Based Finance

Roy E. Johnson
Co-Founder, Vanguard Partners; Currently D/B/A Corporate Strategy

T he material in this chapter incorporates a process and set of analytic techniques that delve into the true economic characteristics and performance of companies, as well as business units within companies. There are two major building blocks of value-based finance (VBF) that will be explored:

1. Indicators of shareholder value creation, neutrality, or destruction.
2. Measurements of actual or potential value created, maintained, or destroyed.

The chapter is divided into the following segments:

- **Introducing Value-Based Finance (a Transition from Accounting to Economics).** An example is given to display the potential differences between accounting and economic returns, along with implications.
- **Valuation Perspectives: Economic Profit (EP) and Market Value Added (MVA).** EP is the primary indicator of value creation and at the core of many value-based performance systems implemented by leading-edge companies. MVA is a key measure of shareholder value creation, representing a spread between what financial markets (or investors) judge a business to be worth and what has been invested. This section explains and explores both.
- **Valuation Perspectives: The Magnifier.** This segment illustrates the value-creating impact of growth, which works in positive and negative directions.

- **Valuation Perspectives: Financial Drivers and Value Profit Margin (VPM).** This segment lays out a template of high-level metrics that are at the heart of many well-known ratios used in measuring financial performance, and then provides a simple and insightful profit margin that links to return on investment.
- **Value Analysis: The Proper Focus.** Many companies spend a lot of time establishing the ingredients of a value-based system, but then misapply them—analyzing stand-alone projects (which are usually part of a larger endeavor) instead of major strategies and investment programs. This misapplication can waste time by performing irrelevant evaluations, confuse management as to what's really important, and, at the extreme, lead to bad investment decisions.

This material provides useful concepts and tools for financial and operating professionals and managers in major corporations, plus owners and key managers of privately held businesses. The reader is taken through a process of:

- Making a transition from traditional accounting-based perspectives and measures to those focused on business economics—centered around the concepts of economic profit, return on investment, and cash flow.
- Developing a template of financial drivers—a set of measures that help business managers and owners instill value creation as a discipline— along with an understanding of how value is created from a financial point of view.
- Establishing analytic tools and techniques to evaluate and measure value creation.
- Focusing all the concepts, tools, techniques, and metrics for the most effective utilization—demonstrating how to avoid common misapplication traps.

Knowledge of this subject is essential for those who work in corporate America, because the value of any for-profit enterprise is linked to its underlying economics and cash flow, which can differ from what is reported through an accounting-based financial system. Virtually all research on public stock markets supports this premise, and knowledgeable investors in privately owned firms employ economic principles in their valuations and decisions about buying and selling businesses.

For anyone involved in commercial or investment banking, the material will provide insight into how to evaluate the performance of client businesses, which should impact the nature of relationships and financing policy, along with financing alternatives and opportunities. This material should enhance the expertise and professionalism of bankers in the area of corporate finance—part of the world their clients live in. For those in merchant banking or equity financing, the material should provide a solid foundation for business valuations and investment selections.

INTRODUCING VALUE-BASED FINANCE
(A TRANSITION FROM ACCOUNTING TO ECONOMICS)

The movement from accounting to economic metrics is at the core of value-based finance (VBF)—driven by the fact that the real profitability of a business is not always reflected in the traditional accounting measures that focus on net earnings. An example using a hypothetical firm—Growthstar Inc.—will illustrate the dilemma. The company has a core business, expanded three years ago by the acquisition of Newco. The purchase price was $55 million, financed with excess cash and new debt. Off-balance-sheet leases of $15 million were assumed. Thus, the total investment was $70 million, none of which impacted the book value of Growthstar Inc. stockholders' equity. Financial highlights of the three most recent historical years plus the current year will be presented, to provide a comparison of the accounting versus economic framework.

Exhibit 6.1 gives a summary for the accounting scenario, noting that year 3 is the most distant and year 1 is the most recent historical period. The Newco deal was closed at the end of year 3. Thus, it had no effect on the company's operations for year 3.

Has this acquisition benefited Growthstar's shareholders? Based on the accounting scenario, the answer would seem to be a resounding yes! Revenue has doubled and net income has grown nearly fourfold—using year 3 as a base—through the current year. Return on equity has almost doubled, from 12 percent to 22 percent, during this time period.

Under an economic framework, however, the key indicators paint a somewhat different picture. The economic scenario entails some important adjustments:

- Interest expense is eliminated from the profit and loss (P&L) statement and is factored into a weighted average cost of capital (WACC). Thus, the P&L is focused on operating profit.
- The acquisition reserve in year 3 (accounting write-off of the "purchased R&D" portion of goodwill) is reversed—added back to both the P&L and the balance sheet—reflecting the sunk cost nature of acquisition investments. Write-offs reduce acquisition prices on the books.

EXHIBIT 6.1 Growthstar Inc. Accounting Summary

$ Millions	Historical Period—3 Years Actual			Current Year Forecast
	Year 3	Year 2	Year 1	
Revenue—Core	$220	$250	$280	$300
Newco	—	75	100	150
Total Co.	$220	$325	$380	$450
Operating Costs	$203	$302	$349	$408
Interest Expense	3	3	4	5
Amortization Expense	—	1	1	1
Acquisition Reserve	5	—	—	—
Income Before Tax	9	19	26	36
Provision for Taxes (at Rate = 36%)	3	7	9	13
Net Income After Tax	$ 6	$ 12	$ 17	$ 23
Earning (N.I.) Growth	—	100%	42%	35%
Stockholders' Equity*	$ 51	$ 53	$ 80	$103
Return on Equity* *Beginning Equity	12%	19%	21%	22%

- All capital invested in the company—not just equity capital—becomes the basis for return measures. This includes working and fixed capital, goodwill, and assets financed by operating leases. A capital charge will be assessed to the total invested capital.
- Deferred taxes are analyzed, to calculate an effective tax rate based on taxes paid.

Exhibit 6.2 gives a tabular summary for the economic scenario. The highlights of Exhibit 6.2 are:

- Net operating profit (NOP) is up about 240 percent during the analysis period versus a 380 percent increase of net income in the accounting scenario. NOP growth is higher than revenue growth, as operating profit margins have increased to 9 percent from their year 3 level of 8 percent. The accounting reserve—related to the acquisition—distorts the real profit in year 3, and affects the comparative indicators for subsequent years in the accounting scenario.
- Return on capital is the same in the current year as it was in year 3, the most distant year. In year 2, this return decreases to below the cost of capital level as the total acquisition investment is absorbed into company operations. Year 1 indicates progress toward getting back to the

EXHIBIT 6.2 Growthstar Inc. Economic Summary

$ Millions	Historical Period—3 Years Actual			Current Year Forecast
	Year 3	Year 2	Year 1	
Revenue-Total	$220	$325	$380	$450
Operating Costs	302	302	349	408
Interest—Eliminate	—	—	—	—
EBITA[a]	17	23	31	42
Cash Taxes—*Rate*	25%	26%	26%	26%
Amount	4	6	8	11
Net Operating Profit	$ 13	$ 17	$ 23	$ 31
Profit (NOP) Growth	—	*31%*	*35%*	*35%*
Invested Capital (IC)*	$ 90	$170	$190	$220
Return on Capital*	14%	10%	12%	14%
Return on Equity*	12%	19%	21%	22%
Economic Profit				
Net Operating Profit	$ 13	$ 17	$ 23	$ 31
Capital Charge[b]	(10)	(19)	(21)	(24)
Economic Profit	$ 3	$ (2)	$ 2	$ 7
*Beginning Equity				

[a]Earnings before interest, taxes and amortization.
[b]The capital charge is based on a weighted cost of capital of 11% for this company and is charged against IC for each year. This charge is an indicator of whether NOP is sufficient to

year 3 return. The message here is that the company is now no better or worse off than it was before it made the acquisition. This is quite a contrast to the return on equity results from Exhibit 6.1, influenced by accounting entries and only the equity portion of invested capital incorporated into the return metric.

■ Economic profit goes from positive in year 3 to negative in year 2, and then rebounds as the firm moves through year 1 and the current year. As with NOP, the current year is a bit more than double the year 3 level, versus a fourfold increase of net income.

Whether the shareholders will benefit long-term from this acquisition will depend on the strategy and future profitability of Newco. This year's economic profit is a good sign.

To conclude, accounting metrics often do not provide good shareholder value indicators. Thus, much of the business world is turning to economics for value analysis. Exhibit 6.3 gives a graphic portrayal of profit growth

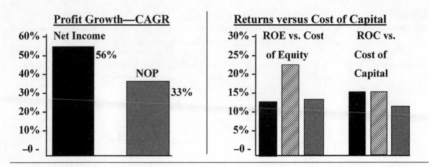

EXHIBIT 6.3   Shareholder Value Indicators

(compound annual growth rate [CAGR]) and returns versus cost of capital. In the "Returns versus Cost of Capital" graph, the left bar (black) is distant year 3 return, the middle bar (striped) is current year return, and the right bar (gray) is cost of capital.

As future segments will discuss, accounting earnings and their growth have little correlation with stock market returns. One of the reasons is that accounting has its origins in credit and liquidation analysis, not in valuation. Most valuation techniques are founded in cash flow–based measures, and many successful investors use accounting-based results as a starting, not an ending, point. Thus, we introduce value-based finance with a transition from accounting to economics—to set the stage for critical valuation perspectives and the proper application of VBF concepts and techniques.

VALUATION PERSPECTIVES: ECONOMIC PROFIT AND MARKET VALUE ADDED

A simple, yet powerful, phrase sets a tone for the second segment. Analyzing shareholder value is mainly about determining what managers have done, or are expected to do, with the capital they have been entrusted with. An important element of the analysis is to measure the value impact of past and present financial performance, along with strategies and future investment programs. Exhibit 6.4 establishes a framework that, through three companies (A, B, and C), provides a basis for determining, first, a key indicator of shareholder value (economic profit) and then two of the most important expressions of value creation (market value added and the magnifier).

EXHIBIT 6.4   Economic Profit Example

Base Period	Company A	Company B	Company C
Revenue (Sales)	$1,000	$1,000	$1,000
Net Operating Profit (NOP)	$ 100	$ 100	$ 100
	10%	10%	10%
Invested Capital (IC)	$ 600	$ 800	$1,000
Cost of Capital (CCAP)	12%	12%	12%
Economic Profit			
NOP (from above)	$ 100	$ 100	$ 100
Capital Charge (CCAP)	(72)	(96)	(120)
Economic Profit (EP)	$ 28	$ 4	$ (20)

Economic profit (EP) is a concept right out of basic economics—the course many people took in college. EP is what any business owner (shareholder) should be concerned with, since it takes into account the cost of all the capital invested in the business. EP is the residual (what's left over) after all the costs of running a business have been accounted for and the suppliers of capital have been provided with a fair return on their investment. A problem with accounting profit—most commonly expressed as net income or earnings per share (EPS)—is that it only includes a charge for debt financing; thus it misses a cost for equity capital, the most expensive and prevalent form of capital for a typical industrial company. The cost of equity capital is what a common shareholder expects to earn annually as a rate of return on investment. The cost of equity capital formula adds a premium to the current return on a long-term risk-free security, such as a 10-year U.S. government bond.

Because of this condition and another important one—the gap between accounting profit and cash flow—there is virtually no correlation between net income and/or EPS growth and key stock market indicators (e.g., market-to-book ratios).

As stated earlier, economic profit (EP) is a residual—the amount of profit available after *all* suppliers of capital have been given a fair return for their investment. The example in Exhibit 6.4 shows how three companies, all with the same accounting profit, can have significantly different economic profits.

If we start with the upper portion of Exhibit 6.4, we have the essence of the accounting profit model, reflecting the traditional P&L summary shown here:

Base Period	Company A	Company B	Company C
Revenue (Sales)	$1,000	$1,000	$1,000
Net Operating Profit			
– $	$ 100	$ 100	$ 100
– %	10%	10%	10%

Historically, this is what Wall Street has published and what most companies have geared themselves to. The questions to ask are: What is different about these companies? Can you make any type of investment decision based on this information?

Two critical factors are missing, from a financial perspective, to begin to make shareholder value judgments. These two factors get at the heart of the shortcomings of using the traditional accounting profit model, based on net income or earnings per share as the key determinant for stock prices. Using earnings alone as a proxy for value misses the following:

- The *risk* of the earnings.
- The *capital* needed to generate the earnings.

Economic profit begins the same as accounting profit—that is, with revenue (or sales). All the operating-related expenses and taxes are then subtracted to arrive at net operating profit (NOP). The EP model, in its unending quest to get close to the economics of the business, makes some adjustments to the typical accounting P&L, as follows:

- Nonoperating charges such as restructuring and other one-time or extraordinary expenses (often *not* related to cash flow) are usually reversed.
- Expenditures for advertising and/or R&D may be capitalized, depending on how such treatment affects the cash flow characteristics of the business. The determining factor (rule of thumb) is whether capitalization/amortization versus expensing affects the calculation of EP by more than 10 percent, on average, over a multiyear period. If so, capitalize. If not, keep the more simple expensing treatment.
- Taxes are based on actual/projected cash payments rather than accounting provisions for statutory tax rates.
- The charge for debt financing (interest expense) is excluded, since this will be picked up in the overall corporate cost of capital (CCAP), which is 12 percent in the example.

The rule for making adjustments is very straightforward and is based on the concept of *simplicity with integrity*. If an adjustment is needed to maintain the economic integrity of the performance measure, then make it. If not, use information as reported.

A major enhancement in the EP model is the explicit recognition of balance sheet investment. The major categories are working capital (receivables, inventory, payables, etc.) and fixed capital (property, plant, and equipment). In some companies, goodwill and intangibles are important investments and so are included in the invested capital. Another important item, ignored in the accounting model, is one found in the footnotes: operating leases. This off-balance-sheet item accounts for assets leased—thus, a financial obligation similar to other secured debt—but falling below an arbitrary hurdle defined by a generally accepted accounting principles (GAAP) formula to determine whether an asset should appear on the balance sheet. In some companies, operating leases represent a significant portion of assets and debt. A rule of thumb is: If the present value of operating leases comprises more than 10 percent of invested capital, then they should be included. If less than 10 percent, they are not material and can be left out of the calculation of EP—again, *simplicity with integrity*.

Charging a cost for the capital invested in a business approximates the desires of investors. What this means is that the capital charge (CCAP)—12 percent in our example—is the minimum annual return that investors, in the aggregate, expect from each of these three companies. (As a note, some refer to this return as the weighted average cost of capital—WACC.) Thus, the closest we can come to replicating the capital market perspective is to assess profitability after charging for this (minimum) return on capital requirement. The term *hurdle rate* is used widely with respect to the analysis of capital investments. CCAP is the hurdle for these three firms. In this case, it is expressed as a dollar amount, but can also be a percentage. While not perfect, this approach captures the expectations of the financial markets.

As seen in Exhibit 6.4, all the firms are *not* profitable from an economic, or rate of return, perspective. In fact, only Company A is truly profitable, with an EP of $28 million. Note the EP of $4 million (just above break-even) in the Company B column and the negative EP of $(20) million in the Company C column. A variation on this format, in which the minimum return is expressed as a percentage, rather than a dollar amount, and the comparison is to a percentage CCAP, can be illustrated as follows:

Base Period	Company A	Company B	Company C
EP Expressed as *return on capital (%)*			
Net Operating Profit (NOP)	$100	$100	$100
Invested Capital (IC)	$600	$800	$1,000
Return on Capital (ROC)	17%	12.5%	10%
Cost of Capital (CCAP)	12%	12.0%	12%
Spread: ROC minus CCAP	5%	.5%	−2%

The point for now is that, conceptually, virtually all economic measures are based on the notion of ascribing a cost (minimum rate of return) to the capital invested in a business. While companies produce a balance sheet when the books are closed, most people don't evaluate it thoroughly, nor do they make the balance sheet a focus of their analysis.

The EP status of a business positions it as a value creator (Company A) or destroyer (Company C)—or, as with Company B, being value neutral. This has major implications for what growth will produce in terms of shareholder value. If we apply a growth scenario, with a very limited number of assumptions, to the three firms (A, B, and C), we can begin to get an appreciation of why EP is so important in the value creation process.

Market Value Added

The simple scenario that follows provides a useful foundation for looking into the future for a business.

Market Value Added—Sample Scenario
Valuation Summary: Assumptions

- All companies maintain the same invested capital-to-revenue ratio.
- All companies continue to earn the same profit margin on revenue.
- All companies increase revenue by 10 percent per year for four years.

The assumptions in this scenario, while simple and few in number, are representative of a forward-looking financial model, which investors use to value companies and businesses within companies. They are also indicative of the type of thinking necessary to value strategies. The value we're describing here—market value added (MVA)—is what the market is adding to or subtracting from what has been invested in the company, based on its evaluation of past/present financial performance and its perception about where the company is going in the future. A goal of any for-profit business is to increase the spread between what has been invested and what the market feels is warranted based on performance. So, both EP and MVA are spreads or residuals.

We could expand these assumptions into a more robust scenario, but the ones given will suffice to illustrate the concept: a numerical expression of these assumptions for our three companies—A, B, and C. Exhibit 6.5 provides an illustration.

Company A increases its EP throughout the forecast period—in this case, four years. If you think about the consistency of performance implied in the assumptions (which, again, are probably oversimplified) you should understand the EP forecast results for Company A—EP increases each year at the 10 percent growth rate for revenue—$31 million in future year 1 to $41 million in future year 4. The "Years 5 on residual" is a typical way that the years after the forecast horizon are treated, which capitalizes the year 4 EP at the CCAP rate (in this case, 12 percent). This assumes that the plan can produce *no incremental EP* even if the business continues to grow, which is equivalent to saying that, after year 4, the company will just earn its cost of capital on new investment. The MVA for this growth scenario is the sum of the EPs for the four-year growth period plus the residual value.

The example is oversimplified, at this point, in that it doesn't (yet) account for *discounting* of the future values. However, it does show that Company A is creating shareholder value with its growth plan. Therefore, the total warranted market value of Company A (again, before discounting the future year EPs) is the base period invested capital (IC) of $600 million (from Exhibit 6.4) plus the MVA of $485 million—for a total of nearly $1.1 billion. Obviously, the real MVA and total warranted value for Com-

EXHIBIT 6.5 Market Value Added Example (10 Percent Growth, $ Millions)

Pro Forma	Company A	Company B	Company C
EP—value impact			
Year 1	$ 31	$ 4	$ (22)
Year 2	34	5	(24)
Year 3	37	5	(27)
Year 4	41	6	(29)
Subtotal (4 years)	143	20	(102)
Years 5 on residual	342	50	(242)
Sum of EPs + residual before discounting	$485	$70	$(344)

pany A will be less when we apply the 12 percent discount rate to future year EP and residual values, but for now we can see that Company A should command a premium over its invested capital when valued in the financial markets. Why? Because management is earning more than the cost of capital and is growing the business. You should be able to visualize that if Company A can increase its revenue growth, then it will generate more MVA—and, thus, should experience a greater warranted total market value.

One of the interesting features of this analysis is that we get approximately the same MVA result as we would with the traditional free cash flow (FCF) approach. Once we factor in an appropriate discount rate—which we will do after we get through with this nondiscounted example—MVA (under the EP approach) is *about the same* as the net present value (NPV) calculated using the free cash flow (FCF) technique. One reason that the EP model is receiving widespread application in corporations and the financial institutions that invest large sums in the equity markets is that it is the conceptual equivalent to the FCF approach, with the result (MVA) equal or very close to the NPV. Further, with the EP approach, we can determine meaningful period-by-period financial results—indicative of value creation, destruction, or neutrality—which is usually not possible with the free cash flow technique. The FCF model provides a credible value-based end result, but is typically *not* very useful in assessing value creation progress along the way.

Company B presents a somewhat different scenario. Even though it grows and maintains its 10 percent after-tax profit margin, the company does not produce any significant future year EPs. By now this should be apparent, since Company B just earns its CCAP. Company B may get bigger, but it doesn't get much better, at least in terms of shareholder value creation. Notice the very modest $70 million MVA, which is less than 10 percent of its $800 million invested capital. This is noteworthy because it indicates that B-type companies should be valued (in the financial markets) fairly close to their economic book value. They simply don't return much more to the shareholders than what was invested in the first place—and are not expected to do much more with new investment.

Company C is truly a problem. It cannot grow out of its dilemma of earning a return *below* the cost of capital without radically changing the way it conducts its business. Yet the business world is littered with C-type companies and businesses, thinking that they can grow and be successful without changing their fundamental structures. This is a very serious situation in corporate America since a significant percentage (in excess of 25 percent according to some research) of publicly traded companies in the United States fall into the C category. Whatever assumptions we may make, the impact is clear—growth destroys shareholder value for C-types—and more growth means more value destruction!

The next segment presents an example to illustrate the value-creating potential for A-type companies and businesses, along with how C-types destroy shareholder value.

VALUATION PERSPECTIVES: THE MAGNIFIER

One of the most powerful concepts in value-based finance is the Magnifier. Whereas previous topics give good indications of shareholder value creation or destruction, the magnifier provides a "more bang for the buck" type of evaluation—especially regarding the impact of growth, which is still the most important determinant of share price movement.

The focus of this analysis will be on Company A and Company C from the previous segment since value-neutral firms, such as Company B essentially run in place and really don't go anywhere from a shareholder value perspective. The point to be illustrated is that the EP position of a business helps to dictate what its future actions should be if the objective is to create shareholder value.

Company A has a positive EP and a return on capital higher than its cost of capital. With these positive indicators, the following gives an overview of what Company A should do.

How to Increase Shareholder Value for Company A

- Invest capital in growth-oriented strategies/programs, with high return potential.
  - Go for growth. Instill growth as a driving force throughout the organization.
  - Emphasize staying close to existing margins and capital intensity, with room for some deterioration if the opportunity is significant.
- Growth adds value. Bigger is better!

This set of directive actions says a lot. Growth is what most companies want. You just have to make sure that the business is in the A category in terms of its sustainable economic profit. If *not* there now, then the near and longer-term strategy has to get it into an A position before embarking on a growth strategy.

The potential for shareholder value creation of this "go for growth" goal for Company A can be illustrated in Exhibit 6.6.

$ MVA

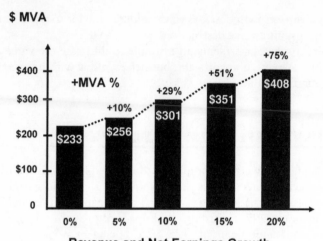

EXHIBIT 6.6   The Magnifier Effect for Company A

Exhibit 6.6 needs careful explanation. We start with the horizontal axis, which plots annual compound growth rates (CGRs) for revenue and net earnings. These are the same, since we're assuming a steady profit margin (10 percent). The growth rate scenarios over a four-year future time horizon are in increments of five percentage points—from 0 percent (no growth) to 20 percent. These are annual CGRs.

Next, the vertical axis plots MVA in millions of dollars. The MVA is the net present value (NPV) of the various growth scenarios, based on the assumptions for invested capital intensity (ICI)—the capital needed for each new revenue dollar—and the NOP margin. Thus, MVA measures shareholder value created—the NPV for each growth plan.

The magnifier effect is the impact on MVA (shareholder value) for the selected revenue growth rates. Starting with the no growth (0 percent) scenario, if the business stays at its base period level of revenue and earnings, it will create $233 million of MVA. This results from the company (A) generating an economic profit (EP) of $28 million. Under a no growth scenario, this level of EP would continue forever. MVA (equivalent to the shareholder value added) is simply the EP capitalized at the 12 percent cost of capital. Finally, $28 million divided by 12 percent is approximately $233 million. What this means is that management has created a warranted MVA of $233 million. This is the amount of market value that management has added to the economic book value of $600 million.

Now, let's assume that a 5 percent growth plan is communicated to the investors. With the assumptions we have made, this 5 percent growth in revenue and earnings translates into a 10 percent increase in MVA. In essence, growth in revenue and earnings is magnified into increasingly higher growth rates for MVA. As we continue along the horizontal axis, to higher growth rates for revenue and earnings, look at what happens to the height of the (vertical) MVA bars. They rise at even higher rates—again, in a magnified fashion. At the peak of this example, a 20 percent CGR for sales and earnings over a four-year future time period produces a 75 percent increase in shareholder value. Extending the time horizon or further increasing the growth rate would magnify the situation even further.

Many CEOs and business unit heads have had this intuitive feeling about the impact of growth. However, many think it's driven by earnings per share (EPS). What this example shows is that value creation is dependent on EP (drop the S from EPS) and profitable growth—beating the cost of capital with old and new investments. This example also explains why some of the great names we know in business have produced incredible gains in their stock prices. They generated positive economic profit—which translates into a high return on their invested capital (well in excess of their cost of capital)—and they grew rapidly!

A picture is often worth a thousand words, and Exhibit 6.6 gives a picture that people at all levels in a business should embed into their minds. In order not to interrupt the discussion flow, two tables placed at the end of this segment show the key calculations for the 15 percent and 20 percent growth cases—this, after all the major scenarios have been presented.

The situation for Company B can be covered rather quickly, per the following:

Company B

- Earn more operating profit with the same capital.
  - Squeeze additional profit from the existing capital base (selective pricing and/or cost cutting).
  - Emphasize margin improvement.
- Growth is secondary, as it adds minimal value!

Company B needs to become more efficient, not bigger. Its predicament is rather straightforward. Many of the conglomerates are in the B category. They buy firms that are sometimes in different businesses, with very little in the way of common marketing, distribution, or other functions. They are running what amounts to a portfolio of companies—in essence, a miniature mutual fund. What they fail to realize are some important shortcomings. First, most institutional investors want to construct their own portfolios, not one that a CEO or management group has chosen. Second, focus—not diversification—has usually produced the highest total shareholder returns (TSRs) in the stock market. This is partly due to the management complexity that conglomerates or diversified companies are subject to. It's very difficult to be an expert at everything! Finally, growth by acquisition alone creates obstacles to value creation in that it's hard to avoid the "transfer of wealth" phenomenon—the payment of a premium to gain control of another company through a purchase. Unless an acquisition target has been mismanaged and a turnaround opportunity exists, or a truly synergistic combination can be implemented, or the seller is not very astute (a rare situation today with the involvement of boards of directors and shareholder activists), it is hard to hit a home run with acquisitions. Companies may do much better with internally developed products and/or services, new marketing channels, distribution methods, manufacturing techniques, and so on. Therefore, without greater efficiency (thus, higher EP) many B-type firms will continue to tread water. They may grow, but they won't add much value if they don't become more efficient with the capital they currently employ.

A real challenge for business is outlined as follows.

Company C

- Reduce the level of capital employed.
  - Streamline/re-engineer/re-structure operations.
  - Validate capital invested in major lines of business.

. . . Noting that Growth destroys value!

C-type firms or businesses can *not* grow and create value without a fundamental—perhaps radical—change in the way they manage their invested capital. The points noted previously are clear. The C businesses are those where major restructuring or reengineering efforts have the potential for a big payoff.

For our example, Exhibit 6.7 quantifies the impact of growth without any change in the operating dynamics for a C-type business.

This illustration conveys a powerful and cautionary message for growth-minded executives. Since the structure of this chart is somewhat different from the magnifier effect for Company A (as illustrated in Exhibit 6.6), the elements require an explanation.

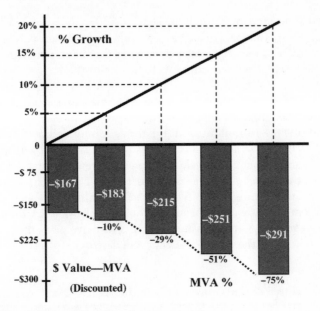

EXHIBIT 6.7   The Magnifier Effect for Company C

The growth rate scenarios for revenue and net earnings are plotted in an upward direction in the top portion of the vertical axis. The diagonally sloped line with points of intersection at 5 percent growth rate increments represent the traditional picture of rising revenue and earnings, the implication being that shareholder value and stock prices rise accordingly. It's fair to say that this is probably the view of many, since the earnings growth model has driven many valuations, or at least valuation perceptions, for a long time.

However, as the bottom portion of the chart indicates, this is *not* the case. What's happening is that every percentage point of compound growth will cost Company C more in a capital charge (CCAP) than it will produce in net operating profit (NOP), thus eroding EP. This is despite the fact that Company C is generating a profit—at least in the traditional accounting method of calculation. As we saw in Exhibit 6.5, however, Company C is actually producing an economic loss. If firms with this performance characteristic signal to the financial markets that the pattern (that is, too much capital) will continue, then the markets should, in theory, respond with valuations that would follow the progression of the MVA bars in the lower portion of the graph.

Let's take them one at a time. In the no growth scenario, the negative EP of −$20 million (the real bottom line from Exhibit 6.4) would be capitalized at negative $167 million. That's −$20 million divided by 12 percent (CCAP). This management has got some fixing to do before thinking about growth. You may have seen some firms that have actually contracted (gotten smaller) and created value. Well, this is why!

Now, assume that management communicates a 5 percent growth plan to investors, maintaining the same NOP margin and invested capital intensity (ICI) as in the base period. The investors should respond by shaving an additional $16 million from the firm's economic book value. Thus, negative MVA grows (how's *that* for misuse of a word?) by 10 percent to −$183 million. The magnifier effect is now working in reverse.

Follow the progression of scenarios to the 20 percent growth level for revenue and earnings. MVA (shareholder value) has been destroyed by 75 percent. By now, the message should be clear: Regardless of their accounting earnings, C-type businesses will destroy value as they grow, and the more they grow, the more value they will destroy!

EXHIBIT 6.8   Fifteen Percent Growth for Company A

($ Millions, Except ICI)	Valuation via Economic Profit (EP)					
	Base	Year 1	Year 2	Year 3	Year 4	Residual
Revenue	1,000	1,150	1,323	1,521	1,749	
Invested capital (IC)	600	690	794	913	1,049	
Economic Profit (EP)						
NOP	100	115	132	152	175	
Capital charge (CCAP)	(72)	(83)	(95)	(110)	(126)	
Economic Profit (EP)	28	32	37	43	49	49

Valuation	Total Market Value	Base IC	MVA – Base + Growth*
Net present value (NPV)	951	600	351

*Discounted (EPs + Residual)
Assumptions:
Annual growth rate (CGR) = 15%
Annual profit (NOP) margin = 10%
Invested capital intensity (ICI) = $0.60
Cost of capital (CCAP) = 12%

Before ending this discussion, we should briefly address start-up businesses. Generally, they should be placed in a special category (A-prime). They may technically be C-type businesses, based on start-up losses, but the expectation is to become an A. These (start-up) businesses have to be valued totally on future prospects with an attempt made to establish a base-level EP and set of financial drivers—margins, investment requirements, and so forth that will carry them into the future.

In conclusion, the following highlights what has been presented and discussed:

- Economic profit incorporates the income statement, balance sheet investments, and a capital cost, making it more robust than accounting earnings.
- A firm's EP category (A, B, or C) provides an important indicator for what a value-creating strategy should focus on and encompass.
- Economic profit translates into market value added through a future outlook.

EXHIBIT 6.9 20 Percent Growth for Company A

($ Millions, Except ICI)	Valuation via Economic Profit (EP)					
	Base	Year 1	Year 2	Year 3	Year 4	Residual
Revenue	1,000	1,200	1,440	1,728	2,074	
Invested capital (IC)	600	720	864	1,037	1,244	
Economic Profit (EP)						
NOP	100	120	144	173	207	
Capital charge (CCAP)	(72)	(86)	(104)	(124)	(149)	
Economic Profit (EP)	28	34	40	48	58	58

Valuation	Total Market Value	Base IC	MVA – Base + Growth*
Net present value (NPV)	1,008	600	408

*Discounted (EPs + Residual)
Assumptions:
Annual growth rate (CGR) = 20%
Annual profit (NOP) margin = 10%
Invested capital intensity (ICI) = $0.60
Cost of capital (CCAP) = 12%

■ Growth magnifies value creation positively or negatively, depending on whether economic returns are above or below the cost of capital.

Exhibits 6.8 and 6.9 provide pertinent details for the MVA/NPV calculations in Exhibit 6.6, regarding the higher-growth scenarios for Company A.

VALUATION PERSPECTIVES: FINANCIAL DRIVERS AND VALUE PROFIT MARGIN

This segment begins with a perception many people in publicly owned companies and investment firms embrace—that steadily rising earnings (defined as net income or earnings per share [EPS]) will produce stock price gains and improved valuation ratios and indexes (for example, price-earnings ratio and/or market-to-book ratio). While pervasive, these beliefs are, in fact, not true. The following two charts are indicative of a vast amount of research that disputes and disproves the emphasis on EPS and growth (alone) as key drivers of stock market performance.

For those who may be a bit rusty on statistics, Exhibit 6.10 is referred to as a scatter diagram—the plots are all over the place and there is no correlation for the variables. In this case, there is no correlation of increasing EPS growth rates and market-to-book ratios for the companies in the research. A great deal of analysis produced by some of the best-known investment

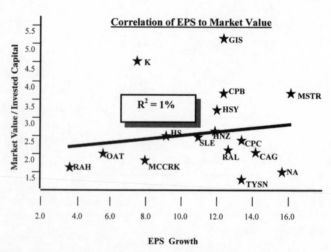

EXHIBIT 6.10 Accounting Profit—Stock Market Test
Source: Credit Suisse First Boston.

EXHIBIT 6.11 Accounting Profit—Stock Market Test (Revenue Growth, ROI Spreads, and Market Multiples)

Revenue CGR (%)	Average Market Multiples—S&P Industrials				
>16%	0.7	*1.1*	*2.1*	*2.2*	*4.2*
12% to 16%	0.9	*1.1*	*1.5*	*1.5*	*2.5*
8% to 12%	1.0	0.9	*1.2*	*1.7*	*3.2*
4% to 8%	0.7	0.9	*1.2*	*1.7*	*3.1*
1% to 4%	0.7	*1.0*	*1.0*	*1.4*	*2.2*
<1%	0.9	*1.1*	*1.1*	*1.2*	*1.6*
	<−4%	−4% to −2%	−2% to 2%	2% to 4%	>4%

Return on Investment "Spread" . . . ROI less Cost of Capital
Source: Hewitt Associates.

research firms during the past 20 or so years yields results similar to what is displayed in Exhibit 6.10. Note that MV/IC is market-to-book.

Exhibit 6.11 presents a similar conclusion from a slightly different perspective.

The key message from Exhibit 6.11 is that revenue growth alone does not create shareholder value. There must also be a return on capital.

To highlight the table, the average market multiples inside the matrix that are *italicized and greater than 1.0* indicate a market value greater than book value (thus creating value for investors). Numbers *equal to 1.0* indicate a market value that is equal to book value (call this being value neutral). Numbers *less than 1.0* portray a shareholder's nightmare—a market value below the firm's book value, which can be translated as destroying value.

Looking into the matrix, it is apparent that, except for a few outliers (two 1.1 multiple rapid-growth groups and two 1.1 multiple negative-growth categories with returns below the cost of capital), the pattern for the value-creating firms—those italicized and >1.0—is consistent in that the return on capital exceeds the cost of capital. This is where we see a payoff for growth in terms of market multiple. In terms of the 1.1 multiple outliers, it's possible that the stocks are being priced on the expectation of higher returns—two resulting from growth and two from shrinking the business and using capital more effectively. Most of the firms in the two columns on the left side of the matrix—those with returns below the cost of capital—have either a <1.0 or a 1.0 number for a market multiple. The market is astute and looks beyond growth to the return that a company generates on the capital that has already been invested and also the new capital expected for the future.

In spite of this evidence, a large contingent of corporate managements and Wall Street analysts seem wedded to revenue growth, along with net income and/or EPS, as their primary performance metrics. This presents a dilemma. On one side are those corporate managers, strung along by a significant number of sell-side analysts evaluating these managers, who pursue accounting-based measures—typically with a short time horizon. On the other (buy) side, an increasing number of sophisticated investors—those with the greatest influence on the financial markets—value common stocks through economic analysis over a longer term (often several years). To complicate the situation, some of the people (on each side) are fairly entrenched in their views.

Fortunately, there is a solution to this problem. Within a set of financial drivers that all companies should have as part of their management scorecards, there is a measure that incorporates the mentality of investors while allowing a company to maintain a simplistic growth and profit margin focus.

To begin, we'll run through the set of financial drivers embedded in value analysis. Our main topic—value profit margin (VPM)—is the final element in the set, preceded by:

- Growth rates.
- Invested capital intensity (ICI)—an ingredient of VPM.

Most of the corporate world is focused on revenue and profit growth. Another important component—growth of invested capital—is usually not given much attention, however. In fact, my experience over the past 30 years leads me to believe that most managers don't know the level of invested capital in their business, never mind its growth rate. Those who do understand how shareholder value is created recognize that what's important is the *relationship* among revenue, profit, and invested capital growth (their *relative* rates). Over the long run, the ideal pattern is for profit to grow the fastest, followed by revenue and invested capital. This ideal long-term pattern can be illustrated as in Exhibit 6.12.

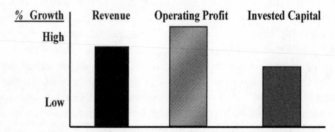

EXHIBIT 6.12   Percent Growth of Revenue, Profit, and Invested Capital

The rationale is straightforward. If operating income (profit) grows faster than revenue, then profit margin will increase. If both revenue and operating profit grow faster than invested capital, then the return on capital—by any of the well-known calculations—will increase. As the previously cited research indicates, higher returns on capital combined with revenue growth are usually rewarded in the financial markets through increased measures of performance (e.g., market-to-book ratios). While the pattern illustrated is ideal for the long run, a business strategy may dictate a different pattern in the short or near term. Such a strategy needs to be tested to see when it will produce the optimal pattern. If the recent history of a business produces a different pattern, then management needs to determine when they will get on track with the optimal pattern.

Growth is an important issue in most firms, and is often overanalyzed. The problem with much of the traditional analysis, however, is that it excludes or deemphasizes the invested capital element. The type of analysis discussed, and illustrated in Exhibit 6.12, is the *only* one that can translate growth into shareholder value impact.

Corporate managements need to communicate this message. Lenders and other capital suppliers should understand the performance of their clients. Sophisticated investors look for signals that profit margin expectations will be at, below, or above historical levels, and estimate the pattern of future investment—especially as related to the past few years.

The second element in the set of financial drivers—a very useful tool in financial analysis and planning—is the ratio of invested capital to revenue. This indicator is focused on how much capital is required (or expected) to generate one dollar (or other currency unit) of revenue. Invested capital intensity (ICI) is the inverse of the well-known turnover ratio.

One application is to compare business units of different size on a standard basis. Another is to estimate capital needs for new business ventures, acquisitions, and other corporate development programs. ICI is looked at in the aggregate and also, as appropriate, by discrete categories (e.g., working and fixed capital). As we'll discuss later, ICI is a key input to the value profit margin.

Companies growing by acquisition need to consider goodwill and intangibles in addition to the traditional hard assets, since these items can have investment and credit rating implications. Obtaining credible ICI indicators may involve detailed evaluations. One important element of the analysis is to determine which investments move in a trend line versus a step pattern. Further, a given investment category (such as inventory or physical plant space) may exhibit different patterns as the business moves along a growth curve (or alternatively, as it contracts). The insights derived from this type of analysis are helpful in assessing the financial impact of a strategy or an acquisition. Since the more sophisticated investors use ICI, it should be part of management's tool kit.

Having highlighted growth and balance sheet drivers, we can now bring them together and provide an earnings performance measure linked to value creation. This measure is the *value profit margin (VPM)*. The overriding thought here is that if operating managers are going to have profit targets, let's give them one or two that correlate to value creation. There is a "pre" and "post" tax profit margin that, for any business, is a minimum requirement for the creation of shareholder value. We incorporate key perspectives from the notion of earning a return on capital that exceeds the cost of capital in a way that expresses the result in a traditional profit margin on sales (revenue). The good news is that it's not difficult to calculate.

The value profit margin (VPM) is derived by integrating:

- Invested capital intensity (ICI).
- Cost of capital (CCAP).
- The effective (or cash) tax rate.

Multiplying ICI by the cost of capital (CCAP) and then dividing by 1 minus the cash tax rate (some use the expression $1 - T$ for this rate) produces a pretax operating income (EBIT, EBITA, or EBITDA) margin that will sustain the value of the business, but not increase it. On an after-tax basis, multiplying ICI by CCAP calculates the value net operating profit (NOP) margin. Margins above the VPM level will increase value, while margins below this level are destructive. Why? Because margins below the VPM level do not cover the cost of capital employed in the business.

Invested capital intensity has been previously discussed. Cost of capital is the weighted (or blended) cost of debt and equity, the basis for the capital charge in economic profit measures. Think of CCAP as the average annual rate of return that you, as an investor, would expect to earn on capital you provided to a business or invested into a portfolio of common stocks, mutual funds, and bonds. Cash tax rates incorporate deferrals and may differ from accounting (book) provisions found on the income statement. Most public companies disclose this effective cash tax rate in the footnotes to their financial statements in 10-K and annual reports. Some analysis may be involved in calculating these capital cost and tax rates, a normal part of any value-based approach to planning and performance review.

The following table—incorporating data presented earlier in the segment on valuation perspectives (EP and MVA) and referred to in the discussion of the magnifier—establishes a framework that allows us to work through the individual financial drivers and then arrive at the value profit margin (VPM):

Base Period	Company A	Company B	Company C
Revenue (Sales)	$1,000	$1,000	$1,000
Net Operating Profit (NOP)			
$	$ 100	$ 100	$ 100
%	10%	10%	10%
Invested Capital (IC)	$ 600	$ 800	$1,000
Cost of Capital (CCAP)	12%	12%	12%
NOP (from above)	$ 100	$ 100	$ 100
Capital Charge (CCAP)	(72)	(96)	(120)
Economic Profit (EP)	$ 28	$ 4	$ (20)

To reiterate what was stated in an earlier segment, economic profit (EP) is a concept from basic economics taught in college. EP is what any business owner (shareholder) should be concerned with, since it takes into account the cost of all the capital invested in the business. EP is the residual (what's left over) after all the costs of running a business have been accounted for and the suppliers of capital have been provided with a fair return on their investment. A problem with accounting profit—most commonly expressed as net income or earnings per share (EPS)—is that it includes only a charge for debt financing; thus, it misses a cost for equity capital, the most expensive and prevalent form of capital for a typical industrial company. The cost of equity capital is what a common shareholder expects to earn annually as a rate of return on investment. The cost of equity capital formula adds a premium to the current return on a long-term risk-free (or close to risk-free) security, such as a 10-year U.S. government bond.

Because of this condition and another important one—the gap between accounting profit and cash flow—there is virtually no correlation between net income and/or EPS growth and key stock market indicators, as illustrated in Exhibit 6.10.

The preceding information can be used to delve into the key financial drivers.

It's important in any business to get a handle on invested capital intensity (ICI). Using the numbers shown in the following table (for the A, B, and C firms), we can see the differences in the amount of fuel needed to maintain and drive the businesses forward:

Base Period	Company A	Company B	Company C
Revenue (Sales)	$1,000	$1,000	$1,000
Invested Capital (IC)	$ 600	$ 800	$1,000
Invested Capital Intensity (ICI)*	$ 0.60	$ 0.80	$ 1.00

*ICI is expressed as cents per dollar; in this case, cents per sales dollar.

This analysis yields an important dynamic regarding the value-creating performance for these three companies, which is that Company A requires the least amount of capital and Company C needs the most. This knowledge is useful in this example, and essential when we're dealing with businesses of different sizes, since it is sometimes the only way we can make comparisons and arrive at meaningful perceptions about the use of capital. So, all things being equal, Company C needs to produce a higher profit margin versus both Company A and Company B to generate the same return on capital. As illustrated next, this is not the case and results in Company C producing an unacceptable return on invested capital—resulting in negative EP—and, thus, being classified as a value destroyer.

Now, let's see how we get to the same conclusion using the value profit margin (VPM) technique, beginning with a summary of its definition and usefulness.

Value Profit Margin (VPM)

- What is it?
  - A minimum profit margin—in essence, a beginning point for value creation.
  - A pre- and/or posttax financial performance benchmark.
- Why use it?
  - Allows for profitability comparisons for businesses of different sizes.
  - Is simple to calculate and easy to communicate, especially to operating managers.
  - Provides managers with a threshold; generating a positive spread creates shareholder value.
  - Is effective for planning—strategies, acquisitions, major investments.
  - Provides an earnings measure linked to value creation.

We can refer back to Company A in the economic profit example earlier in this chapter to illustrate the derivation of the value profit margin. The calculations are:

- *Pretax basis:* Multiply ICI by CCAP; then divide by 1 minus the effective tax rate.
- *After-tax basis:* Multiply ICI by CCAP.

Example—Company A

Revenue (Sales) = \$1,000

IC = \$600 (ICI = \$.60)

CCAP = 12%

Effective tax rate = 30%

- VPM: Pretax basis:
  .60 × 12% = 7.2%/70% = 10.3%
- VPM: After-tax basis:
  .60 × 12% = 7.2% (vs. actual NOP = 10.0%)

Multiplying ICI by the cost of capital and then dividing by 1 minus the cash tax rate produces an operating income (EBIT, EBITA, or EBITDA) margin that will sustain the value of the business. On an after-tax basis, multiplying ICI by CCAP calculates the value profit margin on a net operating profit basis. Margins above the VPM will increase value, while margins below this level are destructive. Why? Because margins above VPM beat CCAP, while those below VPM do not cover the cost for the capital employed in the business. Profit margins at the VPM level maintain the current level of shareholder value.

Invested capital intensity has been discussed. Cost of capital is the weighted (or blended) cost of debt and equity, the basis for the capital charge in the economic profit (EP) measures. "Cash" tax rates incorporate deferrals and, as we have noted, may differ from accounting ("book") provisions.

There is a direct connection of VPM to EP which makes this measure particularly useful. Referring back to Exhibit 6.5, notice that EP for "Company A" is \$28 million . . . derived as NOP of \$100 million minus CCAP of \$72 million. If we compare the VPM for "Company A" (7.2 percent) with the actual NOP margin (10.0 percent), a positive spread of 2.8 percentage points is the result. Multiplying the 2.8 percentage points spread by the \$100 million revenue for "Company A" equals *\$28 million of EP* – the same result as when calculated under the traditional method.

We can make the same calculation for "Company C". Under the traditional EP calculation, NOP of \$100 million minus CCAP of \$120 million yields a negative (\$20) million. VPM for "Company C" is calculated as follows:

Example—Company C

Revenue (Sales) = $1,000

IC = $1,000 (ICI = $1.00)

CCAP = 12%

Effective tax rate = 30%

- VPM: Pretax basis:
    1.00 × 12% = 12.0%/70% = 17.1%
- VPM: After-tax basis:
    1.00 × 12% = 12.0% (vs. actual NOP = 10.0%)
    Spread: 10.0% actual minus 12.0% VPM = (2.0)% (negative)
- EP: $100 million revenue times (2.0)% = $(20) million (negative)

This connection is very important, since it demonstrates the value-driven nature of this metric, and enables us to construct an earnings type of measure that is linked to shareholder value creation. This should be an operating manager's dream—a P&L metric that's basically a percent-to-sales ratio—with key drivers of value creation supporting and standing behind it.

The value profit margin (VPM) is thus one of the most powerful, yet simple, measures for management focus and communication to investors. When VPM is combined with growth, we have the key ingredients of a value-driven measurement system for almost any business. Further, we can work within the P&L (i.e., the earnings framework that people seem fixated on) despite all the evidence (cited earlier) about little or no correlation to stock market value.

To conclude, VPM is the P&L (earnings) measure indicating shareholder value creation or destruction. In fact, it is the only P&L metric with a direct link to value creation! The benefit of developing the VPM input and implementing the technique is well worth the effort, since no other P&L metric has such a direct link to shareholder value.

VALUE ANALYSIS: THE PROPER FOCUS

The final segment explores the unfortunate fact that, in the world of corporate finance, few activities are more entrenched than capital project evaluations. This focus on individual projects often comes at the expense of identifying and analyzing major programs, the building blocks of a strategy. Valuing the strategy itself, the ultimate indicator of future business success, can also be overlooked in the pursuit of net present value (NPV) or internal rate of return (IRR) calculations for individual investments. Project evaluation keeps countless financial analysts hard at work (I have memories of my early years in finance) and consumes a significant amount of time for corporate managers and directors—much of which is nonproductive. Taken to an extreme, bad decisions can result.

A review of project analysis and what it accomplishes, in light of what's really going on in any business, can be revealing. In this appraisal, we need to be willing to raise some candid questions about certain traditions in finance.

Do we really need to be assured that, say, a $750,000 machining center for a $3 billion (in sales) manufacturing company is economically viable? Or that a $300,000 computer-aided design/manufacturing (CAD/CAM) system for the engineering department will have a payoff? When such small investments are put in their proper context, capital project evaluations can appear virtually meaningless—as, in reality, they usually are.

Is this an exaggerated claim? Let's assume that our $3 billion company has three business units (BUs), each with approximately $1 billion of sales. Further, assume that the machining center and CAD/CAM projects are in BU 1, which has a strategy of growing at 15 percent per year and offering a combination of high product quality and competitive cost. BU 1, therefore, plans to grow sales by approximately $150 million next year. Its current year balance sheet reflects the following for fixed assets:

Gross fixed assets	$300 million
Accumulated depreciation	($100) million
Net fixed assets	$200 million

Comparing the gross fixed assets (GFA) and net fixed assets (NFA) amounts to sales, we can calculate the following ratios:

GFA: $300 million (assets) divided by $1 billion (sales) equals $0.30, or 30 percent.

NFA: $200 million (assets) divided by $1 billion (sales) equals $0.20, or 20 percent.

The GFA and NFA ratios reflect capital intensity—that is, how much capital is required to generate each dollar of sales. If we determine that the growth strategy will be in line with past experience, then BU 1 will need to invest about $45 million next year—30 percent of its new sales. After depreciation, the net new investment will be approximately $30 million (20 percent of $150 million) if the strategy replicates recent investment patterns.

Even if the strategy can leverage the existing assets and require less new capital, on a relative basis, we're still dealing with annual investments of many millions of dollars to support the strategy. Since strategies usually require more than one year to execute, the aggregate amount of new capital over the next few years, necessary for BU 1 to grow and prosper, could be $100 million or more.

So what is the point of financially justifying the investment in the machining center or the CAD/CAM system? Why drive people crazy by requiring elaborate evaluations on relatively small projects that have no purpose or life of their own, and are only pieces of a much larger puzzle?

The job of management is to put the puzzle together, not to place each piece under a microscope. I'd be willing to bet that many companies performing extensive capital project evaluations have not quantified the shareholder value impact (that is, the NPV/IRR) of their overall strategy. The key points are: If a strategy has value, then the individual projects should have value, since they are part of the strategy; and further, these projects cannot, and should not, be separated out for purposes of analysis.

The purpose of value-based analysis, regardless of which metric you prefer (since they are all extensions of NPV/IRR), is to determine value creation at appropriate levels in the business hierarchy—the company, business unit, strategy, and major program. *The major program* (for example, an important operational or strategic initiative) *is the absolute lowest level for which value-based analysis should be performed.*

The strategy for BU 1 may encompass *growth via high quality and competitive cost.* A supporting program might be one to *enhance product quality* and, at the same time, *contain or reduce costs.* This type of initiative would seem logical; in fact, it may be an essential program. Let's assume that this program encompasses 10 machining centers averaging $1 million each plus a CAD/CAM system. At this level, value analysis can be meaningful, as it may well represent a building block of the strategy or operating plan, or both. As we present a numerical example, we will highlight the impact of focusing on the program versus the 10 individual machining center projects. It is my belief that too many companies still concentrate on the individual investments, rather than grasping a larger, and more important, link of value to either a strategic or an operational objective. Accepting or rejecting investments are big decisions involving large sums of money.

A walk through the numbers can demonstrate the *valuation hierarchy.* Let's start with the project. Assume that the $750,000 machining center, mentioned earlier, reduces cost, but does not have the throughput capability to increase sales beyond the current level. Therefore, this project is presented as a classic cost-reduction investment. Due to this myopic perspective, we miss the point that the strategy is for growth, through enhanced product quality features, along with competitive cost. Exhibit 6.13

EXHIBIT 6.13 Project Analysis

Invest in a $750,000 N/C Machine Center to Save Costs ($000s Omitted)	Rates/Factors	Year 1	Year 2	Year 3	Year 4	Year 5
Capital Investment (outlay)		$(750)				
Annual Cost Savings (pretax)		$ 150	200	200	200	200
Taxes @ Corporate Tax Rate =	33%	$ (50)	(67)	(67)	(67)	(67)
Tax Shield re: Depreciation:						
Annual Depreciation—Life (years) =	10	$ 75	75	75	75	75
Tax Shield @ Rate =	33%	$ 25	25	25	25	25
Free Cash Flow/Profit After Tax	(FCF/PAT)	$(625)	158	158	158	158

	Rates/Factors	Year 6	Year 7	Year 8	Year 9	Year 10
Annual Cost Savings (pretax)		$ 200	200	200	200	200
Taxes @ Corp. Tax Rate =	33%	$ (67)	(67)	(67)	(67)	(67)
Tax Shield re: Depreciation:						
Annual Depreciation—Life (years) =	10	$ 75	75	75	75	75
Tax Shield @ Rate =	33%	$ 25	25	25	25	25
Free Cash Flow/Profit After Tax	(FCF/PAT)	$ 158	158	158	158	158
Cost of Capital (CCAP) =	11%	. . . Weighted cost of equity and debt				
Net Present Value of 10-year FCF/PAT − Initial Cash Outlay	$227					
Internal Rate of Return (IRR)	21%					

illustrates a typical cost savings analysis to justify spending $750,000. If we take this approach to a ridiculous extreme, we could conceivably have 10 separate evaluations, some growth, some cost reduction, and some maybe combining the two. What a potential nightmare! For some companies, though, this is their analytic world.

Oh, good, we have a winner—at least by some standards. We have produced an analysis that yields a positive net present value (NPV) and a strong internal rate of return (IRR). So what? How can anyone seriously get excited by an NPV of $227,000 in a billion-dollar business? Is this what we want management and the board to concentrate on? Or is there something more important, in terms of achieving the primary goal of any for-profit enterprise—that is, to execute the strategy in order to maximize the value of the total investment that shareholders have made, and will continue to make, in the business? By the way, in one recent research study of institutional investors, strategy execution was one of the most important factors in their investment decision for a particular company; and strategy execution is *two levels* above project returns.

When we elevate our analysis to the program level, we can start to grasp the strategy for this business. The capital investment program alluded to in a previous paragraph is illustrated in Exhibit 6.14.

The highlights of this program are:

- Ten machining centers are to be purchased over a two-year investment period.
- The average investment per machine is $1 million.
- The machining centers have an average useful life of 10 years.
- CAD/CAM systems are to be purchased in years 1 and 6, noting that these systems have a useful life of five years. The first CAD/CAM costs $300,000, and the second is estimated to cost $500,000 in year 6.
- The investment program generates cost savings plus the capability to produce new sales, albeit at a lower throughput ratio. BU 1 generates about $3 of sales for each $1 of gross fixed asset. This equipment reduces manufacturing cost and generates 50 percent of the overall asset base throughput ratio—or $1.50 of sales for each $1 of new capital.

Is there any question as to what is the more relevant message for senior management and the board—the program value of $5.3 million or the project value of $227,000? The project is narrow in scope and presents only a very limited perspective of the goals for the business. The program gets closer to the strategic intent for the business.

EXHIBIT 6.14 Program Analysis

Invest in a $10.8 Million Cost Savings/Quality Program ($000s Omitted)

	Rates/Factors		Year 1	Year 2	Year 3	Year 4	Year 5
Average Cost per N/C Machine Center		$	1,000	1,000	1,000	1,000	1,000
Number of N/C Machine Centers			5	5	—	—	—
Total Capital Investment (outlay) Including 1 CAD/CAM in Year 1		$	(5,300)	(5,000)	—	—	—
Incremental Sales @ per Machine =	$1,500	$	—	7,500	15,000	15,000	15,000
Incremental Profit @ Margin =	12%	$	—	900	1,800	1,800	1,800
Cost Savings (use per-machine impact from Exhibit 6.13)		$	750	1,750	2,000	2,000	2,000
Total Profit Impact		$	750	2,650	3,800	3,800	3,800
Depreciation—N/C Machines (# years)	10	$	(500)	(1,000)	(1,000)	(1,000)	(1,000)
CAD/CAM	5	$	(60)	(60)	(60)	(60)	(60)
Net Taxes @ Rate =	33%	$	(63)	(529)	(912)	(912)	(912)
Free Cash Flow/Profit After Tax	(FCF/PAT)	$	(4,613)	(2,879)	2,888	2,888	2,888

			Year 6	Year 7	Year 8	Year 9	Year 10
Free Cash Flow/Profit After Tax Year 5 Steady State	(FCF/PAT)	$	2,888	2,888	2,888	2,888	2,888
Adjusted for Add'l CAD/CAM in Year 6		$	(500)				
Free Cash Flow/Profit After Tax	(FCF/PAT)	$	2,388	2,888	2,888	2,888	2,888

Net Present Value of 10-year FCF/PAT Net of Initial Cash Outlays $5,300

Internal Rate of Return (IRR)   28%

To appreciate the real value potential for the business, the analysis has to be elevated to a higher level—that of the business strategy itself. This evaluation level is one of the most productive (also, one of the most difficult) for management to work through, because it forces managers to think about their most critical financial drivers and rationalize why they will stay the same or change based on the strategy. These drivers help determine the value potential for the strategy and, ultimately, the entire business.

Exhibit 6.15 gives an example of the financial expectation for BU 1's strategy. It assumes that:

- The business will grow by 15 percent annually for the next four years, maintaining its recent operating profit margin of 12 percent.
- The historical capital intensity ratio will be reduced, from $0.30 gross and $0.20 net to $0.27 and $0.17, respectively, as a ratio to sales, due to the ability to leverage prior years' investment in plant and equipment.
- Detailed assumptions for pricing and cost structure are assumed to be embedded in the summary results presented in Exhibit 6.15.

If you add up the net new fixed capital investments (this is after depreciation) anticipated for the next four years to execute the strategy, you will calculate an amount of slightly over $125 million. How can anyone focus their attention on *analyzing* each $1 million project when the business unit may need to invest $125 million (net) over the next four years? That's not to say we shouldn't *control* the expenditures for capital projects, but we need to move away from *evaluating* them, because they do not provide a meaningful basis or perspective for value analysis. Control systems can, and should be, detailed and specific, but evaluation systems need to be focused at a higher level. To repeat, *the major program is the lowest level for value analysis.*

Look at what we miss if our attention is at the project versus the program or strategy level. BU 1 appears to have a strategy with a very strong value-creating potential, to the tune of over $40 million NPV and total business return (similar to IRR) of nearly 25 percent. And we should be losing sleep over a $750,000 machining center to help execute a major cost-containment objective? Can you imagine going to the board with the capital project and not presenting the value analysis for the strategy? Management needs to know what the strategy is contributing to the overall value (stock price) of the enterprise, and then what the key building blocks (programs) of the strategy are. Major programs are necessary to ensure that the strategy has substance. They also provide a mechanism to prioritize investments and track progress toward

EXHIBIT 6.15 Strategy Analysis

Enhance Product Quality and Control Costs to Grow Sales and Maintain Margins ($ Millions Omitted, Except Ratios)	Rates/Factors; Also, Base #'s	Year 1	Year 2	Year 3	Year 4	Residual
Sales—Total						
New Sales @ Annual Growth =	1,000 15%	$ 1,150	1,323	1,521	1,749	
New Operating Profit (pretax)	120	$ 150	323	521	749	
@ OP Margin =	12%	$ 18	39	63	90	
New Taxes @ Rate =	33%	$ (6)	(13)	(21)	(30)	
New Net Operating Profit (NOP)		$ 12	26	42	60	254
Net New Fixed Investment						
@ Capital Intensity Ratio =	$0.17	$ (26)	(29)	(34)	(39)	
New Working Capital @ Ratio =	$0.20	$ (30)	(35)	(40)	(46)	
Free Cash Flow for the Strategy		$ (43)	(38)	(32)	(24)	254
Net Present Value of 4-Year FCF plus Residual Value	$41					
Total Business Return (TBR)	24%					

The strategy has a present value of $40+ million, assuming a residual that continues year 3 NOP for 6 more years (10-year total time frame for analysis). Equivalent to IRR for the strategy

169

achieving key success elements of a strategy. Projects are a basis for cash control, but provide no foundation for meaningful analysis. Further, project analysis can actually confuse people as to what is really going on in the business. Therefore, project evaluations should be scrapped and replaced with *value analysis focused at the level where value creation occurs!*

A quote from one of the most respected experts on corporate management in the twentieth century will help to drive home the point. Many readers have heard of Peter Drucker. This quote is from one of his books.

> There is one fundamental insight underlying all management science. It is that the business enterprise is a system of the highest order. And one thing characterizes all genuine systems, whether they be mechanical like the control of a missile, biological like a tree, or social like the business enterprise: it is interdependence. The whole of a system is not necessarily improved if one particular function or part is improved or made more efficient. In fact, the system may well be damaged thereby, or even destroyed. In some cases, the best way to strengthen the system may be to weaken a part—to make it less precise or less efficient. For what matters in any system is the performance of the whole; this is the result of growth and dynamic balance, adjustment and integration rather than of mere technical efficiency.[1]

Drucker talks about "interdependence" and "performance of the whole" as key to the functioning of any system. Since financial approaches need to support a company's overall business system, it is hoped that we can come to grips with the notion that financial evaluations have to be done at a level that encompasses the important interdependencies that exist in a business. Think of Drucker's comment about the "performance of the whole" as it might be applied to shareholder value of the whole, in terms of what needs to be accomplished with value-based analysis and performance. The key message here is that managers can do a great job of selecting an overall metric such as EP and all the supporting financial drivers—and then botch the implementation through misapplication. Value analysis must be performed in a logical hierarchy that fits with the way that value is actually created in a business.

We conclude with a summary of which metric(s) to apply at the various levels in the hierarchy.

Value-Based Analysis	Valuation Hierarchy
Total company/operating units/ strategic business units	Full value analysis: EP* and MVA†
Analysis over time	Financial drivers**
Business strategies	MVA† and financial drivers**
Annual operating plans	EP* and financial drivers**
Major programs/strategic	MVA† (linked to a strategy, over an appropriate life cycle)
Major programs/operational	Financial drivers**
Capital projects	No value analysis; focus is on control of appropriations and/or expenditures, part of a program

*EP—Economic profit (similar to economic value added): focus on historical versus future patterns and progression.
†MVA—Market value added (similar to shareholder value creation): focus on an appropriate future growth time horizon.
**Financial drivers—Support (underlying) metrics for EP and MVA.

NOTE

1. Peter F. Drucker, *Management: Tasks, Responsibilities, Practices* (New York: Harper & Row, 1974), 508.

CHAPTER 7

Residual Income and Stock Valuation Techniques

Does It Matter Which One You Use?

Benton E. Gup
Chair of Banking, University of Alabama

Gary K. Taylor
Associate Professor, University of Alabama

Common stockholders are the residual claimants of corporations. It follows that whatever cash flows remain after creditors have been paid are residual cash flows.[1] In essence, all discounted cash flow (including dividends) stock valuation models could be considered residual income valuation models. However, advocates of economic value added (EVA), residual income (RI), and abnormal earnings growth (AEG) valuation methods have a specific definition in mind when using the term *residual income*. For these three models, RI represents earnings above or below normal earnings. Normal earnings are those earnings generated by multiplying the required rate of return by the book value of equity.[2]

All three of these valuation techniques are used on Wall Street and taught in business schools. By way of illustration, consider Stowe et al., *Analysis of Equity Investments: Valuation* (2002). The chapter on residual income valuation states that EVA is a commercial implementation of the residual income "concept." Similarly, Hirst and Hopkins, in *Earnings: Measurement, Disclosure, and the Impact on Equity Valuation* (2000), show that EVA is a specific version of the RI valuation model. However, EVA, RI, and AEG methods of valuation are quite different in their implementation. This chapter clarifies the differences in the use of residual income in the EVA, RI, and AEG methods of valuation. It also calculates intrinsic value using the residual income and abnormal earnings growth valuation models.

The remainder of this chapter is divided into four parts. The first three examine the EVA, RI, and AEG methods, respectively. The last section provides a numerical example of the RI and AEG method of determining intrinsic value.

ECONOMIC VALUE ADDED (EVA)

EVA is trademarked by Stern Stewart & Company. Joel Stern (1998, xi) and G. Bennett Stewart (1991, 742) state that EVA is the residual income that remains after operating profits cover the cost of capital. Stern explains that for debt and equity investors to earn an adequate rate of return, the return must be large enough to compensate them for risk. If the residual income (i.e., EVA) is zero, a firm's operating return is just equal to the return that investors require for the risk they are taking. Thus, EVA is defined by Stewart (1991) and Ehrbar (1998) as:

$$EVA = NOPAT - C\%(TC)$$

where NOPAT = net operating profits after taxes
       C% = cost of capital
       TC = total capital

Based on the EVA model, the value of a firm is equal to the value of its total capital plus the sum of the present value of its projected EVA.[3] Thus, there are three inputs into the EVA model: total capital, net operating profits after taxes, and the cost of capital. The true cost of capital is unobservable but can be estimated from observable data. Stewart (1991, 744) defines TC as total assets less non-interest-bearing current liabilities. However, Stewart suggests the following three adjustments to capital in order to undo the accounting and arrive at a true level of capital: (1) subtract marketable securities; (2) increase property, plant, and equipment by the present value of noncapitalized leases; and (3) increase assets by certain accounting reserves, such as allowance for bad debts, last in, first out (LIFO) reserve, and capitalization of research and development expense. Adjusting TC also requires adjustments to NOPAT. For example, Goldman, Sachs & Company (1997) suggests several adjustments to reported accounting numbers when using EVA. The primary purpose of these adjustments is to calculate a true TC and NOPAT.

Such adjustments to capital and NOPAT require a sophisticated knowledge of accounting rules and procedures in order to perform the necessary adjustments. For example, if not done correctly, these adjustments may eliminate the self-correcting nature of accounting, thereby eliminating one of the advantages of these valuation models. In all three models, overestimating the value of equity causes an over-estimation of normal earnings, causing a simultaneous reduction in residual earnings.

RESIDUAL INCOME METHOD OF VALUATION

Hirst and Hopkins (2000) highlight the benefits of using the RI model, primarily that the RI model is derived from the discounted dividend model and that the model focuses on the creation of value rather than the distribution of value (as in the discounted dividend model). Focusing on the creation of value allows for the RI model to be used as a valuation model and as a tool for determining where business growth will come from and its sustainability via DuPont analysis.[4]

The RI model assumes that future earnings belong to the current shareholders. However, Ohlson (2003) notes that stock options and share buybacks may undermine that assumption.

Penman (2004) shows how the RI model can be used for a parsimonious valuation model. The RI model estimates the intrinsic value of stock by using both the current-period book value of equity on the balance sheet and forecasted earnings. In the RI model, the total equity of the firm is a function of the book value of equity and the sum of the present value of residual income. *Residual income* is the difference between forecasted accounting earnings and normal earnings. Normal earnings are calculated from the book value of equity at the beginning of the period and the cost of capital. Thus, two of the three inputs to the RI model are observable (again, the firm's true cost of equity capital is unobservable but can be estimated by the analyst) and do not require arbitrary adjustments by the analyst.

Formally, *residual income* is defined as the accounting earnings above normal earnings. Normal earnings are the earnings that would be earned given the cost of capital and beginning-of-the-period book value of equity; and the number is calculated by multiplying the book value of equity at the beginning of the period (B_{t-1}) by the firm's cost of equity capital (Ce). The residual income for period t is ($FEPS_t - Ce\ B_{t-1}$), where $FEPS_t$ is the forecasted earnings for period t. An important assumption in the RI model is clean surplus accounting.

The mathematical relationship between the price of a share of stock, forecasted earnings, and book value is:

$$V_0 = B_0 + \sum \left[(1 + Ce)^{-t}(FEPS_t - Ce\,B_{t-1})\right]$$

where V_0 = current intrinsic value of a share of stock
            B_0 = book value of a share of stock
            Ce = cost of equity capital
     $FEPS$ = forecasted earnings per share

As seen by the formulations, the EVA and RI models are similar. In fact, the EVA model is a special case of the more general RI model. Both models have an anchor, total capital in the EVA model and the book value of equity in the RI model. Both models have a residual income component—that is, earnings above what should have been earned by the firm given the book value of equity (total capital in the EVA model) and the cost of capital. The difference between the two models rests in the book value and earnings that are used. The EVA model takes reported accounting numbers and makes several adjustments. These adjustments are based on assumptions made by analysts from reading the financial statements. In essence, the EVA model is trying to undo parts of the accrual accounting process. This then forces the analyst to impose subjective assumptions onto the valuation model. In contrast, the RI model starts with the accounting numbers and recognizes that if the book value of equity is under- or overstated (relative to a true value of equity, which is what the EVA model attempts to calculate) this period, then, due to the nature of double-entry accounting, future earnings will be over- or understated relative to true earnings. This relationship between book and earnings eliminates the effects of conservative or aggressive accounting on firm valuation as long as forecasted earnings are consistent with the firm's accounting choices.

In other words, the RI model utilizes double-entry accounting to address the measurement error associated with the conservative accounting process rather than forcing analysts to undo the effects of the selected accounting policies. Using the RI model allows analysts to focus on predicting future patterns of earnings rather than trying to identify how accounting method selection affects the components of future earnings and the current book value of equity.

ABNORMAL EARNINGS GROWTH MODEL

The abnormal earnings growth (AEG) model is another accounting-based valuation model. The AEG model utilizes capitalized forward earnings as the valuation anchor instead of the book value of equity that is used in the RI model.

$$V_0 = (1/C)\left[FEPS1 + \sum (1 + C)^{-t}(G - C) \times FEPS_{t-1}\right]$$

where V_0 = current intrinsic value of a share of stock
   C = cost of capital
   $FEPS$ = forecasted earnings per share
   G = cum-dividend earnings growth rate

The phrase $(G - C) \times FEPS_{t-1}$ represents abnormal earnings growth, which is the growth in accounting earnings above the cost of capital. In the AEG model, normal earnings represent the earnings growth at the cost of capital. There is no abnormal earnings growth if G is equal to the cost of capital. Similar to the RI model, the addition of value comes only from earnings above normal earnings. Also similar to the RI model, the AEG model allows the analyst to use forecasted earnings rather than an analyst-adjusted earnings number, and focusing on forecasted earnings rather than the individual adjustments to earnings allows the analyst to focus on the growth of earnings. Penman (2004) shows that the RI and AEG models will give the same valuations as long as the inputs (book value of equity, earnings, and dividends) are the same. While the AEG valuation model will yield the same valuations as the RI model, it does not readily lend itself to the financial statement (DuPont) analysis and determination of the creation of firm value.

NUMERICAL EXAMPLE OF RI AND AEG

In this section we calculate Wal-Mart's intrinsic value as of January 1986 using both the RI and AEG valuation models.[5] Wal-Mart is widely used as an example, and has been used extensively in Penman (2004). We assumed that net income is identically equal to comprehensive income, and that realized net income and dividends are identically equal to forecasted net income and dividends. Book value of equity is calculated as the book value of equity at the beginning of the period plus forecasted net income less dividends. Normal earnings are calculated as the cost of capital multiplied by the beginning-of-the-period book value of equity, while residual earnings are the difference between forecasted earnings per share and normal earnings per share. For simplicity we assume that 2002 forecasted earnings will be a perpetuity (see Exhibit 7.1).[6]

Based on this information, Wal-Mart's intrinsic value per share of $5.80 is calculated as the sum of beginning-of-the-period book value of

EXHIBIT 7.1 Wal-Mart Calculation of Components of Residual Income Model

	1987	1988	1989	1990	1991	1992	1993	1994	1995	1996	1997	1998	1999	2000	2001	2002
						Earnings and Dividend Forecast ($)										
Earnings per Share		0.27	0.36	0.47	0.56	0.70	0.87	1.01	1.17	1.19	1.33	1.53	1.93	2.34	2.74	2.90
Dividends per Share		0.03	0.04	0.05	0.07	0.08	0.10	0.13	0.17	0.20	0.21	0.27	0.30	0.39	0.47	0.54
Book Value of Equity per Share	0.73	0.97	1.29	1.71	2.20	2.82	3.59	4.47	5.47	6.46	7.58	8.84	10.47	12.42	14.69	17.05
Normal Earnings		0.09	0.12	0.15	0.21	0.26	0.34	0.43	0.54	0.66	0.78	0.91	1.06	1.26	1.49	1.76
Residual Earnings		0.18	0.24	0.32	0.35	0.44	0.53	0.58	0.63	0.53	0.55	0.62	0.87	1.08	1.25	1.14
Discount Factor		1.12	1.254	1.405	1.574	1.762	1.974	2.211	2.476	2.773	3.106	3.479	3.90	4.363	4.887	5.474
Present Value of Residual Income		0.16	0.19	0.22	0.23	0.25	0.27	0.26	0.26	0.19	0.18	0.18	0.22	0.25	0.26	0.21

equity ($0.73), the sum of the present value of residual income ($3.33), and the present value of the continuing value: [($1.14/0.12)/5.474] = $1.74.[7]

Exhibit 7.2 provides the inputs for calculating Wal-Mart's intrinsic value using the AEG model. In this example, we assume that abnormal earnings growth will be zero after 2002. The intrinsic value based on the AEG valuation model is $5.87.[8] Cum-dividend earnings are defined as earnings after reinvesting the previous period's dividends. In the AEG model, normal earnings are defined as the previous period's earnings growing at the cost of capital. Abnormal earnings growth is the difference between cum-dividend earnings and normal earnings.

As seen in Penman (2004), the RI valuation model allows analysts to forecast those investing activities that will generate value. The AEG valuation model does not lend itself to this type of analysis. However, the AEG valuation model embodies the notion that a firm's intrinsic value is derived from its earnings.

The three models are compared in Exhibit 7.3. As discussed previously, EVA, RI, and AEG valuation models are all derived from the discounted cash flow (including dividends) model. EVA is the residual income model with adjustments to undo the conservative accounting policies of GAAP. The RI model relies on double-entry accounting to adjust for the effect of accounting policies on the reported and forecasted numbers. In other words, if the book value of equity is understated this period relative to a true book value of equity (i.e., not enough earnings have been recorded in previous periods), then forecasted earnings will be higher than true earnings. The AEG model is closer to the concepts discussed on Wall Street, such as the P/E ratio. All three valuation models have an anchor (book value of equity or total capital as in the RI and EVA valuation models, and capitalized earnings in the AEG valuation model) and a residual income component (forecasted earnings above normal earnings). The RI and EVA valuation models allow for financial statement (DuPont) analysis to determine where future growth will arise. The AEG model does not permit this type of analysis.

CONCLUSION

Every stock valuation model that employs discounted cash flows can be considered a residual income model. The EVA model includes analyst assumptions about the book value of equity and future earnings that may not coincide with clean surplus accounting. This process requires analysts to undo the accounting *and* maintain the clean surplus relationship. In contrast to the EVA model, the RI and AEG models utilize observables (current period book value per share, dividends, and forecasted earnings) and allow

EXHIBIT 7.2 Wal-Mart Calculation of Components of Abnormal Earnings Growth Model

							Earnings and Dividend Forecast ($)								
	1988	1989	1990	1991	1992	1993	1994	1995	1996	1997	1998	1999	2000	2001	2002
Dividends per Share	0.03	0.04	0.05	0.07	0.08	0.10	0.13	0.17	0.20	0.21	0.27	0.30	0.39	0.47	0.54
Earnings per Share	0.27	0.36	0.47	0.56	0.70	0.87	1.01	1.17	1.19	1.33	1.53	1.93	2.34	2.74	2.90
Reinvested Dividends (12%)		0.004	0.005	0.006	0.008	0.010	0.012	0.016	0.020	0.024	0.025	0.032	0.036	0.047	0.056
Cum-Dividend Earnings		0.364	0.475	0.566	0.708	0.880	1.022	1.186	1.210	1.354	1.555	1.962	2.376	2.787	2.956
Normal Earnings		0.302	0.414	0.526	0.627	0.784	0.974	1.131	1.310	1.333	1.490	1.714	2.162	2.621	3.069
Abnormal Earnings Growth		0.072	0.061	0.040	0.081	0.096	0.048	0.055	−0.100	0.021	0.065	0.248	0.214	0.166	−0.133
Present Value of AEG		0.064	0.084	0.028	0.051	0.054	0.024	0.025	−0.041	0.008	0.021	0.071	0.055	0.038	−0.023

EXHIBIT 7.3 Comparison of EVA, RI, and AEG Valuation Models

	EVA	RI	AEG
Theoretically derived from discounted dividend model	Yes	Yes	Yes
Can be used if the firm does not pay dividends	Yes	Yes	Yes
Uses an estimated cost of capital	Yes	Yes	Yes
Uses realized accounting data and forecasts	No—Requires analyst to adjust forecasts and accounting data to attempt to arrive at a true total capital and earnings forecast	Yes	Yes
Can be used if future cash flows are negative	Yes	Yes	Yes
On average, the terminal or continuing value makes up a significant portion of the intrinsic value.	No—Total capital is used as the anchor	No—Book value of equity is used as the anchor	No—Capitalized earnings are used as the anchor

the analyst to focus on financial statement analysis to identify growth in earnings rather than undoing the accounting. Having said that, does it make any difference which model is used? The answer appears to be no, because if forecasted earnings and dividends are the same, then the RI and AEG models should yield the same valuation results. The difference between the two models is due to rounding errors. Thus, the choice of the model is a matter of individual preference.

NOTES

1. Damodaran (2001).
2. In the accounting literature, residual earnings have also been called abnormal earnings. See Palepu et al. (1996), Chapter 7.
3. See Stewart (1991), page 320, for further details.
4. See Ohlson (1995) and Feltham and Ohlson (1995) for the detailed explanation of the theoretical formulation of the RI model. See Penman and Sougiannis

(1998) for a comparison of the discounted dividend, free cash flow, and RI models.

5. We use realized earnings and dividends as a forecast for earnings and dividends. We obtained this information from Wal-Mart's published annual reports. We have assumed that there were 2,300 million shares outstanding from 1987 to 2002. We have also assumed a 12 percent cost of capital.

6. See Taylor, Samson, and Gup (2001) for a discussion of how changes in the continuing value will change the intrinsic value calculations.

7. The purpose of this example is to show how to utilize the RI and AEG models in calculating intrinsic value. Obviously, different earnings forecasts will yield different intrinsic values. This example is not intended to discuss market efficiencies and/or the information available to analysts at a point in time.

8. The difference between the two models is due to rounding errors.

REFERENCES

Damodaran, Aswath. 2001. *The dark side of valuation.* Upper Saddle River, NJ: Prentice Hall PTR.

Ehrbar, Al. 1998. *EVA: The real key to creating value.* New York: John Wiley & Sons.

Feltham, G. A., and J. A. Ohlson. 1995. *Valuation and clean surplus accounting for operating and financial activities. Contemporary Accounting Research* 11(2): 689–731.

Goldman, Sachs & Company. 1997. *EVA: A primer.* September 10.

Hirst, D. Eric, and Patrick E. Hopkins. 2000. *Earnings: Measurement, disclosure, and the impact on equity valuation.* Charlottesville, VA: Research Foundation of AIMR and Blackwell Series in Finance.

Ohlson, J. A. 1995. *Earnings, book values, and dividends in equity valuation. Contemporary Accounting Research* 11(2): 661–687.

Ohlson, J. A. 2003. On accounting-based valuation formulae. Working paper.

Palepu, Krishna G., Victor L. Bernar, and Paul M. Healy. 1996. *Business analysis & valuation.* Cincinnati, OH: South-Western Publishing.

Penman, Stephen H. 2004. *Financial statement analysis and security valuation.* 2nd ed. New York: McGraw-Hill.

Penman, S. H., and T. Sougiannis. 1998. A comparison of dividend, cash flow, and earnings approaches to equity valuation. *Contemporary Accounting Research* 15(3): 343–383.

Stern, Joel M. 1998. Foreword. In Ehrbar (1998).

Stewart, G. Bennett, III. 1991. *The quest for value: A guide for senior managers.* New York: HarperCollins.

Stowe, John D., Thomas R. Robinson, Jerald E. Pinto, and Dennis W. McLeavey. 2002. *Analysis of equity investments: Valuation.* Charlottesville, VA: Association for Investment Management and Research.

Taylor, Gary, William Samson, and Benton Gup. 2001. Questrom vs. Federated Department Stores, Inc.: A question of equity value. *Issues in Accounting Education* 16, no. 2 (May): 223–256.

CHAPTER 8

Modern Tools for Valuation

Providing the Investment Community with Better Tools for Investment Decisions

David Trainer
CEO, NEW CONSTRUCTS, LLC

This chapter presents the New Constructs analytical approach for picking stocks. While many firms have claimed to execute similar analytical approaches, no other firm rivals the scale and analytical rigor of New Constructs' research and analytical platform. By removing the accounting distortions found in published financial statements, our methodology enables us to analyze the true economic profitability of businesses. In turn, we demystify stock market valuation by explicitly quantifying the future economic performance that must be attained to justify stock prices.

The founding purpose for New Constructs is to bring more integrity to the function of the capital markets. We fulfill this purpose by delivering to investors more accurate information on the profitability and valuation of stocks. Nevertheless, we cannot accomplish this goal by ourselves. Investors must use the better information, and, for the most part, they do not. After hundreds of meetings, we can report that the analytical rigor of the professional money management community is deplorable. Most of them do not believe they need to understand true economic profits of the business in which they invest. There are three reasons that investors have been successful without conducting their due diligence:

1. They are too rich to care, and believe there is no need for the extra work. Picking stocks has been easy when the market had been going up so much.

2. As interest rates have declined for most of the past 20 years, the rise in the valuation tide has lifted almost all stocks. More of the improvement in valuations has come from lower interest rates than from improved profits. Over time, investors have given less weight to the importance of profitability than of valuation. Until recently, the market has proven them right. I would like to reference the "Sources of Return" slide from the Epoch Investment Partners web site. It shows that the majority of gains in stocks over the past 20 years come from price-earnings (P/E) multiple expansion, not earnings growth or dividends. The point is that valuations have expanded more because of the prosperous economic environment in which we have lived than because the economics of business are better.

3. Most investors do not care much about performance and are closet indexers. (See Exhibit 8.1.)

Perhaps the most alarming reason why more investors do not embrace our research is because they have forgotten the difference between an investor and a speculator. The following quotes define the chasm between the activity of speculating and investing:

> *If you are a speculator, your decision to buy or sell is based on what you believe about the near-term direction of price.*

—Benjamin Graham

> *Speculation is the activity of forecasting the psychology of the market.*

—John Maynard Keynes

> *If you are an investor, your decision to buy or sell is based on the underlying economics of the stock you own.*

—Benjamin Graham

EXHIBIT 8.1 Very Few Investors Are Dedicated Investors

Institutional Investor Category	Percentage Breakdown
Quasi-indexers	61%
Transients	31%
Dedicated	8%
Total	100%

Source: Brian Bushee, "Identifying and Attracting the 'Right' Investors: Evidence on the Behavior of Institutional Investors," *Journal of Applied Corporate Finance* 16, no. 4 (Fall 2004), 28–35.

Investing is an activity of forecasting the yield on assets over the life of the asset.

—John Maynard Keynes

The problem is that most think they are investors when, in reality, they are speculators. New Constructs brings a radical shift to the traditional research paradigm, which is handicapped by the trade-off between analytical rigor and number of companies covered. Traditionally, the more companies a person or a firm covers, the lower the quality of the research. There are exceptions to this rule, but generally and intuitively, this trade-off is easy to understand. By cutting-edge use of technology combined with financial analytical expertise, New Constructs breaks the bonds of this trade-off. (See Exhibit 8.2.)

The accounting rules that govern financial reporting were never designed for equity investors and are suited primarily for credit analysis.[1] Because financial markets place a disproportionate reliance on reported financial statements, many analysts and investors are often misguided by information inappropriate for equity investment analysis. For example, our chapter shows that the cost of annual employee stock option (ESO) issuances is higher than 100 percent of revenues for some companies and a significant operating expense for others. What's more, the liability related to

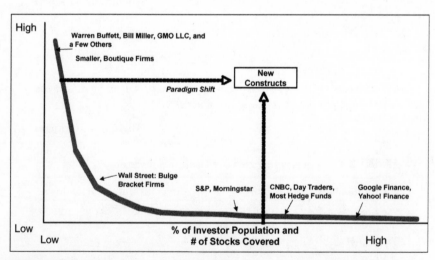

EXHIBIT 8.2 Paradigm Shift: Busting the Mold—Breaking the Trade-Off between Analytical Rigor and Number of Stocks Covered
Source: New Constructs, LLC (www.newconstructs.com).

outstanding ESOs claims as much as 10 percent of the market value of the companies analyzed in our chapter. Unearthing critical financial information buried deep within 10-Q and 10-K filings, we are able to translate accounting statements into economic statements that perform apples-to-apples analysis of the true profitability of businesses despite the accounting policies different businesses may employ.

Folding these economic statements into a valuation framework allows precise quantification of the future economic cash flows required to justify stock prices. We present the stock market's expectations for the future financial performance of the companies in this chapter using intuitive terms.

We do not suggest that basic elements of the investment decision process have changed. We do not present a black box or crystal ball that can predict stock price performance. Our goal is to present analytical techniques that help investors assess the profitability and value of businesses with more reliability and accuracy.

For example, here are some of the key insights presented in our chapter on these companies:

Avalon Bay Communities (AVB)

- *The market has high expectations.* To justify the current market price of $99.45, the company will have to grow its profits by over 6 percent compounded annually for each of the next 45 years.
- *Lifting the accounting veil.* The true profitability of AVB's business is significantly worse than the company's reported financials indicate. Our research shows misleading earnings, which means reported net income is positive and rising while the economic profits of the business are negative and declining.

Accenture Ltd (ACN)

- *Low valuation means low expectations.* To justify the current market price of $36.63, the company need not grow profits at all. The current valuation implies that ACN will never grow its profits above the current level.
- *Strong economics.* Accenture has a top-quintile return on invested capital (ROIC). Over the past five years, the company's ROIC has been rising even while the company grows revenue at a double-digit pace. ACN generates a lot of economic value.

The remainder of this chapter explains how we arrive at our conclusions and presents the detailed information that led us to them.

IDENTIFYING THE PROBLEM

"We still don't know how to value companies."[2]

The problem with popular valuation techniques such as price-to-earnings, price-to-revenues, and EBITDA ratios is twofold: They are shortcuts that fail in their attempt to supplant proper discounted cash flow (DCF) analysis, and they are entirely based on reported accounting data. Too many analysts and investors rely on the face value of reported financial statements and base valuations on those numbers. Financial statements were never designed for equity investors. They were created for accountants and creditors, who have different financial priorities than equity investors. For this reason, it is not unusual that companies with excellent credit ratings are poor stocks.

WHAT DRIVES STOCK MARKET VALUATION?

"The value of any asset equals the discounted present value of its cash flows."

As far back as the 1950s, Professors Merton Miller and Franco Modigliani showed that the stock market equates the value of a firm to the present value of the future cash flows available to the firm's owners. This recipe for valuation seems quite simple, but its execution can be difficult. Although the reported financial statements (e.g., the income statement, balance sheet, and cash flow statement) do not capture the full picture of a company's true financial performance, all of the necessary information is available. The notes to the financial statements found in the 10-K and 10-Q documents provide important disclosures that affect the interpretation of the reported financial statements.

Why haven't more investors followed Warren Buffett's example or Miller and Modigliani's proof? Here are some of the principal reasons:

- The process of removing distortions in accounting statements and arriving at the accurate cash flows of a business is a complex task requiring knowledge of both accounting rules and economic principles.
- Discounting long-term streams of cash flow is computationally cumbersome, even without the additional burden of repeating the process for sensitivity analyses.
- Long before Miller, Modigliani, and Buffett, the large majority of Wall Street analysts and investors had already established a variety of shortcuts, such as price-to-earnings and price-to-revenues ratios, to simplify the information computation process.

■ There has previously been little incentive to modify the practices that have led to unusually high analyst compensation and to investment banks' large share of capital market profits.

OUR VALUATION METHODOLOGY—PROVIDING A SOLUTION

After reviewing and extracting key data from company filings, we perform two key tasks: (1) translation of accounting data from company filings into economic statements that enable an assessment of the economic profitability of the business and (2) quantification of the future financial performance required to justify stock values in terms of revenue growth, cash profits, and sustainability of cash profits.

Translating Accounting Data into Economic Statements

In our view, the true profitability of a business can be derived from the calculation of three key values:

1. *Net operating profit after tax (NOPAT).* This is the after-tax operating cash generated by the business, excluding nonrecurring losses and gains, financing costs, and goodwill amortization and including the compensation cost of employee stock options (ESOs). See Appendix A for a detailed explanation of how we calculate this value.
2. *Invested capital.* This is the sum of all cash that has been invested in a company's net assets over its life without regard to financing form or accounting name. It is the total of investments in the business from which revenue is derived. Common adjustments to this value include the addition of accumulated goodwill amortization, unrecorded goodwill, asset write-offs, unrealized gains and losses in investment securities, loan loss reserves, and capitalizing operating leases. See Appendix A for a detailed explanation of how we calculate this value.
3. *Weighted average cost of capital (WACC).* Weighted average cost of capital (WACC) is the average of debt and equity capital costs that all publicly traded companies with debt and equity stakeholders incur as a cost of operating. The cost of debt capital is equal to the long-term marginal borrowing rate of the business. The cost of equity is calculated using the capital asset pricing model (CAPM). Though there are many other more complicated approaches for arriving at a firm's cost of equity, we do not feel their additional complexity offers commensurate

accuracy. CAPM is simple, gets us close enough, and is easy to implement consistently across all companies we analyze. See Appendix A for a detailed explanation of how we calculate this value.

Samples of these calculations are available in the research section of our web site (www.newconstructs.com). Look for the free snapshot reports.

These three value drivers encompass the comprehensive financial picture of a business and are the foundation for an economic assessment of the profitability of any business. From them we are able to generate the following metrics:

- *Free cash flow.* Free cash flow reflects the amount of cash free for distribution to both debt and equity shareholders. It is calculated by subtracting the change in invested capital from NOPAT.
- *Return on invested capital (ROIC).* This is the best measure of a business's cash return on cash invested. It represents the cash flow derived from all capital invested in the business. It is equal to NOPAT divided by invested capital.
- *Economic profit margin.* ROIC minus WACC equals the truest measure of a business's profitability. This metric accounts for the cash flow returns adjusted for the risk associated with the business model employed to achieve those returns. Economic profit margins precisely measure a firm's ability to create value for its stakeholders.
- *Economic profit.* This metric quantifies the amount of shareholder value a company creates or destroys. It can be calculated two mathematically equivalent ways:
  1. Residual income approach: (ROIC – WACC) × Invested capital = Economic profit.
  2. Refined earnings approach: NOPAT – (Invested capital × WACC) = Economic profit.

These metrics provide investors with insight critical to assessing the merits of business models. Understanding the true economic performance of businesses is the first step in valuing any business model or strategy.

Cash Is King

Our methodology is based on the view that that economic cash flow is the most important driver of asset value.[3] In Exhibit 8.3, we use our discounted cash flow framework to show how ROIC is the key valuation driver value as measured by a price-earnings (P/E) multiple. The results from the 20 different earnings growth and ROIC scenarios show that a company must achieve ROIC greater than the WACC for growth to contribute to the value of a

EXHIBIT 8.3 P/E Ratios That Result from ROIC and Earnings Growth Scenarios

Earnings Growth	ROIC 5%	10%	15%	20%
2%	8.1	10.0	10.6	11.0
10%	−7.3	10.0	15.8	18.6
15%	−29.8	10.0	23.3	29.9
20%	−74.5	10.0	38.2	52.2
35%	−661.5	10.0	233.8	345.8

Assumptions: WACC is 10 percent and the growth appreciation period or DCF forecast horizon is 20 years.
Source: New Constructs, LLC (www.newconstructs.com).

business. Growth has no impact on value if the business's ROIC is equal to its WACC. Growing a business that earns an ROIC below the WACC increases the rate of value destruction. Just left of the middle, the chart shows that when the ROIC equals 10 percent, the same as the WACC, the value of the business does not change no matter how much the company grows. This result stems from the fact that a business with an ROIC equal to its WACC neither creates nor destroys value. Looking toward the left, the chart illustrates that growth from companies not earning ROIC above their WACC destroy value. The faster a business with ROIC less than WACC grows, the more value it destroys, resulting in a lower, eventually negative, P/E multiple. Looking toward the right side of the chart reveals that a company with high revenue growth and an ROIC above its WACC can be very valuable. The takeaway for investors is that understanding the economics of a business is more important than measuring its growth.

Demystifying Stock Market Valuation: Linking Valuation to Fundamentals Once the economic profitability of a business has been accurately evaluated, one can build financial models grounded in bedrock financial theory to compute the value of a business. Exhibit 8.4 illustrates the overall process we employ to value a company's stock.

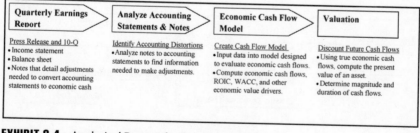

EXHIBIT 8.4 Analytical Process for Equity Valuation
Source: New Constructs, LLC (www.newconstructs.com).

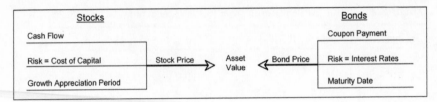

EXHIBIT 8.5 The Basic Valuation Recipe
Source: New Constructs, LLC (www.newconstructs.com).

The Basic Valuation Recipe: Same for Every Asset Exhibit 8.5 shows how the proper approach to value every type of asset is the same. In Exhibit 8.5, we compare bond valuation with stock valuation to show how the relevant terms correspond to each other. Equity cash flows, for example, mirror fixed-income coupon payments. The growth appreciation period (GAP)[4] for stocks is analogous to the maturity date for bonds. Market risk for bond investors comes from interest rate fluctuation. Market risk for equity investors is quantified by the weighted average cost of capital (WACC), which quantifies the risk assigned to the stream of cash flows. Hence, the main key difference between bond and equity valuation is that equity value drivers are based on expectations rather than defined by debt covenants.

We can extend the framework to demonstrate more detailed financial analysis. Exhibit 8.6 shows how business cash flows can be broken down into more intuitive financial terms like revenue growth and return on invested capital (ROIC).

Using Intuitive Terms We can replace the cash flow variable and focus on the three variables with which investors are most familiar. (See Exhibit 8.7.) We can use these three terms (defined in the next section) to quantify the specific financial performance required to justify stock prices for all companies:

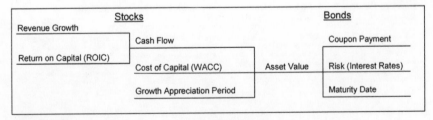

EXHIBIT 8.6 Key Ingredients of the Valuation Recipe
Source: New Constructs, LLC (www.newconstructs.com).

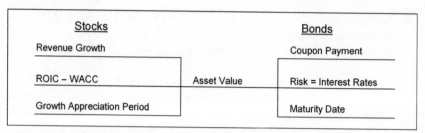

EXHIBIT 8.7 The Valuation Recipe with Core Value Drivers
Source: New Constructs, LLC (www.newconstructs.com).

1. Revenue growth.
2. Economic profit margin (ROIC minus WACC).
3. Growth appreciation period.

THEORY MEETS PRACTICE

Our valuation analyses of Avalon Bay Communities and Accenture apply this methodology to reveal the future financial performance required to justify their stock market values. Exhibit 8.8 presents the results of our discounted cash flow analyses, which offer the results of multiple combinations of the three key value drivers. This valuation matrix shows (gray section) the financial performance required to justify Avalon Bay's current market price of $99.45. Specifically, it shows:

EXHIBIT 8.8 The Valuation Matrix—Avalon Bay Communities (AVB)

| Performance Hurdles | Historical Performance | | | Future Performance | | |
	Past 5-Year Average	Past 3-Year Average	Last FY	−25%	Current Price	25%
Stock values	$47.80	$89.25	$94.14	$74.6	$99.45	$124.3
1. Revenue growth	4.3%	2.1%	8.8%	6.4%	6.4%	6.5%
2. Economic profit margin	−1.4%	−1.5%	−2.4%	2.2%	5.4%	8.8%
3. Growth appreciation period (GAP)	n/a	n/a	n/a	26 years	45 years	75 years

Source: New Constructs, LLC (www.newconstructs.com).

1. *Revenue growth*—the compounded annual growth rate (CAGR) for revenues that must be achieved over the growth appreciation period (GAP—see definition). For the current stock price of $99.45, this hurdle is 6.4 percent.
2. *Economic profit margin*—the excess returns on capital that must be achieved over the growth appreciation period. Note that this number is the average return level during the entire GAP and not the actual level of returns at the end of the GAP. For this reason, the length of the GAP can drive results from this calculation up significantly for longer GAPs and it might seem unusually low for short GAPs. For the current stock price of $99.45, this hurdle is 5.4 percent.
3. *Growth appreciation period (GAP)*—the number of years over which the company must sustain the aforementioned hurdles. For the current stock price, this hurdle is 45 years. We arrive at this number by extending the forecast of our discounted cash flow model as far into the future as needed to calculate a value equal to the current market price.

To the left of the future financial performance required to justify market expectations, we provide a summary of the historical performance of the relevant value drivers.

Exhibit 8.8 also shows the financial performance hurdles required to justify prices 25 percent above and below the current price. All of these calculations are based on market expectations from consensus estimates for revenue. We use this matrix in our valuation analysis of all the companies in this chapter. It is designed to present the reader with a streamlined summary of the financial hurdles the business must meet to justify the market price, or must exceed to drive price appreciation.

Buy Low Expected Cash Flows; Sell High Expected Cash Flows

Material changes in the present value of *expected* cash flows are the key driver of material changes in a stock price. Accordingly, determining the investment merit of a given stock boils down to identifying gaps between the investor's expectations for future financial performance and the market's expectations. Our methodology focuses on comparing the valuation impact of multiple forecast scenarios and measuring the different valuation impacts they create. We offer investors the ability to identify those stocks where the market's expectations are significantly different from their own with greater accuracy and reliability.

We do not see any relevance to the distinction between "growth" and "value" investment strategies. Growth without profit (i.e., value) offers no investment merit. At the same time, value without growth offers little upside incentive for investing in a company. We encourage investors to incorporate the assessment of both the growth and the value of a business into their investment decision-making process.

Providing Context Juxtaposing the historical performance with the required future performance shows how much the expected future performance may or may not diverge from historical performance. The historical information provides insightful context for investors to assess the likelihood of meeting, beating, or underperforming market expectations. In the next section of this chapter, we build on this matrix by adding the results of scenario analyses based on expectations different from those implied by consensus estimates. These scenario analyses enable investors to assess the valuation sensitivity that different companies have to the three key value drivers. Appendix B provides a detailed explanation of how our discounted cash flow model calculates the values in our valuation matrix.

"Better to Be Vaguely Right Than Precisely Wrong"[5] We do not assert that we can define the exact combination of value drivers implied by stock prices. Nevertheless, we attempt to present cogent combinations while offering multiple scenarios that, at the very least, enable investors to calibrate their valuation analyses with greater accuracy and transparency than traditional tools.

Most Attractive Stocks: Methodology

Stocks make our "Most Attractive Stocks" list because they have:

- High-quality earnings based on:
  - ☐ Returns on invested capital are rising.
  - ☐ Economic earnings/cash flows are positive.
- Cheap valuations based on:
  - ☐ Two-year average free cash flow yields[6] are positive.
  - ☐ Price-to-economic book value (EBV)[7] ratios are relatively low.
  - ☐ Growth appreciation periods (GAPs)[8] are relatively short.

These characteristics also qualify stocks for a Very Attractive or Attractive rating, according to our risk/reward rating system. Exhibit 8.9 shows our risk/reward rating analysis, which we apply to the 3,000+ companies that we cover. Stocks get a grade of 1 to 5 for each criterion, 5 being the worst and 1 being the best score. The overall score is based on the average score of all five criteria. Stocks must get an average score of 1.4 or better

EXHIBIT 8.9   New Constructs Risk/Reward Rating for Stocks—Very Attractive

Overall Risk/ Reward Rating	Quality of Earnings		Valuation		
	Economic vs. Reported EPS	Return on Invested Capital (ROIC)	FCF Yield 2-Year Average	Price-to-EBV Ratio	Growth Appreciation Period (Years)
Very dangerous	Misleading trend	Bottom quintile	≤−5%	≥3.5 or −1 to 0	≥50
Dangerous	False positive	4th quintile	−5% to −1%	2.4 to 3.5 or ≤−1	20 to 50
Neutral	Neutral	3rd quintile	−1% to 3%	1.6 to 2.4	10 to 20
Attractive	Positive EP	2nd quintile	3% to 10%	1.1 to 1.6	3 to 10
Very attractive	Rising EP	Top quintile	>10%	0 to 1.1	0 to 3

Source: New Constructs, LLC (www.newconstructs.com).

to be rated Very Attractive. For the most part, only Very Attractive stocks qualify for our "Most Attractive Stocks" lists.

Please see our website (www.newconstructs.com) for a free sample of our Most Attractive Stocks for any given month since July 2004.

Most Dangerous Stocks: Methodology

Stocks make our "Most Dangerous Stocks" list because they have:

- Poor-quality earnings based on:
  - ☐ Misleading earnings: rising and positive GAAP earnings while economic profits are negative and falling.
  - ☐ Low returns on invested capital (ROIC).
- Expensive valuations, based on:
  - ☐ Two-year average free cash flow yields[9] that are very low or negative.
  - ☐ Price-to-economic book value (EBV)[10] ratios that are relatively high.
  - ☐ Growth appreciation periods (GAP)[11] that are relatively long.

These characteristics also qualify stocks for a Very Dangerous or Dangerous rating, according to our risk/reward rating system. Exhibit 8.10 shows our risk/reward rating analysis, which we apply to the 3,000+

EXHIBIT 8.10 New Constructs Risk/Reward Rating for Stocks—Very Dangerous

Overall Risk/ Reward Rating	Quality of Earnings		Valuation		
	Economic vs. Reported EPS	Return on Invested Capital (ROIC)	FCF Yield 2-Year Average	Price- to-EBV Ratio	Growth Appreciation Period (Years)
Very dangerous	Misleading trend	Bottom quintile	≤−5%	≥3.5 or −1 to 0	≥50
Dangerous	False positive	4th quintile	−5% to −1%	2.4 to 3.5 or ≤−1	20 to 50
Neutral	Neutral	3rd quintile	−1% to 3%	1.6 to 2.4	10 to 20
Attractive	Positive EP	2nd quintile	3% to 10%	1.1 to 1.6	3 to 10
Very attractive	Rising EP	Top quintile	>10%	0 to 1.1	0 to 3

Source: New Constructs, LLC (www.newconstructs.com).

companies that we cover. Stocks get a grade of 1 to 5 for each criterion, 5 being the worst and 1 being the best score. The overall score is based on the average score of all five criteria. Stocks must get an average score of 4.25 or more to be rated Very Dangerous. For the most part, only Very Dangerous stocks qualify for our "Most Dangerous Stocks" list.

Please see our website (www.newconstructs.com) for a free sample of our Most Dangerous Stocks for any given month since July 2004.

GENERAL NOTES ON STOCK PICKING

We do not hesitate to admit that our approaches to measuring economic profits and the expectations embedded in stock prices are not novel. We add value, as highlighted in Exhibit 8.2, by not sacrificing any anlytical rigor when applying the approaches consistently to a virtually unlimited number of publicly-traded stocks. New Constructs' ability to gather and apply data from the notes to the financial statements when calculating economic profit gives our clients unprecedented insights into the true profitability and valuation of companies. In our opinion, we are simply applying the proper methodologies for measuring corporate profitability and quantifying market expectations with scale. Our goal is to give investors quick and easy access to better information for making investment deicsions. Despite the rigor and insights delivered by our research, intelligent investing remains a difficult task.

Understanding Our Limitations

Few have articulated the tenets of a sound valuation philosophy as well as Martin Liebowitz:

> At the very most, the modeled result should be taken as delineating the region beyond which the analyst must rely on imagination and intuition.
>
> . . . the results of any equity valuation model should be viewed only as a first step in a truly comprehensive assessment of firm value.
>
> . . . analyzing a firm's future is akin to assessing the value of a continually unfinished game in which the rules themselves drift on a tide of uncertainty.[12]

Our research does not attempt to predict the future performance of businesses or stock prices. Our focus is to present a methodology that empowers investors with information essential to assessing the true profitability and value of companies.

Our models perform no subjective strategic analysis. Instead, we provide the financial context critical to performing subjective analysis more effectively. We offer a methodology that provides a better understanding of the economics of businesses. We hope investors can use these insights to perform a more accurate strategic analysis in order to determine whether a business can exceed the market's implied expectations for future financial performance.

A Good Bargain Is Hard to Find

We underscore that finding undervalued stocks (i.e., good investment opportunities) is not a simple task. Finding overvalued stocks can be simple; however, finding good stocks to short is much more difficult. The market is a very robust pricing mechanism. Consistently finding inappropriately valued stocks is a challenge that few professional investors meet.[13] Indeed, Warren Buffett, one of the most successful contemporary investors, employs an investment strategy that reflects this fact.[14] He has often noted that finding undervalued stocks is difficult, especially at the market heights. Accordingly, his investment strategy focuses on making large investments in the few stocks he considers attractive. The purpose of this chapter is to present a methodology that we believe will help investors more systematically identify those few, rare potential bargains as well as avoid the stocks most likely to decline in value.

Data Sources

There are four sources for the data inputs required to develop a model on each of the companies we analyzed. (1) Companies' 10-K filings are the primary source, and provide all the information required to perform historical analyses. (2) We reference consensus estimates to forecast market expectations where data was available, which primarily includes revenues for two to three years into the future. (3) We extrapolated estimates into future years beyond where consensus provided actual data. (4) In some cases we entered a separate set of forecasts that provide a point of comparison to market expectations. The results of these forecasts demonstrate our ability to perform scenario analyses with our model.

Backup Data

In Appendix D, we provide an example of the NOPAT, invested capital, and weighted average cost of capital (WACC) calculations. We provide free samples of our NOPAT, invested capital, and WACC calculations on our web site: www.newconstructs.com. These backup calculations provide the details behind the calculations that drive our conclusions. Combined with the methodology overview earlier in the chapter, the Appendixes provide readers with additional explanations of how we arrived at all of our results.

One of the 40 Most Dangerous Stocks for September 2008: Avalon Bay Communities— Poor Business Economics with a Rich Valuation

Every month since July 2004, New Constructs publishes its list of the 40 Most Dangerous Stocks comprised of 20 large cap stocks and 20 small cap stocks. All of the reports are available on our website (www.newconstructs. com) along with reports tracking the performance of our Most Attractive and Most Dangerous Stocks as a long/short portfolio and as independent portfolios.

Very Dangerous Risk/Reward Rating[15]

- Avalon Bay Communities (AVB) has an overall risk/reward rating of Very Dangerous because the stock offers much more downside risk than upside potential, in our opinion.

EXHIBIT 8.11 AVB Risk/Reward Rating

Overall Risk/ Reward Rating	Quality of Earnings		Valuation		
	Economic vs. Reported EPS	Return on Invested Capital (ROIC)	FCF Yield 2-Year Average	Price-to-EBV Ratio	Growth Appreciation Period (Years)
Very dangerous	Misleading trend	Bottom quintile	≤−5%	≥3.5 or −1 to 0	≥50
Dangerous	False positive	4th quintile	−5% to −1%	2.4 to 3.5 or ≤−1	20 to 50
Neutral	Neutral	3rd quintile	−1% to 3%	1.6 to 2.4	10 to 20
Attractive	Positive EP	2nd quintile	3% to 10%	1.1 to 1.6	3 to 10
Very attractive	Rising EP	Top quintile	>10%	0 to 1.1	0 to 3
Actual values	−$2.12 vs. $4.38	6.0%	−3.8%	6.2	47

Source: New Constructs, LLC (www.newconstructs.com) and company filings.

- Exhibit 8.11 summarizes the five factors that drive our overall risk/reward rating for AVB. Each factor offers insights into the profitability and valuation of AVB.
- "Misleading trend" means that reported EPS is positive and rising while economic EPS is negative and falling.
- The two biggest adjustments that lower economic EPS and are not captured in reported EPS are reported net assets and off-balance-sheet operating leases.
- The combination of negative economic EPS with a rich stock valuation drives a risk/reward rating of Very Dangerous for AVB.
- Our risk/reward rating system identifies disconnects between the market's expectations for future cash flows and current cash flows.
- This chapter provides a detailed explanation of each diagnostic criterion and each rating for AVB. Appendix C offers an explanation of how our risk/reward rating system works.

Economic versus Reported Earnings: Why Economic profits Matter Economic profits are almost always meaningfully different from GAAP earnings. Economic profits are informative because they provide a truer measure of underlying economic profitability and shareholder value creation than offered by GAAP earnings. Beware of stocks whose economic profits are declining while reported earnings are increasing. Beware of companies whose economic profits differ meaningfully from their accounting earnings.

The Most Attractive stocks have positive economic profits and their returns on capital are increasing. The Most Dangerous stocks have negative economic profits that are declining while reported GAAP earnings are positive and rising.

Exhibit 8.12 highlights the differences between the reported and economic profits for AVB.

Note the misleading trend caused by the company reporting positive and rising GAAP profits while the economics of its business are in decline.

During the past fiscal year, the two biggest drivers of the difference between reported and economic EPS are reported net assets and off-balance-sheet operating leases.

Economic profits and return on capital metrics are significantly more accurate when as-reported financial statements have been adjusted to reverse accounting distortions. The majority of the data required to reverse accounting distortions is available only in the notes to the financial statements, which we analyze rigorously. Our core competency is gathering and analyzing all relevant financial data (from financial statements and the notes) so that we can deliver earnings analyses that best represent the true profitability of businesses. Following is a list of the adjustments we make to a company's reported GAAP profits in order to reverse accounting distortions and arrive at a better measure of a firm's profits:

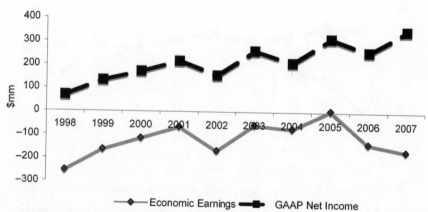

EXHIBIT 8.12 AVB: Accounting Perception versus Economic Reality
Source: New Constructs, LLC (www.newconstructs.com) and company filings.

- Employee stock options.
- Off-balance-sheet financing.
- Pension over-/underfunding.
- LIFO reserve.
- Excess cash.
- Unrealized gains/losses.
- Restructuring charges.
- Goodwill amortization.
- Pooling goodwill.
- Unconsolidated subsidiaries.
- Minority interests.
- Capitalized expenses.

Exhibit 8.13 compares AVB's return on invested capital (ROIC) to its weighted average cost of capital (WACC). This company's ROIC during its last fiscal year ranks in the 4th quintile.

How We Measure Economic profits The metrics we use to measure the economic performance of companies are economic profit margin and economic profits. The economic profit margin for a company equals its return on invested capital (ROIC) minus its weighted average cost of capital (WACC). The economic profits of a company equal its economic profit margin multiplied by its invested capital.

We believe our measures of economic performance to be substantially more accurate than accounting metrics because we make adjustments for all the issues listed in Exhibit 8.5.

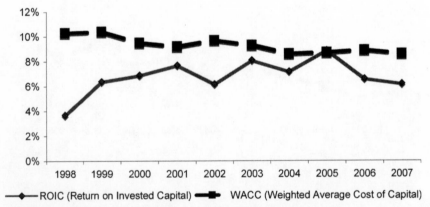

EXHIBIT 8.13 AVB Economic Profit Margin: Return on Invested Capital versus Weighted Average Cost of Capital
Source: New Constructs, LLC (www.newconstructs.com) and company filings.

Free Cash Flow Yield Rigorous back-testing shows that stocks with a free cash flow yield averaging at least 10 percent over a minimum of two years significantly outperformed both the S&P 500 and a survivor-bias-adjusted index. For more detail on free cash flow yield and our back-testing, see our report "Cash Is King," which was published November 30, 2004.

Using free cash flow yields to pick stocks is not a new strategy. However, we believe our strategy yields superior results because we use a better measure of free cash flow (FCF). In the same way that our economic EPS is a better measure of profitability than reported EPS, our measure of FCF is better than traditional accounting-based FCF. We measure free cash flow by subtracting the change in invested capital from NOPAT.

Exhibit 8.14 shows AVB's FCF yield over the past several years. AVB's current two-year average FCF yield is −3.8 percent.

Free cash flow yield equals unlevered FCF divided by enterprise value. The level of FCF does not always reflect the health of a business or its prospects. For example, a large amount of FCF can be a sign that a company has limited investment opportunities and, hence, limited growth prospects. In contrast, negative FCF can be an attractive indication that a company has more investment opportunities than it can fund with cash from operations. Zero FCF could mean that the company generates just enough cash to internally fund its growth opportunities.

Price to EBV per Share Exhibit 8.15 shows the differences between the stock market price and economic book value (EBV) per share of AVB. These differences reflect the portion of the stock price that is entirely dependent on future cash flow growth.

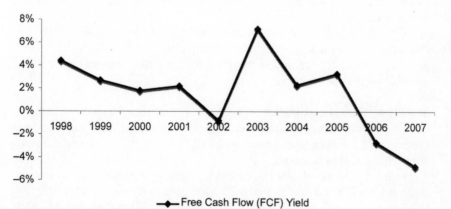

EXHIBIT 8.14 AVB: Free Cash Flow (FCF) Yield
Source: New Constructs, LLC (www.newconstructs.com) and company filings.

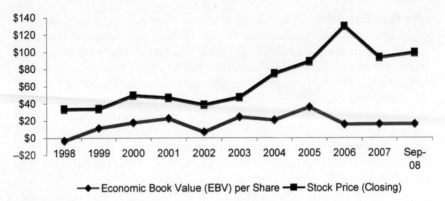

EXHIBIT 8.15 AVB: Stock Price versus Economic Book Value (EBV) per Share
Source: New Constructs, LLC (www.newconstructs.com) and company filings.

When stock prices are much higher than EBVs, the market predicts that the economic profitability (as distinct from accounting profitability) of the company will meaningfully increase. When stock prices are much lower than EBVs, the market predicts that the economic profitability of the company will meaningfully decrease. If the stock price equals the EBV, the market predicts the company's economic profitability will not change.

EBV measures the no-growth value of the company based on the current economic cash flows generated by the business. It is also known as the prestrategy value of the company because it ignores the value attributable to future cash flows, which are, in theory, what business strategies should aim to improve.

The formula for EBV is: (NOPAT/WACC) + Excess cash − Debt (including operating leases) − Value of outstanding stock options − Minority interests ± Over-/underfunded pensions. EBV per share equals EBV divided by basic shares outstanding.

Quantifying Market Expectations We believe this stock has a Very Dangerous risk/reward rating because there is a relatively large difference between the expected financial performance implied by its market price and the company's historical performance.

Exhibit 8.16 compares the future performance required to justify the company's stock market price to its historical performance. Specifically, Exhibit 8.16 shows that to justify the current stock price of $99.45, AVB must grow revenues at 6.4 percent and maintain a 5.4 percent economic profit margin for 45 years.

EXHIBIT 8.16 AVB: Future Performance Required to Justify Valuation

Avalon Bay Communities (AVB) Performance Hurdles	Historical Performance			Future Performance Current Price
	Past 5-Year Average	Past 3-Year Average	Last FY	
Stock values	$47.80	$89.25	$94.14	$99.45
1. Revenue growth	4.3%	2.1%	8.8%	6.4%
2. Economic profit margin	−1.4%	−1.5%	−2.4%	5.4%
3. Growth appreciation period (GAP)	n/a	n/a	n/a	45 years

Source: New Constructs, LLC (www.newconstructs.com) and company filings.

Historically, AVB has generated revenue growth of 4.3 percent, 2.1 percent, and 8.8 percent, and economic profit margins of −1.4 percent, −1.5 percent, and −2.4 percent over the past five years, three years, and one year. For the future, the market expects AVB will achieve revenue growth of 6.4 percent and economic profit margins of 5.4 percent for 45 years.

GAP measures the number of years implied by the stock price during which the company must maintain an edge over its current and future competitors. Specifically, GAP measures the number of years a company will earn returns on invested capital greater than its cost of capital on new investments. The law of competition dictates that a company can only grow its economic profits for the finite period over which it can maintain a competitive advantage.

GAP analysis comes from our dynamic discounted cash flow model, a multistage DCF model that values companies across multiple forecast horizons. Each forecast horizon (i.e., growth appreciation period) assumes the company cannot grow profits beyond the GAP. Our model exclusively uses no-growth terminal value assumptions for calculating the value of the stock for each GAP.

The forecast drivers for our DCF model are: (1) revenue growth, (2) Net Operating Profit Before Tax (NOPBT) margin (i.e., EBIT margin with adjustments), (3) cash tax rate, and (4) incremental net working and fixed capital needs. Our MaxVal models value stocks based on the present value of expected free cash flow, with that free cash flow measured according to our economic (as distinct from conventional accounting) methodology. MaxVal subscribers forecast economic free cash flow by assigning estimates to three value drivers:

1. *Revenue growth*—compounded over the indicated time frame.
2. *Economic profit margin*—the return on invested capital minus the weighted average cost of capital.
3. *Growth appreciation period*—number of years the company can earn a positive economic profit margin on incremental investments (i.e., the number of years it can create economic value).

An alternative way to conceptualize the three value drivers is:

1. "How fast will the company grow?"
2. "How profitable will the company be?"
3. "For how many years will the company grow economic profits or create incremental value?"

One of the 40 Most Attractive Stocks for September 2008: Accenture Ltd—Strong Cash Economics with a Low Valuation

Every month since July 2004, New Constructs publishes its list of the 40 Most Attractive Stocks comprised of 20 large cap stocks and 20 small cap stocks. All of the reports are available on our website (www.newconstructs. com) along with reports tracking the performance of our Most Attractive and Most Dangerous Stocks as a long/short portfolio and as independent portfolios.

Very Attractive Risk/Reward Rating[16]

- ACN has an overall risk/reward rating of Very Attractive because the stock offers much more upside potential than downside risk, in our opinion.
- Exhibit 8.17 summarizes the five factors that drive our overall risk/reward rating for ACN. Each factor offers insights into the profitability and valuation of ACN.
- Rising EP means that economic EPS are positive, the company's ROIC is greater than WACC, and ROIC is rising.
- The biggest adjustment that lowers economic EPS and is not captured in reported EPS is reported net assets.
- The combination of positive and rising economic EPS with a cheap stock valuation drives a risk/reward rating of Very Attractive for ACN.

EXHIBIT 8.17   ACN: Risk/Reward Rating

Overall Risk/ Reward Rating	Quality of Earnings		Valuation		
	Economic vs. Reported EPS	Return on Invested Capital (ROIC)	FCF Yield 2-Year Average	Price-to-EBV Ratio	Growth Appreciation Period (Years)
Very dangerous	Misleading trend	Bottom quintile	≤−5%	≥3.5 or −1 to 0	≥50
Dangerous	False positive	4th quintile	−5% to −1%	2.4 to 3.5 or ≤−1	20 to 50
Neutral	Neutral	3rd quintile	−1% to 3%	1.6 to 2.4	10 to 20
Attractive	Positive EP	2nd quintile	3% to 10%	1.1 to 1.6	3 to 10
Very attractive	Rising EP	Top quintile	>10%	0 to 1.1	0 to 3
Actual values	$2.35 vs. $1.44	50.0%	17.7%	1.0	<1 year

Source: New Constructs, LLC (www.newconstructs.com) and company filings.

- Our risk/reward rating system identifies disconnects between the market's expectations for future cash flows and current cash flows.
- This chapter provides a detailed explanation of each diagnostic criterion and each rating for ACN. Appendix C offers an explanation of how our risk/reward rating system works.

Economic versus Reported Earnings: Why Economic profits Matter   Economic profits are almost always meaningfully different from GAAP earnings. Economic profits are informative because they provide a truer measure of underlying economic profitability and shareholder value creation than is offered by GAAP earnings. Beware of stocks whose economic profits are declining while reported earnings are increasing. Beware of companies whose economic profits differ meaningfully from their accounting earnings.

The Most Attractive stocks have positive economic profits and their returns on capital are increasing. The Most Dangerous stocks have negative economic profits that are declining while reported GAAP earnings are positive and rising.

Exhibit 8.18 highlights the differences between the reported and economic profits for ACN. ACN is one of the few companies in our coverage

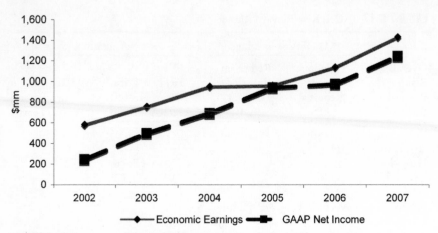

EXHIBIT 8.18 ACN: Accounting Perception versus Economic Reality
Source: New Constructs, LLC (www.newconstructs.com) and company filings.

universe of over 3,000 companies whose economic profits exceed their accounting earnings. During the past fiscal year, the two biggest drivers of the difference between reported and economic EPS are reported net assets and off-balance-sheet operating leases.

Economic profits and return on capital metrics are significantly more accurate when as-reported financial statements have been adjusted to reverse accounting distortions. The majority of the data required to reverse accounting distortions is available only in the notes to the financial statements, which we analyze rigorously. Our core competency is gathering and analyzing all relevant financial data (from financial statements and the notes) so that we can deliver earnings analyses that best represent the true profitability of businesses. Following is a list of the adjustments we make to a company's reported GAAP profits in order to reverse accounting distortions and arrive at a better measure of a firm's profits:

- Employee stock options
- Off-balance-sheet financing.
- Pension over-/underfunding.
- LIFO reserve.
- Excess cash.
- Unrealized gains/losses.
- Restructuring charges.
- Goodwill amortization.
- Pooling goodwill.

- Unconsolidated subsidiaries.
- Minority interests.
- Capitalized expenses.

Exhibit 8.19 compares ACN's return on invested capital (ROIC) to its weighted average cost of capital (WACC). This company's ROIC during its last fiscal year ranks in the 1st quintile.

How We Measure Economic profits   The metrics we use to measure the economic performance of companies are economic profit margin and economic profits. The economic profit margin for a company equals its return on invested capital (ROIC) minus its weighted average cost of capital (WACC). The economic profits of a company equal its economic profit margin multiplied by its invested capital.

We believe our measures of economic performance to be substantially more accurate than accounting metrics because we make adjustments for all the issues listed in Exhibit 8.5.

Free Cash Flow Yield   Rigorous back-testing shows that stocks with a free cash flow yield averaging at least 10 percent over a minimum of two years significantly outperformed both the S&P 500 and a survivor-bias-adjusted index. For more detail on free cash flow yield and our back-testing, see our report "Cash Is King," which was published November 30, 2004.

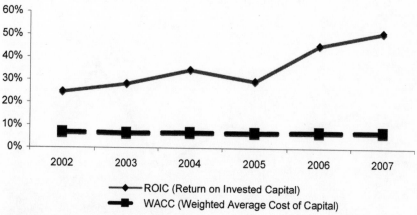

EXHIBIT 8.19   ACN: Economic Profit Margin—Return on Invested Capital versus Weighted Average Cost of Capital
Source: New Constructs, LLC (www.newconstructs.com) and company filings.

Using free cash flow yields to pick stocks is not a new strategy. However, we believe our strategy yields superior results because we use a better measure of free cash flow (FCF). In the same way that our economic EPS is a better measure of profitability than reported EPS, our measure of FCF is better than traditional accounting-based FCF. We measure free cash flow by subtracting the change in invested capital from NOPAT.

Exhibit 8.20 shows ACN's FCF yield over the past several years. ACN's current two-year average FCF yield is 9.5 percent.

Free cash flow yield equals unlevered FCF divided by enterprise value. The level of FCF does not always reflect the health of a business or its prospects. For example, a large amount of FCF can be a sign that a company has limited investment opportunities and, hence, limited growth prospects. In contrast, negative FCF can be an attractive indication that a company has more investment opportunities than it can fund with cash from operations. Zero FCF could mean that the company generates just enough cash to internally fund its growth opportunities.

Price to EBV per Share   Exhibit 8.21 shows the differences between the stock market price and economic book value (EBV) per share of ACN. These differences reflect the portion of the stock price that is entirely dependent on future cash flow growth.

When stock prices are much higher than EBVs, the market predicts that the economic profitability (as distinct from accounting profitability) of the company will meaningfully increase. When stock prices are much lower than EBVs, the market predicts that the economic profitability of the company will meaningfully decrease. If the stock price equals the

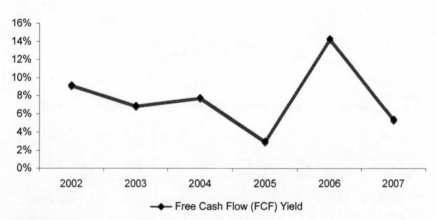

EXHIBIT 8.20   ACN: Free Cash Flow (FCF) Yield
Source: New Constructs, LLC (www.newconstructs.com) and company filings.

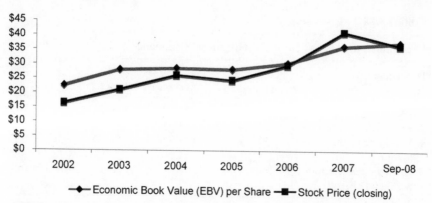

EXHIBIT 8.21 ACN: Stock Price versus Economic Book Value (EBV) Per Share
Source: New Constructs, LLC (www.newconstructs.com) and company filings.

EBV, the market predicts that the company's economic profitability will not change.

EBV measures the no-growth value of the company based on the current economic cash flows generated by the business. It is also known as the prestrategy value of the company because it ignores the value attributable to future cash flows, which are, in theory, what business strategies should aim to improve.

The formula for EBV is: (NOPAT/WACC) + Excess cash – Debt (including operating leases) – Value of outstanding stock options – Minority interests ± Over-/underfunded pensions. EBV per share equals EBV divided by basic shares outstanding.

Quantifying Market Expectations We believe this stock has a Very Dangerous risk/reward rating, because there is a relatively large difference between the expected financial performance implied by its market price and the company's historical performance.

Exhibit 8.22 compares the future performance required to justify the company's stock market price to its historical performance. Specifically, the table shows that to justify the current stock price of $36.63, ACN need not grow its profits at all. In other words, the current stock price implies no profit growth. This finding correlates with our preceding price to economic book value analysis, which shows that ACN's stock price equals its economic book value.

Historically, ACN has generated revenue growth of 12.5 percent, 12.0 percent, and 17.7 percent, and economic profit margins of 30.9 percent, 35.0 percent, and 43.9 percent over the past five years, three years, and one year. For the future, the market expects ACN will achieve no profit growth.

EXHIBIT 8.22 ACN: Future Performance Required to Justify Valuation

Accenture Ltd (ACN)	Historical Performance			Future Performance
Performance Hurdles	Past 5-Year Average	Past 3-Year Average	Last FY	Current Price
Stock values	$21.16	$24.40	$41.21	$36.63
1. Revenue growth	12.5%	12.0%	17.7%	—
2. Economic profit margin	30.9%	35.0%	43.9%	—
3. Growth appreciation period (GAP)	n/a	n/a	n/a	< 1 year

Source: New Constructs, LLC (www.newconstructs.com) and company filings.

APPENDIX A: DEFINITIONS OF KEY TERMS USED IN OUR VALUATION MODELS

We did not invent any of the terms or definitions below. We add value by implementing these calculations with high analytical rigor for a virtually unlimited number of publicly-traded companies.

Invested Capital

Invested capital is the sum of all cash that has been invested in a company over its life without regard to financing form or accounting name. It is the total of investments in the business from which revenue is derived. It can be calculated two mathematically equivalent ways:

Operating	Financing
Current Assets	Short-Term Debt
– NIBCLs*	+ Long-Term Debt
Net Working Capital	+ All Leases
+ Tangible Assets[†]	Total Debt and Leases
+ Intangible Assets	+ Equity Equivalents
+ Other Assets	+ Common Equity
Invested Capital	Invested Capital

*NIBCLS stands for non-interest-bearing current liabilities.
[†]Includes leased assets.
Source: New Constructs, LLC (www.newconstructs.com).

The following are the primary accounting distortions in reported financial statements that require economic translation and adjustment for the invested capital calculation. Appendix D reflects the degree to which these distortions affect the calculations for a specific company.

- Capitalized expenses.
- Excess cash.
- LIFO reserve.
- Other noncash reserves.
- Deferred revenues.
- Operating leases.
- Accumulated goodwill amortization.
- Unrecorded goodwill derived from acquisitions recorded under the pooling method of accounting.
- After-tax portion of asset write-downs.
- Investments in unconsolidated subsidiary/minority interests.
- Unrealized gains/losses on investments.
- Over-/underfunded pensions.

NOPAT

Net operating profit after tax (NOPAT) is the after-tax operating cash generated by the business, excluding nonrecurring losses and gains, financing costs, and goodwill amortization, and including the compensation cost of employee stock options (ESOs). It can be calculated two mathematically equivalent ways:

Operating	Financing
Net Revenues	Net Income
– Operating Expenses	+ Adj. for Capitalized Expenses
– Value of ESOs	Adjusted Net Income
EBIT	+ Increase in Equity Equivalents
+ Goodwill Amortization	– Value of ESOs
EBITA	Income Available to Common
+ Adj. for Capitalized Expenses	+ Other Income
+ Income Equivalents	+ Interest Expense After Taxes
NOPBT	NOPAT
– Cash Operating Taxes	
NOPAT	

The following are the primary accounting distortions in reported financial statements that require economic translation and adjustment for the NOPAT calculation. Appendix D reflects the degree to which these distortions affect the calculations for a specific company.

- Capitalized expenses.
- Income from unconsolidated subsidiaries.
- Restructuring/nonrecurring charges.
- All nonoperating items are below EBIT.
- All after-tax items.
- Value of employee stock options (ESOs) issued in a given year.
- Operating leases.
- Over-/underfunded pensions.

Free Cash Flow

Free cash flow (FCF) reflects the amount of cash free for distribution to both debt and equity shareholders. It is calculated by subtracting the change in invested capital from NOPAT.

ROIC

Return on invested capital (ROIC) is the true measure of a business's operating profitability. It represents the cash flow derived from all capital invested in the business. It is equal to NOPAT divided by invested capital.

WACC

Weighted average cost of capital (WACC) is the average of debt and equity capital costs that all publicly traded companies with debt and equity stakeholders incur as a cost of operating. We provide the details behind our WACC calculations:

Cost of Equity

- Our cost of equity calculation is based on the capital asset pricing model methodology.
- Though there are many other more complicated approaches for arriving at a firm's cost of equity, we do not feel their additional complexity offers commensurate accuracy. CAPM is simple, gets us close enough, and is easy to implement consistently across all companies we analyze.

- The market value of equity is used when calculating the debt to total market capital ratio that is used in the cost of equity calculation.
- The equity risk premium is based on a forward-looking dividend discount model.
- Beta can come from many sources (Value Line, Ibbotson, Yahoo! Finance, etc.). We try to use fairly consistent estimates for beta to avoid this variable having an inappropriately large impact on WACC calculation.

Cost of Debt

- The cost of debt capital is equal to a business's long-term marginal borrowing rate.
- The risk-free rate (RFR) is approximated by the 30-year Treasury bond.
- To the RFR, we add the debt spread associated with the debt rating on the company's long-term debt.
- The resulting pretax cost of debt is then multiplied by $(1 - $ Marginal tax rate[17])
- Debt rating, as per Moody's or S&P.

Formula for Weighted Average Cost of Capital (WACC)

$$WACC = K_e \times (1 - D/TC) + [K_d \times (1 - T)] \times (D/TC)$$

where K_e = cost of equity

D/TC = debt to total adjusted market capital ratio
K_d = cost of debt
T = tax rate

Economic Profit Margin

ROIC minus WACC equals the truest measure of a business's profitability. This metric measures the net cash flow returns to shareholders adjusted for the risk associated with the business model employed to achieve those returns. In essence, economic profit margins directly measure a firm's ability to create actual value for its shareholders.

Growth Appreciation Period (GAP)

The growth appreciation period is the amount of time (usually expressed in years) that a business can be expected to earn positive economic profit margins (ROIC greater than WACC) on new investments. Put simply, GAP is the amount of time a business can grow its economic cash flow. After the GAP, it is assumed that incremental investments by the business earn ROIC equal to WACC. Warren Buffett refers to GAP as the moat around a company's castle. It is also known as the competitive advantage period (CAP) and the forecast growth horizon.

Our dynamic DCF model calculates share prices attributable to multiple GAP scenarios.

For example, the value of the company with a 20-year forecast horizon assumes the company will enjoy a 20-year GAP. Without a model that encompasses this long-term approach, we may not be able to capture the market's true expectations for many companies.

Growth Depreciation Period (GDP)

GDP is the amount of time a business destroys value by allocating capital to projects that earn negative economic profit margins (ROIC below WACC).

Market-Implied GAP

The market-implied growth appreciation period (MIGAP) is the number of years that a company's stock market price implies it will earn ROIC greater than WACC on incremental investments.

Provided that the estimates entered on the forecast page are based on consensus projections, the MIGAP represents the forecast horizon needed in a DCF model to arrive at a value equal to the current market price.

Economic Profit or Economic Cash Flow

Economic profit quantifies the amount of shareholder value a company creates or destroys. It can be calculated two mathematically equivalent ways:

Residual income approach:

$$\text{Economic profit} = (\text{ROIC} - \text{WACC}) \times \text{Invested capital}$$

Refined earnings approach:

$$\text{Economic profit} = \text{NOPAT} - (\text{Invested capital} \times \text{WACC})$$

Consistency and Integrity for All Key Calculations

It is important to note that our model ensures consistent treatment of all adjustments, especially the calculations of NOPAT, invested capital, and WACC. In other words, the model guarantees that any adjustment made to NOPAT is properly reflected in the calculation of invested capital. For example, when goodwill expense is removed from NOPAT, the related accumulated goodwill amortization is added to invested capital. This methodology ensures that no adjustment to the financial statements is double-counted and that the ROIC calculation has maximum integrity.

APPENDIX B: HOW OUR DYNAMIC DISCOUNTED CASH FLOW MODEL WORKS

Dynamic DCF modeling compares closely to the "T" horizon concept in Stern Stewart EVA® and the "fade" rates employed by the Callard, Madden offshoots in cash returns. We did not invent the Dynamic Discounted Cash flow model, but we are among the first to apply this valuation technique to more than five thousand publicly-traded companies.

State-of-the-Art Discounted Cash Flow Analysis

Our discounted cash flow model calculates the value attributable to stock prices based on the forecasted financial performance entered into the model.

In turn, the model harnesses state-of-the-art computing power to calculate a value per share for every year up to 100 years into the future. Notably, we do not believe that we can forecast the future performance of a company into the future with any special accuracy. Our model focuses on the market's expectations for future financial performance by matching the market price of a stock with values calculated by the DCF model. In turn, we leverage our model to tease out of the stock price the stock market's expectations for the future financial performance of a company. This insight enables investors to calibrate their valuation assessment around the market's expectations. The burden of predicting the specific performance of the core value drivers shifts to the market. Investors are positioned to determine only if they feel market expectations are too high, too low, or about right.

Calculating the Value of the Business

Free Cash Flows

Cumulative free cash flow generated during the business's GAP discounted by WACC to present value

Plus:

Perpetuity value of free cash flows generated at end of the business's GAP discounted by WACC to present value.

Basic formula:

Present value of free cash flow during GAP
+ Residual value of free cash flows at end of GAP
= Present value of the business's total cash profits

Economic Profits

Cumulative economic profits generated during the business's GAP discounted by WACC to present value

Plus:

Perpetuity value of economic profits generated at end of the business's GAP discounted by WACC to present value

Plus:

All capital invested in the business prior to the creation of future economic profits.

Basic formula:
  Present value of economic profits during GAP
  + Residual value of economic profits at end of GAP
  + Beginning invested capital
  = Present value of the business's total cash profits

Consistency and Integrity in Our Valuation Model

To ensure absolute consistency and maximum integrity in our valuation model, we calculate the present value of the business's total cash profits by both the free cash flow and economic profit methods. In theory these calculations should provide identical results. In our model they always match perfectly, giving us high confidence in both the consistency and the integrity of our calculations. In addition, they provide the analyst with a choice between metrics and enhance the clarity of model assumptions.

Determining the Value Attributable to Shareholders

Once the model calculates the present value of the business's total cash flows, we know the present value of cash flows available to all stakeholders. The next step, detailed as follows, is to determine the value available to shareholders by adding the value of any nonoperating assets and deducting the value of any senior claims to the cash flows. Remember that value attributable to equity investors is residual to that available to creditors and minority interests. In addition, we must account for the value of outstanding options attributable to employees to determine the net value for current or prospective shareholders.

  Present value of the business's total cash profits
  + Excess cash

+ Current value of unconsolidated subsidiaries

− Current value of preferred stock

− Current value of total debt owed creditors

− Current value of minority interests

− Current value of outstanding employee stock options

= Shareholder value

Divide shareholder value by current number of basic shares outstanding

= Value per share in the business

See Exhibit 8A.1 for a graphic representation of how our model's dynamic discounted cash flow analysis calculates the value of a business and the attendant value available to shareholders for multiple growth appreciation periods. This chart shows how the value of the company analyzed in this example rises as its GAP increases. The market-implied growth appreciation period (MIGAP) is the GAP as implied by the current market price. Our model calculates the MIGAP by matching the current stock price with the year that the DCF value matches that of the current stock price. For example, the MIGAP for the company in Exhibit 8A.1 is 45 years. Our model can also calculate the GAP implied for target prices as well as any other stock prices no matter how great or small they may be. The analysis

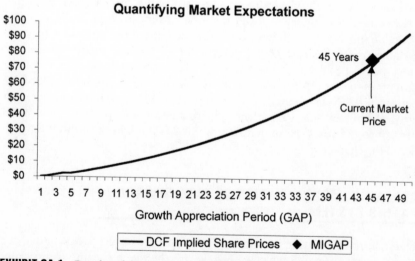

EXHIBIT 8A.1   Results of the Dynamic Discounted Cash Flow Calculations
Source: New Constructs, LLC (www.newconstructs.com).

EXHIBIT 8A.2   The Valuation Matrix—Avalon Bay Communities (AVB)

Performance Hurdles	Historical Performance			Future Performance		
	Past 5-Year Average	Past 3-Year Average	Last FY	−25%	Current Price	25%
Stock values	$47.80	$89.25	$94.14	$74.60	$99.45	$124.30
1. Revenue growth	4.3%	2.1%	8.8%	6.4%	6.4%	6.5%
2. Economic profit margin	−1.4%	−1.5%	−2.4%	2.2%	5.4%	8.8%
3. Growth appreciation period (GAP)	n/a	n/a	n/a	26 years	45 years	75 years

Source: New Constructs, LLC (www.newconstructs.com)

in Exhibit 8A.1 shows DCF values for only 50 years, though the model can value companies over an indefinite time period.

Exhibit 8A.2 provides a more numerical summary of our dynamic DCF analysis of Avalon Bay Communities. This table shows the specific growth rates and profitability levels required to justify the current stock price and prices 25 percent higher or lower than the current stock price. Specifically, the table shows that AVB must grow revenues at 6.4 percent and achieve an economic profit margin of 5.4 percent for 45 years to justify the current stock price of $99.45. To justify a stock price of $74.60, the company must grow revenues at 6.4 percent and achieve an economic profit margin of 2.2 percent for 26 years. To justify a stock price of $124.30, the company must grow revenues at 6.5 percent and achieve an economic profit margin of 8.8 percent for 75 years. Note that Exhibit 8A.2 is the same as Exhibit 8.8 earlier in the chapter.

APPENDIX C: EXPLANATION OF RISK/REWARD RATING SYSTEM

Our risk/reward rating system assigns a rating to every stock under our coverage according to what we believe are the five most important criteria for assessing the risk versus reward profile of stocks. See Exhibit 8A.3 for details.

EXHIBIT 8A.3 New Constructs' Risk/Reward Rating System

Overall Risk/Reward Ranking	The overall risk/reward ranking provides a final rating based on the equal-weighted average rating of each criterion.
Very Dangerous	Two-year average FCF yield is not included in the average.
Dangerous	Two-year average FCF yield is not included in the average.
Neutral	All criteria are equal-weighted in the average calculation.
Attractive	All criteria are equal-weighted in the average calculation.
Very Attractive	All criteria are equal-weighted in the average calculation.
Economic versus Reported EPS	Rates stocks based on how their economic earnings compare to their reported earnings. Values are based on latest fiscal year.
Very Dangerous	Negative and declining economic profits despite positive and rising reported earnings.
Dangerous	Same as above except reported earnings are not rising or reported earnings are not positive.
Neutral	Negative economic and reported earnings.
Attractive	Economic earnings are positive.
Very Attractive	Economic earnings are positive and rising.
Return on Invested Capital (ROIC)	Rates stocks based on their ROICs. Values are based on latest fiscal year.
Bottom Quintile	Very Dangerous = in the bottom 20 percent of all companies.
4th Quintile	Dangerous = in the bottom 40 percent of all companies.
3rd Quintile	Neutral = in the middle 20 percent of all companies.
2nd Quintile	Attractive = in the top 40 percent of all companies.
Top Quintile	Very Attractive = in the top 20 percent of all companies.
FCF Yield Two-Year Average	Rates stocks based on their two-year average free cash flow yield. Values are based on latest closing stock price and latest fiscal year.
$\leq -5\%$	Very Dangerous = less than or equal to -5%.
-5% to -1%	Dangerous = more than -5% but less than or equal to -1%.
-1% to 3%	Neutral = more than -1% but less than or equal to $+3\%$.
3% to 10%	Attractive = more than $+3\%$ but less than or equal to $+10\%$.

(Continued)

EXHIBIT 8A.3 (*Continued*)

>10%	Very Attractive = more than +10%.
Price-to-EBV Ratio	Rates stocks based on their price-to-economic book value ratio. Values are based on latest closing stock price and latest fiscal year.
≥3.5 or −1 to 0	Very Dangerous = greater than or equal to 3.5 or less than 0 but greater than −1.
2.4 to 3.5 or ≤−1	Dangerous = greater than or equal to 2.4 but less than 3.5 or less than or equal to −1.
1.6 to 2.4	Neutral = greater than or equal to 1.6 but less than 2.4.
1.1 to 1.6	Attractive = greater than or equal to 1.1 but less than 1.6.
0 to 1.1	Very Attractive = greater than or equal to 0 but less than 1.1.
Growth Appreciation Period (Years)	Rates stocks based on their market-implied growth appreciation period. Values are based on latest closing stock price and default forecast scenario.
≥50	Very Dangerous = greater than or equal to 50 years.
20 to 50	Dangerous = at least 20 years but less than 50.
10 to 20	Neutral = at least 10 years but less than 20.
3 to 10	Attractive = at least 3 years but less than 10.
0 to 3	Very Attractive = less than 3 years.

APPENDIX D: NOPAT, INVESTED CAPITAL, AND WACC CALCULATIONS FOR ACCENTURE

Exhibits 8A.4, 8A.5, and 8A.6 provide examples of calculations for Accenture. Note that readers can access more examples of our NOPAT, invested capital, and WACC calculations on our web site: www.new constructs.com.

EXHIBIT 8A.4 Accenture's NOPAT ($ Millions)

	2005	2006	2007
Operating Revenues			
Net Sales Revenue	$15,547.03	$16,646.39	$19,695.81
Other Revenue	$ 1,547.40	$ 1,582.00	$ 1,756.90
Total Operating Revenue	$17,094.42	$18,228.37	$21,452.75
Operating Expenses			
Cost of Sales	$12,002.22	$13,234.33	$13,654.34
Cost of Licensing Revenue	—	—	—
Cost of Service Revenue	—	—	—
Other Cost of Revenue	—	—	$ 1,756.90
Total Cost of Sales	$12,002.22	$13,234.33	$15,411.27
Gross Profit	$ 5,092.20	$ 4,994.04	$ 6,041.47
Gross Margin	29.80%	27.40%	28.20%
General and Administrative	$ 1,511.95	$ 1,492.69	$ 1,618.50
Sales and Marketing	$ 1,558.30	$ 1,708.30	$ 1,904.00
Losses from Unconsolidated Subsidiaries (Operating)	—	—	—
Other Operating Expense	—	—	—
Total Operating Expense	$15,072.44	$16,435.27	$ 18,933.76
EBIT	$ 2,021.98	$ 1,793.09	$ 2,518.98
Adjustments			
Goodwill Amortization	—	—	—
EBITA	$ 2,021.98	$ 1,793.09	$ 2,518.98
(ESO) Expense Employee Stock Options	$ 208.30	—	—
ESO Expense as % of Revenue	1.20%	0.00%	0.00%
Adjusted EBITA	$ 1,813.66	$ 1,793.09	$ 2,518.98
Change in Total Reserves	$ 0.00	$ 0.00	$ 0.00
Implied Interest for PV of Operating Leases	$ 68.40	$ 68.60	$ 64.70
Capitalized Items Net Adjustment	$ 68.42	$ 68.59	$ 64.73
Net Operating Profit Before Tax (NOPBT)	$ 1,882.08	$ 1,861.68	$ 2,583.72
NOPBT Margin	11.00%	10.20%	12.00%
Taxes			
Income Tax Provision	$ 697.10	$ 490.53	$ 895.86
ESO Tax Shield	$ 65.80	$ 0	$ 0
Net Nonoperating Expense Tax Impact	($ 58.20)	($ 33.30)	($ 34.20)
Implied Interest for PV of Operating Leases Tax Impact	$ 21.60	$ 17.50	$ 22.10

(Continued)

EXHIBIT 8A.4 (*Continued*)

	2005	2006	2007
Normalized Change in Deferred Taxes	($ 32.10)	($ 32.10)	($ 32.10)
Cash Operating Tax	$ 626.82	$ 506.81	$ 915.90
NOPAT (Net Operating Profit After Tax)	$ 1,255.26	$ 1,354.87	$ 1,667.81

Source: New Constructs, LLC (www.newconstructs.com).

EXHIBIT 8A.5 Accenture's Invested Capital ($ Millions)

	2005	2006	2007
Current Assets			
Cash and Equivalents (Nonoperating)	$ 2,483.99	$3,066.99	$ 3,314.40
Short-Term Investments (Nonoperating)	$ 463.50	$ 353.00	$ 231.30
Long-Term Investments (Nonoperating)	$ 262.90	$ 125.10	$ 81.90
Company-Owned Life Insurance (Nonoperating)	—	—	—
Total Cash and Investments	$ 3,210.32	$3,545.06	$ 3,627.61
Required Cash as % of Revenue	5.00%	5.00%	5.00%
Excess Cash	$42,355.60	$2,633.60	$ 2,555.00
Required Cash	$ 854.70	$ 911.40	$ 1,072.60
Restricted Cash	—	—	—
Accounts Receivable	$ 1,752.90	$1,916.40	$ 2,409.30
Inventory	—	—	—
Current Deferred Taxes	$ 121.40	$ 187.70	$ 318.20
LIFO Reserves	—	—	—
Other Receivables	—	—	—
Other Current or Investment Assets	$ 1,863.50	1,829.70	$ 1,698.00
Total Current Assets (adjusted)	$ 4,592.54	$4,845.30	$ 5,498.14
Current Liabilities			
Accounts Payable	$ 807.32	$ 856.09	$ 985.07
Accrued Expenses	—	—	—
Accrued Compensation	$ 1,431.00	$1,693.80	$ 2,274.10
Accrued Other Taxes	—	—	—
Income Taxes Payable	$ 831.40	$ 722.10	$ 942.30
Deferred Income Taxes	$ 42.60	$ 49.90	$ 39.10
Accrued Restructuring Charges	—	—	—
Current Deferred Revenue	$ 1,284.30	$1,511.30	$ 1,785.30

	2005	2006	2007
Other NIBCL or Investment Liabilities	$ 434.70	$ 958.60	$ 913.00
Non-Interest-Bearing Current Liabilities (NIBCL)	**$ 4,831.32**	**$5,791.69**	**$ 6,938.82**
Net Working Capital	($ 238.78)	($ 946.39)	($1,440.68)
Fixed Assets			
Property, Plant, and Equipment (PPE)	$ 693.71	$ 727.69	$ 808.07
Net Goodwill	$ 378.50	$ 527.60	$ 643.70
Net Combined Intangibles	—	—	—
Deferred Tax Assets	$ 291.00	$ 392.20	$ 389.90
Unconsolidated Subsidiary Assets (Operating)	—	—	—
Other Fixed Assets	$ 646	$ 291.60	$ 852.40
Off-Balance-Sheet Operating Leases	$2,123.90	$1,837.50	$1,952.10
Asset Write-Offs After Tax	97.30	$ 121.50	$ 136.20
Accumulated Unrecorded Goodwill	0	0	0
Accumulated Goodwill Amortization	0	0	0
Accumulated OCI (Other Comprehensive Income)	$ 232.50	$ 26.50	($ 84.20)
Total Adjusted Fixed Assets	**$4,462.84**	**$3,924.71**	**$4,698.18**
Invested Capital	**$4,224.07**	**$2,978.32**	**$3,257.50**

Source: New Constructs, LLC (www.newconstructs.com).

EXHIBIT 8A.6   Accenture's Weighted Average Cost of Capital ($ Millions)

	2005	2006	2007	Current Values
Cost of Equity Capital According to the Capital Asset Pricing Model (CAPM)				
Risk-Free Rate (10-Year Treasury)	4.2%	4.7%	4.7%	4.0%
Beta Adjusted	77.0%	77.0%	77.0%	77.0%
Expected Market Return	8.5%	8.5%	8.5%	8.5%
Equity Risk Premium	4.3%	3.8%	3.8%	4.5%
Cost of Equity	7.5%	7.6%	7.6%	7.4%
Market Value of Basic Equity	$14,359.50	$17,472.70	$24,896.20	$22,099.00
Equity per Total Adjusted Capital	86.7%	90.2%	92.6%	91.6%
Weighted Cost of Equity Capital	6.5%	6.9%	7.1%	6.8%

(*Continued*)

EXHIBIT 8A.6   (*Continued*)

	2005	2006	2007	Current Values
Cost of Debt Capital				
Risk-Free Rate (10-Year Treasury)	4.2%	4.7%	4.7%	4.0%
Debt Spread Adjusted	0.5%	0.3%	0.3%	0.3%
Income Tax Rate	31.6%	25.5%	34.2%	34.2%
Cost of Debt After Tax	3.2%	3.7%	3.3%	2.8%
Adjusted Total Debt	$2,199.00	$1,889.40	$1,978.50	$2,025.10
Debt Per Total Adjusted Market Capital	13.3%	9.8%	7.4%	8.4%
Weighted Cost of Debt After Tax	0.4%	0.4%	0.2%	0.2%
Cost of Preferred Capital				
Preferred Dividends	—	—	—	—
Preferred Capital	—	—	—	—
Cost of Preferred Capital	0.0%	0.0%	0.0%	0.0%
Preferred Capital/ Total Adjusted Market Capital	0.0%	0.0%	0.0%	0.0%
Weighted Cost of Preferred Capital	0.0%	0.0%	0.0%	0.0%
Weighted Average Cost of Capital (WACC)	6.9%	7.2%	7.3%	7.1%

Source: New Constructs, LLC (www.newconstructs.com), CSI Data, and Standard & Poor's.

NOTES

1. A number of books have been written on the deficiencies of accounting metrics when it comes to equity valuation, for example: A. Rappaport, *Creating Shareholder Value* (New York: Free Press, 1986); B. Stewart, *The Quest for Value* (New York: HarperCollins, 1991); T. Copeland, T. Koller, and J. Murrin, *Valuation: Measuring and Managing the Value of Companies* (New York: John Wiley & Sons, 1994).
2. Matthew Bishop, senior writer for the *Economist*, in a television interview on CNNfn on May 17, 2002.

3. We offer additional information on this topic in the reports, interviews, and article on our web site at www.newwconstructs.com.
4. The growth appreciation period (GAP) refers to the number of years into the future that a business can increase its economic profits or free cash flow. In financial terms, it equals the amount of time during which a business can invest in projects that earn ROIC greater than WACC. It also represents the length of the forecast horizon used in a discounted cash flow model.
5. John Maynard Keynes.
6. Free cash flow yields measure the percentage of the total value of the firm for which the free cash flows of the firm account. The formula is $(FCF_t + FCF_{t-1})/$ (Current enterprise value + Enterprise value$_{t-1}$), where t is the latest fiscal year.
7. Economic book value (EBV) measures the no-growth value of the business based on its annual after-tax cash flow. The formula for EBV is: (NOPAT/ WACC) + Excess cash + Nonoperating assets – Debt (including operating leases) – Value of outstanding stock options – Minority interests.
8. The growth appreciation period measures the number of years, implied by the market price, that a company will grow its economic profits. This measure assigns a numerical value to the width of the moat around a firm's business.
9. Free cash flow yields measure the percentage of the total value of the firm for which the free cash flows of the firm account. The formula is $(FCF_t + FCF_{t-1})/$ (Current enterprise value + Enterprise value$_{t-1}$), where t is the latest fiscal year.
10. Economic book value (EBV) measures the no-growth value of the business based on its annual after-tax cash flow. The formula for EBV is: (NOPAT/ WACC) + Excess cash + Nonoperating assets – Debt (including operating leases) – Value of outstanding stock options – Minority interests.
11. The growth appreciation period measures the number of years, implied by the market price, that a company will grow its economic profits. This measure assigns a numerical value to the width of the moat around a firm's business.
12. Martin L. Leibowitz, *Sales-Driven Franchise Value* (Charlottesville, VA: Research Foundation of the Institute of Chartered Financial Analysts, 1997), 5.
13. Many empirical studies show that the majority of professional money managers earn returns below those of market benchmarks like the S&P 500, which are passively managed.
14. " . . . principles of limited diversification hold only for well-chosen common stocks that carry a margin of safety between price paid and the reasonable value estimated. For those, Buffett believes finding between 5 and 10 stocks would be sensible."—L. Cunningham, *How to Think Like Benjamin Graham and Invest Like Warren Buffett* (New York: McGraw-Hill, 2001).
15. Data in this chapter based on 10-Ks and last closing stock price as of 09/11/ 2008: $99.45.
16. Data in this chapter based on 10-Ks and last closing stock price as of 09/11/ 2008: $36.63.
17. In some cases, applying the effective tax rate may be more appropriate.

CHAPTER 9

The Economic Profit Approach to Securities Valuation

James L. Grant
JLG Research and Professor of Finance, University of Massachusetts Boston

This chapter provides a foundation on the economic profit (EVA®[1]) approach to securities valuation. The EVA model differs from other well-known approaches to securities valuation such as the dividend discount model (DDM) and the free cash flow (FCF) model because it provides a *direct* measure of the value added to invested capital.[2] In financial terms, the wealth added to invested capital is called the firm's net present value (NPV). Assuming market efficiency, the firm's market value added (MVA) will be equal to the intrinsic value added measured by its net present value. As shown by Grant (2003), the firm's NPV is equal to the present value of the anticipated future economic profit stream.[3]

In turn, the question of whether economic profit is positive or negative is of interest to corporate managers and securities analysts, as it relates to the period in which a company can actually generate a return on capital (ROC) that exceeds the opportunity weighted average cost of capital (WACC). Common assumptions about economic profit beyond a forecast period are that (1) EVA is zero due to competitive forces, (2) EVA decays over time to zero, (3) EVA is perpetuity, or (4) EVA is growing at some long-term rate that is less than WACC.

In the next sections, we will look at several economic profit valuation models with the goal of assessing the firm's NPV, corporate value, and the intrinsic value of common stock. During our economic profit journey we will look at similarities and differences of EVA valuation to the traditional free cash flow (FCF) model. We will also look at the sensitivity of economic profit valuation to changes in economic profit assumptions (the so-called numerator effects) and the risky discount rate (the so-called denominator effects). We will also discuss how to estimate EVA with standard accounting adjustments, and we'll apply the EVA valuation model to companies that populate a well-known stock market index.

BASICS OF ECONOMIC PROFIT VALUATION

In the economic profit approach to securities valuation, the firm's enterprise value can be expressed as:

$$V = C + NPV$$

In this expression, V is enterprise value, C is net invested capital,[4] and NPV is net present value. As shown by Grant (2003), the firm's NPV can be expressed as a discounted stream of economic profit according to:

$$NPV = \text{Present value of EVA}$$
$$= \sum EVA_t / (1 + WACC)^t \quad (t = 1 \text{ to } \infty)$$

In turn, EVA is the estimated economic profit at time period t, and WACC is the familiar weighted average cost of debt and equity capital.

In practice, EVA is expressed in two forms: in NOPAT form and in EVA spread form according to:

$$EVA = NOPAT - WACC \times \text{Capital}$$
$$= (ROC - WACC) \times \text{Capital}$$

In the first expression, EVA is equal to NOPAT (net operating profit after tax) less the dollar cost of capital. In the second expression, EVA is equal to the EVA spread (after-tax return on capital less the cost of capital) times the amount of invested capital.

Assuming other things the same,[5] we see that managers create wealth by making discounted positive economic profit—positive NPV—decisions. They destroy wealth by making discounted negative EVA—negative NPV—decisions. Moreover, the firm's economic profit is positive when the estimated after-tax return on capital, ROC, exceeds the cost of capital, WACC. That is, EVA is positive when the EVA spread is positive. However, economic profit—and its discounted NPV equivalent—is negative when corporate managers invest in assets (both tangible and intangible) having an after-tax return that falls short of the WACC.

For example, if we assume a NOPAT of $14.95, initial (net[6]) capital of $40, and a cost of capital of 10 percent, we see that the firm's assessed economic profit is $10.95:[7]

$$EVA = NOPAT - WACC \times C$$
$$= \$14.95 - 0.10 \times \$40.00 = \$10.95$$

We can also express the EVA of \$10.95 in terms of a return on capital of 37.38 percent (\$14.95/\$40), a cost of capital of 10 percent, and the assumed invested capital of \$40 (noted as C):

$$
\begin{aligned}
\text{EVA} &= (\text{ROC} - \text{WACC}) \times C \\
&= (\text{NOPAT}/C - \text{WACC}) \times C \\
&= (14.95/40 - 0.10) \times 40 \\
&= (0.3738 - 0.10) \times 40 = \$10.95
\end{aligned}
$$

We will use this EVA figure as a one-step-ahead forecast in the following discussion of the constant growth EVA valuation model and the variable growth EVA valuation model. In the latter valuation model, we look at EVA valuation with forecast and residual value periods, whereby EVA is forecasted during a horizon period and a residual period.

ECONOMIC PROFIT MODELS

Like any discounted cash flow (DCF) model, there are several ways of expressing the EVA valuation model. In this section, we discuss and apply four conventional EVA valuation models:

1. Constant growth EVA model.
2. Variable growth EVA model.
3. Forecast EVA valuation model.
4. T-period EVA model.

We also look at reconciliation of EVA valuation models. Following that, we see how EVA valuation relates to the traditional free cash flow model. We also discuss how to estimate EVA with standard accounting adjustments, and we apply EVA valuation to a well-known stock market index.

Constant Growth EVA Model

We will begin our EVA valuation journey with the constant growth EVA valuation model. Rather than estimating the annual economic profit during forecast and residual periods, EVA growth models are used as a convenient way to simplify the discounted cash flow process. There are two well-known EVA growth models that are used in practice: (1) the constant growth EVA valuation model (a variation of the classic Gordon model) and (2) the variable growth EVA valuation model. We begin with the constant growth EVA model.

The constant growth EVA valuation model makes the simplifying assumption that the estimated one-step-ahead EVA is growing at some long-term rate of growth (g) per period, where, of course, g is less than WACC. In the constant growth EVA model, the firm's NPV can be expressed as:

$$NPV = EVA(1)/(WACC - g)$$

In this expression, EVA(1) is the estimated economic profit one year from the current period, and g is the *annualized* EVA growth rate, where g is less than WACC. As an application, suppose that the one-step-ahead EVA forecast of $10.95 (our prior example) is expected to grow at a rate of 6.17 percent each year, forever (we assume this growth rate for illustrative purposes only). With constant long-term growth, the firm's estimated NPV is equal to $285.90.

$$NPV = \$10.95/(0.10 - 0.0617)$$
$$= \$285.90$$

Equivalently, the *implied* constant EVA growth rate that is embedded in the above NPV equals:

$$g = WACC - EVA(1)/NPV$$
$$= 0.10 - 10.95/285.90 = 0.0617$$

In this expression, g is the implied constant EVA growth rate, EVA(1)/NPV is the EVA yield, and WACC is the cost of capital. In turn, with initial capital at $40, the firm's enterprise value is $325.90.

$$V = C + EVA(1)/(WACC - g)$$
$$= \$40 + \$285.90 = \$325.90$$

Note that at $285.90, the estimated NPV with constant growth is considerably higher than EVA perpetuity (or zero-growth assumption) of $109.50 ($10.95/0.10). This presumes that a company not only has the ability to earn positive economic profit (whereby ROC is greater than WACC), but that it can actually grow economic profit at some long-term rate. Generating economic profit is difficult for any company, let alone growing EVA at some constant rate (forever!). Moreover, in terms of price multiples, the term (WACC − g) in the constant growth EVA model can be interpreted as the EVA cap rate, while 26.11 [1/(WACC − g)] can be viewed as the EVA multiplier (or EVA capitalization factor). Hence, EVA-linked NPV analysis reconciles to price multiple analyses.

Variable Growth EVA Model

The variable growth EVA valuation model is another form of the discounted cash flow model. In the two-phase variable growth model, there are two growth rates that serve to capture the pattern of EVA flows during horizon and residual periods. In this context, it is common to assume that EVA is growing at a relatively high rate during the horizon years (due to competitive or comparative advantages) while EVA growth settles down to either zero or a mature growth rate during the residual years.[8] We can make a simple change to the EVA assumption in the previous constant growth example to see how this model works.

Specifically, suppose that a company's *one-step-ahead* economic profit, EVA(1) of $10.95, is expected to grow at 7.5 percent for just one year, followed by a long-term or mature growth rate of 6.17 percent. In this case, there are two steps to estimating the firm's NPV (and enterprise value) with variable growth assumptions:

Step 1: Calculate the present value of the estimated EVA generated during the first growth phase—we'll interpret this result as the NPV generated during the horizon period (forecast period), NPV-HV.

Step 2: Calculate the present value of the EVA earned during the mature growth phase. We'll express this value as NPV-RV. Then, calculate the present value of the firm's residual (or terminal) NPV value.

With variable growth, the present value of EVA during the horizon years can be expressed as:

$$NPV\text{--}HV = \sum EVA_t \times (1 + g_{NT})^{t-1}/(1 + WACC)^t$$
$$(t = 1 \text{ to } N)$$

In this expression, EVA_t is the estimated economic profit at period t, g_{NT} is the *near*-term growth rate in EVA during the horizon period, and WACC is the discount rate or cost of capital. With just two periods ($N = 2$) during the horizon period, we can express the NPV horizon value as:

$$NPV - HV = EVA(1)/(1 + WACC) + EVA(2)/(1 + WACC)^2$$
$$= EVA(1)/(1 + WACC) + EVA(1)(1 + g_{NT})/(1 + WACC)^2$$

The net present value of the estimated EVA flow for the two-year horizon period is $19.68:

$$NPV - HV = \$10.95/(1.10) + \$10.95(1.075)/(1.10)^2$$
$$= \$9.95 + \$11.77/1.21$$
$$= \$9.95 + \$9.73$$
$$= \$19.68$$

In turn, the firm's residual NPV at the end of period 2, NPV-RV(2), can be calculated by noting that (1) the EVA forecast for period 3 can be viewed as EVA(2) growing at the *long*-term EVA growth rate, and that (2) the one-step-ahead forecast for period 3 is growing at the mature or competitive growth rate, g_{LT}. With these assumptions, the *three-step-ahead* economic profit, EVA(3), can be estimated according to:

$$
\begin{aligned}
\text{EV}(3) &= \text{EVA}(2)(1 + g_{LT}) \\
&= \text{EVA}(1)(1 + g_{NT})(1 + g_{LT}) \\
&= \$10.95(1.075)(1.0617) = \$12.50
\end{aligned}
$$

With constant EVA growth for the residual period, the firm's residual NPV value at the end of the two-year horizon period can be expressed as:

$$
\text{NPV} - \text{RV}(2) = \text{EVA}(3)/(\text{WACC} - g_{LT})
$$

Upon substituting the estimated EVA for period 3, EVA(3) of $12.50, into the preceding expression yields NPV-RV(2), at $326.37:

$$
\begin{aligned}
\text{RV}(2) &= \$12.50/(0.10 - 0.0617) \\
&= \$12.50/0.0383 \\
&= \$326.37
\end{aligned}
$$

Moreover, upon combining the NPV results for horizon and (discounted) residual periods, we obtain the total NPV, at $289.41:

$$
\begin{aligned}
\text{NPV} &= \text{NPV} - \text{HV} + \text{PV of NPV} - \text{RV}(2) \\
&= \$19.68 + \text{NPV} - \text{RV}(2)/(1 + \text{WACC})^2 \\
&= \$19.68 + \$326.37/(1 + 0.10)^2 \\
&= \$19.68 + \$326.37/1.21 \\
&= \$19.68 + \$269.73 \\
&= \$289.41
\end{aligned}
$$

Notice that the variable growth NPV of $289.41 differs by a *small* amount from the 6.17 percent constant growth EVA model result of $285.90.[9] This minor difference in net present value results because we assumed only a 7.5 percent rate of growth in EVA for year 2. All other EVA values were assumed to be growing at 6.17 percent, as in the previous constant growth example. With initial capital of $40, the firm's estimated enterprise value is $329.41.

Forecast EVA Valuation Model

In practice, corporate managers and securities analysts like to forecast the annual economic profit over some discrete time period, say five or ten years. They then assess the residual value of economic profit based on varying assumptions about EVA during the so-called out years, particularly in light of the firm's presumed competitive or comparative advantages, *if any*. As before, the NPV of economic profit over the horizon years *plus* the present value of the residual NPV determines the firm's overall net present value—or net creation of wealth. The firm's enterprise value is equal to invested capital *plus* the present value of all future EVA (which is NPV).

To illustrate the forecast EVA valuation model, we use the EVA estimates (NOPAT, capital, and WACC) obtained from a revenue forecasting model described by Grant (2003). Later on, we will look at the details of economic profit estimation with standard accounting adjustments. For now, let's see how economic profit estimates during a forecast period get rolled up into the firm's enterprise value and intrinsic value of common stock. In this context, Exhibit 9.1 shows EVA estimates over a 10-year forecast or horizon period. As before, with NOPAT(1) at $14.95, initial capital of $40, and a cost of capital of 10 percent, the firm's assessed economic profit for year 1 is $10.95:[10]

$$EVA(1) = NOPAT(1) - WACC \times C(0)$$
$$= \$14.95 - 0.10 \times \$40.00 = \$10.95$$

Likewise, economic profit for year 2, at $12.74, is just NOPAT less the capital charge on invested capital at the end of year 1 (or BOY capital at year 2).

$$EVA(2) = NOPAT(2) - WACC \times C(1)$$
$$= \$17.19 - 0.10 \times \$44.50 = \$12.74$$

At $44.50, the capital at the start of year 2 is a reflection of the initial capital, C(0) of $40, *plus* the net investment in capital (including physical and intangible capital) of $4.50 that occurred during year 1.

EXHIBIT 9.1 Forecasting Economic Profit (EVA)

Year	Yearly Net Investment	Total Net Capital	NOPAT	Capital Charge*	Economic Profit
0		40.00			
1	4.50	44.50	14.95	4.00	10.95
2	5.18	49.68	17.19	4.45	12.74
3	5.95	55.63	19.77	4.97	14.80
4	6.84	62.47	22.74	5.56	17.18
5	7.87	70.34	26.15	6.25	19.90
6	9.05	79.39	30.07	7.03	23.04
7	10.41	89.80	34.58	7.94	26.64
8	11.97	101.77	39.77	8.98	30.79
9	13.77	115.54	45.73	10.18	35.55
10	15.83	131.37	52.59	11.55	41.04
11 Plus			54.17	13.13	41.04

*WACC = 10 percent.

Exhibit 9.1 shows how to estimate economic profit for the rest of the horizon period, covering years 3 to 10. Notice that the estimated economic profit for year 11 is $41.04 (actually 41.036). This figure equals the assessed NOPAT for year 11, at $54.17, less the capital charge, at $13.13, on the beginning of year 11 (or end of year 10) invested capital. Moreover, the one-step-ahead EVA figure for the residual period results because of a simplifying (yet reasonable) assumption that the marginal return on invested capital (MROC) at the end of the horizon period equals the (marginal) cost of invested capital, namely WACC. Equivalently, the economic profit (and resulting NPV) on new invested capital at year 10 equals zero, such that the overall projected EVA remains unchanged, at $41.04 (or 41.036).[11] We'll use these EVA estimates to estimate the NPV generated during the forecast period.

Exhibit 9.2 shows how to roll up the economic profit estimates in Exhibit 9.1 into the NPV generated during the horizon (or forecast) years and the NPV generated during the residual (or terminal value) period. The sum of these two NPV figures is the total net creation of wealth (NPV) that has been added to the firm's invested capital. Holding market forces constant, this is a reflection of the wealth that has been created (or destroyed) by the firm's internal (organic) and external (corporate acquisitions) investment decisions.

Exhibit 9.2 shows that the cumulative present value of the estimated economic profit stream during the horizon period is $127.63. This figure can be interpreted as the NPV generated from economic profit during the forecast years. Assuming economic profit perpetuity of $41.04 commencing in year 11, we see that the firm's residual EVA value (or NPV at year 10) is $410.40 (or $410.36 when internally generated). With our simplifying assumptions, this NPV figure is calculated as:

$$NPV - RV(10) = EVA(11)/WACC$$
$$= \$41.04/0.10 = \$410.40$$

Upon discounting the residual NPV value back to the current period, we obtain the NPV of the economic profit stream generated during the post-horizon years, at $158.21. As before, upon adding up the NPV of economic profit generated during horizon *and* residual years, we obtain the firm's overall net creation of wealth from existing and anticipated future assets *not* currently in place:

$$NPV(0) = NPV(\text{Horizon years}) + NPV(\text{Residual years})$$
$$= \$127.63 + \$158.21 = \$285.84$$

With an initial capital base of $40, the firm's estimated enterprise value is (again[12]) $325.84:

EXHIBIT 9.2 Valuation of Economic Profit

Year	EVA	Present Value*	Cumulative PV(0)
1	10.95	9.95	9.95
2	12.74	10.53	20.48
3	14.80	11.12	31.60
4	17.18	11.73	43.34
5	19.90	12.36	55.69
6	23.04	13.00	68.70
7	26.64	13.67	82.37
8	30.79	14.36	96.73
9	35.55	15.08	111.81
10	41.04	15.82	127.63
Residual Value		410.36	158.21
		(at year 10)	
NPV			285.84
Capital			40.00
Corporate Value			325.84
Long-Term Debt			12.00
Equity			313.84
Shares Outstanding			5.00
Price			62.77

*WACC = 10 percent.

$$EV = C + NPV$$
$$= \$40.00 + \$285.84 = \$325.84$$

Moreover, with debt at say $12 and five shares of common stock outstanding, the firm's intrinsic stock price is:

$$\text{Intrinsic stock price} = (EV - Debt)/Shares$$
$$= (\$325.84 - 12)/5 = \$62.77$$

As explained earlier, the EVA approach to enterprise valuation provides managers and investors with a *direct* assessment of the wealth that is being added—via discounted economic profit on existing and anticipated future growth assets—to the firm's invested capital. As we will see later, the enterprise value and the intrinsic stock price are the same figures that would be obtained using the traditional free cash flow approach to securities valuation.

Investment Opportunities and the *T*-Period EVA Model

In the EVA valuation model, the firm's enterprise value is defined as invested capital *plus* aggregate net present value. With a simple rearrangement, we can see the part of the firm's enterprise value that is attributed to economic profit generated by existing assets *and* the EVA contribution due to future investment (or growth) opportunities. Taken together, the two economic profit sources determine the firm's total net present value.

In this context, the firm's enterprise value can be split into two components: (1) the present value of a NOPAT perpetuity generated by existing assets, NOPAT/WACC, and (2) the net present value of the firm's anticipated investment opportunities, G_f, according to:[13]

$$V = \text{NOPAT}/\text{WACC} + G_f$$

The obvious question at this point is how to estimate the NPV contribution of the firm's anticipated investment opportunities, G_f. While several DCF approaches exist to estimate the market value of future investment opportunities, we will estimate growth opportunities with a simplified version of the *T*-period EVA model.[14]

Growth Opportunities and the *T*-Period EVA Model

In the *T*-period EVA model, the investor makes an assessment of the number of periods that the firm can generate positive economic profit on its anticipated future assets. This boils down to an estimate of the number of positive EVA periods (if any) that managers and investors perceive that the firm can invest in real assets having an after-tax return on capital (ROC) that exceeds the opportunity weighted average cost of capital, WACC. Whether or not a company can actually earn positive (or negative) EVA in the residual years (or out years) is determined by the competitive nature of the industry as it relates to the firm's potential competitive or comparative advantage. We will assume that the length of the economic profit period, T, is greater than zero, at least for illustrating how this EVA valuation model works.

In formal terms, the *T*-period economic profit model can be expressed as:

$$G_f = [\text{Avg. EVA(Future)}/\text{WACC} \times T] \times 1/(1 + \text{WACC})$$

In this expression, Avg. EVA(Future) is an economic profit perpetuity generated on new investment opportunities, T is the number of periods that a firm can realistically earn positive economic profit on future investments, and WACC is the cost of capital, assuming risk constancy of future cash flows.

To illustrate the T-period EVA model,[15] we make the simplifying assumption that economic profit earned during the horizon years is attributed entirely to existing assets,[16] while any economic profit generated during the residual period is due to future assets *not* currently in place. Also, we will make the simple assumption that the estimated economic profit for year 11, at $41.04, can be used to proxy the average economic profit generated during the residual years. Based on these simplifications, the T-period EVA model suggests that a large portion of the firm's NPV and enterprise value can be determined by estimating the number of periods that it can generate positive economic profit during the residual years.

For example, with no restriction on the number of years that the firm can earn economic profit of $41.04 during the residual period, we found that the firm's estimated NPV at year 10 was $410.40 [$41.04/0.10]. This residual EVA value has a current NPV of $158.21. Notice, too, that in the absence of economic profit growth during the residual years the NPV of $158.21 is the maximum *current* value of the firm's estimated EVA stream during the post-horizon years. This, in turn, sets upper limit values on both the firm's aggregate NPV and its intrinsic enterprise value. Drawing values from before, we have $285.84 and $325.84, respectively.

In general, the T-period EVA model assumes that a firm's opportunity to earn positive economic profit during the residual period is limited by technological obsolescence and/or competition in the market for goods and services. In this model, managers and investors must make an assessment of the number of periods that a company can *realistically* earn positive economic profit for the future. By implication, we can say that investors will not pay for negative EVA generated during the residual period covering years $T + 1$ to infinity. Moreover, if the return on future investment opportunities is equal to the cost of capital, then growth opportunities per se make no contribution whatsoever to the firm's overall NPV. In this case the firm's NPV is solely driven by the EVA generated on its existing assets.

In lieu of these restrictions, Exhibit 9.3 shows how the NPV of the firm's future growth opportunities varies as the number of positive EVA periods goes from (say) 5 to 100 years. At $410.40 (rounded), the exhibit shows the upper limit value of the economic profit stream generated during the residual period. Notice how the residual value changes as T varies from 5 to 100 years of positive economic profit. Based on present value dynamics, we see that the residual value function, RV (T), *asymptotically* approaches a line that represents the value of an EVA perpetuity.

EXHIBIT 9.3   T-Period EVA Model

Residual Period	Annuity	RV(T)	RV(0)	NPV (0)*	EV	Stock Price	Price Ratio %
5	41.04	155.56	59.97	187.61	227.61	43.12	68.70
10	41.04	252.15	97.21	224.85	264.85	50.57	80.56
20	41.04	349.36	134.69	262.33	302.33	58.07	92.51
30	41.04	386.84	149.14	276.78	316.78	60.96	97.11
40	41.04	401.29	154.72	282.35	322.35	62.07	98.89
50	41.04	406.86	156.86	284.50	324.50	62.50	99.57
60	41.04	409.01	157.69	285.32	325.32	62.66	99.83
70	41.04	409.84	158.01	285.64	325.64	62.73	99.94
80	41.04	410.16	158.13	285.77	325.77	62.75	99.98
90	41.04	410.28	158.18	285.81	325.81	62.76	99.99
100	41.04	410.33	158.20	285.83	325.83	62.77	100.00
Infinite	41.04	410.36	158.21	285.84	325.84	62.77	100.00

WACC = 10 percent; horizon years = 10.
*NPV(0) reflects present value of EVA during horizon and residual years.

Exhibit 9.3 shows that with just five years of positive EVA in post-horizon years, the NPV of future EVA opportunities is only $59.97. When expressed in terms of the firm's enterprise value and its warranted stock price, we obtain $227.61 and $43.12, respectively. In contrast, with 20 and 30 years of positive economic profit during the residual period, the NPV values of future EVA opportunities are $134.69 and $149.14. The exhibit also shows that with T of 20 and 30 years, the firm's enterprise values are $302.33 and $316.78. Also, the corresponding stock price estimates are $58.07 and $60.96, respectively.

With *unlimited* positive economic profit in the residual years, we see that the firm's estimated enterprise value is $325.84 and its intrinsic stock price is $62.77. These are the values that we obtained before. Notice that with five years of positive EVA in residual years that the estimated stock price is only 69 percent ($43.12/$62.77) of the price obtained with unlimited positive economic profit. With 20 and 30 years of positive economic profit in post-horizon years, the intrinsic stock prices are 93 percent and 97 percent, respectively, of the price obtained with unlimited positive economic profit.[17] Thus, managers and investors must make an accurate assessment of the number of periods that a company can earn economic profit for the future in order to have a realistic view of enterprise value and stock price.

Market-Implied Investment Period

In practice, the T-period EVA model can be rearranged to solve for the market-implied number of years of positive economic profit on future investment opportunities. The following inputs are required to solve for market-implied T that is embedded in a firm's NPV and enterprise value:

- Enterprise value (outstanding debt plus equity values[18]).
- NOPAT perpetuity (or annualized equivalent of periodic NOPAT on existing assets).
- Average economic profit on new investments.
- Cost of capital (WACC).

Upon solving for the market-implied number of growth periods, T, that the firm expects to earn positive economic profit, we obtain:

$$T = [G_f \times \text{WACC} \times (1 + \text{WACC})]/\text{Avg. EVA (future)}$$

Upon calculating market-implied T, managers and investors can assess whether this figure is consistent with a company's intrinsic number of periods to earn positive economic profit on future investments.

Based on our previous illustration, if the actual number of positive EVA periods were, say, 10 years rather than 30 years, then the firm's enterprise value and stock price would be *overvalued* in the capital market. Based on the figures supplied before, the firm's stock price would fall over time from $60.96 to $50.57—unless of course the firm's managers could preempt the decline by surprising investors positively about the number of periods that firm could earn positive economic profit on its investment opportunities. Conversely, a company's stock would be *undervalued* if investors incorrectly perceived that the number of positive EVA periods was, say, 10 years when in fact the intrinsic EVA period was longer.

RECONCILIATION OF EVA MODELS

While examining the EVA model, we focused on two general formulations of the firm's enterprise value. In this context, we said that the firm's enterprise value is equal to (1) invested capital, C, *plus* aggregate NPV and (2) the present value of a NOPAT perpetuity on existing assets *plus* the NPV of all future investment opportunities—as captured by G_f. We can reconcile these EVA valuation models for the firm's enterprise value as follows.

To begin, note that NOPAT can be expressed as a capital charge earned on the firm's existing assets *plus* the EVA generated by existing assets already in place. From this, we see why the firm's enterprise value is equal to invested capital, C, plus the NPV of all future economic profit arising from both existing assets, EVA/WACC, and expected future assets, G_f, according to:

$$V = \text{NOPAT}/\text{WACC} + G_f$$
$$= (\text{WACC} \times C + \text{EVA})/\text{WACC} + G_f$$
$$= C + (\text{EVA}/\text{WACC} + G_f)$$
$$= C + \text{NPV}$$

Thus, the firm's enterprise value is in fact equal to invested capital *plus* aggregate NPV. In turn, the firm's aggregate net present value is equal to the present value of all future economic profit.

COST OF CAPITAL EFFECTS

Based on the preceding developments, we see that a company's NPV has two primary sources: (1) the present value of economic profit generated by the firm's existing assets—namely, EVA/WACC—and (2) the NPV contribution attributed to economic profit improvement from anticipated future assets not currently in place, as captured by G_f in the enterprise valuation model. Moreover, economic profit—whether earned on existing or future assets—is positive *if and only if* the firm invests in real assets having and after-tax return on capital that on average exceeds the weighted average cost of capital.

As with future growth opportunities, the cost of capital is an EVA factor that is central to enterprise valuation. In practice, it is important to recognize that seemingly small changes in WACC can have a large impact on enterprise value and intrinsic stock price. Exhibit 9.4 shows what happens to the key components of enterprise value—including the NPV of economic profit generated during the horizon and residual years—when the cost of capital rises by 100 basis points due to unforeseen raises in interest rates and/or heightened business uncertainty[19] or falls by 100 basis points due to declining interest rates and/or reduced business risk.

With a 10 percent cost of capital, we found that the firm's enterprise value was $325.84. This figure includes the initial $40 capital investment *and* the NPV of economic profit generated during the horizon and post-horizon years—at $127.63 and $158.21, respectively. At that discount rate, the firm's warranted stock price is $62.77. However, Exhibit 9.4 reveals (actual values not shown) that if the cost of capital were to decline from 10 percent to 9 percent—due perhaps to a general decline in interest rates or a decline in the required business risk premium—then the firm's enterprise value and intrinsic stock price would rise to $376.98 and $73.00. This 100

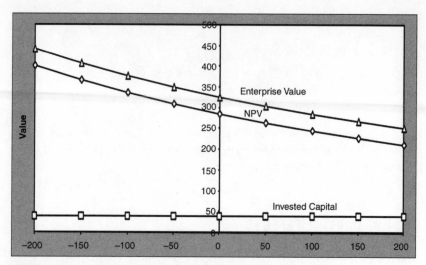

EXHIBIT 9.4   Enterprise Value and the Cost of Capital: EVA Model

basis point change in WACC translates into a 15.69 percent rise in the firm's enterprise value.

However, if the firm's cost of capital were to rise by 100 basis points—from 10 percent to 11 percent—then Exhibit 9.4 shows that the firm's enterprise value and intrinsic stock price would decline to $284.92 and $54.58, respectively. This in turn represents a 12.56 percent decline in the firm's warranted enterprise value. As with the present value impact of changes in a company's future investment opportunities, we see that enterprise value and intrinsic stock price are impacted in a *non*linear way by fluctuations in the firm's cost of capital. This valuation result is the essence of equity duration when viewed through an economic profit lens.

PRICING IMPLICATIONS

The investment opportunities and cost of capital illustrations provide some strategic pricing insight for managers and investors. Specifically, we see that uncertainty about the number of years that a firm can generate positive economic profit on new investments and/or uncertainty about the firm's *true* cost of capital can have a material impact on both its enterprise value and its intrinsic stock price. These valuation effects arise from so-called numerator and denominator effects. Moreover, there are changes in T and WACC that can produce the same impact on the price of any company's stock. For example, the intrinsic stock price—see Exhibits 9.3 and 9.4, respectively—drops from \$62.77 to about \$51 when T declines to 10 years or the cost of capital, WACC, rises to 11.5 percent.[20] Hence, anything that managers can do to increase the positive EVA investment period and/or decrease the opportunity weighted average cost of capital will surprise investors positively and have a meaningful impact on both enterprise value and stock price.

EVA ACCOUNTING ADJUSTMENTS

In practice, there are several value-based accounting adjustments that can be made to calculate economic profit. While a detailed treatment of VBM accounting adjustments is beyond the scope of this chapter, there are several standard accounting adjustments that are often made by corporate managers and securities analysts when estimating economic profit. In this context, Exhibit 9.5 shows the standard income statement adjustments that are made to basic NOPAT (tax-adjusted operating earnings), while Exhibit 9.6 shows the corresponding balance sheet adjustments that are made to basic EVA capital (balance sheet debt and equity capital).[21] As shown, there are equivalent top-down and bottom-up approaches to estimating NOPAT, while there are equivalent assets and financing approaches to estimating EVA capital.

NOPAT Estimation

Exhibit 9.5 shows the bottom-up approach to estimating NOPAT. In this approach, the analyst begins with net operating profit before taxes. This is just the familiar earnings before interest and taxes (EBIT) figure on a company's income statement.[22] To this amount, several value-based accounting adjustments are made to move toward a better representation of the firm's pretax cash operating profit. For example, the increase in LIFO reserve account is added back to operating profit to adjust for the overstatement of cost of goods sold (COGS)—due to an overstatement of product costing—in a period of rising prices (inflation), while the *net* increase in research and development expenditures is added back to pretax operating profit to recognize that R&D expenditures should be capitalized (meaning put on the EVA balance sheet), as they presumably generate a future stream of economic benefits.[23]

Likewise, the increase in accumulated intangibles amortization is added back to pretax cash operating profit to reflect the fact that intangibles (patents, copyrights, etc.) are a form of capital investment that need to earn a cost of capital return just like expenditures on physical capital. The *net*

EXHIBIT 9.5 Calculation of NOPAT from Financial Statement Data

A. Bottom-up approach

Begin:	Operating profit after depreciation and amortization (EBIT)
Add:	Implied interest expense on operating leases
	Increase (decrease) in equity reserve accounts, including:
	Increase in LIFO reserve
	Increase in accumulated intangibles amortization
	Increase in bad debt reserve
	Increase in capitalized research and development
	Increase in cumulative write-offs of special items
Equals:	Adjusted operating profit before taxes
Subtract:	Cash operating taxes
Equals:	NOPAT

B. Top-down approach

Begin:	Net sales
Subtract:	Cost of goods sold
	Selling, general, and administrative expenses
	Depreciation
Add:	Implied interest expense on operating leases
	Increase (decrease) in equity reserve accounts (see listing above)
	Other operating income
Equals:	Adjusted operating profit before taxes
Subtract:	Cash operating taxes
Equals:	NOPAT

increase in bad debt reserve is added back to pretax operating profit to more accurately reflect a company's expected default experience. In addition, the implied interest expense on operating leases is added back to operating results to remove the effects of debt-related financing decisions. Moreover, the rise in reengineering and restructuring expenditures is added back to pretax operating profit because these expenditures are viewed in the value-based realm as reengineering or restructuring investments.

Exhibit 9.5 also shows the top-down approach to estimating NOPAT. In this approach, the manager or investor begins with net sales and then adds the increase in several equity reserve accounts, including the LIFO reserve and accumulated intangibles accounts, the bad debt reserve account, and the rise in other equity reserve accounts noted earlier. As with the bottom-up approach to estimating NOPAT, the implied interest expense on operating leases is added to the EVA-based income statement. Information on LIFO (and other) reserve and leasing accounts is generally found in the footnotes to financial statements. In the top-down approach, the manager or investor subtracts from net sales the usual accounting income statement items such as cost of goods sold (COGS); selling, general, and administrative expenses (SG&A); and depreciation. Also, other operating income (if any) shown on the income statement is included in the calculation of pretax cash operating profit while other *non*operating income is excluded.

In the EVA tax calculation, the manager or investor begins with reported income tax expense on the income statement. To this amount, one subtracts (or adds) the increase (or decrease) in the deferred income tax account obtained from the balance sheet. The tax benefit received from interest expense (tax rate × interest expense) and the tax benefit received from implied interest expense on operating leases is added to the reported income tax figure to remove the tax benefit obtained from debt-related financing decisions. Also, taxes on *non*operating income (or tax benefits received from nonoperating expenses) must be subtracted from (or added to) reported income taxes to obtain an accurate measure of cash operating taxes. Upon subtracting cash operating taxes from pretax net operating profit (from either the bottom-up or top-down approach), one obtains net operating profit after taxes (NOPAT).

INVESTED CAPITAL

Exhibit 9.6 shows the EVA accounting adjustments that are necessary in the equivalent asset and financing approaches to estimating invested capital. In the assets approach, the manager or investor begins with net short-term operating assets (basically, net working capital). This reflects moneys tied up in current assets like accounts receivables and inventories as well as a normal amount of cash needed for operations.[24] Current liabilities such as accounts payable, accrued expenses, and income taxes payable are of course netted from the short-term operating asset accounts. Short-term notes payable (a current liability account) are excluded because they represent a source of debt financing. Interest-bearing debt is reflected in the sources of financing approach, and the debt-interest tax subsidy is reflected in the calculation of a company's (dollar) cost of capital.

Capital Estimation

Net plant, property, and equipment; goodwill; and other assets are then added to net short-term operating assets. As shown in Exhibit 9.6, several equity reserve accounts are added to basic invested capital, including LIFO

EXHIBIT 9.6 Calculation of Capital from Financial Statement Data

---

A. Asset approach

Begin:	Net short-term operating assets
Add:	Net plant, property, and equipment
	Other assets
	Goodwill (net)
	Equity reserve accounts, including:
	LIFO reserve
	Accumulated intangibles amortization
	Bad-debt reserve
	Capitalized research and development
	Cumulative write-offs of special items
	Leased operating assets (Present value of operating leases from debt equivalents)
Equals:	Capital

B. Sources of financing approach

Begin:	Book value of common equity
Add other equity and equivalents:	Preferred stock
	Minority interest
	Deferred income tax
	Equity reserve accounts (see listing above)
Add debt and debt equivalents:	Interest bearing short-term debt
	Current portion of long-term debt due
	Long-term debt
	Other liabilities
	Capitalized lease obligations
	Present value of operating leases
Equals:	Capital

---

reserve, accumulated intangibles amortization (from patents, copyrights, etc), net capitalized research and development, cumulative bad debt reserve, and the cumulative write-off of special items like reengineering and restructuring costs. Also, the present value of operating leases (shown as leased operating assets) is added back to arrive at invested capital on the EVA balance sheet.

In the sources of financing approach (Exhibit 9.6), the manager or investor begins with the book value of common equity. This is just the familiar common at par, capital surplus, and retained earnings amounts on the balance sheet net of treasury stock (if any). To this sum, one adds several equity equivalent accounts, including those already listed on a company's balance sheet—such as preferred stock, minority interest, and deferred income taxes—as well as the companion equity reserve accounts mentioned in the assets approach to estimating invested capital—namely, LIFO reserve, accumulated intangibles amortization, net capitalized research and development, bad debt reserve, and the cumulative write-offs of special items.

Debt and debt equivalents are then added to arrive at an EVA-based figure for invested capital. These debt-related accounts include those listed on the balance sheet—including interest-bearing short-term debt, long-term debt, other liabilities, and capitalized lease obligations—and off-balance-sheet debt items[25] such as the present value of operating leases. With the engagement of several EVA accounting adjustments, we see that the asset *and* financing approaches to estimating invested capital produce a robust measure (compared with basic EVA capital, or on-balance sheet capital) of economic capital that is actually tied up in a business.

EVA APPLICATION: JLG DOW FUNDAMENTAL

To illustrate the results of an EVA valuation in practice, Exhibit 9.7 shows a snapshot of the JLG Dow Fundamental[26] versus the Dow Jones Industrial Average (DJIA) from February 20 to May 1, 2008. The JLG Dow Fundamental provides a bottom-up, EVA-based assessment of where the market should be trading based on underlying economic profit and risk characteristics. While past performance is not indicative of future returns, the JLG

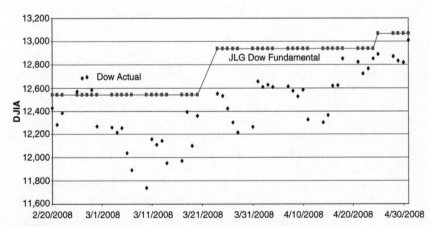

EXHIBIT 9.7 JLG Dow Fundamental versus Dow Actual

Dow Fundamental during the reporting period was a leading fundamental indicator of stock market performance.

Specifically, Exhibit 9.7 shows convergence between the Dow Jones Industrial Average and the JLG Dow Fundamental. In terms of valuation statistics, the estimated cost of capital for the Dow Industrials was 7.77 percent, while the EVA-based future growth component of NPV for the market index was 36 percent. This suggests that 64 percent of estimated NPV was due to economic profit generated by existing assets while the balance of intrinsic value added was due to the presumed EVA generated from future growth opportunities (NPV from assets *not* currently in place). As of April 25, 2008, there were 10 active buy opportunities and 10 active sell or short-sell opportunities within the JLG Dow Fundamental.

Due to the onset of the global financial crisis, stock market performance in the summer and fall of 2008 was impacted negatively by several adverse financial events, as reflected in an unprecedented rise in the base equity risk premium to an all-time high of 9.0 percent.[27] As of January 12, 2009, the JLG Dow Fundamental stood at 8736, some 3% higher than the quoted value of the Dow Jones Industrial Average, at 8474. However, due to the lingering effects of the global financial crisis the market continued to abate until reaching the lows of early March 2009, and did not reach the January value indicated by the JLG Dow Fundamental until June 1, 2009.

EVA LINK TO FCF VALUATION

Given the preceding developments on EVA, it is helpful for managers and investors to know how EVA valuation relates to other DCF approaches such as the free cash flow model. There are a couple of things to keep in mind regarding the similarities and differences between economic profit valuation and, say, free cash flow valuation. The first observation is obvious—namely, that EVA and FCF valuation models (as well as DDM models for that matter) *must* produce the same intrinsic value of the firm and its common stock. That is, the value of the firm is driven by the present value of a cash flow stream generated by the firm's existing assets and its future growth opportunities (assets *not* current in place). Having said that, it is worth emphasizing that EVA valuation provides managers and investors with a *direct* measure of how the firm creates or destroys shareholder value as reflected in NPV.

The second observation about EVA versus FCF valuation pertains to the capital charge on invested capital. Specifically, in the economic profit approach to securities valuation an *explicit* charge on the beginning of year (BOY) capital is assessed each year and deducted from NOPAT. In contrast, in free cash flow model, the present value of the capital charge on the firm's periodic investment is *implicitly* recognized in the year that the capital expenditure is incurred. To see this, suppose that a company spends $4.50 in capital improvement during a particular year. In the free cash flow model, the entire net investment would be subtracted from the net operating profit (NOPAT) in the year incurred. As mentioned, this is equivalent to recognizing the present value of the yearly capital charge that would be assessed in the EVA model. Assuming the capital charge can be expressed as perpetuity, this yields:

$$\text{Net investment (year 1)} = \$4.50$$
$$= (\$4.50 \times \text{WACC})/\text{WACC} = \$4.50$$

Hence, the free cash flow model subtracts the entire investment of $4.50 from NOPAT. In the EVA approach, the periodic capital charge of $0.45 (assuming a 10 percent cost of capital) would be deducted from each year's NOPAT, beginning in the first year *following* the capital expenditure. Of course, the investment expenditure (assumed at $4.50) is added to the end of year 1 capital base to arrive at beginning of year (BOY) capital for the second year.

Free Cash Flow Valuation

For comparative purposes, let's take a look at free cash flow valuation.[28] In this widely used model, the enterprise value of the firm can be expressed as the present value of the anticipated cash flow stream generated by the firm's existing assets and its expected future growth assets not currently in place. In general, the FCF model is expressed as:

$$V = \sum \text{FCF}_t/(1 + \text{WACC})^t \qquad (t = 1 \text{ to } \infty)$$

In this expression, V is the firm's enterprise or corporate value, FCF_t is the assessed free cash flow for year t, and WACC is the weighted average cost of debt and equity capital. In turn, the firm's assessed free cash flow at year t, FCF_t, can be viewed as the anticipated net operating profit after tax, NOPAT, *less* the annual net investment, INV, to support the firm's growth. If, as before, NOPAT is $14.95 and the net investment is $4.50, then the one-step-ahead FCF is $10.45.

$$\text{FCF}(1) = \text{NOPAT}(1) - \text{INV}(1)$$
$$= \$14.95 - \$4.50 = \$10.45$$

Note that net investment refers to gross capital expenditures at year t less the required maintenance expenditures (measured by economic depreciation) on the firm's existing assets. As with gross investment, net investment includes the required change in working capital (measured by the year-over-year change in operating current assets less the associated change in operating current liabilities) to support a growing revenue and earnings stream.

FCF VALUATION: HORIZON YEARS

To illustrate FCF valuation, we'll use the 10-year stream of free cash flow estimates produced by the revenue-forecasting model used by Grant (2003). Exhibit 9.8 shows how to roll up the 10 years of free cash flow estimates for the horizon years. The exhibit reports NOPAT, net annual investment, free cash flow, the present value of free cash flow for any given year, and the *cumulative* present value of the free cash flow estimates over the horizon period. Using a cost of capital (discount rate) of 10 percent, we see that the $10.45 free cash flow estimate for year 1 has a currently assessed market value of $9.50.

Upon calculating the present value of the 10 years of free cash flow estimates and cumulating these values, we see that the firm's horizon value is $116.98. However, stopping here in the enterprise valuation process would be unduly conservative because it presumes that the firm is unable to generate discounted positive free cash flow beyond the horizon period. Such an unfortunate state of affairs might exist for a company's shareholders if (1) the firm's existing capital assets at that time (year-end 10 in our case) were completely obsolete, and if (2) the NPV on all future investments were zero; since the EVA on future investment opportunities is zero when the marginal return on future investments equals the cost of capital.

EXHIBIT 9.8 FCF Valuation: Horizon Years

Year	NOPAT	Net Investment	FCF	Present Value*	Cumulative PV
1	14.95	4.50	10.45	9.50	9.50
2	17.19	5.18	12.01	9.93	19.43
3	19.77	5.95	13.82	10.38	29.81
4	22.74	6.84	15.90	10.86	40.67
5	26.15	7.87	18.28	11.35	52.02
6	30.07	9.05	21.02	11.87	63.88
7	34.58	10.41	24.17	12.40	76.29
8	39.77	11.97	27.80	12.97	89.26
9	45.73	13.77	31.96	13.55	102.81
10	52.59	15.83	36.76	14.17	116.98
11 Plus*	54.17				

*WACC = 10 percent.

FCF VALUATION: RESIDUAL YEARS

While several assumptions can be made about free cash flow generation during the post-horizon years,[29] we'll make the simplifying (and economically consistent) assumption that the marginal return on the *net* investment at end of the horizon period earns a cost of capital return. This is tantamount to saying that (1) free cash flow for post-horizon years is equal to the one-period-ahead estimate of NOPAT, and (2) that economic profit generated by the end-of-horizon period net investment (and the EVA on any future investment) is equal to zero. With this zero-NPV assumption, the firm's residual (or continuing) value at year T can be expressed in simple terms as:

$$V_T = NOPAT_{T+1}/WACC$$

While the resulting perpetuity is a convenient way out of a complex terminal value pricing process, we still need to estimate the *one-step-ahead* NOPAT as of the end of the horizon period. Fortunately, we can obtain this forecast with knowledge of (1) the firm's plow-back or net investment-to-NOPAT ratio, and (2) the marginal return on invested capital (MROC). With this information, we can express the firm's growth in NOPAT, g_N, as:

$$g_N = PBR \times MROC$$

In this expression, g_N is the estimated year-over-year growth rate in NOPAT from the end of the horizon period, PBR is the plowback ratio, measured by *net* investment during the last year of the horizon period over the end-of-horizon period net operating profit after tax, $NOPAT_T$.[30]

Assuming that the investment at year 10, at $15.83 (again, Exhibit 9.8), earns a cost of capital return, we obtain an estimated NOPAT growth rate for the residual or continuing period of 3 percent.

$$g_N = (\$15.83/\$52.59) \times 0.10$$
$$= 0.3010 \times 0.10 = 0.0301 \text{ (or 3.01\%)}$$

It is now a simple matter to estimate the one-step-ahead NOPAT according to:

$$NOPAT_{11} = NOPAT_{10} \times (1 + g_N)$$
$$= \$52.59 \times (1.0301) = \$54.17$$

Note that this is the same continuing value for NOPAT as indicated in Exhibits 9.1 and 9.8. Thus, the firm's residual value at year 10 is equal to $541.73. This is obtained by discounting the one-step-ahead NOPAT perpetuity by the 10 percent cost of capital. Equivalently, this residual value figure is obtained by multiplying the estimated NOPAT perpetuity of $54.17 by a price-to-NOPAT multiplier of 10 (equal to 1/WACC).

$$V_{10} = \$54.17/0.10$$
$$= \$54.17 \times 10 = \$541.73$$

Moreover, upon discounting the residual value back 10 periods, we obtain the intrinsic value, at $208.86, of the free cash flow generated during the residual or continuing years. As summarized in Exhibit 9.9, we see that the enterprise value of the firm is $325.84. This value consists of $116.98 in horizon value *plus* $208.86 of current residual value. With long-term debt at $12, and five shares of common stock outstanding, the warranted stock price is $62.77. Not surprisingly, the firm's enterprise value of $325.84 and its intrinsic stock price of $62.77 are the *same* values that we obtained in the EVA valuation model.

EXHIBIT 9.9   FCF Valuation: Residual Years

Year	NOPAT	Net Investment	FCF	Present Value*	Cumulative PV
1	14.95	4.50	10.45	9.50	9.50
2	17.19	5.18	12.01	9.93	19.43
3	19.77	5.95	13.82	10.38	29.81
4	22.74	6.84	15.90	10.86	40.67
5	26.15	7.87	18.28	11.35	52.02
6	30.07	9.05	21.02	11.87	63.88
7	34.58	10.41	24.17	12.40	76.29
8	39.77	11.97	27.80	12.97	89.26
9	45.73	13.77	31.96	13.55	102.81
10	52.59	15.83	36.76	14.17	116.98
11 Plus	54.17				
Residual Value				541.73 (at year 10)	208.86
Corporate Value					325.84
Long-Term Debt					12.00
Equity					313.84
Shares Outstanding					5.00
Price					62.77

*WACC = 10 percent.

Before concluding, it is interesting to see that the current residual value, at \$208.86, makes up some 64 percent of the firm's warranted corporate value. This large residual value impact is a common finding among discounted cash flow approaches—whether dividend discount model (DDM), free cash flow (FCF), or economic profit approaches—to estimate enterprise value and stock price. In practice, the residual value (or terminal value) impact is especially pronounced for growth-oriented companies.[31] Examples include companies operating in the technology and health care sectors of the economy since most of their enterprise value comes from distant—and often very difficult to predict—free cash flow and EVA generated on current and future R&D investments.

SUMMARY

Like any DCF model, the EVA valuation model has both attractive features and some limitations. On the positive side, the economic profit model provides a *direct* means by which managers and investors can assess the NPV contribution from existing assets as well as future growth opportunities. In this context, the firm's wealth creation—as measured by its NPV—is equal to the present value of all future economic profit generated by existing assets and anticipated future assets (growth opportunities) not currently in place. With discounted positive economic profit, a company is a wealth creator, while with discounted negative economic profit a company is—unfortunately–a wealth destroyer.

While EVA valuation is intuitively appealing, managers and investors need to realize that the resulting estimates of enterprise value and intrinsic stock price are highly sensitive to the model inputs. We found that a seemingly small change in the length of the firm's economic profit period (T) and/or its cost of capital (WACC) via equity duration effects can have a meaningful impact on the value of the firm and its outstanding shares. With uncertainty about model inputs, it is clear that managers must do everything within their responsibility and control to (honestly!) surprise investors *positively* about key economic profit drivers such as the return on capital, the cost of capital, and the length of the economic profit period.

We recognized several value-based accounting adjustments that should be taken into consideration when estimating economic profit. We also provided an application of EVA valuation in the context of the JLG Dow Fundamental. Finally, we argued that EVA valuation must reconcile to other well-known discounted cash flow approaches such as the dividend discount model and the traditional free cash flow model.

NOTES

1. EVA® is a registered trademark of Stern Stewart & Co.
2. However, this does not mean that the EVA approach to securities valuation gives a better answer than that obtained from other valuation models.
3. Grant (2003).
4. As explained later, invested capital or EVA capital can be obtained using an equivalent assets or financing approach.
5. When evaluating companies, investors must be keenly aware of economic profit influences from industry, sector, and general market effects.
6. Since NOPAT is net of depreciation on the EVA income statement, we must use net (of accumulated depreciation) operating assets on the EVA balance sheet. Equivalently, we could use gross operating profit after tax (GOPAT) and gross investment to obtain the same EVA results.
7. The dollar units assumed in the EVA illustration are a matter of detail rather than substance.
8. Some investors use a three-stage EVA growth model, with transitional or decay rate of cash flow growth between horizon and residual stages. The so-called "H (or half-life)" model is popular in this regard.
9. A variable-growth EVA model can produce an answer that is substantially different from that obtained with a constant-growth model. The goal here is to show that the present value dynamics of a variable-growth model are different from those of a constant-growth model.
10. Again, the dollar units assumed in the illustration are a matter of detail rather than substance.
11. In other words, if MROC equals WACC, then the change in EVA from period T to $T + 1$ is zero because the change in NOPAT, at $1.58, is equal to the dollar capital charge on the end-of-horizon-period net investment of $15.83.
12. With long-term growth of precisely 6.1692 percent in the constant-growth EVA model, we obtain the same value—at $285.84—as that shown in the two-stage variable-growth model. This NPV value is marginally different from the $285.90 figure that we obtained before with the assumed constant EVA growth rate of 6.17 percent.
13. The enterprise valuation model presented here is based on the classic "investment opportunities approach to valuation" described by Fama and Miller—see Eugene F. Fama and Merton H. Miller, *The Theory of Finance* (New York: Holt, Rinehart & Winston, 1972).
14. For an insightful discussion of the T-period EVA model, see G. Bennett Stewart III, *The Quest for Value* (New York: HarperCollins, 1991).
15. In the previous EVA illustration, we assumed no future investment opportunities beyond the horizon period. While we utilize the same numbers in the T-period EVA illustration that follows, the goal here is to shed basic insight on EVA investment opportunities (or periods) without getting bogged down in detailed formulas that model the firm's investment opportunities.

16. This simplification presumes that the firm's existing capital is worthless at the end of the 10-year horizon period.

17. Notice, too, that with 50 years of positive EVA during residual years the stock price is virtually the same as the perpetuity result, at $62.77. While wealth-creating managers should focus on long-term EVA rather than just short-term EVA, this sheds some interesting light on how long is "long."

18. In practical application of enterprise valuation models, long-term debt is often measured at book value while equity capitalization—number of shares of stock outstanding times stock price—is used for the common stock.

19. As a real-world example, one would expect a significant rise in the equity risk premium (a component of the cost of equity) due to the tragic events of September 11, 2001. If correct, this would go a long way in helping to explain the sharp decline in stock prices that occurred in the aftermath of 9/11.

20. Specifically, if T falls from infinity to 10 years, or WACC rises from 10 percent to 11.5 percent, then the stock price declines from $62.77 to about $51—actually, the price is $50.57 with T at 10 years, and $51.09 with WACC at 11.5 percent, separately.

21. See JLG Research at www.jlgresearch.com for software that calculates EVA with standard value-based accounting adjustments.

22. Net operating profit before taxes (EBIT) is also the same as operating profit after depreciation and amortization.

23. R&D expenditures should be capitalized and amortized over a useful time period such as five years, rather than expensed on the current year income statement as if these expenditures have no future cash flow benefit.

24. Estimates of a normal amount of cash required for operations vary by industry—such as 0.5 percent to 2 percent of net sales. Also, one can make a distinction between invested capital and operating capital. Operating capital is generally viewed as invested capital net of excess cash and marketable securities and goodwill arising from premiums paid in corporate acquisitions

25. The EVA recognition of *all* forms of debt including off-balance-sheet debt is important. While EVA accounting uses information that is deemed accurate from a company's published financial reports, EVA cannot possibly reflect off-balance-sheet debts arising from hidden liabilities or fraudulent accounting transactions as in the notorious case of Enron.

26. See www.jlgresearch.com for equity valuation software and updates on the JLG Dow Fundamental.

27. For explanation of the base equity risk premium on an "approximately-certainty-earnings (ACE) portfolio," see Abate, Grant, and Rowberry, "Understanding the Required Return under New Uncertainty," *Journal of Portfolio Management*, Fall 2006.

28. See Alfred Rappaport, "Strategic Analysis for More Profitable Acquisitions," *Harvard Business Review* (July/August 1979) for a pioneering application of the free cash flow model.

29. Such possibilities include constant growth in free cash flow during the residual years (at a growth rate less than WACC) and some form of competitive decay in the estimated free cash flow during post-horizon years.
30. The growth in NOPAT, g_N, can be expressed as the product of the net investment plow-back ratio (PBR) times the marginal return on net invested capital, MROC, because (1) PBR measures net investment over NOPAT (at end of the horizon period), and (2) MROC equals the change in NOPAT over net investment.
31. The term *growth-oriented companies* is taken to mean companies that can earn substantially positive EVA on future investment opportunities. They do so because the estimated after-tax rate of return on future investment opportunities widely exceeds the WACC.

REFERENCE

Grant, James L. *Foundations of economic value added*. 2nd ed. Hoboken, NJ: John Wiley & Sons, 2003.

CHAPTER 10

Valuation for Managers

Closing the Gap between Theory and Practice

Dennis N. Aust
Managing Director, CharterMast Partners

O ver the past three decades, creating shareholder value has been widely adopted as a principal objective for publicly held corporations, at least in theory.[1] In practice, the results have been mixed. The long-term secular increase in corporate sector profits is consistent with the image of hard-nosed corporate executives diligently working to increase shareholder value. Yet a continuing stream of corporate miscues suggests otherwise. Whether because of overpriced acquisitions and bad strategic decisions, or because of flagrant, Tyco-type abuses, a significant number of major firms still fail to create value for their shareholders. Numerous benchmarks document this consistent underperformance over both long-term and short-term horizons. For example, during 2007, even though the S&P 500 index increased by 3.5 percent, nearly half of the firms in the index (249 firms, according to statistics provided by Ativo Research LLC) ended the year with their stock prices lower than when they started.

Of course, there are numerous reasons for falling stock prices. External factors such as adverse business cycles, market dynamics, and sector rotation regularly drive down stock prices in any given year. Even when executives diligently work to create value for shareholders, they can still be undermined by competitors that push back, staff who fail to execute, and business conditions that move against them. And yet, while these may seem like reasonable excuses, there's much more to this story of why so many firms perform so poorly.

This chapter asserts that value management experts, whether external consultants or internal financial executives, have unintentionally sabotaged their causes. These experts have provided senior executives with increasingly sophisticated, but ultimately unworkable shareholder value enhancement solutions. These solutions almost always produce one of two results. One type of firm, ambitious and aggressive, initially adopts the best, most sophisticated metrics and methodologies. However, most such ambitious initiatives eventually fail, as the difficulty of implementing an overly complex approach undermines its usefulness and acceptance throughout the organization. The other type of firm, cautious and practical, sticks with a tried-and-true approach that is more easily understood, but ultimately proves inadequate for the task. Executives in these firms diligently execute to meet their targets, but fail to deliver shareholder results because the performance metrics and targets employed are flawed.

From the corporate management perspective, the challenge for valuation experts is not so much to devise a methodology that correlates perfectly with the market, but rather to apply a framework that provides reasonably accurate insights and guidance within the framework of an easily understood package. We, as experts, need to know when to say, "That's good enough."

This doesn't mean we should simply discard the powerful (but complex) models linking operating performance to stock prices, particularly when the alternatives are simplistic rules of thumb with marginal links to value creation. Rather, the challenge is to rework or streamline these sophisticated valuation models so that they become more accessible and practical to executives and managers at all levels of an organization. Carefully paring back complexity while preserving (or substituting) core capabilities can produce valuation models that retain sufficient market linkages, while still providing useful insights and incentives for corporate management. It is often difficult, even painful, to leave out sophisticated adjustments and nuances that are supported both by financial theory and empirical evidence. However, in the long run, leaving out nuances is often a better decision. This is particularly true if the ultimate choice is between a near-perfect methodology that is eventually discarded and a reasonably good approximation with the staying power to provide long-term, market-linked discipline and insights.

CURRENT ENVIRONMENT

Consider this contrast between theory and reality:

Any expert in business strategy must have a superior understanding of what drives financial value creation in the first place. Such a strategy expert must thoroughly understand the differences and nuances between relative valuations and discounted cash flow analyses. . . . In short, he or she must be an expert in business valuations.

Littman, J. and Frigo, M. (2004)

In the classroom, value-based management (VBM) programs sound seductively simple. Theoretically, they involve just two steps. First, adopt an economic profit metric, such as Stern Stewart's Economic Value Added (EVA), as a key measure of performance. Second, tie compensation to agreed-upon improvement targets in that metric. For large companies with flagging share prices, this looks like a miracle cure. All they have to do to boost their market value is call in consultants to revamp their accounting system, install the new measure of performance, align their incentive systems, and voilà! Managers and employees will march along like good foot soldiers and start making all kinds of value-creating decisions.

If only it were that easy. As recent reports in the press indicate, almost half the companies that have adopted a VBM metric have met with mediocre success. Some have even abandoned the system altogether after three to five years, reverting to traditional performance measures such as earnings per share.

Haspeslagh, Noda, and Boulos (2001)

Haspeslagh, Noda, and Boulos conclude that effective value management isn't so much about numbers and metrics, but rather is centered on cultural change. At one point they quote Cadbury Schweppes CEO John Sunderland: "Managing for value is 20% about the numbers and 80% about the people . . . because people create value." Successful VBM adopters build on existing accounting systems, avoid complexity, and adopt methodologies that can be widely understood and embraced throughout the organization.

Unfortunately, as valuation experts we have often embraced a different perspective.

Of course, a highly precise and nuanced approach to valuation is important in certain contexts. A few percentage points in investment returns can make the difference between success and failure for institutional portfolio managers, so they employ highly trained financial specialists who use the most sophisticated models in an attempt to realize as much alpha as possible from each portfolio. Highly sophisticated models are also justified in mergers, acquisitions, divestitures, and related financial transactions, where 1 percent of improved accuracy on a $10 billion deal is worth $100 million. Even so, the success of most acquisitions depends more on understanding the business, getting the forecast right, effectively executing the postmerger integration, and having the confidence and judgment to walk away from a bad deal. Having a sound valuation model is undoubtedly important and appropriate. The risk increases when that model becomes so complex that it diverts attention from more critical issues.

The key challenge when choosing a valuation model/methodology is to match the tool to the objective. Institutional portfolio managers can profit from highly complex models. Executives making major deals can gain insights from sophisticated analysis. But for ongoing corporate performance management and value creation, the objectives are considerably different. Does the model provide managers with directionally accurate incentives and insights so that they make the right decisions? Is it relevant to managers' day-to-day activities and responsibilities? Is it sufficiently clear and straightforward that it can be implemented throughout the organization?

In his 1996 Chairman's Letter, Warren Buffett described Berkshire Hathaway's key principles for executive compensation: "Goals should be (1) tailored to the economics of the specific operating business; (2) simple in character so that the degree to which they are being realized can be easily measured; and (3) directly related to the daily activities of plan participants." (Buffett 1996) If one slightly rephrases the first principle as "tailored to the economics of how the specific operating business creates value," then these principles provide excellent guidance for the corporate executive seeking to implement a value creation framework throughout his organization. Buffett also cautioned against arrangements that are "totally out of the control of the person whose behavior we would like to affect," observing that such schemes "may actually discourage the focused behavior we value in managers." For example, consider the all-too-common situation when the valuation framework leads operating managers into extended debates about intricacies such as alternative cost of capital estimates. There is absolutely no question that operating managers need to know that capital has a cost, and they need to know approximately what that cost is. But most *operating* managers have effectively zero control over their cost of capital. As long as they have an answer that is approximately right, effort dedicated to refining the estimate is effort diverted from running the business. (One particularly savvy client addressed this problem by stating cost of capital as a 3 percentage point range. Operating units and projects that were above this range were clearly exceeding the cost of capital, while those below this range were clearly underperforming. For those within the range, a senior executive observed that he was satisfied that the operation was "close enough" to meeting the cost of capital, and the operating manager's time would best be spent on improving operating performance rather than trying to justify a lower cost-of-capital estimate.)

From a managerial perspective, the purpose of valuation is to provide proper insights, incentives, and control processes. For managers, valuation is concerned with *change*. If I choose among actions X, Y, and Z, the issue is which will increase value and which will destroy value. Once I have made my choice, how do I evaluate whether the financial results provide the shareholder value impact I expected? Valuation is also about *relative* value, and its direction. It is important to know which business units add value, which are neutral, and which destroy value, as well as how these relationships are changing over time.

ALTERNATIVE MEASURES OF VALUE CREATION: A QUICK REVIEW

So, if the goal is to create value, what *should* you measure?

Stock price, or more precisely total shareholder return (TSR), is the gold standard. By definition, TSR *is* the return actually earned by shareholders. Unfortunately, TSR is affected by many factors, including broader market movements, investor sentiment, rumors, and so on that have little or nothing to do with what management accomplishes in running the business. TSR measures expectations, not results. It also provides an unclear link between management actions and objectives. Although management might budget a sales or profit increase of, say, 20 percent, with some degree of confidence, budgeting a stock price increase of 20 percent is considerably riskier. Furthermore, compensation based on stock price has directly led to many of the excesses of the past decade. First, stock options paid off exorbitantly during the technology bubble, even when completely unjustified by firm-specific financial performance. Then, when the bubble burst, firms turned to backdating and repricing options, an attempt to salvage returns for hardworking executives as a falling market slammed both good and bad companies alike. Corporate cultures emerged where employees had one eye on their work and the other on the stock ticker, watching to see how quickly their "lottery tickets," otherwise known as stock options, would make them rich.

Another traditional measure is discounted cash flow (DCF) valuation. The key problem with DCF is its dependence on projections, which makes it an inherently subjective measure. Also, DCF (as normally implemented) is a point-in-time measure. A manager typically constructs a detailed cash flow forecast, which is then discounted back to determine a specific net present value of the business unit (or project) as of some specific point in time. Rarely do managers construct a time series of DCF estimates showing how business value has changed over extended multiyear time periods. (Although Thomas and Atra describe a creative methodology for automated DCF valuations in Chapter 11 of this book, such techniques have not yet been widely adopted.) In current practice DCF remains primarily a point-in-time calculation, so it doesn't show how value is being created or destroyed. In cases when a time series of actual market values is available (e.g., historical stock prices for publicly traded firms), using a single point-in-time DCF value misses an important opportunity to confirm that the trend in calculated value is consistent with the trend in actual value.

Other traditional metrics (sales growth, earnings per share (EPS) growth, etc.) are relatively simple, but empirically unrelated to value creation. Earnings before interest, taxes, depreciation, and amortization (EBITDA), for example, is widely used. It reflects the cash-generating performance of a business, but not the investment required to support that cash generation. Although EBITDA multiples are used to relate EBITDA to valuation, multiples vary widely between firms over time. EBITDA multiples implicitly recognize the importance of cash generation, but don't incorporate the assets required to generate that cash flow.

Residual income metrics, such as economic value added (EVA), which have been adopted by a significant number of firms, have both advantages and disadvantages. An explicit capital charge reflects the impact of managing assets, and the structure of the metric addresses issues such as scale and leverage. The biggest disadvantage is that residual income is not directly comparable to stock price, so it can be difficult or impossible to confirm how reliably operating changes impact valuation. Although the metric itself is reasonably straightforward, we've seen clients who have abandoned the metric because too many complex adjustments undermined its usefulness. Consistent with the theme of this chapter, firms using residual income need to focus on practical utility rather than theoretical purity.

Return metrics (sometimes flippantly characterized as "return on whatever") provide only a partial answer at best. In our experience, when such a metric comes closer to representing the underlying cash flow economics, it does relate more closely to value creation. A traditional accounting metric like return on equity is computed using two synthetic and often suspect inputs, net income and equity, so it isn't surprising that return on equity has little relation to value creation. Return metrics that focus on cash generation and total investment are more closely linked to value creation. One highly sophisticated measure was developed at Callard, Madden & Associates in the 1970s. Using an internal rate of return format, cash flow return on investment (CFROI) balances inflation-adjusted assets against cash generation to compute the economic rate of return actually earned by any firm or business. Various organizations have introduced refinements and variations on this metric, but Bart Madden provides a thorough description of the basic concept and calculation in his book on CFROI valuation (Madden 1999).

Even though carefully constructed metrics like cash flow return on investment provide powerful insights when examining trends or comparing different firms, like all "return on" metrics, they can prove a treacherous foundation for making decisions about value creation. Jensen (2001) succinctly explains the problem of using return and ratio measures:

> *Here I can be blunt: Don't do it. Using ratios, such as sales margin or return on assets, inevitably produces gaming. That's because managers can increase the measure in two ways: by increasing the numerator or decreasing the denominator. If, for example, a company tracks performance according to margin as a percentage of sales, managers can increase their pay by simply cutting back sales (selling only the highest margin products) instead of working to increase the margins on all products. The result: Total dollars of profit fall, and company value erodes.*

Using a return measure as a surrogate for value creation inevitably introduces a bias to reduce assets. Although focusing growth on high-return businesses *is* a powerful value-creation strategy, and redeploying underperforming assets often *does* make economic sense, *arbitrarily* shedding assets (or underinvesting) to boost returns can easily diminish the long-term cash flow, ultimately destroying value.

The underlying problem with return metrics is that they simply fall short of the ultimate goal, which is value creation. Over the years, we have observed a number of firms embracing goals such as earning a return on investment (however measured) in the top quartile (or top quintile, or top third) of the S&P. These goals usually tie to some incentive compensation framework that links specific payouts to some range of performance, but as long as the firm meets its overall return on investment goal, management earns a substantial bonus. That problem is that return on investment isn't the same thing as value created for shareholders. For many slow-growing, mature firms, what drives value creation isn't the *level* of returns, but the *trend* in returns. Even if management continues to meet its top quartile target and earns a hefty bonus, flat returns translate to minimal value creation, and eroding returns destroy value. (In fact, firms with subpar returns regularly create substantial value, and are often more attractive investments than consistent high-return firms. They create value by improving return on investment, as successful turnaround specialists have demonstrated over and over. But once the turnaround is accomplished, maintaining the same rate of improvement becomes significantly more difficult.)

Measuring return on investment is not the same as measuring value creation. If the objective is to increase the value of a company or business unit, rather than focusing on surrogates like return on investment, the ideal metric should be some reasonably direct measure of value. If it is used as a performance measure, it should measure actual achieved performance, rather than forecasts. And it should be routinely and consistently computed over time, because value creation is defined as *change* in value. One such framework is described in the Valuation Equation Solution section. Cash flow ROI models project a stream of cash flows, which are then discounted back to present value. The cash flow profile is adjusted based on projected asset growth rates and standardized hold/fade parameters. The original model was developed at Callard, Madden & Associates in the 1970s, then heavily promoted by HOLT Planning Associates, formed by departing Callard, Madden employees in 1985. Since Madden documented the methodology (Madden 1999), variations of these models have been developed and promoted by various offshoots of the Callard and HOLT organizations.

Cash flow ROI models have been accepted by a large number of institutional investors, but have been less widely adopted in the general business community. Adherents (including the author) believe these models have a very strong link to value, and therefore can serve as powerful tools for the operating manager seeking to increase the value of the firm.

One particular advantage of this type of valuation model is its ability to produce a stream of point-in-time value estimates. Exhibit 10.1 shows how the Ativo/CharterMast valuation model produces annual value estimates for United Technologies Corporation. Many practitioners (see Chapters 2 and 7, Hass, Pryor 2006) believe this type of chart is essential for the systematic implementation of any valuation model. There are two major advantages. First is the ability to identify value creation trends (or value destruction trends). Second is the ability to assess how well the model compares to market value. This is not to imply that the values generated by any valuation model should always mirror stock prices. Stock prices contain a significant amount of noise, and can depart from intrinsic value for extended periods of time. But significant and extended discrepancies do identify the need for a closer look at valuation details.

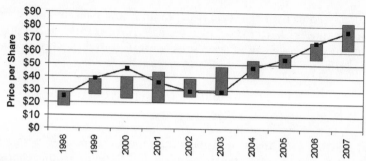

EXHIBIT 10.1 United Technologies Corporation Intrinsic Equity Value with Annual Trading Range (Bars)

The major problem with cash flow ROI models, and return-driven valuation models in general, has been a level of complexity that impedes wider corporate-sector adoption. While finance specialists are often comfortable running and interpreting such models, the fact that someone even needs to run the model introduces an extra step into decision making and management. Unfortunately, running the model has almost always been a requirement, because the internal calculations are extremely detailed, with cash flow projections reflecting asset growth, asset replacement, and carefully sculpted fades to ROI and growth rates over a period of 30 to 50 years, or even longer. In addition, these models are built in such a way that they often require numerous inputs, so the linkage to operating results can be indirect and obscure. In our experience, the learning curve has been extremely steep, requiring significant effort before a manager starts to develop an intuitive feeling for how operating performance drives value.

The Value Equation Solution

It is unfortunate, but not surprising, that the complexity issue has prevented wider usage of sophisticated valuation models in corporate performance management. Executives and managers need clear performance measures that can be understood throughout an organization, so they have generally settled for traditional metrics and ratios that are inferior measures of value creation. The ideal solution would be to implement a value-based framework that clearly links operating performance to value creation, doing so in a direct manner so that managers at any level of an organization can easily understand their contribution to value without having to consult the finance department wizards.

One method of solving the complexity problem with cash flow ROI models is to rearrange the cash flow projection equations to compute functionally equivalent results in a streamlined and conceptually straightforward manner. CharterMast uses a simple three-factor Value Equation that, in everyday usage, provides results equivalent to the complete (but intricate) cash flow projection model:

$$\text{Value} = F1 \times \text{Cash profit} + F2 \times \text{Depreciating assets} \\ + F3 \times \text{Nondepreciating assets}$$

In practice, the three major operating inputs are specified with a level of precision appropriate to the application and to the economic characteristics of the business. For example, cash profit can be defined as EBITDA (or operating income before depreciation) minus cash taxes. If operating management doesn't have visibility into cash tax payments (which depend on year-end tax filings, and may not be available until several months after the fiscal year closes), it often makes sense to substitute a normalized tax provision based on long-run cash tax rates, or to use reported tax expense. Depreciating assets include gross property, plant, and equipment. Nondepreciating assets include net working capital plus other long-term assets (including intangibles and investments but excluding goodwill). The three multiples, F1, F2, and F3, which are equivalent to present value multiples adjusted to reflect the growth/hold/fade profile, are computed by the valuation model.

Exhibit 10.2 shows details of how the simplified Value Equation applies to United Technologies Corporation.

In addition to providing a straightforward value derivation, the Value Equation framework also provides a direct linkage showing how changes in the three main inputs affect enterprise value. In this particular example, a dollar of incremental tax profit is worth $17 in enterprise value, while a dollar of working capital reduces enterprise value by 20 cents. Adding the Value Equation calculation into a financial reporting system provides ongoing visibility into the value contribution of any business unit. Incorporating the Value Equation into a DuPont-style financial model is a quick way to show the linkage between value creation and basic inputs such as pricing, volumes, margins, and other financial variables. In order to support a corporate-wide value creation program, the Value Equation can be applied at any level of an organization, as long as basic income statements and balance sheets are available.

Although changes to the discount rate and long-term growth rate will affect the three multiples, these multiples are not affected by changes to the three main operating inputs. This is a critical observation for operating purposes. To a large degree, the discount rate is an external variable beyond the direct control of operating management. Although the long-term growth

EXHIBIT 10.2   United Technologies Corporation ($ Millions)

	2005	2006	2007
Operating Profit Before Depreciation	6,217	7,165	8,178
− Taxes	−1,253	−1,494	−1,836
= Cash Profit	4,964	5,671	6,342
× Cash Multiple	× 17	× 17	× 17
= Value Impact of Cash Profit (A)	84,388	96,407	107,814
Working Capital plus Other Assets (Excluding Goodwill)	14,255	12,956	15,823
× Nondepreciating Asset Multiple	× −0.2	× −0.2	× −0.2
= Value Impact of Working Capital (B)	−2,851	−2,591	−3,165
Gross Property, Plant, and Equipment	13,328	13,738	14,877
× Fixed Asset Multiple	× −1.4	× −1.4	× −1.4
= Value Impact of Fixed Assets (C)	−18,659	−19,233	−20,828
Enterprise Value (Sum of A + B + C)	62,878	74,583	83,822
− Debt	−8,240	−7,931	−9,148
= Equity Value	54,638	66,652	74,674
Divided by Shares Outstanding	1,014	996	984
= Value per Share	54	67	76
Actual Calendar Year High Price	58.89	67.47	82.50
Actual Calendar Year Low Price	48.42	54.20	61.85

Source Data: Ativo Research LLC, company reports.

rate is certainly influenced by management, changing it is a long-term process: Over periods of a few years, holding long-term growth constant (absent a compelling demonstration to the contrary) is usually a reasonable assumption. The other input that changes the three multiples is the average life of depreciating assets. Significant asset life changes are often associated with changes to the business model (outsourcing manufacturing, for example) or technological overhaul. Asset life changes are more often incremental, since replacing the existing stock of assets for most businesses is a process that can take a decade or more.

This formulation separates operating considerations from strategic considerations. The three operating inputs to the value (cash profit, depreciating assets, and nondepreciating assets) are predominately (although not completely) under the influence of operating management. Changes in these variables represent the levers operating management can pull to change the

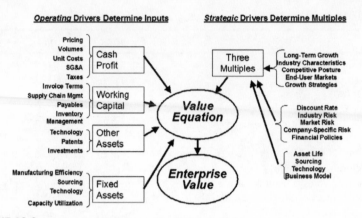

EXHIBIT 10.3   Operating Drivers versus Strategic Drivers

value of the firm. The three multiples are less directly influenced by management, being more closely related to long-term and strategic drivers such as long-term growth, the business model, and market characteristics. Exhibit 10.3 summarizes some of these relationships.

The Value Equation provides a powerful way to focus management's attention on managing three key operating drivers that directly determine the value of the firm—cash profit, working capital, and fixed assets. The result of the equation is a direct measure of value, so if the goal (for example) is to increase the value of the business by $100 million, it is a straightforward task to calculate the combination of cash profitability, working capital, and fixed asset changes required to accomplish that change. Although the computations behind the Value Equation incorporate the full power of the cash flow ROI model, the Value Equation itself requires no math beyond multiplication and addition (or subtraction).

For practical purposes, the Value Equation gives the same answers as the full cash flow ROI model. From a study of 1,249 nonfinancial firms in the S&P 1500, the result calculated by the Value Equation is within ± 2 percent of the value calculated by the full cash flow type model for 95 percent of firms. (It is within ± 1 percent for 86 percent of firms.) Of the remaining 5 percent of firms where the Value Equation differed by more than 2 percent, four out of five were extremely low-return firms (cash flow ROI less than 4 percent), which are typically priced as turnarounds, using alternative valuation methodologies.

The specific multiples vary by firm, depending on current discount rates, long-term growth, and asset mix. As a benchmark, multiples for an average firm with typical growth rates would be between 10 and 25 times cash profit, between −1.0 and −3.0 times gross fixed assets, and between

+0.4 and −0.4 times nondepreciating assets (working capital and other investments, excluding goodwill). Exhibits 10.4, 10.5, and 10.6 show how each of the multiples changes with respect to real (inflation-adjusted) growth and discount rates.

The response to changing assumptions is consistent with financial theory. The multiples decrease as discount rates rise, reflecting that both positive and negative future cash flows have smaller present values at higher discount rates. The absolute value of the multiples increases with growth rates, reflecting the proportionally greater importance of future cash flows at higher compound growth rates.

In certain respects, the Value Equation framework is highly similar to widely used EBITDA multiples. Both approaches recognize that the primary source of value is the ability to generate cash from ongoing operations. The

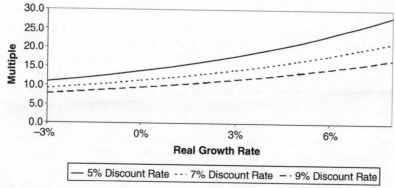

EXHIBIT 10.4   Relationship between Cash Profit Multiple and Growth, Discount Rate

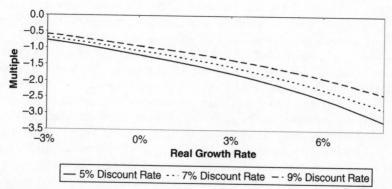

EXHIBIT 10.5   Relationship between Fixed Assets Multiple and Growth, Discount Rate

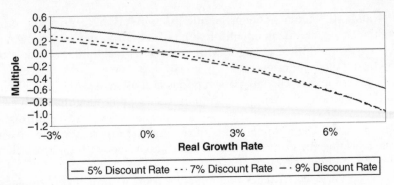

EXHIBIT 10.6 Relationship between Nondepreciating Assets Multiple and Growth, Discount Rate

Value Equation framework refines this principle by recognizing that the positive value of cash generation is offset by the assets required to support the business. For any given level of cash profit or EBITDA, firms that are highly asset intensive have lower EBITDA multiples reflecting lower return on investment. The EBITDA approach also ignores the effect of taxes, consistent with their wide use in restructuring analysis, where tax rates are highly variable in response to changing financial structures. Even so, one might observe that EBITDA multiples are just another form of Value Equation (as long as you are willing to ignore the balance sheet and tax return!).

Another important difference between the Value Equation and EBITDA multiples is that EBITDA multiples are typically *descriptive*, while the Value Equation is designed to be *predictive*. In other words, EBITDA multiples are typically obtained by calculation based on the current market value and estimated EBITDA for a given firm, or for a set of comparable firms. In contrast, the Value Equation is derived from a systematic cash flow valuation model, explicitly incorporating important value drivers such as growth, investments, and the discount rate. As a result, while one can *observe* a given firm's EBITDA multiples at any given point in time, the Value Equation framework allows the manager to *predict* how the various multiples will change under different sets of assumptions.

Examining the Value Equation for various firms yields some useful insights. For example, working capital, by itself, contributes little to value. This is consistent with conventional business wisdom. Working capital is an investment with some optimal level required to generate cash profit, and higher levels generate additional costs, such as warehousing, obsolescence, and write-offs, which depress cash profits. But a dollar of working capital (including cash) on the balance sheet almost always contributes considerably less than a dollar to enterprise value, so it makes sense to aggressively manage working capital to generate cash for debt reduction, dividends, or alternative investments. The key insight comes when considering trade-offs.

One of our clients was recently under pressure from a very large customer to provide extended payment terms. The client's direct competitors were subsidiaries of large firms that were highly resistant to such extended payment terms, while the client had both financial and management flexibility to adjust terms to some degree. This framework allowed the client to directly and easily calculate the trade-off between the incremental investment required and the impact of incremental sales and profits on the client's stock price. A conventional focus on cash flow management would have discouraged any flexibility, as evidenced by how the client's competitors reacted. A sales- or profit-driven strategy would have provided the opposite incentive. The Value Equation quantified the trade-off, so that the client could balance the incremental cash profit realized against the required investment. Understanding the dimensions of this relationship helped the client exploit a profitable growth opportunity it would have otherwise missed.

Measuring Value *Creation*

A good framework for measuring *value* is essential, but one final input is needed to measure value *creation*. Understanding value creation requires understanding the incremental investment (or incremental cash released) in conjunction with the change in value. Consider a mutual fund account. Simply comparing the opening and closing balance doesn't give an accurate picture of performance. You also need to incorporate any interim investments into or disbursements from the account. An account balance that increases from $10,000 to $11,000 appears to indicate a 10 percent positive return, but only if there were no interim transactions. If the investor added $2,000 to the account in the interim, the apparent 10 percent gain masks an actual 10 percent loss.

Such a refinement may seem obvious, but is overlooked by a surprising number of professionals who focus simply on change in enterprise value. Just as in the mutual fund example, true performance is more than just the difference between opening and closing value. To get an accurate measure of value creation, it is essential to incorporate any net cash invested in or released by the business. The end result provides a valuation measure directly comparable to total shareholder return, representing the true economic return provided by the business.

One additional benefit of measuring value creation is that a focus on *change* in value reduces the impact of nonoperating inputs that frequently present unjustified distractions for managers. For example, the discount rate (cost of capital) is a critical valuation input. Managers who want to justify a higher (or lower) business valuation frequently dispute the choice of discount rate as one more way of achieving their goal. Yet, if the focus is on *change* in value, the specific discount rate used is not highly significant. Consider one hypothetical example of a business earning slightly improving returns averaging 7.5 percent (inflation-adjusted). If the inflation-adjusted discount rate is 7 percent, then the business is exceeding its hurdle, but if the discount rate is 8 percent, the business is falling short. At a 7 percent discount rate, the value of the business increases from $691 million to $750 million, or 8.6 percent. If we keep all inputs exactly the same but use an 8 percent discount rate, the value of the business increases from $630 million to $684 million, for the same 8.6 percent increase. A similar result holds for other non-operating inputs, such as long-term growth rate. As long as nonoperating inputs are constant over the measurement period, they have little impact on the calculation. Unlike other measurement frameworks where there is often an incentive to game the system, management focus is right where it should be, on improving operating performance.

In a *Harvard Business Review* article, Jensen (2001) describes the pervasive problems of management attempting to circumvent incentive systems. If good performance is defined as hitting the budget, managers sandbag their projections so that they are assigned a lower budget target. In contrast, measuring value creation performance as a percentage return from one period to the next provides a metric that is directly comparable to the market. The process of setting targets becomes less an issue of subjective negotiation, and more a matter of objectively determining what rate of value increase is required for the stock to hold its own relative to the market. In practice, linking the targeted value creation percentage to the firm's cost of capital provides an objective and market-based method for setting performance objectives.

CONCLUSIONS

Running a business is difficult. Stockholders demand results, yet by definition, 50 percent of firms underperform the average. Executives and managers at all levels of an organization need to balance conflicting demands and challenges from customers, shareholders, suppliers, competitors, and employees. Creating value requires simultaneous success in several dimensions:

- Correctly identifying industries/segments with the potential for significant value creation.
- Developing effective strategies for achieving and sustaining competitive superiority.
- Keeping attention focused on effective execution for value creation.
- Employing value creation metrics that provide accurate and actionable insights on a timely basis.

Expecting busy executives to master the minutiae of an overly complex value management process significantly increases the risk that such a process will ultimately fail. Yet valuation is a complex and sophisticated topic, and overly simplistic approaches will also fail (for different reasons).

The fundamental objective in establishing value creation goals and metrics is to increase the value of the firm. Highly sophisticated frameworks fail when they are too complex to be effectively implemented throughout the organization. Simplistic frameworks that provide inaccurate insights and incentives fail because they give the wrong answer. Either way, having the wrong incentives leads to substantial amounts of value destruction.

For value management, successful execution requires keeping the framework sufficiently straightforward that it can be broadly deployed and embraced throughout the organization as a long-term tool. Simultaneously, it must be sophisticated enough to provide accurate insights, support reasonable and productive goals, and provide a measurement system that supports the achievement of these goals.

An effective value management expert needs to carefully balance these conflicting demands. But it doesn't have to be an either/or decision. Rather than choosing between the complexity and simplicity, the optimal answer is to *manage* the complexity, so that the sophisticated solution becomes workable and comprehensible.

In the earliest days of the twentieth century, automobiles were so prone to breakdown that any driver who ventured far from home needed a tool kit and collection of spare parts. Today's automobiles are considerably more complex, yet the complexity has been packaged in such a way that the driver needs only the most basic knowledge to master the fundamentals of operating a motorcar. He or she still needs to visit the mechanic on a scheduled basis to keep the car in top operating condition, but the day-to-day focus of driving is how to get from point A to point B, rather than how to keep the car running.

The challenge for the valuation expert is to keep the value creation engine running smoothly, so that executives and managers throughout the organization can focus on moving the business forward. The Value Equation provides a particularly effective framework for meeting this challenge, providing a mechanism that effectively links operating performance to value creation. Implemented properly, it provides executives with a powerful tool to measure progress in creating shareholder value, while keeping their attention focused on *running the business*. And that's the way to empower managers for long-term value creation.

NOTE

1. The author wishes to thank Ativo Capital Management LLC (Ricardo Bekin, chief investment officer, and Ram Gopal Gandikota, senior financial analyst) for their assistance and insights in preparing this paper.

REFERENCES

Buffett, W. 1996. Chairman's letter, Berkshire Hathaway annual report.

Haspeslagh, P., T. Noda, and F. Boulos. 2001. Managing for value: It's not just about the numbers. *Harvard Business Review* (July-August).

Hass, W., and S. Pryor. 2006. *Building value through strategy, risk assessment, and renewal*. Chicago, IL: CCH, Inc.

Jensen, M. 2001. Corporate budgeting is broken—Let's fix it. *Harvard Business Review* (November).

Littman, J. and M. Frigo."When Strategy and Value Meet," *Strategic Finance* (August 2004).

Madden, B. 1999. *CFROI Valuation—A total system approach to valuing the firm*. Woburn, MA: Butterworth-Heinemann.

CHAPTER 11

The LifeCycle Returns Valuation System

Rawley Thomas
President, LifeCycle Returns, Inc.

Robert J. Atra
Chair of the Finance Department, Lewis University

"It's simple," exclaimed an academic at a recent conference. "The value of a firm is the present value of the firm's cash flows." Practitioners, however, understand that valuing a firm is anything but simple. Though most would agree with the soundness of valuing a firm by a discounted cash flow (DCF) methodology, the details of the process become a source of much debate. Consider, for instance, the issue of computing *what* cash flows to discount. Ask a dozen valuation experts what the firm's future cash flows are and those experts will likely reveal a dozen different answers.

This chapter presents an overview of the LifeCycle Returns system for computing valuations. We say "system" for several reasons. First, *system* refers to the process by which a builder develops and improves a model. We do not expound on that process since Chapter 3 presents that procedure in detail.

Second, *system* also refers to the way LifeCycle considers theory and practice to interact.[1] Traditionally, theories are developed and then tested. When theories fail empirically, theoreticians develop substitute theories and the testing process begins once again. LifeCycle's research system treats observations of actual data as the starting point of the system, not the initiation of an untested theory. Once the model builder observes a phenomenon, the builder initiates a pragmatic solution while offering consistently sound economic explanations. For example, we observed that models employing traditional theory could not value start-ups effectively. Consequently, we developed a special fade function for start-ups to solve the problem. Option theory provided both the economic explanation and the adjusted fade function to produce more accurate valuations for start-ups. This chapter illustrates that fade function later.

Finally, *system* refers to the reality that valuation becomes just a part of a process that begins with information and ends with decisions by investment or corporate professionals. We portray that process as follows:

Accounting information → Economic returns → Intrinsic values → Decisions

Each part of the process represents a critical element of the LifeCycle valuation system. Though the following sections sequentially present the concepts in the arrow diagram, the modeling process does not follow a strictly linear path. As the model builder compares intrinsic values to actual market prices for accuracy, the builder revises the model. Excellent models can always be improved. Encouraging models to learn from their own output forms a core philosophy of the LifeCycle valuation system. We begin where most analysts must start—by restating the accounting statements to what, we think, represents the true economic performance of the firm.

CONVERTING ACCOUNTING INFORMATION TO ECONOMIC RETURNS

Accounting information → Economic returns → **Intrinsic values → Decisions**

Ultimately, the value of any asset derives from the economic returns of that asset. An analyst first forecasts the cash flows and then discounts those flows at an appropriate discount rate to produce a value for the asset. For example, assume a firm considers purchasing a machine to fabricate a product. Once it is purchased at a known initial cost, the firm expects the machine to produce less certain positive cash flows over a finite life. A diagram representing those cash flows appears in Exhibit 11.1. Note that the down arrow represents a cash outflow and the up arrows represent cash inflows. A typical capital budgeting analysis nets the present value of the inflows against the cash outflow, resulting in a net present value (NPV). Traditionally, if the NPV exceeds zero, the firm funds the project. Alternatively, the analysis can rely on an internal rate of return (IRR) where a rate is found that will equate the present value of the cash inflows and the cash outflow. The company then compares the IRR to its cost of capital and decides whether to accept the project, accepting the project if the IRR is at least as great as the cost of capital.

Analysts should follow a similar approach when valuing a firm. Of course, the plot thickens when valuing a firm, since, unlike the machine, the

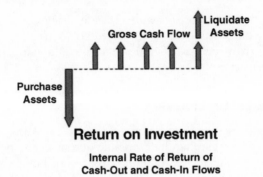

Return on Investment

Internal Rate of Return of
Cash-Out and Cash-In Flows

EXHIBIT 11.1   Corporate Investment

firm does not necessarily have a finite life. One way an analyst can handle the complication of a firm with an infinite life is to assume that the firm is a string of projects, whereby the firm purchases new machines when the old machines wear out—a process that could go on perpetually. Valuing the string of projects is not so simple, though. If a machine is valuable, other firms are likely to enter the market by purchasing similar machines. Competition for the equipment will cause firms to invest larger initial outlays in the replacement machines. Furthermore, the cash inflows produced by the replacement machines are likely to decrease as firms reduce prices to gain market share. In other words, returns from the replacement machines will tend to *fade* due to competition—an issue we address in detail later.

Another complication that analysts encounter when valuing firms is that firms do not operate a single string of projects but simultaneously manage many projects. Exhibit 11.2 represents the cash flows from several projects. The firm now becomes a nexus of cash flows as it invests in,

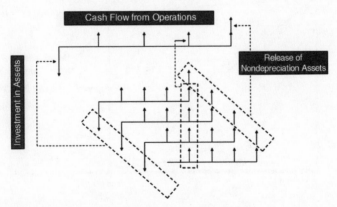

EXHIBIT 11.2   The firm's cash flows from several projects

operates, and terminates projects with a release of nonoperating assets such as working capital. Despite the complicated set of arrows in the diagram, analysts armed with such specific information could value the firm as if it were a single project.

The Economic Output of Assets

Given that an analyst can value a firm as if it were a project, what is a reasonable assumption regarding the economic output of the project? We believe that assets produce a nearly level output until failure, instead of the output implied by the straight-line or declining balance depreciation, as in Exhibit 11.3. For example, if a person's car achieved 25 miles per gallon the first year, 20 the second, 15 the third, 10 the fourth, and 5 the fifth, or if the transmission worked perfectly the first year but only 20 percent of the time by the fifth year, then one would likely seek another car manufacturer who produced reliable vehicles until the end of their useful economic life.[2] The consumer expects some modest increase in maintenance expenses, but most assets produce high output levels throughout their lives. In fact, well-designed assets incorporate systems that are designed to fail simultaneously, so one is not overdesigned relative to the others. If one major system fails, it is logical to say, "Now is the time to trade in the car to avoid the other major systems failing."

Exhibit 11.3 displays four output curves to illustrate the principles just discussed. The top line shows constant output or a constant dollar level annuity until the asset reaches its economic life, when failure causes that

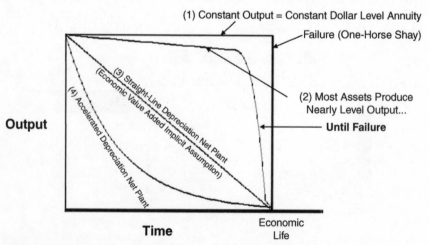

EXHIBIT 11.3 Output from assets under different assumptions

output to fall immediately to zero, as in the classic one-horse shay example. The second line down from the top displays the high output for most assets until failure at the end of their economic lives. The third line, a diagonal from the upper left to the lower right, exhibits the net plant under straight-line depreciation. Economic value added (EVA) models implicitly assume this line of output, unless they adjust each asset's depreciation schedule from the one reported. The fourth line, curved from the upper left to the lower right, reveals the net plant under declining-balance accelerated depreciation. Of course, not all assets produce constant output, equivalent to a constant dollar level annuity; however, their output line (2) more closely resembles line (1) than the depreciated net plant line (3). Therefore, the constant output assumption is closer to reality than the depreciated net plant output assumption.

Little research exists on output curves, although an abundance of research on optimum asset replacement policy appears in the literature.[3] As mentioned before, substantially complicating the analysis is competitive reaction. Most new assets produce higher output and have less down time than older assets. Some face declining prices. The relevant issue is how much of the higher output, less down time, and lower prices flow through to investors and how much flows through to customers in the form of lower prices and margins from competitive pressures.

For example, consider the output curves of personal computers. Consistent with the previous example, the output produced by the PC remains constant as it ages. Despite increased capacity and speed with lower prices, no one purchases a new computer each month. Even computers have a design life, reflecting the amortization of their costs with benefits given the usage application and over which output is reasonably stable. Some purchase new computers every 12 to 18 months, if speed and capacity are critical. The rest make do with replacements every three to five years.

Future research will likely investigate asset output, lives, and competitive price reaction, as the importance of this field and data becomes more obvious and relevant to economic performance measurement. Of particular importance will be how these principles apply to capitalizing expenses associated with creating intellectual intangible property—software, customer acquisition, employee training, advertising, and R&D—all critical to the proper economic performance measurement in service industries. *All* businesses follow this fundamental cash-out, cash-in project pattern with a finite life of the depreciating or amortizable assets. The challenge is identifying the fundamental underlying projects and properly accounting for them so measuring cash economic returns becomes possible. As business continues the shift from hard assets to intangible assets in a more service-oriented economy, the more important solutions to these measurement issues will become.

Unfortunately for practitioners, companies generally do not provide information for specific projects, only for the firm overall. Therefore, the challenge presented to the analyst is how best to convert information provided by the financial statements into cash flows as if they arose from the underlying projects. In terms of our system approach, this is the idea of converting accounting information to economic returns.

Accounting statements provide information, not valuation. Accounting academics have known for many years that annual accounting rates of return—return on equity (ROE), return on net assets (RONA), return on capital employed (ROCE), and return on assets (ROA)—do not reflect the economic or internal rate of return of necessary for the valuation of the underlying projects. Ezra Solomon (1966), Gerald Salamon (1982), and Richard Brief (1986) wrote some of the classic articles on the problem of relating economic to accounting returns. The difference between the accounting returns and economic returns relates to the pattern of cash flows within the project, the depreciation method, the growth rate of the projects, the project life, and inflation, making the problem almost insolvable. But, if one can make the simplifying assumption that most assets produce constant output and follow a constant dollar level annuity, one can create an annual performance measure—gross cash flow return on gross assets with a finite life—which precisely equals the economic or internal rate of return of all the underlying projects. Then one need only apply Ijiri's (1980) insight on the proper method for accounting for inflation: simply to translate all cash flows from the income statement and balance sheet into units of the same constant dollar purchasing power. This appropriate treatment relates to investors' objectives to receive a return for their investment, all expressed in the same purchasing units. The type of assets or their replacement cost matters little to investor rate of return objectives.

To illustrate these principles, consider a project consisting of a depreciating asset costing $10,000, which produces cash flows of $1,740 for eight years with no salvage value. This project produces an internal rate of return (IRR) of 8 percent. Assume for the moment no inflation. Exhibit 11.4 displays the project and the accounting for each year. The income is constant, but the net plant declines from $8,750 in year 1 to zero in year 8. The return on net assets (RONA = Net income ÷ Net plant) begins at 5.71 percent in year 1, rises to 40 percent in year 7, and becomes infinite in year 8. Only in year 3 does the RONA precisely equal the 8 percent IRR economic rate of return, known for the project. With inflation, the RONA bias becomes worse, as cash flows tend to rise with the price level, while the historical dollar net plant declines with depreciation accounting.

The annual performance measure, the cash economic return (CER), explained in detail in the following section, precisely equals the 8 percent

EXHIBIT 11.4 Annual Performance Measure of Project

	Year							
	1	2	3	4	5	6	7	8
Income	$ 500	$ 500	$ 500	$ 500	$ 500	$ 500	$ 500	$ 500
Depreciation	1,250	1,250	1,250	1,250	1,250	1,250	1,250	1,250
Gross Cash Flow	1,750	1,750	1,750	1,750	1,750	1,750	1,750	1,750
Gross Plant	10,000	10,000	10,000	10,000	10,000	10,000	10,000	10,000
Accumulated Depreciation	1,250	2,500	3,750	5,000	6,250	7,500	8,750	10,000
Net Plant	$8,750	$7,500	$6,250	$5,000	$3,750	$2,500	$1,250	$ 0
Return on Net Assets (RONA) = Income/Net Plant	5.71%	6.67%	8.00%	10.00%	13.33%	20.00%	40.00%	∞
Cash Economic Return (CER)	8.00%	8.00%	8.00%	8.00%	8.00%	8.00%	8.00%	8.00%
Difference	−2.29%	−1.33%	0.00%	2.00%	5.33%	12.00%	32.00%	∞
Return on Gross Assets	17.50%	17.50%	17.50%	17.50%	17.50%	17.50%	17.50%	17.50%

economic return each and every year, because it relates the gross cash flow to the gross assets over the eight-year life as an IRR calculation. Another simplified annual performance measure, return on gross assets (ROGA = Gross cash flow ÷ Gross plant) remains constant at 17.5 percent and avoids the upward bias of RONA.

Any performance measure that relies on an accounting return of net income divided by net assets after depreciation suffers from the same biases. Only where output declines with depreciated net plant does the annual RONA approximate the project IRR.[4]

It is possible that new projects counterbalance old projects, so RONAs average out. While true directionally, this hypothesis is not supported by client work or empirical work with company financial statements. In the late 1980s, unpublished research by Rawley Thomas sought to quantify how frequently the accounting returns provided the wrong strategic direction for the company compared to the economic returns. The answer was 30 percent. Thirty percent of the time, accounting RONAs exceeded their cost of capital hurdle while the economic returns fell below the investor's required real returns or vice versa.

Examples of the failure to address the material differences between accounting returns and cash economic returns (CERs) abound in academic research studies. For instance, some observed level to declining returns on assets during the 1990s. Actually, economic returns increased significantly during the 1990s because of declining inflation and more noncash charges for amortization of goodwill. The increase in economic returns helps to explain superior stock price performance; the nominal accounting returns do not. Most academic researchers should pay much closer attention to the material differences between CERs and accounting returns. Insights on market performance arise from understanding these differences in depth; however, these insights are not available from calculating simple accounting returns.

The following paragraphs describe corporate planning applications. Referring to case B in Exhibit 11.5, ponder the chemical company, under investor pressure, that sold its new plants because they showed the lowest returns on net assets, while retaining the older, inefficient plants with higher RONAs. Or consider the tire company, case A, whose strategic plan showed increasing RONAs barely reaching the cost of capital as the company let its plants age, while the economic returns remained substantially underwater. A management group, who realized complacency was not an option, acquired the tire company in an unfriendly takeover. Dramatic restructuring would be required.

Examine case C in the diagram, where the credit operation was acquired for its very high returns and then starved by the board of directors because its low RONAs, including goodwill, were not making the cost of

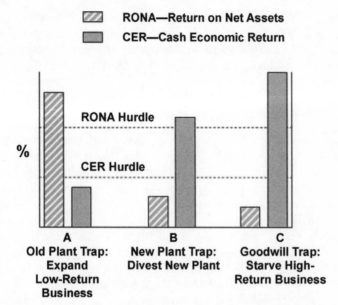

EXHIBIT 11.5   Accounting Return Measures Encourage Poor Decisions

capital. Accounting for goodwill in performance measurement is a controversial subject. Many include goodwill in the asset base, as this company did, in order to penalize the unit for the price paid. In contrast, the new theory would treat goodwill as a valuation item, not a performance one. It would exclude goodwill from the gross cash investment base to calculate the economic returns *on the operations*, so the acquirer could feed it more sensible market extension investment to justify the purchase price paid. Then the firm would value the business, demanding that the increase in value exceed the purchase price paid plus new investment. The new theory would not let low RONAs including goodwill discourage new investment.

Exhibit 11.5 illustrates how accounting measures encourage poor decisions, because the nominal RONA suggests one strategy, while the economic return suggests precisely the opposite.

The previous discussion and chart covered corporate planning applications. Following are some portfolio investment examples in narrative form. Consider the mature paper company with rising earnings per share (EPS). Traditional approaches would treat this firm as a buy candidate. However, the company's investment in assets is rising faster than EPS—its cash economic return is falling. It should be sold.

In contrast, consider the low-P/E timber firm that appears to be a bargain purchase. However, if the cash economic return is less than the cost of capital and management is growing the assets, it should be sold.

Last, reflect on the aerospace company with level EPS, whose stock investors normally avoid. Nevertheless, if the management is restructuring the asset base by eliminating unprofitable operations and the cash economic return is rising, the company should be a buy candidate.

Computing a Cash Economic Return

As demonstrated in the preceding paragraphs, accounting information may not always provide an accurate picture of the economic condition of a firm. The problem is not just a theoretical one. The examples show how both corporate and investment managers could make erroneous decisions based on the accounting information alone.

Traditionally, analysts adjust the information from the financial statements to better reflect the economics of the firm. This is the first step toward deriving a value. We cannot provide here an exhaustive set of adjustments used by LifeCycle, but will present a nice sample along with some economic intuition. The key to understanding the adjustments used by LifeCycle is that we are attempting to create a "cash on cash" or cash economic return (CER) from the financial statement information. As with cash flows generated by projects, the return on an investment in a company can be computed as cash flows returned to the firm (gross cash flow) divided by the capital investment in the firm (gross investment). We now turn to a particular example of the computation of CER.

Exhibit 11.6 displays the details of the cash economic return for Super-Valu, a major grocery store chain, in 2001.[5] The method transforms the $206 million of income and $5,825 million of assets into $781 million of gross cash flow and $5,704 million of gross cash investment, all expressed in the same units of investor purchasing power—2001 current dollars. Details on the computations follow:

A: To income, LifeCycle Returns adds $33 million in extraordinary items after tax and subtracts $16 million in nonoperating expenses. To assets, LifeCycle subtracts $137 million of nonoperating assets and $1,531 million of purchase goodwill. These two adjustments focus the results on the operations.

B: Noncash charges of $333 million in the numerator consist of depreciation, amortization, and changes to the allowance for doubtful accounts. In turn, adding back reserves for receivables, LIFO (inventory), and accumulated depreciation—$23 million, $141 million, and $1,580 million respectively—returns to the original investor cash investment in the denominator assets.

C: To reflect inflation and restate all historical dollars to 2001 dollars, LifeCycle computes a $14 million gain on nonfixed assets in the numerator (GDP deflator change × nonfixed assets—payables and other nondebt liabilities for SuperValu exceed assets of receivables, operating cash, inventories, and other assets) and a $249 million adjustment to land, gross plant, and deferred taxes to the denominator. Using the plant life and age enables approximate restatement of historical cost for plant to 2001 dollars without knowing internal company records.[6] When tested against internal company records from selected clients, the algorithm is accurate within 5 to 10 percent, unless capital expenditures have been extremely large in the past one to two years.

D: Capitalizing $1,202 million of operating leases in the denominator and adding back $134 million of after-tax interest on debt and leases along with the $77 million principal portion of rental payments to the numerator make the measure independent of financial leverage.

E: If SuperValu disclosed advertising and research and development (R&D), those elements would be capitalized in the denominator, while adding back the after-corporate-tax effect in the numerator.

F: Last, LifeCycle subtracts $1,648 million of non-interest-bearing liabilities, in order to effectively reconcile to the cash investment made by all the equity holders, debt holders, and landlords.

The ratio of $781 million gross cash flow to $5,704 million is not yet a proper return measure, because it erroneously assumes the assets will last forever. To reflect the finite life of depreciating assets, LifeCycle transforms the CER into a project 9.09 percent internal rate of return (IRR) format, according to Exhibit 11.7. The $5,704 million down arrow reflects the current-dollar investor gross cash investment expressed in 2001 dollars. The 11.55 years up arrows of $781 million reflect the current-dollar annual gross cash flow available to all the investors and to the business for reinvestment.

Life equals a weighted average of the operating leased asset life of 15 years and the plant life from gross plant/depreciation. Of all the estimates, plant life merits the greatest scrutiny in client assignments to ensure it reflects the economic life over which the assets produce cash flows until failure and to ensure the proper fixed asset inflation adjustment.

The capability to relate annual performance measures derived from accounting data to capital budgeting project internal rates of return represents an extremely powerful way of monitoring firm economic performance. This capability enables comparison of economic performance across

EXHIBIT 11.6 Cash Economic Return Example: Accounting to Cash—SuperValu, 2001 ($ Millions)

		Income
		$206
$206 Income	A: Eliminate Nonoperating Items	
	Special Extraordinary Items After Tax	33
	(−) Non-operating Expense After Tax	(16)
	B: Translate to Cash	
	Noncash Charges	333
	C: Restate for Inflation	
	Inflation Gain on Nonfixed Assets	14
	D: Eliminate Leverage	
	After-Tax Interest (Debtand Operating Leases)	134
	Rentals—Principal Payments	77
	E: Capitalize Expenses	
	(−) Advertising and R&D After Tax	(0)
		$781 Current-Dollar Gross Cash Flow

Assets $5,825	A: Eliminate Nonoperating Items	
	Total Assets	$9,825
	(−) Nonoperating Assets	(137)
	(−) Purchase Goodwill	(1,531)
	B: Translate to Cash Invest.	
	Receivables Reserve	23
	LIFO Reserve	141
	Accumulated Depreciation	1,580
	C: Restate for Inflation	
	Inflation Adjustments to Land, Gross Plant, and Deferred Taxes	249
	D: Eliminate Leverage	
	Gross Leased Property from Operating Leases	1,202
	E: Capitalize Expenses	
	Capitalized Advertising, R&D	0
	F: Capital Owner Cash Invest.	
	(−) Operating Non-Interest-Bearing Liabilities	(1,648)
		Current-Dollar Investor Gross Cash Investment **$5,704**

Source: Raw data from Standard & Poor's Compustat; inflation adjustments from LifeCycle Returns, Inc.

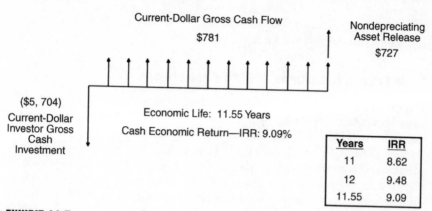

Current-Dollar Gross Cash Flow

$781

Nondepreciating
Asset Release

$727

($5, 704)
Current-Dollar
Investor Gross
Cash
Investment

Economic Life: 11.55 Years

Cash Economic Return—IRR: 9.09%

Years	IRR
11	8.62
12	9.48
11.55	9.09

EXHIBIT 11.7 Cash Economic Return Example: Cash to Economics—SuperValu, 2001 ($ Millions)

firms through time, without the cash distortions arising from accounting conventions, depreciation, purchase goodwill, or varying inflation. Is it perfect? No. Is it much better than other performance measures, such as accounting returns or EPS growth? Yes.

The CER represents a practical method for translating accounting information to economic real internal rates of return with imperfect, noisy data. Critics who take issue with the constant dollar level annuity assumption bear the responsibility, if not the obligation, to propose a better, practical alternative applicable to real-world company data, which is equally correct theoretically.

CONVERTING ECONOMIC RETURNS TO INTRINSIC VALUES

Accounting information → Economic returns → Intrinsic values → Decisions

Once LifeCycle converts accounting information to an economically meaningful form, the next step is to convert the CER to an intrinsic value for the firm of interest. Two key elements play a role in converting the CER to an intrinsic value. The first is how the cash economic returns appear on the time line as cash flows. Recall that the value of a firm is the present value of *all* the cash flows received in the future by that firm. Critical to the valuation process is the timing of the expected cash flows and their duration, since, theoretically, the firm *may* live forever but also attempts to survive a competitive environment. The second key element is the rate used to discount the cash flows. We address timing of the cash flows first and the discount rate computation later.

From Economic Returns to Firm Cash Flows

Intuitively, the cash flows a company is able to generate are a function of its asset base and the rate of return on those assets. In LifeCycle terms, a company will produce cash flows consistent with its gross assets and its CER. In forecasting CERs and asset growth, one thing is certain—neither is immune from competition. Competition will cause firms to decrease prices, thus reducing CERs. Competition will also cause market saturation, trimming asset growth in attractive industries. The manner in which LifeCycle factors in competitive effects is a process called fade. Academics often describe a very similar concept: regression toward the mean.

Research confirms that CERs and asset growth rates regress over time toward the mean of all companies. Exactly how the CER and asset growth rates fade is an empirical question. LifeCycle recomputes fade parameters each year so that 50 percent of the firms in the universe are overvalued and 50 percent are undervalued. Exhibit 11.8 shows fade patterns representative of those that appear in the LifeCycle model for CERs.

A couple of key points stand out in the exhibit. First, our research reveals that fade patterns differ by firm size. Larger firms, whose CERs tend to fall in a narrower band, have less extreme adjustments, while smaller firms experience greater adjustments as their extreme returns move toward the average for all companies. Second, firms currently earning low returns should actually expect their returns to fade *up*; that is, the poor returns will not persist forever. A peculiar case is the small firm that has a low return.

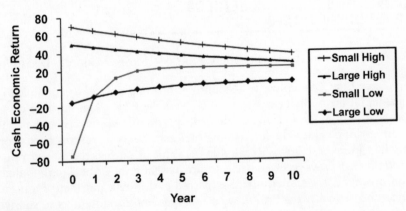

EXHIBIT 11.8   Fade Patterns

EXHIBIT 11.9 Fade Procedure for Asset growth

Year	Future Growth Rate	Constant Dollar Gross Investment
2004	5.67%	21,779
2005	3.54%	22,549
Increase		770

Small start-up firms are an exception in that the market prices those firms as though the average survivors will achieve superior returns above the average. Effectively, investors purchasing small start-ups are buying an option on economic performance, where the initial public offering (IPO) cash invested in operating assets is the premium.

The numerical example in Exhibit 11.9 illustrates an example of a fade procedure used for both asset growth and CER. Assume a firm in 2004 employs constant dollar gross investment of $21.779 billion. Furthermore, assume the firm's sustainable growth rate is 5.67 percent. LifeCycle computes the sustainable growth rate using a proprietary model that factors in historical data on asset size, capital expenditures, and dividend payments. Fading the growth rate toward the 3 percent economy growth rate at an assumed 80 percent rate results in a 3.54 percent growth rate for the following year. The calculation is as follows: $(5.67\% - 3.00\%) \times .80 + 3.00\% = 3.54\%$.

The calculated growth rate applies each year to the expected growth in assets to determine the required amount of new annual asset investment and the resultant total gross investment. Therefore, by applying the 3.54 percent asset growth rate in 2005, the model anticipates that the $21.779 billion 2004 investment will grow to $22.549 billion in 2005. The growth rate results in new asset investment of $770. The fading of asset growth continues in the LifeCycle model for 50 years, at which point the remaining assets wind down and are not replaced. The life of a firm, therefore, in the Life-Cycle model is 50 years plus the life of the assets at that time—firms do not continue into perpetuity.

The second fade adjustment made by the model is to the CER. Assume the company achieves a CER of 20.17 percent in 2004. Also, assume the model fades the CER *toward*, but not all the way to, the universe average of 8 percent at a 50 percent rate. Instead, assume this particular firm fades to a rate of 12.57 percent.[7] The computation of the CER for 2005 is: $(20.17\% - 12.57\%) \times .50 + 12.57\% = 16.56\%$. The faded CER results in a constant dollar gross cash flow of $5,977 for 2005, demonstrated in Exhibit 11.10.

To arrive at constant dollar net free cash flow—the cash flow available to investors—we need to deduct replacement investments and growth investments as shown in Exhibit 11.11.

EXHIBIT 11.10 Fade Procedure for Cash Economic Return

Year	Constant Dollar Gross Investment	Cash Economic Return	Constant Dollar Gross Cash Flow
2004	$21,779	20.17%	$6,462
2005	$22,549	16.56%	$5,977

EXHIBIT 11.11 Constant Dollar Net Free Cash Flow

Gross cash flow	+$5,977
Replacement investments	−$1,973
Growth investments	−$ 770
Constant dollar net free cash flow	+$3,234

The model repeats this procedure for each year in the future, assuming a life for the firm of 50 years plus the life of the assets in place at the time. The present values of the 50+ years of cash flows determine the firm's intrinsic value.

The Market Derived Discount Rate

Financial theory dictates that the value of an asset is the present value of the cash flows discounted at an appropriate rate. Traditionally, valuation books suggest a weighted average discount rate based on the capital asset pricing model (CAPM) for equity and an after-tax cost of debt. The weighted average cost of capital (WACC) represents the appropriate discount rate to use to discount cash flows available to the entire firm. Equity values result by subtracting the value of the debt from the total firm value.

Although elegant, using the CAPM presents theoretical and practical problems. We will focus here on the practical issues and address the theoretical problems of the CAPM in this chapter's appendix. The CAPM accounts for risk, for example, via its use of the systematic risk measure beta. Computing beta, however, presents a valuation conundrum for the analyst. The primary practical problem facing the use of beta as a risk measure is a timing problem—the analyst must estimate beta based on *historical* data, while the discount rate determines the present value of *future* cash flows. The beta computed from historical data may not be consistent with the risk of future cash flows.

Another CAPM problem arises when estimating the market risk premium. Most estimates from historical data have relied on Ibbotson data of 1926 to the present.[8] The geometric mean of large company returns less long-term government securities from 1926 to 2007 was 4.90 percent and 6.70 percent over Treasury bills. Large company returns over long-term government securities over the past 20 years averaged 2.54 percent while over the past 10 years they averaged −1.35 percent. The run-up in stock prices during the 1990s caused the *measured* equity risk premium to increase, while, in contrast, financial theory suggests prices increase with declining costs of capital. The theory's application appears inconsistent.

Contrast these *historical* equity risk premium numbers generally in the 5 to 7 percent range with those *forward*-looking ones derived recently from dividend discount models, which lie in the 2 to 3 percent range. The premiums derived from dividend discount models generally rely on finding the equity discount rate that equates the price to the present value of a perpetual stream of dividends, growing at various growth rates to reflect recent trends.[9]

It behooves analysts to find a forward-looking discount rate that captures investors' required rates of returns given the current investment environment. Actually, forward-looking rates are common. Take, for example, the WACC discussed earlier. Practitioners almost universally determine a cost of debt by estimating a yield to maturity on the company's current debt, where the yield to maturity is the discount rate that equates the future cash flows from the debt to its current price. In other words, yields to maturity are forward-looking discount rates.

Can one compute costs of equity similarly? Peruse a corporate finance text and it generally makes several suggestions to compute a cost of equity (discount rate). For example, Brigham and Houston (2007) present three approaches to estimating the cost of equity: (1) CAPM, (2) dividend discount model (DDM), and (3) bond yield plus a premium. The DDM approach takes the familiar Gordon constant growth model of $P_0 = D_1/(k_e - g)$ and solves for the cost of equity, $k_e = D_1/P_0 + g$. The bond yield plus a premium approach adds a premium of 3 to 5 percent to the yield to maturity of the bonds of the firm. The constant growth approach uses *future* dividends and growth rates, and the bond yield approach uses *future* bond cash flows. Indeed, two of the three methods suggested are forward-looking discount rates!

As with the DDM approach and bond yield approach, we consider a forward-looking discount rate the appropriate way to determine the discount rate. The DDM approach, however, is limited since many firms pay either no dividends or arbitrarily low dividends. Furthermore, dividends are only flows to equity. Instead, LifeCycle uses cash flows estimated from the earlier section as the first step in determining the discount rate. As previously explained, the model computes cash flows to firms from the CER, asset base, and fade patterns. Once LifeCycle estimates cash flows for all firms in the universe, the model iteratively selects a discount rate to equate the present value of cash flows to the current values of debt and equity. Critics may claim that the discount rate procedure just described is circular. Those critics would be correct if the model computed a separate discount rate in this fashion for each company in every year. The model, however, uses a single discount rate for all companies after appropriately adjusting for risk, which is the topic we turn to next.

Bart Madden, author of Chapter 3, once offered a keen insight on valuation models. Traditionalists place risk dimensions in the denominator discount rate of present value calculations, but more insights arise from placing those same effects in the model's numerator cash flow descriptions. For example, yield to maturity measures on bonds assume investors receive all the cash interest and principal payments. They do not—some bonds default. A model including 1 minus the probability of default times the interest and principal payments would enable the comparison of the *realized* yield between bonds of differing credit quality. Similarly for stocks, some models assume no default. A more insightful model, however, would incorporate the probability of dropout from acquisition or bankruptcy and the capital released at the dropout date. The no-default models would have to incorporate equity risk premiums for leverage, but the more complete dropout models would not. LifeCycle Returns' research process places more and more of the traditional risk effects into the cash flow model, so the costs of capital remain within a very narrow range across companies. Tests of successful refinements require reduced errors between actual prices and DCF model values. Tests also require reduced ranges of costs of capital between companies and industries.

In contrast to the research process just described with one unified model, many would prefer separate parameters for each industry. Adding additional degrees of freedom can increase *apparent* accuracy, but often at the expense of conceptual soundness. Ijiri (1980) had this insight: Investors should not focus on what assets (or markets) the corporation invests in, only the gross investor cash outlays and gross cash flows generated, all expressed in the same units of purchasing power.[10] The industry should not make any difference to the investor, unless the *distribution* of potential returns is fundamentally different from other industries.

Definitely following differing fundamental distributions are the three sectors: financial firms, unregulated firms, and regulated firms (utilities, telephones, railroads, and to a lesser extent oils and autos). Regulation tends to narrow the economic rate of return distribution of companies. Consequently, we treat the three sectors of financials, regulated utilities, and unregulated firms fundamentally differently—with different cash economic return distributions and different market derived discount rates applied to the cash flows. Adjusting the structure of the valuation model is preferable to treating industries within the unregulated sector differently from each other.

Our empirical work suggests several adjustments to the *cash flows* in order to employ a uniform discount rate each year. The most salient adjustments are based upon CER levels and the amount of leverage a firm uses. CER levels (and hence the risk they imply) are accounted for by the fade procedure in the earlier section. The less transparent leverage adjustment requires additional explanation.

This risk of a firm clearly increases with the amount of debt used. However, relevant questions remain—what is the best way to measure debt usage, and what is the precise effect on firm value? Our measure of a firm's debt usage is the percentage of debt to debt capacity. We compute debt capacity as the present value of cash flows from existing assets. Clearly, this approach is superior to simply measuring debt as a percentage of book value of assets, which does not reflect the ability of firms that generate high cash flows to incur additional debt. The approach also avoids the inaccuracies of book value.

Exhibit 11.12 demonstrates the effect of debt on firm intrinsic value. We have found that debt effects differ by firm size. Therefore, we divide the universe into the smallest, midsize, and largest firms. The shapes of the lines in the exhibit reveal core insights into how debt impacts intrinsic value in the LifeCycle model. For the smallest firms, the impact of any debt becomes immediate—as the firm adds debt, a loss of enterprise value occurs. For largest firms, increased debt usage correlates with decreases in intrinsic value, but only after the firm crosses an empirically derived debt threshold. Medium-sized firms are a weighted average of the smallest and largest firms, using constant dollar gross investment as the weight.

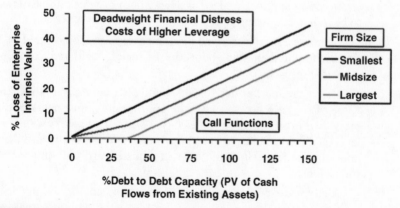

EXHIBIT 11.12   Effect of Debt on Intrinsic Value

In summary, LifeCycle bridges the gap between price matching intrinsic value and accounting information in a structured, empirically supported system. Starting with adjustments to balance sheet and income statement accounts to reflect cash economics, the LifeCycle model computes an expected cash economic return on the firm's assets. Because our philosophy assumes that "competition does not wait," both CERs and asset growth rates fade toward sector averages depending on whether the firm is in the financial sector, a regulated sector, or an unregulated sector. The combination of CERs and expected gross assets produces expected cash flows, which the model discounts at a uniform rate for each sector to present value, resulting in an enterprise value. The equity intrinsic value results from deducting debt and adding net nonoperating assets to the present value of the cash flows. In practice, the model does not stop with the computation of intrinsic value. LifeCycle continually updates both the structures and the information contained in the models to improve their performance. Chapter 5 describes the process we follow for analyzing and improving the models. In that sense, the model never rests. The following list summarizes LifeCycle's entire process of converting accounting information to intrinsic values.

Step 1: Adjust accounting information to treat the firm as a series of projects.

Step 2: Place gross cash flows on a time line for the expected life of assets, including a cash flow expected from the release of nonoperating assets at the end of time line.

Step 3: Compute a cash economic return by finding the internal rate of return for the time line.

Step 4: Create expected cash flows for the firm by taking the product of cash economic return and gross assets, both of which are assumed to be fading toward economy-wide averages.

Step 5: Compute a market derived discount rate from the expected cash flows computed in step 4 for the financial, regulated, and unregulated sectors.

Step 6: Using the market derived discount rate, compute the present value of the cash flows, and make appropriate adjustments to the individual firms' intrinsic values based on the risk analysis, such as leverage. To the adjusted enterprise value, add nonoperating assets and subtract debt. The result is a risk-adjusted intrinsic equity value for each firm.

Step 7: Analyze the performance of the model by comparing intrinsic values to actual market prices. Repeat the process, making adjustments to both the model structure and its parameterization as necessary to improve its accuracy.

CONVERTING INTRINSIC VALUES TO INVESTMENT DECISIONS

Accounting information → **Economic returns** → Intrinsic values → Decisions

To many practitioners, intrinsic values represent the beginning, not the end of a process. Security analysts, portfolio managers, corporate executives, and regulators, among others, can benefit from the information provided by the intrinsic values produced from LifeCycle models. This section focuses on how investment professionals and corporate managers can use the results in their decisions. Investment professionals may find that investing in securities where the price is lower than intrinsic value will produce that often-elusive combination of lower risk and higher returns. Corporate managers may use the models to better understand the true underlying value drivers of their stock, irrespective of the noise that clouds the information in market prices.

Exhibit 11.13 illustrates one of the most powerful tools in the LifeCycle valuation system—value charts. Value Line introduced value charts in the 1930s to display the capitalization of its cash flow model. Later, Callard, Madden and Associates (CMA) employed the value chart to demonstrate

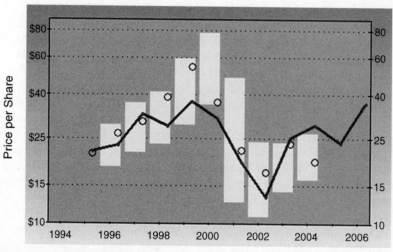

EXHIBIT 11.13 Value Chart Example

its model's results. Subsequently, HOLT Planning, HOLT Value, the Boston Consulting Group, and others illustrated their models with value charts. In 2001, we began using value charts to illustrate the results of multiple models.

The value chart represented in Exhibit 11.13 incorporates bars representing the trading range for fiscal year prices, small circles representing the closing price at the end of the fiscal year plus three months (allowing for a disclosure lag), and a solid line connecting the intrinsic values determined by the valuation model. The value chart serves two core purposes. First, the chart represents a convenient visual way to determine the relative position of prices to the intrinsic value. Analysts can easily determine the under- or overvaluation of the security and how the relative positions behaved over time. Consider, for instance, the example in Exhibit 11.13. In the early years of the chart, the actual prices and intrinsic values remain relatively close, suggesting that the market fairly valued the stock. In the middle years, the price rises substantially above the intrinsic value, indicating the stock became overvalued. Supporting this overvaluation signal is that the intrinsic value tracks not only below the current stock price but also at the low end of the trading range. In later years, both the stock and intrinsic values begin to drop, though the market valuation appears generally fair. In the final year, once again the price and intrinsic value diverge, but this time the value chart indicates an undervaluation, portending future stock price increases.

The second core purpose of the value chart is to examine the effectiveness of the model itself—or even compare the effectiveness of several models, as LifeCycle does. Let's assume the value chart indicates that the price remains consistently very distant from the intrinsic value for a particular security. Under- or overvaluation signals from that model for that security may be suspect, since the model appears to lack accuracy in tracking the actual price. While one would never expect a model to perfectly track all market prices, a model that produces intrinsic values that are never close to the actual price is most likely facing serious trouble valuing that particular security. Exhibit 11.14 demonstrates the use of a value chart to compare multiple valuation models. In the exhibit, the LifeCycle (LCRT) model produces intrinsic values much closer to actual market prices than the other two models, one based on a simple rule of eight times EBITDA and another based on net free cash flow. Both non-LifeCycle models consistently underestimate the market price, suggesting that they are misspecified and therefore would not likely lead to accurate, wealth-producing decisions.[11]

A model that consistently under- or overvalues firms in the universe is biased. Dividend discount models, for example, tend to produce intrinsic values that are consistently too low when using typical assumptions about discount rates. LifeCycle continually examines its intrinsic values to ensure

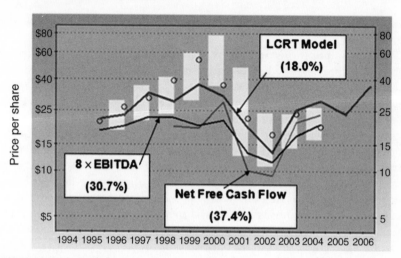

EXHIBIT 11.14 Value Chart with Three Models

they are, on average,[12] unbiased and accurate. A most important analyst role, however, addresses situations where the automated model fails to track prices well in order to investigate why the breakdown occurs.

In contrast to security analysts, portfolio managers seek to select *combinations* of securities to produce the best risk/return trade-off. Life-Cycle back-tests the model's predictive ability by ranking the securities according to their under-/overvaluation in order to construct decile portfolios. Portfolio managers expect the top decile (most undervalued) to outperform the bottom decile (most overvalued) if the model is functioning properly. Though the back-test is no guarantee of future performance, Exhibit 11.15 presents a sample. In this sample, the model works well, as

EXHIBIT 11.15 Sample Back-Test: Undervalued Stocks, Overvalued Stocks, and S&P 500

undervalued stocks greatly outperform the overvalued stocks as well as the S&P 500.

Two complications arise in examining portfolios constructed from a model's intrinsic values. First, some of the most under- or overvalued firms may not possess sufficient trading liquidity to enter a portfolio. Portfolio managers should filter out illiquid firms prior to back-testing. In this example, we included only firms with greater than $1 billion market capitalization and prices greater than $10 per share. Second, since no model is perfect, some of the model under- or overvaluations may result from model error instead of market mispricing. To avoid securities where the model may not perform well, LifeCycle filters out securities where the firm's tracking error is high. Tracking error is the absolute percentage value of the difference between the intrinsic value and the stock price. On average, if that tracking error exceeds 40 percent, the model is not performing well enough to include those securities in the back-test.

For investment analysts and portfolio managers who would like to peek under the hood, LifeCycle also examines the key value drivers for any firm, the CER and asset growth rates. Utilizing Hewlett-Packard as an example, Exhibit 11.16 presents key information on exactly *why* a firm's intrinsic value may be increasing or decreasing. The top chart in the exhibit compares Hewlett-Packard's CER with the market derived discount rate discussed earlier. The CER exceeds the discount rate for the entire period—

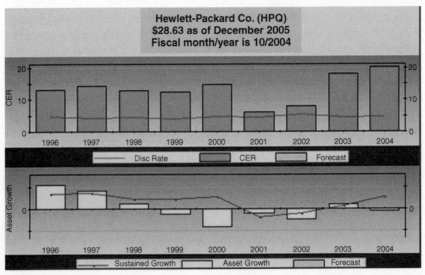

EXHIBIT 11.16   Economic Drivers: Hewlett-Packard Co. CER and Asset Growth

substantially so in the later years. Will the excess of the CER above the discount rate lead to a substantial increase in intrinsic value? Not necessarily, as the bottom of the exhibit reveals. Since cash flows are a product of the CER and asset base, we must consider the growth in assets as well. In this case, the asset base is growing far below what the firm could sustain and therefore restrains increases in intrinsic value. The firm is finding profitable product niches, but fewer than the number supportable from its sustainable cash flow.

Exhibit 11.16 presents the economic drivers of the intrinsic values computed by the model. We can easily see that the intrinsic values for Hewlett-Packard respond significantly to the jump in CER in 2003. Furthermore, though the asset growth rate is small, there was a substantial change from 2002 to 2003, rising from a negative rate to a small positive one. Now examine the data in 2003 and 2004. Hewlett-Packard experienced an even stronger CER in 2004, yet the intrinsic value rose only slightly. Why? Once again, the asset growth did not justify a large increase in intrinsic value as the rate dropped back to approximately zero in 2004. Despite the flattening of the intrinsic values during that 2003–2004 period, the market still undervalued the stock, according to the LifeCycle model. (That undervaluation quickly evaporated, though, as the stock steadily rose in 2005 and 2006.) The example demonstrates how effective charts, such as the value chart and economic driver chart, complete a model. They provide the user with easy-to-access information on pricing and economic performance.

Despite the fact that the LifeCycle platform is fully automated, the system encourages analyst input. In fact, an analyst with superior insight substantially improves the predictive results through an override procedure. For example, assume the analyst correctly believes that the firm will experience above-average sales due to a new product introduction. The LifeCycle model encourages the analyst to override the automated computations with this forecasted data. The analyst's short-term insight should lead to a more accurate intrinsic value than one estimated purely from the automated process based purely on historical data. In our opinion, though, certain areas of the model should remain off limits to the analyst. Extensive empirical analysis, for example, underlies the fade procedure built into the model. The analyst is not likely to add much value in that fade area of the model. Other areas, such as incorporating information from the footnote data, may prove much more fertile ground for analysts. Also, recall that the LifeCycle model—or any other model—cannot value every security accurately. Those securities not tracking well, such as heavily leveraged firms or those in financial distress, may provide the greatest opportunity for analyst intervention and subsequent superior risk/return portfolio performance.

Understanding their firm's economic performance and the resulting intrinsic values should appeal to corporate managers as well. While an investment manager may want to peek under the hood, the corporate manager *lives* under the hood. Investors expect their agent corporate managers to pull the correct levers to maximize shareholder value in the long run. These valuation models now provide a laboratory in which the manager can examine the impact of corporate investment and operating decisions on the firm's intrinsic value. What is the likely impact on stock value from a reduction in accounts receivable? What effect will an increase in leverage have on firm value? A well-functioning, empirically validated, automated model should assist the manager in answering those questions instantly.

A valuation model can also provide additional benefits to corporate managers on compensation issues. Stock-related compensation helps cure one of the stickiest problems associated with the corporate form of business ownership, the agency problem. Stock compensation based on a noisy (and possibly manipulated) stock price produces the primary difficulty. An accurate model offers an alternative to the noisy stock price in the form of an intrinsic value. Compensation tied to the economic drivers of a model's valuation encourages managers to pull the right levers to increase shareholder value since they directly benefit from their actions with higher compensation. To accomplish shareholder value creation, however, requires empirical validation of theoretically sound models and deep manager understanding of the strategic economic drivers of those models.

Of course, the *actual* change in stock price, not the change in intrinsic value, compensates shareholders, so examining whether a model has *explanatory* power in addition to *predictive* capability becomes critical. The difference between those two concepts relates to timing. Predictive capability implies that the model's calculations of under- and overvaluation forecast changes in future stock prices. Explanatory power means that the model's intrinsic values correlate with movements in current stock prices. In other words, if a manager takes an action that increases intrinsic value, on average that action should also increase stock price. Without that correlation, the use of a valuation model for compensation purposes remains dubious.

Determining compensation from a complete analysis of valuation models extends beyond the scope of this chapter. Our brief discussion here, however, highlights the role of the valuation model as an integral part of a *system* as opposed to simply producing valuations as a product or manual process. The LifeCycle valuation system processes accounting information in a mathematically rigorous and empirically supported program to provide tools for managers—from Wall Street investment firms to corporate boardrooms, all the way down to the shop floor—to make better decisions.

SUMMARY

This chapter presented an introduction to the LifeCycle Returns valuation system. We refer to it as a system as opposed to simply a model, since it provides a comprehensive, automated way to:

- Translate data from accounting statements into economic returns.
- Compute an intrinsic value based on those economic returns and extensively empirically validate the intrinsic values against actual stock prices.
- Present the information to decision makers in simple charts and graphs that are easy to digest.

The LifeCycle Research platform also possesses a systems mind-set, whereby it observes valuation phenomena to develop solutions that professionals can pragmatically implement in a robust fashion—that is, one applicable to a wide variety of securities within the universe.

The LifeCycle system employs publicly available financial data to create economically sound adjustments to avoid much of the distortions inherent in financial statements. The financial data converts to a cash economic return—a return similar in concept to an internal rate of return on a project. Then the model forecasts that return and the associated cash flows for the life of the company. Companies naturally face competitive pressures. To reflect competition, LifeCycle uses its proprietary computations of fade, which trend both the cash economic return and asset growth toward economy averages. The fade process is not arbitrary, but rather an empirically researched method designed to ensure that the model, on average, produces valuations consistent with actual market prices in an unbiased way.

LifeCycle employs a market derived discount rate to determine the present value of cash flows produced by the model. The LifeCycle system iteratively determines the uniform market derived discount rate across sectors by equating cash flows produced by the model to current prices. The system adjusts individual securities' values for risk, such as leverage, by modifying the expected cash flows instead of the discount rate.

Analysts and portfolio managers utilize the intrinsic values in security selection and portfolio construction. Based on its evidence that market prices tend to migrate toward intrinsic values, under- and overvaluations signaled by the LifeCycle model present an opportunity to reduce risk while increasing return. Value-based corporate managers can incorporate the model into an analysis of the economic drivers impacting their shareholders' value. In addition, targeting intrinsic values for executive compensation avoids the serious problems of noisy prices when measuring how much value managers actually added.

An estimate of value can come from conjecture or be derived from empirical analysis. Our philosophy represents an approach to determine value in an empirical and structured way. We hope the chapter provided insights into the process of LifeCycle's system. Though not simple, the automated system produces intrinsic values on thousands of securities at the touch of a ticker symbol. In addition, it provides numerous tools for decision makers to whom the concept of value proves critical.

APPENDIX: MARKET DERIVED DISCOUNT RATES AND CAPM BETA COSTS OF CAPITAL

All discounted cash flow (DCF) models require a discount rate or cost of capital to discount the cash flows to present value. Determining the best rate to use, however, can be challenging, in part because the issue is fairly complex and in part because competing theories exist on how best to deal with these complexities. Two theories in use are the well-known capital asset pricing model (CAPM) and the much less known market derived discount rates.

All knowledgeable finance professionals know that a CAPM total cost of capital arises from a weighted average of debt and equity. The nominal equity rate derives from multiplying a beta times an equity risk premium and adding a risk-free rate.

While at Callard, Madden (CMA) in the early 1980s, author Thomas first experienced the benefits of replacing a CAPM cost of total capital with a market derived discount rate. The market derived discount rate applies to *both* stock valuation and corporate finance for capital projects. It also extends to business unit valuation in value-based strategic planning applications.

All CMA offshoots chose the road less traveled between CAPM and market derived discount rates. All chose a market derived discount rate[13] because we wanted the rate to be derived from the cash flow model itself, using a system mind-set to assure internally consistent assumptions. Although it is less frequently employed, the finance and investment professions do use market derived discount rates. For one example, market derived discount rates represent the only method commonly accepted for calculating yields to maturity on bonds from the price, the coupon cash flows, and the principal repayments. For a second example, some finance professionals reverse the Gordon dividend discount model to calculate a market derived cost of equity: Price = Dividend/(Equity discount rate − Growth rate), so Equity discount rate = Dividend/Price + Growth. Utility rate-making cases often use this reversal approach to estimate the required rate of return.

We found zero *empirical* correlations between market derived equity rates from the cash flow models and CAPM betas. Zero! The accompanying Atra-Thomas Chapter 5 *empirically* found a beta of 1 produced more accurate and more predictive dividend discount rate models than traditional betas. Consequently, incorporating non-1 actual betas added noise to both the models' accuracy for price level and their predictive capability for future price change. (Refer to Chapter 5.)

With these two strong empirical results, a system mind-set and sound theory testing require reevaluating the assumptions of these two choices for discounting.

A market derived discount rate assumes:

- A methodology based on price *level*, not price *change*.
- A structure of a discounted cash flow model equating price to the present value of cash flows.
- Risks may be incorporated into either the discount rate or the cash flows. For one example, the discount rate may measure the price effect of financial leverage risk. For another example, the cash flow model specification may capture the risk of competitive fade of the firm's operating returns on capital employed toward a corporate average.

From our perspective, a CAPM beta cost of capital relies on six assumptions—either explicitly or implicitly. Following are those six assumptions and our observations on each. Unfortunately, marrying CAPM beta discount rates with automated discounted cash flow models—both dividend discount models and Callard, Madden offshoot enterprise DCF models based on constant dollar real cash flows—produces less accurate and less predictive results than market derived discount rates. These empirical failures to explain actual price levels caused us to question the assumptions underlying the CAPM beta cost of capital by building on the shoulders of non-CAPM giants in the profession.

CAPM Assumptions

1. *A methodology based on price change, not price level.* In simple practitioner terms, although CAPM theoretically looks forward, its estimates traditionally rely on backward data to calculate risk measures based on price *change*. In contrast, market derived discount rates look forward to calculate risk measures based on price *levels*, not price changes.

2. *Investors seek to avoid stock price variability relative to market varia-bility.* Thaler (1987) and others suggest loss aversion as more appropri-ate than variability aversion.

3. *A risk-free rate exists to form one anchor.* Since even Treasury index-linked bonds vary in price and can therefore lose money in the short term, no risk-free asset exists in real terms. Recall that Treasury bills lost 18 to 20 percent of their purchasing power in 1946–1947 with the unexpected inflation resulting from relaxing price controls after World War II. Consequently, T-bills were not a risk-free asset.

4. *A portfolio of assets exists to form the other anchor,* so the capital mar-ket line can be drawn between the two (Sharpe 1970). Richard Roll (1977) questions the existence of the market portfolio to form the other anchor to the risk-free asset in the CAPM.

5. *Investors are indifferent between the loss and gain tails of the price dis-tribution,* as implied by the variance statistic. Variance treats both tails of the price change distribution as equally undesirable. Markowitz him-self (1959) recognized that this assumption may not reflect investor behavior.

6. *Firm stock price changes follow lognormal distributions with finite var-iances,* so co-variances with the market can be calculated with confi-dence. Mandelbrot and Hudson (2004), McCulloch (1986), and Thomas (2006) all demonstrated that price changes follow stable Pare-tian distributions with infinite variances, so the statistical measurements assumed in the CAPM fail to exist.

Cracks in CAPM began to appear after publication of Fama and French's 1992 paper.

For our own continuing empirical research and personal portfolio in-vestments, we choose to marry market derived discount rates with the cash flows instead of CAPM-based discount rates, in order to assure a systems mind-set of internal consistency between the price level and the cash flows. This marriage with market derived discount rates creates more accurate and predictive DCF models. Consequently, these models prove more useful to portfolio manager clients of all Callard, Madden's offshoots for stock selection decisions than employing CAPM beta. For consistency, these dis-count rates should also apply to corporate capital projects and business unit valuations.

NOTES

1. We owe this insight to Bart Madden, who presents the concept in Chapter 3.

2. See Oliver Wendell Holmes's poem, "The Deacon's Masterpiece or, the Wonderful 'One-Hoss Shay': A Logical Story" (Holmes 1895). The "one-hoss shay" was designed to last precisely a hundred years to the day, on which day it fell apart to dust.

3. A classic is Terborgh (1958).

4. Using beginning-of-year assets eliminates this RONA/IRR difference.

5. Source: Raw data from Standard & Poor's Compustat; inflation adjustments from LifeCycle Returns, Inc.

6. Lewis, Stelter, Casata, and Reiter (1994).

7. Although the exact computation of the 12.57 percent is beyond the scope of this section, recall from Exhibit 11.8 that the fade patterns indicate that high-CER firms fade, but they fade to a higher than average level. Low-CER firms may fade to a lower than average level of CER.

8. Ibbotson Associates (2008). For a longer time horizon, see Siegel (1992).

9. Arnott and Bernstein (2002), Fama and French (2002), and Lawson (2002). The last article employs the dividend discount model and surveys of portfolio managers and chief investment officers.

10. Ijiri (1980).

11. The numbers in parentheses in the exhibit represent the models' tracking error—a statistical measure for how well the model is performing. Models with lower tracking errors produce better results, as discussed in Chapter 5.

12. By "on average" we mean 50 percent of the firms are undervalued and 50 percent are overvalued. That is, the median firm is valued correctly by the market.

13. This market derived discount rate is a weighted average cost of debt and equity, since the valuation is based on the enterprise, not the equity. Consequently, the market derived rate may be decomposed into its debt and equity components, unlike the CAPM, which provides only the cost of equity component for the cost of capital.

REFERENCES

Arnott, R., and P. Bernstein. 2002. What risk premium is "normal"? *Financial Analysts Journal* (March/April): 64–84.

Brief, Richard P. 1986. *Estimating the economic rate of return from accounting data*, New York and London, Garland Publishing, Inc.

Brigham, E., and J. Houston. 2007. *Fundamentals of financial management*. 11th ed. Mason, OH: Thomson-Southwestern, 335–340.

Fama, E., and K. French. 1992. The cross section of expected returns. *Journal of Finance* 43: 153–194.

Fama, E., and K. French. 2002. The equity premium. *Journal of Finance* (April): 637–659.

Holmes, O. 1895. *The complete poetical works of Oliver Wendell Holmes*. Boston: Houghton Mifflin. http://rpo.library.utoronto.ca/poem/1028.html.

Ibbotson Associates. 2008. *2008 Ibbotson stocks, bonds, bills, and inflation classic yearbook*. Chicago, IL: Morningstar.

Ijiri, Y. 1980. Recovery rate and cash flow accounting. *Financial Executive* (March): 54–60.

Lawson, S. 2002. *The equity risk premium: It's lower than you think. Goldman Sachs CEO Confidential* 14 (November).

Lewis, T., D. Stelter, T. Casata, and M. Reiter. 1994. *Steigerung des unternehamenswertes (Total value management)*. Landsberg am Lech, Germany: Verlag Moderne Industrie, 244–247.

Mandelbrot, B., and R. Hudson. 2004. *The (mis)behavior of markets: A fractal view of risk, ruin, and reward*. New York: Basic Books.

Markowitz, H. 1959. *Portfolio selection: Efficient diversification of investments*. New Haven, CT: Cowles Foundation, 94.

McCulloch, J. 1986. *Simple consistent estimators of stable distribution parameters. Communications in Statistics Simulation and Computation* 15(4): 1109–1136.

Roll, R. 1977. A critique of the asset pricing theory's tests. Part 1: On past and potential testability of the theory. *Journal of Financial Economics* 4: 129–176.

Salamon, Gerald L. 1982. Cash recovery rates and measures of firm profitability, *The Accounting Review*, April, 292–302.

Soloman, Ezra 1966. *Return on investment: the relation of book yield to true yield, research in accounting measurement, American Accounting Association*, 232–244.

Sharpe, W. 1970. *Portfolio theory and capital markets*. New York: McGraw-Hill, 83.

Siegel, J. 1992. The equity premium: Stock and bond returns since 1802. *Financial Analysts Journal* (January-February): 28–46.

Terborgh, G. 1958. *Business investment policy: A MAPI study and manual*. Washington, DC: Machinery and Allied Products Institute and Council for Technological Investment. 1958.

Thaler, R. 1987. The psychology of choice and the assumptions of economics. In *Laboratory Experimentation in Economics: Six Points of View*, ed. Alvin Roth, 99–130, especially 106. New York: Cambridge University Press.

Thomas, R. 2006. Advanced DCF valuation measurement methodology: Predictive capability, accuracy, and robustness. Presented at the Midwest Finance Association Annual Meeting. www.LCRT.com. Slides 33–36.

CHAPTER 12

Morningstar's Approach to Equity Analysis and Security Valuation

Pat Dorsey
Director of Equity Research, Morningstar

At Morningstar, we take an unusual perspective toward equity analysis, relative to much of the industry. Instead of setting price targets and guessing what others might pay for a stock 12 months hence, we forecast cash flows and value businesses. In fact, our estimates of intrinsic value are the anchor for the five-star rating system we use for equities. If a company's share price is roughly in line with our estimate of its intrinsic value, the stock receives a three-star rating—essentially a "neutral" or "hold." When share prices diverge markedly from our estimates of intrinsic value, our ratings become more bullish or bearish.

We focus on intrinsic—rather than relative—valuation because it centers our thinking on the business that we are analyzing, as opposed to the market's current opinion of that business. We use a discounted cash flow (DCF) approach to arrive at our intrinsic value estimates because it allows us to separate economic reality from accounting-based noise. Also, we believe that shareholder value creation is a more complex process than simply increasing earnings per share, and a cash flow–based approach lets us unpack concepts like growth, investment, and returns on capital.

By modeling the relationships between these three concepts, DCF allows our analysts to better understand the value drivers for the companies that we cover. We can quickly isolate the variables most likely to have a large impact on a company's intrinsic value, in addition to gaining insight on the effect of corporate capital allocation. If, for example, slower growth and less internal reinvestment would actually increase shareholder value, a DCF model will reveal this fact more clearly than an earnings-based model.

We use a standardized DCF model at Morningstar, which has a number of advantages relative to using individually customized models. It ensures consistency across our analyst staff, which means we're always treating various line items and calculations in the same way. Having a standardized model also gives our analyst staff a common language, which makes internal debate more efficient as we are able to discuss what matters—our cash flow assumptions—rather than wasting time understanding the vagaries of individualized models. Finally, standardized models make it relatively easy to roll up our data by sector or industry, which allows us to ensure that our bottom-up forecasts make sense in the aggregate.

Of course, our models are standardized only to a certain extent, since it would be silly to attempt to forecast sales for a retailer in the same way that you would forecast sales for a large pharmaceutical firm. So, our analysts build company-specific front-end models to help them forecast sales and margins, and then link the output to our standardized model. Essentially, it's as if all of our analysts drive cars with V-6 engines, but the cars may look quite different from the outside. We think this process gives the best balance of company-specific flexibility and across-the-board consistency.

Intrinsic value is the first pillar of our investment approach. The second is margin of safety—we always look for a material discount from our intrinsic value estimates before we recommend a security, as an insurance policy against being wrong. The size of that discount varies depending on how confident we are in the accuracy of our cash flow forecasts, since it's much easier to bound the intrinsic value of some companies than others. The greater the spread of likely future outcomes, the larger the margin of safety we demand before recommending a stock.

We try to think about the valuation of companies as points along a continuum of possible outcomes, rather than as definitive point estimates. So, we employ scenario analysis as a way of gauging how large a margin of safety we should attach to the companies that we follow. If we can plausibly envision scenarios in which a company could be worth one-half or two times our base case scenario, we'd look for a reasonably large discount to our intrinsic value estimate before recommending the shares. (Imagine a small biotech company, or a levered auto-parts company.) By contrast, if the range of reasonably likely outcomes is fairly narrow, we can have some degree of confidence that investors purchasing the shares at even a modest discount are likely to have a good expected return.

The third concept around which we organize our research is competitive analysis. In any reasonably unregulated capitalist economy, capital seeks the area of highest prospective return, which forces down above-average returns on invested capital over time. Our valuation framework explicitly assumes that firms with high return on invested capital (ROIC) eventually revert to their cost of capital. We think this assumption is critical to disciplined valuation—trees don't grow to the sky, and the natural human tendency is to extrapolate recent trends too far into the future. Good valuation requires a framework that is strict enough to rein in the potentially overly enthusiastic analyst, but flexible enough to encompass a wide variety of companies.

Of course, it's an empirical fact that some firms post supranormal ROICs for very short periods of time before returning to terra firma, while others manage to maintain high returns on capital for many decades. But which is which? We think that we can add a lot of value to the analytical process by prospectively sorting companies into groups based on their economic moat or competitive advantage.

We divide our coverage universe into three groups—wide moat, narrow moat, and no moat—depending on our assessment of the strength of the company's competitive advantage. Exhibit 12.1 shows some summary statistics from our coverage universe. As you can see, we think that companies with very strong competitive advantages—wide economic moats—are quite rare, accounting for less than 10 percent of our coverage universe. We think this is consistent with both the lessons of economic history and the assumption of excess returns regressing to the mean over time.

In our view, the wider a company's economic moat—that is, the stronger its competitive advantage—the longer it will be able to keep competitors at bay and post high returns on capital. And if returns on capital regress to cost of capital at a slower pace, a company has the potential to create more economic value for shareholders over time.

Given that moat analysis is central to how we value companies and is also the most unique aspect of our valuation process at Morningstar, we'll first dig further into that topic. We'll then circle back to the details of how and why we use discounted cash flow analysis at Morningstar—and when we think DCF is less useful than alternative valuation techniques. Finally, we'll discuss how we attempt to systematically incorporate uncertainty and

EXHIBIT 12.1 Economic Moats in Morningstar's Coverage Universe

Type of Moat	Number Covered	As % of Total Coverage	Average ROIC	Median ROIC
None	1,116	52%	9%	9%
Narrow	835	39%	18%	13%
Wide	183	9%	27%	19%

scenario analysis into our margin of safety process, and then conclude with some lessons that we've learned from several years of applying DCF analysis in a real-world setting.

APPLYING ECONOMIC MOATS TO SECURITY VALUATION

We think that identifying economic moats is an important part of the analytical process for several reasons, chief among them the simple fact that moats add intrinsic value. After all, a company that has a high likelihood of generating returns above its cost of capital for many years will create more economic value in the future than a company that has a high likelihood of short-lived excess returns.

Schematically, this is shown in Exhibit 12.2, which places time on the x-axis and return on invested capital on the y-axis. Here, we assume three companies with equal starting ROICs, but with different levels of competitive advantage. ROIC declines linearly in all three examples, but does so over a longer time frame for the wide-moat business than for the no-moat business. A slower rate of decline leads to a higher level of economic value creation, which is represented by the areas of the three triangles.

When comparing two businesses with similar growth rates, returns on capital, and reinvestment needs, the business with the moat should have a higher intrinsic value. From an investment perspective, this has two important implications: First, underestimating a moat can result in opportunity cost, because the investor will assume a shorter competitive advantage period than actually comes to pass, and may not estimate an intrinsic value high enough to make the security appear attractively priced. After all, if excess returns are likely to persist, and a business can reinvest capital at a high rate of return for a substantial period of time, what looks expensive may actually be quite a bargain.

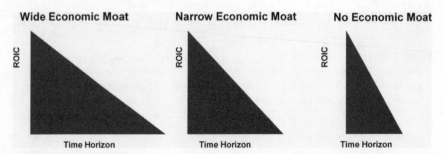

EXHIBIT 12.2   Schematic Illustration of the Value Created by Economic Moats

Bob Goldfarb, co-manager of the famed Sequoia Fund, summarized this concept nicely at the 2004 Sequoia shareholder meeting: "Time is the friend of the wonderful business, affording it the opportunity to reinvest capital at favorable rates and increase the value of the enterprise. Over time, the price you paid for a terrific company looks cheaper and cheaper. For the inferior business at the cheap price, time may turn out to be the fell destroyer."

The second important implication of the notion that moats add intrinsic value is that overestimating a moat can result in capital loss or investment underperformance, since the investor pays up for sustained value creation that fails to materialize. Given that moats add value only over time, while investors can become overexcited about securities for all kinds of transient reasons—such as a hot product or a celebrity CEO—we can see how thinking about economic moats can be valuable by enforcing investment discipline.

After all, high returns on capital will always be competed away eventually, and for most companies—and their investors—the regression to the mean is fast and painful. Economic moats give us a systematic framework for thinking about which businesses have a reasonable probability of sustaining high returns, and which do not.

Finding Moats

Morningstar's process for identifying economic moats is both qualitative and quantitative. We begin with a strong belief that sustainable competitive advantage should be demonstrated in excess returns on capital—to paraphrase Jerry Maguire, "Show us the money." Corporate managers may tell a good story about a company's strong market share, well-regarded brand name, or superior strategy, but we take these blandishments with a large grain of salt if there is not accompanying financial evidence.

Yet even businesses that have posted high returns on capital in the past do not necessarily have a moat. A hot product may enable a company to generate substantial returns on capital for a time, but such sudden popularity is rarely enduring—as investors in one-hit wonders from Iomega to Krispy Kreme to Crocs all discovered to their chagrin.

So, what is a moat? In our view, an economic moat is a structural business characteristic that allows a firm to generate excess economic returns for an extended period of time. Moats must be structural because the basic economics of businesses do not tend to change quickly, so we can more confidently forecast sustained excess returns if they can be tied to some structural attribute of the business.

We're skeptical that smart managers and good strategies constitute sustainable competitive advantages, simply because we cannot predict their future with a high degree of confidence. Managers can come and go, while strategies can be implemented, tweaked, or abandoned.

Moreover, managers in structurally disadvantaged companies fight an uphill battle. Certainly, some succeed against the odds, and these cases get plenty of attention (how many books have been written about Herb Kelleher and Southwest Airlines?). But investing is all about stacking the odds in one's favor, and we believe that while it is easy to anchor on the exceptions—such as Southwest—the hard truth is that companies with economic moats and undistinguished managers are more likely to post excess returns on capital than companies with poor economics and savvy managers. As Warren Buffett has famously said, "When a management team with a reputation for brilliance meets a business with a reputation for bad economics, it is the reputation of the business that remains intact."

Make no mistake—we are not blind to the value that can be created through intelligent capital allocation by a skilled team of managers, and we fully recognize that some strategies are more likely to succeed than others. Management and strategy do matter. However, they matter less than most managers think, since some businesses are simply better (that is, more likely to post sustainable excess economic returns) than others.

We would also argue that managerial skill and strategic success are easier to recognize ex post than ex ante. Smart managers are generally lauded only in hindsight, and strategies that may work well in one competitive environment can easily fail in another. Structural advantages, by contrast, can be identified prospectively with greater confidence because they are less subject to change.

Types of Moats

At Morningstar, we categorize economic moats into four groups: intangible assets, customer switching costs, the network effect, and cost advantages.

Intangible Assets   In this group, we look specifically for brands, patents, and regulatory approvals, all of which typically confer some kind of sustainable advantage on their owners.

Brands are an interesting case study. Those that are well-known don't necessarily confer competitive advantage on their owners. Brands are valuable only if they increase a consumer's willingness to pay (think Tiffany) or if they reduce a consumer's search costs by delivering a predictable experience (think McDonald's).

Sony, for example, has a very well-known brand, but it fails both tests. Consumer electronics is a cutthroat business, and even if Sony can command a small premium over a second-tier brand such as Goldstar, that premium is not large enough to offset the company's enormous investment in maintaining its brand through extensive advertising and expensive showcase stores. Moreover, consumers do not buy electronics frequently enough to need to rely on a brand name to reduce the time they spend deciding which product to buy; instead, they compare features, consult experts such as *Consumer Reports*, and then make their purchase decision.

Now contrast Sony with Tiffany, which can charge substantially higher prices for virtually the same products as competing jewelers. Or Bayer aspirin, which is the exact same chemical formulation as other aspirins, but which costs twice as much as generic aspirin. These brands confer competitive advantage because they enable the company to charge more for a good with reasonably similar production costs, leading to higher returns on invested capital.

Brands attached to goods and services with a high frequency of consumption may not necessarily have pricing power (McDonald's does not charge more than Burger King), but they can create customer loyalty by delivering a highly consistent experience. This reduces consumer search costs, leading to habitual purchase behavior that drives sales volumes. Most people don't compare the price of Colgate and Crest when they're out of toothpaste. They simply buy the product they have previously used and enjoyed.

Brands can create powerful economic moats, but they are subject to constant threat, and need to be prudently managed if they are to last. Kraft used to dominate the market for processed cheese, but overplayed its hand on price, allowing private labels to show consumers that Kraft processed cheese didn't taste any different than store brands. Tommy Hilfiger used to charge premium prices for its preppy designer clothing, until the company flooded department stores with too much product that had to be discounted, damaging the brand's high-end image.

Patents can create obvious economic advantages—potential competitors are legally enjoined from selling identical products. However, patents have finite life spans and are frequently subject to challenge, so we think carefully about a company's entire patent portfolio before deciding whether it has an economic moat. We find that companies with a long track record of producing valuable intellectual property, and whose revenues are well diversified across many patents (3M, for example, qualifies on both counts), have stronger competitive advantages than companies that are too reliant on a small number of patents.

Regulatory approvals, like patents, can increase the scarcity of a good or service by limiting the number of companies that can provide it. These are also vulnerable to challenge, though usually through a political process rather than a legal one. However, a company with a durable regulatory approval can nonetheless often extract high economic rents.

Consider, for example, the pedestrian but profitable industries of waste hauling and aggregate production. In both cases, the key economic asset—a landfill or gravel quarry—requires municipal approval, and municipalities typically are not eager to hand out licenses for new landfills or quarries, because they reduce adjacent property values. Customers in any given area thus have fewer choices than they would otherwise, so they wind up paying higher prices.

This pricing power is enhanced by the low value-to-weight characteristics of waste and gravel. The further one has to travel to a landfill, or from a quarry, the more transport costs eat into profit margins, giving customers a strong incentive to use the closest landfill or quarry. This combination can lead to quasi-monopolies within a certain geographic radius.

Of course, regulatory approvals can be withdrawn, but the incentives are such that this is less common with regulatory approvals than with patents. Smart lawyers have incentives to challenge profitable patents, and courts can often find consumer benefits by leveling the playing field. But a municipality has little incentive to approve a new landfill close to a population center—precisely where it would be most valuable—because doing so could harm neighboring property values.

The caveat to regulatory approvals is that they're most valuable when output is regulated, via licenses, but pricing is not. Utilities, for example, must get reams of approvals to build new power plants and transmission lines, but pricing is regulated precisely to cap the economic returns available to shareholders. Monopolies are best for shareholders when they're not regulated like monopolies.

Switching Costs   The second broad category of competitive advantage that we look for when assigning economic moats is customer switching costs, which can increase pricing power. If the cost for a consumer to switch from one company's products or services to those of a competitor is greater than the benefit from doing so, odds are good that the company will be able to charge higher prices and earn excess profits.

We frequently see this type of economic moat in the software industry, which can lock in customers by requiring them to invest substantial amounts of time to become proficient in a particular program. New entrants would need to induce users to discard months or years of hard-won expertise with the incumbent platform, and then invest still more time learning the new software. This can happen, but we have found it's more the exception than the rule.

Adobe's Photoshop image-management software and Autodesk's AutoCAD computer-aided design software are perfect examples of this phenomenon. Designers and engineers are often trained on these two platforms in college, so employers would need to bear the cost of retraining and at least a temporary loss in productivity if they chose to use different software. Of course, if a new entrant offered image-management or CAD software that was tremendously better than Photoshop or AutoCAD, companies might be induced to move away from the incumbent—but the new software would need to offer benefits that compensated for the high switching costs.

A similar phenomenon can occur when the cost of switching is relatively low, but the perceived benefit from switching is even lower. Intuit's TurboTax is not terribly complicated, and it's not markedly better than competing products. Yet Intuit has maintained a high level of market share in the tax-prep software market simply because users don't see very large benefits to switching. As long as TurboTax is good enough, that's all most users need.

Switching costs are not limited to the software industry, of course. Companies that provide back-office data-processing services to financial institutions—like Fiserv, DST, and Jack Henry—often benefit from the same economic moat. Their services are so vital to the smooth operation of their customers' businesses that renewal rates of 90 percent to 95 percent are quite common, since switching to a competitor would incur known monetary and labor costs to manage the change, as well as unknown costs in the form of potential business disruption. (How do you put a price on your customers receiving accurate account statements every month?) In this industry, the challenge is not making money—data processors tend to be phenomenally profitable—but wisely allocating the resulting free cash flow.

Finally, switching costs needn't be explicit and burdensome in order to create an economic moat. The explicit cost for consumers to move their accounts from one asset manager to another is quite low; competing managers even offer to do most of the legwork for a new customer. Yet consumers routinely leave their money parked in funds that have high costs or abysmal performance.

The reason for this seemingly odd consumer behavior is that, while the cost of switching may be relatively low, the benefit of switching is highly uncertain. Maybe the new mutual fund will perform better—but maybe it won't. Moreover, selling shares in an underperforming fund and investing the proceeds elsewhere requires the consumer to admit a mistake and possibly recognize taxable gains, something most people are loath to do. So, assets in the fund industry—especially for funds that are sold through financial advisers—tend to be sticky, and high returns on capital are the industry norm.

Network Effects   The third type of economic moat we look for is in some ways a type of switching cost, but it's powerful enough that we think it merits a separate category. Network effects occur when the value of a product or service increases with the number of users, and broaching a moat based on network effects can be very difficult, making it a very robust type of competitive advantage.

Credit cards are a perfect network-effect industry. More cardholders mean more businesses are likely to be persuaded to accept the card, and higher merchant acceptance makes consumers more likely to own a card. Given these dynamics, it's not hard to understand why 85 percent of all credit card transactions in the United States pass through just four credit card networks—Visa, MasterCard, American Express, and Discover. There's little incentive for merchants or consumers to bear the additional hassle of marginal cards, so transaction volume naturally concentrates around a few networks.

To get an idea of how powerful this competitive advantage can be, imagine that a large venture capitalist offers you substantial funding to start a new credit card brand. With no consumers, how would you convince merchants to accept the card? And even if you could convince a few large merchants to accept your new card by offering them attractive pricing, how would you convince consumers to use it? Perhaps you offer below-market interest rates for a time, but what would prevent customers from dumping your card as soon as you raised rates to an economically sustainable level?

Any business that benefits consumers by providing a pool of liquidity can be a strong candidate for network effects, which is why financial exchanges tend to have economic moats. The strength of that moat, however, can vary tremendously depending on how captive the liquidity pool is to a particular network.

For example, contrast the New York Stock Exchange (NYSE) and the Chicago Mercantile Exchange. While the NYSE still has a very profitable business collecting listing fees, it makes far less from bread-and-butter equity trading than it did 20 years ago. Competitors like Archipelago created lower-cost businesses that stole volume and reduced pricing, which was possible because equities are fungible across different exchanges— there's nothing to prevent an investor from purchasing a share on exchange A and selling it on exchange B.

Futures are quite different. Since futures contracts require settlement in cash or in kind, users require a clearing agent to reduce counterparty risk; so most futures exchanges have in-house clearing operations. A futures contract must be closed on the same exchange on which it was opened, making customers captive to a particular exchange and giving the exchange much greater pricing power. Pricing, profit margins, and returns on capital for futures exchanges like the Chicago Merc are far higher than those for equity-based exchanges.

Network effects, though rare, are not limited to financial services firms, of course. Think about Adobe's Acrobat Reader software, which is installed on over 600 million PCs and has become the industry standard for creating portable documents. The more PCs that have Reader installed, the more attractive it becomes to create documents in Adobe's PDF format, because the creator has a high level of confidence that the recipient will be able to read the file. Network effects based around industry standards are certainly subject to technological disruption (getting a royalty on VHS tapes isn't much good if everyone is buying DVDs), but they can provide a strong competitive advantage nonetheless.

Cost Advantages The fourth and final group of moats we look for at Morningstar are structural cost advantages, but we think it's vital to analyze the _source_ of a company's cost advantage when assessing the durability of this competitive advantage. We sort these sources into better processes, advantageous locations, access to unique assets, and/or traditional economies of scale.

Process advantages are the least durable type of cost advantage, since rivals or new entrants are generally able to replicate a given process with time. However, this type of advantage can last longer than one might initially expect. When we analyze process-based cost advantages we consider not just the theoretical feasibility of replication, but the practical likelihood. Most incumbents are typically skeptical of radical departures from business as usual, which also slows their competitive response.

Dell and Southwest are both good examples of process-based cost advantages that enabled each company to generate high returns on invested capital for surprisingly long periods. In both cases, processes that delivered products or services at a markedly lower cost were neither secret nor patented, but competitors would have had to throw away their existing business models in order to copy them. In Dell's case, selling direct would have required other computer manufacturers to anger their largest distribution partners. Southwest's competitors faced capital costs that were prohibitively high to standardize on a single plane type, and junking the hub-and-spoke model would have risked losing lucrative international traffic.

It may be inevitable that process-based advantages will be replicated given enough time, but the competitive advantage period may last longer than one would initially suppose.

Location can also serve as the basis for a sustainable cost advantage, most commonly in commodity industries with high weight-to-value ratios, for which transportation is a large component of the final cost to the consumer. The aggregate quarries mentioned earlier, as well as cement plants, often enjoy mini-monopolies in the areas close to the facility, because a competing supplier further away simply can't overcome the higher transport costs and still be price competitive. The numbers for aggregate quarries in particular are quite powerful. Transporting a truckload of stone, sand, or gravel 10 miles from the quarry site in mid-2007 would increase the cost to the end user by 15 percent to 20 percent. If one quarry is 10 miles from a construction site and another is 20 miles away, the former has a 20 percent pricing advantage right off the bat.

Another type of cost advantage that we see mainly in commodity industries is access to a unique, world-class asset. If a company has access to natural resource deposit that is markedly cheaper to extract—located closer to low-cost transportation, or composed of a richer grade that is cheaper to refine—it can have a sustainable edge. Granted, this competitive advantage is subject to disruption if a deposit is discovered lower on the cost curve, but low-cost deposits are not discovered every day, and the high weight-to-value nature of many commodities makes transport costs a big factor.

Finally, we come to the fourth type of cost advantage—scale—which is often the most durable and the most applicable across a wide swath of industries. Manufacturing scale (spreading fixed costs across a large volume of widgets) is the type of scale that we're most familiar with from Econ 101. However, it's also the most vulnerable to a globalized economy that constantly incorporates newer, cheaper pools of labor. Size alone cannot generate excess profitability (just ask General Motors).

By contrast, scale advantages based on large or dense distribution networks can be very durable. Although the cost to establish a sizable distribution network is high, the marginal cost of delivering an extra package on that network is quite low. If an incumbent has built out a distribution system which covers its fixed costs, it's likely earning large incremental profits as volumes increase, making it very difficult for a competitor to scale up profitably. And because these advantages are geographically defined, they're less vulnerable than manufacturing scale to foreign competition.

We see this phenomenon with package delivery in the United States, which is essentially a duopoly between UPS and FedEx. In the medical waste disposal industry, Stericycle is 15 times larger than its closest competitor, giving it unrivaled route density. More stops per route leads to more profitable routes and higher overall returns on capital—in addition to the ability to underprice a potential competitor, should one emerge. In food distribution, Sysco exhibits similar characteristics, and in uniform rental, Cintas has far lower costs than its peers due to a larger delivery network.

The final type of cost advantage that we look for is single-scale efficiency, which occurs when a company dominates a market that is too small for competitors to justify the cost of competing. We see this advantage in niche providers of software solutions, such as Blackbaud, which dominates the market for fund-raising software used by nonprofit organizations. This is a relatively small market, so large competitors like Oracle or Salesforce.com pass it by, and Blackbaud is entrenched enough that a new entrant would need to incur large losses before establishing itself as a credible player. Moreover, the new entrant would then need to split a relatively small profit pool with Blackbaud, reducing its potential return on investment.

INTRINSIC VALUE

Given that legions of investors rely solely on multiple-based and comparable-company valuation to make their decisions, what is it about intrinsic value that we find useful?

To start, it's important to note that we don't view discounted cash flow analysis as a magic bullet. Poor assumptions fed into a DCF model will produce results just as inaccurate as will assigning a too-high or too-low price-earnings (P/E) ratio to an accurately estimated earnings stream. And in fact, the complexity of DCF models relative to multiple-based analysis can lead to a false sense of analytical confidence, since it is easy for analysts to conflate more detail with greater accuracy.

Why DCF?

However, we do think DCF modeling is valuable for a number of reasons. First, the end result is an intrinsic value that's not dependent on comparison with a benchmark. For example, if you know that a stock trades for $20 per share and has a P/E of 15, you're still in the dark, since that P/E means very little in a vacuum. Fifteen times earnings might be wildly expensive for a deeply cyclical steel company that can barely earn its cost of capital over a cycle, but it could be the bargain of an investing lifetime for a company with low capital needs, high returns on capital, and ample opportunities to reinvest future earnings. You need to know more about the business—or at a minimum, you need to know the multiples of comparable companies—in order to make an informed decision about valuation.

But if you know that a stock trades for $20 and its intrinsic value is estimated to be $30, you can reasonably say that the shares are undervalued, especially if that intrinsic value has been estimated using a model that incorporates factors like the value-creating potential of a high ROIC. Moreover, you've estimated the *value* of the business based on the cash it can generate, rather than estimating the potential *price* of the business based on what other market participants might pay for it. This last point is important, and underscores a key difference between DCF valuation and multiple-based valuation. DCF relies on accurately forecasting the economics of a business, while multiple-based valuation frequently relies on accurately predicting changes in market opinion.

Forecasting the economics of a business, in fact, is the second reason we use DCF. Modeling the intrinsic value of a company forces the analyst to think through the cash economics of a business—a valuable process regardless of the result.

For example, DCF allows the analyst to better appreciate the inflection points brought on by operating leverage—when an average-seeming business suddenly starts gushing cash, or vice versa. When MasterCard went public in mid-2006, it looked like a solid business, with good margins and reasonable growth prospects. However, it was also a business that should have had extremely high operating leverage, since the cost of managing a global payment-processing network is relatively fixed. Using DCF, we were able to model the effect of rapidly increasing margins, and initiate coverage with an intrinsic value roughly twice the offering price.

DCF disaggregates cash flow from generally accepted accounting principles (GAAP) earnings, and requires the practitioner to clearly understand how money flows in and out of the business to create value for shareholders. This process can be overlooked when an analyst simply forecasts year-ahead earnings per share and assigns a multiple.

We also think that DCF is valuable because it incorporates the empirical relationship between growth and return on capital. As Warren Buffett said in another context, "Growth is always a component in the calculation of value, constituting a variable whose importance can range from negligible to enormous and whose impact can be negative as well as positive." Growth is valuable *only* if a company earns a return on capital greater than its cost of capital, and it can in fact *subtract* value if ROIC is below cost of capital. Redeploying shareholder capital into a low-ROIC business to increase earnings per share is the height of economic lunacy, yet it can produce the growth so prized by Wall Street.

DCF also enables the user to perform diagnostics on the intrinsic value. Because you're forecasting full pro forma financial statements, you can analyze forward operating ratios to ensure that the revenue growth you're forecasting is actually feasible given the economics of the business. Ratio outputs allow for quick sanity checks that would be more difficult with a rough-and-ready multiple analysis.

Fourth, DCF modeling enables the analyst to reverse-engineer market expectations in a detailed fashion. We often find ourselves asking: What revenue growth or margin assumptions do we have to plug into our DCF models in order to arrive at the current market price? And do those assumptions seem reasonable? From an investment perspective, making a reasonable estimate of intrinsic value by forecasting cash flows is just one part of making an accurate stock call. Understanding the expectations implied by the current market price is also important, since it can help gauge how rational or irrational those expectations may be.

DCF modeling also facilitates scenario analysis, enabling an expected-value approach to security valuation. We'll discuss the importance of scenario analysis later in this chapter, but we think DCF is tailor-made for thinking about the future in a probabilistic fashion, since the analyst can easily change a large number of variables to see which has the largest impact on valuation.

Finally, DCF modeling provides consumers of our research—both internal and external—an easy way to see how we derive our intrinsic value estimates. This facilitates conversation with clients, for example, since the discussion can zero in on why we're making certain operating assumptions, versus spending time going over exactly what those assumptions are.

Nuts and Bolts

The mechanics of Morningstar's DCF model are conceptually quite simple, though we have bolted on a number of bells and whistles that we'll describe here. At the end of the day, we think we can add more analytical value by closely following the companies we cover, and developing greater insight into their competitive positions and ability to generate cash, than we can by developing a better DCF mousetrap.

We use a free cash flow to the firm approach because is allows us to focus on the cash flows generated by operations without the noise of capital structure movement in our analysis. We think it's simpler to subtract out debt at the end of the analysis, rather than attempting to forecast interest expense. Granted, this simplification can cause problems when a firm's capital structure is not currently at a steady state, but we can accommodate these cases by forecasting a long-run capital structure. For example, if a firm is sold to the public by a leveraged buyout firm with a large slug of debt and plans to quickly delever, we will estimate a reasonable long-run mix of debt to equity and use that in our model.

Our model has three stages: an explicit forecast period, a "moat value" period, and a perpetuity period. In the first stage, we make explicit financial forecasts for a wide variety of variables—sales, margins, working capital efficiency, capex, and so forth—typically for five years. We extend the length of the first stage if we think that a company is unlikely to reach something approaching a steady state by year 5.

For example, a company may have a very long product cycle. Boeing would be a good example of this case—the commercial aerospace cycle is typically longer than five years, and the company may carry two to three years of fairly firm backlog on its books at any given time. We'll also extend our stage 1 forecast horizon for pharmaceutical companies, for which we may need to forecast patent expirations and new drug approvals beyond year 5. Biotech firms would fall into the same category, since they may have only marginal cash flows until approval of their first product, which could be many years in the future.

Finally, if we think a fast-growing company with a large addressable market is likely to continue generating profits at supranormal rates past year 5, we'll extend our explicit forecast horizon. Chipotle would be a good current example; we think the firm has a very long runway ahead of it, and even though we project growth to slow after year 5, we think margins will continue to expand as the firm gains scale.

The second stage of our model is straightforward in some respects; for example, we assume that marginal returns on invested capital—the return of a new dollar invested in the business—converge to the company's cost of capital during this stage, consistent with the observation that high ROICs attract competition. However, we differ from some other three-stage models in one important manner, which is that we tie the length of the second stage of our model to the analyst's assessment of the company's economic moat. Wide-moat firms can defend their franchises against competitive threats, so we assume a lengthy ROIC-WACC convergence period. Firms without competitive advantages should see their high returns on capital quickly competed away, so we assume that marginal ROIC declines to WACC very soon after year 5 of our explicit forecast.

We use a variable-length second stage for a number of reasons. First and foremost, we think it reflects reality—some companies are able to maintain high returns on capital in the face of strong competition, many are not, and the distinction is usually company-specific. The second reason is that we can explicitly value the company's moat. By changing the length of the second stage from zero to, say, 20 years, we can see just how much of the company's current intrinsic value hinges on its ability to successfully maintain high returns on capital for an extended time.

There are a few main drivers to our second stage: a starting growth rate for earnings before interest (EBI), an investment rate taken from the initial forecast stage, and an incremental ROIC in the first year of the second stage. The values of these drivers can vary across our coverage universe depending on an analyst's perception of the company's growth prospects, profitability, operating leverage, and capital intensity. Exhibit 12.3 shows values for these three drivers for three industrial companies.

EXHIBIT 12.3 Second-Stage Value Drivers

	Waste Management	Landstar	Boeing
Growth of earnings before interest	5%	9%	5%
Investment rate	10%	5%	19%
Incremental ROIC	25%	130%	13%

A mature company like Waste Management may have a starting growth rate for EBI in the middle single digits, while a young, fast-growing firm like Fastenal could see a level well north of this, perhaps in the mid-teens. An asset-light firm like logistics services company Landstar, which is essentially a broker for truck cargo, would have a very low investment rate of perhaps 5 percent, while a manufacturing company like Boeing would be plowing back a much higher percentage of its EBI into investment.

During the second stage, the investment rate and marginal ROIC decline until a firm's marginal ROIC hits its real cost of capital (WACC minus inflation). At this point, we apply a standard perpetuity formula, assuming that the firm will no longer be able to invest in projects that earn a profit greater than its cost of capital. However, because the perpetuity value is essentially unknowable (how do you forecast forever with any accuracy?) we simply assume that all companies grow at 3 percent, and don't spend much time thinking about company-by-company tweaks to that value.

Our model outputs a table that summarizes the present value of each of the three stages, which is helpful for understanding the model's mechanics. You can see in Exhibits 12.4, 12.5, and 12.6 the distribution of values between stages for a variety of companies. Expeditors International is an asset-light logistics company that we think has a wide economic moat, so our second stage—during which we assume that marginal returns on capital converge to cost of capital—is quite long. As a result, the present value of cash flows from the second stage of our model accounts for a substantial proportion of the company's total estimated intrinsic value. So, if we're right about the moat, we're likely going to be at least roughly on target with our valuation.

EXHIBIT 12.4 Expeditors International

Present value of future cash flows:	
Present value of years 1 to 5	$ 875,178
Present value of years 6 through the perpetuity	$3,425,042
Present value of the perpetuity	$3,808,638
Total value	$8,109,856

EXHIBIT 12.5   Lululemon Athletica

Present value of future cash flows:	
Present value of years 1 to 10	$275,229
Present value of years 11 through the perpetuity	$ 26,538
Present value of the perpetuity	$341,671
Total value	$643,438

Contrast Expeditors with Lululemon Athletica, a young, fast-growing chain of stores that sells yoga-inspired apparel. We do not think this company possesses an economic moat, so our second stage is almost nonexistent, accounting for a very small proportion of the total value. Although we explicitly model a longer first stage than we do for Expeditors (the company is growing quickly, and has a large addressable market), we assume that growth and returns on capital decline very rapidly after the first stage. If the company does manage to pull off the rare retailing feat of creating an economic moat and generating sustainable excess economic returns, we will have undershot the valuation.

EXHIBIT 12.6   General Motors Valuation ($ Millions)

Present value of future cash flows:	
Present value of years 1 to 7	($4,641)
Present value of years 8 through the perpetuity	$ 5,547
Present value of the perpetuity	$20,565
Total value, future cash flows	**$21,472**
Balance Sheet Items:	
Excess cash and marketable securities	$25,171
Cash and equivalents	$ 5,000
Short-term debt	($ 6,047)
Total long-term debt	($36,384)
Net balance sheet impact	**($12,260)**
Value before adjusting for hidden assets/liabilities	**$9,212**
Hidden assets (liabilities)	($6,081)
Estimated market value of preferred	$0
Equity value	**$3,131**
Diluted shares	566
Equity value per share	**5.50**

Adjustments to the DCF Value

Once we have forecasted cash flows and arrived at a base intrinsic value for the business, we then adjust that value for hidden assets and liabilities, such as pensions and stock options. Although the amount of value being subtracted by options is less today than it was a few years ago (options issuance declined once companies actually had to recognize the expense), it's still a meaningful deduction to our valuation for some companies.

We start with the premise that options are a potential transfer of economic value away from existing shareholders to holders of the options. Although one can model this value loss by diluting the stake of current shareholders, we think it's more intuitive to quantify the dollar value being transferred. This approach also better matches companies' actual behavior, since most firms use cash to buy back shares in an effort to mitigate—or negate—option-driven dilution.

In valuing options, we assume that all options already issued with exercise prices below our fair value are in the money, and that the shares issued upon exercise are immediately repurchased by the company with cash. Options with strikes well above our fair value do not impact valuation, as they are unlikely to be exercised. We also adjust for the cash received by the company as proceeds from the options, the tax benefits of the grants, and a discount factor for buybacks that take place in future years.

Until recently, this was the easy part of our options adjustment; we also had to estimate the cost of options not yet granted, which was a tricky exercise given that companies did not have to expense them on the income statement. Now that options are expensed, we generally assume options are a fixed percentage of expenses going forward, and incorporate that assumption into our forecasts for sales, general & administrative costs, or cost of goods sold when we project cash flows.

Compared with stock options, our pension adjustment is relatively simple. We take the present value of all future pension payouts, and compare them with the assets set aside to pay for them. We do the same with other postemployment benefits (OPEBs) such as health care, since this liability can often dwarf the pension liability for companies with a large number of retirees and a relatively small number of active workers.

We also make adjustments for companies that lease a material portion of their operating assets to reflect the economic reality of leasing transactions. Long-term contractual leases are in many ways economically equivalent to a purchase of the underlying asset, so we want to reflect them as such to get a more accurate picture of companies' true financial health. So, we often remove the lease payments associated with these contractual arrangements from the income statement and replace them with the corresponding interest and depreciation component of rent expense that would have been created if the leased assets were financed with debt and purchased outright in the first place. This adjustment tends to boost free cash flow to the firm (FCFF) because a key component of operating expenses (rent) is now interest expense, which is not removed from the FCFF calculation. However, because the capitalized lease obligations are deducted from the firm's equity value (similar to debt), and the cost of capital is modified to reflect both the adjusted capital structure and the cost of leases, the valuation impact could vary depending on the company.

We also adjust for off-balance-sheet debt such as special purpose entities, as well as potential legal liabilities. The latter are often eye-opening, since the huge numbers thrown around by the popular press in the wake of a high-profile story (think Vioxx) are generally paid out over a lengthy time period, rather than as an immediate lump sum. When you take a reasonable estimate of potential liability, adjust it for time, and then factor in a probability that a jury will reduce the award, the actual economic impact can be surprisingly small.

For example, when the Vioxx news broke in November 2004, we estimated a total legal liability of about $15 billion. We based this estimate on Wyeth's phen-fen settlement of $375,000 per patient, multiplied by a rough number of potential Vioxx claimants, which yielded an estimate of $10 billion. We then added an additional $5 billion in possible liability to account for uncertainty, and assumed that the payments would occur in 2006–2008 after legal wrangling was completed. At the time, the present value of that $15 billion liability was only about $7.5 billion, which was the amount we deducted from our intrinsic value estimate.

We adjusted this liability estimate as new information became available regarding Food and Drug Administration (FDA) decisions and the unfolding legal picture, finally knocking it down to just $600 million in March 2008 once most claimants had signed on to a proposed settlement. It's interesting to note that although we initially overestimated the eventual legal liability, we were on target with our assumption that payments would not take place for some time after the news broke; in fact, Merck made its first payments in August 2008. Also, despite our (in hindsight) draconian liability estimates, the stock market assumed things would be even worse.

We finish out this section with an example of a company for which our cash flow–based fair value was overwhelmed by adjustments: General Motors. (Note that this example is from late summer, 2008, just before the company went off a cliff. By early November, our intrinsic value estimate for GM was less than a dollar.) You can see in Exhibit 12.6 that our first-stage DCF value is actually negative—a wonderful industry, automobiles—

and our total cash flow–based value is about $21 billion. After adding in $30 billion in cash and securities and netting out $42 billion in debt, we're left with about $9 billion in value.

That's before we adjust for hidden assets and liabilities, however—and as you can see in Exhibit 12.7, those make quite a difference. The pension plan is overfunded by about $8 billion, but the company owes far more money to retirees in the form of health care and other benefits than it has assets to pay for those benefits, which knocks over $21 billion off of enterprise value. Then we have about $3 billion in net operating losses (NOLs), about $1.5 billion attributable to the company's financing arm, and about $2 billion in cash that the company expects to receive from some asset sales. It's an interesting commentary on General Motors that estimating how many cars it will sell and for what prices is only a small part of the whole story when valuing the company.

When DCF Fails

No valuation method is perfect, of course, and there are times when we find that DCF modeling needs to be set aside in favor of other tools. We think DCF works very well in most cases, but we're aware of its limitations.

The most common reason that we turn to alternative valuation tools is when a company's survival is at risk. We've found that relying on a DCF model for these types of companies frequently results in an overestimation of the company's worth, because implicit in a DCF is the assumption of a perpetuity, which generally comprises a large chunk of the total intrinsic

EXHIBIT 12.7 General Motors' Hidden Assets and Liabilities

Pensions:	
Fair value of plan assets less projected benefit obligation	$ 8,348
Fair value of OPEB* plan assets less accumulated OPEB	($21,022)
Total pension + OPEB value	($12,674)
Other Adjustments to Enterprise Value:	
Present value of net operating losses (NOLs)	$ 3,068
49% of GMAC's book value at P/B multiple of 0.2	$ 1,525
Cash for Hummer and other asset sales	$ 2,000
Balance sheet impact	$ 6,593
Net hidden assets (liabilities)	($ 6,081)

*OPEB = Other postretirement employee benefits.

value. Needless to say, the value of perpetuity is completely moot if a company is at risk of going belly-up.

In these cases—usually brought on by a liquidity crunch—we run various scenarios focused on two questions: What are the odds that the company will survive? And what is it worth if it does? Generally, this means detailed analysis of capital ratios, debt covenants, and a look at whether parties high in the capital structure have a vested interest in survival versus failure. (As the saying goes, if you owe the bank $10,000, it's your problem; if you owe the bank $10 billion, it's the bank's problem.)

We also shift our focus from long-run to short-term operational performance. We have a long-term focus at Morningstar, and one of the things we like about DCF valuation is that it matches that focus, since we have to project several years of financial results and estimate the length of a company's competitive advantage period. But when a company's survival may be determined by its ability to generate cash or pare losses over the next several quarters, its long-term prospects become much less relevant.

We also use alternative valuation tools when a company is being broken up, or when it has placed itself on the auction block. In this case of breakups, we may not have enough financial information to perform a DCF valuation, so we'll look at industry multiples, recent transactions, and so forth. When a company has either put itself up for sale or is in play as a potential target, we will typically blend an upside scenario based on a takeout price with DCF-derived scenarios that value the company on a stand-alone basis.

There are many cases in which a company's value to an acquirer can be legitimately higher than its value as an independent firm—perhaps due to the acquirer's ability to leverage a larger distribution platform, for example—and we take this into account when estimating our upside scenario. For example, we cover a small medical device company called Insulet, which makes a novel type of insulin pump that is selling very quickly. Unfortunately, Insulet is competing with giants like Medtronic and Johnson & Johnson with vastly greater resources.

So, in valuing the company, we blend three scenarios: one based on a DCF model that assumes the company is successful as a stand-alone entity, one that assumes that the competition rolls out a better insulin pump and drives Insulet's equity value to zero, and one that assumes the company is purchased at a premium by a larger competitor. The diabetes device field has undergone a lot of recent consolidation, and buyouts are fairly common, so we're comfortable with the assumption that this is a plausible scenario.

Uncertainty and Margin of Safety

Physicist Niels Bohr once said, "Making predictions is hard, especially about the future." We're very cognizant of Bohr's words at Morningstar, and we recognize that any forward-looking estimate of intrinsic value is really better thought of as a range of possible outcomes. For this reason, we try to look at the future in a probabilistic way as much as possible.

After all, the future of any company can follow a number of different paths. In estimating an intrinsic value, we think the analyst's job is to assess which of those paths have some likelihood of occurring, assign reasonable probabilities to the least implausible scenarios, and thus reach an expected intrinsic value for the company's shares.

Practically, this means we encourage our analysts to spend time thinking about the range of possible outcomes for the companies that we value, even though the fair values we publish are, of necessity, point estimates. For example, we use scenario analysis and other tools to estimate a variety of fair values given different combinations of plausible future events.

Why do we think it's so important to consider a range of possible future fair values, rather than a single most likely fair value? Although it's very easy to think about the future in a linear fashion, in reality events rarely play out in such a neat and orderly manner. Major structural changes in an industry or a company are inherently hard to predict, but thinking about the future probabilistically allows us to at least open our minds to the possibility of outcomes that, though unlikely, can have a huge impact on fair values.

A second reason we believe it's important to think about fair values as points along a distribution of potential outcomes is that it improves the decision-making process. If you think about only a single fair value, you've anchored yourself to a particular outcome and the pathway that leads to it, which means you're likely to discount new information that doesn't support the answer to which you have already mentally committed. However, if you consider a range of possible outcomes, you essentially commit to the possibility that the future could play out in a wide variety of ways, so you're more likely to assess new information in a less biased fashion.

Our scenario analysis typically focuses on a few key value drivers that are often company-specific. For example, we cover a small company called Fuel-Tech that manufactures a product that makes coal-burning power plants much more efficient. As far as we can tell, it has minimal competition and offers a compelling return on investment to utilities that use it. However, Fuel-Tech is a small company with a limited sales force, and the purchasing decisions of utilities are often hard to forecast because they're so heavily regulated. So, our scenarios range from a low of $14 to a high of

EXHIBIT 12.8 Valuation Scenarios for Fuel-Tech

Scenario	Base	Pessimistic	Optimistic
Air Pollution Control annual growth rate	20%	8%	25%
Share of addressable U.S. coal-fired market	35%	10%	50%
Share of addressable China coal-fired market	33%	3%	50%
Share of addressable India coal-fired market	20%	3%	50%
Share of addressable EU coal-fired market	15%	2%	50%
Share of addressable Russian coal-fired market	10%	0%	50%
Total 8-year revenue CAGR	33%	14%	41%
Total 8-year EBIT CAGR	44%	20%	48%
Fair value estimate	$55	$14	$92

$92 depending on what share of various markets the company is able to get. Exhibit 12.8 shows these scenarios.

Because Fuel-Tech is such a young company, estimating its eventual market share is the best way to tackle various scenarios. For a company operating in a long-cycle market like Boeing, the key variables may be how long the current cycle lasts and what kind of cost efficiencies can be achieved. So for Boeing, we forecast sales of different key products, roll them up into an overall estimate of aircraft deliveries, and forecast cost of goods sold (COGS) as a percentage of sales. Exhibit 12.9 shows our possible scenarios for Boeing, with the current commercial aircraft cycle peaking in 2009, 2010, or 2012, depending on the level of optimism.

We believe that thinking about what could happen is just as useful as thinking simply about what is most likely to happen—or perhaps more so. This is why we believe it's very useful to embed multipath thinking in an analytical tool kit. To reflect this aspect of our research process, we have a fair value uncertainty rating on every stock that we cover, assessing each company's uncertainty as low, medium, high, very high, or extreme. In assigning the rating, we ask ourselves, "How tightly can we bound the fair value of this company? With what level of confidence can we estimate its future cash flows?" What we're essentially attempting to do is to estimate the size of the confidence interval for the values of the companies we analyze.

For example, a small biotech company with a promising drug in clinical trials could plausibly be worth anywhere from $50 (if the drug is approved and gains a reasonable amount of market share) all the way down to $2 (if things do not pan out and the company is left with nothing but the cash on its balance sheet and some interesting research ideas). Such a company would land squarely in our very high uncertainty bucket.

EXHIBIT 12.9 Valuation Scenarios for Boeing (Number of planes delivered.)

	2008	2009	2010	2011	2012	2013	2014	2015	2016	2017
Expected case, value = $84										
Commercial deliveries	475	502	523	518	498	486	481	421	391	$386
COGS, as % of sales	79.9%	81.6%	82.2%	83.9%	83.2%	83.0%	83.8%	85.0%	84.8%	84.5%
Worst case, value = $56										
Commercial deliveries	475	502	444	414	399	389	385	337	313	$309
COGS, as % of sales	79.9%	81.6%	84.7%	86.4%	85.7%	85.5%	86.3%	87.5%	87.3%	87.0%
Best case, value = $124										
Commercial deliveries	$477	$502	$549	$571	$597	$583	$577	$505	$469	$463
COGS, as % of sales	79.9%	81.6%	78.7%	80.4%	79.7%	79.5%	80.3%	81.5%	81.3%	81.0%

EXHIBIT 12.10 Valuation Scenarios for MannKind

Probability	Description		Fair Value Estimate
20%	Drug on market in 2010 with 10% peak share in 2020	On track	$12.00
40%	Drug on market in 2012, with 5% peak share in 2020	Additional studies	$ 7.00
40%	Failure	Rejected	$ 0
			$ 5.00

For example, we cover a small biotechnology company called Mann-Kind that is developing a form of insulin that can be inhaled, rather than injected. This could potentially be a blockbuster product, but the high-profile failure of a competing product early in 2008 could also cause physicians to be wary of recommending it without data from further studies, which would be both expensive and time-consuming for MannKind. Or, despite the promising data that has been released so far, the company's application for approval could simply be rejected by the FDA. It should come as no surprise, then, that the company could be worth anywhere from zero to $12 per share, as you can see in Exhibit 12.10.

At the other end of the spectrum, consider a company like McCormick, which dominates the spice and seasoning industry. The spice market neither grows nor shrinks very much over time, and McCormick's strong brands give it pricing power that no competitor can match. Unless Americans suddenly shift their tastes en masse to desire much more heavily flavored or much blander food, there's not a very wide range of plausible outcomes for the fair value, so McCormick would get a low uncertainty rating.

Of course, precisely quantifying uncertainty is an almost oxymoronically difficult process. So what we do is try to look at a standardized set of factors, all of which affect the dispersion of possible fair values.

For example, we estimate the likely range of sales for a company. Some businesses—such as grocery stores or consumer product companies—have fairly predictable sales, while many others have revenue lines that can swing around quite a bit. A closely related step is thinking about a company's operating leverage. What percentage of each incremental dollar of sales becomes income? The key to this question is often the mix of variables relative to fixed costs at a company.

We also take financial leverage into account, because high levels of debt can amplify equity values in both directions, and we consider whether a specific event in the future, such as a product approval or legal decision, could radically change a company's value.

Finally, we are cognizant of how these factors interact. For example, sales variability and operating leverage work together. A company with sales that don't fluctuate very much, but which has high fixed costs—such as a grocery store—might have the same level of uncertainty as a company with more variable sales but costs that can ebb and flow with the business, such as a consulting firm.

We use these uncertainty ratings to set our margins of safety. A company with a wide range of plausible outcomes and a very high uncertainty rating would need to trade at a very large discount to our estimate of intrinsic value before we would recommend the stock to investors. The reasoning behind this is simple. Although the central tendency of the range of possible intrinsic values may be $30, our confidence in that point estimate is not terribly high, so we look for a large margin of safety as an insurance policy of sorts.

Empirical research into decision making has shown that people are not terribly good at accurately estimating probabilities, and so some may criticize our emphasis on scenario analysis on these grounds. We agree that estimating the likely probabilities of various future scenarios is difficult and imprecise. However, we think that a process that embraces uncertainty and incorporates scenario analysis is more representative of reality than a finely tuned point estimate that considers only a single set of potential outcomes.

Moreover, we think that scenario analysis can improve the decision-making process inside a large research organization when new information needs to be incorporated into an intrinsic value estimate, or when conflict arises over what a company's future may look like. When only one intrinsic value has been estimated, the conversation centers on whether that estimate is right or wrong, and a discussion framed in such terms can lead to inappropriate anchoring on the previous opinion. However, if multiple scenarios were forecasted initially, then the discussion centers on the distribution of probabilities among various scenarios, as well as the appropriate level of optimism/pessimism for upside and downside cases. This can lead to a much healthier debate, in addition to less anchoring.

CONCLUSION

After applying DCF modeling to literally thousands of companies from scores of industries and dozens of companies over several years, we think we have learned a few lessons.

- It's better to be approximately right than precisely wrong. The complexity of DCF models can cause the user to spend too much time making assumptions that have a relatively minor impact on valuation. DCF valuation works best when the user steps back and asks, "How does this company make money? What assumptions are likely to move the needle, and which are not?" before plunging head first into Excel. Greater complexity and greater accuracy are not necessarily joined at the hip; in fact, more complex modeling may cause the analyst to lose sight of the issues likely to have the largest impact on intrinsic value.

■ Look for diminishing returns in the valuation process, since some things either are unknowable or would require too much effort without a corresponding payback in increased accuracy. For example, the right level of capex for a software firm is not going to move the valuation needle relative to the right values for research and development or sales and marketing. Tie the time you spend on each assumption to its likely impact on the firm's overall valuation.

■ Be aware that *how* you model can affect *what* you model. For example, if your assumptions are based on growth rates and margin percentages—as most models are—it's very easy to misestimate operating leverage, because operating margins that increase from, say, 20 percent to 30 percent over a few years look unreasonable. Avoid this mental trap by thinking carefully about how much additional capital a company actually needs to spend to generate an incremental dollar of sales, and by modeling results in absolute dollar terms. Once this process is complete, see what margins are implied by your incremental-cost estimates. The results may surprise you.

■ A corollary to the preceding lesson is that underestimating operating leverage—positive and negative—is one of the most common mistakes analysts can make. Thinking creatively and carefully about a company's cost structure is one of the most fruitful avenues for uncovering companies with intrinsic values that are dramatically higher or lower than the current market price.

■ Don't forget the importance of checks and balances. About three-quarters of Morningstar's DCF model is devoted to ratios, pro forma financial statements, and other output meant to provide context and gut checks to our analysts. This output is tremendously helpful in pinpointing where a model may be too optimistic, too pessimistic, or simply inconsistent. Even more importantly, it helps us have confidence in value estimates that seem too high or too low, but which are actually likely to be reasonable estimates of the future.

We've performed detailed DCF valuations on something close to 3,000 stocks over the past eight years, and our experience has been that DCF works well in the vast majority of cases, however tempting it might be to opt for a shortcut. At the end of the day, the value of an asset is dependent on the cash it can generate in the future, and DCF is generally the best tool available for forecasting and valuing those cash flows. Of course, no valuation tool is perfect, and there are times when we eschew DCF in favor of other approaches.

Finally, we think it's vital to remember that any valuation approach is only as good as its inputs, and even the most complex or cutting-edge valuation tool cannot compensate for a poor understanding of the asset being valued. We spend a great deal of time understanding the companies that we cover so we can attempt to forecast their future cash flows with an appropriate level of confidence, and we think any user of DCF should do the same. Understanding your valuation tool kit is important, but understanding the assets you're valuing is paramount.

CHAPTER 13

Valuing Real Options

Insights from Competitive Strategy

Andrew G. Sutherland
Vice President, Stern Stewart & Co.

Jeffrey R. Williams
Professor of Business Strategy, Tepper School of Business at Carnegie Mellon

Growth opportunities and future strategies can comprise a significant proportion of a firm's valuation. At the end of 2006, the median companies in the S&P 500 and the Russell 3000 had 25 percent and 40 percent of their valuations, respectively, attributed to Future Growth Value (FGV®), the capitalized value of future profit growth.[1] Acquisition premiums can also be interpreted as estimates of value creation attributed to new tactics and operational improvements under a new regime. Unfortunately, managers often find static net present value (NPV) tools and trading multiples to be too rigid to evaluate the contingent nature of strategic decisions and the cash flow recovery profiles associated with possible outcomes. For example, Microsoft was willing to develop its Xbox platform at a loss because it expected subsequent game and peripheral offerings linked to it to generate significant profits. Similarly, commodities producers frequently choose to delay extraction until output prices swing in their favor. Academics and practitioners have recognized the similarities of payoff functions between such contingent decisions about real assets, classic examples of so-called real options, and those of financial securities whose values are derived from the price of something else. The Black-Scholes model and binomial lattices have emerged as the most frequently prescribed and used tools for evaluating real options within both capital budgeting and enterprise valuation contexts. With the classic real option decision growing increasingly complex, and managers becoming more sophisticated, a frank assessment of modern valuation tools is timely.

The first section provides an overview of commonly used approaches for pricing contingent claims on financial securities. We then review how practitioners and academics have extended these approaches to the basic application of real option pricing. The next section, the core focus of this chapter, scrutinizes the assumptions made in the extension of models built for financial securities to real projects. A number of refinements are presented that attempt to better address the strategic realities of the firm and, in doing so, generate a more robust valuation. A summary and discussion of areas of future research conclude the chapter.

OVERVIEW OF OPTION PRICING FOR FINANCIAL SECURITIES

Options give an investor the right, but not the obligation, to buy or sell a security according to predetermined terms during some period or at some specific point. Stock option contracts can be divided into two categories: calls and puts. A call option gives the holder the right to purchase (call) stock from a counterparty at a fixed exercise price at or before a specific date. A put option gives the holder the right to sell (put) stock to a counterparty at a fixed exercise price at or before a specific date. At contract expiry, the call holder makes money when the price of the underlying is above the exercise price, while the opposite holds for the put holder. When the exercise is only permitted upon option contract expiry, it is termed European; when exercise is permitted at any point up to and upon expiry, it is termed American. Exhibit 13.1 depicts the payoff function for call and put option positions where the exercise price is $100.

Stock options can serve three important purposes:

1. Given their low price relative to the underlying stock, call and put options can be used to make a leveraged bet on future returns. For the same up-front cost as a single stock, a number of call options can be purchased, resulting in more than a dollar-for-dollar change in wealth for each dollar change in stock price.
2. Call and put options can provide an inexpensive way to hedge positions in firms with similar exposures, or holdings in the stock itself. An investor locked into a long position in a stock can purchase insurance on the position by purchasing a put option.
3. Finally, call options are instruments frequently used in executive compensation to align the long-term interests of management and the firm.

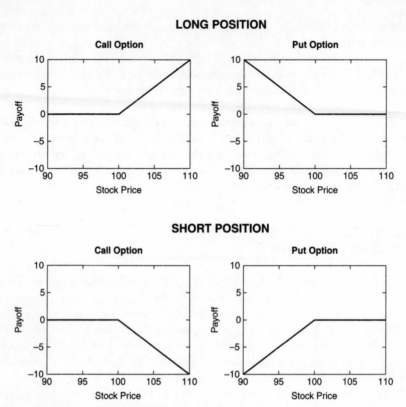

EXHIBIT 13.1 Payoff Diagrams for Stock Options

For example, Exhibit 13.2 shows that FedEx disclosed in its 2007 annual report the granting of options to its management (SEC 2007).

Options contracts are written on all sorts of other underlying assets and variables such as bonds, interest rates, exchange rates, and commodities. They also have been tailored in their mechanics, with options termed Asian, barrier, Bermuda, and digital characterizing different payoff rules.

The Black-Scholes Model

The growth of innovation and volume in option trading has coincided with advances in pricing approaches for stock options. One of the most influential approaches was published by Fischer S. Black and Myron S. Scholes in 1973. The Black-Scholes model employed geometric Brownian motion, a domain of stochastic calculus, to simulate the price path of the underlying

EXHIBIT 13.2   FedEx Option Grants

	2007	2006	2005
Expected lives	5 years	5 years	4 years
Expected volatility	22%	25%	27%
Risk-free interest rate	4.869%	3.794%	3.559%
Dividend yield	0.3023%	0.3229%	0.3215%

The weighted-average Black-Scholes value of our stock option grants using the assumptions indicated above was $31.60 per option in 2007, $25.78 per option in 2006 and $20.37 per option in 2005. The intrinsic value of options exercised was $145 million in 2007, $191 million in 2006 and $126 million in 2005.

The following table summarizes information about stock option activity for the year ended May 31, 2007:

	Stock Options			
	Shares	Weighted-Average Exercise Price	Weighted-Average Remaining Contractual Term	Aggregate Intrinsic Value (in Millions)
Outstanding at June 1, 2006	17,099,526	$ 60.82		
Granted	2,094,873	110.25		
Exercised	(2,333,845)	49.55		
Forfeited	(270,153)	89.12		
Outstanding at May 31, 2007	16,590,401	$ 68.22	5.9 years	$696
Exercisable	10,418,072	$ 54.75	4.6 years	$577
Expected to vest	5,678,543	$ 90.97	8.0 years	$109

stock. Options had been traded on exchanges as far back as the seventeenth century, but it wasn't until the Black-Scholes model and equally important research by Robert C. Merton (1973) was published that the market truly took off. (See Exhibit 13.3.)

The Black-Scholes model prices stock options with five variables:

■ The price of the underlying (S).
■ The exercise (strike) price (X).

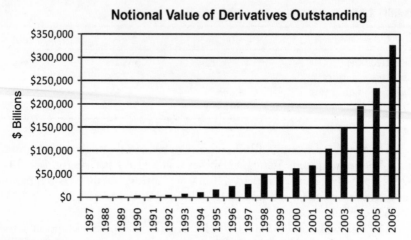

EXHIBIT 13.3   Size of the Derivatives Market
Source: International Swaps and Derivatives Association (2008). Derivatives include interest rate swaps, currency swaps, credit default swaps, and equity derivatives.

- The risk-free rate (r).
- The option contract horizon, in years (T).
- The annual return volatility of the underlying (σ).

Exhibit 13.4 summarizes how the option value responds to changes in these variables.

Consider the logic behind the valuation relationships in Exhibit 13.4. The right to buy (call) stock is worth more when you can pay less than what it's worth; and the right to sell (put) stock is worth more when you are entitled to receive more than what it's worth. This refers to the *intrinsic value* of the option, or the current spread between the stock and exercise price. Since option contracts endow a right but not an obligation of exercise, having a more uncertain underlying price path increases the possible upside, while the potential downside (you forfeit the cost of the call when exercise is not worthwhile) remains limited. Finally, having more time to enjoy price swings in your favor increases the value of the option to you. Black-Scholes synthesizes the relationships between these inputs to produce European call (C) and put (P) option values as follows:

$$C = S \times N(d_1) - X \times e^{-rt} \times N(d_2)$$

$$P = X \times e^{-rt} \times N(-d_2) - S \times N(-d_1)$$

where $d_1 = [\ln(S/X) + ((r + \sigma^2)/2 \times)t]/\sigma \times \sqrt{t}$
$d_2 = d_1 - \sigma \times \sqrt{T}$

	CALL OPTION		PUT OPTION	
	Increase	Decrease	Increase	Decrease
S	Increase	Decrease	Decrease	Increase
X	Decrease	Increase	Increase	Decrease
r	Increase	Decrease	Decrease	Increase
T	Increase	Decrease	Increase	Decrease
σ	Increase	Decrease	Increase	Decrease

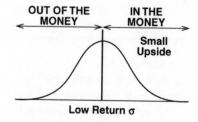

OUT OF THE MONEY ← → IN THE MONEY

Small Upside

Low Return σ

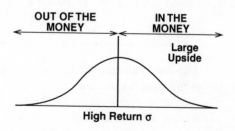

OUT OF THE MONEY ← → IN THE MONEY

Large Upside

High Return σ

EXHIBIT 13.4 Drivers of Option Value

One significant finding of Black and Scholes is that there is a relationship between the option value, the current value of the underlying stock, and the return on a risk-free security. The put-call parity relationship is:

$$C + X \times e^{-rt} = P + S$$

Exercise 1

1. Price a European call option issued on stock with an exercise price of $15, value of $13, annual return volatility of 25 percent, and horizon of one year. Assume the risk-free rate is 5 percent.
2. Use the put-call parity relationship to price a put option on the same stock.
3. Another one-year European call issued on a different stock is priced at $1.20. It has an exercise price of $20 and a current value of $17, and the risk-free rate is still 5 percent. Use the Black-Scholes model to calculate the annual return volatility implied by the current price.

Solutions

1. $0.81
2. $2.08
3. 28.74 percent

EXHIBIT 13.5 Option Valuation When Dividends Are Paid

	Call Option	Put Option
Stock price, predividend	$100	$100
Exercise price	$100	$100
Intrinsic value, predividend	$100 − $100 = $0	$100 − $100 = $0
Dividend	$X	$X
Stock price, postdividend	($100 − $X)	($100 − $X)
Intrinsic value, postdividend	($100 − $X) − $100 = − $X	$100 − ($100 − $X) = $X

The configuration of the Black-Scholes model assumes that no dividends are paid on the underlying stock. When dividends are paid, call option holders suffer because they don't participate in the payment, and the underlying stock price falls by approximately the amount of the dividend. For this same reason, put holders are better off—the spread between the exercise and underlying price increases. Exhibit 13.5 outlines the effect of dividends on call and put option values.

To handle cases where the underlying stock has a nonzero dividend yield, the Black-Scholes model can be applied as follows:

$$C = S \times e^{-yt} \times N(d_1) - X \times e^{-rt} \times N(d_2)$$

where y = the annual dividend yield (dividend divided by S)
$d_1 = [\ln(S/X) + ((r - y + \sigma^2)/2 \times)t]/\sigma \times \sqrt{t}$
$d_2 = d_1 - \sigma \times \sqrt{T}$

The value of the put can be determined using the same put-call parity relationship for non-dividend-paying stocks outlined earlier. Note that the dividend yield represents a continuous payment, consistent with the time mechanics assumed in the Black-Scholes model.

Exercise 2

Refer back to the excerpt from the FedEx annual report at the beginning of this section. Use the horizon, volatility, risk-free rate, and dividend yield assumptions from the 2007 column to price a call option on FedEx stock issued at the money ($S = X$) when the stock is worth $108.75.

Solution

$31.57

Binomial Lattices

Whereas the Black-Scholes model applies continuous time dynamics, binomial lattices use discrete time dynamics. This approach, developed by Cox, Ross, and Rubinstein (1979), is particularly useful for analyzing the effects on option values of one-time events such as bankruptcies or mergers and recurring events such as quarterly dividends, in addition to modeling the American option exercise. The same five variables (price of the underlying, strike price, risk-free rate, option contract horizon, and return volatility of the underlying) play a role in valuing the option. In fact, as the binomial lattice is geared with smaller and smaller time increments, the option price will converge to the Black-Scholes value.

A binomial lattice works as follows. The period leading up to option expiration is split into subperiods, marked by nodes. Price discovery for the underlying occurs at each node—the stock rises or falls by a specific amount depending on its return volatility. The stock increase scalar "u" that sets the magnitude of the price rise is equal to $e^{\sigma\sqrt{t}}$ and the stock decrease scalar "d" equals $1/u$. Readers familiar with decision trees will recognize the mechanics of this framework, presented in Exhibit 13.6.

Exercise 3

Using the volatility assumptions of Exercise 1.1, model the price path of the stock for one year using a binomial lattice with nodes every three months.

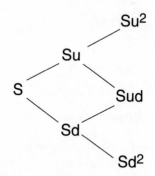

EXHIBIT 13.6 Simple Binomial Lattice for Stock

Solution

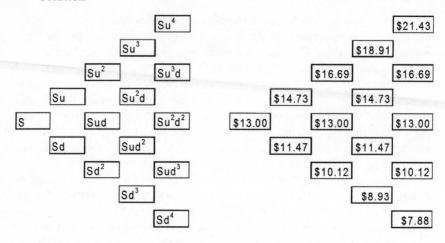

Once the price path of the underlying has been simulated, the option can be valued at each ending node.

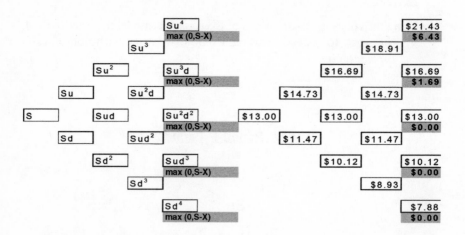

For the call option, the value is the greater of 0 and S-X: for the put option, the value is the greater of 0 and X-S.

The option value today is then estimated by working recursively through the tree, assuming risk neutrality. This means that future payoffs are discounted at the risk-free rate, where the probability of a "u" step in the underlying is:

$$p_u = \left[e^{(r-y)} - d \right] / (u - d)$$

And the probability of a "*d*" step is simply $1 - p_u$.

The value of the options at each of the second-to-last nodes can be calculated:

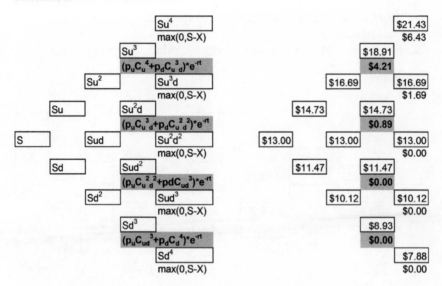

For each node prior to the second-to-last node, using the same recursive approach:

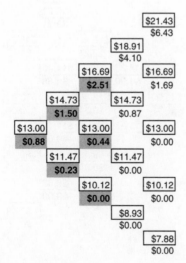

When the stock pays a discrete dividend (as the vast majority of dividends are paid in practice), it can be modeled in the lattice by simply subtracting the dividend from the underlying when it is paid.

Exercise 4

1. The stock from Exercise 3 pays a dividend of $0.10 at the end of each quarter. Recalculate the price path of the stock using the binomial lattice approach.
2. How does the new price path change the value of the call option?

Solutions

1.

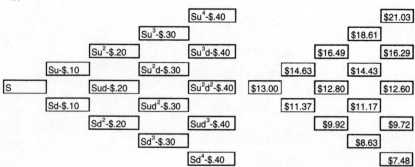

2.

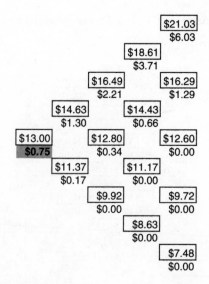

The call is worth $0.13 less.

BASIC OPTION PRICING APPLICATIONS FOR REAL ASSETS

The pricing tools for call and put options have been extended to the valuation of all sorts of other contracts, including interest rate derivatives, futures contracts, and exotic variations of vanilla calls and puts. Largely because of the explicit modeling of state-dependent decisions, they have also proven useful for evaluating real options, where the firm holds the right but not the obligation to make some business decision. Traditional valuation approaches such as NPV and internal rate of return (IRR) are useful for application to the as-is perspective of the firm. However, the total worth of a firm comprises not just the value of the current operations, but also the value derived from the ability to expand projects progressing successfully; abandon ones revealing themselves to be unsuccessful; and take advantage of the learning, information, and market position gained in both scenarios. Net present value (NPV) and internal rate of return (IRR) analyses often are too rigid to maneuver the dynamic and flexible nature of such strategic options.

The classic capital budgeting exercise involves discounting expected cash flows at an appropriate risk-adjusted rate. When only point estimates of the most likely scenario are used in valuation and the payoffs from dynamic and flexible strategies are ignored or improperly measured, the valuation exercise is incomplete (Myers 1977, 1984). How can the ability to expand, abandon, and collect information be priced? What is the conceptual connection to the options framework?

Production Flexibility and Platform Investments

Let's start with a call option. There are many situations where possessing the right, but not the obligation, to make a production or investment decision creates value for the firm. Consider the investment and extraction opportunities of an oil company. While spot (current) market prices are a major determinant of project valuation, the possibility of delaying production until prices may be higher can be a material source of value as well. The greater the uncertainty in the output market, the more the right to delay is worth. The value of this flexibility, combined with the present value of the project in current conditions, can be compared to the fixed investment cost. A manufacturer may look at its capacity decisions with a similar perspective. Maintaining excess capacity or inventory can allow the firm to capture enormous profits during periods of peak demand that more than offset holding costs and the opportunity cost of the capital tied up.

Yet another analogy can be made to companies that invest significant amounts in intangible assets. Much of their focus is on searching for growth opportunities where platform investments, often developed at considerable expense, spawn profitable offspring. For example, Microsoft's ownership of the Windows platform allowed it to develop follow-on products such as the Office software, the MSN Messenger application, and subsequent versions of Windows. Had Microsoft overlooked the value of follow-on products and made the decision to develop the first Windows product based solely on its stand-alone profits, the company might not have invested so heavily or placed so much faith in the development of what would be one of the richest real-option platforms in history. Note that Microsoft succeeded with another platform investment in the Xbox video game system, sold at a considerable loss (as described in Exhibit 13.7), expecting to more than recover through the sale of games and hardware that are linked exclusively to the system (Ivan 2007).

EXHIBIT 13.7 Xbox's Real Options

"There are three ways to make money on an Xbox. Generally it's not on the hardware itself: we'll probably be gross margin neutral on that over the life cycle of the product and try to break even on that. The second thing you try to do is you make money on the games themselves, and there are two models there. One is first-party games that Microsoft produces. The other is games that Electronic Arts or an Activision produces, and we get paid a royalty on those games. The third place you make money is on Live, and where we actually have a very nice service that's scaling very well, and that is a business model that's subscription, ad-based, and download-based. It kind of has the full gamut of business models associated with it, and I think you're going to continue to see that grow. And then the final place you make money is on peripherals, so game controllers, cameras, steering wheels, a whole other set of things."

—Robbie Back, President of Microsoft's Entertainment and Devices Division

Estimates of Microsoft's development spending on the system varied, but the company recorded significant operating losses in its Home and Entertainment segment, comprised primarily of Xbox offerings, leading up to its release:

Home and Entertainment (In millions, except percentages)	2006	2005	2004	Percent Change 2006 versus 2005	Percent Change 2005 versus 2004
Revenue	$ 4,256	$ 3,140	$ 2,737	36%	15%
Operating loss	$ (1,262)	$ (485)	$ (1,337)	(160%)	64%

Information and Organizational Learning

There are scenarios in which the information revealed or the organizational learning following a decision can be used to maximize the potential of platform investments. Sometimes the uncertainty surrounding the future success of a new product release can be managed in such a way to make even the biggest Hail Mary offerings worth taking on. A film studio can phase its investments in advertising, distribution, and development of sequels for a movie by staging its expenditures pending the reaction of critics and other viewers at early screenings. While new releases tend to have a low probability of success, successful releases generate vast payoffs not just from screening revenues, but from DVDs, merchandise, and sequels. Therefore, being able to accelerate or decelerate spending *after* the results of early screenings are known is like letting the studio participate in a real options lottery, and keeping the cost of their participation at a minimum. Exhibit 13.8 provides a hypothetical investment-decision road map for film studios.

The investments made by a pharmaceutical company can be thought of in terms of embedded real options as well. Like the film studio, it can similarly stage the research and development of drugs pending clinical trials and regulatory approval. Furthermore, it attaches value to learning, often firm-specific and proprietary, that occurs even when a given product fails to make it to market. The research and development for one project may generate knowledge and capabilities useful for others that would not have necessarily been enjoyed had the initial project not been carried out. Breakthroughs and patents spawned from a losing effort can be applied to support related projects, and mistakes made in previous trials can be avoided.

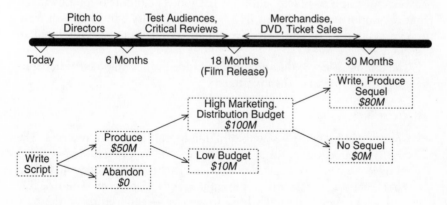

Cost of option exercise in italics

EXHIBIT 13.8 Real Options Embedded in a Film Project

Project Abandonment as an Option

The right to abandon or scale back an investment is also worth something to the firm, and this is what typifies the put variety of real options. Take a minerals company that gets hit with an extended period of declining prices for its output. Rather than continue to operate at a loss, it can sell its property and equipment, and use the proceeds to invest elsewhere. There are many analogous situations in which shutting down a business that runs into hard times is a much better alternative to letting it ride.

Each of the aforementioned investment scenarios can be characterized by a common element. Being able to make or unwind an investment at a future date, pending the realization of some event, is a valuable right. When relating the realization to the price path of the underlying security for a call or put option, the analogy between the real investment and the financial derivative, for the purpose of real option pricing, is complete. To the extent one can model the variables that determine the value of the investment—be it the price path of oil, the popularity of a movie, or the success of follow-on projects—either the Black-Scholes or the binomial lattice framework can be applied. The remainder of this section demonstrates how the trade-offs between the benefits and costs of investment flexibility and information are quantified in each of these frameworks.

Using the Black-Scholes Model to Value Real Assets

Recall the example of the oil company that possesses reserves, and thinks about market price volatility in timing extraction. This situation naturally extends itself to Black-Scholes valuation. The inputs originally taken from the opportunity to invest in a financial security can be drawn from the characteristics of the real investment opportunity as illustrated in Exhibit 13.9.

The option values (calls and puts) are added to the static NPV in determining the total worth of the investment.

Exercise 5

1. Consider an oil company with 400,000 barrels of known reserves. The company can extract and produce the reserves at a cost of $25 per barrel over the next five years. Oil is priced in the market today at $100 a barrel, and the contribution margin averages 45 percent. The risk-free rate is 5 percent, and volatility of oil prices—believed to be the only source of uncertainty influencing the value of the reserves—is estimated at 25 percent per year. What is the value of producing the oil today?

EXHIBIT 13.9 Real Option Valuation Drivers Using Black-Scholes

Black-Scholes Input	Stock Option	Real Option
S	Stock price	Value of reserves today, given quantity and price of oil, and variable cost structure
X	Exercise price	Fixed cost of extraction and production (no variable costs counted here)
r	Risk-free rate	Risk-free rate
T	Contract horizon	Investment option horizon, given maintenance costs, depletion, and competitive forces
δ	Return volatility	Return volatility resulting from future price uncertainty, reserve uncertainty, etc.

2. Use the Black-Scholes framework to estimate the value of the reserves.
3. How much is the ability to delay production worth to the company?

Solutions

1. $8,000,000
2. $18,401,139
3. $10,401,139

Exercise 6

1. Consider a company that is bidding on a mine. For various reasons, the company cannot delay or ramp up production given the evolution of commodity prices in the market, but it can abandon the investment in three years by selling off the property and equipment for $5 million. It estimates the value of the mine today to be $10 million. The risk-free rate is 5 percent, and the volatility of commodities prices—believed to be the only source of uncertainty influencing the value of the reserves—is estimated at 20 percent per year. Use the Black-Scholes framework to estimate the maximum acceptable bid for the mine.
2. How much is the ability to abandon worth to the company?

Solutions

1. $10,405,352
2. $405,352

Using Binomial Lattices to Value Real Assets

The binomial lattice approach can be applied to price the option to expand, delay, and abandon using the very same inputs required for the Black-Scholes model, as discussed in the first section.

An interesting application of the binomial lattice valuation has the lattice pricing the securities in the firm's capital structure using the principle of limited liability. Shareholders cannot lose anything more than their initial investment, but must pay off outstanding debt before realizing the value of their equity. In this sense, their stock is like a call option on the firm's assets—by paying off the debt outstanding, they earn the right to receive the cash flows from the underlying assets. They will only "exercise" when the value of the assets exceeds the debt outstanding. The position of lenders can be looked at through an options lens as well. They essentially hold risk-free debt, and have sold shareholders the option to default on the loan—a put option.

Exercise 7

1. A firm's assets, currently valued at $500, vary with an annual volatility of 30 percent. If the risk-free rate is 5 percent and the firm holds $250 of debt, is bankruptcy likely? Use a one-year horizon with three-month steps.
2. Price the stock as a call option on the firm's assets using the binomial lattice.

Solutions

1. The firm's equity is worth $262.19. Even in the worst projected outcome, the firm is solvent and the stock is worth $24.41.
2.

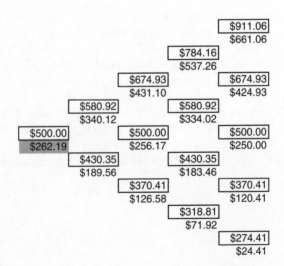

ADVANCED OPTION PRICING APPLICATIONS FOR REAL ASSETS

Academic research continues to advance the quantitative techniques for pricing contingent claims on financial and real assets alike, but the use of such techniques remains found within a very small, sophisticated audience. A 2003 *CFO* magazine survey found that just 9 to 11 percent of senior executives are using the valuation technique, and a large proportion of early adopters have abandoned it (Teach 2003). The well-publicized demise of Enron, once considered to be championing the integration of real-option decision making into the twenty-first century, has only served to build an aura of distrust around the field.

While such preconceptions will wane over time, there are bona fide objections to refocusing the strategic investment process that will need to be overcome. The most significant of these is the divide between what many perceive to be the worth of their investment opportunities and what the basic application of pricing models tells them. This often results when the assumptions underlying the financial pricing techniques do not hold in a corporate investment setting. The intent is not to critique the extension of pricing financial derivatives to real options, but rather to understand where the underlying conditions differ and to adjust pricing models as well as possible. This section provides commentary on the critical strategic and economic considerations surrounding investment opportunities—areas where much of the existing literature has been agnostic. The aim is to equip students and practitioners with a set of approaches that address the discrepancies between financial market and corporate investment settings. The most relevant discrepancies include:

- The manner in which volatility is estimated.
- The act of option exercise.
- The legal right to option payoffs.

Volatility

According to the Black-Scholes model, the value of a financial option is influenced by the uncertainty of returns on the underlying stock. Even though many systematic and nonsystematic factors influence returns, a reasonable estimate of volatility for the purposes of computing the option value can be calculated by simply measuring the variation in historical returns on the traded stock. Techniques for doing this may vary, but the volatility implied by call or put prices set in a competitive financial market is most likely going to reflect some reasonable estimate of future return volatility. However, there is no market exchange for real option opportunities that can be referenced to produce an implied volatility. Though some models of estimating volatility using certainty equivalents have been proposed (Copeland and Antikarov 2005), there is no widely accepted technique that captures the systematic and nonsystematic risks affecting the cash flows of real investments. The lack of a simple, practical method for getting the volatility input makes price estimates more likely to drift from their economic value to the firm, and therefore be less credible.

Exercise

Financial investors can exercise options almost instantaneously by calling their broker or using an online trading account. Real investment opportunities can be much more complex and time- consuming to act on. The investment decisions we identified earlier—extracting a commodity from a mine; ramping investment in advertising and research; and releasing follow-on products—all involve a certain level of time and resources to follow through. Companies, for many reasons, maintain varying degrees of agility or control; and this will affect their ability to exercise and capture the option payoffs from their project.

Capturing Option Payoffs

A related and equally important distinction between financial and real investment settings rests in the ownership of option payoffs. Whereas financial investors hold legal rights to the profits on their options, the same protection does not exist for firms in competitive corporate markets. Firms can converge on one another's markets with little or no recourse for the loser. This can be prevented in markets where physical property rights (the commodities seller owns its mine) or intellectual property rights (the pharmaceutical company files patents) exist and are enforced but, in many cases, the information and competitive setting are available for all rivals to capitalize on. While employees are being mobilized, marketing programs launched, and distribution channels filled during the exercise process, rivals are reacting and new information is arriving in ways that make the original option value estimate meaningless.

Intel's initial processor releases surely generated demand for faster subsequent releases, but the company ended up sharing much of the profits from these future releases with Advanced Micro Devices and others. The risk of such convergence happening is especially high when there are weak isolating mechanisms, and competitors have varying degrees of agility to act on their investment opportunities. Another competitive factor that heavily influences option payoffs is the extent to which a firm can cope with the very uncertainty that drives (at least mathematically) option values (Williams 2006). Those such as Wal-Mart and McDonald's that compete on the basis of scale are more likely to see risk as disruptive rather than as a source of value creation within their process-driven organizations. In light of these more prominent discrepancies, we have attempted to modify and expand upon traditional models to better capture the strategic realities of the firm.

Black-Scholes Model: Dividend Yield Adjustment

In many settings, possessing a first mover or organizational learning advantage may enhance the value of future projects. Then, as barriers to entry decline and competing firms enter the market, the profitability of these projects becomes less secure and more uncertain. Extreme forms of convergence to commodity status of products and services occur in so-called fast-cycle markets, where cash flow half-life is on the order of one year or less (Williams 1999). Examples include microchips (Intel), hard drives for computers (Seagate), cell phones (Nokia), the fashion industry (Benetton), and innovation-driven sports markets such as golf (Callaway). These markets experience high marginal utility of early adoption, but simultaneously are characterized by weak isolating mechanisms, with the result that considerable profit can be made for companies that move quickly. At the same time, delays in production or distribution are typically very costly, as competitors quickly enter first mover markets with look-alike products at a fraction of the first mover's price.

One way to model the trajectories of such fast-cycle option payoffs is to assess a dividend yield that erodes the value of the expected underlying cash flows (Damodaran n.d.). In a similar sense that dividend payments represent forgone income for the financial call option holder, the assessed dividend yield captures the economic cost of having to share option payoffs with fast-following competitors.

Exercise 8

Future releases for a microchip manufacturer are expected to be worth $25 million, with development costs of $25 million, a two-year investment horizon, and an annual volatility of returns on the investment of 25 percent. Competitors are likely to follow the releases with lower-quality, knock-off products in an attempt to capture market share. What do various dividend yields imply about option values?

Solution

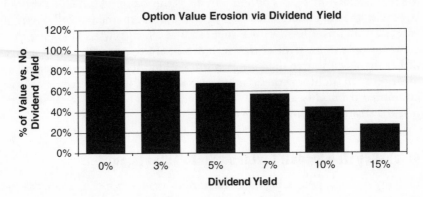

Option Value Erosion via Dividend Yield

While assessing a dividend yield on a real asset may seem opaque, to the extent investment value erosion can be estimated, the approach can be informative. Estimates may be drawn from projections of excess returns or monopoly profits available during the competitive advantage period, consumer demand and price forecasts, and past investment experience.

Stochastic Variables

For many financial derivatives, market conditions evolve by a sufficient margin to justify modeling the inputs to the pricing model dynamically. Volatility can increase over time, or vary with the price of the underlying security. The underlying may tend to exhibit mean reversion—common in interest rate derivatives—or experience random shocks from time to time, as in energy markets. Traders have reverse-engineered the Black-Scholes model, stripping out the assumed static volatility and geometric Brownian motion assumptions and recalibrating their models for assumptions more relevant to the given security.

The variables that drive real option value may change over time as well. An excellent example of this in the context of real options is the tipping of the high-definition video storage market toward the Blu-ray Disc platform, where the HD DVD Optical Disc platform ultimately lost out. Preceding the release of the machines, both Sony and Toshiba invested heavily in research and development and spent significant time courting movie studios and distributors for exclusivity deals. The money spent on these endeavors was expected to be more than recovered on the discs that would be sold in the future and used on the platform. Given the high stakes and uncertainty for both Sony and Toshiba at this stage, their development options were both likely in the money. However, the subsequent events—the rate of consumer adoption and the level of success in landing exclusivity deals—would determine the ultimate payoffs. The degree of uncertainty would decrease as these events were to unfold, and one competitor would surpass the other. However, managers at Sony or Toshiba don't have a crystal ball, and must ex ante do their best to capture the possibilities and state-dependent outcomes in their decision tools. To the extent they are equipped with quantitative approaches rooted in dynamic rather than static settings, they will be making more informed decisions.

Quantitative Approaches

Monte Carlo simulations have proven to be a popular and useful tool for conducting scenario analysis for investment decisions. The tool allows for a wide variety of variables to be modeled with a distribution, and the range of option payoffs are produced over hundreds or thousands of trials. Managers may be adept at forecasting the cash flow drivers of their businesses, but there are further adjustments to the underlying price process and volatility assumptions worth incorporating into the simulations.

Recall that the Black-Scholes model assumes stock prices are governed by geometric Brownian motion, a form of continuous-time stochastic process. In order to look at the option in a binomial lattice or assign a different stochastic process to the underlying, the continuous price path must be converted into a discrete step-by-step model. The Euler discretization allows for the price changes to be simulated in small time increments as follows:

$$dS_t = \mu S_t dt + \sigma S_t dw_t$$

where dS_t = the change in value of the underlying from one period to the next

μ = the annualized mean return

dt = the time increment

σ = the annualized standard deviation of returns

S_t = the present value of the underlying at time t

dw_t = the instantaneous increment to a Wiener process, which captures the random arrival of information

Exercise 9

1. Model the price path over 12 months of a stock with μ 8 percent, dt of one month, initial price of $24, and annual σ of 20 percent using the following random numbers generated from a normal distribution:

Period	1	2	3	4	5	6	7	8	9	10	11	12
Random Normal	0.2369	2.3593	1.1456	–1.0193	0.1606	1.8706	–0.8572	0.3757	–1.9000	0.8581	0.9516	0.9795

2. The strike price on a 12-month call option is $23.50. Assuming the underlying stock follows the path from Exercise 9.1, determine the value of the option at expiration.

Solutions

1.

Period	0	1	2	3	4	5	6	7	8	9	10	11	12
Price	$24.00	$24.45	$28.16	$30.24	$28.65	$29.06	$32.54	$31.13	$31.97	$28.79	$30.40	$32.28	$34.33

2. $Max(0, S - X) = \$10.83$

There are alternative processes that can be modeled for situations where a normally distributed return process or constant volatility does not apply.

A Markov Ito price process allows for changing annual returns and heteroscedasticity by:

$$dS_t = \mu(S_t, t)S_t dt + v(S_t, t)S_t dw_t$$

where v = the annual variance of returns

An Ornstein-Uhlenbeck process allows for mean reversion by:

$$dS_t = \alpha(\theta - S_t)dt + \sigma dw_t$$

where α = the parameter denoting the speed of mean reversion
θ = the mean

Exercise 10

1. A mining company has 10,000 tons of XYZ deposits that it can bring to market at any point. The current market price per ton is $650, and prices tend to mean revert with properties $\alpha = .005$ and $\theta = \$580$. If the annual price volatility is 20 percent, model the price path using one-month steps with the following randomly generated numbers:

Period	1	2	3	4	5	6	7	8	9	10	11	12
Random Normal	0.4990	0.5115	–1.5999	1.1199	–0.7580	1.0363	–1.0604	–0.0068	1.9674	0.5088	–0.5629	–1.1259

2. Assuming that the contribution margin is 60 percent and the fixed cost of extraction per ton is $300, value the opportunity to bring the metals to market at the end of 12 months using the price path in Exercise 10.1.

Solutions

1.

Period	0	1	2	3	4	5	6	7	8	9	10	11	12
Price	$650.00	$697.58	$735.78	$500.72	$647.46	$540.96	$676.46	$525.63	$536.94	$810.22	$814.97	$660.28	$509.81

2.

$$Max(0, S - X) = Max[0, 10,000 \times (\$509.81 \times 0.60) - \$300] = \$58,844$$

A stochastic variance model allows for variance to evolve according to some specified relationship:

$$dS_t = \mu(S_t, t)S_t dt + v(S_t, h_t, t)S_t dw_t$$

where h_t = secondary volatility factor where heteroscedasticity is not driven by t or S_t

A Poisson jump diffusion process allows for spikes and regressions in price path:

$$dS_t = \mu(S_t, t)S_t dt + v(S_t, t)S_t dw_t + A_t S_t dq_t$$

where A_t = the variable accounting for random jumps
dq_t = the change in the level of a Poisson process, which is either 1 or 0

Managers can configure their business case simulation with the appropriate statistical underpinnings and evolving decision rules or payoff functions that reflect competitive dynamics. For example, the achievement of a certain level of customer adoption can serve as the market tipping point, where volatility and the risk of competitive convergence severely dissipate. Such a payoff rule resembles that of a barrier option in financial markets, where payoffs kick in only when a predetermined threshold has been reached.

Introducing even the most basic forms of scenario analysis requires training and planning process redesign. Yet despite the negative sentiment surrounding real options expressed in senior executive surveys, some promising trends have emerged. The use of sensitivity analysis and scenario analysis is widespread, appearing in 85 percent and 67 percent of companies, respectively, in the aforementioned *CFO* magazine survey (Teach 2003). While managers may perceive real option pricing exercises to be occurring in black boxes, they may soon realize that, by incorporating sensitivity analysis and scenario analysis into the decision process, they are indirectly assigning a value to the firm's real options. We hope the approaches outlined in this section bring them closer to embracing more explicit assessments of real options.

Advanced Binomial Lattice Approach—Cost of Delay

For some firms, it is particularly important to be able to maintain flexibility to ramp and shutter operations, because the goal is to match production capacity of the firm to rapidly shifting changes in supply and demand. The case of Pulse Engineering is illustrative here. In 1982, Pulse became a component supplier to IBM in the rapidly growing personal computer industry, and could build delay lines at a rate of 15,000 units a week. But demand quickly jumped to 35,000 units per week, leaving Pulse unable to meet demand. Management responded with investment to increase available capacity until late 1984 when demand shrunk to 6,000 units per week, requiring Pulse to lay off much of its production force and take large inventory write-offs. Then, in 1986, demand for a second-generation PC component rose from 20,000 units per week to 120,000 units per week over a nine-month period, only to fall off in demand by 1988 in a pattern similar to what occurred in 1984. Yet during this period spanning rapid growth and volume decline, Pulse Engineering enjoyed several years of profits, due in no small part to its ability to rapidly adjust its capacity to changing market demand.

In situations like these, rather than using Monte Carlo simulations to simulate the underlying price path and payoffs, managers can explicitly model decision-triggering events in a binomial lattice. This technique is particularly useful for estimating the cost of delayed exercise, and provides a useful visual road map for tracking the life of the investment. The critical step of this approach is to distinguish between the exercise decision point and when the exercise actually happens. The decision point occurs when the organization commits to following through with investment. *Exercise* can be defined as the point at which the firm has made the necessary resource allocations to make the investment possible, as discussed earlier in this section. The wider the gap between decision and exercise, the greater the *expected* option value lost because of the firm's inability to react quickly and capture payoffs before competitors do.

Exercise 11

1. A mobile phone maker has the option of releasing an extension of an existing model with new Web browsing and music applications. Fixed development costs are $1 billion, and the present value of expected cash flows from the extension is $850 million, with annual volatility of 35 percent. The applications and features built into the phone are anticipated to be popular for 15 months before future releases make the model obsolete. Price the option using a binomial lattice, assuming the risk-free rate is 5 percent.
2. Now assume that the company plans on making its exercise decision three months from now, but will only have the wherewithal to mobilize on the decision in nine months. It expects to have forgone income of $300 million at the six-month point, and an additional $115 million at the nine-month point due to missing out on sales to early adopters. Retrace the project value through the binomial lattice.
3. What is the cost of delay to the firm?

Solutions

1.

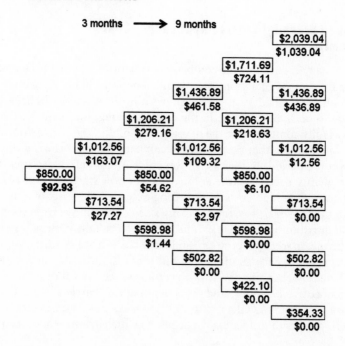

NORMAL CONDITIONS

3 months ⟶ 9 months

					$2,039.04
					$1,039.04
				$1,711.69	
				$724.11	
			$1,436.89		$1,436.89
			$461.58		$436.89
		$1,206.21		$1,206.21	
		$279.16		$218.63	
	$1,012.56		$1,012.56		$1,012.56
	$163.07		$109.32		$12.56
$850.00		$850.00		$850.00	
$92.93		$54.62		$6.10	
	$713.54		$713.54		$713.54
	$27.27		$2.97		$0.00
		$598.98		$598.98	
		$1.44		$0.00	
			$502.82		$502.82
			$0.00		$0.00
				$422.10	
				$0.00	
					$354.33
					$0.00

2. The forgone income can be subtracted from the project value at the six-month and nine-month nodes, similar to the dividend yield treatment in Exercise 4 (8th lattice).

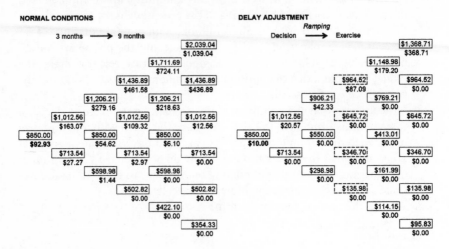

3. The cost of delay is $82.93 million.

Advanced Binomial Lattice Approach—Cost of Commitment

Firms in many industries face competitive situations where it is necessary to commit to a course of action over extended periods. In his pioneering work on commitment, Ghemawat (1991) shows how the strategies of firms have a tendency to persist over time. In the case of Boeing, for example, the company was fully committed to the development of the 747 because of the high levels of investment that precluded the company from developing other aircraft over the period. In the case of Reynolds Aluminum, a decision to shut down a facility precluded the company from ever starting up that facility again because the high costs of restarting exceeded the costs of a newer facility. In the case of Coors, the company's decision to move from regional to national distribution would take a full decade to be fully realized due to lags in marketing, market penetration, and large-scale facilities start-up.

During these periods of inertia and irreversibility, decision making is complicated by changing levels of uncertainty, the arrival of new information, competitive behavior, and compounding exit barriers associated with decisions over time. As Ghemawat (1991) makes clear, an important factor over periods of commitment is the degree to which investment decisions can be reversed. If, during the gap between decision and exercise, information arrives that makes the investment no longer worthwhile (or worthwhile escalating), option value can be recovered only when the firm can act on the new information. The ex ante difference between the traditional option price and the price accounting for exercise and decision reversal constraints can be interpreted as the cost of commitment.

Exercise 12

1. A pharmaceutical company has the right to develop a drug at any point over the next two and a half years. The present value of expected cash flows and the exercise price related to development are both $200 million, the annual volatility of expected cash flows is 20 percent, and the risk-free rate is 5 percent. Price the option.
2. Now assume the company plans to make a decision on option exercise, and stick with it six months from now. In what scenarios will the firm wish it had made a different decision, and how (qualitatively) will this affect the real option value?
3. What is the cost of commitment to the firm?

Solutions

1.

NORMAL CONDITIONS

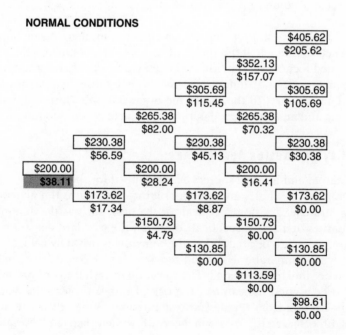

2. When decisions can't be reversed, the firm will regret exercising when subsequent information is unfavorable, and not exercising when subsequent information is favorable. The inability to act on new information makes the possibility of development less valuable to the firm (10th lattice).

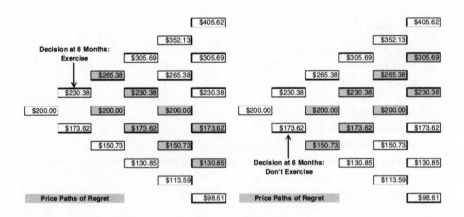

3. The cost of commitment is $16.56 million.

The scale orchestration constraints common in oligopolistic industries serve to decrease much of the appeal of real option investments. Such a control-oriented focus may lead firms to be unable to quickly react to favorable developments, or to abandon investments that subsequently turn for the worse. Furthermore, to the extent the organization's culture discourages risk taking and innovation, real option thinking may be discouraged.

Volatility Estimation Approaches

Both external and internal sources can be tapped for the volatility input required for Black-Scholes and binomial lattice valuation. If a given investment or strategic decision is typical for the firm, such as the development opportunities of a pharmaceutical company, the standard deviation of the enterprise value can be used. When the company is privately held, a peer set of firms with comparable assets and activities can be constructed, and volatility can be similarly estimated. The variation in cash flows of past projects may also be a good indicator of the risk of future projects, as would the implied variation from Monte Carlo simulations. When there are multiple sources of project risk that can be readily identified and estimated, a

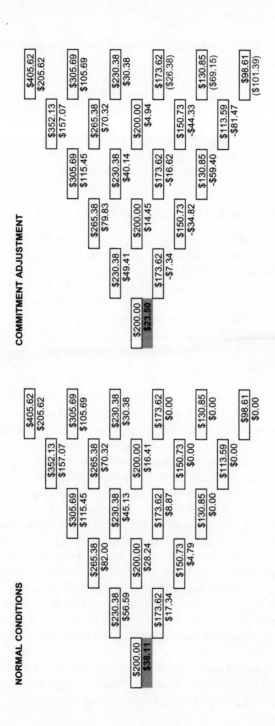

NORMAL CONDITIONS

COMMITMENT ADJUSTMENT

portfolio variance model can be introduced to estimate volatility:

$$\sigma_p^2 = \sum_{i=1}^{N} w_i^2 \sigma_i^2 + \sum_{i=1}^{N} \sum_{j=1}^{N} w_i w_j \sigma_{ij} \sigma_j \rho_{ij}$$

where σ_p = the project volatility
$\quad \sigma_i$ = the volatility of factor i
$\quad w_i$ = the weighting of volatility factor i
$\quad \rho_{ij}$ = the correlation between factors i and j

Do All Investments Have Embedded Options?

The bulk of this section highlights investment opportunities where real option pricing tools focus and empower valuation exercises. When can these same tools be misleading or inappropriate to apply? One of the biggest credibility barriers preventing real options valuation from being adopted on a widespread basis is the notion that any project can be justified by supplementing the stand-alone NPV with the option value for an unlimited number of projects. While part of embracing real option thinking is looking for sources of project value outside of the expected course of action, some warnings are in order:

■ Favorable market settings alone do not necessarily mean a given investment has option value. If a company is unwilling to pursue a new strategy regardless of the potential payoffs, that strategy has no value to it. Similarly, if a firm lacks the agility or competence to capture potential option payoffs available, no option value exists. Retail chains with substantial real estate investments such as McDonald's should not be including the option value of selling underlying property if prices rise when they have no intention or capability of relocating or leasing.

■ Premeditated strategic moves do not count as options. When a firm has dedicated itself to escalating or unwinding an investment, the very right to react to new information that characterizes real options does not exist. This situation resembles the commitment setting discussed earlier, with the important difference that with commitment it isn't option exercise that is certain, but rather the follow-through if exercise occurs. Premeditated moves should be evaluated with NPV analysis of most likely outcomes and Monte Carlo simulations, but not options analysis.

Being skilled at identifying when *not* to apply real options valuation tools will help prevent managers from attempting to justify unprofitable projects, and prevent investors from overvaluing shares.

CONCLUSION AND FUTURE RESEARCH

Advances in pricing methods for financial securities have served to benefit managers in the valuation of the strategic options of their firms. Research in asset pricing is rapidly evolving, and the development of valuation models driven by quantitative software platforms is transforming the capital markets. There is great potential for leveraging asset pricing technology to the evaluation of real investments, and for helping managers make capital allocation decisions, value their businesses, and assess performance. Pricing real options arguably involves as much art as science, and the application of traditional models can produce misleading output. This chapter has outlined a number of valuation approaches designed to bring about heightened understanding of strategic capabilities and limitations of the firm in relation to its real option opportunities. By incorporating insights from competitive strategy into the valuation exercise and by using a variety of approaches to triangulate on investment values, the real options management process will be better informed.

NOTE

1. FGV is calculated as Enterprise value – Capital in place – Current year's EVA®/ WACC. S&P data for the 2006 year-end was downloaded from Bloomberg; and Russell 3000 and WACC data was pulled from the 2007 Russell 3000 EVA/MVA Annual Ranking Database (Russell 2007).

REFERENCES

Black, F., and M. Scholes. 1973. The pricing of options and corporate liabilities. *Journal of Political Economy* 81(3): 637–654.

Copeland, T., and V. Antikarov. 2005. Real options: Meeting the Georgetown challenge. *Journal of Applied Corporate Finance* 17(2): 32–51.

Cox, J, S. Ross, and M. Rubenstein. 1979. Option pricing: A simplified approach. *Journal of Financial Economics* (7): 229–263.

Damodaran, A. N.d.The promise and peril of real options. http://pages.stern.nyu .edu/~adamodar.

Ghemawat, P. 1991. *Commitment: The dynamic of strategy.* New York: Free Press.

International Swaps and Derivatives Association. 2008. ISDA market survey results, 1987-present.

Ivan, T. 2007. The Xbox turnaround. *BusinessWeek,* May 7. www.businessweek .com/innovate/content/may2007/id20070507_071106.htm?chan=search.

Merton, R. 1973. Theory of rational option pricing. *Bell Journal of Economics and Management Science* 4(1): 141–183.

Myers, S. 1977. Determinants of corporate borrowing. *Journal of Financial Economics* 5: 147–175.

Myers, S. 1984. Finance theory and financial strategy. *Interfaces* 14(January-February): 126–137.

Russell. 2007. EVA dimensions: The 2007 Russell 3000 EVA/MVA annual ranking database.

SEC. 2007. *Annual report on Form 10-K for FedEx Corporation.* Commission File Number 1-15829, United States Securities and Exchange Commission, Washington, D.C.

Teach, E. 2003. Will real options take root? *CFO.*

Williams, J. 1999. *Renewable advantage: Crafting strategy through economic time.* New York: Free Press, 46–47.

Williams, J., and A. Sutherland. 2006. Options pricing of dynamic strategies. Tepper Working Paper 2006-E20. http://business.tepper.cmu.edu/facultyAdmin/upload/wpaper_27770882620405_2006-E20.pdf.

United States Securities and Exchange Commission. 2006. *Annual Report on Form 10-K for Microsoft Corporation* (Commission File Number 0-14278), Washington, D.C.

CHAPTER 14

GRAPES

A Theory of Stock Prices

Max Zavanelli
President, ZPR Investment Research, Inc.

Max Zavanelli developed the Growth Rate Arbitrage Price Equilibrium System (GRAPES) theory of stock prices in 1986. ZPR Investment Management, Inc. has since recorded what may be the best performance of any diversified U.S. equity manager from 1988 to 2007 with an 1897 percent return net of fees measured according to the Global Investment Performance Standards (GIPS®). From 2001, the audited returns are shown in Exhibit 14.1.

Since 2001, ZPR also has had a global investment product (see Exhibit 14.2), which is also audited, net of fees, and according to GIPS. (Full details of the composites can be found on the company's web site www.zprim.com.)

Both investment products set a record for the most consecutive times (12) on Morningstar's top 10 managers list for the categories of World Stock and U.S. Value for the trailing five years.

ZPR Investment Research, Inc. provides quantitative research to mutual fund families and institutional investors. Over $21 billion invested in U.S. equities uses its databases and models.

A NEW THEORY OF ASSET PRICES

The field of microeconomics has established the theory for a price of a good. It is the intersection of supply and demand. This is further overlaid with utility preference theory related to consumption. In the field of investments, we use risk and expected returns instead of demand and supply. Utility

EXHIBIT 14.1 ZPR Investment Management, Inc. Small Cap Value
Performance Analysis

Year	ZPR Small Cap Value	Russell 2000	S&P 500
2001	28.02%	2.49%	−11.88%
2002	33.67%	−20.48%	−22.10%
2003	55.36%	47.25%	28.68%
2004	17.32%	18.32%	10.88%
2005	16.47%	4.55%	4.92%
2006	29.87%	18.37%	15.80%
2007	3.35%	−1.57%	5.49%
Compounded	387.65%	72.95%	25.53%
Annualized	25.40%	8.14%	3.30%

preference is based on our tolerance for risk and the trade-off with return. A
new dimension is advanced with the concept of diversification. We can minimize risk and maximize return per Harry Markowitz's optimizations and his
famous 1950 book defining the efficient frontier. This began modern portfolio theory (MPT) and greatly eclipsed the thinking of Benjamin Graham
and David Dodd, the fundamentalists, who argued for value but were folksy
in their philosophy; they set guidelines, not theory or mathematics, for what
value was; but they were at least concerned about the price.

The next great leap forward was the capital asset pricing model and
theory by William Sharpe, also approached in another way by Eugene
Fama, who championed efficient market theory. These expositions were
brilliant and insightful, but completely missed the most important ingredient (price), resulting in a pizza without cheese, a hamburger without beef.
We simply assume that in equilibrium all prices are efficient. You buy the
market portfolio (index), as you can't beat the market. The price at any

EXHIBIT 14.2 ZPR Investment Management, Inc. Global Equity
Performance Analysis

Year	Global Equity	S&P 500	MSCI-EAFE
2001	18.62%	−11.88%	−21.21%
2002	28.46%	−22.10%	−15.66%
2003	55.34%	28.68%	39.17%
2004	11.78%	10.88%	20.70%
2005	9.48%	4.92%	14.02%
2006	27.69%	15.80%	26.86%
2007	9.29%	5.49%	11.62%
Compounded	304.25%	25.53%	80.22%
Annualized	22.09%	3.30%	8.78%

time reflects all expectations, so price doesn't matter: extraordinary and remarkable logic.

As a result, we have stock prices built on air. You can pay anything and be right. No wonder many have gone back to Graham and Dodd, follow squiggly lines on charts, are concerned about astrology (alignment of the prices), or follow waves, cycle vibrations, and the like. The investment world at large has been left to its own arcane devices. Every university across the land in its undergrad, MBA, and PhD programs fails to clearly explain two basic elements: value and price. What should we pay for a stock today? Next year? Is there any wonder investors react nervously to changes in price when academia has failed to build a theory on the foundation of price? The United States completed a wild bubble in the year 2000 with extreme swings in style. Before that there was also the stock market crash of 1987 caused by MPT and portfolio insurance. If we don't know what something is worth, we are left to our emotions of panic and greed, or the bigger fool theory. We hope to find someone else to sell to at a higher price.

We need a real theory of price using the best concepts of efficient markets and of Franco Modigliani and Merton Miller (cost of capital theory and value of the firm). We can borrow from the bond market mechanics, where we indeed have an excellent idea of the relationships of price.

The first task is to establish normative theory—what would be under perfect conditions. The second task is to establish positive theory—how it works in practice given the rest of the world's behavior. This is the adaptive and applicative form of the theory. The application has many variants and exceptions and must fit reality and behavior to be useful for our investing. It would take many pages to expound upon the application, and the variants can be subject to improvement, debate, substitution, and continuing discoveries of investor behavior. That behavior itself may be dynamic and adaptive over time. Our normative theory is different. It must be built like geometry, like the calculation of the circumference of a circle or the sides of a triangle.

Its foundation must be made in granite to withstand all challenge. Our theory must stand for a thousand years. We present it here.

As we are writing this to a general audience, we need to establish some basic concepts and definitions so everyone can follow.

Concept of Value and Price

Existing modern portfolio theory (MPT) uses only expected return. It is missing one of the most important elements and the first investment rule, which is: *return of my money* (not return *on* my money).

(MPT handles this indirectly by assuming a principal payment at the end, or it is incorporated into risk.)

The stock market is a tug-of-war between two classes of investors: growth and value. Growth investors follow the income statement—sales and earnings. Value investors follow the balance sheet—book value, cash, and tangible assets.

There is a third group of investors that we will call "hope" (hype?). They are the group that follows tech and biotech stocks without earnings or assets. They don't pay attention to the balance sheet or the income statement, but are only interested in product and research development announcements. This speculative class has grown over time to become a major one and can dominate the market. It is the main cause of volatility and bubbles. For now, we will ignore this very important group. They are akin to the Mongols and Huns of old who only want to pillage, burn, and plunder. They are out for the quick buck and care not for civilized investing. Risk has a completely different meaning for them, as does casino risk versus investment risk.

We first define our theory for traditional growth and value investing. Our theory must link the income statement to the balance sheet and bridge these two classes of investors. It must find the hidden equilibrium price.

ARBITRAGE

Our key tool for mathematical proof of our tenets will be arbitrage. What do we mean by growth rate arbitrage? (Recall that GRAPES stands for Growth Rate Arbitrage Price Equilibrium System.)

Assume that you have two identical companies except for price-earnings (P/E) ratio.

Company A	25% growth	10 P/E
Company B	25% growth	15 P/E

Everything else is equal. Which company's shares do you buy? Everyone will keep buying A (and selling B) until the prices are the same, which is what we call equilibrium. Here the P/E would be 12.5—proof by arbitrage.

But P/E is a spurious measure. It has mathematical holes and discontinuities. How do you evaluate a negative P/E, zero earnings, or the companies with only pennies for earnings? (Note that we didn't define growth. Growth of what?) If we use historical or current P/E, we have violated efficient market theory, which implies that historical earnings have less influence on today's prices as it is an expectational market.

THE BEGINNING OF ALL THINGS

We assume that risk is the same for our two companies A and B—that tangible value is identical to accounting value. We make all the favorite disclaimers of economists to begin our theory by assuming away all possibilities by choosing two identical firms to compare price and value.

Postulate 1: Price should be a function of future returns to investors.

Future returns may be received by investors either as a collection of dividends received in perpetuity or by selling (or liquidating the company) at any time.

$$\text{Stock price} = \phi \, (\text{Investor returns}) \qquad (\text{P}\,1.0)$$

$$P = \phi \, (r)$$

If we are a for-profit firm or investor, we must accept Postulate 1.

Postulate 2: The stock price must be a function of earnings.

If you are the sole owner of a private company, your earnings are indeed your investor returns.

$$P = \phi \, (e) \qquad (\text{P}\,2.0)$$

We know that growth is a factor and we must deal with growth of earnings, which directly translates to investor returns for the private company. But: earnings growth relative to what?

Let us again use a sample of two companies:

	Earnings		
	Year 1	Year 2	Growth
Company A	$1.00	$2.00	100%
Company B	$1.00	$2.00	100%

What if the net worth is:
$$A = \$10$$
$$B = \$100$$

We submit that the 100 percent increase in earnings is far more important to Company A (or Investor A if we consider returns). Another way to look at it is that an extra dollar means more to a poor man than to a rich man. We cannot simply look at earnings growth. It must be relative to the size of the investment—the net worth of our investment. We must introduce a scaling factor.

We define *net worth* as book value. (Our actual investment as an investor needs the stock price; here we are first trying to establish the value of the company and its relationship to what we will pay for it.) So we have earnings scaled by book value, which happens to also be the definition of return on equity (ROE).

Definition 1.0

$$\text{ROE} = \frac{\text{Earnings}}{\text{Book value}} \tag{D 1.0}$$

where book value is simply assets – liabilities = equity. (We can assume no liabilities. Then assets = equity.) We can further define this as common equity.

For a private firm, book value is the sum of all paid–in capital and retained earnings.

We can express both earnings and book value in per-share terms since:

Definition 2.0

$$\text{Price} \times \text{Shares outstanding} = \text{Book value} = \text{Capitalization} \\ \text{for a private company} \tag{D 2.0}$$

For a partnership, we would use percentage ownership instead of shares. As a sole owner of several companies, I was legally required to issue shares according to the paid-in value of the start-up capital and issue additional shares for when additional capital is added. (Otherwise it is considered a loan.)

Now that we have shares, we have **Postulate 2.1**:

$$\text{Stock price} = \oint (\text{Earnings per share}) \tag{P 2.1}$$

And now we will divide both sides of the equation by book value (BKV) per share to get the relative importance of size.

Postulate 3

$$\frac{\text{Price}}{\text{BKV per share}} = \oint \left(\frac{\text{Earnings per share}}{\text{BKV per share}} \right) \tag{P 3.0}$$

We can also assume there is only one share if you wish.

The right-hand equation is also the definition for ROE—equation (**D1.0**). So our equation is now:

$$P/BKV = \oint (ROE) \qquad\qquad (\textbf{P3.1})$$

But the stock market is built on expectations, so this should be *future* return on equity (FROE).

$$P/BKV = \oint (FROE) \qquad\qquad (\textbf{P3.2})$$

Note that we can at any time convert this to per-share values by multiplying the equation by BKV. To demonstrate:

$$\frac{Price}{BKV}(BKV) = \oint (FROE)(BKV)$$

$$\frac{Price}{BKV}(BKV) = \oint \left(\frac{Future\ earnings}{BKV}\right)(BKV)$$

and since BKV/BKV = 1, we get back to:

$$Price = \frac{Future\ earnings}{BKV}(BKV)$$

which becomes:

$$P = \oint (Earnings)$$

which is **Postulate 2**.

Our equation so far is mathematically granite. But prices in the stock market are relative to each other. We introduce one more concept that is critical and the solution to the long-standing riddle.

Let us take any asset. Let us use the example of a $1,000 Treasury bond. When this bond was first issued (the original investment), this bond had a coupon of 10 percent.

Price	Income	Return
$1,000	$100	10%

It was issued at par, and the expected market return was 10 percent at that time. (Bond prices are quoted in a unique way, as the last figure is dropped. This bond would be considered having a price of 100.) Let us assume this bond has infinite maturity, as does the legal life of a corporation and its common stock. (Bond mechanics are such that a 100-year maturity approaches infinite maturity and a 30-year bond mathematically app-roaches 100 years when issued, so any asset with a long life approaches the infinite case. (Continuously compounding interest acts similarly.)

Now assume that one day later the rate on new bonds issued of the same risk class, everything else being equal, falls to 5 percent.

Why buy a new bond at par ($1,000) yielding 5 percent when we can buy the old bond at 10 percent? To be sure, no one will buy the new bond if they are rational[1] and aware of the first bond until both are in equilibrium, which occurs only when the price of the old bond doubles.

	Price	Coupon	Income	MRRET
New bond #1	$1,000	5%	$ 50	5%
Old bond	$2,000	10%	$100	5%

The market requires the rate of return of 5 percent. We use (MRRET) to represent the Market Required Rate of Return. And if on the next day, rates suddenly go to 20 percent and new bonds are again issued at par, the price of our first bond will plunge to be in equilibrium with the new bond since you will sell it and buy the new bond to double your income at 20 percent.

	Price	Coupon	Income	MRRET
New bond #2	$1,000	20%	$200	20%
Old bond	$ 500	10%	$100	20%

It is not the firm's cost of capital that determines the stock price; it is the required market rate of return! We will also call this the investor's cost of capital.

Prices therefore can swing wildly while the underlying asset, company, and structure (return on equity, earnings and book value, etc.) remain fixed.

To be sure this is the case for Treasury bonds as every professional investor including myself will step in and arbitrage for profit until the opportunity on the old bond is gone. Note that the value and coupon when issued do indeed affect the nominal price, so prices cannot be the only function of future returns. Our bond analogy takes us a quantum leap forward to understand market valuation levels.

Postulate 4: The required rate of return by the market directly affects the price of the stock.

We define the required rate of return as KOC: the investor's cost of capital.

From equation (**P 3.2**):

$$P/BKV = \oint (FROE)$$

We insert KOC to give comparative meaning to FROE:

$$P/BKV = \oint (FROE/KOC) \qquad \text{(P 4.1)}$$

Proof: the arbitrage of bond prices and interest rates; and after multiplying both sides by BKV we get:

$$P = \oint (FROE/KOC)BKV \qquad \text{(P 4.2)}$$

which is the normative GRAPES model.

If an investment is expected to earn twice the required rate of return, it should sell for twice its book value. If it can't make the required rate of return, it should sell at a discount exactly like a bond that has a lower coupon or a higher coupon.

The positive theoretical version will introduce behavioral risk and different risk classes of the firm and deal with two period outcomes. (Assumed in the normative model is that the same FROE continues forever.) The normative model captures all the key elements but risk. Risk is subject to individual preference.

We have assumed a riskless asset. We can extend this to securities of the same risk class, which allows us to do a comparative evaluation.

We present Postulate 4.2 as the correct theory of price—to withstand all time. It establishes the true value of the firm. It adjusts to market conditions. It captures future expectations. It connects and gives meaning to value and growth. It shows that the firm's structure (book value) is still important. It explains huge premiums to book value and discounts. It explains the role of interest rates and their competing influence on cost of capital of investors. It explains volatility of the markets, contraction and expansion of P/E rates, and levels of market valuation. It removes the confusion over the firm's cost of capital, which is merely a latent determinant of the profitability of the firm and its earnings.

Summary of The Theory

Academia has addressed well the issue of risk and return, but it has all but ignored concepts of value and price. Yes, there are dividend discount models, but they lie outside MPT and cannot tell us what the price should be today even under a host of assumptions. What is an asset worth?

We have solved the problem for three of the four elements; value, price, and return. We sidestep the issue of risk by assuming a riskless security, or securities of the same risk class. Academia provides no useful basis for relative evaluation of securities—except for security market line (SML)—in risk/return space by saying all prices are efficient. Specific risk can be diversified away, so only systematic risk (beta) is important. It is a very clever and diabolical argument signifying nothing about the price and value of an asset.

We want a theory that will tell us what we should pay for a company in a rational context. When we begin to overlay the characteristics of investor behavior (the most dangerous form of risk is how investors react to greed and fear), we get very close to explaining today's stock price. Knowing what the price should be gives us an awesome tool for turning GRAPES into fine wine. It is one major reason why we have had the best performance in the world the past seven years. It is also why we think we will continue to have exceptional performance. Of course we are subject to the usual extreme style swings and moods of the general investing public. And we must add the mandatory disclaimer that past performance is not an indicator of future performance (just in case Big Brother is watching).

But we can invest with great confidence that we know what the price should be given all publicly available information and that we will not overpay for anything. That gives us an advantage over thousands of other investment managers who are essentially clueless.[2]

GRAPES is a simple equation, like $E = mc^2$. It is elegant, and a theory of relativity for investing that will stand the test of time.

THE MODEL AND SYSTEM

The GRAPES model is a sophisticated, dynamic, and powerful investment management tool. It addresses both value and growth of an investment by relating the earnings growth with the size of the firm and cost of capital. In so doing, it resolves the controversy of having to make a choice between value and growth. In reality a stock price is affected by both the company's balance sheet and its earnings potential. The GRAPES theory makes this important link by integrating the two. The model, driven by the theory, becomes the practical application of identifying the efficient price of a stock.

The value of a firm has to be linked to some general cost of capital, and the concepts of capital budgeting theory should apply to investor decisions as well as to projects. Price should be a function of future returns to investors. We would pay a premium for a company if returns were above average and a discount if returns were below average. Earnings of a company are viewed by investors as being earnings available to the owners or shareholders. We assume that stock price is a function of earnings.

The efficient market hypothesis states that consensus expectations and historical information are fully reflected in stock prices. Historical earnings have no significant influence on stock prices except as a potential aid for forecasting future earnings patterns. Also, an important piece of nonexpectational data is the immediate liquidation value of the firm. If an investment fails to earn its cost of capital, the investment will sell at a discount to its book value or liquidation value. If it earns more than its cost of capital, it will sell at a premium to its book value.

$$\frac{\text{Price}}{\text{Book value}} = \frac{\text{Forecasted return on equity}}{\text{Cost of capital}}$$

A particular company's unique cost of capital is considered irrelevant to an investor's decision to buy or sell with the exception of the implicit effect of that unique cost of capital on calculating future return on equity. Investors determine stock prices and it is *their* cost of capital that is important. If the cost of capital of investors change, they would be able to raise more or less funds. They would now take advantage of more profitable situations or be forced to sell positions that are no longer profitable. All new opportunities created by a change in the cost of capital will be exploited until a new market equilibrium is reached.

In capital market theory, a key of price equilibrium is the security market line (SML), shown in Exhibit 14.3. In equilibrium, an asset's expected return is a positive linear function of its covariance of returns with the market. Every individual security's expected return and risk will be on this SML. Proof is by arbitrage. If we assume that all securities are of the same risk class, by proof of arbitrage all stock prices will be on the SML in order of expected return on equity after scaling for the size of the firm.

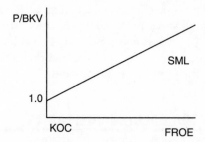

EXHIBIT 14.3 GRAPES Security Market Line (SML)

The SML slope coefficient or regression coefficient is a measure of systematic risk, universally known as beta. The slope coefficient of the GRAPES SML is defined as the ratio of the future return on equity and the cost of capital. We will call this the GRAPES coefficient multiplier (GCM). When GCM is 1, the company is expected to earn exactly the cost of capital and will sell at book value. To find the theoretical price of a stock on the SML, we multiply both sides of our relationship by book value:

$$\frac{\text{Price}}{\text{Book value}} = \frac{\text{Forecasted return on equity}}{\text{Cost of capital}}$$

$$\frac{\text{Price}}{\text{Book value}}(\text{Book value}) = \frac{\text{FROE}}{\text{KOC}}(\text{Book value})$$

$$\text{Price} = \frac{\text{FROE}}{\text{KOC}}(\text{Book value})$$

where KOC is the investor's cost of capital and FROE is the theoretical return on equity.

In summary, the GRAPES theory links the balance sheet with the earnings statement of a firm, the size of the firm, and the cost of capital in the marketplace. The model adjusts for investor's perceptions and risk preferences. The model is:

$$\text{Price} = \text{Zeta}(f)\frac{\text{FROE}}{\text{KOC}}(\text{BKV}) + \text{Chinese wall}$$

Zeta is the investor's preference function that is a transformation to the GRAPES Coefficient Multiplier (GCM). The Zeta function accommodates not only high-growth stocks but also speculation in turnaround cases and even bankruptcy situations. The Chinese wall is a nonparametric item that we add to our model; it reflects the investor time horizon. We use the Chinese wall concept (there are two: current wall and future wall) to explain and understand stock prices that are temporarily much lower than the theoretical price per investor behavior. They are not used in the actual calculation of theoretical price or the adjusted theoretical price, and they are considered temporary behavioral anomalies.

GRAPES SYSTEM FOR VALUING COMPANIES

This is the practical data you need to apply the theory.

Definitions

KOC = Cost of capital = Long-term government bond yield

FY1 = Consensus EPS estimate for current fiscal year

BKVPS = Book value per share (one year ago from FY1 date)[2]

FROE = Forecast ROE = **FY1/BKVPS**

ZETA = $[(1 + FROE)^2 - (1 + FROE)]/KOC$

GRAPES = GRAPES company value = **ZETA** $\times$ **BKVPS**

Special Situations

■ If FROE < KOC, use the following GRAPES calculation:

$$GRAPES = BKVPS \times [1 - (KOC - FROE)]$$

■ When no forecast for EPS (FY1) is available:

$BKVPS_{-1}$ = Year ago book value per share = Latest book value per share − Latest EPS12 + Dividends/share throughout the year (*EPS12 = trailing 12 months earnings per share*)

ROE = Latest $EPS12/BKVPS_{-1}$

ZETA = $[(1 + ROE)^2 - (1 + ROE)]/KOC$

GRAPES = GRAPES company value = ZETA $\times BKVPS_{-1}$

GRAPES Adjustments

This section not only handles extreme cases, but deals with financial companies – especially banks.

For Excessive Risk of Default or Bankruptcy In our model and theory, we assume there is no long-term debt. These companies are debt free. Companies that are highly leveraged will obtain a high return on a small level of equity, but have greater risk. For companies in a normal risk range, we don't need a special adjustment. However, the following can be used for all companies – especially financial companies.

GRAPES Long-term debt coefficient (GLT) is:

$$GLT = 1.0 - \left(\frac{\text{Long term debt}}{\text{Common equity}} \times 0.10 \right)$$

| a limit of ≥ 0.50

Some foreign banks do not report long-term debt. The ratio to use for these banks is:

$$GLT = 1.0 - \left(\frac{\text{Loans to customers}}{\text{Current account deposits}} \times 0.10 \right)$$

| a limit of ≥ 0.50

So if long-term debt is equal to common equity, we discount the GRAPES price by 10 percent. If long-term debt exceeds common equity by double, then it is 20 percent. This adjustment should also be used with the next one:

GRAPES current liabilities coefficient (GCL) is:

$$GCL = 1.0 - \left(\frac{\text{Current liabilities}}{\text{Common equity}} \times 0.10 \right)$$

| a limit of ≥ 0.50

So if current liabilities are equal to common equity, there is a 10 percent discount. Note that almost all companies have some current liabilities, and we may add a condition that if current liabilities are at some minimal percent we can ignore them. Note that this measure penalizes low-margin companies, as it should. We also stay away from using current assets since this would use inventories, and unsold bloated inventory is often a cause of bankruptcy.

Adjusted formula for the GRAPES price (GP) is:

$$GP = [\text{Zeta} f(ROE/KOC) \times BKV] \times GLT \times GCL$$

For Extreme ROEs from Tiny Book Values When a company has losses, its book value can approach zero (still positive) or go from negative to positive when turning around. This can create infinite ROE mathematically, and we need to fix this.

Conditions:

- If book value is ≤ 1.00 and EPS12 is > than half of BKV (50% ROE), then substitute total assets instead of common equity for the ROE calculation (ROA instead).
- If book value >1.00 and < 10.00 and ROE >100%, and book value is < .20 of total assets, also substitute ROA.
- If you use ROA, do not use GLT and GCL adjustments.

Special Cases There are two other special cases that create mathematical problems:

1. Negative book value and positive earnings.
2. Negative book value and negative earnings.

These have a more complicated solution using the analyst's long-term growth rate forecast and assets. For extreme negative cases, one can substitute the Black-Scholes option pricing model to come up with a price that reflects speculation without any underlying value. For simplicity, we suggest excluding these cases when solving for KOC treating them as N/A or not appropriate.

Class Stock To reflect your true ownership, you need to adjust class stocks for their true voting power.

Grapes Procedure for Handling Class Stocks All class stocks (over 10% of all companies) need to be manually investigated by looking up their shares outstanding for both classes and the voting rights from each company's 10-K or 10-Q and proxy statement (DEF-14A).

Then FY1 or EPS12 needs to be manually reduced before doing GRAPES theoretical price calculation.

The ratio by which FY1 or EPS12 need to be multiplied is:

Total number of shares for both classes/Total number of votes

Illustrated by example:

Richardson Electronics, Ltd.

Common stock	14.865 million shares	Entitled to one vote
Class B stock	3.048 million shares	Entitled to 10 votes

Adjustment ratio to FY1 or EPS12:

14.865 + 3.048 = 17.913 million total shares available
3.048 × 10 = 30.48 + 14.865 = 45.345 million votes available
Total number of shares/Total number of votes = 0.40

The company's FY1 or EPS12 needs to be multiplied by 0.40 before doing the GRAPES calculation.

THE PRICING OF RISK

While the CAPM is totally concerned with risk to the extent there is no price, there is no direct pricing of risk in the GRAPES model. The

GRAPES model best applies to securities of the same risk class. Stocks that lie outside the normal range of leverage, including financials, have their own variants of measurement. There should be some further discount or premium for quality, stability, or reliability, perhaps in accordance with bond ratings. However, bond ratings are badly skewed to market capitalization.

There is no evidence that a large company with a stable business will survive longer than a small company with a stable business. In fact, there may be evidence to the contrary. Nevertheless the larger, more politically powerful company will get a substantially higher credit rating although the products that got it there are more likely to become obsolete and are under greater competition, more cyclical influence, and less sustainable growth by the very nature of its size.

Another issue is the use of consensus forecasted earnings when agreement could be either unanimous or wide among analysts. The size of the forecast error, the correlation of future errors, and the behavior of analysts are more important than agreement.

In the commodities market, risk is often not priced. The future prices normally trade at less than the spot price or close to the spot price. Oil, for example, rarely has a futures premium where it pays to store current oil for future delivery even though there are always high geopolitical risks. Basic crops such as corn and wheat are at high risk to the weather, which tends to have many extremes, yet future prices often seem to only reflect that the sun is always shining.

The investors' required cost of capital can change rapidly, and this, too, should be a risk (gain or loss), but like forecasting the stock market, perhaps the most practical forecast is today's price as the best guess for the future (at least according to efficient market theory), so we don't need to further adjust the prices for general risk. You can solve for KOC at any point in time across the market since that is the only unknown variable in the GRAPES model. Prices are set by marginal sellers and buyers—in some way linked to those of an auction where the highest bid wins or the most extreme opinion generates a buy or sell. The pricing of risk will be a function of investment behavior affected by fear, greed, and overreaction. Such an overlay function will explain the differences between the GRAPES theoretical price and the actual price.

The model does an excellent job of explaining most stock prices. Like Adam Smith's *Wealth of Nations*, the market invisibly finds its equilibrium. GRAPES goes a very long way in clearly explaining and understanding this invisible process.

APPENDIX: EXAMPLES OF MCDONALD'S AND WAL-MART

GRAPES System for Valuing Companies McDonald's Corp. (MCD)

Cost of Capital = 2/28/2008 Corporate AAA Bond Yield

$$KOC = 5.55\%$$

Consensus EPS Estimate for Current Fiscal Year

$$FY1 = \$3.18$$

Book Value per Share One Year Prior to FY1 Date*

$$BKVPS = \$13.11$$

Forecast ROE = FY1/BKVPS

$$FROE = 0.2425$$

$$Zeta = [(1 + FROE)^2 - (1 + FROE)]/KOC$$

$$Zeta = 5.43$$

GRAPES Company Value = Zeta × Full Year Ago BKVPS

$$GRAPES = \$71.19$$

GRAPES Adjustments:

$$GLT = 1.0 - \left(\tfrac{\text{Long-Term Debt}}{\text{Common Equity}} \times 0.10 \right)$$

Long-Term Debt = $7,310   (million)
Common Equity = $15,280   (million)

$$GLT = 0.95$$

$$GCL = 1.0 - \left(\tfrac{\text{Current Liabilities}}{\text{Common Equity}} \times 0.10 \right)$$

Current Liabilities = $4,499   (million)
Common Equity = $15,280   (million)

$$GCL = 0.97$$

GRAPES Price = $65.79

Last Price = $53.16   (3/3/2008)
GRAPES Return = 23.76%

*FY1 is for fiscal year ending 12/31/2008; book value per share is as of 12/31/2007.

On December 12, 2007, McDonald's was at $63.69 (almost its GRAPES price) when the stock market began a sharp decline.

GRAPES System for Valuing Companies Wal-Mart Stores Inc. (WMT)

Cost of Capital = 2/28/2008 Corporate AAA Bond Yield

$$KOC = 5.55\%$$

Consensus EPS Estimate for Current Fiscal Year

$$FY1 = \$3.40$$

Book Value per Share One Year Prior to FY1 Date*

$$BKVPS = \$16.18$$

Forecast ROE = FY1/BKVPS

$$FROE = 0.2101$$

Zeta = $[(1 + FROE)^2 - (1 + FROE)]/KOC$

$$Zeta = 4.58$$

GRAPES Company Value = Zeta × Full Year Ago BKVPS

$$GRAPES = \$74.13$$

GRAPES Adjustments:

$$GLT = 1.0 - \left(\frac{\text{Long-Term Debt}}{\text{Common Equity}} \times 0.10\right)$$

Long-Term Debt = \$29,799   (million)

Common Equity = \$64,608   (million)

$$GLT = 0.95$$

$$GCL = 1.0 - \left(\frac{\text{Current Liabilities}}{\text{Common Equity}} \times 0.10\right)$$

Current Liabilities = \$58,153   (million)

Common Equity = \$64,608   (million)

$$GCL = 0.91$$

GRAPES Price = \$64.35

Last Price = \$49.89   (3/3/2008)
GRAPES Return = 28.98%

*FY1 is for fiscal year ending 1/31/2009; book value per share is as of 1/31/2008.

Wal-Mart made a new 52-week high of \$51.57 on February 27, 2008, as it has defied a sharply declining stock market.

NOTES

1. In practice, bond salespeople do indeed manage to sell new bonds to Joe Investor when better opportunities from older bonds can be purchased directly in the market.
2. Example: If FY1 is for fiscal year ending 12/31/2009, book value per share should be as of 12/31/2008. Similarly, for fiscal years not ending in December, book value per share should be one year back from the FY1 date.

REFERENCE

See any investment textbook for the existing Capital Asset Pricing Theory, the Capital Asset Pricing Model (CAPM), and dividend discount models.

CHAPTER 15

Portfolio Valuation

Challenges and Opportunities Using Automation

Randall Schostag
President, Minnesota Business Valuation Group,
LLC. Olsen Thielen & Co., Ltd. subsidiary

Business development companies, hedge funds, and other fund managers face new, intensive scrutiny over periodic valuations of portfolio securities. From a funds management/compliance standpoint, it is essential to have reliable sources for this security valuation, especially with privately owned holdings. For multiple reasons, business valuators who value these funds must simultaneously value numerous securities rapidly. To accomplish this laborious task may require the employment of new types of technological tools. Automating aspects of the process might offer a new solution.

Divided into two major groups of topics, this chapter explores the various aspects of partial automation. The first segment summarizes background rules and procedures currently developing for portfolio valuation. Included is a detailed history that reviews how valuation evolved from a narrow domestic focus to an international application. This segment concludes with the effect of these events on appraisers and their portfolio valuations. The chapter then reviews the application of the evolving portfolio valuation regulations. Finally, it concludes by proposing that current methods may also need to evolve to be timely, cost effective, and (most important) defensible.

BACKGROUND

Changes in the value of underlying securities from one period to the next not only determine the net asset value of holdings, but in addition measure portfolio managers' performance. Further, the valuation and periodic review of a portfolio should also provide information about risk to the investor.

Accurate security valuation becomes significant because open-end mutual funds must buy and sell shares daily. Unlike other industries, where directors may be conservative and simply mark down a security, mutual fund directors don't have that alternative (Investment Company Institute 2001).

The most important contributors to U.S. portfolio valuation theory include the Securities and Exchange Commission (SEC), the Financial Accounting Standards Board, the Investment Company Institute, and the Private Equity Investment Guidelines Group (PEIGG).[1] The Chartered Financial Analysts Institute (formerly the Association for Investment Management and Research) has been the most visible contributor of valuation issues from valuation practitioners.[2]

The task of fulfilling new best practices and regulations will eventually become the responsibility of certified valuators and appraisers who perform the work. Client companies and valuation specialists will be the ones who may be sanctioned for failing to comply with new directives.

Valuation practitioners have the knowledge, skill, and experience to appraise company securities for multiple purposes. The resulting appraisals provided a primary source of case law, creating legal precedent of accepted methods and procedures. Courts examine appraisers using the Federal Rules of Evidence for admissibility of expert testimony, test their methods, subject them to peer review, and determine if the methods are accepted within the valuation community.

Appraisers understand that the most problematic securities are those that are not publicly traded or where trading prices do not reflect true value. Certified business appraisers specialize in valuing private business. The certifying bodies have adopted standards, developed over time, to assure complete work product.[3]

Business appraisal experts can benefit from emerging recommended practice. A partial listing includes addressing acceptable modeling/methods, portfolio holdings liquidity, and economical/timely reporting. Although emerging procedures consider acceptable modeling/methods, later in the article a closer inspection reveals that the enumerated procedures may fail in real-world application.

METHODS ADOPTION IMPLICATIONS

Accurate reporting by registered funds is paramount. Failure to provide defensible portfolio valuations can have significant consequences. In August 2007 the SEC issued a cease and desist order[4] against Allied Capital

Corporation in determining the fair value of specific portfolio securities for which market quotations were not readily available (SEC 2007). Internal personnel completed the appraisals instead of engaging an independent third party.[5]

Registered fund organizations are not the only ones sanctioned. In September 1998, the SEC issued a cease and desist order after establishing an aiding and abetting violation against certain individuals who did not use appropriate methods to determine the fair value of certain holdings (SEC 1998).

Portfolio management, as defined in the United States, is the management of funds for fees or commissions. Managers decide on investments and earn fees based on the size and/or overall performance of the portfolio. Participants include managers of trusts, mutual funds, pension funds, and other portfolios.[6]

About 90 percent of the portfolios are managed by organizations or persons registered with the SEC under the Investment Company Act of 1940 (ASA 2003). Such professionals have at least minimum standards of periodic reporting. However, in the past 10 years, hedge funds have demonstrated blistering growth. Consequently these funds receive little oversight or have few reporting requirements. Unregistered investment pools (venture capital funds/private equity funds/commodity pools) and registered funds/hedge funds are all often referred to as hedge funds. Some regard business development companies as part of registered investment companies, although the primary accounting challenge remains valuation.

For funds registered under the 1940 Act, IBISWorld estimated that about $10.4 trillion existed in assets under management at the end of 2006. Of the totals, institutions invested about $3.06 million and individuals invested about $7.35 trillion. Growth averages about 9.1 percent a year, increasing from $7.1 trillion at the end of 2002 to about $11 trillion by the end of 2007.

Funds management is a fragmented industry. IBISWorld estimates the four largest managers of registered funds comprise about 20 percent of the market. IBIS assessed that there are approximately 1,170 enterprises and 12,300 establishments in the registered funds industry, which employ 212,000 individuals (IBISWorld 2007).

Hedge funds grew rapidly and consequently became virtually unregulated. No universally accepted definition of hedge fund exists. It typically refers to an entity that holds a pool of securities (and/or other assets) that is not sold in a registered public offering. Also key to the definition is that the fund is not registered as an investment company. In 2003 the SEC determined that approximately 6,000 to 7,000 hedge funds and funds of hedge funds (FOHFs) existed in the United States, managing assets of $600 billion to $650 billion. The SEC expected hedge fund assets to exceed $1 trillion by 2008 (Implications 2003). By 2007 the hedge fund industry had increased to nearly 9,000 companies (Hedge 2007).

The SEC report and resulting actions focused on (1) an increase in hedge fund enforcement, (2) limited ability to obtain basic information, (3) emergence of FOHFs that do register but hold securities that are not registered, (4) hedge fund disclosure/marketing practices, (5) valuation practices, and (6) conflicts of interest.

The Financial Services Authority in 2005[7] issued a discussion paper in which it listed valuation weaknesses in hedge fund methods. It assigned the weaknesses to skill shortages and potential conflicts of interest that created significant potential for ill-informed investment decisions and harm to market confidence (Financial Services Authority 2005).

Several groups attempted efforts to set up guidelines and standards for funds as a result of rising investor, regulator, accountant, and other stakeholder concerns.

ACCOUNTING PRONOUNCEMENTS

The pivot point for valuing investments is the Financial Accounting Standards Board (FASB). On one side are the certified public accountants (CPAs) who must sign off on the audit and the appraisers who must sign off on the values. By issuance and enforcement of new requirements, the SEC is on the other side.

The Investment Company Act of 1940 drives the SEC. The 1940 Act determines policy encouraging the SEC to take certain positions that have had significant influence on how the FASB determined its definition of fair value. The SEC influenced many of the FASB's decisions by referring to the 1940 Act. Auditors and appraisers have had much less influence.

Begun in 1924, mutual funds were quickly and extensively accepted by investors. Just five and a half years later the stock market crashed. To renew market confidence, Congress enacted the Securities Act of 1933 and the Securities Exchange Act of 1934 to regulate the securities industry.

Investment companies were still new in 1940. To give investors confidence in this unique offering, Congress passed the 1940 Act to regulate conflicts of interest between investment companies and securities exchanges. Furthermore, it protected the public by requiring disclosure of material details about the investment companies.

The 1940 Act applies to all investment companies, but exempts several types of investment companies from coverage. Sections 3(c)(1) and 3(c)(7) contain the most common exceptions and include hedge funds. The Act (as amended) requires open-end investment companies to sell and redeem their shares at a price based on "current net asset value," defined as the amount that reflects calculations made substantially as follows:

- Managers must value portfolio securities for which market quotations are readily available at current market value.
- Managers must value at fair value other securities and assets for which market quotations are not readily available, and the board of directors must determine fair value in good faith.
- Managers must reflect changes in portfolio holdings by the first business day following the trade date.

The 1940 Act did not define "readily available market quotations," "fair value" or "good faith" for valuation (Ake and Hays 2007). As the gatekeeper responsible for enforcing the 1940 Act, the SEC became responsible for oversight and made interpretations.

SEC GUIDANCE

Issues may arise even if market quotations are readily available on a specific security. For example, restricted securities differ materially from unrestricted securities, so the market-quoted price is not applicable. The following chronology summarizes important SEC guidance, starting with the question of restricted securities and then addressing fair value considerations and overall supervision by fund boards of directors (Ake and Hays 2007).

> *1969.* Accounting Series Release No. 113 (October 21, 1969) provides guidance on fair valuation determinations for restricted securities. It defines fair value as "the amount which the owner might reasonably expect to receive for [the securities] on their current sale." Although there can be no "automatic formula" by which an investment company can value restricted securities, ASR 113 requires that a fund's board of directors consider all relevant factors. These factors include the operations of the issuer, changes in general market conditions, and the extent to which the inherent value of the securities may have changed.
>
> *1970.* In ASR No. 118 (December 23, 1970), the SEC sought to provide more general guidance regarding how funds should value portfolio securities. Where market quotations are not readily available,

including where existing quotations are unreliable or invalid, a fund must price its securities at fair value. ASR 118 describes several nonexclusive methods of valuation a board may use to value securities: a multiple of earnings, a discount from the market price of a similar freely traded security, a yield to maturity for debt issues, or a combination of these principles. In addition, a fund's board of directors should consider several general reasons when choosing a valuation method, including (1) the fundamental and analytical data about the investment, (2) the nature and duration of any limits on disposition of the securities, and (3) an evaluation of the forces that influence the market in which the securities are purchased and sold.

1999. The staff issued an interpretative letter to the Investment Company Institute (December 8, 1999). The letter was an effort to clarify and provide more guidance on pricing issues in an emergency or other unusual situations.

2001. A second interpretative letter (April 30, 2001) supplemented advice in the 1999 letter about valuing foreign securities. Paraphrasing, "where a fund board knows or has reason to believe that its fair value determination does not reflect the amount the fund might reasonably expect to receive for the security upon its current sale, or where a board acts with reckless neglect about its fair value determination, a fund board would not be judged to have acted in good faith."

2003. The SEC adopted Investment Company Act Rule 38a-1 (ICA Rel. No. 26299, December 17, 2003), which requires invested companies to adopt, and boards of directors approve, written compliance policies and procedures, including procedures covering the pricing of portfolio securities.

The preceding SEC directives explain how the SEC's interpretations following implementation of the 1940 Act have expanded what investment companies and appraisers must now consider when making fair value determinations. These directives have become part of generally accepted accounting principles (GAAP) through the FASB.

ACCOUNTING PRONOUNCEMENTS AND THE FASB

The SEC has statutory authority to establish financial accounting and reporting standards for publicly held companies under the Securities

Exchange Act of 1934. Throughout its history, the SEC relied on the private-sector FASB for this role.

Created in 1973, FASB is independent of all other business and professional organizations. Before FASB, the Committee on Accounting Procedure of the American Institute of Certified Public Accountants (AICPA) (1936–1959), and then the Accounting Principles Board, also a part of the AICPA (1959–1973), set up the financial accounting and reporting standards.

The standards and interpretations rendered by FASB are considered authoritative not only for the SEC, but for AICPA as well, where GAAP rules apply to all audits, reviews, and compilations, regardless of whether the companies are public or private, unless otherwise stipulated. For example, through the Uniform Accountancy Act the FASB has encouraged these rules to be broadly adopted (AICPA 2007).

The FASB's mission is "to establish and improve standards of financial accounting and reporting for the guidance and education of the public, including issuers, auditors, and users of financial information." It is a seven-member, independent board consisting of accounting professionals in a private, not-for-profit organization.

FASB standards (GAAP) govern the preparation of corporate financial reports. The Financial Accounting Foundation (FAF) funds, oversees, administers, and decides governance issues at the FASB, including determining the criteria for a sufficient majority for adopting new rules (Financial Accounting Foundation 2002). FAF is also responsible for the Governmental Accounting Standards Board (GASB) and advisory councils for both FASB and GASB. Founded in 1972, FAF consists of 16 trustees (Financial Accounting Foundation 2006). The following organizations determine who is on the FAF Board of Trustees:

- American Accounting Association.
- American Institute of Certified Public Accountants.
- CFA Institute.
- Financial Executives International.
- Government Finance Officers Association.
- Institute of Management Accountants.
- National Association of State Auditors, Comptrollers and Treasurers.
- Securities Industry Association.

As part of its role in providing guidelines for U.S. accounting, FASB participates in a convergence project with the International Accounting Standards Board (IASB). The project's goal is to move toward intercontinental uniformity in financial statements. Therefore, U.S and international companies would no longer need to complete separate financial statements. Another vital element of the convergence project for the FASB was to begin to transition from the principle of historical cost to fair value.

The 1940 Act referred to fair value, and the SEC's history of enforcement has in part involved evaluating methods to get fair value. IASB also incorporated language and set forth definitions using fair value and has been moving toward substituting fair value for historical cost accounting. Although there are many places that referred to fair value within past accounting statements and interpretations,[8] FASB did not assemble to resolve these various pronouncements about fair value until 2006.

Effective November 15, 2007, FASB's Statement of Financial Accounting Standard (SFAS) 157 became effective. It defines fair value and addresses fair value measurement protocols, financial statement disclosure, and measurement techniques. With the market melt-down in 2008, the FASB has been under pressure to revise the SFAS 157. Modest changes were made in interpretations in 2008-2009, mostly relating to securitized debt holdings, not equity.

Auditors must use the SFAS when examining financial statements, including those funds that hold multiple securities.[9] Because the SEC considers this work authoritative, it references the new statement and integrates the SFAS into its requirements. Consequently, for registered funds or other audited reporting entities, SFAS 157 is a critical determinant in how appraisers should value funds and report to users.

The FASB history, composition, and principle mandate highlights its focus on politics and its concentration on fulfilling requirements for the SEC, the 1940 Act, and publicly traded securities. There is less evidence of contributions from the private valuation community (although the FASB valuation resource group seems to offer some broader perspective). Court decisions also differ in some respects from that considered important to public companies.

Forbidding the application of a blockage discount when valuing a large position in an unrestricted security represents one troublesome feature proposed by SFAS 157. This prohibition fails to recognize that the valuation community and courts accept the blockage discount concept.[10] Strong empirical evidence exists for the effect of blockage discounts. Many now believe appraisers should divide the traditional idea of a "discount for lack of marketability" into a "discount for lack of marketability" and a "discount for lack of liquidity." Lack of liquidity effects represent the essence of a blockage discount (Abbott 2004).

Investors who trade thinly traded public stocks (or who own a proportionately large position in a stock that otherwise has reasonable trading activity) recognize the difficulty of selling blocks of stock in a timely manner. Most experience a discount or must conduct a costly secondary registration (Pratt 1996). The failure to provide a discount for liquidity of large block holdings thus potentially rewards portfolio managers who acquire thinly traded equities. The portfolio manager's buys may increase the quoted price of the stock, while also failing to describe to fund investors the potential risk of selling stock.

The FASB's proposed position reflects positions upheld in the past by the SEC. In SEC Accounting Series Release (ASR) 118 (SEC 1970) the Commission stated that for securities listed or traded on a national securities exchange, market value is the last quoted sales price on the valuation effective date. In that ASR, modification for commissions (other selling expenses) or for other adjustments (liquidity) was not provided.

The SFAS uses "exit price" and has thus avoided the question of commissions or selling costs. It uses the bid price of a security, when available, rather than its offer or last selling price. The writing of SFAS 157 caused a debate. Some became concerned about using the bid price rather than the ask price or other measure (e.g., an average of the bid and ask). The Investment Company Institute expressed apprehension that this "could cause funds to undervalue their shares, to the detriment of shareholders" (Investment Company Institute 2000). The 1940 Act established the ASR rules. The ASR requires, where market quotations are available, that securities be valued at market value, and all other securities be valued at fair value. The fund's board of directors estimates fair value "in good faith."

The SFAS 157 established a three-tiered fair value hierarchy, which prioritizes techniques for valuing the portfolio securities. It facilitates a more uniform interpretation of "good faith":

- Level 1 uses quoted prices in active markets of the subject securities. FASB considers active markets those where transactions occur with sufficient frequency and volume to provide reliable pricing information.
- Level 2 are prices other than those quoted in Level 1 that are observable either directly or indirectly. Included are prices for similar investments in active markets, quoted prices for identical or similar assets in markets that are not active, or drawn from or corroborated by observable market data.
- Level 3 pricing considers unobservable inputs (entity inputs). Includes projections used for discounted cash flow analyses.

Understanding the escalating levels is essential because they affect not only the methods used but the documentation auditors require for working papers/disclosure footnotes to financial statements. The cost of auditing and valuation progressively increases from the first to the third level.

Although appraisers still need more clarification, the SFAS 157 recognizes that a market quote in a thinly traded or inactive stock may not reflect fair value. Therefore, it may need more analyses before simply marking the price to market.

XBRL FORMAT

Another linkage between the FASB and the SEC has been their recent advocacy of eXtensible Business Reporting Language (XBRL), an XML-based, standards-based format to define and exchange business and financial information.[11] Metadata defines these communications set out in taxonomies. Taxonomies define individual reporting concepts as well as the relationships between concepts.

An international consortium, XBRL International, governs and markets the XBRL format. The consortium consists of about 600 organizations that encompass companies, regulators, government agencies, "infomediaries," and software vendors. The consortium promotes the format to transfer business information from paper-based/proprietary electronic formats to Internet-oriented processes.[12]

Availability of financial and other information through XBRL in the future will have a significant impact on use of public company information for analysts as the SEC reporting adopts its use.

EMERGING BEST PRACTICES

Regulation and accounting history are equally vital to understanding how valuing portfolios best practices evolved. Because those establishing the standards expect findings of value to be used in the context of the 1940 Act, the standards have been created for public company reporting. The appraiser must rethink the kinds of methods and procedures to use and how to report such findings.

The American Society of Appraisers (ASA) College of Fellows in 1989 (Opinion 1989) stressed defining the standard of value pertinent to a specific valuation. The Fellows noted there are many different standards of value, including fair market value, fair value (which now has two definitions, as one relates to shareholder oppression and dissenting rights), intrinsic value, and investment value. Also, the standard of value may vary among legal jurisdictions, such as in matters of divorce where states may depart from the standards of other states. It is important to know that when we appraisers apply a different standard of value, it may produce a different final value in the security.

Issued in 1959, the seminal standards work is IRS Revenue Ruling 59-60. It remains the most important reference for valuing ownership interests in closely held businesses (Lieberman and Anderson 2008). RR 59-60 applies to federal gift, income, and estate tax valuations, and the U.S. Department of Labor has incorporated it into requirements for employee stock ownership plans. Matrimonial dissolution is an example of another valuation standard that has referenced RR 59-60.

In 2006 the IRS issued general business valuation standards, applicable to all Internal Revenue Service (IRS) employees and to those who provide or review valuation services valuations for the IRS. Revenue Ruling 59-60's continuing influence is also obvious in the comprehensive business valuation standards that began to appear in the late 1980s. The most important of these was the Uniform Standards of Professional Appraisal Practice (USPAP), issued by the Appraisal Foundation in 1987, followed by standards from professional associations such as the American Society of Appraisers (ASA) in 1992, the Institute of Business Appraisers (IBA) in 1993, and the National Association of Certified Valuation Analysts (NACVA).

These appraisal associations have a history of developing valuation as a profession. This effort is independent of accounting/analyses of public securities, and establishing accepted methods/procedures for work. The valuation profession includes certification to ensure members possess uniform standards of knowledge, skill, and experience to enhance public confidence in work product. To complete the requirements, each association offers education/continuing education programs to obtain and maintain certification. The AICPA formally recognized the existence of business valuation and embraced it in 1996 by establishing the accredited business valuator designation.

The Appraisal Foundation and USPAP are outgrowths of fraudulent and poor real estate appraisals that ended with several savings and loan failures. The first edition of USPAP appeared in 1987 and the most recent edition for 2008–2009 was effective January 1, 2008.

The several business valuation standards have much in common, including the dependence on Revenue Ruling 59-60, which discusses eight factors to consider in valuations. USPAP Standard Rule 9-4 incorporates the eight factors from Revenue Ruling 59-60, and this USPAP Standard Rule remains essentially unchanged from its first issuance. The eight factors from RR 59-60 also appear in ASA Standard I–iii, IBA Standards section 5.3, and NACVA's Development Standards 3.4, as well as in the IRS Standards under "Analyzing."

Although the SEC and FASB do not directly cite the ASA, IBA, or NACVA, FASB issued a new standard, effective January 1, 2008. It reflects, in part, this body of knowledge. The Statement on Standards for Valuation Services No. 1 has incorporated most of these established principles. Since the FASB's directives are authoritative to the SEC, industry organizations are now integrating the new standards into the analyses of public companies.

INTERNATIONAL STANDARDS

The FASB's influence extends to the international community. In coordinating with the IASB, its guidelines become part of the broader discussion; increasingly parties are originating or holding portfolios outside the United States. While GAAP are the rules issued within this country, the IASB's International Financial Reporting Standards (IFRS) are the ones now most accepted outside the United States.[13]

In 2002, the FASB and the IASB agreed to integrate their standards in the Norwalk Agreement. The first paragraph of the Norwalk Agreement reads: "At their joint meeting in Norwalk, Connecticut, USA, on September 18, 2002, the FASB and the IASB each acknowledged their commitment to the development of high-quality, compatible accounting standards that could be used for both domestic and cross-border financial reporting." At that meeting, the FASB and the IASB pledged to use their best efforts to (1) make their existing financial reporting standards fully compatible as soon as is practicable, and (2) coordinate their future work programs to ensure that once achieved, compatibility is maintained.

Before finalizing SFAS 157 in January 2007, the FASB formed a valuation resource group (VRG) to provide the FASB with input for clarifying the guidance related to the application of the principles in SFAS 157. The VRG is comprised of a cross section of constituents in addition to major accounting firms. Representatives from the valuation community include:

- American Appraisal.
- Duff & Phelps.
- Financial Reporting Advisors.
- FVG International.
- Houlihan Lokey.

Users who are participating include the CFA Institute and Moody's, along with regulators. Standard setters include: AICPA, Appraisal

Foundation, International Valuation Standards Council (IVSC), Public Company Accounting Oversight Board (PCAOB), SEC, and IASB.

Simultaneous to the joint efforts by the IASB (IVSC) and the FASB (with its VRG), several other international groups have emerged and are now engaging. Many reflect the U.S. concerns about hedge funds. Valuing private security holdings and other difficult-to-value securities (e.g., derivatives) is a universal concern.

In October 2007, the International Organization of Securities Commissions issued its Policy Statement on Hedge Fund Valuation, Principles for the Valuation of Hedge Fund Portfolios. The Association Française des Investisseurs en Capital, the British Venture Capital Association, and the European Private Equity and Venture Capital Association produced International Private Equity and Venture Capital Valuation Guidelines to reflect the need for greater comparability across the industry and for consistency with IFRS and U.S. GAAP. In March 2007 the Private Equity Industry Guidelines Group issued its Updated U.S. Private Equity Valuation Guidelines.

Far from inclusive, the foregoing list demonstrates a global understanding of the changes in GAAP applicable to portfolio valuation. A deluge of ideas and preferences on valuing private securities exists. Formulating such rules is political. The rules must address the multiple international stakeholders. Additional interpretations and associated changes will likely occur within the next few years as FASB, the SEC, the IASB, and others balance the political concerns.

The domestic valuation community, which deals only with privately held companies, may possibly never appraise hedge funds or other passive investor portfolios. Appraisers and their clients will, however, experience the impact of decisions in this arena.

PRODUCING PORTFOLIO VALUATIONS

Producing portfolio valuations requires a deep understanding of the background of SFAS 157. This knowledge provides a clearer basis for fair value and the wide-ranging impact on both domestic and international communities. Business appraisers must apply their acquired knowledge, skill, and experience. However, the SEC and diverse international groups will become increasingly significant in establishing focus/standards for a broad spectrum of financial valuation assessments and, more specifically, for portfolio valuations.

Practitioner Considerations

A thoughtful review of the requirements of the various organizations indicates that political compromising may have overlooked 10 very real considerations that will directly affect the business appraiser:

1. In some practical cases, the definition of fair value departs significantly from fair market value (a critical basis for U.S. business valuations).
2. Apart from its tax purposes, the use of fair market value was influential in formulating much of U.S. case law.
3. The business valuation community has become much more reliant on using methods other than the market approach for much of its work. The use of a discounted cash flow analysis, for example, has become much more common with the advent of digital technology. Models can be thoroughly constructed. Back-tested models become more visually dramatic and require less explanation compared to using potentially problematic public guideline companies.
4. A typical valuation for a valuation engagement (AICPA definition of a complete valuation) may cost from \$8,000 to \$50,000 or more. Therefore, for a fund with multiple securities, a high cost to obtain defensible values may likely result.
5. An ordinary valuation for a typical valuation engagement may take a month or more for each security analyzed. For a fund with multiple securities, this process creates a significant delay between the effective date of a valuation and the delivery of findings. Given the use of these findings for pricing and compliance reporting, such delays will fail to meet investor needs.
6. The valuation community has traditionally employed capital market theory in a modified form to build portfolio risk from individual security risk. When performing portfolio valuations, should the appraiser measure the diversification effect of the interaction of securities to determine portfolio risk and aggregate valuation?
7. In addition to other investments, hedge funds (and other funds) not only hold private common stocks, but also hold private debt, real estate, specialized equipment for leasing, derivatives, and hybrid securities. Often valuing these various securities requires unique, specialized skills. These skill requirements raise another management issue for delivering high-quality and timely reports from potentially multiple sources of expertise.
8. Practically, the time/cost factors for valuation confirm the need for automated systems use. However, automation becomes antithetical to the hands-on analysis that currently represents the greatest strength of

business valuation. *One essential reservation remains: how can auto-mated tools be evaluated to ensure new standards compliance?*

9. The hierarchy levels set forth in SFAS 157 increase the need for documentation and support for both appraiser and auditor as the methods shift from Level 1 through Level 3. For cost and timely reporting purposes, avoiding Level 3 with its substantial analyst intervention and subjective judgment becomes likely. Given the "implied lower credibility" (FASB language), investors may be less confident if analysts use "unobservable" data (e.g., discounted estimated future cash flows). Analysts may therefore favor one method over another, because the conclusions retain more support from the rule makers.

10. The AICPA Statement of Standards for Valuation Services No. 1 lists two forms for valuation services: a full valuation engagement or a valuation calculation. Using the market approach for portfolio securities may technically represent only a calculation and therefore not reflect thorough due diligence. A valuation calculation retains much less weight than a full valuation engagement.

In summary, the following topics were reviewed:

- Background on the expanding rules and regulations.
- Protocols for portfolio valuation.
- Shift in focus from domestic to international applications.
- Ongoing debate among the stakeholders concerning the appropriate procedures to use in portfolio valuation.

USING AUTOMATION IN VALUATIONS

The remainder of the discussion examines how technology might minimize analyst intervention to solve the issues of valuing multiple securities within a rigid time constraint for compliance applications. Finding a solution is timely in light of mark-to-market concerns expressed by the Federal Reserve chairman, the insurance industry, and others.[14] This chapter now explores "marking to model."

The Financial Accounting Standards Board (FASB) issued Statement of Financial Accounting Standard 157 (effective after November 15, 2007) on fair value, which defines what auditors must now evaluate to accept appraisals of securities in portfolios. The international community, through the International Accounting Standards Board (IASB), accepts the FASB leadership on the fair value definition. The standard remains consistent with accounting series releases from the SEC to fulfill its responsibility for supervision over the Investment Company Act of 1940. The FASB has delayed some interpretations for financial assets. However, appraisers, portfolio managers, and auditors can no longer use simple cost or rule of thumb to value securities in portfolios for audit and compliance purposes.

Issues

For compliance purposes, significant, multiple issues will impact valuing portfolio securities. Appraisers must plan the work or anticipate problems when reviewed by auditors. To avoid audit difficulties, the work plan should address the following issues:

- Business appraisers consider three approaches to value: the market approach, the asset-based approach, and the income approach. A robust appraisal should evaluate all three. In contrast, the FASB defines a three-level hierarchy in valuing securities. Each higher tier—from bucket 1 to bucket 3—requires more auditors' footnotes.
- Each advanced level consumes more time, is more expensive, and is more vulnerable to rejection by an examiner. Since both the appraiser and the auditor need greater certainty, appraisers will want to achieve values for private securities by using Level 2 methods whenever possible, thereby avoiding Level 3.
- The FASB may reconsider whether publicly traded securities' prices should be reevaluated based on size of blocks relative to trading volume. At present, however, appraisers utilize a publicly traded price quote as the safest measure, despite the potential failure of the current price to reflect true value.
- The FASB and prior SEC accounting series releases stress prices quoted in public markets. Focusing on price remains consistent with the IRS. Historically, the IRS encouraged using the market approach, while discouraging other methods.
- Using publicly traded securities to benchmark the values of private securities only amplifies the problem of the mark-to-market approach, which fails to consider intrinsic value.
- The business appraisal community uses methods other than the market approach for much of its work. Appraisers face problems identifying what, if any, public companies are comparable. Consequently, subjective, discretionary selection of guideline public companies occurs.
- Managers of private equity and those engaged in mergers and acquisitions use discounted cash flow analysis. Sophisticated computer software calculates values that are transparent and easier to evaluate than previous methods.

■ Given the implied lower credibility for Level 3 analyses, investors may be less confident if the valuation uses "unobservable" data, such as discounted estimated future cash flows from analysts. Consequently, appraisers may favor a Level 2 method, even if the findings are less certain, because the conclusions receive more support from the rule makers.

■ A valuation engagement (AICPA definition of a complete valuation) may cost $8,000 to $50,000 or more. For a fund with multiple securities, significant costs exist to obtain defensible values.

■ A valuation engagement could take a month or more for *each* security analyzed. For multiple securities, substantial delay occurs between the effective date of a valuation and the delivery of findings. Given the use for compliance reporting, such delays fail to meet stated requirements.

■ The AICPA Statement of Standards for Valuation Services No. 1 lists two forms for appraisal services: a full valuation engagement or a valuation calculation. Using the market approach for portfolio securities may technically represent only a calculation and therefore not reflect thorough due diligence. A valuation calculation holds much less credibility than a valuation with thorough due diligence to users.

THREE-LEVEL HIERARCHY FOR FAIR VALUE

SFAS 157 set up a "fair value hierarchy" of three levels, which prioritizes valuation techniques for valuing portfolio securities. It promotes the understanding of "good faith":

Level 1 uses quoted prices in active markets of the subject securities. The FASB considers active markets those where transactions occur with enough frequency and volume to provide reliable pricing information.

Level 2 uses prices other than those quoted in Level 1 that are observable either directly or indirectly. It includes prices for similar investments in active markets, quoted prices for similar assets in markets that are not active, or drawn from or corroborated by observable market data.

Level 3 pricing considers unobservable inputs (entity inputs). This includes projections used for discounted cash flow analyses.

■ Appraisers use capital market theory in an adjusted form to build port-folio risk derived from individual securities. Although the SEC and the FASB prescribe approaches for valuing individual securities, the SFAS 157 and the SEC fail to address the interaction of securities within a portfolio. Portfolio construction, however, has a proven effect on the risk and value of a portfolio.

Promising Solutions

The time and cost for delivering valuations, coupled with advancing tech-nology and data availability, indicate the potential use of automated or semiautomated work flow. However, automation is antithetical to the hands-on analysis that currently is the greatest strength of business valua-tors. Appraisers and rule makers should assess how to evaluate automation tools to conduct defensible work to comply with the new standards for mul-tiple-securities valuations.

Various sellers offer software to value businesses, but the programs rely on subjective input by analysts for appraising nonpublic securities. Most software solutions do cash flow projections and analyses, producing a dis-counted present value. Although discounted cash flow (DCF) evaluation gives intrinsic value estimates, thus marking to model rather than marking to market, a human analyst must estimate various inputs. These inputs in-clude growth rate, capital structure, risk, and other factors. A few, such as the Automated Valuation Service (AVS) of the National Association of In-surance Commissioners Securities Valuation Office, keep a computerized database for members only.[15] The database updates securities prices for in-surance company portfolios, but only for traded bonds and preferred stocks—namely, securities that are filing-exempt.[16]

To establish the inputs, analysts use a labor-intensive process to select specific data and models. This analyst process incorporates personal bias. The process also increases cost and delays opinion delivery time. Most im-portant, findings based on analyst intervention escalate the valuation to Level 3 (SFAS 157). Therefore, the findings are subject to the misgivings and costs associated with Level 3. Maximizing automation to minimize an-alyst intervention may save time and cost. Therefore, partial automation could become an ideal solution. Using publicly traded guideline companies to set parameters for public companies cash flow projections to apply to a private company combines the best attributes of the market approach and the DCF income approach models. Such automation may also shift findings from Level 3 to Level 2 if the conclusions result from observable data and replicable models.

Market and Income Approaches

Certified appraisers now value private companies with a mark-to-model approach to valuation. They continue to evaluate the market approach, but also consider the income approach. The asset-based approach is usually reserved only for holding companies or companies with minimal value added from management. Because the income approach employs so many assumptions not observable in the market, its conclusions rely on Level 3 inputs, requiring substantial documentation.

Designing an automated model with minimal analyst intervention for business valuation first raises the question of what is state-of-the-art and how models have developed. Aswath Damodaran[17] stated that "the research into valuation models and metrics in finance is surprisingly spotty, with some aspects of valuation, such as risk assessment, being deeply analyzed and others, such as how best to estimate cash flows and reconciling different versions of models, not receiving the attention that they deserve" (Damodaran 2006). Yet Damodaran argues that DCF forms the basis for all other valuation.

Susan Mangiero, CFA, AVA, MBA, FRM, has said that "model-related issues are relevant as never before. Anyone using a financial model must be prepared to defend it, warts and all. No one can afford to look at output alone. Valuation professionals will be under even more pressure to explain what goes into the black box, how it gets assembled, and whether the output makes sense."[18]

An automated model needs to incorporate SEC, FASB, AICPA, and USPAP, as well as valuation certifying body rules. Therefore, an ideal model should:

- Use accurate and replicable data relevant to the effective date.
- Be sufficiently transparent so users can effortlessly interpret and justify conclusions.
- Select comparable public guideline companies based on quantitative criteria without subjective input to avoid cherry-picking.
- Select a sufficient sample of companies to reduce unique influence.
- Apply accepted methods within the academic and practitioner communities to function as a model for both.
- Focus on the market approach, using information from publicly traded companies to benchmark the value of private companies. Application includes thinly traded firms because their quoted prices may not represent intrinsic value.
- Incorporate an income approach solution, which can be applied to a subject company with minimal or no user intervention.

- Incorporate past inflation and future economic growth based on quantitative, nonsubjective input.
- Measure risk based on quantitative reasons gained from the public market to lessen analyst judgment and bias.[19]
- Provide a conclusion of value to reported equity (asset-based approach) for a reasonableness assessment and evaluation of intangible assets.
- Conduct back-testing to estimate an error rate in findings.

The preceding depicts minimum obstacles for any software answer to overcome. Focusing on those criteria, these should be goals for any automated solutions:

- Base identifying comparable guideline public companies on economics rather than arbitrary industry and size filters.[20]
- Compare companies even if in different industries. Many companies within the same industry are not comparable, depending on capital structure and operating differences.
- Understand the tools' strengths and limitations. This includes the required amount and distribution of data when developing value and confidence measures.[21] The data, for example, might not be normally distributed.[22]
- Base the income approach method, if developed, on information gained from the guideline public companies and applied to unique quantitative information pertinent to the subject company. A measure of income should be determined (earnings, gross cash flow, net free cash flow, or cash economic return) that can be used across multiple industries (Schostag and Thomas 2006).
- Normalize company financial statements to a common standard. For instance, make capital investment adjustments to normalize fixed assets and make excess cash adjustments (Schostag and Thomas 2006, 37).
- Test model measurement conclusions against the public guideline companies historically to demonstrate how well the model's intrinsic value compares with historical pricing. Back-tests should allow the analyst to gain an error estimate for findings.

In a working paper presented at the Financial Management Association conference in Texas in October 2008, authors Robert J. Atra and Rawley Thomas[23] describe a system for developing and evaluating an automated DCF model based on the fundamental measurement principles of robustness, accuracy, minimum bias, and predictability.

"Finding the 'economic drivers' is an essential result of developing a DCF model," the authors write. A well-specified DCF model can avoid the criticisms of other models, including data mining. "Since the model of price level has a foundation of DCF at its base, there is a built-in economic explanation of why different inputs alter the intrinsic value. Theoreticians should be more comfortable with a process that begins with an economic model as opposed to one that is an artifact of massive statistical analysis" (Atra and Thomas 2008).

To test existing computerized models of publicly traded common stock, Atra and Thomas used proven statistical techniques to assess whether models were robust, accurate, unbiased, and predictive. Basing the work on the assumption that market prices of publicly traded common stock represent errors around intrinsic values, the intrinsic values determined by the various models were then compared to actual market prices. Models that produce intrinsic values close to actual prices are deemed more accurate.

Atra and Thomas investigated several versions of dividend discount models for the study, as those models represented actual cash flows received by investors. The three particular models were the Gordon model, the GROW model, and the ROPE model. The Gordon model is a one-phase model, not considering future changes in payout. The GROW and ROPE models are multiphase, where growth regresses toward a mean over time.

The Atra and Thomas study results demonstrated that models differ significantly in terms of accuracy. Model accuracy can be improved in a systematic manner, however. For instance, the authors found that including firm-specific betas actually created a bias in the models, reducing accuracy. Removing bias by incorporating a uniform beta of 1 actually improved the accuracy of the model. The more accurate models also predicted future returns, as prices migrate toward intrinsic values. In other words, undervalued securities from the model provided greater returns than overvalued firms.

Atra and Thomas concluded that models can be built that are accurate and predictive. However, they also stated that models require developers to systematically remove bias arising from the model's economic drivers.

Data Sources

Business valuation professionals are fortunate to have high-quality publicly traded company information—both pricing and fundamental data. Unlike data for real estate specialists, the data available are not only high-quality but consistent nationwide as well.

There are several sellers that supply historical public company information, both pricing and financial. Some important vendors are:

- Hemscott Data[24]: fundamental and pricing data.
- Center for Research in Security Prices (CRSP)[25]: pricing data.

- Compustat[26]: fundamental data; a joint venture of CRSP and Compustat[27] combines fundamental and pricing data.
- EDGAR Online: pricing and fundamental information.[28]

The SEC's EDGAR is a primary source of information. EDGAR Online and other vendors use the reported information directly from EDGAR, while sellers like Compustat adjust the reported information. EDGAR is available because the SEC mandates that reporting companies, including all exchange-traded firms, file financial statements in accordance with its Regulation SX, which governs the actual form and content of financial statements of publicly traded securities.[29] Since 1972, the SEC requires companies that report to it to use Regulation SX formatting.[30] However, many provisions of Regulation SX have since been modified by Regulation S-T, which governs the preparation and submission of documents in electronic format. Subsequently, Regulation S-T is currently undergoing modifications with new and future provisions to mandate substantial new methods by which companies submit the data, thus making it easier to utilize the information.

Among those changes, in February 2008 the SEC launched on its web site the Financial Explorer to help investors rapidly and more easily analyze financial results of public companies. Users can examine corporate performance by viewing diagrams and charts. They can use the financial information provided to the SEC as interactive data in eXtensible Business Reporting Language (XBRL).

Many expect the SEC's mandate for using XBRL in financial reporting will encourage more uniform charts of accounts and, therefore, ensure consistency among reported financial statements. EDGAR Online partnered with XBRL and has a database that is now consistent with the reporting (and downloading) of the new format.

Valuation Automation History

Real estate appraisal use of automated valuation technology provides some insight into challenges and opportunities for business appraisal. Automated valuation models (AVMs) have been one answer for property assessors, insurance underwriters, and lenders to obtain timely and economical values. Acceptance of the models has encountered conflict.

After a 30+-year history, a regulator in late 2006 noted, "While AVM technology can augment the appraisal process, it is not a substitute for an appraisal or independent valuation." Later the regulator states, "The appraisal rule contemplates the involvement of an experienced, disinterested individual who prepares the written estimate of value."[31] In this case, the regulator subsequently backed away from the first tough stance. In early 2007 the regulator wrote that AVM use is acceptable in "conjunction with review by a loan officer or an individual with knowledge, training, and experience in the real estate market where the loan is being made."[32] The regulator referred to a legal opinion necessitating human involvement in the valuation work for tax assessment (National Credit Union Administration 1994).

The correspondence on automated real estate valuations does not relate to the FASB or the SEC. However, it illustrates concern about automated models and insists on continuing professional oversight. The critical takeaway from this example remains that even if automation is developed for securities analyses, a continuing need exists for certified professionals to exercise strict oversight.

AVM technology is an outgrowth of multiple regression analysis (O'Rourke 1998). Many econometric models use multiple regression analysis to identify statistically significant variables and, therefore, predictors.

In statistics, regression analysis epitomizes a method for explaining occurrences and predicting future events. Multivariate regression analysis uses many variables to predict some unknown variable. It produces a method not only to measure the correlation between variables but also to assess confidence in those findings. For real estate, the variables may include square footage, lot size, age, quality, and other measures (O'Rourke 1998).

After identifying statistically significant measures (square footage, lot size, etc.), the real estate appraiser may use an adjustment grid to set forth the variables. The appraiser then adjusts for a specific subject property (Gordon n.d.). An analyst who feels that growth rate, debt to equity, or yield of a stock might be useful in predicting a price-earnings ratio may use multiple linear regressions and produce a range of possible price-earnings ratios (Multiple n.d.). Business appraisers also use grids, often for assessing factors, when comparing a subject company to public guideline companies or private transactions.

Access to a reliable database is essential to AVM to produce real estate values. The Federal Home Loan Mortgage Corporation and the Federal National Mortgage Association, for example, use their proprietary internal databases for pricing.[33] Vendors that build databases rely chiefly on public records from those states making disclosure of information. If unavailable, tax assessment information (adjusted for percent of market value considered in locations) and Multiple Listing Service data may also be used for benchmarking.

Many vendors use multiple sources and methods for confirmation. However, some states, for example, do not make tax assessment information available. Often in rural areas no data is available. When required information is not available, the real estate appraiser is unable to use AVM.

Automated Valuation Model Lessons

The Uniform Standards of Professional Appraisal Practice (USPAP)[34] lists five critical questions the real estate appraiser should answer affirmatively before using AVM in an engagement for valuing real estate.[35] Appraisers who can give positive answers to the following questions are likely competent to perform an appraisal using AVM:

1. Does the appraiser have a basic concept of how the AVM functions?
2. Can the appraiser operate the AVM appropriately?
3. Are the AVM and the data it uses suitable given the intended use of assignment results?
4. Is the AVM output credible?
5. Is the AVM output sufficiently reliable for use in the assignment?

Further, according to the USPAP advisory opinion, the appraiser must specify if the scope of work is to:

- Perform an appraisal.
- Conduct an appraisal review.
- Provide appraisal consulting service.
- Supply AVM findings only.

This real estate appraisal criterion is consistent with the AICPA Statement of Standards for Valuation Services No. 1 (effective January 1, 2008) for business appraisal to define if the work is a valuation engagement or a valuation calculation.

Past historical examples reveal why the appraiser prefers the market approach; the SEC, FASB, and IRS all support it. Therefore, the analyst should first ascertain if an automated solution exists to expedite the valuation and reduce cost. Second, the appraiser should try to either locate or develop an automated solution. Third, and finally, the appraiser must comprehensively learn the model to assure reliable, defensible determinations of value.

Business Valuation Software

For appraisal solutions not related to real estate, software developers that create software to discover the intrinsic value of publicly traded companies for investor buy/sell decisions should be one source of possible programs. An Internet search of "business valuation software" produced the following:

- Business ValuExpress.[36]
- Business Valuation Model (BizPrep).

- ValuSource Pro (MBAWare).
- BizPricer (Business Book Express).
- DealSense Plus (MoneySoft).
- Business Valuation Specialist (Thompson).
- Business Valuation Manager Pro (the National Association of Valuation Analysts).
- Business Valuation (Ball Park).
- VALUware (Deal Maker's Resource Center).
- Business valuation software (PriceYourBusiness.com, Value Adder, Business Valuer, Urgent Business Forms).
- Numerous programs to run on Excel (available as shareware or freeware).

In the institutional investor market, the following products approach minimal analyst intervention criteria:

- Stock Screener by Credit Suisse: analysis by sector, market, momentum, price to earnings, return on equity, price to book, dividend yield, and other measures.
- Value Line Investment Survey products.
- Programs from Zacks, Schaeffer's Research, StockTrak, Haugen Custom Financial Systems.
- DeMarche Associates ranking system.
- Numerous other valuation software sellers.

First, all available software listed, however, contains a universal flaw: The user must make numerous subjective decisions concerning which factors to input. User judgments include growth and margin forecasts for expected future performance using the income approach. Second, the few software packages that include the market approach require analyst screening to select public guideline companies for market comparables. Third, none of the various models currently available contains back-testing to supply confidence intervals of statistical reliability. Finally, none of the listed models apply the findings for use against private securities for an enhanced market approach method.

Software can be designed to follow accepted valuation methods for:

- Fitting standards.
- Eliminating mathematical errors.
- Avoiding information after the valuation effective date.
- Discovering objectively capitalization rates and long-term growth capacity.

- Avoiding subjective use of comparable company data.
- Giving consistent analyses across different companies and industries.

The aforementioned type of solution remains weak, however, relying only on numbers. For example, the automated software solution excludes company visits. These limitations must be fully disclosed. Procedures must contain sufficient information so the conclusion of value can rise above the limitations. Any reporting must contain adequate information so results can be reproduced by another analyst. A certified appraiser must remain responsible for a review and sign the conclusion. Output and reporting with an automated model implies peers within the professional community should be able to test and endorse a model. Certifying organizations like the National Association of Certified Valuation Analysts (publisher of the *Value Examiner*) should establish a certification program for appraisers.

CONCLUSION

Compliance reporting research confirms the central importance of valuation. Mark-to-market and mark-to-model approaches represent core issues facing the profession today. The growing concern of the SEC, FASB, IASB, and domestic/international private equity groups for consistent, independent valuation of portfolio securities has created opportunities within the business valuation community. Strict new rules necessitate increased appraisal quality in financial and regulatory reporting.

Believers of instantaneous, strong-form efficient markets *always* demand a mark-to-market approach. However, both behavioral finance and automated DCF research confirm the noise of market overreaction that occurs around intrinsic valuation as the anchor. Heretofore, the ability of any empirically validated model to separate with confidence the effects of anchor and noise has been inadequate. However, valuation professionals should no longer *assume* that DCF refers only to the labor-intensive approach of one company at a time for the current year.

Historically, valuing companies has evolved from an art based solely on analyst assumptions to an increasing reliance on scientific methods. Personal computers with sophisticated software have dramatically revolutionized the world, including our very own profession. Digital information about publicly traded companies is now readily available. Accessibility makes in-depth research and analysis much more cost-effective. Today's comprehensive programs should surmount the difficulties of solely marking to model. Companies must disclose *both* mark-to-market capability (when a market exists) and mark-to-model capability while describing the empirical validation of their model(s). Empirical validation needs to incorporate the measurement principles of:

- Robustness or percentage of total company years for which model(s) calculates.
- Lack of bias on driver variables of under or over intrinsic valuation.
- Accuracy of intrinsic valuations relative to achieving market prices.

Software exists today to value public securities to assist investors in selecting publicly traded common stocks to buy and sell. The foundation now exists to transform the use of these software programs into sophisticated models for a market approach. Based on empirical data that can minimize analyst intervention and produce robust values for privately held common stock, the next generation of software has the potential for revolutionizing valuation employed in the business world.

NOTES

1. PEIGG was formed in February 2002 and is comprised of a volunteer group of industry-wide representatives (www.peigg.org).
2. The CFA Institute contribution is most noteworthy for its Global Investment Performance Standards.
3. The Appraisal Standards Board of the Appraisal Foundation has been authorized by the U.S. Congress as the source of appraisal standards and appraisal qualifications with respect to certain appraisal for government purposes. The ASB issues these standards in the Uniform Standards of Professional Appraisal Practice (USPAP), the most current edition of which is effective from January 1, 2008, through December 31, 2009. At present the only certifying organization that requires adherence to USPAP is the ASA. All of the certifying organizations, however, have standards; the most recent issuance was by the AICPA through the Statement of Standards for Valuation Services, No. 1, effective January 1, 2008, which is consistent with USPAP but in greater detail for business valuation. The other certifying body standards contain provisions that are similar to those issued by the AICPA.
4. If the SEC finds, after notice and opportunity for hearing, that any person is violating, has violated, or is about to violate any provision of Section 21C, the Commission may publish its findings and enter an order requiring such person, and any other person that is, was, or would be a cause of the violation, due to an act or omission the person knew or should have known would contribute to such violation, to cease and desist from committing or causing such violation and any future violation of the same provision, rule, or regulation.
5. See also "An Analysis of Allied Capital: Questions of Valuation Technique," Greenlight Capital, June 17, 2002.

6. This activity is generally reported under North American Industry Classification 52392.
7. The FSA is an independent United Kingdom nongovernmental body, given statutory powers by the Financial Services and Markets Act of 2000, limited by guarantee and financed by the financial services industry.
8. Jim Hitchner, "Fair Value Measurement: Understanding and Applying SFAS 157, 141, & 142," 7th Annual MNCPA Business Valuation Conference, October 17, 2007, said that SFAS 157 amends 28 Opinions, Statements, Interpretations, and other official pronouncements of FASB and applies to another 39 pieces of accounting literature.
9. Although effective in late 2007, the FASB has delayed implementing many of the portions that treat financial assets.
10. See, for example, *Edwin A. Gallun*, 1974, 33 T.C.M. 1316.
11. See Wikipedia discussion regarding XBRL at http://en.wikipedia.org/wiki/XBRL.
12. Besides the SEC, the U.S. Federal Deposit Insurance Corporation, in coordination with the Federal Reserve Board and the Office of the Comptroller of the Currency, launched an XBRL project in October 2005.
13. Many of the standards forming part of IFRS are known by the older name of International Accounting Standards, which were issued between 1973 and 2001 by the board of the International Accounting Standards Committee.
14. See www.ft.com and other articles for discussion of Fed Chairman Bernanke's Congressional testimony. See also "Liquidity and Leverage" (2007) by Tobias Adrian, Federal Reserve Bank New York, and Hyun Song Shiin, Princeton University, for argument that the mark-to-market approach is procyclical and fails to give evidence of value.
15. See "Automated Valuation Service User's Manual," www.naic.org/documents/svo_AVS_user_guide.pdf.
16. The securities should be SEC-registered for reporting and have Committee on Uniform Securities Identification Procedures (CUSIP) identification. The CUSIP number identifies most securities, including stocks of all registered U.S. and Canadian companies and U.S. government and municipal bonds. CUSIP is owned by the American Bankers Association and operated by Standard & Poor's to facilitate the clearing and settlement process of securities.
17. Aswath Damodaran is a professor of finance at the Stern School of Business at New York University, where he teaches corporate finance and equity valuation. He is best known as the author of several widely used academic texts on valuation, corporate finance, and investment management.
18. Susan Mangiero, "Model Risk and Valuation," *Valuation Strategies*, RIA Thompson, March/April 2003, 37. Mangiero is president of Business Valuation Analytics, LLC, and the author of *Risk Management for Pensions, Endowments, and Foundations* (Hoboken, NJ: John Wiley & Sons, 2005).
19. Ibid. See discussion about using certainty equivalent cash flows versus a risk-adjusted discount rate, beginning page 6.
20. This extends the concept of comparables as described in Gilbert E. Matthews's presentation titled "Fairness Opinions," April 2, 2001. (*Estate of Gallo v. Commissioner*, T.C. Memo, 1985-363 [July 22, 1985])

21. See *Fat-Tailed and Skewed Asset Return Distributions: Implications for Risk Management, Portfolio Selection, and Option Pricing,* by Svetlozar T. Rachev, Christian Menn, and Frank J. Fabozzi (Hoboken, NJ: Wiley Finance, 2005).

22. See discussion of Paretian versus Gaussian distributions in "Valuing Foreign Currency Options with the Paretian Stable Option Pricing Model," by Stanley J. Hales, Price Waterhouse, LLP, October 3, 1997.

23. Robert J. Atra, PhD, is professor and chair of the finance department, Lewis University. Rawley Thomas is co-founder and president of LifeCycle Returns, Inc.

24. Hemscott databases offer historical financial data and stock price information on U.S., Canadian, and international publicly traded companies, 215 industry groups, and major equity markets. Most time series data in the database begins in the early 1970s. It was formed in 2003 from Media General Financial Services and was acquired by Morningstar in early 2008. Morningstar acquired Ibbotson Associates in 2006 and the Standard & Poor's fund data business in March 2007.

25. CRSP is an integral part of the University of Chicago's Graduate School of Business. With a grant of $300,000 from Merrill Lynch, CRSP was established in 1960.

26. Standard & Poor's started Compustat in 1962. Compustat provides unmatched company history back to 1950, providing key restated and unrestated data for back-testing. S&P's Compustat data is standardized to ensure comparability among similar types of data items, as well as financial results in current and prior time frames. Compustat notes that there is much latitude among companies and industries regarding reporting, presentation, and disclosure methods and alleges that its manual adjustments present better data for modeling.

27. See www.crsp.com/products/ccm.htm.

28. EDGAR Online, Inc. makes its information and a variety of analytical tools available via online subscriptions and licensing agreements (www.edgaronline.com/company/about.aspx).

29. All companies, foreign and domestic, are required to file registration statements, periodic reports, and other forms electronically through EDGAR.

30. See www.law.uc.edu/CCL/regS-X/SX1-01.html#history.

31. Letter dated October 31, 2006, to Infinity Federal Credit Union, Westbrook, Maine, from National Credit Union Administration associate general counsel Sheila Albin regarding use of automated valuation models. NCUA is the federal agency that charters and supervises federal credit unions and insures savings in federal and most state-chartered credit unions.

32. Letter dated January 19, 2007, to Infinity Federal Credit Union from NCUA, regarding "Additional Guidance on Using Automated Valuation Methods."

33. See Econbrowser, www.econbrowser.com/archives/2007/03/fannie_freddie.html for discussion of Freddie Mac and Fannie Mae business of holding large mortgage portfolios.

34. USPAP, 2008–2009 Edition, effective January 1, 2008 through December 31, 2009, Appraisal Standards Board, Appraisal Foundation. See Advisory Opinion 18 (AO 18), A-45.
35. This discussion does not pertain to mass appraisal, but to the appraisal of a specific real property. Mass appraisal generally describes a procedure that defines a group of properties with characteristics sufficiently similar so that one model may be applied to all.
36. Business ValuExpress is owned by Mike Adhikari, a principal of the Minnesota Business Valuation Group, LLC.

REFERENCES

Abbott, A. 2004. *Role of liquidity in asset pricing.* West Virginia University.

AICPA. 2007. Standards for regulation, including substantial equivalency. *Uniform Accountancy Act.* New York: AICPA (July).

Ake, J., and M. Hays. 2007. *Regulatory and accounting standards on the valuation of portfolio securities. Wall Street Lawyer* (January).

ASA College of Fellows. 1989. *Opinion of the College on defining standards of value. American Society of Appraisers* (June).

Atra, R., and R. Thomas. The fundamentals of automated DCF modeling. Financial Management Association Annual Conference, Dallas, Texas, October 10, 2008.

Damodaran, A. 2006. Valuation approaches and metrics: A survey of the theory and evidence. Stern School of Business, New York University (November).

Financial Accounting Foundation. 2002. Financial Accounting Foundation changes Financial Accounting Standards Board's voting to increase efficiency. Financial Accounting Foundation press release, Norwalk, CT, April 24.

Financial Accounting Foundation. 2006. Annual report.

Financial Services Authority. 2005. Briefing note BN008/2005. FSA (June 23). www.fsa.gov.uk/pages/about/media/notes/bn008.shtml.

Gordon, W. N.d. Appraisers, buyers and adjustment grids. www.aicanada.ca/e/articles/appraisal_principles_related_to_market_value_and_injurious_affection.cfm.

Hedge fund management. 2007. *First Research, Quarterly Update* (November 12).

IBISWorld. 2007. Portfolio management in the US: 52392 (July 30).

Implications of the growth of hedge funds. 2003. Staff report to the United States Securities and Exchange Commission (September).

Investment Company Institute. 2000. Comment letter ICI Director-Operations/Compliance & Fund Accounting to FASB. ICI (May 31).

Investment Company Institute. 2001. Valuation issues for mutual fund directors. Investment Directors Conference.

Lieberman, M., and D. Anderson. 2008. Will the real business valuation standards please stand up? New York Society of CPAs (January).

Multiple linear regression. N.d. www.trade10.com/Linear_Regression.html.

National Credit Union Administration. 1994. NCUA Office of General Counsel Opinion 94-0909 (October 7).

Initiation Chair Responsibility. Volume 34, No. 2.

O'Rourke, A. 1998. *Automated valuation models*—Threat and opportunity. *Appraisal Today.* www.appraisaltoday.com/avms.htm.

Pratt, S. 1996. *Valuing a business.* Chicago, IL: Irwin Professional Publishing, 324.

Reilly, R. 2000. *Handbook of advanced business valuation.* New York: McGraw-Hill, 140.

Schostag, R., and R. Thomas. 2006. *Discounted cash flow method, using new modeling to test reasonableness. Valuation Strategies, Thompson RIA* (September/October), 24–41.

SEC. 1970. Investment Company Act Release No. 6295, December 23.

SEC. 1998. Administrative Proceeding File No. 3-9317. *In the matter of: Parnassus Investments, Jerome L. Dodson, Marilyn Chou, and David L. Gibbon; and Western Asset Management Co. & Legg Mason Fund Advisor, Inc.,* IAA No. 1980, September 28, 2001; and *Hammes* (ICA Rel. No. 26290), December 11, 2003.

SEC. 2007. Administrative Proceeding File No. 3-12661; Securities Exchange Act of 1934 Release No. 55931; and Accounting and Auditing Enforcement Release 2618.

CHAPTER 16

The Valuation of Health Care Professional Practices

Robert James Cimasi
President, Health Capital Consultants

Todd A. Zigrang
Senior Vice President, Health Capital Consultants

The valuation of professional practices, such as medical practices, requires an understanding of the economic and market forces—that is, the reimbursement and regulatory environment in which the professional practice operates. Specifically, this chapter discusses the selection and application of the methodologies and approaches utilized in the valuation of professional practice enterprises.

The valuation of professional practices can be examined within the framework of the *four pillars*: *regulation, reimbursement, competition,* and *technology.* (See Exhibit 16.1.)

BASIC ECONOMIC VALUATION TENETS

Market perceptions of the value of an enterprise are based on investors' knowledge of the *historical* and *current status*, but more important, the *future trends* of the industry and transactional/capital marketplace within which the subject professional practice operates. An understanding of the importance of future trends to the valuation process is illustrated by the following basic valuation tenets:

- All value is the expectation of future benefit; therefore, value is forward-looking.
- The best indicator of future performance is usually the performance of the immediate past.

EXHIBIT 16.1   The Four Pillars of Valuing Professional Practice Enterprises

- Historical accounting and other data are useful primarily as a road map to the future.

Traditional professional practice valuation methodologies have relied on the analysis of historical accounting and other data as predictive of future performance and value. However, circumstances surrounding the specific industry in which the professional practice operates may have the potential to make the historical past a less reliable indicator of the future financial performance of the practice. For example, in the case of a medical practice, the turbulent status of the health care industry over the past three decades has introduced intervening events and circumstances that may have a dramatic effect on the revenue or benefit stream of the subject medical practice. In that event, the road map of historical performance becomes less predictive of future performance. An example of how events may change the prediction of future performance for a subject medical practice is set forth in Exhibit 16.2.

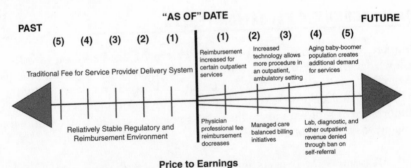

EXHIBIT 16.2   Reliance on Historical Data

THE VALUE PYRAMID

Key value drivers of professional practice enterprises may be viewed within the context of the Value Pyramid; that is, the process related to the financial valuation of these enterprises can generally be discussed within the context of two determinants: "I," the determination of the appropriate *income/earnings/benefit stream* for the subject enterprise, and "R," the development and selection of the appropriate *risk-adjusted required rate of return*, typically expressed as a discount rate, capitalization rate, or multiple, to apply to the income stream selected. (See Exhibit 16.3.)

When assessing the amount of risk associated with the given professional practice enterprise being valued, it is important for the valuator to keep the following items in mind:

- Since uncertainty breeds the perception of risk, under which circumstances a higher rate of return is demanded by potential purchasers, even high-quality, risk-averse, stable-growth, highly profitable and eminently transferable professional practices may have the potential to be "tar-brushed" by the perception of overall market uncertainty, as well as risk related to the particular subject enterprise's industry sector.
- Other market motivating factors often drive transactional pricing multiples; for example, investors' fear of being shut out of their ability to legally maintain or sell their investment represents an undue stimulus

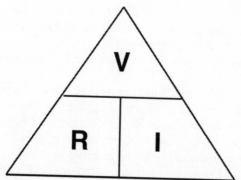

I ➡ Income/earnings/benifit stream as defined by appraiser and appropriate to assignment

R ➡ Risk-adjusted discount rate/cap rate/multiple risk-adjusted and applicable to selected income stream

V   VALUE

EXHIBIT 16.3 The Value Pyramid

or special motivation and synergy that may drive the deal, resulting in prices below or above value.

■ The selection of risk-adjusted rates to capitalize an earnings or benefit stream into value requires more than just a cursory analysis of underlying data related to market systematic risk, as a nonsystematic, subject enterprise risk adjustment may also be appropriate.

The valuation expert must be aware that the assessment of risk by investors is related to both the *actualities* and (perhaps more substantially) the *perceptions* of the market; it is related to external economic, demographic, and industry conditions, as well as aspects of the specific subject professional practice and the prospective transaction.

BUY OR BUILD? VALUE AS INCREMENTAL BENEFIT

Another important value concept is driven by the economic *principle of substitution*, which states that the cost of an equally desirable substitute (or one of equivalent utility) tends to set the ceiling of value; that is, it is the maximum price that a knowledgeable buyer would be willing to pay for a given asset or property. As applied to the professional practice valuation process, this concept is embodied in selecting and applying valuation methods in a manner that recognize that the fair market value of a professional practice (e.g., a medical practice) is the aggregate present value of the total of all future benefits of ownership to be derived, in excess of (incremental to) the level of net economic benefits that may be projected to accrue from an alternative, hypothetical, start-up entity of the same type, setting, format, and location. This benefit of *buying* rather than *building* is referred to as the *incremental benefit*. (See Exhibit 16.4.)

The equally desirable substitute that is required by the principle of substitution is more difficult to hypothecate or project at a time when historical trends and assumptions may no longer be deemed valid by prospective purchasers or investors. Measuring the depth of the marketplace's perception of the probability of success for start-ups being diminished by reimbursement and regulatory pressures is subject to similar uncertainties.

STANDARD OF VALUE AND PREMISE OF VALUE

At the outset of each valuation engagement, it is important to appropriately define the *standard of value*, which defines the type of value to be

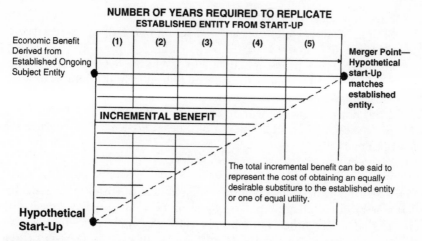

EXHIBIT 16.4 Value as an Incremental Benefit

determined (e.g., fair market value, fair value, market value, investment value, book value, etc.), and is often described as answering the question, "Value to whom?"; each type of value its own specific meaning to investors. It is also imperative that the *premise of value*, an assumption further defining the standard of value to be used and under which a valuation is conducted, be determined at the outset of the valuation engagement. The premise of value defines the hypothetical terms of the sale and answers the question, "Value under what further defining circumstances?" (e.g., going concern, orderly disposition, forced liquidation, etc.).

The Standard of Value and the Universe of Typical Buyers

The standard of *fair market value* is defined as the most probable price that the subject interest should bring if exposed for sale on the open market as of the valuation date, but exclusive of any element of value arising from the accomplishment or expectation of the merger or consolidation. This standard of value assumes an anticipated hypothetical transaction in which the buyer and seller are each acting prudently with a reasonable equivalence of knowledge, and that the price is not affected by any undue stimulus or coercion. Implicit in this definition are the following further assumptions:

- The hypothetical transaction considered contemplates a universe of typical potential purchasers for the subject property and not a specific purchaser or specific class of purchaser.

- Buyer and seller are typically motivated.
- Both parties are well informed and acting in their respective rational economic self-interests.
- Both parties are professionally advised, and the hypothetical transaction is assumed to be closed with the typical legal protections in place to safeguard the transfer of ownership of the legal bundle of rights that define and encompass the transacted property or interest.
- A sufficiently reasonable amount of time is allowed for exposure in the open market.
- Payment is made in cash or its equivalent.

When the professional practice being valued operates in an industry that is subject to further regulatory restraints defining what is meant by fair market value, other assumptions may also apply that the valuator should be aware of: For example, in the case of a medical practice, the following assumptions implicit in the definition of fair market value also apply:

- The anticipated hypothetical transaction would be conducted in compliance with Stark I and II legislation prohibiting physicians from making referrals for "designated health services" reimbursable under Medicare or Medicaid to an entity with which the referring physician has a financial relationship.[1] Stark II defines *fair market value* as the "value in arm's-length transactions, consistent with the general market value."[2] The transaction falls within Stark II's specific exception for "isolated financial transactions" when the amount of the remuneration under the employment (1) is consistent with fair market value of the services, (2) is not determined in a manner that takes into account (directly or indirectly) the volume or value of any referrals by the referring physician, and (3) is provided pursuant to an agreement that would be commercially reasonable even if no referrals were made to the employer; and (4) the transaction meets such other requirements as the Secretary [of the Department of Health and Human Services] may impose by regulation as needed to protect against program or patient abuse.[3]
- The anticipated hypothetical transaction would be conducted in compliance with the Medicare Anti-Kickback Statute making it illegal to knowingly pay or receive any remuneration in return for referrals.[4] The Medicare Anti-Kickback Statute requires the payment of "fair market value in arm's-length transactions . . . [and that any compensation is] not determined in a manner that takes into account the volume or value of any referrals or business otherwise generated between the

parties for which payment may be made in whole or in part under Medicare, Medicaid or other Federal health care programs."[5]

- Related to the aforementioned, the following definitions of terms apply. "In an excess benefit transaction, the general rule for the valuation of property, including the right to use property, is fair market value."[6] "A disqualified person, regarding any transaction, is any person who was in a position to exercise substantial influence over the affairs of the applicable tax-exempt organization at any time during [a five-year period ending on the date of the transaction]."[7] An "excess benefit transaction" is a "transaction in which an economic benefit is provided by an applicable tax-exempt organization, directly or indirectly, to or for the use of a disqualified person, and the value of the economic benefit provided by the organization exceeds the value of the consideration received by the organization."[8]

The Premise of Value and the Investment Time Horizon

The premise of value under which a valuation is conducted is an assumption further defining the standard of value to be used. The premise of value defines the hypothetical terms of the sale and answers the question, "Value under what further defining circumstances?" Two general concepts relate to the consideration and selection of the premise of value: *value in use* and *value in exchange*.

Value in Use   *Value in use* is that premise of value that assumes that the assets will continue to be used as part of an ongoing business enterprise, producing profits as a benefit of ownership. For example, in valuing the assets of a surgical hospital, the valuator must determine whether it is appropriate to value simply the tangible assets or to consider the enterprise as a going concern and incorporate the potential value of intangible assets. Orderly liquidation value involves assuming that the equipment is sold, perhaps separately, over a reasonable period of time. Forced liquidation assumes that the equipment is sold as quickly as possible to the first bidder.

Value in Exchange   *Value in exchange* describes an orderly disposition of a mass assemblage of the assets in place, but not as a going concern enterprise. While value in exchange is often referred to as liquidation value, the liquidation can be either on the basis of an orderly disposition of the assets where more extensive marketing efforts are made and sufficient time is permitted to achieve the best price for all assets, or on the basis of forced liquidation where assets are sold immediately and without concern for obtaining the best price. Costs of liquidation should be considered in the value estimate when using this premise of value. Shortening the investment time horizon may have a deleterious effect on the valuation of the subject entity, as it presents a restriction on the available pool of buyers and investors and the level of physician ownership, as required under the standard of fair market value.

VALUATION ADJUSTMENTS FOR RISK

The selection of the appropriate risk adjustment to market-derived required rates of return utilized in the development of selected discount rates, capitalization rates, and/or market multiples in health care valuation requires a thorough understanding of several underlying investment concepts. In developing a discount/capitalization rate to be applied in income approach methods, the following should be considered:

- Investors in professional practices have alternative investments available to them. Therefore, the investment justification for a given professional practice should be considered in comparison to rates of return available from a broader array of other types of investments.
- High-risk factors are considered to have a greater than average chance of negatively affecting the enterprise's earning power, while low-risk factors are considered less likely to reduce the enterprise's ability to generate profits and cash flow as a future benefit of ownership; accordingly, *elements that increase risk decrease the value of the enterprise*, and conversely, *elements that decrease risk increase value.*
- Knowledgeable investors in a professional practice with an accompanying high degree of risk should require a greater return on investment to compensate for the greater risk.
- There will be differences of opinion as to how much risk is represented by any single characteristic of the professional practice, and the risk tolerance of each individual investor is, to a large extent, dependent upon the return on investment required to compensate for the perceived level of risk.

In addition to informed consideration (i.e., consideration of the four pillars) of the effect of what may be volatile market changes on the perception of risk and resulting adjustment to the required rate of return for investment, the most probable income/earnings/benefit stream that is forecasted to be available for return to the subject practice's investors should also be carefully analyzed to determine appropriate adjustments to reported results derived from historical performance, in order to reflect the most accurate and appropriate information available on the valuation date of the most probable future performance, often referred to as *normalized earnings*. To arrive at an estimate of the normalized earnings for the subject enterprise, the adjustments considered should include, but not necessarily be limited to:

- Actual or expected increase(s)/decrease(s) in fees and reimbursements for services by regulatory edict or competitive market pressures.
- Projected increase(s)/decrease(s) in operating expenses based on new operating parameters and market realities (e.g., provider taxes and disclosure requirements).
- Expectations of the future stability and growth of the revenue streams and the sustainability of the subject practice's earnings within the context of what may be an ever-changing industry and marketplace.

In the final analysis, both the valuator's assessment of an appropriate risk-adjusted required rate of return for investment and the forecast of the most probable income/earnings/benefit stream are inexorably related to, should be based on, and must be carefully correlated to an informed, realistic, and unsparing assessment of a *universe of typical buyers'* current perceptions of the market as to the future performance of the subject enterprise, as well the market's assessment of risk related to an investment in such an enterprise.

Discount for Lack of Control

While a *control premium* is an increase to the pro rata share of the value of the business that reflects the impact on value inherent in the management and financial power that can be exercised by the holders of a control interest of the business, usually the majority holders, a discount for lack of control (DLOC) or *minority discount* is the reduction from the pro rata share of the value of the business as a whole that reflects the impact on value of the absence or diminution of control that can be exercised by the holders of a subject interest.

Discount for Lack of Marketability

There are inherent risks relative to the *liquidity* of investments in closely held, nonpublic companies in that investors in closely held companies do not have the ability to dispose of an invested interest quickly if the situation is called for (e.g., forecasted unfavorable industry conditions or the investor's personal immediate need for cash). This relative lack of liquidity of ownership in a closely held company is accompanied by risks and costs associated with the selling of an interest of a closely held company (i.e., locating a buyer, negotiation of terms, adviser/broker fees, risk of exposure to the market, etc.). Thus, a discount may be applicable to the value of closely held company due to both the inherent illiquidity of the investment as well as the transactional costs related to its disposition. Such discounts are commonly referred to as *discounts for lack of marketability*.

CLASSIFICATION OF ASSETS AND DETERMINATION OF GOODWILL

The valuator must be careful to define the professional practice entity and interest being valued. The definition and description of the entity should include identification of legal structure, legal name, trade name, address of record, and other descriptors (e.g., type of company), as well as the specific definition and description of the type and size of the interest in the entity being appraised in the engagement (e.g., "100 percent interest in the common shareholders' equity" or "100 percent interest in the total invested capital/assets").

Once the subject entity and interest have been defined, the appropriate classification of assets and the goodwill related to the professional practice is critical to the valuation process. The classification of assets may be initiated by condensing of the existing assets within the context of two categories, tangible and intangible assets. See Exhibit 16.5 for a representative classification of tangible and intangible assets in the context of a professional medical practice.

In the context of the valuation of medical professional practices, the typical focus of the classification of assets begins with determining the existence and quantifiability of intangible assets. Once that existence is established, one type of intangible asset that is often subsequently found is commonly called *goodwill*. This term may appropriately be defined as the propensity of clients/customers (and the revenue stream thereof) to return to the practice. Keep in mind that goodwill is only one of several intangible assets that may be found, not a catchall moniker for all intangible assets in the aggregate.

Intangible assets that may be classified as *goodwill and patient-related* include custody of client charts and records, as well as both personal/professional and practice/commercial goodwill. The custody of client charts and records may create the background that supports the propensity for the continued client-provider relationship, which constitutes goodwill.

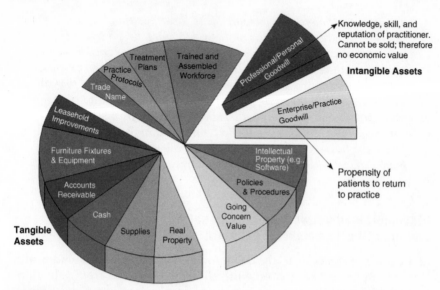

Knowledge, skill, and
reputation of practitioner.
Cannot be sold; therefore
no economic value

Intangible Assets

Propensity of
patients to return
to practice

EXHIBIT 16.5   Classification of Tangible and Intangible Assets of Professional
Enterprise Practices

There are numerous sources for information related to the definition of
the often-misused valuation term *goodwill*. The following is the definition
of "Good Will" [sic] from *Black's Law Dictionary*:

> *The favor which the management of a business wins from the pub-
> lic. Seneca Hotel Co. V. U.S., Ct.C.., 42 F.2d. 343, 344. The fixed
> and favorable consideration of customers arising from established
> and well-conducted business. Colton v. Duvall, 254 Mich. 346,
> 237 N.W. 48, 49. The favorable consideration shown by the pur-
> chasing public to goods known to emanate from a particular
> source. White Tower System v. White Castle System of Eating
> Houses Corporation, C.C.A.Mich., 90 F.2d 67, 69. Goodwill is an
> intangible asset. Something in business which gives reasonable
> expectancy of preference in race of competition. In re Witkind's
> Estate, 167 Misc. 885, 4 N.Y.S.2d 933, 947. The custom or patron-
> age of any established trade or business; the benefit or advantage of
> having established a business and secured its patronage by the
> public. The advantage or benefit which is acquired by an establish-
> ment, beyond the mere value of the capital, stocks, funds, or prop-
> erty employed therein, in consequence of the general public
> patronage and encouragement which it receives from constant or*

habitual customers, on account of its local position, or common celebrity, or reputation for skill or affluence or punctuality, or from other accidental circumstances or necessities, or even from ancient partialities or prejudices. And as property incident to business sold, favor vendor has won from public, and probability that all customers will continue their patronage. It means every advantage, every positive advantage, that has been acquired by a proprietor in carrying on his business, whether connected with the premises in which the business is conducted, or with the name under which it is managed, or with any other matter carrying with it the benefit of the business.[9]

Distinguishing between Professional/Personal and Practice/Commercial Goodwill

Sources for guidance as to the definition of goodwill can be found in IRS Revenue Ruling 59-60 and established judicial opinions from valuation-related case law. In the event that the valuation consultant determines, first, the existence of intangible asset value in the subject practice and, second, the existence of goodwill as one of the intangible assets existing, then the next step is to identify, distinguish, disaggregate, and allocate the relevant potion of the existing goodwill to either *professional/personal goodwill* or *practice/commercial goodwill*.

Professional/Personal Goodwill   Professional goodwill results from the charisma, knowledge, skill, and reputation of a specific practitioner. Professional/personal goodwill is generated by the reputation and personal attributes of the physician that accrue to that individual physician. Professional/personal goodwill may include such characteristics as "(1) lacks transferability, (2) specialized knowledge, (3) personalized name, (4) inbound referrals, (5) personal reputation, (6) personal staff, (7) age, health, and work habits, and (8) knowledge of end user."[10] Since these attributes go to the grave with that specific individual physician and therefore can't be sold, they have no economic value.

Professional/personal goodwill is not, as a practical matter, transferable. Even with long transition periods of introduction for a new acquiring physician-owner, the charisma, skills, reputation, and personal attributes of the seller cannot, by definition, be transferred. It is often stated that with assisted transfer (i.e., an extended transition period), a large portion of professional/personal goodwill may be transferred; however, the transferability suggested is in conflict with the definition of professional or personal goodwill.

Practice/Commercial Goodwill Practice/commercial goodwill should be defined in a medical services enterprise that includes a practice component as "the propensity of patients (and the revenue stream thereof) to return to the practice in the future." That portion of goodwill that may be transferred should be appropriately characterized as practice (or commercial) goodwill as described next. Practice/commercial goodwill may include such characteristics as "(1) number of offices, (2) business location, (3) multiple service providers, (4) enterprise staff, (5) systems, (6) years in business, (7) outbound referrals, and (8) marketing."[11]

Practice/commercial goodwill, as distinguished from professional/personal goodwill, is transferred frequently, and may be described as the unidentified, unspecified, residual attributes of the practice as an operating enterprise that contribute to the propensity of patients (and the revenue stream thereof) to return to the practice in the future. There are several significant factors to consider in determining the existence and quantity of practice/commercial goodwill related value.

There are several significant factors to consider in determining the existence and quantity of practice goodwill related value. In litigation related to valuation engagements, there may be significant legal precedents related to establishing evidence as to goodwill in a specific legal venue or court jurisdiction. The valuator should consult with the attorney in the case to clearly understand these definitional requirements. Also, significant practice transfer activity in the market area can result in marginal practices attaining significant goodwill value.

IMPACT OF COMPETITIVE FORCES

The competitive environment in which the subject professional practice operates is a significant factor to be addressed by the valuator in performing the valuation analysis.

Harvard professor Michael Porter[12] is considered by many to be one of the world's leading authorities on competitive strategy and international competitiveness. In his 1980 book *Competitive Strategy: Techniques for Analyzing Industries and Competitors*[13] he argues that all businesses must respond to five competitive forces, shown in Exhibit 16.6.

1. *Threat of new market entrants.* This force may be defined as the risk of a similar company entering your marketplace and winning business. There are many barriers to entry of new market entrants in health care, including the high cost of equipment, licensure, requirements for physicians and other highly trained technicians, development of physician

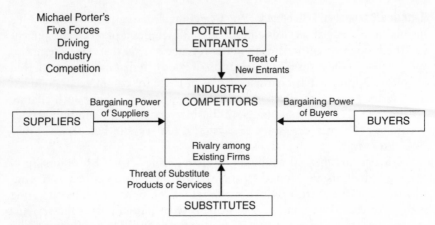

EXHIBIT 16.6   Five Forces of Competition
Source: Michael Porter, *Competitive Strategy: Techniques for Analyzing Industries and Competitors* (New York: Free Press, 1980), 4.

referral networks and provider contracts, and other significant regulatory requirements.

2. *Bargaining power of suppliers.* A supplier can be defined as any business relationship you rely on to deliver your product, service, or outcome.

3. *Threats from substitute products or services.* Substitute products or services are those that are sufficiently equivalent in function or utility to offer consumers an alternate choice of product or service.

4. *Bargaining power of buyers.* This force is the degree of negotiating leverage of an industry's buyers or customers.

5. *Rivalry among existing firms.* This is ongoing competition between existing firms without consideration of the other competitive forces that define industries.

VALUATION APPROACHES, METHODS, AND TECHNIQUES

There are numerous generally accepted health care valuation approaches, methods, and procedures. The choice of approaches or methods depends primarily on the purpose of the valuation report and the specific characteristics of the entity to be appraised. The objective and purpose of the valuation engagement, the standard of value, the premise of value, and the availability and reliability of data must all be considered by the valuator in the selection of applicable approaches and methods

Revenue Ruling 59-60

Among the wide array of sources of guidance with which business valuation consultants should be familiar to conduct an accurate business valuation, the pronouncements of the IRS may be most widely cited. The IRS provides insights regarding its positions on business valuation issues through various mediums: the Internal Revenue Code, the Treasury Regulations to the Code, Technical Advice Memorandums, Private Letter Rulings, and various Revenue Rulings. Revenue Ruling 59-60 (RR 59-60) has been a significant topic of discussion in the valuation community, as it provides basic guidance for the valuation of closely held common stocks. RR 59-60 provides a general outline and review of "the approach, methods, and factors to be considered in valuing shares of the capital stock of closely held corporations for estate tax and gift tax purposes."[14]

In the valuation of the stock of closely held corporations or corporate stock that lacks market quotations, all available financial data along with significant factors impacting the fair market value should be considered.

The following contains fundamental factors that require vigilant analysis in each business valuation:

- The nature of the business and the history of the enterprise from its inception.
- The economic outlook in general and the condition and outlook of the specific industry in particular.
- The book value of the stock and the financial condition of the business.
- The earnings capacity of the company.
- The dividend-paying capacity.
- Whether or not the enterprise has goodwill or other intangible value.
- Sales of stock and the size of the block of stock to be valued.
- The market price of stocks of corporations engaged in the same or similar line of business having their stocks actively traded in a free and open market, either on an exchange or over the counter.[15]

The choice of methodology depends primarily on the purpose of the valuation report and the specific characteristics of the professional practice. For example, the standard of value to be estimated in a divorce case is often fair market value; however, the standard may be different from state to state; that is, some states set a standard of fair value that is either judicially or legislatively defined. For example, the state of Michigan has developed a concept known as the holder's interest theory of value. The value to the holder concept is most often associated, although not frequently articulated, with investment or intrinsic value. Application of this standard of value contemplates value to the holder (or particular buyer) rather than value to a potential hypothetical buyer; that is, investment value is distinguished from fair market value in that investment value provides a going concern value to the current owner and thereby identifies assets that have an intrinsic worth to the owner, which may not be transferable to another person.[16]

It is also important that the valuation consultant determine the premise of value. For example, value in use considers the subject practice on the basis of an ongoing professional practice enterprise. Value in exchange denotes a liquidation of the practice on either an orderly or a forced basis.

Once the valuation consultant clearly understands the purpose of the appraisal assignment, has determined the standard of value and the premise of value, and has determined the availability and reliability of data, he or she must select one or more applicable methods. These methods can be classified by three major valuation approaches: income, cost, and market.

Income Approaches

The following methods may be utilized under the income approach.

Discounted Cash Flow Method   The discounted cash flow method is based on a multiperiod discounting income approach that estimates the present value of normalized expected cash flows distributable to the owners of the entity being appraised, with a residual or terminal value ascribed to all periods beyond the projection.

The value of an investment in an operating company is often considered to be equal to the present value of all its expected future cash flows. Therefore, when selecting the discounted cash flow method (an income approach method), the valuation consultant recognizes that the fair market value of a medical practice is the aggregate present value of the total of all cash flows likely to be achieved from the practice in the future.

The net present value is calculated by applying a weighted average cost of capital (WACC) or a risk-adjusted built-up discount rate to the total net cash flow generated by the practice.

This total net cash flow is the gross collected revenues of the practice less all noncash and non-owner/officer-compensation-related expenses adjusted for depreciation, capital expenditures, and working capital. This represents the real cash flow of the practice.

These cash flows are then discounted over the selected years of the projection at the risk-adjusted discount rate. All cash flows from the final year of the projection through infinity are accounted for in the terminal period and calculated by utilizing the adjusted cash flow of the final year capitalized at the selected capitalization rate (discount rate less growth rate) and then discounted at the selected risk-adjusted discount rate to arrive at the present value of all of these future terminal-period cash flows. The total present value of all the cash flows will be equal to the estimated fair market value of the practice under this method.

As the discounted net cash flow method results in a C corporation equivalent level of value due to both the tax structure typically used in projections as well as the use of a buildup method to develop a discount rate derived from empirical market transactional data of publicly traded C corporation interests, an adjustment to reflect a pass-through entity level of value may be appropriate. An adjustment to reflect the additional incremental net economic benefits derived from an entity's pass-through status may also be applicable to the indicated results derived from other methods, including the guideline public company method and the direct market comparable transactions method, discussed further later.

Single-Period Capitalization Method　　The single-period capitalization method estimates the present value of the entity being appraised by capitalizing a single year of benefits.

Cost Approaches

The following methods may be utilized under the cost approach.

Asset Accumulation Method　　In valuation engagements where there is no significant income stream to capitalize, a cost approach method such as the asset accumulation method is often used. This method identifies, distinguishes, disaggregates, and appraises each of the component assets, both tangible and intangible, within the practice.

Challenges with this method include determining which assets can legally be sold and to whom; determining fair market value of goodwill and other intangible assets requires the use of some type of capitalization of earnings method, with the same difficulties noted earlier.

Liquidation Value Methods　　Liquidation methods, either by orderly disposition or by forced liquidation, estimate the value of an entity by determining the present value of the net proceeds from liquidating the company's assets and paying off liabilities. The orderly method describes a situation in which the sell-off process is conducted in an organized and systematic fashion under a reasonable time line constructed by the seller. In this scenario a lesser degree of urgency exists. Under the forced method the seller no longer is in a situation to proceed at his or her own discretion. All, or the majority, of the assets will be sold at approximately the same time in a relatively quick fashion. Generally, the orderly liquidation method value will be greater than the forced liquidation value.

Excess Earnings Method   The excess earnings method, also called the treasury method or the IRS formula method based on Revenue Ruling 68-609, does not fit neatly into any of the three approaches. This method is considered by many valuators to be a hybrid method, combining elements of the asset-/cost-based approach with elements of income approach methods.

The excess earnings method first values the intangible assets of the entity being appraised utilizing a residual technique, whereby a portion of the benefit stream (e.g., net free cash flow or net income) is first attributed to a return on net tangible assets utilizing a market-derived cost of capital for similar tangible assets; second, an appropriate portion of the benefit stream is attributed to the fair market value of the replacement cost of services provided by the owner as owner compensation; and finally, the dollar amount of the benefit that remains after the deduction of these two amounts (the residual) is then presumed to be attributable to the intangible assets. This amount of the benefit stream, which has been determined to be attributable to the intangible assets of the subject entity, is then capitalized using a risk-adjusted equity rate of return and the resulting indicated value of the intangible assets is then combined with (added to) the value of the tangible assets of the entity being appraised to arrive at an estimate of overall asset value for the subject entity as a going concern.

Market Approaches

The following methods may be utilized under the market approach.

Direct Market Comparable Transactions Method   The direct market comparable transactions method, also known as the market data comparable or analysis of transactional data method, is often selected because conceptually an analysis of actual transactions of comparable health care practices and a comparison in the aggregate to the practice make good sense.

However, because of the developing and unreliable nature of reported comparable transactional data for health care practices and the significant and substantive dissimilarity and individual uniqueness of health care practices (which tend to be unique enterprises lacking easily disaggregatable, homogenous units for comparison), the abstraction of useful and valid data is problematic.

The lack of publicly traded physician practice management company (PPMC) purchasers has reduced the number of reported sales.

Guideline Publicly Traded Company Approach   This method compares publicly traded companies in the same industry and line of business as the subject practice. Comparable companies for medical practices are physician practice management companies (PPMCs) that contract with practices within the same medical specialty as the subject practice. The current price-to-revenue and price-to-earnings ratios of these guideline companies are used in the computation of an estimated fair market value for the practice. Because these guideline companies are publicly traded on the various exchanges, these two ratios represent a minority-marketable position of their investors, as compared to a controlling-interest closely held, nonmarketable position of the subject practice. Therefore, appropriate adjustments need to be made before calculating the indicated value.

Previous Subject Practice Transactions   Previous sales of the subject practice, whether partially in its entirety, can provide a very good estimate of value. However, depending on how long ago the practice sold, market and practice changes may discount the validity of such data.

ANALYSIS OF RISK

As discussed earlier, it is important to first analyze and reach a supportable conclusion as to the relationship between risk and return for a specific type of practice investment that is characteristic of the specific dynamics of the market in which it operates at any point in time, before selecting a discount/capitalization rate.

It should be kept in mind that while this estimate of investor-perceived risk is, in the end, necessarily based, to a great degree, on the subjective judgment of the valuation consultant, objective methods and teachings are available and will be employed to the extent possible to arrive at a valid and supportable discount/capitalization rate. The assessment of risk is inexorably related to and should be based on an informed consideration of the most probable expectations and perceptions of a universe of typical buyers as to the future performance of the subject entity, as well as material changes in substantive value drivers.

In the final analysis, the assessment of risk must be carefully correlated to an informed, realistic, and unsparing assessment of current buyer perceptions in the market.

Comparative Financial Data and Development of Discount Rates

Information used to compare the subject practice's financial statements with industry averages is available through a variety of industry studies. Some of the standard sources that cover all industry categories include *RMA Annual Statement Studies*, published by the Risk Management Association; *Financial Studies of the Small Business*, published by Financial Research Associates; and *Statistics of Income: Partnership Source Book* and *Statistics of Income: Sole Proprietor Source Book*, available through the IRS. Other sources of this data include trade associations and various industry studies.

Benchmarking techniques are often used to determine the degree to which the subject entity varies from comparable health care industry norms, as well as to provide vital information regarding its trends in internal operational performance and financial status. An appropriate and successful application of benchmarking techniques generally reveals both favorable and unfavorable areas of the business operation of the subject entity, which may in turn require further examination to determine causality and the effect, if any, on the subject entity's value. Thus, benchmarking often assists valuators not only in identifying the existence of nonstandard performance and anomalies in costs, levels of productivity, and financial ratios, but also in discovering the underlying causes of these anomalies. When the causes for aberration from the norm are identified, they should be further investigated and assessed as to the potential weaknesses and risk factors (as well as the potential strengths) they pose for the subject entity.

As illustrated by the preceding discussion, the benchmarking process is not only essential for internal managers seeking to adjust business methods to optimize performance, but is also an invaluable tool for valuators and financial analysts. Common methods of applying the results of benchmarking analysis include:

- Adjusting operating expense and capital items, as well as capital structure, to industry norms (when valuing a control position).
- Adjusting the indication of a discount rate or cost of equity as derived from the market (subject entity specific risk premium).
- Selecting the appropriate financial multiples or ratios (e.g., price-earnings, price-to-revenue, price-to-EBITDA, etc.).
- Selecting the appropriate discounts and premiums, based on the level of value sought (e.g., discount for lack of marketability, control premium, discount for lack of control, etc.).

Return on Investment: Discount Rate/ Cost of Equity

The discount rate, at which the measured expected future stream of economic benefit of ownership is discounted to present value, is selected by the valuation consultant to represent the rate of return a typical investor in the professional practice would require in discounting the expected stream of the economic benefits of equity ownership of the subject professional practice, given the systematic risk of the market, as well as the unsystematic risk of investment in the subject professional practice. In contrast, the capitalization rate is the rate by which a single estimate of benefit is divided to determine value. Inherent in this single-period capitalization formula is the assumption of continuity of the benefit stream in perpetuity. Typically, the capitalization rate is calculated by deducting the projected annual long-term growth rate of the subject medical practice from the selected discount rate:

$$\text{Discount rate} - \text{Growth rate} = \text{Capitalization (cap) rate}$$

As mentioned earlier, the discount rate is a measure of return required of an equity investor, thus, in effect, is the cost of equity of a specific business enterprise. The cost of equity, combined with the cost of debt, comprise the weighted average cost of capital (WACC) of a specific business enterprise, which is utilized when estimating the return on investment of total invested capital (both equity and debt).

The discount rate or cost of equity, selected by the valuation consultant may be developed by building up the aggregate elements of several rates and risk adjustments as illustrated in Exhibit 16.7.

Risk-Free Rate

The starting point for developing an appropriate discount rate is the alternative investment opportunities in risk free or relatively risk-free

EXHIBIT 16.7 Determination of the Discount Rate

Discount Rate/Cost of Equity Components	Rate
1 Risk-free rate	3.05%
2 Investment alternative (equity risk premium)	6.05%
3 Health care risk premium adjustment	−0.79%
4 Size premium	5.82%
5 Subject enterprise company-specific risk premium	5.00%
6 Total discount rate/cost of equity	19.13%

438

THE VALUATION HANDBOOK

investments. The interest paid by U.S. government securities are the closest substitute or proxy available for a risk-free rate.

Investment Alternative (Equity Risk Premium)

This adjustment reflects the extra return, or premium, that is expected by the typical equity investor in large company stocks in excess of the return on a riskless asset. Ibbotson has studied and estimated the historical (since 1926) realized equity risk premium (ERP) associated with the risk of investment in common stock in its *Stocks, Bonds, Bills and Inflation Yearbook* *(SBBI)*.

According to several recent published articles and papers in the valuation profession, the *realized* returns on equity reported by Ibbotson, as mentioned earlier, have been overstated as compared to the ERP that must have been *expected* by investors given the underlying economics of the economy (i.e., expected growth in gross domestic product) and the underlying economics of public companies (i.e., expected growth in earnings and/or dividends). These studies suggest that investors would not reasonably have expected as large an ERP as what was actually realized, and it may be appropriate to adjust downward a historical *realized* ERP to estimate an expected ERP,[17] based on the aforementioned studies and recent research.

Company-Specific Risk Premium

The combination of the risk-free rate and the equity risk premium estimates the return required by the investor in large company stocks. Ibbotson measures the additional return of small company stocks over the market as a whole.

This adjustment is somewhat more subjective in that it reflects the valuation consultant's informed assessment of the various risk factors that are inherent and specific to the subject professional practice. Additional risk factors specific to a subject medical practice include but are not limited to: operational performance, market/competition, technological obsolescence, revenue stream, risk related to key persons, and depth of management.

Research challenges related to determining the appropriate discount rate/cost of equity include: (1) finding research to support the quantification of subject medical practice risk premiums, (2) obtaining size premium data for small companies, and (3) determining industry risk adjustments for certain professional practice industry subsectors.

Keith Pinkerton and Peter Butler have released a calculator to measure total cost of equity and public company-specific risk.[18] It provides empirical benchmarks for selecting the correct company-specific risk premium (CSRP) for the subject entity, mixing subjective and objective techniques. This process begins by reviewing the public company's form 10-K to understand the disclosures related to company-specific factors. The valuator can then place the private company within, above, or below the calculated benchmarks based on the degree to which the private company faces the same risks as the public company. Also, while Pinkerton and Butler do not recommend using the NASDAQ index as a proxy, it is available in their calculator. The calculator can only be used to calculate implicit volatilities exactly matching the private company's total cost of equities (TCOE). Canadian public companies can also be used in the calculator. If the companies are publicly traded in the United States, pricing data will be available. Otherwise, historical data must be utilized. The calculator pulls indexes' closing prices, and can handle pricing either adjusted for dividends or not. Data is available for the previous five years or 261 weeks, and the creators recommend using at least the past three years when calculating beta. Also, selecting public company comparables in the model using the calculator does not differ from selecting them for the market approach.

One of the most innovative abilities of the calculator is the way it pulls the prior 261 days of closing prices for a particular company. For example, if the effective date is Monday, the calculator will return 261 Mondays of closing prices. The technique has not been reviewed by the SEC or IRS.

Pinkerton and Butler were questioned about the necessity of having good public company comparables when using the calculator for a $40 million entity when the opposing party valued it at $90 million. They responded by explaining that the calculator has empirical data whereas alternatives to calculating company-specific risk (CSR) lack this type of data. While the calculator may have "not so great guidelines," the component observation method offers no empirical data. Since the calculator computes the CSR from the same publicly traded companies as the income approach, it should not be thrown out when there are no good guideline companies to use, since the income approach is not abandoned when this occurs.[19]

LEVEL OF VALUE: DISCOUNTS AND PREMIUMS

With each method utilized, certain adjustments should be considered based on the specific requirements of each engagement and the inherent indication of value (i.e., the level of value that results from each method).

When a closely held level of value (in contrast to a freely traded, marketable, or publicly traded level) is sought, the valuation consultant may need to make adjustments to the indicated valuation results. There are inherent risks relative to the liquidity of investments in closely held, nonpublic companies that are not relevant to the investment in companies whose shares are publicly traded (freely traded). Investors in closely held companies do not have the ability to dispose of an invested interest quickly if the situation is called for (e.g., forecasted unfavorable industry conditions or the investor's personal immediate need for cash). This relative lack of liquidity of ownership in a closely held company is accompanied by risks and costs associated with the selling of an interest of a closely held company (i.e., locating a buyer, negotiation of terms, adviser/broker fees, risk of exposure to the market, etc.). By contrast, investors in the stock market are most often able to sell their interests in a publicly traded company within hours and receive cash proceeds in a few days. Accordingly, a discount may be applicable to the value of a closely held company due to the inherent illiquidity of the investment. Such a discount is commonly referred to as a discount for lack of marketability.

Over the years, there have been several empirical studies performed attempting to quantify a discount for lack of marketability, typically in three categories: (1) transactions involving restricted stock of publicly traded companies, (2) private transactions of companies prior to their initial public offerings (IPOs), and (3) an analysis and comparison of the price-earnings (P/E) ratios of acquisitions of public and private companies published in the *Mergerstat Review* study.

With a noncontrolling interest, in which the holder cannot solely authorize and cannot solely prevent corporate actions (in contrast to a controlling interest), a discount for lack of control (DLOC) may be appropriate. In contrast, a control premium may be applicable to a controlling interest. While a control premium is an increase to the pro rata share of the value of the business that reflects the impact on value inherent in the management and financial power that can be exercised by the holders of a control interest of the business, usually the majority holders, a discount for lack of control is the reduction from the pro rata share of the value of the business that reflects the impact on value of the absence or diminution of control that can be exercised by the holders of the minority interest.

Several empirical studies have been done to attempt to quantify DLOCs from their antithesis, control premiums. The studies include the *Mergerstat Review*,[20] an annual series study of the premium paid by investors for controlling interest in publicly traded stock, and the *Control Premium Study*,[21] a quarterly series study that compiles control premiums of publicly traded stocks by attempting to eliminate the possible distortion caused by speculation of a deal.

CONCLUSION

There is *no* single approach or method, or combination thereof, that is universally correct or that applies to every engagement. Each case must be considered as a unique exercise of informed judgment, based on careful analysis and supported by documented evidence and reasoned argument. All the sophisticated arithmetic and brilliant theoretical constructs in the valuation world will not support a credible valuation if the appraiser does not have a thorough understanding of the market sector within which the subject entity exists and operates (i.e., the four pillars). In addition, the valuator should remember to question everything and everyone, but be prepared to utilize reasoned, informed professional judgment to review the valuation report. In the end, in arriving at your opinion of value, remember to "love everyone, trust no one, and paddle your own canoe!"

NOTES

1. 42 U.S.C.A. 1395nn(a); Social Security Act 1877(a).
2. 42 U.S.C.A. 1395nn(h)(3); Social Security Act 1877(h)(3).
3. 42 U.S.C.A. 1395nn(e)(6); Social Security Act 1877(e)(6).
4. 42 U.S.C.A. 1320a-7b(b).
5. 42 C.F.R. 1001.952(d)(5).
6. "Intermediate Sanctions—Excess Benefit Transactions," Internal Revenue Service, www.irs.gov/charities/charitable/article/0,id=123303,00.html (accessed 9/2/08).
7. "Disqualified Person," Internal Revenue Service, www.irs.gov/charities/charitable/article/0,id=154667,00.html (accessed 9/2/08); "Lookback Period," Internal Revenue Service, www.irs.gov/charities/charitable/article/0,id=154670,00.html (accessed 9/2/08).
8. "Intermediate Sanctions—Excess Benefit Transactions," Internal Revenue Service, www.irs.gov/charities/charitable/article/0,id=123303,00.html (accessed 9/2/08).
9. *Black's Law Dictionary*, 5th ed. (St. Paul, MN: West, 1979), 625.
10. *In re Marriage of Alexander*, 368 Ill.App.3d 192, 199 (2006).
11. Ibid.
12. Michael Porter is the recipient of the Wells Prize in Economics, the Adam Smith Award, three McKinsey Awards, and honorary doctorates from the Stockholm School of Economics and six other universities. He is also the author of 14 books, including *Competitive Advantage*, *The Competitive Advantage of Nations*, and *Cases in Competitive Strategy*.
13. Michael Porter, *Competitive Strategy: Techniques for Analyzing Industries and Competitors* (New York: Free Press, 1980), 4.

14. Shannon P. Pratt, Robert F. Reilly, and Robert P. Schweihs, *Valuing a Business* (New York: McGraw-Hill, 2000), 585.
15. Ibid.
16. J. Fishman et al., *Standards of Value: Theory and Applications* (Hoboken, NJ: John Wiley & Sons, 2007), 167, 181.
17. Roger J. Grabowski, "Equity Risk Premium: What Valuation Consultants Need to Know About Recent Research," *Valuation Strategies* (September/October 2003).
18. Keith Pinkerton and Peter Butler, "Using the Butler Pinkerton Model—Total Cost of Equity and Public Company Specific Risk Calculator," Business Valuation Resources (March 6, 2008).
19. "Butler/Pinkerton Update Questions on Comparables," *BVUpdate*, March 5, 2008, www.bvlibrary.com.
20. Published by FactSet Mergerstat, LLC.
21. Compiled by Mergerstat/Shannon Pratt's Business Valuation Resources.

CHAPTER 17

Valuing Dental Practices

Stanley L. Pollock
Professional Practice Planners, Inc.

Over the past decades, the appraisal of dental practices has become popular and the number of appraisers involved in dental practice appraisal has increased greatly. During the decades, dental practice appraisal has developed from a rather crude, formula-driven art form into a mature, multimethod process. By way of example, in the 1970s and 1980s dental practices were valued and sold at 100 percent of the latest 12 months equals gross revenues. In the 1990s, values of dental practices continued upward and sold at inflated numbers. Shortly thereafter, the dental practice bubble began to leak. Cox (1995) reported on the subject; as a rule, dental practices sold at around 65 percent of collected revenues, which was the price/gross ratio. After extensive research, I reported in the 2006 and 2007 supplements of *Valuing Professional Practices & Licenses* (Pollock 2006, 2007) that general dental practices sold in arm's-length deals at 57 percent of the latest gross revenues. Gross revenues, of course, were higher than in previous decades, and operating expenses were creeping up; certain pockets across the United States were not affected to any great extent, while other pockets were greatly affected.

What became apparent during the decades was that certain appraisers were still seeking simple guideline formulas while other more studious ones gained a great deal of relevant and applicable appraisal information. Many appraisers maintained a great deal of local data. Data banks, most notably those of the Institute of Business Appraisers (IBA),[1] Pratt's Stats,[2] the Goodwill Registry, the American Dental Association,[3] the National Society of Professional Business Healthcare Consultants, and the Risk Management Association, gathered and published a great deal of important data, which became available for astute and eager dental practice appraisers to use. The Appraisal Foundation published the Uniform Standards of Professional

Appraisal Practice (USPAP 2008), which certain appraisal societies and individuals recognized; certain others proudly declared they would not, but conscientious appraisers do follow them (far too many unconscientious ones do not).

What also became apparent during the decades is that dental practices, especially specialty practices, have turned into large business organizations. Although professional practices generally are not thought of or classified as small businesses, they are, nevertheless, generating gross and net revenues in six and seven figures. For appraisal and business matters and all intents, dental practices are and must be treated as not-so-small businesses.

Appraisers value practices differently depending on the purpose and function of the valuation; their training, experience, style, and integrity; the location of the subject practice; the size and type of practice; the business form of the practice; and other reasons. Despite being not-so-small businesses, dental practices and their valuations pose many differences from other businesses and even from other professions. This chapter addresses differences that have transpired over the past few decades and includes my and others' relevant suggestions and comments. The first few are:

Over the years multiple organizations have seen the value and applicability of accumulating data. Foremost is the data bank of the Institute of Business Appraisers located in Plantation, Florida. Other significant data banks for dental practices are Pratt's Stats of Business Valuation Resources in Portland, Oregon, and the Goodwill Registry in Plymouth Meeting, Pennsylvania. Raymond C. Miles, ASA, FIBA, one of the founders and the mainstay of the Institute of Business Appraisers and its vast market data bank, promulgated the direct market data method (DMDM). The DMDM has become a highly relevant standard to assist appraisers in implementing the market approach, especially for dental practices. At this time the IBA data bank has accumulated data on close to 3,000 transactions of general and specialty dental practices. Interestingly, the category of dental practices is the second largest category of transactions in the IBA data bank (nonethnic restaurants are number one). The following are important data points for the appraiser of dental practices to have as background in today's dental practice environment:

- Dental practices are heavily involved and controlled by third-party, managed care, and government sources.
- Certain practices participate in managed care and other programs completely or partially, while others do not.
- Although corporate ownership of dental practices is possible and encouraged, the actual care of patients is limited to licensed dentists.
- There is a major decreasing supply of dentists.

- Within certain limits, there are few barriers in dentistry to free market competition. Professional or personal and practice or entrepreneurial goodwill, as well as noncompetitive covenants, play a large part in the valuation and transition processes.
- Acquiring a dental education and advanced training is long-term and extremely expensive.
- The cost of starting a dental practice is extremely expensive.
- The cost of operating a dental practice is very high.
- Technology plays a large part in dental practices.
- Efficient management, more than ever, is required to operate a dental practice.
- The average dental practice staff today consists of four to five skilled individuals per dentist.

NORMALIZATION

Normalization is the adjustment of financial statements for items that are not representative of the present going-concern status of the practice. Normalization addresses and characterizes unusual, over- or understated, and nonrecurring items. In other words, normalization brings reasonableness and consistency into the valuation process. Adjusting financial statements is one of the first steps an appraiser of a dental practice addresses. The sources of the data are the latest three to five years' tax reports, financial statements, depreciation, amortization, and Section 179 schedules.

First, of course, are gross receipts or collections (which are not production). Both are important, but the practitioner can't spend money that is not yet collected and deposited. Also, comparing collections to production provides an initial and meaningful way to see if the practice is operating efficiently. The collection ratio (collections divided by production) is crucial to the financial health and security of a dental practice and should run in the mid 90 percent range. Practices heavily involved and reliant upon third-party and Medicaid participation will have a lower percent. It is important to know how much the practice is producing and actually collecting. Certain write-offs and discounts are normal, but they must be controlled and they affect bottom lines and valuations.

A major normalization is in owners' or professional compensation. For valuation purposes, all practice or professional income should be classified as compensation, that is, income of officers, associates, independent contractors, employees, hygienists, and others. The appraiser is looking for the professional income and its sources that the practice entity provides. Frequently, the appraiser has to search for this income, especially if associates, employees, and independent contractors are involved. Obtaining the complete revenue stream is crucial. A major difference between most dental practices and regular businesses is that most dental practices will balance out at the end of the year and will show little or no profit or taxable income.

In regard to the matter of compensation, the appraiser must question if there are family members or others on the payroll who are nonproductive employees. In such hiring matters, family education, Social Security, retirement, and other funding show up and require appropriate adjustment. Marketing, advertising, promotion, meals, club memberships, and entertainment are major and legitimate factors in a dental practice today. However, a great deal of such expenses are personal, which can run from 50 to 75 percent of the deductions. Many appraisers automatically adjust out 100 percent for professional continuing education. Today, in all states and in many professional organizations, continuing education is required and is very expensive. Therefore, appraisers should allow a reasonable amount for legitimate continuing education, for meetings and travel, and for personal allocation, and 50 percent, generally, is reasonable (but can run higher). Vehicles and vehicle expenses can be quite large for many practitioners, and deductions may be difficult to substantiate. However, for those practitioners with multiple facilities, hospital privileges, and reasons to attend professional meetings and visit accountants and consultants, banks, referrers, and laboratories, vehicle expenses are legitimate and can run around 50 percent of the listed expenses.

Cash and cash equivalents normally (but not always) are not included in most dental practice appraisals. Accounts receivable and payable and liabilities may or may not be included. In most practice sales, they are not; in divorce matters and associate buy-ins and buyouts they are. In mergers and acquisitions, they may or not be included yet play an important role. Most of the time, they are handled separately. If handled separately or included in an appraisal, accounts receivable and payable should be properly adjusted or aged. A reasonable approach to such aging of accounts receivable is:

Up to 30 days	92%
31–60 days	85%
61–90 days	75%
91–120 days	65%
120+ days	25% or more

Beyond 120 days, collection usually drops off rapidly.

For accounts payable, unless specifically listed, 50 percent of one month's true operating expenses is reasonable. Current or short- and long-term liabilities should be those listed in the financial reports. Orthodontic practices have an added current asset to address—contracts receivable, the amount that the orthodontist and patient or patient's family have contracted for services that have not been completed but that are still under contract to be paid. They are tricky to calculate. Mr. William Sutton,[4] a seasoned appraiser of orthodontic practices (located in Highpoint, North Carolina), developed a method to value contracts receivable and has given me permission to include his practical method and example in this chapter.

Total amount of contracts receivable	$650,000
Less normal overhead (62%)	−$403,000
Less cost of professional to complete at 30%	−$195,000
Value of contracts receivable	$ 52,000

Over the decades, normal operating overhead expenses in a dental practice have increased considerably and today run between 50 percent (specialists) to 65 percent (generalists). Staff expenses range from 15 percent to 30 percent plus $3\frac{1}{2}$ percent for benefits of gross collected revenues depending on type of practice and staff longevity. Normal rent and occupancy costs run around 7 percent of gross collected revenues. Laboratory expenses are critical in a general dental practice and run around 7 percent also. In dental practices today, the amount paid for normal operating supplies is quite large and can run from 8 percent to 12 percent of gross revenues. A reasonable method of determining the value of such expenses, considered inventory, is to calculate the amount actually paid during the past 12 months and divide by 6, which is the equivalent of two months' inventory. Appraisers can reasonably vary this amount from one to three months' supply. If a practice has a large inventory of implant materials, precious metals, costly injectibles, and medications or other specialty items, an actual count may be in order.

Rent is a major expense in most professional practices, and normally runs from 3 to 6 percent of gross receipts. Rent is a frequent cause for adjustment, particularly for owners of the property or facility. Solo practitioners frequently do not charge their practices for rent; rather they allocate and include mortgage payments, taxes, interest, and other expenses. Other owners will charge their corporation or limited liability company an excessive rental. Both cases require adjustments to the area's fair market rental, which sometimes is difficult (but necessary) to obtain.

It is essential that the valuator be aware of nonrecurring expenses, especially in divorce and employment and professional liability situations. In such situations, dental practices not infrequently exhibit strange and exceptional legal and other expenses and practice trends, which the appraiser must recognize and accommodate.

Not only are many types of insurance necessary in a dental practice, but also they usually need to be adjusted. Most of the time practices lump all of the practice's insurance into one category. The appraiser, then, must examine the grouping and make appropriate business, fringe, and personal deductions. Generally, life and buyout insurance is not deductible. Disability income insurance may or not be deductible depending on the accountant's and doctor's inclinations. The professional's health care, although deductible most of the time, can still be considered a fringe benefit and the appraiser should adjust it appropriately.

A final adjustment that I do not see very often but that I feel is noteworthy is an allowance for future replacement of equipment and furniture. In modern dental practice today, equipment, especially computer systems and other technology assets, instruments, furniture, and furnishings require frequent replacement and updating, which are terribly expensive. Therefore, it is best to include an allocation and adjustment for them in normalizing financial statements. Reviewing the depreciation schedule and being aware of today's cost of equipment and furnishings provides a good starting point and, generally, $10,000 to $30,000 per year is reasonable.

It is obvious and absolutely necessary, then, that the appraiser must meticulously review and adjust the financial statements. This painstaking activity reveals a great deal about the practice and practitioner and, normally, makes a considerable impact on the valuation process and final estimate of value. It is, to a large extent, a matter of being perceptive, reasonable, and realistic.

FIXED ASSET APPRAISAL

For years, appraisers utilized simple methods to come up with the value of the tangible assets of the practice for an appraisal. A few are: (1) calculating book values shown on the balance sheet (original costs less accumulated depreciation) and adding one-half of the accumulated depreciation to the book value, (2) calculating the major equipment on a 10-year depreciation schedule and the furniture and furnishings on a five-year depreciation schedule rather than the more rapid accountant's depreciation or economic schedule, and (3) engaging the services of a dental supply company or equipment dealer to determine the value of the tangible assets. It is imperative that the doctor or appraiser explain the purpose of the engagement, what is and is not included, and what she or he needs and expects. All too often, the equipment dealer values only those items that the dealer originally sold or that are obvious in the office but overlooks the expensive computer, telephone, communication, technology, anesthesia, vacuum and other systems, cabinetry, certain leasehold improvements, and the expensive office and digital equipment. It is imperative that all major and minor tangible assets are included in the fixed asset appraisal.

Computer systems and office equipment fall into a five-year depreciation schedule. Dental practices have a great deal of so-called minor equipment, including hand instruments, handpieces, implant systems, blood pressure apparatus, forceps, typewriters, television and stereophonic systems, and others that are exceedingly expensive, which must be included in a comprehensive valuation and which are overlooked most of the time. If the practice appraiser or tangible asset appraiser cannot determine detailed or specific valuations, the appraiser can determine their values at 15 to 20 percent of the value of the major items, which can be a reasonable estimation to include in the normalized balance sheet. Be aware that with the rapid and large Section 179 write-offs today, many major items do not appear on the balance sheets but should be included in the fixed asset appraisals. Genuine antiques, certain artwork, and special and personal items are generally not included, and are valued at original cost or have to be valued by a competent personal property appraiser.

In dental practices, leasehold improvements are extensive, expensive, and amortized over 30 years. For normalization, however, a 15-year amortization write-off is appropriate. Additionally, reviewing the depreciation and amortization schedules provides the appraiser an opportunity to determine the age, condition, and obsolescence of the various tangible assets and if replacement may be indicated.

However, like dental and professional practice appraisal, the appraisal of tangible assets has progressed, has become specialized, and has risen to a higher level. Comprehensive dental practice valuation includes a detailed tangible asset valuation. John Harris, president and founder of the National Equipment and Business Brokers Institute (NEBB Institute) in Wichita, Kansas, has been a leader, advocate, and instrumental proponent in training professional appraisers in the specialized field of machinery and equipment appraisal, which certainly is appropriate in a comprehensive valuation of a dental practice. NEBB Institute training is particularly valuable for appraisers experienced in business appraisals. The American Society of Appraisers in northern Virginia also trains and certifies machinery and equipment appraisers.

The NEBB Institute addresses the appraisal of dental equipment. NEBB Institute trains, certifies, and supports certified machinery and equipment appraisers (CMEAs). CMEAs prepare and deliver comprehensive and detailed Certified Appraisal Reports consistent with the ethics and guidelines mandated by the Uniform Standards of Professional Appraisal Practice (USPAP 2008). USPAP, promulgated by Congress and the Appraisal Foundation, is the leading authoritative source for appraisals and appraisers. Many appraisal assignments may be solely tangible asset appraisals. A USPAP-compliant Certified Appraisal Report includes, but is not limited to:

- Purpose, function, and type of appraisal.
- Scope of services, including economic factors that affect property.
- Data research.
- Type and extent of analysis applied in arriving at opinions and conclusions.
- Onside inspection and its depth.
- Highest and best use.
- Statement of limiting conditions.
- Definitions.
- Methods of valuation.
- Additional and special considerations.
- Final value summary and reconciliation.
- Appraiser's certification and qualification.
- Additional.

RATIO ANALYSIS

Ratio analysis involves establishing a relationship between specific pairs of figures found in financial statements. Ratios reveal trends, comparisons, strengths, and weaknesses of the practice and provide an additional guide to assist in establishing an estimate of value. Many ratios are available to assist the appraiser. A few of the more important and applicable ratios for a dental practice are:

- *Liquidity ratios*. Liquidity ratios indicate the practice's ability to pay its current bills and liabilities, including unexpected ones. The current ratio (total current assets divided by current liabilities) indicates solvency of the practice. The quick ratio (total current assets less inventory and supplies) indicates liquidity or the ability of the practice to pay off short-term obligations and, similarly, indicates its solvency. The ratios show the liquid assets available to cover every dollar of current debt.
- *Profitability ratio*. The profitability ratio is net cash flow divided by total revenues; it indicates how effectively the practice has been managed,

the relative amount of net cash flow that the practice has generated, and how much profit had been made on every dollar earned. Today, profitability ratios range from 35 percent (generalists) to 50+ percent (specialists), indicating that dental practices earn 35 to 50 cents for every dollar collected.

■ *Debt to net worth ratio.* The debt to net worth ratio is total liabilities divided by tangible net worth; it indicates the debt structure or margin of safety and the long-term solvency of a practice. This leverage ratio indicates the practice's ability to deal with financial problems and opportunities as they arise, and indicates whether a practice has a favorable debt structure.

TREND ANALYSIS

After completing normalization; reviewing and analyzing the tax returns, financial statements, and other data over a number of years; and conducting ratio analysis, an appraiser observes certain trends. By way of example, are the collected revenues, cash flows, and overhead increasing? Or are they decreasing? By how much or by what percentage? Are they ahead of or below the consumer price index (CPI), inflation, and those of other similar practitioners? It is imperative that the appraiser comprehend fully the financial status of the practice, what the practice has or has not accomplished financially, and what it is expected to do in the future. After the appraiser has thoroughly reviewed and analyzed the data and has a knowledgeable and comfortable impression of the practice, the appraiser can contact the owner to arrange that central, personal, confidential on-site inspection and interview.

Exhibit 17.1 is an outline to assist in the revealing trend analysis, which illustrates:

■ Gross revenues and net cash flows of an oral and maxillofacial surgeon (OMFS) compared to an average surgeon across the country.
■ Dollar differentials between the two.
■ Percent differentials between the two.
■ Annual increase and averages in gross revenues and net cash flows for most recent years.

Exhibit 17.1 shows that the practice and practitioner have gross revenues 41 percent greater and net cash flows 43 percent greater than the average oral and maxillofacial surgeon across the country. It also demonstrates that average annual gross revenues increased 5 percent and the net cash flows increased 10.5 percent annually.

EXHIBIT 17.1   Differentials

Oral and Maxillofacial Surgeon—Gross Revenues

	2007	2006	2005	Total
Gross Revenues	$1,309,506	$1,257,165	$1,183,059	$3,749,729
Average OMFS	−$943,554	−$881,826	−$839,834	−$2,665,214
Differential	$365,952	$187,670	$343,225	$896,847
			Differential %	41%

Annual Increase/Decrease

	2006/2007	2005/2006	Average
	+4%	+6%	+5%

Oral and Maxillofacial Surgeon—Net Cash Flows

	2007	2006	2005	Total
Net Cash Flow	$669,031	$588,549	$557,277	$1,814,857
Average OMFS	−$453,180	−$421,563	−$392,141	−$1,266,884
Differential	$215,851	$166,986	$165,136	$547,973
			Differential %	43%

Annual Increase/Decrease

	2006/2007	2005/2006	Average
	14%	+7%	+10.5%

Source: National Society of Certified Healthcare Business Consultants.

USPAP STANDARDS

The Uniform Standards of Professional Appraisal Practice (USPAP) Standards Rule 9-4 states: "In developing an appraisal of an interest in a business enterprise or intangible asset, (a) an appraiser must develop value opinion(s) and conclusion(s) by use of one or more approaches that are necessary for credible assignment results." Nowhere is this rule more appropriate than in the valuation of a dental practice. Proficient practice appraisers follow USPAP 9-4(a) and its multi-approach edict. At this time there are specific differences or variations in the performance and application of the approaches and methods in valuing dental practices.

Capitalization of Income Method

In this method, also called the capitalized economic income method, capitalization of benefits method, cash flow method, and other names, gross and net revenues, overhead, and benefits play a large part in the valuation of a dental practice and require exquisite adjusting. For most business appraisals in this single-period method, the appraiser reviews and analyzes three to five years of financial statements. In dental practice valuations today, more particularly because of the accelerated changes in the dental health care environment, three years of financial statements generally are appropriate and sufficient. The six-step outline of the method is:

1. *Gross revenues:* In applying the methodology, the latest year's gross revenues are reasonably projected based on the previous years' increase or decrease and other business and economic factors.
2. *(Less) true operational expenses:* Expenses and adjustments to expenses are highly pertinent in the valuation of dental practices and are, to some degree, substitutes for income and dividends. In additional to the adjustments mentioned before, others are depreciation, amortization, retirement and profit-sharing contributions, certain insurance, telephones, and loans to and for shareholders. Interest still is optional, and the inclination is to allocate it as an operating expense and not as a personal adjustment.
3. *(Less) professional compensation:* Appraisers are frequently looking for reasonable professional compensation, which is the amount the practice would have to pay a professional or professionals to produce the intended gross revenues of the practice. Data derived from the Practice Valuation Study Group, a national group of professional practice valuators, the American Dental Association, and other reliable sources indicate that reasonable professional compensation for most dental practices today is around 35 percent of gross revenues plus certain fringe benefits. By using this realistic percentage or modest variations, the appraiser does not have to spend a great deal of time, and sometimes money, in attempting to procure so-called reasonable professional compensation. This is also case-specific as compared to researching the various data from certain organizations. To emphasize, dental practices pay out most of the practice earnings as salaries, benefits and perquisites; and all professional compensation—that is, owners', associates', and employed professionals' compensation—must be included. In surveys of dental and other professional practices, owners' compensation is and must be considered net profit or income.

4. *Equals profit:* Simply, then, gross revenues minus true operational expenses, minus reasonable compensation, equals pretax profit.

5. *Capitalization rate determination:* Capitalization rate deserves special attention. Besides being the bane of many appraisers, determining the capitalization rate is extremely important. The buildup method is most frequently used in dental practice valuations and deserves a few comments. The first element is the long-term government or 20-year bond rate, and the next two elements are the common study equity and the small stock equity derived from the Ibbotson Associates annual reports (Ibbotson 2008) or the latest Duff & Phelps data. Since the multiple risk factors in a dental practice are large, the risk premium is large and ranges from 5 to 10 or more percent. Finally, in the buildup capitalization rate, usually there should be an amount for management burden, which can range from 4 to 10 percent. Capitalization rates, then, for modern dental practices and their pretax profits generally run between 25 and 30 percent. Depending on the uniqueness of each practice and practice situation, however, the appraiser must build up a realistic, workable capitalization rate.

   James A. Schilit, editor of *Business Valuation Review*, listed and described guidelines for risk management premiums, classified businesses into categories, and assigned risk premiums (Schilit 1987). His category 5, "small businesses of a personal service nature," has a risk premium (capitalization rate) of 26 percent to 30 percent and is applicable today.

6. *Profit divided by capitalization rate equals practice value:* In this investment value appraisal method, the appraiser converts the determined profit into value. The value reflects a broad interpretation of the important principle of substitution, which simply states that the value of a practice is determined by the cost of an equally desirable practice or the cost of starting a new one. The process of capitalization is the conversion of this profit into value and involves dividing the profit by the determined capitalization rate (Profit ÷ Capitalization rate = Practice value).

Discounted Future Cash Flow Method

For many years, courts were skeptical about an appraiser's use of this method regardless of the purpose of appraisal, but they have recently shown a major inclination for its use. At the same time, this method has become popular and applicable in the valuation of dental practices. The concept of the method is that the value of a dental practice is the value of its sum of expected future economic income or cash flows *discounted* to present values. The discount rate generally is the previously determined capitalization rate *plus* an allowance for growth (the growth rate), which is usually 5 percent. Conversely, the capitalization rate is the determined discount rate *less* the growth rate.

In dental practice valuation, the problems in this method are (1) the determination of the discount rate, (2) the number of years to project the cash flows, and (3) the so-called terminal, residual, or perpetuity value. An appraiser can build up a reasonable discount rate as described earlier. For dental practices, five years is a reasonable projection time. Many years ago, Robert J. Cimasi[5] of Health Capital Consultants in St. Louis taught that not only was five years a normal time frame for purchases, buy-ins, and payouts for dental practices and dental practice valuations, but also that including a terminal or residual value unrealistically increases the estimate of value. Further, the five-year time frame eliminates the necessity to add the unrealistic terminal value. Mark Dietrich,[6] a noted health care consultant and valuator, has suggested that the time frame for medical practices currently could even be two to three years.

I have found that the five-year time frame without the terminal value is exceedingly applicable. I apply this excellent method and find it useful to assist in the determination of value in most dental practice valuations. I have found abuse in its use when certain valuators have extended the time frame for an inordinate number of years. Going beyond five years is unreasonable in most cases, and including a terminal or residual value is impractical almost all of the time in dental practice valuation.

Excess Earnings Method

For whatever reasons, some appraisers will not use this method, while others (and I am one) find it very useful and applicable. This so-called formula method is considered a hybrid method by many appraisers; it originated in the 1920s, pronounced in Revenue Ruling 68-609, and, like other appraisal and business factors, it is entitled to current revision. The applicable concept of this method is that the goodwill of a dental practice entity is determined by capitalizing the net earnings of the entity over the fair rate of return on its tangible assets. Determining goodwill of a dental practice is crucial in that goodwill normally is the largest single asset in the valuation of the practice. The difficulties lie in interpreting the IRS's 1968 definition of tangible assets, fair rate of return, and the capitalization rate.

The value of the tangible assets should be the actual, realistic determined values of the major and minor equipment, furniture and furnishings, and other assets that the appraiser prepared and presented from the adjusted balance sheet and is simply labeled the tangible asset value (TAV).

This is another important reason for a highly competent tangible asset valuation. The TAV can command a 10 percent rate of return. Assets such as cash, accounts receivable, supplies, and leasehold improvements less all liabilities simply cannot and should not command a 10 percent assessment and should not be included. As mentioned earlier, dental practices are generating large net cash flows today, especially after appropriate adjustments. The net cash flows are quite large relative to the tangible assets of the practices. Therefore, it should not be necessary or appropriate to capitalize the excess earnings, which saves the agony of trying to determine another capitalization rate and negates an unrealistic final estimate of value. By way of example, the following is close to an actual valuation:

Latest year's net cash flows	$2,400,000
Tangible asset value (TAV)	$ 475,000
Reasonable rate of return	× 10%
Return on investment	$ 47,500
Excess earnings	$2,352,500
+ Net tangible asset value (adjusted balance sheet)	$ 775,000
Practice value	$3,127,500

Revenue Rule 68-609 states that "the formula approach may be used in determining the fair market value of intangible assets of a business (or practice) only if there is no better basis available for making the determination." Strangely, the IRS issued this ruling in 1968 when no (or few) data banks existed so that it would have been extremely difficult to value the goodwill of a professional practice by any method other than simple rules of thumb or formulas. Notwithstanding the goodwill factor, the excess earnings method is an excellent method to assist the appraiser in the valuation of a dental practice, especially as modified.

Adjusted Net Asset Method

In simple terms, the value of a dental practice should be the current fair market value of the tangible and intangible assets of the practice. The valuation of the tangible assets is not simple and requires the expertise of an individual skilled in the valuation of dental practice tangible assets. This leaves the appraiser with the important determination of the intangible value, which consists of personal and entity goodwill, going concern, and other values.

When the appraiser procures the two values, she or he adds them and derives the value of the practice.

Market Approach

Although there have been many, the greatest difference over the years in the valuation of dental practices is in the market approach. Fortunately, multiple organizations have seen the value and applicability of accumulating data. Foremost was the data bank of the Institute of Business Appraisers. (See Exhibit 17.2.) Significant data points from this data bank are annual gross revenues and earnings, owner's compensation, sale price, price to gross revenues, price to earnings, and year/month of sale.

Many years ago, Dr. Shannon P. Pratt believed that accumulating and recording certain transaction data was imperative to assist appraisers in their application of the market approach in the valuation of businesses and professional practices. Dr. Pratt founded Pratt's Stats. Dental practice data comprise a large portion of Pratt's Stats. This excellent data bank encompasses income data, asset data, transaction data, and relevant additional data. (See Exhibit 17.3.) Income data includes net sales, cost of goods sold, gross profit, operating and other expenses, owner's compensation, earnings before taxes, and net income. Asset data is listed according to purchase price allocations, which include current assets of cash equivalents, accounts receivable, inventory and fixed assets, real estate, intangibles and nonrecurring assets, liabilities, and stockholder's equity. Pertinent transactions data include sale and asking price, business form of entity, amount of down payment, whether stock or asset sale, details about employment/consulting agreement, leases, and others. The form further lists certain information in regard to valuation multiples and financial ratios. With 88 data points, Pratt's Stats is a reliable, major source of pertinent data that greatly assists today's appraisers in the valuation of dental practices.

Raymond C. Miles, a founder and the mainstay of the Institute of Business Appraisers and its vast market data bank, promulgated the direct market data method (DMDM). The DMDM has become a highly relevant standard to assist appraisers in implementing the market approach, especially for dental practices. At this time the IBA data bank has accumulated data on close to 3,000 transactions of general and specialty dental practices. In contrast to the aforementioned guideline methods, which strive to use five to ten comparable transactions, the DMDM stresses, uses, and thrives on data from many transactions. Interestingly, the category of dental practices is the second largest category of transactions in the IBA data bank (nonethnic restaurants are number one).

With the accumulation and availability of data from the multiple data banks over the decades, the use of the market approach in valuing dental practices has become extremely meaningful. The market approach to

EXHIBIT 17.2 Market Comparison Data—IBA Data Bank, Sample Form

SIC CODE: 8021

Notice: This information is to be used only with the Direct Market Data Method or a similar method of appraising closely held businesses. It is not to be used with the Guideline Company Method.

The information below is supplied in response to your request for data to be used in applying the "Market Data Approach" to business appraisal. Because of the nature of sources from which the information is obtained, we are not able to guarantee its accuracy. Neither do we make any representation as to the applicability of the information to any specific appraisal situation.

The following is an explanation of the entries in the data table:

Business Type	Principal line of business.
SIC CODE	Principal Standard Industrial Classification number applicable to the business sold.
Annual Gross	Reported annual sales volume of business sold.
Discretionary Earnings	Reported annual earnings, excluding owner's compensation and before interest and taxes.
Owner's Comp.	Reported owner's compensation.
Sale Price	Total reported consideration; i.e. cash, liabilities assumed, etc. excluding real estate.
Price/Gross	Ratio of total consideration to reported annual gross.
Price/Earnings	Ratio of total consideration to reported annual earnings.
Yr/Mo of Sale	Year and month during which transaction was consummated.

Business Type	Annual Gross $000's	Discretionary Earnings $000's	Owner's Comp. $000's	Sale Price $000's	Price/ Gross	Price/ Earnings	Geographic	Year/Month of Sale
Dentist, General	276		125	210	0.76		PA	97/12
Dentist, General	237		157	95	0.40		WV	97/12
Pededontal	587		300	500	0.85		PA	97/08
Dentist, General	135		25	35	0.26		PA	97/10
Oral Surgeon	1,100		610	600	0.55		CA	97/10
Oral Surgeon	1,000		485	500	0.50		NC	97/01
Dentist, General	256		105	145	0.57		PA	97/08
Orthodontia	1,096		535	700	0.64		PA	97/10
Oral Surgery	780		442	600	0.77		MA	97/09
Oral Surgery	721		423	600	0.83		MA	97/09
Oral Surgery	1,918		978	1400	0.73		PA	97/09
Oral Surgery	460		215	300	0.65		MD	97/08
Oral Surgery	738		341	500	0.68		ID	98/01
Oral Surgery	925		373	500	0.54		KS	97/11
Oral Surgery	250		204	265	1.06		NC	97/12
Oral Surgery	1,024		591	550	0.54		NC	97/11
Orthodontia	265		126	175	0.66		PA	97/09

(Continued)

EXHIBIT 17.2 (*Continued*)

Business Type	Annual Gross $000's	Discretionary Earnings $000's	Owner's Comp. $000's	Sale Price $000's	Price/ Gross	Price/ Earnings	Geographic	Year/Month of Sale
Dentist, General	732		258	400	0.55		PA	97/02
Oral Surgery	1,361		700	1000	0.73		MI	97/12
Oral Surgery	310		140	175	0.56		NC	97/06
Oral Surgery	776		417	550	0.71		PA	97/07
Oral Surgery	1,620		1042	1200	0.74		MI	97/10
Oral Surgery	1,110		562	700	0.63		ID	97/10
Oral Surgery	2,500		1500	2000	0.80		OH	97/03
Dentist, General	238		108	150	0.63		PA	97/05
Oral Surgery	605		320	440	0.73		FL	97/09
Oral Surgery	766		430	500	0.65		CO	97/05

Source: Institute of Business Appraisers.

Pratt's Stats® Subscriber Detail Results

Seller Details			Source Data	
Target Name:	N/A		Broker Name:	Pollock, Stanley L.
Business Description:	Oral and Maxillofacial Surgery		Broker Firm Name:	Professional Practice Planners, Inc.
SIC:	8021 Offices and Clinics of Dentists			
NAICS:	621210 Offices of Dentists		Contact Broker (Retrieve broker contact information from BVR's	
Sale Location:	VA, United States		"Find a Broker" database.)	
Years in Business:	N/A	Number Employees: N/A		

Income Data		Asset Data		Transaction Data	
Data is "Latest Full Year" Reported	Yes	Data is Latest Reported	Yes	Date Sale Initiated:	1/1/2008
		Data is "Purchase Price		Date of Sale:	4/1/2008
Data is Restated (see Notes for any explanation)	No	Allocation agreed upon by Buyer and Seller"	No	Asking Price:	$2,000,000
Income Statement Date	12/31/2007	Balance Sheet Date	12/31/2007	Market Value of Invested Capital*:	$1,700,000
Net Sales	$2,619,011	Cash Equivalents	$15,811	Debt Assumed:	N/A
COGS	$0	Trade Receivables	$264,850	Employment	
Gross Profit	$2,619,011	Inventory	$42,639	Agreement Value:	N/A
Yearly Rent	$104,294	Other Current Assets	$152,771	Noncompete Value:	N/A
Owner's Compensation	$1,345,031	Total Current Assets	$476,071	Amount of Down	
Other Operating Expenses	$1,103,085	Fixed Assets	$313,944	Payment:	$200,000
Noncash Charges	$59,068	Real Estate	$0	Stock or Asset Sale:	Asset
Total Operating Expenses	$2,611,478	Intangibles	$1,085,883	Company Type:	C Corporation
Operating Profit	$7,533	Other Noncurrent Assets	$0	Was there an Employment/Consulting	No
Interest Expenses	$7,533	Total Assets	$1,875,898	Agreement?	
EBT	$0	Long-term Liabilities	N/A	Was there an Assumed Lease in the sale?	No
Taxes	$0	Total Liabilities	$175,898		
Net Income	$0	Stockholder's Equity	$1,700,000	Was there a Renewal Option with the Lease?	No

*Includes noncompete value and interest-bearing debt; excludes real estate, employment/consulting agreement values, and all contingent payments.

Additional Transaction Information	
Was there a Note in the consideration paid? No Terms:	Was there a personal guarantee on the Note? No
Assumed Lease (Months): N/A	Terms of Lease: N/A
Noncompete Length (Months): 24	Noncompete Description: 20 mile radius
Employment/Consulting Agreement Description:	
Additional Notes:	
Owner's compensation was for two doctors.	

Valuation Multiples		Profitability Ratios		Leverage Ratios	
MVIC/Net Sales	0.65	Net Profit Margin	0.00	Fixed Charge Coverage	1.00
MVIC/Gross Profit	0.65	Operating Profit Margin	0.00	Long-Term Debt to Assets	N/A
MVIC/EBITDA	25.53	Gross Profit Margin	1.00	Long-Term Debt to Equity	N/A
MVIC/EBIT	225.67	Return on Assets	0.00		
MVIC/Discretionary Earnings	1.20	Return on Equity	0.00		
MVIC/Book Value of Invested Capital	N/A				

Earnings		Liquidity Ratios		Activity Ratios	
EBITDA	$66,601	Current Ratio	N/A	Total Asset Turnover	1.40
Discretionary Earnings	$1,411,632	Quick Ratio	N/A	Fixed Asset Turnover	8.34
				Inventory Turnover	61.42

Copyright © 2008 Business Valuation Resources, LLC. All rights reserved.
(503) 291-7963

EXHIBIT 17.3 Pratt's Stats, Sample Form
Source: Pratt's Stats.

valuing dental practices is powerful in that the compilation and organization of accumulated data permit comparison of prices at which similar practices have actually exchanged hands at arm's length.[7] Courts, appraisers, buyers, sellers, brokers, lenders, and others rely on this method a great deal. Revenue Ruling 59-60 and IRS Code Section 2031(b) emphasize the use of the market approach, especially in estate, income, and gift tax cases.

In comprehensive appraisal practice, the market approach comprises multiple methods—the market value multiple method, the guideline merged and acquired company method, and the guideline public company method. The market value multiple method is based on multiples derived from publicly traded security prices and transactions. The appraiser obtains, computes, and applies the multiples of public companies to multiples of the subject company. The two basic categories of multiples are equity multiples and invested capital multiples, and the most commonly used market values are price to earnings, price to gross cash flow, and price to pretax income. After organizing the pertinent multiples, the appraiser computes and applies the multiples of the public companies to multiples of the subject company. Such data is normally not available or applicable for dental practice appraisals despite dental practices today being considered not-too-small businesses.

Today, there are many dental practice mergers and acquisitions. In the business world, particularly, the guideline merged and acquired company method is a relatively popular market appraisal method. However, with mergers and acquisitions, there is little or no organized trading of shares, reporting of data, or accessibility of multiples, especially in dental practices. For dental and other professional practices, the guideline merged and acquired company method is not applicable. It is used in a variety of general business appraisals, especially large ones, but I have not seen or read of its being used in the appraisal of dental practices. Similarly, there is little to no data available for dental practices.

The guideline public multiple method deals with public companies that are similar to the subject company that trade daily and actively in the public environment. In this method, the appraiser is working with data of major and large companies in comparing certain relationships and analyzing smaller nonlisted companies. The object of the guideline public multiple method is to develop multiples that are applicable to the subject company. This method is used extensively in the valuation of almost all types of businesses but, like the market value multiple method and guideline merged and acquired company method, it is hardly ever used in the valuation of dental practices.

All methods are used in a variety of general business appraisals, especially midsize to large ones, but have not been used to any great extent in the appraisal of dental practices. The comparability between dental practices, even ones with large gross and net revenues that are publicly traded companies, is just too vast to be meaningful.

Direct Market Data Method (DMDM)

This method, developed, promulgated, and advanced by Raymond C. Miles, has become a highly relevant standard to help appraisers to determine values of small and midsize businesses and professions, more particularly in their application of the market approach. In the DMDM, all transactions for which market data are available are considered as a statistical ensemble that defines the market for businesses and professions of the same general type and classifies them under their Standard Industrial Classification (SIC) codes. Dental practices are classified under SIC 8021 or the North American Industrial Classification System (NAICS) 621210.

The appraiser determines by conventional means the economic, industry, financial ratios, and other analyses and the desirability of the subject practice relative to the overall market and specific situation. The appraiser further determines whether the practice is more or less desirable than the typical market transaction and by approximately how much. This provides useful insight into the practice and its value. The appraiser then estimates the market value of the target practice from the prices for which other similar practices or practice entities have been sold at arm's length.

The DMDM's use of a statistical ensemble is representative of the entire market instead of a limited number of publicly traded similar practices for which there is little data available. This is a major difference between the direct market data method and other market valuation methods. While other methods based on comparison are about *practices*, the DMDM is about *markets*. (See Exhibit 17.4.)

EXHIBIT 17.4   Outline of the DMDM Method

1. Gather data on large number of actual, arm's-length sales and transactions—SIC 8021, NAICA 621210.
2. Select performance measure—usually, price to gross revenues.
3. Analyze the transactional data:
   A. Number of transactions.
   B. Mean (average) ratio.
   C. Median ratio.
   D. Gross revenues.
   E. Net profit and cash flow.
   F. Additional.
4. Compare the subject practice and data to the transacted practices and data.
5. Estimate the fair market value of the practice:
   A. Apply all appropriate methods from the three approaches—income, assets, and market.
   B. Weight the methods.
6. Justify the value estimate.

Source: IBA Tutorial, Institute of Business Appraisers, P.O. Box 1741, Plantation, FL 33318.

Price to Earnings (P/E)

In the valuation of most dental practices, earnings are central and critical and the price-earnings (P/E) ratio is highly relevant. Results gleaned from the IBA transactional data bank revealed that (1) practical problems in data gathering and interpretation limited the usefulness of the P/E ratio as a measure of market performance, and (2) the most implausible number from an economic perspective on the financial statements of a closely held business is net income or profit. The same is true of dental practices.

Price to Gross Revenues (P/G)

Empirical data from the IBA transactional data bank indicate that in the valuation of dental practices, price to gross revenues (P/G) is the most significant ratio. Mr. Miles calls the P/G a "significant surrogate." He states that "the selling price to gross sales is a more reliable measure of market value than is price to earnings." The DMDM considers the data a statistical ensemble that defines the market for businesses and professions. The DMDM's use of the statistical ensemble is representative of the entire market instead of a limited number of publicly traded same or similar businesses or practices. This is the major difference between the DMDM and other valuation market methods.

Once the appraiser selects the large number of transactions and determines the price-to-gross ratio, the appraiser simply multiplies the ratio times the latest gross revenues of the practice. This, then, calculates the value of the practice. If the data in the data bank does not include accounts receivable and payable and liabilities—which most of the time it does not—and if it is indicated, the appraiser must include this determined amount to arrive at the estimate of value. The formula is:

Gross revenues × P/G ratio + Accounts receivable − Liabilities
= Practice value

Significant facts in the direct market data method are:

- The appraisal effective date is the key date for an appraisal.
- Price to gross revenues and net earnings of sales of dental practices are not influenced by the dates of the transactions.
- Events occurring after the appraisal effective date should not be considered in the estimated value of the dental practice.
- Fair market value defined in Revenue Ruling 59-60 and the Internal Revenue Service's *Business Valuation Guidelines* is the value normally determined and used in dental practice valuations.

- The DMDM employs as many transactions as possible to assist in the determination of value; other methods use a relatively small number of transactions.
- The DMDM is about *ranges*; other methods are about *individual* transactions.
- With fewer than five transactions, regardless of source, an appraiser should not or cannot properly draw upon the market approach.
- Dental practices are unique and most are not average, although appraisers and others refer to and like to use the term *average*. Average is difficult to define.
- Correlation between Price/Revenue ratios and down payment is very low to negligible.
- DMDM transactions and applications are relatively inexpensive to acquire.
- DMDM transactions and applications are relatively simple to explain to individuals not trained or experienced in the appraisal process.
- Finally and importantly, the best evidence of the market value is direct observation of the marketplace.

Empirical data from the IBA data bank indicate that in the valuation of a dental practice, price to gross revenues (P/G) is the most significant ratio. I have assessed the IBA dental data and have come up with the following pertinent price to gross revenue statistics in 2008.

Type of Practice	Price/Gross
General dentistry	61%
Oral and maxillofacial surgery	65%
Orthodontics	63%

The data indicate that the average of these practices actually sold at arm's length for the listed price-to-gross ratio. It does not mean that every practice is worth or should sell for such average, but it is a significant guideline. Each practice and each appraisal must stand on its own merits. Not only is the direct market data method an excellent market method, but also its resultant P/G ratio can serve as a reasonable checkpoint or guideline when an appraiser attempts to justify a final estimate of value. The results serve as excellent aids to the perceptive appraiser.

Many appraisers who value dental practices for multiple reasons and practice brokers maintain their own market data banks. This is excellent as different communities, areas, and portions of states have indigenous market characteristics that deserve specific recognition. Western Pennsylvania, where I practice, falls into this pattern, and the price to gross revenues and sale prices, like many factors in the region, are lower than national averages. Following the pattern of simply multiplying previous or weighted net income by some percent has been popular with many dental practice appraisers in the past and currently. Regrettably, the source of this percent is self-determined, and unprincipled appraisers use their sources in a self-serving manner to arrive at an unsubstantiated conclusion of value.

Revenue Multiplier Method

Another method under the market approach is the revenue multiplier method. In this method, the appraiser multiplies the latest gross revenues of the practice by a goodwill factor. In most cases, intangible asset value is important and generally is the largest asset in the valuation of a dental practice. In divorces cases in certain states, personal goodwill is not a marital asset, while enterprise goodwill may be. Many appraisers have accumulated data of actual arm's-length transactions, while others look for reliable data banks of accumulated data. The Goodwill Registry, located in Plymouth Meeting, Pennsylvania, has accumulated data contributed by appraisers, certified public accountants, business and practice brokers, attorneys, and others who have submitted data for many years. The Goodwill Registry records the reason for the valuation—sale/purchase of the practice, divorce, buy-sell arrangement and agreement, and reevaluation. It also lists the state and practice location as urban, suburban, or rural. Interestingly, this data bank actually lists the methods that the appraiser used in determining the estimate of value. The methods listed are the comparable sales market, gross revenue multiplier, discounted cash flow, excess earnings capitalization, and capitalization of earnings/income methods. In its annual survey, the Goodwill Registry requests and tabulates:

- *Gross revenues*— the practice's cash-basis gross receipts for the past 12 months.
- *Overhead percent*— the overhead rate, excluding doctors' compensation and benefits.
- *Practice price*— the total value/sales price for 100 percent of the practice, normally without accounts receivable.
- *Goodwill value*— allocated as the portion of the total value/sales price, including charts, patient lists, records, restrictive covenants, and so on.
- The simple formula is:

$$\text{Goodwill value} \div \text{Gross revenues} = \text{Goodwill percent}$$

EXHIBIT 17.5 Cumulative Goodwill Statistics, 1998–2007

	Goodwill	No Goodwill*	Goodwill as a Percentage of Gross Revenues			
			Mean	Median	Low	High
Endodontia	24	1 (4%)	50.05%	52.63%	16.00%	69.49%
General dentistry	1,857	23 (1%)	44.48%	45.62%	0.06%	163.50%
Oral and maxillofacial surgery	301	4 (1%)	43.24%	42.86%	2.35%	100.00%
Orthodontia	63	2 (3%)	45.61%	43.19%	4.41%	76.52%
Pedodontia	30	1 (3%)	49.21%	49.93%	15.52%	69.98%
Periodontia	44	1 (2%)	37.67%	38.18%	6.19%	67.24%
Prosthodontia	4	0 (0%)	37.73%	34.45%	27.82%	54.18%
Total/Average	**2,323**	**32 (1%)**	**44.33%**	**45.34%**	**0.06%**	**163.50%**

*Includes instances of negative goodwill.

In its copyrighted 2008 edition, the Goodwill Registry lists the significant data shown in Exhibit 17.5.

The accumulation of reliable data and the sources of such data over the years have made the foremost difference in the valuing of dental practices during the past decades. There are multiple excellent data banks available today, three of which I have addressed. The vast data bank of the Institute of Business Appraisers, the respected Pratt's Stats, and the long-term Goodwill Registry are outstanding sources and provide outstanding data. Each has its major and appropriate data points and, some appraisers believe, weaknesses; yet each greatly assists appraisers in their approaches to estimating the value of dental practices. Each data bank is relatively easy and inexpensive to access. The data banks encourage participants to contribute data, and by submitting sufficient data, participants have free access to the data banks. Access to and proper use of data from the multiple collection sources provide appraisers with a tremendous tool in the appraisal of dental practices.

Buy-Sell Agreement Method

Around 15 percent of general dentists and 65 percent of specialists are in multiperson practices. Over the years, and especially recently, there have been frequent and numerous buy-in and payout transactions in this large number of practices. In the case of group practices, buy-sell agreements are crucial. No multiperson practice should be without one. The terms of the agreements should be reasonable, realistic, and fair to all parties and, of course, committed to writing. The agreements should be reviewed and, if appropriate, revised annually. Valuing dental practices today is common and necessary for buy-sell transactions, and the terms of buy-sell transitions are highly relevant. The terms can be considered a form of market method. However, not all buy-sell agreements include a value or a method to value the practice and intangible assets. Many actually state that there is no intangible asset value, which may cause a problem in certain contentious valuation cases. It is imperative that the appraiser request information concerning whether there have been previous sales, principally recent ones, and the terms of them. Having realistic data available from practice buy-sell transactions in general and the subject practice particularly goes a long way in the valuation process regardless of the purpose and function of the appraisal.

Corporate-owned insurance plays a large part in funding buy-sell agreements. As a matter of fact, it is the major source of funding of the agreements. Death and other benefits and cash values are highly relative to the funding process. The planned steps in case of premature death and permanent disability are: (1) The corporation owns the policies. (2) Tragedy sets in. (3) The corporation arranges to collect the benefits. (4) The corporation collects the benefits. (5) Money is deposited into the corporation's account. (6) The corporation pays the deceased or disabled partner's estate or beneficiary the entitled benefits. (7) The corporation owns additional stock or units.

There is a flaw in this process, however, which professional partners and appraisers must be aware of and address. Recently, there have been problems in certain cases. When the corporation receives and deposits the benefits (steps 4 and 5), the corporation then actually adds hundreds of thousands of dollars to its bank accounts and balance sheet even though this may (or may not) be on a short-term basis. However, two major conditions now exist: (1) If the corporation owes any debts or other payables, in most cases the lenders and creditors have first lien on the collected benefits and the corporation legally cannot distribute the beneficiary's intended funds until the liabilities are satisfied or the lenders and creditors give permission to do so. (2) Importantly, certain individuals, more particularly the heirs and their attorneys, may conclude that the value of the corporation may have increased considerably and the heirs are entitled to a larger payout. Any amount collected that is greater than the amount that will be paid to the beneficiaries is another factor. Timing of the insurance collection, the payout, and the appraisal is pertinent. Therefore, what we are seeing and suggesting is that the parties insert a clause in their buy-sell and other agreements such as: "The death benefits of a deceased or permanently disabled Shareholder which the Corporation shall receive shall not in any manner affect nor alter the total value of the Company."

Relative to sales today, there are two types of dental practices—solo and group practices. A dentist in a solo practice may plan and want to retire, and the practice on paper has considerable value; but there are no buyers and the departing doctor cannot sell the practice. This is mainly due to the tremendous shortage of dentists. Potential buyers of both general and specialty practices feel that although goodwill and other intangible assets may be present, they simply are not going to pay for them. Buyers may explain their reasons for perceiving no intangible value, whereas others will simply refuse to pay for it. Modern technology, equipment, and techniques are extensive and expensive in dental practices today, and many seasoned, financially rewarding practices have not caught up with them. Modern dentists believe they cannot practice without them. Taking these crucial points one step further and in pointed contrast, group practices definitely have a great deal of valuable intangible assets. Wise seasoned and neophyte practitioners alike and astute appraisers must become aware of these recent practice phenomena and appropriately consider and accommodate them in practice buy-ins, payouts, transactions, and appraisals.

Discounts and Premiums

Discounts and premiums are frequently applicable and used in determining the final estimate of value in businesses. Similarly, they should be used in selected dental practice cases to determine the final estimate of value, especially specialty and group practices. Common discounts are for lack of marketability and lack of control. Having and maintaining control can be a reason for a premium. When applicable, discounts and premiums widely run from 10 to 50 percent. Marketability refers to (1) the market of individuals or practice entities available to purchase a practice or practice interest and (2) the ability to convert the value of a dental practice into cash in a short time (also known as liquidity). Today, more than ever, most dental practices are highly illiquid. The typical time involved in the sale of a dental practice has increased and runs between 8 and 12 or more months, if a sale occurs at all.

Control simply refers to the power and ability to have power over the operation, decisions, and management of the practice entity. Most dentists are frightfully aware of control and abhor losing it, which can considerably affect the true value of noncontrolling dentists. Some group practice entities have voting and nonvoting stock or units that handle control, compensation, and other matters. Very few valuators tack on a premium for control, although they may find an occasion where it is indicated. Conversely, it is entirely appropriate in valuations and sales of a minority interest in a dental practice to apply a discount for lack of control as well as lack of marketability. The purpose and function of the appraisal play a large part in the decision for the application.

Discounts for lack of marketability are more common and appropriate in valuations and sales of solo and group dental practices. Over the years there have been multiple studies, much disagreement, and a great deal of authorship on marketability, control, and other discounts, more particularly the lack of them. Therefore, in aptly applying discounts or premiums, appraisers must be able to justify and document adequately their basis for determination of either. The appraiser may apply the appropriate discount or premium to the final estimate of value and not to selected methods only.

Weighting

Section 7 of RR 59-60 states that "no useful purpose is served by taking an average of several factors and basing the valuation on the result. Such a process excludes active consideration of other factors, and the end result cannot be supported by a realistic application of the significant facts in the case except by mere change."

In each appraisal method, present and future earnings and market comparables are significant. Like appraising in general, weighting is subjective, is not always exact, and may change over time. Weighting is presented in mathematical terms to assist in determining the relevance of the different methods.

Earnings-based methods are significant and proper methods for the valuation of a dental practice. The capitalization of income method, to a great extent, is dependent on the built-up capitalization rate and certain projections. The result, advantageously, incorporates both tangible and intangible values. This method is a well-established and relied-upon appraisal method. The discounted cash flow method is dependent on reasonable cash flow projections for a number of years with allowances for taxes and future replacement of tangible assets and the built-up discount rate. This method is a highly recognized and acceptable method in today's appraisal environment of dental practices.

Derived from IRS Revenue Ruling 68-609, the IRS and certain appraisers use this method to calculate goodwill and to value closely held businesses and health care entities. The basic concept is to determine intangible value as a reasonable return on invested tangible assets subtracted from net cash flow or earnings of the practice, the excess earnings, which is then added to the value of the adjusted balance sheet or net tangible asset value. The ruling states that modification permits application for the valuation of a dental practice. This is a reliable method to assist an appraiser in the estimation of value of a dental practice.

The comparable market sales method is meaningful and addresses the facts of the marketplace, that is, the actual prices at which dental practices have changed hands at arm's length. Having data available from the Institute of Business Appraisers, Pratt's Stats, and other reliable data banks enables an appraiser to estimate the value of a dental practice in a realistic and reasonable manner.

The revenue multiplier method multiplies previous gross revenues by an intangible factor to determine the intangible asset value. The resultant intangible or goodwill value is added to the adjusted balance sheet or net tangible asset value, which calculates the estimated value of the practice.

There are other recognized and unrecognized valuation methods available and used today. After reviewing the calculated results of all methods and determining which are applicable and which are not, appraisers have to call upon their meticulous skill and experience to determine the various weights of the accepted methods.

SUMMARY

During the past few decades, dental practice appraisal has developed from simple formulas and rules of thumb. Glenn Desmond's 1987 *Handbook of Small Business Valuation Formulas and Rules of Thumb* was a classic. His formulas were based on monthly net revenues (MNRs) for tangibles and intangibles, which ranged widely from 50 percent to 100 percent. Today, appraisers have many training and educational programs leading to various certifications. Continuing education is a must for current-day appraisers. Most important, multiple organizations have accumulated and made available extensive and significant data.

Dental practice appraising has become a mature, established, businesslike, skillful art. Appraisers apply modern appraisal techniques derived from a plethora of methods and follow established guidelines. Attorneys, courts, lenders, the Internal Revenue Service, and other interested parties are aware of and look for appraisals that are properly prepared, adequately documented, reasonable, and realistic, and the examine the methodology applied in achieving the results. They are aware of, understand, and expect reliable, comprehensive appraising that includes application of the three approaches and multiple methods, whether or not they eventually end up in the final estimate of value. In cases where bias, unreasonableness, and unrealistic estimates appear, appraisers and their appraisals will be legitimately challenged.

In this chapter, relevant to the valuation of general and specialty dental practices, I have shown the overall enormity of the appraisal specialty of dental practices; the development, importance, and uniqueness of the special field; and its relationship with, differences from, and similarities to business and other appraising. I pointed out the important guidelines for responsible appraisers of the Uniform Standards of Professional Appraisal Practice (USPAP). I pointed out today's importance, reliability, and availability of certified machinery and equipment appraisers and their importance in tangible asset appraisals. I showed the method and the applicability of the direct market data method.

There are, however, major and important differences between the valuation of dental practices and other businesses. I pointed out such pertinent differences in the recognized and most commonly used appraisal methods— the capitalization of income method, the discounted future cash flow method, the excess earnings method, the comparable market data method, and the revenue multiplier method. I presented general and specific guidelines that may provide appraisers of dental practices with additional information, data, and suggestions, which, I hope, will be helpful to appraisers who already apply sound appraisal techniques.

Although each appraiser, each appraisal, each dental practice, and each dental practitioner is elegantly unique, with proper application of the basic and unique characteristics, each appraiser will be able to prepare, publish, and defend his of her professional appraisal.

NOTES

1. Institute of Business Appraisers, P.O. Box 1741, Plantation, FL 33318.
2. Pratt's Stats, Business Valuation Resources, 7412 SW Beaverton Hillsdale Highway, Portland, OR 97225.
3. American Dental Association, 211 East Chicago Avenue, Chicago, IL 60611.
4. William Sutton, 3 McAllister Place, Greensboro, NY 27455.
5. Robert J. Cimasi, MHA, ASA, CBA, AVA, CM&AA, CMP, Health Capital Consultants, LLC, 9666 Olive Blvd., St. Louis, MO 63132.
6. Mark O. Dietrich, CPA, ABV, 801 Water Street, Framingham, MA 01701.
7. Arm's length transaction—a transaction negotiated by *unrelated* parties each acting in his or her self interest; a good faith transaction. A basis for fair market value determination. (*Black's Law Dictionary*).

REFERENCES

Cox, H.A., 1995. Are you prepared to retire? *Dental Economics* 85(7): 36–45.

Ibbotson. 2008. *Stocks, bonds, bills & inflation: 2008 yearbook*. Chicago, IL: Ibbotson Associates.

Pollock, Stanley L. 2006, 2007. *Valuing professional practices & licenses: A guide for the matrimonial practitioner*. 3rd ed., supplements. Ed. Ronald L. Brown. Austin, TX: Wolters Kluwer.

Schilit, James H. 1987. Relevance of financial analysis to standard appraisal methodology. *Business Valuation Review* (September): 110.

USPAP. 2008. Uniform standards of professional appraisal practice, 2008–2009 edition. Washington, DC: Appraisal Standards Board, Appraisal Foundation.

CHAPTER 18

Measures of Discount for Lack of Marketability and Liquidity

Ashok Abbott, Ph.D.
Associate Professor of Finance, West Virginia University

Fair market value is defined as the price at which an asset will change hands between a willing buyer and a willing seller, neither party being under compulsion to buy or sell, and both having reasonable knowledge of relevant facts. It is generally accepted that equity interests in small, closely held businesses are not readily marketable and may be relatively illiquid. Estimating the loss in value due to lack of marketability and liquidity is not merely an academic issue. Investors, owners of small businesses, and tax authorities frequently need to make an estimate of realizable value in the case of a willing buyer not being readily available.

In fact, a better theoretically sound, empirically validated model framework on illiquidity effects can provide immense economic understanding of the recent market turmoil induced by the freeze-up and meltdown of markets. This chapter addresses this model framework.

PUBLICLY TRADED EQUIVALENT VALUE

Public markets based approaches in business valuation practice are designed to convert a stream of anticipated cash flows from ownership of a closely held business to a present value. This conversion can be achieved by using a multiple, such as a price-to-sales ratio, or a more sophisticated, but functionally equivalent, application of capitalizing a cash flow stream using a required rate of return. These multiples or required rates of return are frequently calculated using public markets based data. The steps involved are simple; after selecting a risk-free rate and an appropriate risk premium, required rate of return for the subject company being valued is determined. A variety of approaches are used to develop the appropriate risk premium. These may include estimates based on the capital asset pricing model (CAPM) beta or a buildup method where premiums based on different risk, size, industry, or other parameters are added to the risk-free rate to estimate the required rate of return. This approach results in an income approach estimating the publicly traded equivalent value (PTEV) of the privately held company.

DISCOUNTS FOR LACK OF MARKETABILITY AND DISCOUNT FOR LACK OF LIQUIDITY

The issues of discounts for lack of marketability (DLOM) and liquidity (DLOL), therefore, need to be identified and addressed in the valuation analysis. PTEV assumes inherently that the interests in closely held businesses being priced are freely tradable in open-outcry liquid markets. In reality, nothing could be further from the truth. Even in the public markets for freely traded stocks, liquidity is not always available. Smaller market value stocks suffer from significant lack of liquidity and the observed high buy-and-hold returns may be masking considerable transaction costs that an investor desiring liquidity would face. Loeb (1983), for example, documents that the total cost of trading (the spread plus price concessions and brokerage commissions) increases significantly as the size of the firm decreases and the block size increases. "The roundtrip trading cost on a $5,000 block of small capitalization issues (under $10 million) will consume 17.3 per cent of the price; the spread/price cost for an equivalent block of large capitalization issues (over $1.5 billion) will be 1.1 per cent." These results suggest that it would be unreasonable to ignore the role of liquidity in asset pricing.

Pratt (2009) suggests that understanding the difference between marketability (legal ability to sell an asset) and liquidity (ability to sell an asset without delay or loss of value) is critical to identifying the appropriate level of applicable discounts. Emory (2003) defines a "gold standard" of marketability for stock as "being actively traded on a public market, where an investor can receive a predictable amount of cash three business days after deciding to sell, with minimal transaction costs." Such acceptance provides a simple starting point where any price differences between this "gold standard" and the price of the unregistered/restricted security is accepted as a measurement of the discount for lack of marketability. In practice this distinction appears to have been largely ignored. Liquidity is different for different classes of assets and can change relatively quickly in response to market conditions. Recent events in the financial markets have amply illustrated how much the financial system depends on the ability to trade assets continuously. Even though traditional business valuation literature has used marketability and liquidity interchangeably, it is important for us to make clear the important distinction between the two concepts. While the concepts of marketability and liquidity are closely aligned, they are quite separate and distinct, and the presence of one does not automatically confer the other.

Marketability, as defined by Pratt, denotes the ability to sell a block of securities in an established and efficient public capital market, whereas liquidity denotes the ability to sell an asset within a reasonable time, with relatively low transaction costs, and with minimal effect on that asset's public market price. Liquidity denotes the ability to convert an asset into cash. Marketability is discrete with well-defined different stages, whereas liquidity is a continuous and varying spectrum. A block with high liquidity will have low transaction costs, a short liquidation period, and minimal discounts (e.g., bid-ask spread). A block with low liquidity will have opposite characteristics. In summary, marketability relates to the right to sell something, whereas liquidity refers to the speed with which an asset may be converted to cash without diminishing its value.

Marketability and liquidity vary across a fairly wide range. There are varying degrees of marketability as well as liquidity. Registering a security, incurring a defined registration cost, can cure lack of marketability, allowing the original holders to offer the security in public capital markets. Liquidity, however, is a function of multiple factors, at least some of which are outside the control of the management. As marketability and liquidity get impaired, larger value adjustments need to be made. For example, marketability may be ranked from highest to lowest in the following order.

1. Registered stock in an exchange-listed publicly traded firm capable of being transferred without any limitations.
2. Registered stock in an exchange-listed publicly traded firm subject to Regulation 144 or similar contractual restrictions.
3. Unregistered stock in an exchange-listed publicly traded firm.
4. Unregistered stock in a closely held unlisted large firm (potential to go public).
5. Unregistered stock in a closely held unlisted small firm.

Each of these marketability stages after the first one will require deeper discounts for lack of marketability. Further, liquidity can differ significantly within each marketability class, based on the attributes of the asset. For example, a significant block of a large stock may be liquidated relatively easily, whereas stock of a small over-the-counter (OTC) firm may find few buyers in the short run without offering significant discounts.

Prior business valuation literature has focused on the lack of marketability, without making an explicit effort to identify and address the cost of liquidity, which is the focus of our analysis in this chapter.

BENCHMARKING METHODS

It has been suggested that the length of expected holding period is a critical variable in determining an appropriate discount for lack of liquidity. The observed changes in price differentials for recent studies of restricted stocks issued after reduction of holding period by the Securities and Exchange Commission (SEC) have been ascribed to the new shorter holding period. Similarly, a growing body of initial public offering (IPO) underpricing studies suggests that the observed underpricing is explained, at least in part, by the level of expected post-IPO liquidity. Therefore, the results from publicly traded firm data may be helpful in explaining the liquidity behavior of unlisted closely held firms. Pratt (2009) provides a summary of research suggesting the importance of expected holding period in explaining observed discounts for restricted stock. The three groups of empirical studies identified by Pratt are:

1. Studies comparing private placements of restricted securities with publicly traded securities of the same company, known as restricted stock studies.
2. Studies comparing prices received in sales of closely held stock with subsequent initial public offerings, known as pre-IPO studies.
3. Studies measuring equity returns around events causing increase in liquidity

The business valuation community has generally used results of restricted stock valuation studies and pre-IPO studies as benchmarks for estimating discounts for lack of marketability. A myriad of studies, ranging from comparing pre- and post-IPO prices, observed discounts in private placements of registered and unregistered stocks, and differences between prices of restricted and unrestricted securities of the same issuer, have been conducted and published. There are two problems with this benchmark approach. The mean or median of observed sample discounts appears to have been used as an estimate of the general discount for lack of marketability (DLOM), without exploring causal relationship between the observed discount and the characteristics of the subject company. The second problem arises from the failure to distinguish between the returns attributable to changes in liquidity and the combined effects of market conditions and other confounding factors.

Restricted stock studies compare the prices observed in placement of restricted stock issued to corporate insiders during an initial public offering or to company executives as a result of exercising incentive stock options. Restricted stocks of publicly traded companies are identical to their freely tradable counterpart securities except that they are restricted from public trading. Under SEC Rule 144 a holder of restricted stock is allowed to sell limited quantities of stock in any three-month period (the greater of 1 percent of the then outstanding shares of the company or an average of the prior four weeks' trading volume) after an initial period that has been gradually reduced over time. These restrictions on free reselling of restricted stock were originally set to expire two years after initial acquisition. In February 1997 these guidelines were revised to reduce the period of trading restrictions to one year. Further changes in applicable restrictions occurred in February 2008, reducing the period of the initial no-trading restriction to six months for registered reporting companies.

Since restricted stocks are not freely tradable, they suffer from a relative lack of marketability when compared with the equivalent publicly tradable stock of the same firm. The relative price difference between a trade of restricted and unrestricted stock in a similar time frame has been used to provide a measure of DLOM. The mean and median discounts for most of these studies fall between 30 percent and 35 percent. The mean discounts from these studies have been widely used by the business appraisal profession as an indication of applicable DLOM. This analysis does not usually distinguish between the characteristics of the individual firms, and the samples show wide variation in observed discounts, reducing statistical significance of these results. This variation indicates a need for further investigation of causal factors.

Empirical analysis of the price differences between restricted stocks and their tradable counterparts provides an indication of the significant discount for lack of trading ability. Wruck (1989) reports an average discount of 14 percent in a sample of 83 sales of New York Stock Exchange (NYSE) and American Stock Exchange (AMEX) firms making private sales of restricted shares between July 1979 and December 1985. In contrast, a sample of 45 sales of registered securities during the same period reveals a premium of 4 percent. This paper does not provide any analysis of systematic differences in the characteristics of firms issuing registered and restricted shares. A regression model developed by Silber (1991) analyzes a sample of 69 private placements. The average discount for restricted stocks analyzed in this study was 33.75 percent. The sample analysis indicates that the firm revenue, relative size of the restricted block, firm profitability, and the buyer's relationship with the selling firm are significant in explaining the level of the observed discount, which ranged from 84 percent to a premium of 12.7 percent.

The estimated regression is:

$$LN\,(RPRS) = 4.33 + 0.036\,LN\,(REV) - 0.142\,LN\,(RBRT)$$
$$+ 0.174\,DERN - 0.332\,DCUST$$

where LN (RPRS) is natural logarithm of the relative price of restricted stock expressed in percentage terms $[(p^*/p) \cdot 100]$. The explanatory variables are LN (REV), the natural logarithm of the firm's revenues (in millions); LN (RBRT), the natural logarithm of the restricted block relative to total common stock (in percent); DERN, a dummy variable equal to 1 if the firm's earnings are positive and equal to zero otherwise; and DCUST, a dummy variable equal to 1 if there is a customer relationship between the investor and the firm issuing the restricted stock and zero otherwise.

Hertzel and Smith (1993) analyze a sample of 106 private placements made between January 1980 and May 1987 and find that firm size, fraction placed, financial distress, book to market equity, restricted shares, single investor, and management buyer are all significant in explaining the amount of discount observed in private placements. Their results indicate that firms in financial distress and engaged in speculative development of new products are more likely to place equity privately, and that observed discounts tend to be higher for these types of firms. In their opinion, discounts are not caused solely by the lack of marketability, but also may be caused by these factors. After controlling for nonmarketability determinants of private placement discounts in a multivariate regression framework, the observed mean discount for restricted shares in the Hertzel-Smith study was 20.14 percent and the median discount was 13.25 percent.

Bajaj et al. (2001) also provides empirical analysis of data sets involving restricted stock placements for identifying factors influencing the level of discounts related to lack of marketability. This study analyzed a sample of 88 private placements occurring between January 1, 1990, and December 31, 1995. In conformity with prior literature, the size of the block, financial condition, and riskiness of the firm's cash flows were found to be significant. This regression also tested a dummy variable for the registration status of the issue and found a significant effect. The estimated regression is:

$$Discount = a + 0.40 \times Fraction\ of\ shares\ issued - 0.08 \times Z\text{-}Score + 3.13$$
$$\times Standard\ deviation\ of\ returns + b_4 \times Registration\ indicator$$

The coefficients are as expected and significant. Every percentage point by which the block size increases (relative to the total shares after the issue) is accompanied by an increase in the discount by 0.40 percent. Similarly, for every unit increase in the Z-Score (indicating better financial health), the discount decreases by 0.08 percent. For every percent by which the standard deviation of monthly returns increases, indicating greater business risk in the issuer, the discount increases by 3.13 percent. Lack of registration increases the discount by 7 percent.

These models present a significant theoretical advance in understanding the causal nature of the discount for lack of marketability. The results provide a theoretical justification for the observed discount and are appealing as a relatively simple approach for quantifying DLOM for a specific firm. While the models provide an explanation for the observed discounts and identify causal factors that may explain the level of discount, the estimated coefficients may be time-sensitive, as underlying economic conditions are not accounted for in the model specification. In addition, any model that seeks to explain gross returns from an event may suffer from confounding events. More recently, FMV Opinions, Inc. has started providing FMV Restricted Stock Study^{TM}, a database of transactions involving stock restricted under SEC Rule 144 that can be used to create a customized study to determine discounts for lack of marketability (DLOM).

Pre-IPO studies have been used to provide another set of benchmarks for DLOM adopted by the business valuation community. These studies compare prices received in sales of closely held stock with subsequent initial public offerings. SEC rules require all firms registering their stock to disclose all transactions in the stock as a private company for a period of three years prior to the registration. A comparison of the pre-offering transfer prices with the IPO price has been used as an estimate of the marketability discount. Two series of such studies have been published. Robert W. Baird & Co., Inc. studies compare transaction prices up to five months before the IPO. These studies are regularly updated by Emory Business Valuation LLC. Willamette Management Associates studies compare transaction prices up to three years prior to the IPO with the IPO prices. These studies are also updated periodically. Valuation Advisors, LLC published another pre-IPO study in 2000. These studies have shown mean and median discounts in the range of 42 percent to 46 percent. The discounts reported in the Valuation Advisors study were considerably higher, reaching 77 percent for transactions dated one year and more prior to the date of the IPO.

EMPIRICAL STUDIES

Academic empirical studies are inconclusive about the effects of listing on shareholder wealth. Such studies disagree about whether prelisting gains offset postlisting losses. Sanger and McConnell (1986) and Edelman and Baker (1993) find abnormally positive returns before listing, especially during the interval between application and listing, but abnormally negative returns immediately afterward. Researchers often attribute the positive reaction to listing announcements to expectations of increased liquidity and to signaling effects. Long-run post-IPO performance has been studied, and the aftermarket stock and operating performances are found to be negative, falling short of initial expectations. The extent of the actual postissue growth was lower than the ex ante estimations by financial analysts, whose valuations were systematically upwardly biased. Affiliated analysts are found not to be more overly optimistic than the unaffiliated analysts (e.g., Paleari 2007).

A corollary to pre-IPO studies is to study the change in value when a public stock is delisted. Such an event allows us to directly observe the value lost as a result of the lost access to public markets. Abbott (2004) analyzed delisting events specifying lack of liquidity as the reason for delisting during the years from 1982 to 2001. NASDAQ listing rules require active participation of a minimum number of market makers to ensure liquidity for the listed stocks. If the number of active market makers falls below the required minimum (two active market makers for smaller firms and four active market makers for larger firms), the firm receives a notice of deficiency. If the firm fails to cure this deficiency within a period of 90 days, the firm is delisted from NASDAQ. The data sample consists of a total verified sample of 324 delistings due to lack of liquidity and a smaller sample of 179 delistings due to lack of liquidity without any confounding events occurring during the year leading to delisting. This selection procedure resulted in a final sample of 175 firms for which adequate information is available. The mean observed cumulative negative excess returns during the period of delisting were 22.75 percent, ranging from a loss of 86.67 percent of value to a gain of 64.25 percent of value.

The mean market value of the firms on the day of the delisting announcement was $3.08 million and values ranged from $115,000 to $65 million. The firms included in this sample had a mean annual stock turnover of 1.27 times, ranging from firms that were practically not traded during the preceding year to highly liquid firms with a stock turnover of 18 times per year. The firms in the sample had trailed the market by an average of 18.29 percent during the year leading to delisting announcement. The average value of transactions during the year leading to the delisting was $4 million, and ranged from $14,000 to $7 million. A clear pattern emerges when we compare the observed variables across different size categories. The excess negative returns observed during the period of delisting are largest for the smallest firms, with the lowest quartile showing a mean of 39.9 percent, reducing to 28.56 percent for the second quartile, 17.51 percent for the third quartile, and becoming an insignificant 4.19 percent for the largest firms in the sample. The firm performance relative to the market also changes with size. The average annual total transactions value for the firms also changes with the firm size. The observed variables are all statistically significantly different from zero, with the exception of the observed excess returns for the period of delisting for the firms in the largest quartile.

Discount for lack of marketability is found to be a function of market value of the firm, firm performance relative to the market, and the level of liquidity measured by the annual turnover of the stock.

The estimated model equation for DLOM according to this model is:

$$\text{DLOM} = -0.22220 + 0.39571 \times \text{Cumexret} + 1.146 \times \text{Cap90X10}^\wedge - 5 + 0.02491 \times \text{Turnover}$$

The results indicate that DLOM gets smaller as the firm becomes larger and more profitable, and the volume of trades taking place during the year increases as less market value is lost by delisting. For highly profitable and heavily traded firms, there may not be appreciable loss of value due to delisting, as buyers are likely to be available for such firms. Conversely, smaller firms with performance trailing the market and a small number of transactions or no transactions would suffer a larger loss in value as a result of the delisting event.

More recently, Macey, O'Hara, and Pompilio (2008), analyzing a sample of stocks delisted from the NYSE in 2002, report that share prices fall by half, percentage spreads on average triple, and volatility almost doubles at the announcement of delisting.

LIQUIDITY AS A PRICING FACTOR

The role of liquidity has not been explicitly empirically recognized in business valuation literature. One common feature of all of the restricted stock and pre-IPO studies is that liquidity is presumed to exist for all degrees of marketability. A review of this literature suggests that the assumption of unlimited instantaneous liquidity for all registered marketable securities has been accepted without question. This omission is not surprising since the vast majority of equilibrium asset pricing models do not consider trading and thus ignore the time and cost of transforming cash into financial assets or vice versa. We can get considerable help from prior academic finance research, which, in contrast, has concentrated on the issue of liquidity and its cost for publicly traded equity securities. Since the data from publicly traded markets have been used, the marketability assumption has been satisfied in the data used for this research.

A small but growing body of market microstructure finance literature explores the relationship among liquidity, marketability, and the bid-ask spread. Various empirical and theoretical studies, such as Amihud and Mendelson (1986, 1991) and, more recently, Garvey (2000), have argued and documented that the yield to maturity, or investment returns, on less liquid financial instruments might be higher compared to their identical liquid counterparts. Studies measuring equity returns around events causing increase in liquidity (e.g., inclusion in the S&P 500 index, or switching registration between different exchanges) generally report a gain from this increase. Liquidity pricing is also evident in event studies analyzing changes in liquidity as a result of exchange migration or inclusion in an index. For example, the studies on additions to the S&P 500 (e.g., Harris and Gurel 1986; Shleifer 1986) find a 2 percent to 3 percent excess return when a stock is added to the S&P 500 index. Other recent studies, such as Beneish and Whaley (1996, 2002) and Lynch and Mendenhall (1997), establish that there is a permanent excess return when a stock enters the heavily traded S&P 500 list. Furthermore, these studies show that this permanent increase in value is closely related to improvements in the stock's liquidity. Exchange migration listings of NASDAQ stocks provide another opportunity for monitoring the effects of a major liquidity event. Studies such as Kadlec and McConnell (1994) find an average excess return of approximately 5 percent to 6 percent when a stock listing moves from NASDAQ to the NYSE. Kadlec and McConnell further claim that this excess return is weakly associated with the reduction in the bid-ask spread that follows the listing.

Academic finance literature recognizes four dimensions of liquidity:

1. Width (availability of a large number of buyers).
2. Depth (ability to absorb large volume).
3. Immediacy (ability to complete the transaction quickly).
4. Resiliency (ability to absorb a large volume of trades without moving the price).

The market for small firms suffers from lack of liquidity in each of these four dimensions. A small number of potential buyers decreases the competition inherent in an auction market; therefore, lack of depth and resiliency force a higher price impact of trading. Consequently, the seller has to choose between a long liquidation period (lack of immediacy) with attendant price risk and the immediate price pressure attributable to lack of depth and the attendant likelihood of market failure. It is important to note that price risk is not only the risk of a decline in selling price, but also the risk of not being able to realize the higher prices that might occur during the period of liquidation. The two components of the discount for lack of liquidity can, thus, be identified as the price pressure caused by additional supply of the stock and the price risk faced by the holder as a result of the long liquidation period. The optimal trading strategy for a seller is to minimize the total cost of the price pressure and the price risk by selecting an appropriate level of trade size and frequency over the anticipated liquidation period.

DISTINCTION BETWEEN HOLDING PERIOD AND LIQUIDATION PERIOD

At this point it is useful to make a clear distinction between holding period and liquidation period. A holding period is discretionary; investors elect to hold an asset for a certain period based on their investment preferences and expected returns. In contrast, a liquidation period is the time needed to liquidate a position in a manner that minimizes the total cost of the price pressure and price risk faced by the seller in response to the prevailing market conditions. The price concession offered by the seller (discount for lack of liquidity) is therefore determined by the liquidation period faced by the seller, and not the intended holding period of the buyer. This externally determined constraint is a major factor for determining the discount for lack of liquidity. The second piece of the DLOL puzzle is the variability of asset returns, which creates the price risk faced by the investor during the period of liquidation. Since this risk consists of both the risk of decline in value as well as the inability to realize the gains from an increase in value, it is appropriate to use a path-dependent option (look-back put) to capture the entire value of the price risk, as opposed to a Black-Scholes put option, which captures only the risk of the decline in value during the liquidation period. Longstaff (1995) provides an expectations form of the look-back put that uses only two inputs, the variance of asset returns and the liquidation period, to determine the discount for lack of liquidity.

Translating these concepts to the business valuation arena requires substantial adjustments. Business valuation assignments typically deal with negotiated transactions for significant blocks between a very small number of potential buyers and sellers for a particular business. In contrast, public trading involves markets where minuscule interests in relatively large firms are traded among a very large number of potential buyers and sellers. Using rates of return derived from small at-the-market transactions of high-trading-volume public securities approaching immediate execution to price transactions in the closely held business marketplace induces large distortions that need to be corrected.

QUANTITATIVE APPROACHES BASED ON CAPM AND TIME VALUE

One approach used in business valuation literature to account for delayed value realization has been to adapt the traditional CAPM-based discounted cash flow models. Four notable discounted cash flow models commonly recognized in business valuation literature are:

1. Quantitative Model of Discount for Marketability (QMDM) proposed by Z. Christopher Mercer and Travis W. Harms (1997).
2. Time Value Model proposed by John J. Stockdale (2006).
3. CAPM-based approach to calculating illiquidity discounts that deals with lack of diversification proposed by David I. Tabak. (2002)
4. Meulbroek model for cost of lack of diversification proposed by Lisa K. Meulbroek (2002).

The primary mechanism for the first two papers is to adjust the parameters of present value calculation by varying the required rate of return and the anticipated period of liquidation. The second set of papers incorporates the notion of lack of diversification in addition to the time dimension of delayed liquidation and consequent ability to diversify.

The QMDM was the first model to attempt to identify the parameters for the discussion of marketability discounts. This model introduced some specificity to the rather murky qualitative benchmarking practices of the time. An additional advantage of this framework is to make explicit the implicit (and unspecified) assumptions used by practitioners. The model estimates a difference in value if immediately realizable versus the present value of the expected delayed realization. The parameters used are:

Expected holding period (HP).

Expected distribution yield (D%)

Expected growth in distributions (GD%).

Projected terminal value.

When appraisers use a DCF model to value an enterprise, they forecast expected enterprise cash flows and estimate an appropriate discount rate, inclusive of specific risks attributable to the enterprise not otherwise accounted for by their CAPM-related discount rates. The enterprise value is the sum of the forecasted cash flows discounted to the present at the estimated discount rate. The role of the discount rate in the QMDM is no different from in any other DCF model. Any increase in the discount rate is accompanied by a decrease in the present value and therefore a higher DLOM. QMDM has been criticized by some practitioners for the sensitivity of the estimated DLOM to the input parameters. This sensitivity, however, is not unique to QMDM. Any equation will change its value when the inputs are changed. QMDM application provides a midrange DLOM value as well as a range of values with an analysis of the anticipated changes in DLOM when the required rates of return and period of liquidation are varied.

The Stockdale model was published in 2006 and presents an additional level of flexibility. The model's major contribution is that it explicitly incorporates the inherent uncertainty in the estimated liquidation period. While the paper assumes a linear liquidation probability, the model is flexible enough to accommodate any selected probability distribution. It also allows for the starting point for the period of liquidation to be any time in the future rather than the present time period. This makes it easy to incorporate the initial delays in liquidation mandated by the Regulation 144 requirements or lockout periods provided in restricted stock and IPO allotments.

The CAPM-based model proposed by David Tabak treats the stockholder restricted from selling the security interest as an undiversified investor subject to an increased risk due to the lack of diversification and treats this incremental cost of lack of diversification as a proxy for the cost of marketability.

The model is simple and relatively easily computed:

$$\text{DLOM} = 1 - e^{\wedge}\left(\sigma_S^2/\sigma_m^2\right) \times \text{RP} \times \text{T}$$

where the equity risk premium is multiplied by the ratio of variance of the asset's returns with the variance of the market and the time to anticipated liquidation.

Thus, the discount is a function of the total risk of the security to market risk, the market risk premium, and the time at which the security would be sold.

The Meulbroek model is similar in concept, except it uses the difference between the asset beta and the ratio of standard deviation of returns for the asset and the market as a measure of the incremental risk taken by the undiversified holder during the period of restricted marketability:

$$\text{DLOM} = 1 - [1/(1 + R)^n]$$

where R is the product of the market risk premium multiplied by the difference between the asset's beta and the ratio of standard deviation of returns for the asset and the market, a measure of incremental risk.

Both of these models assume that the total wealth of the holder is tied up in the undiversified asset. Kahl, Liu, and Longstaff (2001) present a similar model in which the value of restricted stock is a function of stock volatility, beta, the holder's risk aversion coefficient, fraction of illiquid wealth to total wealth, and time to hold the stock. The model is not easy to implement.

HISTORICAL MARKET LIQUIDITY STATISTICS

It has been suggested that the length of expected holding period is a critical variable in determining an appropriate discount for lack of liquidity. Theoretical underpinnings of the QMDM model, for example, hinge on the notion of an estimated holding period. A longer holding period implies the existence of a larger discount for lack of liquidity. It is important to note that all of these present value models use a specific time to sale as one input into the model. As Stockdale (2006) points out, this assumption results in neglecting the uncertainty as to future time of sale and suggests that each of these models should be used in connection with a time probability distribution when used to compute a DLOM. The observed changes in price differentials for recent studies of restricted stocks issued after reduction of holding period by the SEC has been ascribed to the new shorter holding period. Similarly, a growing body of IPO underpricing studies suggests that the observed underpricing is explained, at least in part, by the level of expected post-IPO liquidity. Further, the liquidity characteristics of securities pre- and post-IPO have been shown to be comparable. Therefore the results from publicly traded firm data may be helpful in explaining the liquidity behavior of unlisted closely held firms. Pratt (2009) provides a summary of research suggesting the importance of expected holding period in explaining observed discounts for restricted stock.

Market data show a very striking difference between the observed liquidity for large and small stocks. Large stocks, defined as the largest market value decile, exhibit a high degree of liquidity, as shown in Exhibit 18.1.

The largest decile stocks (median market value $15 billion) trade on a regular basis, the mean bid ask spread is less than 0.1 percent,, and the cost of trading as measured by the difference between the buy-and-hold and buy-and-sell returns is less than one- percent. Positive returns dominate negative

EXHIBIT 18.1 Measures of Liquidity for Large Market Capitalization Stocks

Variable	Minimum	Maximum	Mean	Median	t	Pr > |t|
Market Value '000	4,833,845	25,967,708	14,299,716	15,263,634	31.61	<.0001
Trading Cost	0.02%	2.61%	0.77%	0.94%	18.17	<.0001
No Trade Days	0.00%	0.30%	0.08%	0.05%	12.17	<.0001
Spread	0.000753	0.0127176	0.0074236	0.0093479	6.02	<.0001

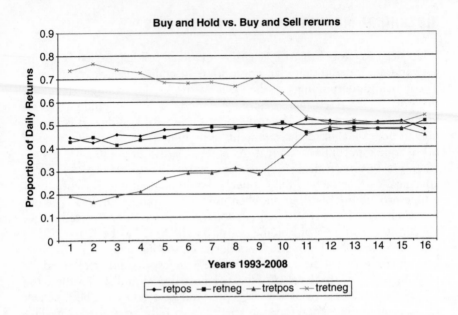

returns, and even after factoring in trading costs there is not a significant difference between the likelihood of positive and negative returns.

Small stocks, defined as the smallest market value decile, (median market value $6.75 million) exhibit a very low degree of liquidity, as shown in Exhibit 18.2.

The small stocks do not trade frequentlymean bid ask spread, while it has declined significantly from the very high levels of early 1990s, is still more than 10 percent,, and the cost of trading as measured by the difference between the buy-and-hold and buy-and-sell returns is more than 9 percent. A very large part of the incremental small stock returns can be explained by the higher trading costs. Negative returns dominate positive returns, and

EXHIBIT 18.2 Measures of Liquidity for Small Market Capitalization Stocks

Variable	Minimum	Maximum	Mean	Median	t	Pr > |t|
Market Value '000	3,783	21,467	9,144	6,751	24.95	<.0001
Trading Cost	1.38%	19.62%	9.11%	9.33%	25.46	<.0001
No Trade Days	8.47%	41.85%	21.44%	21.20%	35.53	<.0001
Spread	2.24%	19.25%	10.18%	10.32%	6.97	<.0001

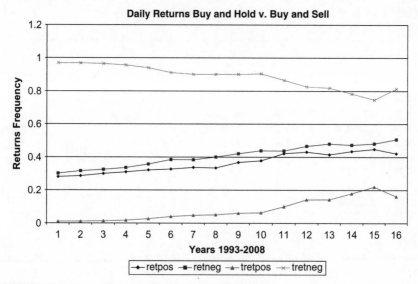

EXHIBIT 18-2-A   Market Liquidity Changes over Time

this difference is exaggerated after factoring in trading costs as there is a very significant difference between the likelihood of positive and negative returns.

PRICE PRESSURE AND MARKET FAILURE

Small stocks are very susceptible to price pressure. We calculate incremental price pressure by regressing trading costs over volume, and find that increasing volume is accompanied by increasing trading costs. Exhibit 18.3 presents the incremental price pressure calculated for increasing block sizes during 1993–2007.

We find that the incremental price pressure can reduce the bid price to zero for a substantial number of cases. Exhibit 18.4 presents the likelihood of market failure for small firms during the 1993–2007 period.

It is therefore unlikely that large blocks of small market value firms can be sold as such. It would be necessary to dribble out even unrestricted securities over extended periods of time, exposing the holders to considerable price risk. Such a high level of trading cost indicates that the market for small, publicly listed (marketable) firms is not quite liquid and the commonly reported small stock premium may be a reflection of this liquidity cost.

Market prices are formed in a dynamic equilibrium between supply and demand. The observed trading price is the market clearing price for the

EXHIBIT 18.3 Price Pressure Changes over Time- Small Market Capitalization Stocks

	Block Size					
	1	5	10	20	30	40
Year	Percent	Percent	Percent	Percent	Percent	Percent
1993	14.83%	21.08%	30.09%	46.98%	63.57%	80.05%
1994	13.88%	18.84%	26.50%	40.97%	55.21%	69.05%
1995	16.05%	28.84%	46.21%	80.57%	MF	MF
1996	11.67%	14.07%	18.63%	27.50%	35.82%	43.86%
1997	12.45%	15.50%	20.97%	31.52%	41.49%	51.24%
1998	17.04%	44.29%	79.55%	MF	MF	MF
1999	12.00%	22.89%	36.99%	65.22%	93.30%	121.24%
2000	9.23%	12.25%	17.21%	26.60%	35.86%	45.02%
2001	11.68%	20.60%	31.88%	53.96%	75.96%	97.91%
2002	11.11%	26.79%	45.95%	84.11%	MF	MF
2003	7.93%	14.47%	23.40%	40.07%	56.67%	73.21%
2004	4.02%	5.10%	6.80%	9.86%	13.14%	16.25%
2005	4.34%	6.14%	8.63%	13.63%	18.52%	23.46%
2006	3.38%	4.46%	5.89%	8.99%	12.02%	15.02%
2007	2.14%	3.02%	4.11%	6.35%	8.56%	10.66%

EXHIBIT 18.4 Likelihood of Market Failure- Small Market Capitalization Stocks

	Block Size					
	1	5	10	20	30	40
Year	Percent	Percent	Percent	Percent	Percent	Percent
1993	0.36%	2.04%	4.00%	7.13%	8.95%	11.21%
1994	0.39%	1.09%	3.35%	6.85%	9.27%	12.31%
1995	0.32%	1.67%	3.42%	7.79%	10.17%	12.16%
1996	0.00%	1.01%	1.74%	4.03%	5.95%	7.69%
1997	0.09%	0.95%	2.94%	5.11%	7.01%	9.38%
1998	0.36%	1.28%	3.19%	6.93%	9.95%	12.32%
1999	0.48%	1.74%	3.78%	6.98%	9.11%	10.95%
2000	0.00%	0.63%	1.77%	4.94%	6.84%	10.38%
2001	0.27%	2.74%	5.47%	11.13%	14.78%	17.15%
2002	0.21%	2.47%	4.93%	8.53%	11.20%	14.39%
2003	0.28%	1.38%	2.90%	4.97%	6.34%	7.59%
2004	0.00%	0.00%	0.00%	2.75%	4.28%	4.28%
2005	0.00%	0.00%	1.20%	2.79%	3.59%	5.18%
2006	0.00%	0.00%	0.47%	1.86%	1.86%	2.33%
2007	0.00%	0.31%	0.63%	0.94%	0.94%	1.57%

stock. That is, the current volume of stock traded represents the total matched demand and supply at the prevailing price. Market makers post bid (price available to the seller) and ask (price payable by the buyer) quotes for small trading lots and revise these quotes frequently, and without cost, in response to changes in demand (buy orders) and supply (sell orders) of the stock. An examination of the trade and quote data from NYSE shows that while the bid-ask spread for single-lot quotes (100 shares) is usually small, it increases rapidly for larger blocks and is very sensitive to changes in trading volume. As additional supply enters the market, it increases the volume that needs to be traded and the price decreases to stimulate demand. Conversely, if additional demand enters the marketplace, increasing the volume that needs to be traded, the price increases to stimulate supply. There is considerable empirical evidence that large block trades tend to occur outside the posted bid-ask spread.

Using a variety of liquidity measures, finance researchers have demonstrated that generally less liquid stocks have higher average returns (lower prices). Amihud and Mendelson (1986), Constantinides (1986), Heaton and Lucas (1996), Vayanos (1998), and Lo, Mamaysky, and Wang (2001), among others, explore the relationship between liquidity and asset prices and show that significant price discounts exist for less liquid but otherwise comparable assets. While liquidity has many facets, existing measures of liquidity typically focus on one dimension of liquidity. For example, the bid-ask spread measure used in Amihud and Mendelson (1986) relates to the trading cost dimension; the turnover measure of Datar, Naik, and Radcliffe (1998) captures the trading quantity dimension; and Amihud (2002) and Pastor and Stambaugh (2003) construct their measures based on the concept of price impact to capture the price reaction to trading volume. Abbott (2006) extends this research to develop a continuous time model for measuring liquidity. This approach provides a measure of liquidity that is based on two observable variables—the quantity of outstanding stock and the observed trading volume at the current quoted bid-ask spread. This measure allows us to directly estimate the liquidation period for a specific block of stock that is specific to the asset class, size, and prevailing market conditions.

There is a general consensus regarding the positive relationship between liquidity and observed asset prices, but the precise measurement of liquidity and, by extension, measurement of an appropriate discount for lack of liquidity have posed a problem for valuation practitioners.

Any analysis of liquidity and its impact on the asset needs to consider current conditions surrounding the asset. An alternative mechanism for determining the expected liquidation period is proposed in Abbott (2006). Follwing, the proposed direct measure of liquidity is defined.

MEASURING ASSET LIQUIDITY

Given:

The stock holding at time t is S_t.

Volume for one time period time t is V_t.

The stock holding at time $t + 1$ is $S_{t+1} = S_t - V_t$.

Assuming that the rate of deal flow is constant λ

at time t

$$S_{t+1} = S_t e^{-\lambda}$$

$$\text{Or} \quad \lambda \text{Log}_n (S_t) - \text{Log}_n (S_t + 1)$$

λ is a measure of the observed level of liquidity, with higher levels signifying that the current order flow in the market can absorb larger volumes of trading without impacting prices. An additional advantage of this specification of λ is that the expected half-life or average holding period can be calculated directly by dividing the value of lognormal (2) by the calculated value of λ. If 50 percent of the stock changes hands over a period n,

$$\text{Log}_n (S_t) - \text{Log}_n (S_{t+n}) \text{ is Log}_n (S_t/0.5\,S_t) = \text{Log}_n (2)$$

The observed liquidity levels for different market value deciles are significantly different from each other and vary across time, indicating that the level of liquidity and consequently the time to liquidation are variable and should be estimated for the period of analysis. Using a sample of 715,785 firm-month observations spanning all listed securities for the three equity markets (NYSE, AMEX, and NASDAQ) for January 1993 to December 2007, we find that the observed average holding period (half-life) for listed securities is much longer than the standard of instantaneous liquidity assumed in existing literature. Market-level liquidity varies over time, and the average holding period for individual stocks is significantly influenced by the size of the firm, the level of holding period returns, and the systematic liquidity of the markets. It has been suggested by Chordia, Roll, and Subrahmanyam (2000) that market index moves are accompanied by corresponding changes in market liquidity.

Prior finance literature suggests that larger firms tend to be more liquid as a result of enhanced analyst following and institutional portfolio investment. A similar market capitalization effect appears to be significant in explaining the observed liquidity for listed firms. The average holding period appears to decrease as market capitalization increases. Each month the firms in the sample are partitioned into 10 equal (decile) groups, ranked by the size of market capitalization. Mean, median minimum, and maximum

EXHIBIT 18.5 Observed Half Life (Average Holding period) in Months- Small Market Capitalization Stocks

Year	N	Minimum	Maximum	Mean	Median	t	Pr > |t|
1993	8240	0.106626	27039.32	146.0706	28.72826	19.31	<.0001
1994	9091	0.15011	23559.73	135.8086	24.63378	18.64	<.0001
1995	9381	0.143805	23746.88	98.47306	20.57023	18.84	<.0001
1996	9857	0.138335	14347.8	81.9523	17.6965	19.43	<.0001
1997	10258	0.113984	19754.35	67.58244	14.64149	15.76	<.0001
1998	10014	0.119041	11117.73	45.75571	12.90686	16.86	<.0001
1999	9229	0.124116	45587.94	54.11297	14.30336	8.65	<.0001
2000	8574	0.109128	7624.27	49.17992	14.0678	17.89	<.0001
2001	7011	0.146613	14472.57	94.74068	28.28889	18.65	<.0001
2002	6701	0.161453	13301.15	89.23909	31.83736	21.27	<.0001
2003	6128	0.15791	34518.38	83.63157	26.45441	11.95	<.0001
2004	5724	0.128788	6407.8	52.11892	19.31529	21.61	<.0001
2005	5374	0.13232	8078.28	46.74653	18.60425	20.54	<.0001

holding periods are calculated for each of the decile portfolios. Summary annual results for the smallest and largest deciles are presented in Exhibit 18.5 and 18.6. While each decile portfolio shows a wide dispersion from a low of less than one day to 20 years or beyond, the mean holding period decreases from a high of 47 months for smaller firms to 14 months for the largest firms in 2005. Abbott's (2006) results confirm this relationship. In Exhibit 18.5 it is seen that market liquidity increased and the holding period

EXHIBIT 18.6 Observed Half Life (Average Holding period) in Months- Large Market Capitalization Stocks

Year	N	Minimum	Maximum	Mean	Median	t	Pr > |t|
1993	8645	0.277218	100134	38.36299	13.66489	3.29	0.001
1994	9498	0.197619	75479.22	51.45356	13.07885	4.89	<.0001
1995	9669	0.169446	15095.57	35.17457	11.98269	12.37	<.0001
1996	10187	0.140644	8247.97	30.85015	11.17565	15.92	<.0001
1997	10527	0.175407	3323.83	21.88812	10.36773	24.18	<.0001
1998	10158	0.195504	462097.8	67.84834	9.585681	1.49	0.136
1999	9269	0.132759	74999.48	34.85971	8.190064	4.16	<.0001
2000	8360	0.1055	8119.22	24.13534	5.902787	11.15	<.0001
2001	7641	0.101258	10146.86	17.45331	5.805328	10.74	<.0001
2002	7771	0.087806	3478.91	14.3471	5.666866	16.15	<.0001
2003	7125	0.151554	1264.35	14.035	5.93147	21.09	<.0001
2004	6830	0.13616	3162.24	16.00685	6.370044	14.65	<.0001
2005	6720	0.138856	3450.34	14.06328	5.851912	12.79	<.0001

decreased during the monetary expansion from 1994 to 2000, and thereafter market liquidity sharply declined in 2001 in response to market conditions, recovering somewhat in 2004.

Penny stocks have been anecdotally linked with low liquidity. The results show that there is a significant difference between observed liquidity for the stocks priced at less than $1 per share (penny stocks, not eligible for continued listing), priced between $1 and $5 per share (small-cap market), and shares priced at $5 or above (see Exhibit 18.7).

These results are in line with the prior studies of liquidity behavior for stocks. The next step is to estimate a predictive equation for calculating the average holding period faced by the holders of a publicly traded stock. Using a standard multivariate ordinary least squares procedure, the coefficients for the hypothesized variables are tested for significance. Economic theory suggests that the individual security liquidity is a function of the systematic liquidity and security-specific attributes.

Prior literature suggests the following security attributes as significant factors:

EXHIBIT 18.7   Observed Half Life (Average Holding period) in Months—Penny Stocks

Price per Share	N	Min	Max	Mean
Less than $1	27,033	0.064274	551.0211	32.11198
Price between $1 and $5	164,337	0.05721	552.1212	27.09066
Price greater than $5	524,415	0.057029	562.1384	21.94253

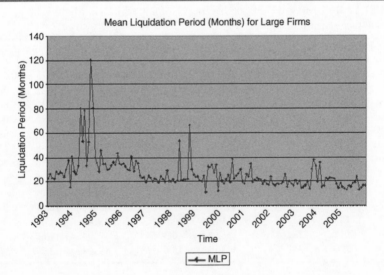

- *Market liquidity:* equally weighted average of holding period for all securities in the sample during the estimation month.
- *Stock returns, excluding dividends:* proxy for expected growth in value.
- *Dividend distributions:* proxy for cash distributions received.
- *Market capitalization:* proxy for relative size.
- *Stock price per share:* proxy for continued listing ability.

The regression results show that all of the hypothesized variables are highly significant, and the regression equation is also significant in explaining the observed holding period.

The estimation equation for the average holding period in months for a security is given by:

$$
\begin{aligned}
\text{Estimated half-life} = {} & 3.67 + 0.95 \times \text{Market average holding period} - 6.42 \\
& \times \text{Returns excluding dividends (\%)} + 202.23 \\
& \times \text{Dividend returns (\%)} - 0.00000121 \\
& \times \text{Market capitalization (\$'000)} - 0.10 \\
& \times \text{Price per share (\$)}
\end{aligned}
$$

The expected holding period for individual stocks rises and falls with the observed average market (systematic) levels, and decreases as the stock price and size of the firm increase and as the firm provides higher returns. However, as the level of dividends paid by the firm increases, willingness to hold the firm stock for longer periods rises sharply. (See Exhibits 18.6 and 18.7.)

These results provide an interesting insight for valuation practitioners.

Markets appear to be relatively illiquid, especially for smaller firms, and the prior assumption of costless unlimited trading does not appear to hold even for relatively large firms. These results suggest that applying a benchmark discount for lack of liquidity based on restricted stock studies assuming a holding period of 12 or even 24 months for stocks in small firms may be a serious underestimation of the true discount for lack of liquidity applicable for smaller illiquid firms with much longer holding periods. In the next section we present an introduction to three empirically sound option based methods for determining the applicable discount for lack of liquidity.

APPLICATION OF TIME/VOLATILITY (OPTION) MODELS TO DISCOUNT FOR LACK OF LIQUIDITY

Business valuation profession is moving toward a consensus that development and application of empirically rigorous methods for determining and defending discounts and premiums is warranted. Increased availability of affordable good-quality public markets data has contributed to this move toward empirical analysis. Time/volatility models use options theory to estimate the appropriate discounts for lack of liquidity, are conceptually easy to understand, and are relatively simple computationally. The parameters are directly observable from market data, making them easy to defend. This following section presents three major put option models and illustrates their applications for estimating appropriate discounts for lack of liquidity.

The "gold standard" for liquidity is cash in hand. When the holder of an illiquid asset wants to exchange the asset for cash in hand, the intending buyer offers a cash price and by implication an option to liquidate the asset. The price of this option is the difference between the seller's asking price for the asset as if liquid and the buyer's offered price recognizing the relative illiquidity of the asset. The buyer assesses the potential illiquidity of the asset and seeks compensation for the potential discount that may have to be offered if and when the buyer in turn needs to liquidate the asset.

It is important to identify the two components of the price risk faced by the buyer due to the lack of liquidity. If the price of the asset goes down during the period of illiquidity and the realized price is lower than the price at which the asset was purchased, there is a realized loss. This is the first component, and is well understood (Loss I). Potentially, a second and much larger component of the price risk is the opportunity loss that occurs when the asset increases in price during the period of illiquidity, and then declines to a lower value by the time the asset can be liquidated (Loss II). Thousands of dot-com paper millionaires faced the tax nightmare when they had to treat the value of restricted securities granted during the year as taxable compensation based on the post-IPO prices reached. Subsequently, as the bubble burst, the stocks become worthless and these grantees ended up with tax liabilities on the phantom gains that were never realizable by them.

Valuing the option to liquidate the asset is an important and interesting issue for valuation practitioners. Option-based models are being increasingly employed by practitioners to measure the price risk associated with lack of liquidity. The value of an option premium, estimating the cost of liquidity, is frequently presented as the discount for lack of liquidity. Neglecting to convert from the option premium to the applicable discount may create the illusion that the estimated discounts are greater than 100 percent, an impossible solution. Stockdale (2008) makes an important point: "Models providing results that equal or exceed 100 percent may have a theoretical problem because it seems logical that a discount would not reduce a value to zero or less." It appears that this conclusion may have been reached by interpreting the estimated option premiums as discounts for lack of liquidity. This section presents the underlying models and their application to estimating the applicable discounts for lack of liquidity. In order to keep the analysis simple, an assumption is made that the asset does not pay any dividends during the period of illiquidity. The analysis presented in this chapter can accommodate dividend payments, but the equations become slightly more complex.

THREE OPTION BASED MODELS

The three models most commonly used in valuation practice are:

1. Black-Scholes put (BSP) (Chaffee 1993).
2. Average-price Asian put (AAP) (Finnerty 2002).
3. Maximum price strike look-back put (LBP) (Longstaff 1995).

The underlying concepts and a method for computing discounts for lack of liquidity using these three put option–based models are very basic. A put is a simple contract that allows the holder to liquidate the underlying asset at a predetermined price at a certain date. The price of the option, commonly called the premium, is the present value of the expected payout at maturity. Each of the three models is briefly described next.

BLACK-SCHOLES PUT (BSP)

The Black-Scholes put (BSP) is a simple contract. It provides protection against any realized loss in value at maturity of the contract (Loss I). The minimum value any asset can reach is zero. Therefore, the maximum value payable under a BSP contract is the exercise price for the put. As the time to maturity and volatility of the underlying asset increase, the likelihood of lower asset values being realized and higher option payouts being received increases. The value of the BSP put increases as the price of the underlying asset decreases, but there is no increase in value of the BSP put if the value of the underlying asset increases. Further, since there is an upper bound for the payout (the exercise price), the present value of this bounded payout decreases as the risk-free rate and the time to payout increases. Therefore, the premium for an option on an asset with a fixed level of volatility is a parabola. The price of the option increases as the volatility of the asset and the time to maturity increase, until the maximum likely payout is achieved (projecting the probability of the asset value reaching zero). At the same time as the time to maturity and the risk-free rate increase, the present value of this payout starts declining. BSP provides protection against a decline in value of the asset as compared to the current price, but does not address the opportunity cost of not being able to liquidate the asset at the intermediate high price reached but not realized (Loss II).

The underlying equation for the price of a BSP put option is:

$$P(S, T) = K e^{-rT} N(-d_2) - S N(-d_1)$$

where

S = the current asset price

K = the exercise price

T = the time to maturity (for our purpose, time to liquidation)

r = the risk-free rate

e = the natural constant, approximately 2.71828

σ = the standard deviation for the returns computed for the same

$d_1 = [\text{lognormal}(S/K) + (r + \sigma^2/2)T]/\sigma\sqrt{T}$

$d_2 = d_1 - \sigma\sqrt{T}$

$N(-d_1)$ and $N(-d_2)$ = the normal cumulative distribution probabilities

Setting the exercise price K to be the same as the current asset price S and assuming $S = K = 1$, we can compute the option premium as a fraction of the current asset price.

The BSP put option premium equation collapses to

$$P(T) = e^{-rT} N(-d_2) - N(-d_1)$$

where $d_1 = [(r + \sigma^2/2)T]/\sigma\sqrt{T}$

$d_2 = d_1 - \sigma\sqrt{T}$

Thus an asset selling for a price of 1, if liquid would sell for $1 + P(T)$. The estimated BSP discount for lack of liquidity then becomes $P(T)/[1 + P(T)]$.

AVERAGE PRICE ASIAN PUT (AAP)

The Finnerty model is an application of the average-price Asian put (AAP). This contract provides a payout based on the average price achieved for the asset during the life of the option. The price of the option increases as the volatility of the underlying asset and the time to maturity increase. Initially, the value of an AAP is lower than the corresponding BSP, as the payout is based on the average of gains and losses. It increases slowly with volatility, as the likelihood of achieving lower values and higher values is symmetric. Once the lower bound for negative returns (-100 percent) is reached, the entire increase in value comes from the potential increase in the value of the underlying asset. For larger values of the asset volatility and the time to maturity, the potential increase in value of the underlying asset dominates the growth in value. An Asian put option provides partial coverage of the opportunity cost for not being able to liquidate it at the higher prices reached during the life of the option by averaging it with the potential losses.

The equation for an Asian put premium for a non-dividend-paying asset is:

$$D(T) = V\left[e^{rt} N\left(r/v\sqrt{T} + v\sqrt{T}/2\right) - N\left(r/v\sqrt{T} - v\sqrt{T}/2\right)\right]$$

and

$$v^2 = \sigma 2\, T + \text{Ln}\left[2\left(e^{\sigma 2 T} - \sigma 2\, T - 1\right)\right] - 2\,\text{Ln}\left[e^{\sigma 2 T} - 1\right]$$

Once again setting V to 1, $D(T)$ becomes:

$$e^{rt} N\left(r/v\sqrt{T} + v\sqrt{T/2}\right) - N\left(r/v\sqrt{T} - v\sqrt{T/2}\right)$$

and the corresponding discount for lack of liquidity becomes:

$$D(T)/1 + D(T)$$

LOOK BACK PUT (LBP)

The Longstaff model is an application of the look-back put (LBP), a contract that pays out based on the highest value for the underlying asset achieved over the lifetime of the option. The price of the option increases as the volatility of the underlying asset and the time to maturity increase. An LBP option addresses the risk of loss in value of the asset as well as providing full coverage of the opportunity cost for not being able to liquidate at the highest price reached during the life of the option. From the perspective of a buyer of an asset, the price risk is the value given up by buying an asset that cannot be liquidated over a defined period of time. An LBP is the ultimate no-regret contract, as it fully compensates the buyer for the inability to sell during the period of the contract protecting against a realized loss in value, as well as the opportunity cost of not being able to sell at the intermediate high price reached (Loss I + Loss II). This property makes it highly desirable for the buyer to demand a discount that fully compensates for the lack of liquidity.

The simplified estimation equation for an LBP involves only two parameters: T, the time to liquidation, and σ, the standard deviation of returns. The equation defines the potential maximum value reached during the period to liquidation as:

$$V(2 + \sigma2T/2)N\left(\sqrt{\sigma2}T/2\right) + V\sqrt{\left(\sigma2T/2 \prod\right)}e^{(-\sigma2T/8)}$$

where V = the current value of the asset
         T = the time to liquidation
         σ^2 = the variance of returns on the asset
         $N(-)$ = the cumulative normal distribution

The LBP put option premium becomes:

$$F(V, T) = V(2 + \sigma2T/2)N\left(\sqrt{\sigma2}T/2\right) + V\sqrt{\left(\sigma2T/2 \prod\right)}e^{(-\sigma2T/8)} - V$$

Again, since we are interested in computing a proportional discount for lack of liquidity, we can set V to 1, the LBP option premium becomes:

$$F(T) = (2 + \sigma2T/2)N\left(\sqrt{\sigma2}T/2\right) + \sqrt{\left(\sigma2T/2 \prod\right)}e^{(-\sigma2T/8)} - 1$$

The corresponding LBP discount for lack of liquidity becomes:

$$F(T) = (2 + \sigma2T/2)N\left(\sqrt{\sigma2}T/2\right) + \sqrt{\left(\sigma2T/2 \prod\right)}e(-\sigma2T/8)$$

These theoretical models indicate that for low values of volatility, BSP discounts will dominate AAP discounts as the holder of an AAP contract shares in the lower as well as higher prices achieved during the period of illiquidity. However, as volatility increases, AAP discounts will become larger than BSP discounts. LBP will dominate both AAP and BSP as the exercise price of the put is set to the highest value achieved during the period of illiquidity, compensating the holder for both Loss I and Loss II, defined earlier. In negotiated sales, BSP and AAP represent the discount offered by the seller, and LBP represents the discount demanded by the buyer. Seller-initiated transactions would likely occur at a price incorporating the LBP discount, whereas buyer-initiated offers are likely to be made at prices incorporating the larger of the BSP or AAP discount. The negotiated discount is likely to be in between these bounds based on the relative motivation of the buyer and seller.

Estimated lack of liquidity discounts for a range of inputs using each of the three option based methods are presented in Exhibits 18.8 to 18.10. A comparison of the three subsets, based on volatility, risk-free rates, and time

EXHIBIT 18.8 Estimated DLOL for Low Volatility (Annual σ 0.10–0.30), Low Risk-Free Rate (3%), Short Duration (1 Year)

Annual Standard Deviation	BSP	LBP	AAP
0.10	2.56%	7.61%	4.00%
0.11	2.92%	8.33%	4.19%
0.12	3.27%	9.04%	4.38%
0.13	3.63%	9.75%	4.58%
0.14	3.98%	10.45%	4.77%
0.15	4.33%	11.14%	4.97%
0.16	4.68%	11.83%	5.17%
0.17	5.03%	12.51%	5.37%
0.18	5.38%	13.19%	5.56%
0.19	5.72%	13.86%	5.76%
0.20	6.07%	14.52%	5.96%
0.21	6.41%	15.17%	6.16%
0.22	6.74%	15.82%	6.35%
0.23	7.08%	16.47%	6.55%
0.24	7.41%	17.10%	6.75%
0.25	7.74%	17.74%	6.94%
0.26	8.07%	18.36%	7.14%
0.27	8.40%	18.98%	7.33%
0.28	8.72%	19.60%	7.52%
0.29	9.04%	20.20%	7.71%
0.30	9.36%	20.81%	7.90%

EXHIBIT 18.9 Estimated DLOL for Midrange Volatility (Annual σ 0.40–0.60), Medium Risk-Free Rate (6%), Medium Duration (5 Years)

Standard Deviation	BSP	LBP	AAP
0.40	15.72%	48.38%	33.79%
0.41	16.18%	49.16%	34.22%
0.42	16.64%	49.92%	34.64%
0.43	17.09%	50.68%	35.06%
0.44	17.53%	51.41%	35.46%
0.45	17.97%	52.14%	35.86%
0.46	18.40%	52.85%	36.25%
0.47	18.83%	53.55%	36.63%
0.48	19.25%	54.23%	37.00%
0.49	19.66%	54.90%	37.36%
0.50	20.07%	55.56%	37.70%
0.51	20.47%	56.21%	38.04%
0.52	20.87%	56.84%	38.37%
0.53	21.26%	57.47%	38.69%

(Continued)

EXHIBIT 18.9 (*Continued*)

Standard Deviation	BSP	LBP	AAP
0.54	21.64%	58.08%	39.00%
0.55	22.02%	58.68%	39.30%
0.56	22.39%	59.27%	39.58%
0.57	22.76%	59.85%	39.86%
0.58	23.12%	60.42%	40.13%
0.59	23.47%	60.97%	40.39%
0.60	23.82%	61.52%	40.64%

period for illiquidity confirms our theoretical results for ranking of the estimated discounts. Exhibit 18.11 illustrates the mean calculated Look Back Put discounts for block sizes of five, ten, and twenty percent during the years 1993–2005. The discounts track closely the prevailing levels of liquidity and volatility and illustrate the difference between the behavior of the large and small stocks.

EXHIBIT 18.10 Estimated DLOL for High Volatility (Annual σ 0.70–0.90), High Risk-Free Rate (9%), Long Duration (10 Years)

Standard Deviation	BSP	LBP	AAP
0.70	19.56%	76.91%	59.57%
0.71	19.81%	77.30%	59.57%
0.72	20.07%	77.69%	59.58%
0.73	20.31%	78.06%	59.59%
0.74	20.55%	78.43%	59.59%
0.75	20.79%	78.79%	59.60%
0.76	21.02%	79.14%	59.60%
0.77	21.24%	79.48%	59.60%
0.78	21.46%	79.81%	59.61%
0.79	21.68%	80.14%	59.61%
0.80	21.89%	80.46%	59.61%
0.81	22.09%	80.78%	59.62%
0.82	22.29%	81.08%	59.62%
0.83	22.49%	81.38%	59.62%
0.84	22.68%	81.68%	59.62%
0.85	22.86%	81.97%	59.62%
0.86	23.04%	82.25%	59.63%
0.87	23.22%	82.52%	59.63%
0.88	23.39%	82.79%	59.63%
0.89	23.56%	83.06%	59.63%
0.90	23.72%	83.32%	59.63%

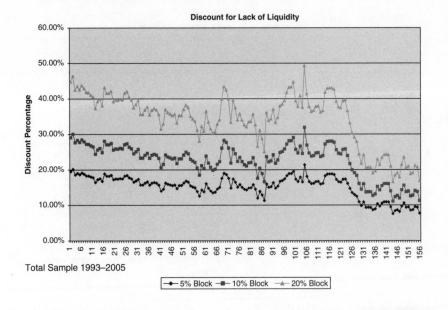

Total Sample 1993–2005

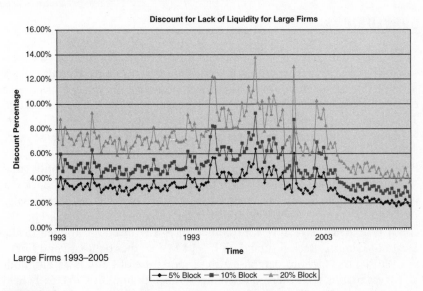

Large Firms 1993–2005

EXHIBIT 18.11 Look Back Put Discounts for Lack of Liquidity Changes over Time

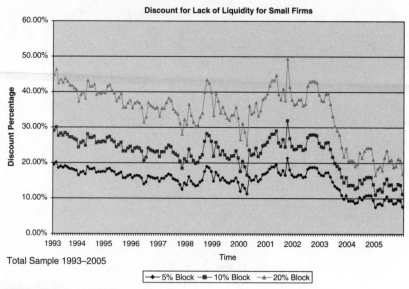

EXHIBIT 18.11   (*Continued*)

CONCLUSIONS

The primary difference between these models is the assumption of risk aversion being priced. A seller would be very willing to negotiate around a Black Scholes Put based discount as the lower bound. A buyer is expected to extract maximum concession from a seller experiencing a need for liquidity. The choice of applicable discounts is therefore a function of the relative negotiating power between the buyer and the seller. As markets become more volatile and less liquid the discounts get larger, shifting towards Look Back Put estimates. It would be appropriate to consider the levels of volatility and liquidity prevailing in the markets at the time of valuation. A Look Back Put provides a simple method to incorporate both of these factors in the analysis. It was shown in Abbott (2007) that the calculated Look Back Put discount provided the closest approximation to the discount applied in the Estate of Gimbel. Back testing data from FMV studies database and Liquistat (Pluris) transactions database also supports use of Look Back Put models for estimating the observed discounts for lack of liquidity. In closely held firm markets where the pool of potential buyers is small, and most negotiations take place without competing bids, the buyer has a strong negotiation advantage. Therefore it is not surprising that the observed discounts tend to be close to the upper bound.

These option based models are conceptually sound, rely on observable empirical data, and are replicable. Therefore they meet the requirements of scientific method for determining the applicable discounts for lack of liquidity. It is expected that their increasing usage will allow the valuation practitioners to have a greater degree of confidence in their discount estimates.

Lastly, these Look Back Put Option based models provide a theoretically and empirically validated foundation for better economic understanding of the recent melt-down in markets induced by liquidity crises.

REFERENCES

Abbott, A. 2004. Estimating the holding period for listed securities. *Valuation Strategies* 8 (September–October).

Abbott, A. 2006. Role of liquidity in asset pricing. Conference Proceedings CAFI. December 2006, Hyderabad, India.

Abbott, A. 2007. A quantitative measure of discount for lack of liquidity. *Business Valuation Review*, April 2007.

Amihud, Yakov. 2002. Illiquidity and stock returns. *Journal of Financial Markets*, 5:31–56.

Amihud, Yakov, and Haim Mendelson. 1986. Asset pricing and the bid-ask spread. *Journal of Financial Economics* 17 (December): 223–249.

Amihud, Yakov, and Haim Mendelson. 1991. Liquidity, maturity, and the yields on U.S. Treasury securities. *Journal of Finance* 46, issue 4 (September): 1411–1425.

Bajaj, Mukesh, David J. Denis, Stephen P. Ferris, and Atulya Sarin. 2001. Firm value and marketability discounts. (February 26). Available at SSRN: http://ssrn.com/abstract¼262198 or DOI: 10.2139/ssrn.262198.

Beneish, Messod D., and Robert E. Whaley. 1996. An anatomy of the "S&P Game": The effects of changing the rules. *Journal of Finance* 51, issue 5 (December): 1909.

Beneish, Messod D., and Robert E. Whaley. 2002. S&P 500 index replacements. *Journal of Portfolio Management* 29, no. 1 (Fall): 51–60.

Chaffee, David B.H., II. 1993. Option pricing as a proxy for discount for lack of marketability in private company valuations. *Business Valuation Review* (December).

Chordia, Tarun, Richard Roll, and Avanidhar Subrahmanyam. 2000. Commonality in liquidity. *Journal of Financial Economics* 56 (April): 3–28.

Constantinides, George M. 1986. Capital market equilibrium with transaction costs. *Journal of Political Economy* 94 (August): 842–862.

Datar, Vinay T., Narayan Y. Naik, and Robert Radcliffe. 1998. Liquidity and stock returns: An alternative test. *Journal of Financial Markets* 1 (August): 203–219.

Edelman, Richard B., and H. Kent Baker. 1993. The impact of company pre-listing attributes on the market reaction to NYSE listings. *Financial Review* 28, no. 3 (August): 431–448.

Emory, John D. 2003. Business valuation discounts for lack of marketability in divorce. *American Journal of Family Law* 17, issue 3 (Fall).

Finnerty, John D. 2002. The impact of transfer restrictions on stock prices. Presented at AFA 2003 Washington DC meetings, October 2002.

Garvey, Gerald T., and Todd T Milbourn. 2000. EVA versus earnings: Does it matter which is more highly correlated with stock returns? *Journal of Accounting Research* 38.

Harris, Lawrence, and Eitan Gurel. 1986. Price and volume effects associated with changes in the S&P 500 list: New evidence for the existence of price pressures. *Journal of Finance* 41, issue 4 (September): 815.

Heaton, John, and Deborah J. Lucas. 1996. Evaluating the effects of incomplete markets on risk sharing and asset pricing. *Journal of Political Economy* 104 (June): 443–487.

Hertzel, Michael, and Richard L. Smith. 1993. Market discounts and shareholder gains for placing equity privately. *Journal of Finance* 48, issue 2 (June): 459.

Kadlec, Gregory B., and John J. McConnell. 1994. The effect of market segmentation and illiquidity on asset prices: Evidence from exchange listings. *Journal of Finance* 49, no. 2 (June): 611–636.

Kahl, Matthias, Jun Liu, and Francis A. Longstaff. 2003. Paper millionaires: how valuable is stock to a stockholder who is restricted from selling it? *Journal of Financial Economics* 67, 385410.

Lo, Andrew W., Harry Mamaysky, and Jiang Wang. 2001. Asset prices and trading volume under fixed transactions costs. (May). EFA 2001 Barcelona meetings; Yale ICF Working Paper 00-35. Available at SSRN: http://ssrn.com/abstract=270733.

Loeb, Thomas F. 1983. Trading cost: The critical link between investment information and results. *Financial Analysts Journal* 39, issue 3 (May/June): 39.

Longstaff, Francis A. 1995. How much can marketability affect security values? *Journal of Finance* 50, issue 5 (December): 1767.

Lynch, Anthony W., and Richard R. Mendenhall. 1997. New evidence on stock price effects associated with changes in the S&P 500 index. *Journal of Business* 70, issue 3 (July): 351.

Macey, Jonathan, Maureen O'Hara, and David Pompilio. 2008. Down and out in the stock market: The law and economics of the delisting process. *Journal of Law and Economics* 51, issue 4 (November): 68.

Mercer, Z. Christopher, and Travis W. Harms. 1997. *Quantifying marketability discounts*. Memphis, TN: Peabody Publishing LP.

Paleari, Stefano, and Silvio Vismara. 2007. Over-optimism when pricing IPOs. *Managerial Finance* 33(6): 352–367.

Pastor, L., and Robert F. Stambaugh. 2003. Liquidity risk and expected stock returns. *Journal of Political Economy* 111:642–685.

Pratt, Shannon P. 2001. *Business valuation discounts and premiums*. New York: John Wiley & Sons.

Pratt, Shannon P., and Alina V. Niculta. 2009. *Valuing a business*. New York: McGraw-Hill.

Sanger, Gary C., and John J. McConnell. 1986. Stock exchange listings, firm value, and security market efficiency: The impact of NASDAQ. *Journal of Financial & Quantitative Analysis* 21, issue 1 (March): 1.

Shleifer, Andrei. 1986. Do demand curves for stocks slope down? *Journal of Finance* 41, issue 3 (July): 579.

Silber, William L. 1991. Discounts on restricted stock: The impact of illiquidity on stock prices. *Financial Analysts Journal* 47, issue 4 (July/August): 60.

Stockdale, John J. 2006. Time is of the essence: A proposed model for computing the discount for lack of marketability. *Business Valuation Review* (Fall).

Stockdale, John J. 2008. A test of DLOM computational models. *Business Valuation Review* (December).

Tabak, David. 2002. A CAPM-based approach to calculating illiquidity discounts. NERA working Paper 11, November 2002.

Vayanos, Dimitri. 1998. Transaction costs and asset prices: A dynamic equilibrium model. *Review of Financial Studies* 11 (Spring): 1–58.

Wruck, Karen Hopper. 1989. Equity ownership concentration and firm value: Evidence from private equity financings. *Journal of Financial Economics* 23, issue 1 (June): 3.

CHAPTER 19

An Economic View of the Impact of Human Capital on Firm Performance and Valuation

Mark C. Ubelhart

Practice Leader, Value-Based Management, and Architect,
Human Capital Foresight, Hewitt Associates

Everyone knows that human capital and intellectual property form the core drivers of our global economic growth today. Consequently, how best to measure these driver effects become paramount to shareholder wealth creation. This chapter explains the measurement of the movement of pivotal employees between firms and their effect on shareholder value return.

In order to examine business valuation implications from a human capital standpoint, cross-company, longitudinal data becomes essential. While making use of such data forms the empirical underpinnings of modern corporate finance, that usage is new to human resources (HR) as a function; consequently, it is unavailable to investors in general.

Of course, investors can obtain a glimpse of the highest-level pay practices from proxy disclosures, but see virtually nothing below or beyond those disclosures. Hewitt possesses an exceptionally rich database. That database includes well over 1,000 companies and 20 million employees derived from compensation and benefit surveys. It also includes the outsourced administration of many HR activities to Hewitt Associates as well. For our research, we gathered and used all the data possible, while carefully preserving company confidentiality and individual privacy. Our intent mirrored accomplishments using data and associated measurements in other disciplines like marketing and finance.

CREATING AND STANDARDIZING METRICS

Once we de-identified individual data covering the 20 million employees by giving them unique numbers, we discovered that some employees in one company one day arose in another company the next. In other words, they changed jobs. We could observe the workings of a microcosm of the U.S. labor market, as employees transitioned between companies.

Knowing we now had the capability to measure the flow of employees into and out of organizations, our next step was to devise a metric—called the Talent Quotient^{TM} (TQ^{TM}). TQ quantified these employee transitions by measuring the relative proportion of employees leaving or joining the company who are pivotal employees. Simply put, pivotal employees produce a disproportionate impact on the business. TQ reveals the proportional magnitude of pivotal employees leaving the organization who are critical to the firm's success.

The standardized definition of pivotal employees relies on incremental investment measured by percentage pay progression, adjusted for age, pay, and tenure. This definition captures management decisions regarding individual employees in a systematic manner applicable to cross-company analysis and linkage to business performance and value creation. The top quartile percentage pay progressors are identified as pivotal. Consequently, a standard TQ score of 100 means 25 out of every 100 departing employees were considered pivotal—equal to the percentage of total employees so defined within the company. A higher score means fewer than 25 out of 100 departing employees were pivotal—that is, a better retention rate for such critical employees—and the reverse, that a lower score means less retention of them. The TQ score is compensation-dollar weighted so that a lower-paid departing person has less impact in the calculation. It is not a head-counting turnover statistic but a financial one.

Of course, one can take issue with the definition; for example:

- What if pay decisions are made poorly such that those so identified as pivotals really are not? The law of large numbers helps out, as some level of poor pay decisions or other anomalies characterize most companies, but with many companies and over time, an element of self-correction occurs. In some cases, we went back 10 years in applying this definition, and for all companies in our database we went back at least five years.
- And even if these pay decisions are poorly made, what does it say about a company where the people receiving the highest pay increases are leaving?

Certainly some companies may have separate internal lists of high potentials and people with the highest performance ratings, but these lists are not available in cross-company data and are not consistently developed. Moreover, in our piloting process, clients encouraged us to rely on pay progression rather than internal lists because they believed their own internal lists were suspect.

PREDICTING FUTURE FINANCIAL RESULTS

With a measure of the flow of pivotal employees in and out of a company, testing its relationship to business value creation became possible. Well-performing companies are likely to retain more of their pivotal employees, and at the same time the retention of more pivotal employees is likely to contribute to subsequent financial performance and value creation. We had to separate these effects. We removed reverse casualty by handicapping company performance—that is, whether a company was performing well was taken into account at the start of the time period analyzed, which used prior-period TQs together with subsequent performance. The process used is illustrated in Exhibit 19.1, and greater detail is available in the article

▣ Quantifying what's been fuzzy

   – Shareholder value

Incremental Cost of Talent
versus
Measurable Business Impact

Data on 1,000 companies, 20 million employees
8 pilot companies (Verizon, Alcoa, JC Penney, Lilly, Nationwide, Sony Electronics, Siemens, MeadWestvaco)

▣ Apples-to-apples results

   – Industry by industry

CFROI and Total Business Return
1997–2007, N = 115 companies

▣ Statistical validity

   – Reverse causality

EXHIBIT 19.1   Linkage to Business Results and Cash Flow Return on Investment (CFROI)

"Optimizing Human Capital Investments for Superior Shareholder Returns" by Samir Raza (*Valuation Issues*, February 2006).

Most readers of this publication will be at least somewhat familiar with cash flow return on investment (CFROI[®1]) and variations of it. For those less familiar, please refer to Rawley Thomas and Robert Atra's Chapter 11, "The LifeCycle Returns Valuation System." Also, refer to Bartley Madden's book (Madden 1999) and his Chapter 3, "Applying a Systems Mind-Set to Stock Valuation." We incorporated CFROI into the analysis because of its measurement advantages—both over time and across industry. CFROI's conceptual validity as an economic return measure of business performance and the prevalence of its use by analysts and inventors add to its advantages.

Research suggests that stock price level links to CFROI level, while stock price change correlates to the market's expectations of CFROI change.

Exhibits 19.2 and 19.3 summarize the results, namely that a 10-point difference in TQ predicts a 0.7 percent and 1.6 percent difference in CFROI for standard industrial companies and financial services, respectively.

Exhibit 19.4 shows a more dramatic picture by comparing the best to worst in TQ and their subsequent financial results on measures other than CFROI.

Two individual company case studies are represented in Exhibits 19.5 and 19.6, to complement and reinforce the results found in the multicompany analysis.

Our results suggest that high-TQ companies tend to outperform low TQ-firms by a factor of 0.7% to 1.6% in CFROI for every 10-point difference in TQ. For example, if a company has $10B in invested capital, a 10-point TQ improvement converts to $70M to 160M in after-tax cash flow on average.

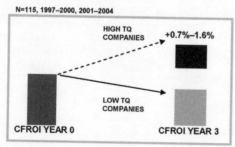

EXHIBIT 19.2 What Is the Impact of Loss or Gain of Talent on Future Business Performance?

For example, we find that the financial services industry group have over 2× CFROI Impact relative to other industry types. In general, we extend the higher leverage to any industry that is more dependent on human and intellectual capital.

CFROI Improvement over 3 Years for High TQ Companies

MANUFACTURING / OTHER — 0.7% ↑

FINANCIAL SERVICES — 1.6% ↑

EXHIBIT 19.3 Is There a Greater Talent Leverage in Industries That Are Relatively More Dependent on Human and Intellectual Capital?

Diagnostic Benchmarking

A crucial characteristic of financial reporting is its standardization through generally accepted accounting principles (GAAP). Credit Suisse HOLT and LifeCycle Returns go beyond conventional reporting to recast results so that they are much more reflective of economic cash flow performance and more accurate for comparison over time and company to company. No such equivalent exists in the domain of human capital. This fact alone stifles accountability and reporting, and that, in turn, stifles HR's use of data in a decision science framework, as there are no external anchors creating pressures on firms to more effectively manage their pivotal employees.

In fact, the development of TQ is a step in the direction of measuring and managing pivotal employees, as any company can report it in the standardized manner used in our analysis. At the same time, any company can compute its own customized TQ, using its own internally

EXHIBIT 19.4 TQ Impacts Business Results—Cross-Industry Study

	Average 2004 TQ		Sales Growth 3 Years Annualized (Ending 7/07)	Total Return 3 years Annualized (Ending 7/07)	Price to Book (at 7/07)
Worst 10 in TQ	84	Median	5.8%	7.1%	1.8
Best 10 in TQ	141	Median	8.0%	13.2%	2.9

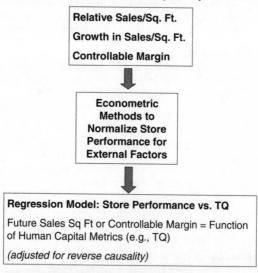

For each 10-point improvement in TQ...

1.5 to 2.0% improvement in sales per square foot

EXHIBIT 19.5 Case Study—Big Box Retail Organization

defined pivotal employees, just like it can define and report non-GAAP financial metrics.

Exhibit 19.7 reveals TQ results for various industries. Please note that most companies score above 100, meaning they do a better job of retaining their own critical employees than retaining all other employees. However, a wide range does exist, and where on this spectrum any individual company (or business unit within the company) lies is telling in an overall human capital performance context. Since the TQ metric predicts future financial performance, its importance is underlined.

ORGANIZATIONAL DECOMPOSITION

Like financial metrics, in order to understand where and what is driving results, drilling down becomes necessary. The top half of Exhibit 19.8 portrays the parallel between financial and human capital metrics.

Just as firms decompose earnings and economic profit by organization unit, so can the Talent Quotient. As an example, Exhibit 19.9 reveals the TQs broken into pay levels—broad employees, management, and executive

Clinical Trials—A Business Case for TQ

To determine if the *flow of talent matters* for a particular pharmaceutical sales force, a detailed analysis was undertaken to measure the impact of TQ on sales performance across 22 sales units over four years. A two-step econometric model was developed to first capture the effect of past sales results on TQ, and then measure the impact of TQ on future sales performance. Not only are the results consistent with the intuition of seasoned HR professionals, but for the first time, this landmark effort quantifies what was previously unmeasurable.

KEY FINDINGS

• TQ reliably predicts future sales performance. In other words, retaining critical talent is a leading indicator of higher sales, and vice versa.

• A 10-point increase in TQ within this sales force translates into approximately $40–$110 million per year in additional pretax operating income.

• Sales unit TQs were startlingly different, making a compelling business case to manage TQ.

EXHIBIT 19.6 Case Study—Major Pharmaceutical Company

TQ retention values are typically over 100, but vary widely from company to company

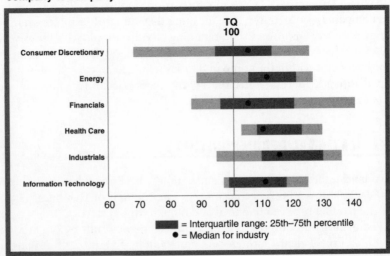

EXHIBIT 19.7 Industry TQ Retention Ranges

A summary metric is needed for overall monitoring, but must be decomposed to identify the organizational sources of these results for interpretation and actionable insights.

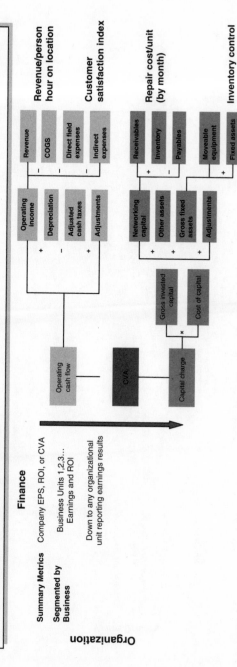

Finance

Summary Metrics Company EPS, ROI, or CVA

Segmented by Business Business Units 1,2,3...
Earnings and ROI

Down to any organizational
unit reporting earnings results

Organization

EXHIBIT 19.8 Drilling Down to Financial and Human Capital Value Drivers

Particular drivers of the overall results, especially those that can be managed, such as inventory control in the financial domain and performance management in human capital, also need determination.

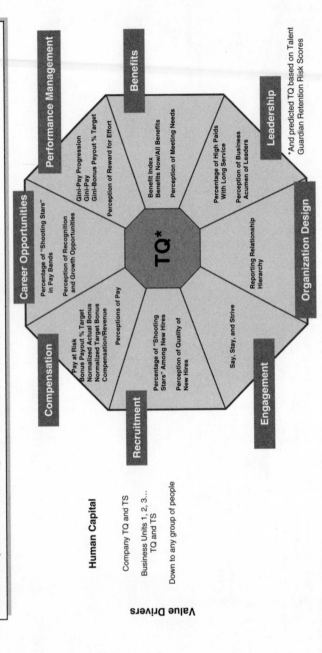

Human Capital

Company TQ and TS

Business Units 1, 2, 3....
TQ and TS

Down to any group of people

Value Drivers

*And predicted TQ based on Talent Guardian Retention Risk Scores

EXHIBIT 19.8 (*Continued*)

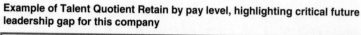

Example of Talent Quotient Retain by pay level, highlighting critical future leadership gap for this company

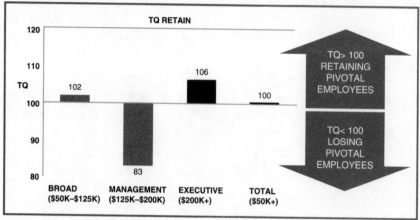

EXHIBIT 19.9 Organizational TQ Retention

groups. Here the particular company is assessed as being deficient in bench strength, as it is disproportionately losing pivotal employees at the level just below executives.

Interestingly, analysts' comments about this particular company raise the same issue by conjecturing that it may not be able to grow organically—but only by acquisition—as it lacks internal management depth. Human capital metrics can be decomposed in many ways, such as according to the demographics of age, pay, tenure, location, ethnicity, and gender. They can also be grouped in categories, such as those who participate in certain training programs or other initiatives and those who do not.

Prescriptive Insights

Once TQ is recognized as a linchpin metric that predicts future financial results, stepping back to examine what drives TQ becomes not only possible but essential to decision making in the human capital arena. All of the dimensions depicted in the octagon in Exhibit 19.8, and many more, can be linked to TQ using data available internally within a company or cross-company information where it exists.

The fundamental building block of such analysis is retention risk at the individual level, as illustrated in Exhibit 19.10.

Each individual is assigned a score representing the risk of leaving the organization within the next 12 months. These proprietary calculations utilize a neural network model continuously trained on:

To help companies understand and manage their critical talent risk, the basic building block is the *individual retention risk score.*

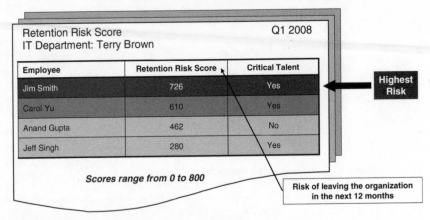

EXHIBIT 19.10   Individual Retention Risk Score

- Human capital data on the behavior of participants.
- Employee demographics such as age, tenure, and gender.
- Employee history, including pay progression and performance.
- Company history of hiring and attrition.
- National economic data such as housing statistics and price inflation or deflation.
- General labor market data such as regional unemployment.
- Local market data such as household income and hiring trends.

This is precisely the methodology used to detect credit card fraud and stop transactions before they occur. It also utilizes concepts applied to develop FICO credit scores, which range from 0 to 800. In this case (as opposed to FICO scores), a higher number means greater risk. Exhibit 19.11 shows the probability that an individual employee with a particular retention risk score will leave the company during the coming year.

Exhibit 19.12 employs the same individual scoring methodology to identify prominent risk clusters of people and their characteristics. Such information can inform talent management strategies to:

- Identify and target at-risk talent.
- Target segments of risk for group interventions.
- Discover retention performance differences across units.
- Inform talent sourcing strategies.
- Benchmark the company.

EXHIBIT 19.11   Attrition Probabilities

Retention Risk Score	Probability of Attrition (within 12 Months)
800	95%
700	85%
620	65%
520	32%
455	16%
400	8%
345	4%
300	2%

A Portfolio View

Mitigating risk is a good thing, but not if it costs too much. The cost of intiatives aimed at improving retention rates can be compared to the resulting improvement in TQ and its estimated financial benefit.

Exhibit 19.13 shows a portfolio view of retention risk incorporating the scoring methodology just described, applied to 75 companies in Hewitt Associates' database. It displays two different charts. The one on the left simply counts people, while the one on the right is compensation-dollar weighted and illustrates greater human capital risk. From the standpoints

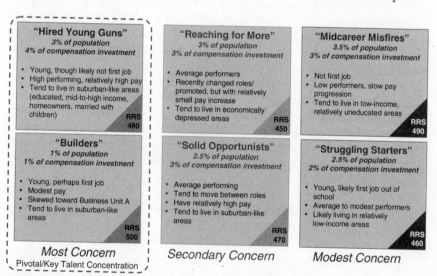

EXHIBIT 19.12   Talent Guardian™—Actual Client, Prominent Risk Clusters

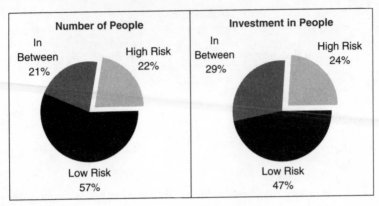

EXHIBIT 19.13   Retention Risk Complexion Benchmarks

of both business valuation and the board of directors' fiduciary responsibility to manage the risk of pivotal employee loss, these retention assessments matter to shareholders.

Clamor for Disclosure

No one denies the impact that human capital has on business valuation. Despite its obvious importance, the absence of commonly accepted measurement and reporting standards creates a vacuum on the availability of human capital metrics that matter. As mentioned previously, that same vacuum inhibits a groundswell of external pressure from focusing its energy on changing these conditions. A perfect storm is gathering and inevitable. Exhibit 19.14 represents just one indication.

In answer to the question posed during a live webcast by the Human Capital Institute, 76 percent of the respondents stated they believed standardized human capital metrics are coming within five years.

Another indication occurred in May 2008 at the joint Credit Suisse/ Hewitt Associates conference—the first-ever joint conference of investment professionals and corporate managements focused on human capital and its impact on valuation.

The Impact of Human Capital on Investment Capital
Tuesday Evening, May 13, 2008

Hewitt and HOLT: Examining human capital metrics that drive corporate performance

Please accept this invitation for this joint conference of Hewitt Associates and Credit Suisse HOLT. This program offers new

When will standardized human capital metrics become a visible practice for leading companies? — 2007 Human Capital Institute Poll:

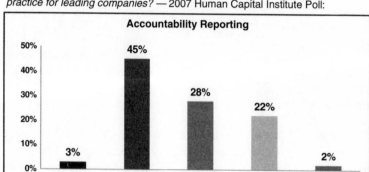

EXHIBIT 19.14 Human Resources Measures . . . Management and Investment Information
Source: Human Capital Institute.

insights on human capital management and the impact on CFROI® *levels.*

   Hewitt Associates has a research database for nearly 20 million individuals, a microcosm of the U.S. labor force. Credit Suisse HOLT's database provides detailed cash flow and valuation analysis for more than 19,000 equities through the lens of the HOLT CFROI® *Performance and Valuation Framework. Hewitt's Human Capital Foresight*™ *(HCF*™*) initiative used the HOLT CFROI*® *framework and database in combination with their extensive employee data to examine the relationships between people-related measures, corporate performance, and valuation.*

   The results of this research project have been quite insightful:

- *Industry-by-industry analysis and trends of the U.S. labor market, and the relevance of key human capital indicators to industries in the HOLT CFROI*® *framework.*
- *The Talent Quotient*™ *metric, a measure that stood out as a leading indicator of future changes in business cash flow returns.*
- *Research results from examining the corporate-level impact of other metrics such as pay differentiation, pay at risk, and rewards mix.*
- *Determining when issues such as employee turnover begin to dramatically impact corporate cash flows.*

- *What companies are beginning to monitor internally, what actions can they take as a result, and what investors may begin requesting from management teams.*

This program provides insights from two perspectives: From the point of view of the investor analyzing company fundamentals with an eye on stock price and from the planning and actions of management looking to improve business performance and valuation.

The goal of business strategy is clear—to invest capital in a way that maximizes shareholder value. Traditional capital budgeting and financial planning frameworks offer very little to guide human capital investment decisions; yet pay and benefits typically constitute 30% to 70% of operating expenses. Hewitt's Human Capital Foresight™ offers factual analysis grounded in data representing more than 20 million people—in effect, a microcosm of the U.S. labor market.

The research based on this data has yielded HR metrics and insights quantitatively linked to business results.

Credit Suisse Conference Center, 11 Madison Avenue, Level 2B, The Club Room, New York, NY 10010

There are two sides to this story. Certainly, investors are clamoring for more disclosure. They seek an enhanced ability to both understand and value the human capital risks and associated circumstances of companies in which they invest. At the same time, managements—particularly leading-edge human resources (HR) functions—seek to apply decision science frameworks to the vast amount of data now available. They know that HR data will provide their firms with a competitive advantage and they welcome the external pressure that will reinforce their efforts.

MATHEMATICAL MODELS GUIDING PRACTICAL ACTION

At the core of Talent Guardian™ is a mathematical model that predicts the likelihood an individual employee will quit within a specified time. Hewitt designed the rest of Talent Guardian to achieve the greatest practical benefit from this basic insight of quitting behavior.

Predicting individual human behavior with a computer represents a notoriously difficult challenge. The Human Capital Foresight team at Hewitt Associates and partner Global Analytics overcame this challenge by a flanking attack: Rather than write a program to mimic the complexity of human decisions, the Talent Guardian team developed a program—a mathematical model—that learns by example from exhaustive trial and error to behave as humans actually do in millions of actual employment histories in Hewitt databases and in histories from subscribing employers.

To capture the complexity of human actions, Global Analytics and Hewitt constructed Talent Guardian models using a proprietary, evolved neural network structure. This approach differs from more traditional model structures like those used in regression models. The model-building process analyzes the impact of both individual variables and the many combinations of variables interacting with one another thereby changing each other's impact on a final outcome. The resulting models recognize complex patterns of behavior and their most probable outcomes.

By dealing directly with the complex relationships in employment decisions, these models avoid misleading, oversimplified, single-cause explanations for complex human outcomes. As a consequence, their predictive performance is superior. (Models for each client vary in technical performance, but are usually in the high 20s to low 30s on the Komogorov-Smirnov—K-S—test statistic.) Exhibit 19.15, based on real-world examples for over 200,000 employees, shows that Talent Guardian retention risk scores accurately predict subsequent actual attrition.

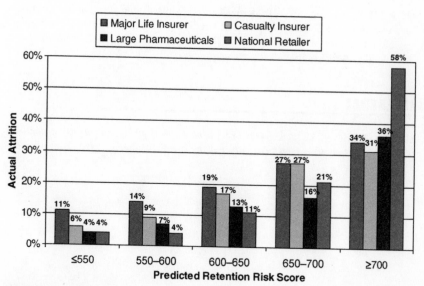

EXHIBIT 19.15 Predicted Retention Risk Scores versus Subsequent Actual Attrition

Talent Guardian not only locates attrition risk in employee populations, it also differentiates between those risks due to employee characteristics and those due to employer actions or policies. It guides intervention by identifying high-risk groups with common characteristics and by accurately monitoring the retention impact of specific interventions and policy actions.

Talent Guardian avoids the guesswork on whether retention successes or problems are due to employee characteristics or to employer actions; whether a group's retention problems are inherent or created; or whether apparent patterns across similar employees are real or random.

Talent Guardian is the most sensitive way to identify retention risks. It represents the best tool to help overcome those risks.

Global Analytics supplies Talent Guardian's predictive analytics. Global's management includes the inventor of neural network fraud detection for bank payment systems and other pioneers in the application of advanced analytics to financial services. One pioneering executive became most responsible for the widespread adoption of consumer credit scores and the way financial services firms manage consumer credit accounts today. Learn more about Global Analytics at www.global-analytics.com.

NOTE

1. CFROI® is a registered trademark in the United States and other countries (excluding the United Kingdom) of Credit Suisse or its affiliates. Credit Suisse HOLT is a division of Credit Suisse. CFROI is adjusted for asset age/life/mix, and allows for comparisons across companies.

REFERENCE

Madden, Bartley J. 1999. *CFROI valuation: Cash flow return on investment—A total system approach to valuing the firm.* Woburn, MA: Butterworth-Heinemann.

CHAPTER 20

EBITDA

Down but Not Out

Arjan J. Brouwer
University of Amsterdam and PricewaterhouseCoopers

Benton E. Gup
Chair of Banking, University of Alabama

O n June 12, 2008, Belgian-Brazilian InBev S.A. published the terms of its initial unsolicited bid for Anheuser-Busch Company of the United States. InBev wanted to pay $47.5 billion, which "represents 12× Anheuser-Busch's 2007 EBITDA."[1] On July 14, 2008, Anheuser-Busch agreed to be taken over for $70 per share in cash. InBev presented the transaction value as $62 billion and stated that the implied enterprise value/earnings before interest, taxes, depreciation, and amortization (EV/EBITDA) multiple of 12.4 was in line with comparable transactions in the industry.[2] InBev financed the transaction primarily with borrowed funds that will be repaid largely from the divestiture of noncore assets from both companies and by temporarily reducing cash dividends. The noncore assets include the Anheuser-Busch theme parks—Busch Gardens, SeaWorld, and others.[3]

This transaction is interesting from many perspectives. Not only does the combination of the two firms result in the world's largest beer company and the third largest consumer products company after Procter & Gamble and Nestlé, but the transaction is one of the examples of the increasing involvement of other economies (Europe, Asia, Middle East) in the U.S. capital market. Companies from these countries bring their own governance, business, and valuation practices and reporting behavior into the U.S. market. Since 2007, the Securities and Exchange Commission (SEC) has allowed foreign companies with a U.S. listing (foreign private issuers) to file their International Financial Reporting Standards (IFRS) financial statements without additional U.S. generally accepted accounting principles (GAAP) information. This will also affect the financial analyst's job to analyze financial information that is reported into the market. Except for the United States, all other major capital markets have already implemented IFRS (for example Europe and Australia) or are in the process of converting to IFRS (for example Japan and Canada), and the influence of IFRS on the U.S. capital markets cannot be ignored. Even the SEC has started talking about whether U.S. public companies should be granted the option of using the IFRS.

Differences in valuation and reporting behavior are also reflected in the InBev–Anheuser-Busch transaction where it appears that InBev placed significant weight on Anheuser-Busch's EBITDA in the valuation of the company. EBITDA is a non-GAAP measure that lost significant ground in the United States after the implementation of the Sarbanes-Oxley Act (SOX) and related SEC regulations, but is still popular in Europe, partly driven by the fact that IFRS allows significant flexibility in the presentation of a company's income statement. The EBITDA acronym was, for example, found 64 times in InBev's 2007 financial statements, whereas it was not found at all in the Anheuser-Busch 2007 10-K.

The EBITDA measure can serve many useful purposes, but if not handled with care it also has the potential to lead the analyst to incorrect conclusions. Therefore, this paper discusses EBITDA, its benefits and shortcomings, and developments in the use thereof in the three largest non-U.S. capital markets that have implemented IFRS: the United Kingdom, France, and Germany.

WHAT IS EBITDA?

As mentioned, EBITDA[4] is the acronym for earnings before interest, taxes, depreciation, and amortization. Some analysts consider EBITDA a measure of operating income. The logic behind this method is that the analysts deducted interest expenses and taxes from a firm's income because they wanted to use their own calculations to determine the costs. They also deducted depreciation and amortization because those do not reflect current cash outlays. The operating income excluded the value of investment activities such as investments in securities, including minority interests in other companies. More will be said about this exclusion in connection with the InBev–Anheuser-Busch merger.

Moody's[5] explains how EBITDA became popular in the mid-1980s among leveraged buyout sponsors and bankers to evaluate cash flow and calculate multiples for companies in a near-bankruptcy state. The idea was that if large-scale capital expenditure programs would not be necessary in the foreseeable future, the noncash depreciation and amortization charges should be available to service debt. At that time EBITDA was thus mainly used in the context of companies' debt and interest (re)payment capacity.

During the dot-com bubble era of the mid-1990s to 2001,[6] EBITDA became a widely used and widely abused measure of profitability and performance. Multiples of EBITDA were used to calculate the enterprise value of companies. Some firms manipulated their financial data in order to inflate their revenues and EBITDAs. WorldCom, a large communications company, capitalized many items that might have been expensed. By "improperly manipulating WorldCom's reported revenue, expenses, net income, earnings before interest, taxes, depreciation and amortization (EBITDA), and earnings per share . . . [WorldCom] materially overstated the income it reported in its financial statements by at least $9 billion."[7] The manipulation of its earnings contributed to its bankruptcy in July 2002. The $103.9 billion bankruptcy was the largest in U.S. history.[8]

Vivendi Universal, S.A., a media and environmental services conglomerate, is another example of the misuse of EBITDA. The Securities and Exchange Commission (SEC) settled civil fraud action against Vivendi that the company "at the direction of its senior executives, made improper adjustments that raised Vivendi's EBITDA by approximately $59 million during the second quarter of 2001 and by at least $10 million during the third quarter of 2001. These adjustments were made so that Vivendi could meet ambitious earnings targets that it had communicated to the market."[9]

However, during the boom part of the dot-com era, Internet and technology stocks soared. Many of the new initial public offerings (IPOs) were not profitable, and were never going to make a profit. Companies, regulators, and investors found out that excessive emphasis on non-GAAP measures like EBITDA may not draw the complete picture that is necessary to make well-substantiated investment decisions, also refer to the section EBITDA in financial reporting. This does not, however, mean that EBITDA is completely gone. As we will see later in this chapter, EBITDA as a performance measure is still widely used in Europe. In addition, EBITDA is often used for valuation purposes, like in the InBev–Anheuser-Busch transaction.

WHO USES EBITDA AND WHY?

EBITDA became a widely used profitability measure in the 1980s and 1990s because it is easy to understand and it is not complicated by different methods of depreciation and taxation. As part of its initial research into performance reporting, the Financial Accounting Standards Board (FASB) interviewed 56 analysts and other users, the results of which were reported in 2002. According to the FASB, "most analysts interviewed focus primarily on operating cash flow/free cash flow or operating earnings. EBITDA, EBIT, return on investment, and measures of leverage or liquidity and revenue growth or market share were among the key metrics."[10]

Also as a basis for the valuation of companies, EBITDA is often referred to as a relevant measure. Camblain (2008) presented the results of an Ernst & Young 2005 survey of 142 European brokers, 88 companies, and 15 investment banks. The survey found that 55 percent of the respondents used EBITDA valuation multiples. In their International Private Equity and Venture Capital Valuation Guidelines (AFIC, BVCA, and ECVA 2006), an international group of private/venture capital associations describe how EBIT- and EBITDA-based multiples are commonly used to estimate the value of an entity. They, however, also note that the particular multiple used should be appropriate for the business being valued, and they warn that if EBITDA multiples are used without sufficient care, "the valuer may fail to recognize that business decisions to spend heavily on fixed assets or to grow by acquisition . . . do have real costs associated with them which should be reflected in the value attributed to the business in question." This indicates that EBITDA multiples are less appropriate for businesses where significant investments are required to grow. In the PricewaterhouseCoopers Outlook (2007) PricewaterhouseCoopers used EBITDA multiples to describe market values and valuation opportunities in the United States and stated that "The average middle market EBITDA multiple for the last twelve months, as of October 15, 2007, was 10.3×, up from 8.6× for the same period in 2006." The PwC data was provided by Thomson Reuters, a company with employees in 19 countries that provides intelligent information for businesses and professionals.[11] Its databases contain EBITDA multiples and other data. The point here is that data about EBITDA is readily available to analysts and investors worldwide.

The references just mentioned indicate that many consider EBITDA a relevant measure to assess a company's performance and as a basis for the valuation of a company. But why would an analyst or a valuator be interested in this measure? Damodaran (2001, 317) states that EBITDA acquired adherents among analysts because:

1. There are fewer firms with negative EBITDAs than negative earnings per share.
2. Differences in depreciation methods across firms will not affect EBITDA.
3. It is easy to compare the EBITDA multiples across firms with different degrees of financial leverage.

Williams (2002), a strategist for Goldman Sachs, stated that analysts can use enterprise value (EV)/EBITDA or EV/sales for looking at a large number of companies "because these measures tend to be less distorted by accounting differences than measures further down the P&L (profit and loss) statement. . . . We have found EV/sales and EV/EBITDA to be superior to both P/E (price/earnings) and required cash flow measures." He also points out that the use of EBITDA "does not solve the problem of how to look at differences in balance sheet measurements."

EBITDA multiples are thus still widely used since they allow comparison between companies that use different depreciation methods or have different degrees of financial leverage. When assessing management's performance, EBITDA also has the potential to exclude expenses that are more or less outside the control of current management since depreciation and amortization often follow from capital expenditures made by prior management in the past, and interest expenses largely follow from financing decisions made in the past as well. In addition, from a valuation perspective, the fact that EBITDA is positive more often than net profit is an advantage because application of a multiple to a negative amount will not result in meaningful results. However, it ignores relevant costs that must be paid to continue doing business (interest, taxes) or to grow the business (capital expenditures), which brings us to some of the shortcomings of EBITDA.

Shortcomings of EBITDA

Although EBITDA can be a useful measure to assess a company's performance, it has a number of shortcomings that should not be ignored when using it, including, but not limited to, the following:

- EBITDA represents debt-free firms, which is not the case for most companies. EBITDA can be helpful for valuation purposes since it can be used to estimate the enterprise value, which is less variable to a company's financing policy. In addition, it can be used to determine a company's ability to repay debt and interest when worst comes to worst. However, when assessing a company's performance it ignores a true cost that must be paid on a regular basis and will result in a cash outflow.
- EBITDA also ignores tax payments, which profitable firms cannot, or cannot always, avoid. Again, EBITDA can be useful in a stress test to assess what room the company has to pay debt holders when results decrease to a break-even point (and taxes are not likely to be paid), but it overestimates a company's capacity to generate future cash flows for profitable firms that generally have to pay their taxes.

- It does not take into account firms with different capital investments, and the depreciation that comes with them. A capital-intensive and growing company may have large depreciation charges but will also have to incur large capital expenditures to continue as a going concern or grow the business as intended, and this cost cannot be ignored when valuing the company. A measure like free cash flow (operating cash flow less capital expenditures) seems more appropriate to estimate relevant future cash flows for these companies. On the contrary, companies with higher depreciation and tax deductions will have smaller tax burdens and higher cash flows.
- EBITDA does not exclude all noncash items such as the allowances for bad debts and inventory write-downs as well as the impact of investments in working capital. It is therefore questionable whether an imperfect measure of cash flows would give more meaningful information to predict future cash flows than the current cash flow itself.

Warren Buffett told Berkshire Hathaway, Inc. shareholders in his 2002 annual letter that:

> *Trumpeting EBITDA . . . is a particularly pernicious practice. Doing so implies that depreciation is not truly an expense, given that it is a "non-cash" charge. That's nonsense. In truth, depreciation is a particularly unattractive expense because the cash outlay it represents is paid up front, before the asset acquired has delivered any benefits to the business. Imagine, if you will, that at the beginning of this year a company paid all of its employees for the next ten years of their service (in the way they would lay out cash for a fixed asset to be useful for ten years). In the following nine years, compensation would be a "non-cash" expense—a reduction of a prepaid compensation asset established this year. Would anyone care to argue that the recording of the expense in years two through ten would be simply a bookkeeping formality?[12]*

Another shortcoming of EBITDA is illustrated in the InBev–Anheuser-Busch transaction. As indicated before, InBev wanted to pay $47.5 billion, which "represents 12× Anheuser-Busch's 2007 EBITDA."[13] However, EBITDA excludes the value of investments in securities, including minority interests in other companies. This includes Anheuser-Busch's income from its 50 percent stake in Groupo Modelo SA, a Mexican beer company, and its 27 percent stake in Tsingtao, a Chinese beer company.[14] The 2007 Anheuser-Busch balance sheet revealed that investments in affiliated companies totaled $4.012 billion, or 23 percent of total assets. Income from affiliates where there is not sufficient ownership to consider them as subsidiaries is listed as "equity income." Equity income is not part of operating income that is the basis of EBITDA. In 2007, equity income net of taxes was $662.4 million, about 23 percent of operating income.[15] Anheuser-Busch noted that the economic benefit from Modelo also could be measured in terms of its fair market value of the investment over its cost. The excess was $8.7 billion.[16] Thus, a valuation measure based on Anheuser-Busch's operating income undervalued the enterprise value because there is substantial equity income.

EBITDA IN FINANCIAL REPORTING

One of the objectives of general-purpose financial statements is to provide information about the performance of the entity. As stated by both the Financial Accounting Standards Board (FASB) and the International Accounting Standards Board (IASB), this information is primarily provided in the income statement. In the income statement, the company's earnings and its components are reported; these numbers are frequently used as a measure of performance or as the basis for other measures.

According to both the FASB's Statements of Financial Accounting Concepts (CON) 2 and the IASB's Framework for the Preparation and Presentation of Financial Statements, the information that is reported in the financial statements should be relevant. Both consider information relevant when it assists users in their economic decision making by helping them evaluate past, present, or future events, or confirm or correct their past evaluations.

In this context and given that many analysts and valuators indicate they find EBITDA a helpful measure, one might conclude that to adhere to these qualitative characteristics a company should disclose its EBITDA explicitly. A question that is difficult to answer, however, is: "Which came first, the chicken or the egg?" Did companies start reporting EBITDA because the users of their financial statements asked for this as a relevant measure, or did the users start looking at this measure because the companies could not stop talking about it?

Many have objected to the use of these so-called non-GAAP measures. The Securities and Exchange Commission (SEC) and the International Organization of Securities Commissions (IOSCO) are among them. At the end of the previous century and the start of this century, the SEC debated this subject in many comment letters that were sent to companies using such measures.[17] In May 2002, the IOSCO also cautioned issuers, investors, and other users of financial information to use care when presenting and interpreting non-GAAP results measures.[18]

Following the passage of the Sarbanes-Oxley Act of 2002, the SEC adopted new rules concerning public companies' disclosure of financial information that is not based on GAAP.[19] Because EBITDA is not an accepted measure under GAAP, firms registering securities with the SEC are required to justify its use and to reconcile it to the most directly comparable GAAP financial measure, such as net income. For example, if EBITDA is presented as a performance measure, it should be reconciled to net income as presented in the statement of operations under GAAP. "Operating income would not be considered the most directly comparable GAAP financial measure because EBIT and EBITDA make adjustments for items that are not included in operating income."[20]

The use and misuse of EBITDA in the United States declined sharply in the post-dot-com era. As shown in the following list, many books that dealt with valuation and were published in the United States after 2000 had little or nothing to say about EBITDA valuation multiples.

Valuation Books Post-2000

Arzac, Enrique R., *Valuation for Mergers, Buyouts, and Restructuring* (Hoboken, NJ: John Wiley & Sons, 2005). EBITDA is not mentioned.

Damodaran, Aswath, *The Dark Side of Valuation* (Upper Saddle River, NJ: Prentice Hall, 2001). Offers favorable comments for comparing firms with different degrees of financial leverage. EBITDA's uses may be industry/sector specific. EBITDA valuation multiples are discussed.

Damodaran, Aswath, *Investment Valuation*, 2nd ed. (New York: John Wiley & Sons, 2002). EBITDA is mentioned as one of several measures of relative valuation. EBITDA valuation multiples are discussed.

Fernández, Pablo, *Valuation Methods and Shareholder Value Creation* (San Diego, CA: Academic Press, 2002). States that EBITDA is a widely used valuation model. EBITDA valuation multiples are discussed.

Ferris, Kenneth R., and Barbara S. Pécherot Petitt, *Valuation: Avoiding the Winner's Curse* (Upper Saddle River, NJ: Prentice Hall, 2002). EBITDA is briefly mentioned.

Koller, Tim, Mark Goedhart, and David Wessels, *Valuation: Measuring and Managing the Value of Companies*, University Edition (New York: McKinsey & Co./John Wiley & Sons, 2005). Briefly discusses both EBITA and EBITDA measures of valuation.

Lundholm, Russell, and Richard Sloan, *Equity Valuation & Analysis with eVal* (New York: McGraw-Hill, 2004). EBITDA is barely mentioned.

Stowe, John D., Thomas R. Robinson, Jerald E. Pinto, and Dennis W. McLeavey, *Analysis of Equity Investments: Valuation* (Charlottesville, VA: AIMR, 2002). Is critical of EBITDA as a substitute for free cash flow. It does not mention EBITDA valuation multiples.

EBITDA IN EUROPE

Until 2004, European Union (EU) companies were subject to local accounting laws and regulations. The national laws regarding financial reporting are based on the fourth and seventh EU directives, which contain detailed formats for the presentation of the income statement. An entity had to apply one of the mandatory formats for the income statement, including the line items as indicated, and in the prescribed format.

Since 2005, all (with a few exceptions) EU listed companies have to apply IFRS in their consolidated financial statements, and EU law is no longer applicable to this part of their financial reporting. IFRS does not give a detailed format for the presentation of the income statement, but gives significant flexibility to managers to present the income statement in what they believe is a relevant and understandable format. In addition, a significant portion of the financial information that is communicated to the market through the financial statements is included in parts other than the income statement itself. The narrative review sections (management's discussion and analysis) are used by management to further explain the development of the results and performance and the drivers behind these developments. IFRS does not yet provide guidance with regard to these narrative review sections. In October 2005, the IASB issued a discussion paper, and an exposure draft is tentatively planned for 2009. The content of these parts is therefore subject to local legislation, which is generally limited. The fourth EU directive only requires that the narrative section give a fair review of the development of the company's business and of its position, an indication of any important events that have occurred since the end of the financial year, and likely future developments and activities in the field of research and development. In addition, the narrative sections outside the audited financial statements are generally not subject to audit requirements. As a result, companies have a large degree of freedom in the presentation of their performance in these sections. Many companies report alternative performance measures in these sections, and these alternative measures seem to become increasingly important.

EXHIBIT 20.1 Number of Financial Statements per Country and Year in the Sample

	1999	2000	2001	2002	2003	2004	2005	Total
France	100	136	163	169	167	169	130	1,034
Germany	233	351	386	378	370	363	325	2,406
United Kingdom	341	538	663	704	723	723	660	4,352
Total	674	1,025	1,212	1,251	1,260	1,255	1,115	7,792

The relative freedom under IFRS gives management the possibility to provide understandable, relevant, and reliable information to stakeholders based on the company-specific situation. However, it also creates an opportunity to present the financial information, and additional performance measures, in such a way that a more positive picture is drawn of the company's performance than would be appropriate under the circumstances.

Although EBITDA fell out of favor in the United States, the messages and warnings about its shortcomings do not seem to have had an impact on the reporting of it by European companies. To gain insight in this matter, we have reviewed the use of EBITDA and similar measures in the financial statements of a large set of companies from the three largest capital markets in Europe—France, Germany, and the United Kingdom—over the period 1999–2005. The study covers the sample of financial statements shown in Exhibit 20.1.

As indicated in Exhibit 20.2, a large portion of the European companies do report EBITDA or a similar measure (like EBITA or profit before depreciation and amortization). After a sharp increase in the use of EBITDA until 2002, the use stabilizes after that. There is a slight decline between 2003 and 2005, but Exhibit 20.3 indicates that this is primarily due to the group of European companies with a U.S. listing.

The results in Exhibit 20.2 indicate that there are significant cross-country differences in the extent to which companies report EBITDA in their financial statements. In the United Kingdom, the use is fairly low at 31

EXHIBIT 20.2 Percentage of Financial Statements That Include EBITDA and Similar Measures

	1999	2000	2001	2002	2003	2004	2005	Total
France	33%	32%	37%	45%	44%	43%	42%	40%
Germany	32%	51%	58%	65%	66%	65%	63%	59%
United Kingdom	16%	22%	27%	31%	30%	30%	31%	28%
Total	24%	33%	38%	43%	43%	42%	41%	39%

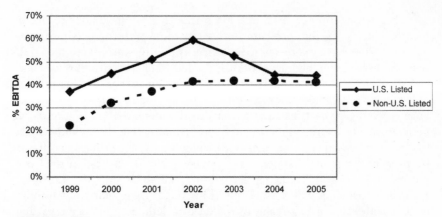

EXHIBIT 20.3   Percentage of Financial Statements That Include Alternative Performance Measures for EU Companies with and without a U.S. Listing

percent in 2005, whereas in Germany as much as 63 percent of the companies in our sample report this measure. This is likely driven by the fact that the German economy has historically been more bank driven than the United Kingdom's economy, which is much more shareholder driven, comparable to the United States. This is in line with the notion that EBITDA is more suitable as a debt service ratio than as a performance measure for shareholders.

Brouwer et. al (2007)[21] also reviewed the income statements in the 2005 year-end financial statements of 250 companies from eight European countries in order to examine EBITDA and similar income measures they used beyond the minimum required by International Financial Reporting Standards (IFRS). The study included companies from Belgium, Denmark, France, Germany, Italy, the Netherlands, Spain, and the United Kingdom. Also in this area, the study found significant national differences. In the Netherlands, EBITDA is rarely reported on the face of the income statement, whereas this is very common in Denmark, Italy, and Spain. These results should be taken with care, though, since sample sizes were small.

This does not, however, mean that the use of EBITDA or other alternative performance measures is without debate in Europe. Already in 2001, for example, the Dutch Accounting Standards Board prohibited the use of EBITDA and EBITA on the face of the income statement. Early in 2004, both the Dutch Institute for Auditors (NIVRA) and the security exchange regulator—Netherlands Authority for the Financial Markets (AFM)—expressed their concerns regarding the use of these measures in financial information.

The introduction of IFRS in 2005 further led to discussions regarding inconsistencies in the presentation of various performance measures. Several parties have expressed their concerns that the introduction of IFRS will not result in the high level of transparency and comparability of financial reporting from all publicly traded EU companies that was the primary objective of this introduction. The IASB, for example, started its performance-reporting project because it regarded the increased use of alternative performance measures as increasingly problematic, but also acknowledged that the bottom-line (comprehensive) income was not sufficiently useful for the users of the financial statements (Newberry 2003). Parties like the Committee of European Securities Regulators (CESR)[22] and the European Financial Reporting Advisory Group (EFRAG)[23] argue that comparability could even decrease as a result of the lack of detailed guidance regarding the presentation of the result of the entity in the income statement and other parts of the financial statements. In the 2006 European Economic Association Congress plenary opening session, M. Hoogendoorn[24] stated that comparability under IFRS is significantly impeded by the lack of standardization of income statement formats and considers this a step backwards compared to the EU directives. He believes that income statements will be prepared in a variety of formats, using a variety of pro forma revenue, cost, and profit measures that will cause great difficulty for analysts attempting to compare financial statements. Newberry (2003), Barker (2004), and Marseille and Vergoossen (2005) have expressed similar concerns.

In October 2005, the Committee of European Securities Regulators (CESR) issued recommendations to encourage European companies to ensure that alternative performance measures are reported in a way that is appropriate and useful for investors' decision making. CESR recommended, among other things, that alternative performance measures be clearly defined, used consistently, and reconciled to defined measures, and that companies explain why alternative performance measures are presented and how they are used internally. The recommendation does not, however, prescribe or forbid the use of certain performance measures and does not have a legal status. As a result, European companies rarely consider these recommendations when preparing their financial statements. This was also noted by European regulators, like the UK, the French, and the Dutch regulator.

Exhibit 20.3 shows the trend in the use of EBITDA by the European companies with (approximately 10 percent of the sample) and without a U.S. listing. It appears that initially EBITDA and similar performance measures were more popular with the companies that were more influenced by the U.S. capital market due to their U.S. listings. In 2002, approximately 60 percent of the U.S.-listed companies reported EBITDA, whereas this was done by approximately 40 percent of the companies with an EU listing only. However, from that moment on, the implementation of Regulation G in 2002 clearly had an impact on EBITDA reporting by the U.S.-listed companies whereas the non-U.S.-listed companies were not affected by this event. The CESR recommendation in 2005 does not seem to have affected either group. As a result, the levels of EBITDA reporting by both the U.S.-listed and non-U.S.-listed companies were at almost the same level in 2005, slightly above 40 percent.

IMPACT ON THE U.S. CAPITAL MARKET

As discussed earlier in the chapter, the impact of IFRS as well as other elements of financial reporting behavior in Europe and other economies on the U.S. capital markets is expected to increase. This means that financial analysts will have to be aware of the consequences thereof. These consequences are widespread and affect elements of recognition and valuation, but certainly also the presentation of financial information. Prior research has indicated that format, emphasis, and transparency in the presentation of financial information do affect investors' decision making. See for example Hirst and Hopkins (1998), and Maines and McDaniel (2000) who study the impact of comprehensive income disclosure formats and Frederickson and Miller (2004) and Elliott (2006) who study disclosure of alternative performance measures in experimental settings. This means that analysts should be aware that their conclusions might be affected simply by management decisions about the format in which information is presented and the decision whether to report certain alternative performance measures.

Should we expect an explicit ban on EBITDA reporting by the U.S. regulators once IFRS is widely accepted in the U.S. market? The first indications are that this will not be the case. In their summary observations from their review of 2006 IFRS financial statements filed by foreign private issuers, the SEC, for example, noted the following:

> *We found that companies based in the same jurisdiction and companies in the same industries sometimes used different income statement formats. IAS 1 provides general guidance of minimum line items a company must include and requires a company to present other items, captions and subtotals "relevant to an understanding of the entity's financial performance." We asked a number of companies to:*
>
> ■ *rename income statement subtotals so it was clear what each subtotal represented;*

■ *explain the accounting policies they followed in determining what items to exclude from the income statement subtotals, including what elements constituted operating income; and*

■ *disclose how they calculated additional voluntary per share measures and how they reconciled these measures to the income statement.*

It is important to note that while we sought further explanation of the relevance of an item a company presented on the face of its income statement or in footnotes, we did not request any company to remove any measure that we would consider a non-GAAP measure under U.S. GAAP.

www.sec.gov/divisions/corpfin/ifrs_staffobservations.htm

This communication, as well as other communications made by the SEC so far related to the acceptance of IFRS, indicates that the SEC is likely to accept IFRS as it stands, including all the options and judgmental areas that come with it.

THE REPORTING PERFORMANCE PROJECT

Discussions about alternative performance measures used and reported cannot be seen separately from the fact that the FASB and IASB do in fact not explicitly state how they define performance other than stating that information about performance is primarily provided in the income statement. The widespread use of alternative performance measures indicates that the current reporting model may not fit very well to the actual information needs of analysts and other users of financial information.

After publication of the reports "Reporting Financial Performance: Current Developments and Future Directions" and "Reporting Financial Performance: Proposals for Change" in 1998 and 1999, already in 2001 both the FASB and the IASB had started their "Performance Reporting" projects, which they combined in 2004 and later renamed (or narrowed in scope) into "Financial Statement Presentation." The project should result in new standards for the presentation of information in annual accounts, including classification, aggregation, and display that improve the usefulness of that information in assessing the financial performance of a company. In October 2008, a Discussion Paper ("Preliminary Views on Financial Statement Presentation") was issued. The Discussion Paper proposes a new financial statements format which "portrays a cohesive financial picture of an entity's activities" and "disaggregates information so that it is useful in predicting an entity's future cash flows". The Discussion Paper proposes to present an entity's financial position, financial performance (comprehensive income) and cash flows in three statements which are consistently disaggregated in comparable categories:

Statement of Financial Position	Statement of Comprehensive Income	Statement of Cash Flows
Business	*Business*	*Business*
■ Operating assets and liabilities	■ Operating income and expenses	■ Operating cash flows
■ Investing assets and liabilities	■ Investment income and expenses	■ Investing cash flows
Financing	*Financing*	*Financing*
■ Financing assets	■ Financing asset income	■ Financing asset cash flows
■ Financing liabilities	■ Financing liability expenses	■ Financing liability cash flows
Income taxes	*Income taxes on continuing operations (business and financing)*	*Income taxes*
Discontinued operations	*Discontinued Operations, net of tax* *Other comprehensive income, net of tax*	*Discontinued operations*
Equity		*Equity*

Although the Boards initiated the joint project to address users' concerns that existing requirements permit too many alternative types of presentation and that information in financial statements is highly aggregated and inconsistently presented, the Discussion Paper does not propose to include additional detailed guidance on the presentation of items within or between the categories presented above. In fact, the Discussion paper proposes a "management approach" which will follow management's classification rationale based on how management views and manages the entity and its resources. This rationale would be presented in the notes to financial statements as part of the accounting policy discussion. The Discussion Paper is silent about the use of EBITDA and similar measures.

This means that both in the current situation and in the expected future situation, analysts and valuators must ensure that they fully understand the definition, relevance and shortcomings of performance measures reported by an entity's management before they use it as the basis for their assessment of an entity's performance or valuation.

CONCLUSIONS

The worldwide adoption of IFRS seems unavoidable and the influences of IFRS, as well as other reporting behavior from outside the United States, are noticeable already in the U.S. capital markets. Given the current IFRS requirements and the proposed direction for a new standard about financial statements presentation, this is expected to result in a larger variety of presentation formats and increased use of what under U.S. GAAP would be considered non-GAAP measures. Many of the measures, including EBITDA, can be very relevant when assessing a company's performance. However, there is no company in the world whose performance can be captured in one single measure. And for different companies the relevant measures can be different. For a telecom company the performance may be best explained by number of customers, churn, and average revenue per user (ARPU); for an oil company, by the development of its oil reserves; and for a biotech company, by the development of its R&D pipeline. Therefore, it is not likely that there will ever be a standard that will make reporting of alternative performance measures disappear.

It is the analyst's responsibility to assess and summarize a company's performance as fairly and comprehensively as possible using all the relevant performance measures. For many companies it is very well possible that EBITDA is one of them. In that case, the analyst should use it to cover the areas where EBITDA is relevant and beneficial for the analysis, but should not shut his or her eyes for the shortcomings that are discussed in this chapter. In addition, the analyst should determine which measures are relevant given the fundamentals of the company, irrespective of the reporting choices made by the company's management.

History has, however, shown that people may easily forget about the shortcomings of EBITDA. Let's make sure that history does not repeat itself!

NOTES

1. "Proposed Combination with Anheuser-Busch: Creating the Global Leader in Beer with Flagship Brand Budweiser," June 12, 2008, www.inbev.com/pdf/Investor_Presentation_080612.pdf.

2. "Anheuser-Busch InBev, Creating the Global Leader in Beer," July 14, 2008, www.inbev.com/pdf/Final_Investor_Presentation.pdf. Data were based on I/B/E/S 2008E EBITDA consensus estimate from Bloomberg.

3. "InBev May Sell US Theme Parks," *CNNMoney.com*, July 18, 2008, http://money.cnn.com/news/newsfeeds/articles/apwire/200359aad711f3f3f669e21c8bb737df.htm.

4. Pronounced E-bit-dah.

5. Moody's Investors Service, Inc. *Putting EBITDA in Perspective: 10 Critical Failings of EBITDA as the Principal Determinant of Cash Flow* (New York: Moody's Investors Service, 2000).

6. The NASDAQ Composite index peaked at an intraday high of 5,132.52 on March 10, 2000. Subsequently, the dot-com bubble burst.

7. "SEC Charges Scott D. Sullivan, WorldCom's Former Chief Financial Officer, with Engaging in Multi-Billion Dollar Financial Fraud," U.S. Securities and Exchange Commission, Press Release 2004-25, March 2, 2004.

8. "Largest Bankruptcies, 1980–Present," Infoplease.com, 2008, www.infoplease.com/toptens/bankruptcies.html.

9. "SEC Files Settled Civil Fraud Action against Vivendi Universal, SA," *SEC News Digest*, issue 2003-244, Enforcement Proceedings, December 2003, 24.

10. Financial Accounting Standards Board (FASB), "Summary of User Interviews—Reporting Financial Performance by Business Enterprises," 2002.

11. www.thomsonreuters.com/about/.

12. Berkshire Hathaway, Inc., Shareholder Letters, 2002, 21. www.berkshirehathaway.com/letters/2002pdf.pdf.

13. "Proposed Combination with Anheuser-Busch: Creating the Global Leader in Beer with Flagship Brand Budweiser," June 12, 2008, www.inbev.com/pdf/Investor_Presentation_080612.pdf.

14. David Kesmodel and Matthew Karnitschnig, "Anheuser to Slash 1,000 Jobs, Raise Prices," *Wall Street Journal*, June 28–29, 2008, B6.

15. Anheuser-Busch, 2007 Annual Report, 44.

16. Ibid., 40.

17. See, among others: Securities and Exchange Commission (SEC), Division of Corporation Finance, "Frequently Requested Accounting and Financial Reporting Interpretations and Guidance," March 31, 2001.

18. IOSCO Technical Committee, "Cautionary Statement Regarding Non-GAAP Results Measures," May 2002.

19. SEC, "Final Rule: Conditions for Use of Non-GAAP Financial Measures," Release No. 47226 (2003); also see: 17 CFR Parts 228, 229, 244, and 249.

20. SEC, "Frequently Asked Questions Regarding the Use of Non-GAAP Financial Measures," June 13, 2003, http://sec.gov/divisions/corpfin/faqs/nongaapfaq.htm#ebit.

21. Brouwer's study (*Presentation of Income under IFRS: Flexibility and Consistency Explored*) was funded and reported by PricewaterhouseCoopers (PwC).

22. Committee of European Securities Regulators (CESR) press release, 2005. CESR consults on recommendations on the use of alternative performance

measures to ensure best practices by companies in the information prepared for investors.

23. European Financial Reporting Advisory Group (EFRAG), "Pro-Active Accounting Activities in Europe—Discussion Paper 2: The Performance Reporting Debate—What (If Anything) Is Wrong with the Good Old Income Statement," 2006.

24. M. Hoogendoorn, "International Accounting Regulation and IFRS Implementation in Europe and Beyond—Experiences with First-Time Adoption in Europe," European Economic Association Congress Plenary Opening Session, 2006.

REFERENCES

AFIC, BVCA and EVCA (2006), International Private Equity And Venture Capital Valuation Guidelines.

Barker, R. 2004. Reporting financial performance. *Accounting Horizons* 18(2): 157–172.

Brouwer, Arjan, Leandrovan Dam and Ian Wright. 2007. *Presentation of income under IFRS: Flexibility and consistency explored.* New York: PricewaterhouseCoopers.

Camblain, Edouard. 2008. Valuation tricks and traps. Microsoft PowerPoint, presented at the Association des EDHEC Business School, Lille-Nice, France, January 15. http://planete.edhec.com/servlet/com.univ.collaboratif.utils.Lecture Fichiergw?ID_FICHIER=9700-.

Continued EBITDA margin expansion in a tough quarter. 2007. InBev press release, November 8. www.inbev.com/press_releases/20071108_1_e.pdf.

Damodaran, Aswath. 2001. *The dark side of valuation.* Upper Saddle River, NJ: Prentice Hall.

Elliot, W.B. (2006), Are Investors Influenced by Pro Forma Emphasis and Reconciliations in Earnings Announcements, in: *The Accounting Review*, Vol. 81, No.1, pp. 113–133.

Frederickson, J.R. and Miller, J.S. (2004), The Effects of Pro Forma Earnings Disclosures on Analysts' and Nonprofessional Investors' Equity Valuation Judgments, in: *The Accounting Review*, Vol. 79, No.3, pp. 667–686.

Hirst E.D. and Hopkins P.E. (1998), Comprehensive Income Reporting and Analysts' Valuation Judgments, in: *Journal of Accounting Research*, Vol. 36, pp. 47–75.

International Accounting Standards Board (2008), Piscussion Paper Preliminary Views on Financial Statement Presentation, October.

Johnson, Jeffrey J. 2002. FASB works with IASB toward global convergence. FASB report, November 27.

Maines, L.A., and McDaniel, L.S. (2000), Effects of Comprehensive-Income Characteristics on Nonprofessional Investors' Judgments: The Role of Financial-

Statement Presentation Format, in: *The Accounting Review*, Vol. 75, No. 2, pp. 179–207.

Marseille, E. A., and R. G. A. Vergoossen. 2005. Het gebruik van alternatieve financiële prestatie-indicatoren in persberichten. *Maandblad voor Accountancy en Bedrijfseconomie* 79(5): 196–204.

Newberry, S. 2003. Reporting performance: Comprehensive income and its components. *Abacus* 39(3): 325–339.

PricewaterhouseCoopers Outlook. 2007. Disruption in the US credit markets to create some favorable valuation opportunities in 2008. (December 12).

Williams, Neil. 2002. Valuation models for cross-border analysis. AIMR Conference Proceedings, Equity Research and Valuation Techniques, August, 26–36.

CHAPTER 21

Optimizing the Value of Investor Relations

William F. Mahoney
Editor, Valuation Issues

The primary purpose of investor relations (IR) is to optimize the understanding of the company by the investment community.

Given the popularity of multifactor models among professional investors, we can think of a good investor relations program as being one of those factors. In this way, an effective IR function contributes to the value of a company.

In this case, *value* doesn't mean that IR adds to revenues or cash flow or margins or other operating drivers. It means that the IR help is being provided by enabling investors to price the stock at its fair value.

That contribution, of course, isn't limited to users of multifactor models. There is a productive role for IR to play for every investor using an active modeling approach, whether it emphasizes earnings or cash, and whether it is built on multiple factors or other approaches. Even indexers and other users of quantitative methods benefit from inputting the best information possible into their models. A really good IR program delivers the best information.

We believe that corporate managements and professional investors have served to limit the role and value of IR. Investor relations people as well can do a better job of educating these two primary audiences on the real value of the function. Stock analysts and fund/portfolio managers still can be heard calling IR "PR" (public relations), and company executives mainly think of it as a service function.

INVESTOR RELATIONS AS A SERVICE FUNCTION

Indeed, investor relations can be divided into two broad categories of activities: (1) service and (2) in an enhanced capacity, value fulfillment.

CEOs, presidents, operating division heads, and CFOs have enough to do. Hire the best IRO you can find and have him or her lead the value fulfillment team.

As we say, still today most managements view IR as a service function, and thus most corporate IR programs essentially provide service to shareholders, analysts, brokers, and institutional and individual investors. Thus, unfortunately, the function continues to accomplish less than it can.

So, let's divide the IR function into its two primary components—service and value fulfillment. Basic service functions are familiar to all practicing IROs as well as CFOs and CEOs. Essentially they consist of six major activities:

1. Produce or participate with the finance and legal groups in preparing disclosure materials and filings. These include the proxy materials, 10-K, 10-Q, 8-K, and similar documents.
2. Prepare news releases, covering both material and nonmaterial information. Quarterly/annual results, dividend declarations, executive and board elections, mergers and acquisitions and divestitures, new facilities, and significant operational and product/service offerings head the list.
3. Lead or participate in preparing the annual report, fact book, and other materials geared for the investment community.
4. Answer requests for information from shareholders, analysts, brokers, prospects among these groups, and maybe the media and other influential parties—by phone, mail, e-mail, and Internet.
5. Maintain the IR web site.
6. Provide information about the investment market to management and the board of directors. Typically, these include analysts' reports and comments, investment market attitudes toward the company, media coverage, and identities of leading analyst and institutional investor prospects.

Frequently, IR programs extend beyond these activities, incorporating a number of proactive efforts in reaching out to the market. Managements have come to consider these as leading activities, conducted primarily by the investor relations office:

■ Enable the CEO, CFO, and other top executives to address analyst and institutional groups, typically professional investment societies and splinter groups and organizations created to bring investment and corporate players together. There also exist today similar opportunities to meet with individual investors, hopefully most times those with large portfolios.

■ Encourage analysts and investors to meet with senior management, either in small groups or individually, and arrange these sessions. IR departments score points with management by being able to attract leading portfolio managers to meet with the CEO and CFO. Likewise, IROs gain credibility when they can get the CEO to take the time to meet with certain fund managers and analysts.

■ Prepare presentations for the top executives to give to these audiences. This work by IROs also includes anticipating and preparing answers to questions most likely to be asked during these sessions.

■ Expand and upgrade the communications flow through the frequency and quality of the content of such materials as releases, fact books, presentations, phone conversations, e-mails, and the company's web site. Striving to improve the quality of information should be an ongoing objective.

■ Run the meetings and give the presentations to analyst and investor groups. At an extensive number of companies, the IRO is the chief spokesperson to the investment community, making the presentations and answering questions. In one way, this is an expansion of the ongoing role of IR pros in handling telephone conversations and Internet contact. Filling this role means management is comfortable with letting the IRO be the prime source of information and confident that he or she is fully able to satisfy investors' information desires.

Confidence that the IRO speaks well for the company is the right attitude for management. But, unfortunately, there are some senior executives who are only too glad to pass along the job to the IRO or CFO for the wrong reasons. There are CEOs who feel they are too busy, or it isn't worth their time, or they fear making mistakes or saying the wrong thing, or they simply are shy and afraid to take on a public persona. That's not good. The market needs to know the people in charge; it is a fundamental piece of analyzing the qualities of management.

■ Advise management and the board of directors on analyst and investor attitudes toward the company, its fundamentals and prospects to grow. Feedback from the IR department can be very helpful in understanding how the market views the company, and it can impact management strategies and decisions. Plus (this is very important), it is critical for that feedback to be on the mark.

THE INVESTMENT RELATIONS OFFICER AS THE RESIDENT INVESTMENT MARKET EXPERT

This last function creates a bridge between investor relations operating as a service function and being vital in the value fulfillment process. Now we are moving into that second and most vital role, that of leading the way in having the investment market price its stock at the level of the company's intrinsic value.

This process starts with understanding the investment market as fully as possible. Your path to achieving fair value begins with having a deep understanding of how this collective group of investors called the equity market goes about its business.

It is logical for the investor relations officer to be the company's *resident expert* on the investment marketplace. Filling this role is a big and important job, and it isn't easy to be wholly knowledgeable. It can take intense study—indeed, study that never ends. The market is highly complex, incorporating a myriad of macro and micro factors, bringing together an array of investment processes, continually refining models, constantly changing.

It should be a fundamental requirement for the IRO to have investment market expertise and to be steadily growing it. It should be the foundation of his or her work. It makes sense that the leader of the value fulfillment team be the person in the company who best understands market dynamics and the investment process. He or she should be viewed that way by the entire management group. Each member should be totally comfortable consulting with the IRO on matters of the stock and bond markets. That high level of respect should exist.

Some IROs today have work to do to reach that level of knowledge and respect. Get to work if you need to. Make the time to be a student of the market to the extent necessary to build your expertise. It should be an integral part of your job description, more so than anyone else in the company.

In taking the chief responsibility for being the resident market expert, the IRO also may have to work at winning management acceptance. Indeed, winning that acceptance can be the hardest part of the job for IROs. Many CEOs and CFOs consider themselves to be the ultimate implementer of the shareholder value mandate.

These executives need to distinguish between the two responsibilities. Managements *create* shareholder value; investor relations teams see to it that the company's full value is recognized by the investment community. Enlightened managements understand the role of investor relations in growing shareholder value.

The best way for IROs to win the acceptance of senior management and the board is through execution. Prove your market knowledge every day and perform the key parts of carrying out the service function and leading the value fulfillment effort at the highest level.

Going full circle, ideally, the investor relations program effectively combines the service function with the pursuit of value fulfillment.

BUILDING INVESTOR RESPECT AS WELL

It's a two-way street. To lead the value fulfillment effort, the investor relations officer must be trusted to successfully handle and manage the role by *both* the executive team and the investment community. The IRO truly is the bridge between the two vital groups.

Security analysts, institutional fund and portfolio managers, institutional and retail brokers, individual investors—all the players need to be comfortable and trustful of the effectiveness of the IR team. The IRO and key members of the staff have to prove themselves to the market through their daily performance.

Once that trust is established, managers and investors are in a position to literally work together to achieve the fair value of the company's securities, working through all the daily market nuances. Wouldn't it be great to reach that high point of progress, multiplied by all the companies in the investment universe!

IT'S ALL ABOUT INFORMATION OF VALUE

As indicated earlier and is obvious anyway, information is the key ingredient in this recipe for fairly valuing a company's securities. The quality of information is what matters. It is information of the highest quality and value that leads analysts and investors first to the knowledge and then to the insights that enhance the accuracy of their decisions.

What each analyst and investor seeks is an information advantage. Professionals in the market work hard to gain that information advantage, recognizing its benefits in the practical process of making investment recommendations and decisions. An information advantage has even become a factor in the models of many investors.

Highest-quality information is elusive—certainly elusive enough to make gaining an information advantage a real factor in understanding a company.

Companies and their IR teams can make an important difference in providing valuable information across the investment market spectrum. Clearly, it should be the goal of every public company to deliver information of the highest value in both their required disclosure filings and their voluntary communications efforts, seeking to reach the widest investment audience effectively.

In reality, there is a huge spread in the range of the quality and value of information made available by companies. Part of the reason for this differential across the spectrum of companies is a lack of professionalism in recognizing the information investors need to make good decisions. The other part is intentional; management prefers to hold back information, usually from fear it might benefit competitors or reveal too much to such interested audiences as investors, the media, government, and others. How many times have we heard a CEO say, "It's none of their damn business!" Well, in fact, it is.

THE INFORMATION ADVANTAGE

As hard as we might try and as effective as we might be, there always will be a limit on the ability of IR departments to extend the information advantage to everyone. It just can't happen; it just isn't human nature; and then there wouldn't be any information advantage.

In fact, building an information advantage is a complex effort, bringing together the willingness and capability of the company and its IR department to provide quality information with the efforts of analysts and investors to gather, analyze, and deeply understand the information and its value.

For the investor, that effort includes a commitment of a significant amount of time and energy involved in processing the information fully. Vital in this commitment: spending time with the IRO and asking probing questions.

Those discussions and questions and answers likely deliver the *difference* in being able to gain an information advantage. This assumes that the IRO (or CFO or CEO) is fully forthcoming, just short of crossing the line in making sure that no material information is being given selectively.

A word about selective material disclosure: Clearly, IROs have to be very careful about not violating the rules, which require disseminating information that likely will cause any or many investors to make buy/hold/sell decisions to the entire marketplace. Providing such material information to one person or a group of people can send an IRO, CFO, CEO, or anyone else to jail.

WORKING WITH ONE KEY INVESTOR AT A TIME

At this point, it is becoming clear that effective investor relations programs involve a considerable amount of one-on-one relationship building.

Thus, overall, the investor relations function is practiced simultaneously on two levels—reaching the investment audience broadly and working with investors and analysts selectively.

The task of building professional, personal relationships with dozens to hundreds of portfolio managers and analysts is formidable, if not impossible. Most corporate IR staffs consist of anywhere from one to a handful of professionals, limiting the number of relationships that can benefit both parties. Perhaps the size of the IR staff should be larger; the mission is important enough to deserve more firepower.

A certain amount of selectivity takes place somewhat naturally. Compatibility impacts decisions by research analysts on which companies to cover, primarily companies within the sector and industry each is assigned or chooses. To some extent, fund and portfolio managers focus on evaluating companies that fit the parameters of their models, such as growth, value, growth at a reasonable price (GARP), and other styles. The models themselves are much more precise in their requirements when evaluating investment prospects.

Thus, selectivity applies on both sides of the equation. Investors and analysts pursue certain companies; investor relations professionals should be about the work of finding them.

For sure, targeting has been a practice of IR departments for a couple of decades now. Most companies use the various targeting services available, and that's okay. These services offer names of institutional investors, identify the specific funds within the investment firm, describe the fundamental compatibility with the company, and give names of managers and analysts, size of holdings, amounts invested in the sector and industry, competitors, and much more information. Collectively, the services range from fairly basic in their analysis of compatibility and detail of data to fairly sophisticated.

By showing levels of compatibility, IROs can better understand the reasons certain institutions and funds currently are shareholders. They can see how the financial and operating characteristics of their companies match up with the factors important in an institution's investing model. Indeed, the elements may indicate a positive or negative match now or could suggest they will turn more positive or negative as strategies and initiatives roll out in the coming months and years. IROs can gauge whether an institution is likely to buy more shares or sell shares as these realities unfold. They can anticipate more buying or selling.

This same information can be used to identify institutions likely to become interested in the company going forward. In this way, targeting is a tool to begin contact and dialogue with these investors.

Collectively, institutional managers have a wide range of models at their disposal. The range of multifactor models, for example, is quite extensive.[1] Models are described in chapters of this book. In every case, the manager is pursuing highest returns; they call it alpha, captured well in the book by Richard Tortoriello (2009), *Quantitative Strategies for Achieving Alpha.*

Understanding the reasons for investing helps the IRO, CFO, CEO, and other spokespersons in the company determine and focus on the information that matters in driving the institution's investing model. This serves as a vital step in being able to provide highest-quality information in helping deliver an information advantage to the investor.

Certainly, institutional and research analyst targeting is worthwhile. It also is a starting point and should be viewed that way. The main problem is that it is working at a superficial level. Its value probably comes more from gaining some limited intelligence on the reasons institutional investors are holding the stock. There likely is some connection between the investor's model and company performance and outlook.

Using the targeting lists, however, companies have found that many of the institutions being contacted have no interest in investing or talking with management at the time. Or their models have driven them to the stock and they are content to apply the data from readily available sources and make their decisions. The latter is especially true among quant investors.

WORKING WITH THE PRIMARY INVESTORS

The key for IROs is to help build an information advantage for those institutions that are having and will have the greatest influence on determining the company's value as measured by stock price.

Given the wide scope of the shareholder base of most companies, these institutions assuredly encompass an extensive collection of investing styles and models. They are active investors, applying growth or value or similar styles and using earnings or cash as a leading measure, versus passive investors, using quantitative and indexing models, even though these quants certainly influence rising/falling stock pricing trends as they are occurring.

We want to focus on active investors who put a high value on having an information advantage. We are far less likely to get audiences with and exert much influence over the multifactor quants.

Ideally, our dialogue centers on the intrinsic value of the company. We should strive for a relationship with each investor and analyst that encourages discussion around intrinsic value. In these discussions, we can share the findings of our models as intrinsic value is calculated and determined. We can talk about how the investor's model calculates intrinsic value and the primary drivers in that process. We can compare that model with our company model.

Perhaps the investor's model is mainly driven by earnings. Or it is a multifactor model, incorporating a number of vital inputs. That's fine. We have lots of information to contribute in working these models. We happen to have a bias toward cash flow modeling. Our model focuses on cash economic return. We want to understand the real cash being generated by the business, how it is being used, and how future cash investments will continue to grow operating performance and intrinsic value.

If the portfolio manager doesn't want to go so far as to share his or her model, okay. You still can discuss the primary inputs and contribute to making the model of the investor or analyst more accurate. You can discuss the company's model. Clearly, it is a successful relationship when the IRO is providing information that enables an investor to run an accurate model in calculating intrinsic value. Accuracy is what every investor wants. You can gain more insight into understanding the work of modeling and the information that's most valuable by reading Chapter 4, "Comparing Valuation Models," by Thomas Copeland, and Chapter 5, "Developing an Automated Discounted Cash Flow Model," by Robert Atra and Rawley Thomas.

Are these discussions in which material information is being provided selectively? We don't believe so. Or at least they don't have to be. Certainly, these conversations can be meaningful without divulging non-public material information. Sharing and describing models is not inherently a material discussion. Certain inputs can be material. Know what they are. Be careful.

Building dialogue around intrinsic value modeling enables investors and analysts to do a better job of identifying the inflection points. These are the key events and developments that begin to change the company's intrinsic value *or* begin to move the investment market toward its fair value. Investors who recognize the inflection point early can begin buying shares before the price starts to rise or begin selling shares before the price starts to fall. An excellent primer on recognizing inflection points is provided in Rawley Thomas, Dandan Yang, and Robert Atra's Chapter 22, "Lower Risk and Higher Returns: Linking Stable Paretian Distributions and Discounted Cash Flow." Refer to that chapter's Appendix B on ranges of bounded rationality.

The goal of a company and its IR professionals is to be engaged in effective relationship building with the highest number of those powerful investors driving valuation.

Identifying those investors requires a considerable amount of hard work and energy.

WHAT IT TAKES TO DO THE JOB

That's why IR professionals need to be students of the investment market and process, learning everything possible, academically and operationally. It's a challenge, requiring substantial intellectual effort to understand the market and all its nuances, combined with hands-on learning of the many investment approaches, styles, and models at work. Add the challenge of maintaining that high level of expertise in a dynamic, always changing investment marketplace.

Success also depends on having a strong personal interest and good skills in growing relationships. The focus here is on conversation. The real understanding of an investor's model results from discussion and demonstration. The portfolio manager needs to be confident that sharing at this level will benefit him or her.

As the company's leading investor relations officer, are you up to the task? Or are you content to fill the various service functions and reach out to shareholders and targeted investors by giving presentations, answering their questions, and lining up sessions with senior management?

Another way of looking at it: To what extent is the investor relations function passive and active? Is IR primarily a response function? Is it 75 percent response and 25 percent proactive?

How time is used is critical in expanding the value of investor relations. Time is limited, especially in one-person and small staffs. Emphasize time management. Be thoughtful about it and plan time usage carefully. Conducting all the service and standard proactive activities should take up less than half of the time available, leaving the bulk of it for the value fulfillment thrust.

Get help if necessary in completing the other activities. It is good to have people inside or outside writing the press releases, annual reports, and other materials and watching over the web site. For sure, be involved in these activities, but don't perform them. They can be distracting.

Also, investor relations professionals need to guard against getting caught up in related functions, key ones being public relations and corporate governance. These are important functions, best left to others having or growing their credentials in these fields. To wit: Let the corporate secretary be the governance guru. Let the PR officer be the media representative.

A footnote: Reducing risk is a big part of every investor's proposition. The investor relations function helps reduce risk for both the investor and the company through the flow of the most valuable information available.

Result: Investors and analysts are confident of the quality and value of the information being inputted into their models. Managements are confident of their ability to fashion a more knowledgeable shareholder base that will retain some loyalty and hold their positions. It is good to have a foundation of longer-term shareholders.

It can be argued that reducing risk is what investor relations is all about.

IDENTIFYING THE INFORMATION THAT DETERMINES INTRINSIC VALUE

Now we come to the information that isn't necessarily obvious in the disclosure documents that can make the difference in fully understanding the value of a company. Of course, a considerable amount of it is in the disclosure filings, with some of it speaking for itself and some benefiting from further explanation and interpretation.

Information is an integral ingredient of the value creation process. Information leads to understanding a company's intrinsic value. While strategies and initiatives and programs successfully implemented create value, information makes those activities understood.

The decision-driving information is unique to each company. We readily can organize all the information into three categories: macro, sector/industry, and company-specific, the latter mainly financial and operational, encompassing physical assets, intangible attributes, and more.

We can put all this information into an intrinsic value context. What is a company's intrinsic value? It is the calculated worth of all the company's assets, incorporating physical and intangible assets.

Thus, intrinsic value is based on calculating a value for plant, property, and equipment; talents of management and employees; scientific and technological capabilities; patents and licenses; products and services and their competitive positions; new products being launched and products in the pipeline; production and administration efficiencies; partnerships; quality and effectiveness of strategies; levels of creativity and leadership; social and environmental leadership; and the list goes on.

Efforts have been growing for years now to put values on intangible assets, especially those included in the preceding grouping.

Add calculating an intrinsic value for revenue generation, cash flow generation, profit margin, and cash available to invest.

We believe that investors are better off seeking an economic number, namely based on cash flow rather than earnings.

Our intrinsic value calculation proposition also must take into account realities that subtract from value. These can include lawsuits, regulatory issues, environmental/social issues, declining competitive positions, product and plant obsolescence, fading markets, and rising and new competition. Add your own.

FOCUS ON THE VALUE DRIVERS

Prioritizing the information leads companies and investors to focus on the value drivers. These constitute the half-dozen (more or less) of the real determinants of a company's intrinsic value. They likely encompass a combination of outside macro/sector/industry drivers and inside operating/financial/intangible drivers.

Availability and cost of a critical raw material may be a macro driver. Being part of a fading or growing industry is another. A sizable and strong new product pipeline can be an inside value driver, and so can running a modern, highly efficient production system, or having a sizable cash reserve to make strategic acquisitions and expand into new markets at highly advantageous times.

There is much to be gained in having the investment market price the stock at levels of intrinsic value. For this to happen, it helps to have management and investors agree on the value drivers. Investor relations professionals have a key role to play in making this happen. Dialogue usually brings it about. Investors have their convictions on which drivers matter the most, and so does management.

Good discussion can be enlightening in enabling the two groups to determine together the primary value drivers and probably even rank and quantify their relative contributions.

In the process, management is gaining a better understanding of investor views on the company and its value drivers, and investors gain important insights into executive thinking.

An ongoing solid communications program detailing the primary drivers of value reaching an ever widening audience can significantly expand the number of investors using an information advantage to make decisions.

Also important, efforts to focus investors and analysts on the most useful information can reduce the amount of the least useful information floating through the marketplace. Superfluous noise distracts investors.

LINKING INTRINSIC VALUE TO STOCK PRICE

As indicated, understanding a company's intrinsic value is the basis for knowing whether its stock at the moment is underpriced, overpriced, or fairly priced. Studies by LifeCycle Returns, Inc. (LCRT), a consultancy that has won high praise for its work to understand investment behavior, show that about half the firms in its 6,000-company universe are overvalued and half are undervalued. By their actions, investors comprising the market move those prices toward fair value. Using their intrinsic value models, investors gain an advantage by identifying the inflection points early that will start the price movement up or down accordingly.

The lesson for managements and their IR officers is to understand where the company stands; compare the current price with your calculation of intrinsic value.

In leading the value fulfillment team, the investor relations officer should focus information and communication on the drivers of value while also providing the other information most important to investors and analysts, and advising and preparing management for what is likely to happen to stock price—higher if the market perceives the stock to be underpriced and lower if the market perceives the stock to be overpriced.

Management must be working always to create more value, especially when the stock is seen as fairly priced.

NUMEROUS VITAL LESSONS FROM THIS BOOK

Investor relations officers, CFOs, CEOs, boards of directors, and other executives reading this book can benefit greatly from studying the chapters and work of the authors describing how the stock market functions, theories, and practices of academics and professional investors that have grown and evolved through the years, insights into investment process and investor behavior, and especially the *new thinking* that is emerging.

To wit, there is the systems mind-set to investing that is described in Chapter 3, "Applying a Systems Mind-Set to Stock Valuation," by Bartley J. Madden, an author and a principal in HOLT Value Associates, later acquired by Credit Suisse. Bart describes how knowledge and understanding grow from inquiry aimed at identifying problems and developing solutions, incorporating solid analysis of the "interactions among variables" and intense use and analysis of data to enhance understanding.

Chapters in the book describe in detail the range of valuation models being employed by the investment community, covering the variations of economic and cash-based models. To gain insight into these various approaches, suggested reading include, in addition to Bart Madden's chapter: Chapter 4, "Comparing Valuation Models," by Thomas E. Copeland, author, consultant, and senior lecturer at MIT; Chapter 5, "Developing an Automated Discounted Cash Flow Model," by Robert J. Atra, professor and chair of the department of finance at Lewis University, and Rawley Thomas, president and co-founder of LifeCycle Returns, Inc. (LCRT); Chapter 6, "The Essence of Value-Based Finance," by Roy Johnson, author, consultant, and educator; and Chapter 9, "The Economic Profit Approach to Securities Valuation," by James Grant, author, president of JLG Research,and a finance professor at the University of Massachusetts–Boston.

Rawley Thomas envisions a future when DCF and multifactor modeling will be brought together by these and other brilliant minds, forming a new and better standard for investing. For those investors, says Thomas, the ability to "harness the combined power of lower-risk automated DCF for higher returns and multifactor models combined with incorporating analysts' insights will create a durable competitive advantage."

The references here highlight just a handful of the gems and opportunity to gain wisdom from thoroughly reading this book.

For corporate executives, another quote from Bart Madden's chapter warrants serious thought.

Referring to continuing new research to overcome current personal bias, he writes, "A better understanding of cause and effect throughout the wealth creation process will lead to better decisions for the long-term, mutual benefit of customers, employees, and shareholders.

"Most especially," continues Madden, "managements and boards of directors need better valuation tools in order to make the right long-term decisions. Their decisions may, at times, disappoint Wall Street's myopic fixation on quarterly earnings expectations. But managements should finally quit playing Wall Street's game. Managers should employ an insightful valuation model and value-relevant accounting information to make sure their decisions make economic sense. Then, they need to clearly communicate to investors the rationale for their decisions."

Now that hits at the essence of investor relations.

WRAPPING IT UP

A quick summary: The service role of the investor relations office is being conducted very professionally with sufficient disclosure of good information taking place; the IRO and management are reaching out to the investment community, offering valuable additional information. Thus, the IR function is being performed quite well. This is the case today at numerous companies across the world.

Then, we add the vital dimension of working toward achieving value fulfillment by enabling the investors who matter to build an information advantage and drive the stock price to match the company's intrinsic value. Job well done.

NOTE

1. For a description of the Schwab multifactor approach with very good perform-ance, see Racanelli (2006).

REFERENCES

Racanelli, Vito J. 2006. The Schwab advantage. *Barron's*, November 27, 22 ff.
Tortoriello, Richard. 2009. *Quantitative strategies for achieving alpha*. New York: McGraw-Hill.

CHAPTER 22

Lower Risk and Higher Returns

Linking Stable Paretian Distributions and Discounted Cash Flow

Rawley Thomas
President, LifeCycle Returns, Inc.

Dandan Yang
President's Research Associate, LifeCycle Returns, Inc.

Robert J. Atra
Chair of the Finance Department, Lewis University

The nonnormality of security returns has reemerged due to the recent crisis in the financial markets. In just October 2008, the Dow Jones Industrial Average experienced five days where the average moved more than ±5 percent. Given a daily standard deviation of around 1 percent, these returns should be extraordinarily rare, if not impossible, assuming the normal distribution (De Grauwe, Iania, Rovira, and Kaltwasser 2008). These rare events traditionally predicted by the normal distribution are not nearly rare enough.

October 2008 is not an isolated event. The crash of October 1987 was approximately a 20 standard deviation event. The 1987 event should never have occurred, not only in our lifetime but in the universe's lifetime, assuming normality. Furthermore, international borders do not confine these extraordinary episodes. The 1987 crash, as well as the recent crisis, represents a worldwide phenomenon. As disastrous as October 1987 was for the U.S. stock market, in reality it performed the fifth *best* of the 23 major country markets (Roll 1989) during that depressing month.

Given the doubt cast upon applications of the normal distribution in finance, two questions arise: (1) What is an accurate assumption regarding the distribution of security returns? and (2) What does the assumption imply for practitioners, especially those in the field of security valuation and portfolio management?

Due to the current economic turmoil, considerable academic research and debate has reignited interest in answering the first question. While a complete analysis of the topic extends well beyond the scope of this chapter, a brief literature review in the next section represents some of the financial research key insights on the distribution of security returns. Academics have expended great effort in researching the first question, but rigorous research has virtually ignored the second question. Therefore, we anticipate that the insights in this empirical research chapter represent a significant contribution to the valuation literature. This chapter endeavors also to provide guidance for practitioners, while revealing the crucial link between valuation and portfolio construction.

Clearly, portfolio managers' beliefs about distributions of security returns closely impact their decisions. For example, consider portfolio managers analyzing the value at risk (VaR) of their portfolios. An individual's belief about risk depends almost entirely on one's assumptions about the left tail of the distribution. If returns are normal, risk is much less than if returns are fat-tailed. Consequently, portfolio managers express keen interest in return distributions and related risk management research. Value at risk (VaR) becomes problematic if it assumes Gaussian normality. If the portfolio manager relies on VaR as a primary risk control tool, assuming normality understates the risk in any fat tails.

Securities do not just magically appear in a portfolio, but typically enter through a security analysis selection process. Admittedly, that process can be passive, as in the case of indexing, but it often follows an active approach. LifeCycle's research focuses on how *active* security selection influences the distribution of returns.[1] Active selection processes affect not only location (expected return) but also shape, including tail thickness. The research concludes that superior security selection may effectively lead to normally distributed returns, placing less of the portfolio at risk.[2]

Security selection traditionally is a labor-intensive process, and, therefore, most challenging to assess empirically. We employ, however, an automated process in identifying over- and undervalued securities, explained briefly in a later section.[3] This automated process produces valuation estimates for thousands of stocks, allowing for diversified portfolios of substantially under- or overvalued securities.

BACKGROUND

Beginning with the Bachelier's (1900) work on modeling Brownian motion of security prices, finance has evolved into a mathematical discipline.

Markowitz (1952) extended mathematical concepts to portfolio construction by quantitatively incorporating risk into the process. Prior to Markowitz, both academic and industry publications presented risk primarily in a qualitative way.

Markowitz's theory assumed that investors desired to achieve a high mean return but with little variation in that return. Markowitz, therefore, employed variance as an appropriate measure of risk.[4] The use of variance as a risk measure later led to the development of the capital asset pricing model (CAPM) by Sharpe (1964), Lintner (1965), and Mossin (1966).

Huang and Litzenberger (1988) observed that the Markowitz mean-variance model, however, is not a general model of asset choice. Theoretical support for the model derives from either an assumption of quadratic utility or normally distributed asset returns. Quadratic utility provides motivation for the mean-variance model, because investors define utility over only the first two moments. In other words, investors with quadratic utility consider only mean and variance when choosing investments. Quadratic utility, however, becomes counterintuitive since it implies satiation and increasing absolute risk aversion. These undesirable facts reduce its application in theoretically supporting the mean-variance model.[5]

Despite quadratic utility limitations, investors may accept the mean-variance paradigm if asset returns follow Gaussian distributions, because the mean and variance completely define the normal distribution. The Markowitz model centers on the assumption of normality. Therefore, if that normality assumption is incorrect, the mean-variance model and all of its derivative theories become subject to question.

Originally, Markowitz conceded the questionability of the normality assumption. Later, Mandelbrot (1963, 1997, and 2004) investigated the normality assumption in depth. Primarily, Mandelbrot contended that random security return processes do not empirically conform to the normal distribution, but to a stable Paretian distribution. Stable Paretian distributions represent a class of distributions of which the normal distribution is a limiting case. Such distributions retain the attractive feature that they are stable in the sense that the distribution of returns does not depend on the time period over which those returns are measured. In other words, stability of scale and location means that daily returns possess the same distribution as weekly returns, monthly returns, annual returns, and so on.[6]

In contrast to the normal distribution, stable Paretian distributions may have more or less "thick" or "fat" tails. As the anecdotal evidence in the introduction stated, extreme stock returns occur with much higher frequency than predictions of the normal distribution. The stable Paretian distribution fat tails better model the extreme behavior of security returns.

The following parameters characterize a stable Paretian distribution:

- α, which determines the peakedness and thickness of the tails, falls in the range $0 \leq \alpha \leq 2$, where 2 is the limiting case of the normal distribution.
- β determines the skewness.
- "c" determines the scale (dispersion).
- δ determines the location.

For the limiting normal case, α is 2 and β is zero. The σ and μ parameters then become the standard deviation and mean of the distribution. As a stable distribution departs from normality, the lower α implies relatively fatter tails and a more peaked distribution.

Stable distributions pose one extremely serious problem: For an α less than 2, any moment of order greater than α is not defined, thus rendering theories relying on variance not useful.[7] Therefore, testing whether a set of securities possesses an α peakedness parameter significantly less than 2 produces useful information about the possibility of extreme returns and the benefits of diversification corresponding to that set.

An undefined variance does not imply that the concept of diversification with greater numbers of securities becomes meaningless. For an α above 1, diversification produces benefits by reducing the dispersion of returns, even if that dispersion is not the variance per se. As the α parameter approaches 1, however, diversification becomes more difficult, with greater numbers of securities required to achieve a certain level of dispersion. Diversification ceases to be meaningful for α peakedness equal to 1, as adding securities no longer reduces dispersion. In the extreme case, when α is less than 1, adding securities to a portfolio actually *increases* dispersion.[8]

Given the preceding discussion, the key question becomes: What is the α of a particular set of security returns? Early work by Fama (1965) indicated that the α parameter of large American companies ranges between 1.7 to 1.9—perhaps close enough to normal to make the concept of Markowitz diversification operational, if not theoretically airtight.

Campbell, Lo, and MacKinlay (1997) computed sample statistics for individual and aggregate stock returns over the period 1962–1994. While not specifically computing the stable Paretian parameters, they did compute excess kurtosis. For daily returns, they found statistically significant excess kurtosis for both stock indexes and individual stocks. While the monthly returns still exhibited excess kurtosis, they were not statistically significant in most cases.

Stoyanov et al. (2005) performed an extensive analysis of daily returns of stocks in the S&P 500 over a 12-year time period beginning in 1992. In addition to an unconditional model assuming independent and identically distributed (IID) returns, Stoyanov et al. modeled returns according to an autoregressive moving average-generalized autoregressive conditional heteroskedasticity (ARMA-GARCH) process, thus allowing for clustering of volatility of the returns. Although the ARMA-GARCH model produced more normally distributed returns, returns for both models were closer to a stable Paretian than normal distribution as measured by the Kolmogorov distance statistic. For the unconditional model, every stock in the sample had an α less than 2, with the majority falling between 1.5 and 2. The ARMA-GARCH formulation produced α parameters closer to 2, with most falling above 1.7. In both models, returns were almost universally positively skewed.

The research on the fat-tailed tendency of security returns is too vast to completely address here. Numerous studies have documented the aforementioned phenomenon; the incidents and applications are wide-ranging. The early work of Mandelbrot (1963) focused on commodity prices. Rachev, Schwartz, and Khindanova (2003) document fat-tailed returns for Treasury and corporate bonds, while Fabozzi, Racheva-Iotova, and Stoyanov (2005) examined fat-tailed returns and value at risk in the mortgage-backed securities market. Stable Paretian distributions also apply in researching option pricing. For example, McCulloch (1986), Carr and Wu (2003), and Hales (1997) found that a stable Paretian model better explains pricing of far out-of-the-money options in order to avoid the "volatility smile" anomaly.

Rietz (1988) and Barro (2005) present yet another interesting application of fat-tailed distributions in analyzing the equity risk premium puzzle. Historically, stocks yield a return too high compared to risk-free investments given standard financial theory. However, if catastrophic events (wars, depressions, etc.) occur with more frequency than predicted by the normal distribution, required returns on risky securities, such as equities, should reflect the possibility of catastrophe in their expected returns.

Despite the plethora of research indicating nonnormal security returns, researchers are not unanimous that the stable Paretian is the only distribution to model the fat tails. Cootner (1964) critiqued Mandelbrot's stable Paretian distribution security return evidence as too casual. More recently, Campbell, Lo, and MacKinlay (1997) criticized stable Paretian distributions use from both a theoretical and an empirical perspective. Much of the development of modern financial theory requires finite higher moments (or at least a finite second moment). As those moments are not defined for the stable Paretian distributions, developing financial theory from them could be extremely challenging. The second criticism relates to stock return empirical behavior that is inconsistent with stable Paretian theory of constant alpha peakedness and beta skewness over different time periods. For example, stable distribution theory predicts that short-term returns would be as nonnormal as long-term returns. Yet empirical work reveals that long-term returns may be less skewed and kurtotic than short-term returns.

Do alternatives to stable Paretian distributions exist to explain stock returns? The *t*-distribution, gamma distributions, and mixtures of normal distributions all present alternatives to the stable Paretian because they can contain more mass in the tails than the normal distribution. None of them, however, has the desirable mathematical property of stability. We therefore examined data using the stable Paretian distribution.

INTRINSIC VALUES AND DISTRIBUTIONS

Much of the research on distributions of returns has focused on indexes of assets or subsets of those indexes, such as the individual stocks of the S&P 500. Research to measure the benefit of stock selection in finding securities with less fat-tailed distributions has been virtually nonexistent, to our knowledge. If avoiding extreme events increases investor utility, then determining which stocks have less thickness in the tails of their return distributions should represent at least a side benefit, if not a primary objective, of security selection.

Historically, security analysts attempt to find stocks that are not properly valued by the market. Stocks that analysts deem to have a greater value than their market price are undervalued and are likely candidates for "buy" recommendations, whereas overvalued stocks would receive "sell" recommendations.

If analysts can accurately determine which stocks are under- and overvalued, then portfolios constructed with undervalued stocks should experience relatively higher returns. Intuitively, not only should undervalued stocks possess different average returns than overvalued stocks, but the *distributions* of their returns should differ as well. If an empirically validated process can detect undervalued securities, then the left tail of the return distribution may become thinner. A thinner left tail results, since the analyst naturally expects a reduction in the probability of an already undervalued stock dropping dramatically.

One key impediment to the distribution of under- and overvalued securities centers on the current labor-intensive process of security valuation. Security analysts most often perform valuation on a company-by-company basis for the current year. Assembling value estimates of a vast number of stocks becomes virtually impossible given the analyst's current suite of tools. One could use crude value measures—such as dividend yields and price-earnings ratios—but as Chen and Zhang (1998) observe, value measures may be more indicative of firms in financial distress than mispricing.

AUTOMATED VALUATION MODELS

To assist analysts in processing the values of thousands of securities, Life-Cycle Returns created unique automated valuation models. Model builders specify automated models a priori and, therefore, can provide empirical validation of the model. Numerous valuation methods appear in the literature for valuing securities. These models include dividend discount models (Rozeff 1990; Penman and Sougiannis 1998); free cash flow models (Francis, Olsson, and Oswald 2000); and earnings-based models (Sougiannis and Yaekura 2001). Most of the research utilizing automated models tends to focus on the model's accuracy. Very few analyze the distributions of returns from portfolios constructed from the automated models. *None*, to our knowledge, performs a stable Paretian analysis of the portfolio returns, except LifeCycle.

Discounted cash flow (DCF) concepts form the basis for LifeCycle's models. These models were based on a concept termed "cash economic return" formulated by LifeCycle to extend current constructs.[9] For the analyst, LifeCycle's system[10] of computing intrinsic values transforms accounting information into valuation. This transformation occurs through a series of empirically validated adjustments and discounted cash flow modeling. First, LifeCycle's system converts raw accounting data into a cash return by adjusting generally accepted accounting principles (GAAP) accounting. One adjustment adds back depreciation while another translates investment in assets into constant dollars. Second, the model converts the cash-on-cash return to an economically meaningful performance measure. This measure estimates the consolidated internal rate of return of all the current projects in which the firm invests.

Third, LifeCycle's system subsequently translates, for the analyst, the firm's real internal rate of return to a lifetime net cash flow stream by utilizing option pricing and regression toward the mean. In valuation terms, company returns fade as returns and growth rates trend toward a long-term average. Fourth, LifeCycle's system estimates the firm's intrinsic value by discounting the cash flow stream at a single, forward-looking "real market derived discount rate." This rate for valuing firms is analogous to the yield to maturity on bonds. Fifth, the automated LifeCycle system examines the intrinsic values for accuracy to provide feedback to the model for refinement. In-house research documents that the cash economic return model is superior to other tested models based on two core measurements. The two core measures relate to accuracy (how closely the intrinsic values approximate market prices) and robustness (the percentage of the stock universe for which the model can produce reasonable values).[11] A third core measure relates to unbiasedness (does the model produce intrinsic value estimates where 50 percent of the firms are undervalued and 50 percent are overvalued across all the model's drivers?).[12] The fourth core measure is predictive capability (can the model predict future returns as prices migrate toward intrinsic values?).

The "intrinsic values" of the securities represent the valuations produced by LifeCycle's models. LifeCycle hypothesizes that intrinsic values produced by a well-functioning model provide an anchor to which market prices migrate. We therefore assume that the market is not instantaneously efficient. Consequently, the market moves toward efficiency as prices that stray too far from their intrinsic values tend to move back over time toward those intrinsic values. Exactly how far is "too far," LifeCycle thinks, is an empirical question. A practical description of "too far" follows in the next section.

RESEARCH DESIGN AND EMPIRICAL RESULTS

To examine the normality of stock returns on the total industrial universe, LifeCycle's initial automated research computed annual returns on 5,500 industrial firms from 1994 to 2003.[13] The natural log of 1 plus the total shareholder return transforms the distribution of logged returns. Over this transformed return data, we superimposed both a normal and a stable distribution. The histogram data and distributions appear in Exhibit 22.1.

As demonstrated in the left chart, the normal distribution cannot account for the high peak or the thicker tails of the shareholder returns. In sharp contrast, the stable distribution demonstrates a very close fit, due to

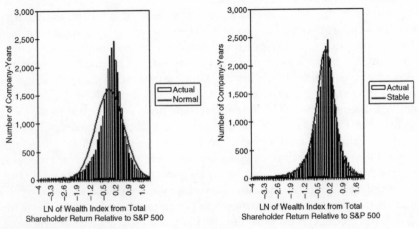

EXHIBIT 22.1 Distributions of Stock Returns

its peakedness and thicker tails. The exhibit also clearly illustrates where the mass that creates the peak and fatter tails arises. The normal distribution reveals a significant gap between the hypothetical distribution and the empirical distribution in the shoulder area, perhaps most significant around one standard deviation.

Based on the data, LifeCycle's system computed the statistics in Exhibit 22.2 for the four stable Paretian parameters. All four parameters confirm the nonnormality of the data. The peakedness of the data is readily obvious from the alpha parameter. The data is also negatively skewed and more dispersed than the normal distribution would imply. Statistically, each and every parameter is significantly different from the normal distribution parameters. These statistical results effectively refute Cootner's (1964) constructive criticism of Mandelbrot's research as "too casual."

The analysis confirms that the normality assumption is likely a flawed one for portfolio management. The analysis is not, however, normative. It only describes to security analysts and portfolio managers what the distribution *is*. It does not describe how they may apply these insights. LifeCycle's research recommends avenues in which both analysts and portfolio managers may avoid fat-tailed returns by more effective security selection.

Using Morningstar's raw data from 2002 to 2006, LifeCycle's system segregates stocks into under- and overvalued stocks via the proprietary Life-Cycle automated discounted cash flow models. In order to ensure that the models analyze *investable* securities, we apply a market capitalization filter to the universe. Selected stocks are greater than the 40th percentile of market capitalization, thereby avoiding thinly traded stocks and the associated liquidity issues.[14] Applying the market capitalization filter reduces the number of securities from the approximately 5,500 in the initial universe to approximately 3,300 firms.

EXHIBIT 22.2 Stable Paretian Parameters of Stock Returns

Results	Value	Standard Error	t-Statistic	
α (peakedness)	1.48	0.01	43.41	Difference from 2.00
β (skewness)	−0.31	0.02	−17.55	Difference from 0.00
"c" (dispersion)	0.39	0.01	50.60	Difference from 0.00
δ (location or average)	−0.16	0.02	−7.32	Difference from 0.00

Sources: 5,500 industrial firms, 1994–2003, total shareholder return (TSR) from FY +3 to +15 months relative to S&P 500, Hemscott Data, LCRT platform calculations; J. Huston McCulloch, "Simple Consistent Estimators of Stable Distribution Parameters," *Communications in Statistics—Simulation and Computation* 15, no. 4 (1986): 1109–1136.

Beyond the market capitalization filter, we chose several other criteria to avoid firms that either do not report clean accounting data or are financially distressed. The resulting filter includes firms with plant life between 4 and 50 years. The plant life filter eliminates firms with suspect fixed assets accounting data. We also eliminated firms with debt in excess of 85 percent of debt capacity.[15] Applying the Miller and Modigliani (1961) insight, Life-Cycle's system computes debt capacity as the "present value of estimated cash flows from existing assets."[16] This definition avoids using a flawed book value debt measurement. Firms that exceed the 85 percent debt filter are likely either start-up firms or those that have experienced recent large losses and are therefore not likely candidates for the typical investment manager's portfolio. Finally, to avoid liquidity and related excessive trading costs, the analysis includes only firms that have a share price greater than $5.

As with any valuation model, LifeCycle's System may not be able to value every firm in the universe. For instance, a Gordon dividend discount model could not value stocks that do not pay dividends. While the models are cash flow based and therefore able to value a substantial portion of the universe, LifeCycle's system utilizes a statistic termed tracking error. Low tracking errors ensure that the analysis employs the model for stocks likely to outperform the market. The tracking error statistic measures how closely the model's intrinsic values compare to actual market prices. LifeCycle's system computes a geometric average of 1 plus the absolute percentage differences between the intrinsic values and market prices. Specifically, Life-Cycle's system weights recent annual results more heavily than distant results with a sum-of-the-years digits method. The sample includes stocks with weighted average tracking errors of less than 45 percent. The aforementioned filters result in a final total sample size of between 500 and 1,000 securities.[17] This filtered universe is between 25 times and 50 times the 15 to 20 stocks currently evaluated by most individual security analysts. Therefore, automation could significantly facilitate analysts' efficiency and effectiveness.

Intrinsic values represent a model's estimate of the value of a security. However, concentrating solely on a point estimate of value could prove unwise. Examining a likely range of prices around intrinsic value as the anchor is much more beneficial. We utilize the behavioral finance technique known as "ranges of bounded rationality." These ranges provide reasonable estimates of where the price of a security could likely fall. Separately for each firm-year, LifeCycle's system applies the economic drivers that influence the dispersion of intrinsic values (size, economic returns, and trading volume) to provide a range of the estimates—a low end and a high end.[18] Consistent with the work of Thaler (1987) on loss aversion, LifeCycle's system uses the lower end of the range to estimate intrinsic values for portfolio construction purposes.

The LifeCycle system first computes intrinsic values. It then ranks the sampled stocks by the percent difference between the current price and the low end of the range of bounded rationality. The ranking assigns stocks to deciles in order to track the deciles' performance over the subsequent quarter. We rebalance at the beginning of each quarter based on the stocks' intrinsic value ranking. The LifeCycle ranking system contains a subtlety: The intrinsic values base themselves only on annual data[19] (after a three-month disclosure lag). Therefore, while this procedure rebalances quarterly, that rebalancing occurs due to price fluctuations rather than changes in intrinsic values. Later, we address this issue again in the analysis of panel data. After ranking the securities, we weight each decile portfolio by market capitalization, thus avoiding small stock bias. Finally, for simplicity, the analysis assumes no transaction or price impact costs.

Exhibit 22.3 represents the return performance of over- and undervalued portfolios. As the chart reveals, the most overvalued securities (on the left-hand side of the horizontal scale) produce a quarterly mean return of approximately −0.5 percent while the most undervalued yield a mean quarterly return of about 4.5 percent. Throughout the entire range of all valuations, returns positively correlate with the degree of undervaluation.

How do returns from the undervalued securities compare to their risk? We first answered that question by reviewing the traditional risk measure, standard deviation. Exhibit 22.4 summarizes the standard deviation of the

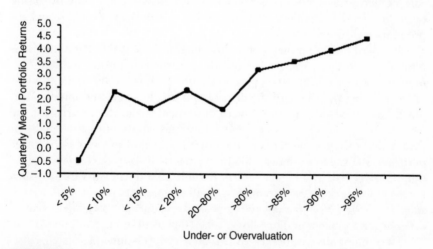

EXHIBIT 22.3 Returns of Overvalued and Undervalued Securities—Quarterly Rebalancing

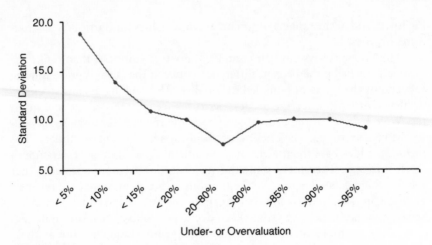

EXHIBIT 22.4 Standard Deviation of Returns of Overvalued and Undervalued Securities—Quarterly Rebalancing

decile portfolios as somewhat of a U shape. The overvalued stocks experience the highest standard deviation while the most undervalued stocks show a standard deviation slightly higher than those in the middle deciles. The results exhibit inconsistency with the higher risk and higher return story, as the portfolios with the poorest return performance display the highest standard deviations. The chart does suggest, however, that trying to earn higher returns from undervalued securities may come only by taking on additional risk, if indeed standard deviation represents a reliable and appropriate measure of risk.

Standard deviation may not be meaningful if the stable Paretian distribution is representative of the portfolio returns. Therefore, Exhibit 22.5 presents stable Paretian alpha parameters for each portfolio decile to assist in determining the shape of the distribution for the over- and undervalued portfolios. According to the (inverted) vertical scale, the returns for the most undervalued securities exhibit returns distributed more normally in their tails. If the thinner tails of the normal distributions represent lower portfolio risk, the most undervalued securities do display the ideal combination of lower risk and higher return. Exhibit 22.6 documents the statistics for the alpha peakedness parameters. Small sample sizes produce quite large standard errors. Nonetheless, two α peakedness parameters achieve significance at the 5 percent and one does at the 10 percent level.

Two major disadvantages to the quarterly rebalancing design exist. First, quarterly data may not produce enough data points to enable robust statistical testing. Second, the limitation of the quarterly analysis relates to

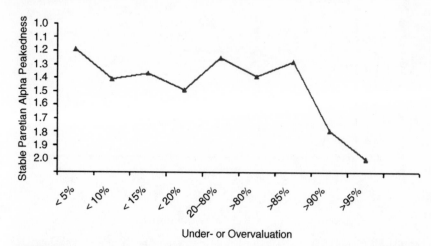

EXHIBIT 22.5 Alpha Peakedness Parameters of Overvalued and Undervalued Securities—Quarterly Rebalancing

LifeCycle models computing intrinsic values only annually. Thus, when LifeCycle's system rebalances, the adjustments relate solely to price changes as opposed to changes in intrinsic value.

To surmount these limitations, a second test creates a panel of data each year by ranking the securities based on their intrinsic values. The test then collects the data across all the years for every security to compute risk and return measures. Each security, therefore, represents one data point of over- or undervaluation to compare to the associated annual return.

EXHIBIT 22.6 Alpha Peakedness Parameters—Quarterly Rebalancing

	Most Overvalued Bottom 5%	Percentiles			20–80%	80%	85%	90%	Most Undervalued Top 5%
		10%	15%	20%					
Alpha peakedness	1.19	1.41	1.37	1.49	1.25	1.39	1.28	1.79	2.00
t-Statistic	<u>1.54</u>	1.23	1.05	0.86	<u>1.74</u>	<u>1.43</u>	<u>1.88</u>	0.29	0.00

Underlined t-statistics are significant at the 10% level.
Quarterly returns on portfolios 2002–2006; 4 < plant life < 50; debt/debt capacity < 85%; price > $5; tracking error < 45%; market capitalization weights > 40th percentile.
Source: Financial statement and price data from Morningstar; calculations from LifeCycle Returns.

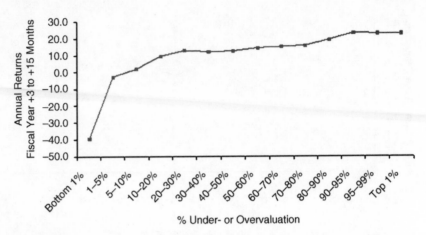

EXHIBIT 22.7 Returns of Overvalued and Undervalued Securities—Panel Data

Exhibit 22.7 presents returns for the panel data. Again, the model appears to be performing well, as returns rise monotonically from the overvalued to the undervalued securities. The extremely overvalued securities again perform very poorly over the period.

The question arises, once again, whether the returns correlate with risk as measured by a traditional metric such as standard deviation. As with quarterly rebalancing, standard deviation compared to over- and undervaluation follows an approximate U shape, with the highest standard deviations produced by the most over- and undervalued securities. These results appear in Exhibit 22.8.

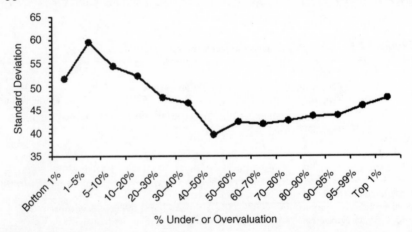

EXHIBIT 22.8 Standard Deviation of Returns of Overvalued and Undervalued Securities—Panel Data

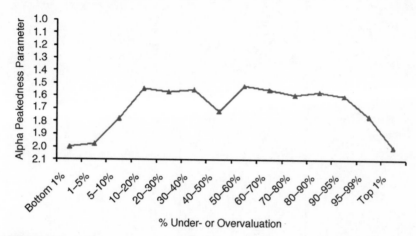

EXHIBIT 22.9 Alpha Peakedness Parameters of Overvalued and Undervalued Securities—Panel Data

In contrast to standard deviation, Exhibit 22.9 displays risk, as measured by the alpha peakedness parameter, as an inverted U when measured across over- and undervaluations. Consequently, the panel data confirm that managers may lessen exposure to extreme events by investing in securities that are extremely over- or undervalued—ironically, the very same securities that possess a very high standard deviation of returns. Therefore, according to the annual data, investment managers may experience higher returns and lower risk (as measured by the normality of the returns) by either going long in undervalued securities or shorting the most extremely overvalued securities.

Statistics for the panel data appear Exhibit 22.10. The t-statistics reveal that securities that are neither extremely overvalued nor undervalued have alpha parameters significantly different from 2. Therefore, the test cannot reject normality for securities that have an intrinsic value very different from market value. *However, extensive stable Paretian distribution analysis confirms that fairly valued securities may actually become more risky than extremely over- or undervalued ones.*

CONCLUSION

LifeCycle's linkage of automated DCF with the stable Paretian alpha peakedness parameter aligns the security selection process with portfolio construction. As extreme returns in the fat tails of distributions are

EXHIBIT 22.10 Alpha Peakedness Parameters—Panel Data

	Most Overvalued				Percentiles							Most Undervalued
	Bottom 1%	1–5%	5–10%	10–20%	20–30%	30–40%	40–50%	50–60%	60–70%	70–80%	80–90%	90–95%	95–99%	Top 1%
Alpha peakedness	2.00	1.98	1.78	1.54	1.57	1.55	1.72	1.52	1.55	1.59	1.57	1.60	1.76	2.00
t-statistic	0.00	0.09	1.17	**4.54**	**4.17**	**4.76**	**2.18**	**4.86**	**4.60**	**4.00**	**3.98**	**2.33**	1.13	0.00

Underlined bold t-statistics are significant at the 5% level.

Quarterly returns on portfolios 2002–2006; $4 <$ plant life < 50; debt/debt capacity $< 85\%$; price $> \$5$; tracking error $< 45\%$; market capitalization weights > 40th percentile.

Source: Financial statement and price data from Morningstar; calculations from LifeCycle Returns.

becoming an increasingly recognized significant risk, managers may try to find securities that produce returns that are more normally distributed while simultaneously attempting to enhance returns. This study's targeted results reveal that an automated discounted cash flow model may well produce the once elusive combination of higher returns and lower risk given that the alpha peakedness parameter evolves as an appropriate risk measure.

Clearly, the importance of the topic warrants additional research. Researchers can easily extend the time frame represented in this chapter to determine whether the results are consistent. A longer time frame would enable analysts to examine the data over subperiods to determine if possible shifts in the hypothesized distributions occur over time.

Another extension of this research would employ various valuation models to rank the securities. While the chapter presented results from the proprietary LifeCycle model, many valuation models appear in the finance and accounting literature. Academics could use these other models to test this chapter's conclusions. Practitioners may wish to employ their own proprietary models with the framework provided in this chapter.

Finally, researchers may need to develop additional risk measures. This chapter's analysis provided some introductory evidence by concentrating on the alpha peakedness parameter of stable Paretian distributions, but others may prove to be appropriate as well. Even for distributions where the variance is not defined, measures of skewness and dispersion exist. Consequently, those measures may provide valuable insight into how risk and return may be measured in a fat-tailed world.

APPENDIX A: SYNTHESIZING THE LIFECYCLE FRAMEWORK

Three chapters (5, 11, and 22) in this *Handbook* embody LifeCycle's valuation philosophy. They represent a unique, integrated examination of the security analysis and portfolio construction process to enhance client benefit, in contrast to current organization structures. LifeCycle's framework best utilizes the strengths of traditional security analysts' insights, the power of statistical testing, and the resulting implications for redefining portfolio construction risk.

A quick glance through Graham and Dodd's (1962) *Security Analysis* and Campbell, Lo, and MacKinlay's (1997) *Econometrics of Financial Markets* reveals the stark differences between traditional security analysis and analyses steeped in econometrics. The strength of traditional security analysis lies in its ability to analyze accounting data to examine the role of corporate decision making in shareholder value creation. The ability to subject large quantities of financial market data to rigorous statistical testing represents the forte of quantitative approaches. Unfortunately, within an organization, security analysts and econometricians may never totally integrate their separate skill sets, which results in a broken bridge that we term the silo effect.

The LifeCycle framework can synergistically bridge across silos. As described in Chapter 11, LifeCycle's system first translates accounting data to economic returns and then derives an intrinsic value through automated discounted cash flow models. While still producing *thousands* of intrinsic value estimates, star analysts with exceptional insights can significantly contribute to the process along three critical dimensions:

1. Produce more accurate decade-long intrinsic value baselines from which to forecast by:
   - Adding missing value-relevant data to the analysis.
   - Overriding plant lives and other variables from GAAP data that do not reflect the economics of the business.
   - Testing empirically analysts' terminal value assumptions with superior model structures. (See Chapter 5 for related measurements and methodologies.)
2. Enhance the automated models with their near-term forecasts based on the deep understanding necessary to accurately model industry competitive conditions.
3. Tackle the formidable task of valuing those firms most difficult to value, such as start-ups or companies in financial distress.

Due to the vast amount of data arising from the process, portfolio managers can now statistically construct portfolios with the best risk and return trade-offs.

Of course, risk will remain elusive to define comprehensively for every individual investor. Building on the pioneering work of Mandelbrot in the current chapter, LifeCycle links the security selection process and an innovative way to evaluate portfolio risk. Thus, we compiled in three chapters a process that transforms raw accounting data to eventually produce path-breaking portfolio risk measurement.

Periodically, "disruptive technologies" emerge which change the way firms within industries must compete. Christensen (1997) cites numerous examples, while documenting how large firms often miss disruptive technologies until too late to change. We consider the LifeCycle process disruptive because investment firms must bridge traditional silos to reexamine the interaction among security valuation, quantitative analysis, and portfolio construction. As the three chapters document, the resulting processes could then combine the greatest strengths of any investment organization to significantly increase customer security and benefit.

APPENDIX B: TECHNICAL NOTE—RANGES OF BOUNDED RATIONALITY

Intrinsic values represent an estimate of the true value of a security. As such, investors best think of them as a point in a range of reasonable estimates for the underlying value. LifeCycle derives this range by examining the dispersion of actual prices over a period and applying a dispersion adjustment to the intrinsic value. Academics call the dispersion around intrinsic valuations "the range of bounded rationality."

Two schools of thought impacted the concept of LifeCycle's ranges of bounded rationality. The first school relates to behavioral finance observations. These observations revealed that dispersions around reasonable estimates of intrinsic valuation were far too wide to support the concept of instantaneous, strong-form market efficiency. Consequently, the market overreacts. Price does not always equal intrinsic value. See Shiller (1981) for dispersion research on the U.S. market around dividend discount model estimates of intrinsic valuation. Also, see Smith (1986) for supporting evidence in a controlled economic laboratory of overreaction by individuals around a dividend discount model intrinsic value as the anchor.

The second school of thought relates to technical analysis, which tries to measure market sentiment or market overreaction of prices. For example, see Bollinger (2002). LifeCycle adapted these two concepts to create models of ranges of bounded rationality. Instead of employing Bollinger's ±1.5 standard errors around the 200-day moving average of stock prices, Life-Cycle developed a model of dispersion that relies on the fundamental economic drivers of size, cash economic return, and trading volume.

Exhibit 22B.1 illustrates the ranges of bounded rationality results with a value chart. The bars represent the fiscal year high/low prices. The dark line in the middle exhibits the intrinsic value. The white line on top and the gray line on the bottom display the high and low ranges of bounded rationality, respectively. The star in the current year represents the latest price. Since the star falls on the lower bound, the stock becomes undervalued. Consequently, the analyst should issue a buy recommendation.

To measure relative dispersion, LifeCycle's system first divides the fiscal year high price for the stock by the fiscal year high value for the S&P 500 to determine a relative high value for the stock. It also computes a relative low value for the stock by the same procedure. Second, LifeCycle's system calculates a geometric mean of the relative highs and lows. Third, taking the

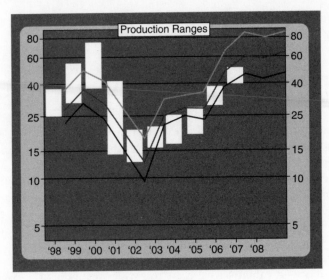

EXHIBIT 22B.1   Ranges of Bounded Rationality

relative high value for the stock divided by the geometric mean then becomes LifeCycle's measure of dispersion for the security. Fourth and last, LifeCycle utilizes that measure as a data point in determining the relationship between dispersion and fundamental drivers across all firms.

LifeCycle's empirical research documents that three fundamental drivers determine dispersions around stock prices: size, economic performance, and liquidity. To measure the underlying empirical relationship, LifeCycle regresses the dispersion measure against proprietary nonlinear functions of constant dollar gross investment (size), cash economic return (economic performance), and trading volume (liquidity). Directionally, all three variables should negatively correlate with dispersion. As firms grow larger, achieve higher economic performance, and trade more deeply, analysts and investors possess more certainty about where the true value of the security should lie.

LifeCycle's system then applies the mathematical relationship determined through the regression to the individual firm's dispersion by entering the fundamentals as independent variables. The result from the regression becomes the dispersion applied to that individual firm. Multiplying the measure of dispersion by the intrinsic value produces a high estimate of value, while dividing the intrinsic value by the dispersion measures produces the low-end estimate of intrinsic value.

LifeCycle documented that the low-end value predicts inflection points in security pricing far more effectively than the high-end value does.

LifeCycle's empirical research reveals that stocks that drift from their intrinsic values tend to bounce off the low-end value. From there, they migrate back toward the intrinsic value, thus providing a return to the theoretically undervalued investment. Prices also bounce off the high-end value as they become overvalued. We expected that the low-end value would become more predictive for buys, while the high-end value would become more predictive for sells. Counter intuitively, the empirical evidence did not support our expectations. In fact, the low-end was more predictive for both the buys *and the sells*. We interpret these empirical results to suggest that investors implicitly sort on the lower-end value to avoid risk (Thaler 1987), because their risk avoidance is asymmetrical. They strongly prefer to avoid losses than achieve gains of the same magnitude.

NOTES

1. Technically, this research employs panel data, which includes both cross-sectional and time series results. LifeCycle utilizes panel data in order to study the significance of effects at the extreme tails of the distributions where few data points exist in time series data.
2. For example, Fabozzi, Focardi, and Jonas (2008, 16) state, "If a modeler is successful in rendering errors truly Gaussian with small variance and also serially independent, the model should be safe." Although that monograph refers to Fama/French multifactor modelers, this chapter applies the same concept of normality to the riskiness of DCF models.
3. A complete description of developing an automated discounted cash flow model for security valuation appears in Chapter 5.
4. Markowitz (1959) extensively discusses other risk measures besides variance. These measures include semivariance, expected value of loss, expected absolute deviation, probability of loss, and maximum loss. Most academic development after Markowitz, however, focuses on mean variance.
5. *Satiation* means that an increase in wealth beyond some point will actually *decrease* utility. Increasing absolute risk aversion implies that risky assets are inferior goods. Theoreticians can assume the point of satiation occurs very far out, thus negating the satiation criticism. However, increasing absolute risk aversion remains a major impediment to using quadratic utility.
6. For an accessible but more complete explanation of stability, please see Rachev, Menn, and Fabozzi (2005).
7. The LifeCycle system does not rely on any mean-variance calculations in determining its intrinsic valuations. Consequently, the system remains consistent with the non-Gaussian methodology of this chapter.
8. If adding securities actually increases risk, it may be wise to follow Warren Buffett's philosophy of putting fewer eggs in your basket, but watching them very closely.

9. For a complete description of the LifeCycle Returns valuation system, see Chapter 11. Callard, Madden and Associates (CMA) first began computing economic performance measures in the 1960s. Calculating an IRR measure of gross cash flow against an inflation adjusted gross investment began with CMA's DCF ROI. HOLT Planning Associates used the term CFROI® to describe this concept in 1985. HOLT Value Associates registered the CFROI term. The Boston Consulting Group may also use the CFROI term. CMA spawned several offshoots. Applied Financial Group (AFG) utilizes a similar concept, calling it economic margin. LifeCycle's name for this concept is cash economic return. Callard, Madden later became Callard Research and then Ativo Research and CharterMast.

10. For an excellent discussion of applying a systems mind-set to the creation of valuation models, please see Bart Madden's Chapter 3, "Applying a Systems Mind-Set to Stock Valuation."

11. Since we are using a proprietary model, LifeCycle permits independent verification of our results by interested parties.

12. For a discussion of unbiasedness, see Atra and Thomas's Chapter 5, "Developing an Automated Discounted Cash Flow Model."

13. Technically, we computed our annual returns from month 3 through 15 in order to allow for a disclosure lag. While not all firms would fit into this window to account for the disclosure lag, our research indicates that it would accurately represent the lag for about 90 percent of firms.

14. Tiny start-up firms tend to possess alpha peakedness parameters close to 1.00 or even less than 1.00.

15. High-leverage firms tend to possess alpha peakedness parameters approaching 1.00 or even less than 1.00.

16. Page 345 states: " . . . the worth of an enterprise, as such, will depend only on: (a) the 'normal' rate of return he can earn by investing his capital in securities held by the firms; (b) the earning power of the physical assets current held by the firm; and (c) the opportunities, if any, that the firm offers for making additional investments in real assets what will yield more than the 'normal' (market) rate of return." Callard, Madden offshoots (see note 9) define (b) as the present value of cash flows from existing assets and (c) as the present value of future investments; (a) is the real investors' market derived discount rate. LifeCycle uses (b) as its measure of the firm's debt capacity.

17. LifeCycle's use of the tracking filter does not mean investment firms must ignore the portion of the universe eliminated by the filter. The filter only means that the *automated* valuation process is not valuing those firms accurately. In fact, security analysts, using firm-specific knowledge and insight, should focus their attention on the securities not covered by the automated model.

18. This chapter's Appendix B presents some of the technical details of computing these ranges of bounded rationality.

19. Some make the case that annual information contains more accurate audited data on cash flows than quarterly data, which may contain suspect accruals to match analysts' interim earnings per share (EPS) expectations and lacks the footnote data included in annual statements.

REFERENCES

Bachelier, Louis. 1900. Theorie de la speculation. Doctoral dissertation, Annales Scientifiques de l'Ecole Normale Superieure. Trans. Cootner, 1964.

Barro, Robert J. 2005. Rare events and the equity premium. Working paper, Harvard University.

Bollinger, John. 2002. *Bollinger on Bollinger bands.* New York: McGraw-Hill.

Campbell, J. Y., A. W. Lo, and A. C. MacKinlay, 1997. *The econometrics of financial markets.* Princeton, NJ: Princeton University Press.

Carr, P., and L. Wu. 2003. The finite moment log stable process and option pricing. *Journal of Finance* 58: 753–778.

Chen, Nai-fu, and Feng Zhang. 1998. Risk and return of value stocks.

Christensen, Clayton M. 1997. *The innovator's dilemma.* Boston: Harvard Business School Press; HarperBusiness, 2000; Harper Business Essentials, 2003; Collins Business Essentials, 2006.

Cootner, Paul,ed. 1964. *The random character of stock prices.* Cambridge, MA: MIT Press, 333.

De Grauwe, Paul, Leonardo Iania, and Pablo Rovira Kaltwasser. 2008. How abnormal was the stock market in October 2008? *Euro Intelligence.* www.eurointelligence.com/article.581+M5f21b8d26a3.0.html.

Fabozzi, Frank J., Sergio M. Focardi, and Caroline Jonas. 2008. *Challenges in quantitative equity management.* Charlottesville, VA: CFA Institute.

Fabozzi, Frank J., B. Racheva-Iotova, and S. Stoyanov. 2005. An empirical examination of the return distribution characteristics of agency mortgage pass through securities. Reported in Rachev, Menn, and Fabozzi (2005).

Fama, Eugene. 1965. Portfolio analysis in a stable Paretian market. *Management Science* 11: 404–419.

Francis, J., P. Olsson, and D. Oswald. 2000. Comparing the accuracy and explainability of dividend, free cash flow, and abnormal earnings equity value estimates. *Journal of Accounting Research* 38: 45–69.

Graham, Benjamin, David L. Dodd, Sidney Cottle, and Charles Tatham. 1962. *Security analysis: Principles and techniques.* New York: McGraw-Hill.

Hales, Stanley. 1997. Valuing foreign currency options with the Paretian stable option pricing model. Working paper, Price Waterhouse, LLP.

Huang, Chi-fu, and R. Litzenberger, 1988. *Foundations for financial economics.* Upper Saddle River, NJ: Prentice Hall.

Lintner, John. 1965. The valuation of risk assets and the selection of risky investments in stock portfolios and capital budgets. *Review of Economics and Statistics* 47: 13–37.

Mandelbrot, Benoit B. 1963. The variation of certain speculative prices. *Journal of Business* 36: 394–419.

Mandelbrot, Benoit B. 1997. Fractals and Sealing in Finance: Discontinuity, Concentration, Risk. New York: Springer.

Mandelbrot, Benoit B. and Richard L, Hudson. 2004. The (Mis)Behavior of Markets: A Fractal View of Risk, Ruin, and Reward. New York: Basic Books.

Markowitz, Harry. 1952. Portfolio selection. *Journal of Finance* 7: 77–91.

Markowitz, Harry. 1959. Portfolio selection: Efficient diversification of investments. The Cowles Foundation, Utility Functions and Measures of Risk, pp. 286–297.

McCulloch, J. Huston. 1986. Simple consistent estimators of stable distribution parameters. *Communications in Statistics—Simulation and Computation* 15(4): 1109–1136.

Miller, Merton H., and Franco Modigliani. 1961. Dividend policy, growth, and the valuation of shares. *Journal of Business* 34, no. 4 (October): 411–433. Reprinted in Stephen H. Archer and Charles A. D'Ambrosio, *The Theory of Business Finance: A Book of Readings* (New York: Macmillan, 1967).

Mossin, Jan. 1966. Equilibrium in a capital asset market. *Econometrica* 35: 768–783.

Penman, S., and T. Sougiannis. 1998. A comparison of dividend, cash flow, and earnings approaches to equity valuation. *Contemporary Accounting Research* 15: 343–383.

Rachev, Svetlozar T., Christian Menn, and Frank J. Fabozzi. 2005. *Fat-tailed and skewed asset return distributions: Implications for risk management, portfolio selection and option pricing.* Hoboken, NJ: John Wiley & Sons.

Rachev, Svetlozar, T. E. Schwartz, and I. Khindanove. 2003. Stable modeling of credit risk. In *Handbook of Heavy Tailed Distributions in Finance*, ed. S. Rachev, 249–328. Amsterdam: North Holland. Reported in Rachev, Menn, and Fabozzi (2005).

Rietz, T. A. 1988. The equity risk premium: A solution. *Journal of Monetary Economics* 23: 117–131.

Roll, Richard. 1989. The international crash of October 1987. In *Black Monday and the Future of Financial Markets*, ed. Kamphuis, Kormendi, and Watson, 35–70. Chicago: MAI.

Rozeff, Michael. 1990. The three-phase dividend discount model and the ROPE model. *Journal of Portfolio Management* (Winter): 36–42.

Sharpe, William. 1964. Capital asset prices: A theory of capital market equilibrium under conditions of risk. *Journal of Finance* 19: 425–442.

Shiller, Robert J. 1981. Do stock prices move too much to be justified by subsequent changes in dividends. *American Economic Review* 71, no. 3 (June): 421–436.

Smith, Vernon, 1986. Experimental methods in the political economy of exchange. *Science* 234, no. 10 (October): 167–173.

Sougiannis, T., and T. Yaekura. 2001. The accuracy and bias of equity values inferred from analysts' earnings forecasts. *Journal of Accounting, Auditing, and Finance* 16: 331–362.

Stoyanov, S., S. Rachev, A. Biglova, and F. Fabozzi. 2005. An empirical examination of daily stock return distributions for U.S. stocks. Data Analysis and Decision Support, Springer Series in Studies in Classification, Data Analysis, and Knowledge Organization. Reported in Rachev, Menn, and Fabozzi (2005).

Thaler, Richard. 1987. The psychology of choice and the assumptions of economics. In *Laboratory Experimentation in Economics: Six Points of View*, ed. Alvin E. Roth, 99–130. New York: Cambridge University Press.

CHAPTER 23

Common Themes and Differences

Debates and Associated Issues
Facing the Profession

Rawley Thomas
President, LifeCycle Returns, Inc.

he Preface suggested that valuations are important simply because they form the basis for making decisions involving significant amounts of money or wealth transferred from one party to another.

The following partial list covers many decision applications for valuation. Valuations are normally done to:

- Buy or sell publicly held stock.
- Buy or sell a privately held business.
- Determine how much estate tax is owed the government.
- Settle a divorce.
- Resolve a dispute with a minority shareholder who wants to receive full value for his or her stock.
- Give a value basis to accounting auditors.
- Determine the compensation amount for executives, division or business unit managers, or employee-owners.
- Determine to proceed (or not) with strategic initiatives and/or major investment opportunities.
- Offer fairness opinions in the purchase or sale of companies.

The Valuation Handbook has provided the unique perspectives from many of today's top practitioners. Some authors covered labor-intensive techniques, in which expert analyst judgment is paramount. Other authors proposed expert or automated systems with minimal analyst judgment. Some described the valuation of publicly held firms. Others displayed techniques utilized on privately held firms to satisfy compliance standards of law and legal precedents. Clearly, the techniques to be used rely on the decisions to be made. The reader now has in one location a compendium from some of the best minds in the world.

With the 2007–2008 market meltdowns, the profession has begun a most healthy debate on the theories, assumptions, and associated practices in valuation. Intrinsic valuations work best when liquid markets are trading. Without liquid markets, no standard of prices exists against which to compare intrinsic valuations. When markets freeze or function much less perfectly, what are decision makers to do? To what extent should intrinsic valuations substitute for prices in frozen or illiquid markets? In addition, how may insights from all the various theories and associated techniques be merged into better ones?

Exhibit 23.1 compares dimensions of efficient markets with inefficient markets. Any effort to establish a comparison like this is destined to be

Exhibit 23.1 Comparison of Efficient and Inefficient Markets

	Efficient Markets	Inefficient Markets
Theories	CAPM, modern portfolio theory	Behavioral finance, discounted cash flow (DCF)
Distributions	Gaussian normal	Fat-tailed: stable Paretian and others
Key contributors	Markowitz, Sharpe, Fama, French, Grinold, Kahn	Graham and Dodd, Mandelbrot, Shiller, Smith, McCulloch, Nolan, Copeland, Stern Stewart, Callard Madden offshoots
Philosophy of knowing (Madden's Chapter 3—first three pages)	Deductive: Theory $\Rightarrow$ empirical testing	Inductive: Data (observations) $\Rightarrow$ patterns $\Rightarrow$ economic theories $\Rightarrow$ anomalies from observations $\Rightarrow$ modified theory
Results—key beliefs	Markets are strong-form, instantaneously efficient, reflecting all current information; no excess returns after	Markets are efficient within ranges of bounded rationality; sometimes markets fail to function due to illiquidity or uncertainty;

Exhibit 23.1 (*Continued*)

	Efficient Markets	Inefficient Markets
	price impact costs can be achieved	excess returns (alpha) can be achieved with information advantages or better modeling
Primary assumptions deserving debate	Homogeneous investors; homogeneous expectations; costless or very low-cost information; rational investors; adaptive learning	Heterogeneous investors and expectations; information and model development costly; investors possess irrational biases, don't always learn from their mistakes
Primary quantitative methods	Price change regressions against factors (may produce excess return from information advantage)	Price levels from DCF or regressions from economic drivers
Risk implications	Higher returns require more risk taking	Lower risk and higher returns may not be mutually exclusive
Corporate finance costs of capital	Based on beta and price variability	Based on fundamental economic drivers like financial leverage *or* uniform discount rate, with risks placed in certainty-equivalent cash flows
Portfolio construction implications	Indexation based on market cap: no benefit to stock selection	Fundamental (size) indexation *or* intrinsic value weights
Existence of intrinsic values	Prices are close to intrinsic values	Prices may differ substantially from intrinsic values; intrinsic values exist; excess returns can be obtained
Implications of beliefs about intrinsic values to disclosure	Mark to market	Mark to model
Traditional dichotomy (Fabozzi et al., *Challenges in Quantitative Equity Management*)	Quant models on price change	Labor-intensive security analysis on price level

(*Continued*)

Exhibit 23.1 (*Continued*)

	Efficient Markets	Inefficient Markets
Alternatives arising from dichotomy	DCF intrinsic value added as addition factor	Security analysts use automated DCF model structures for their terminal valuations
Speculation on evolution	Probabilistic price formation models based on intrinsic valuation as the core, with ranges of bounded rationality, price momentum, EPS surprises of market overreaction, and other information effects modeled with Mandelbrot-type fractional Brownian motion generating functions with memory	

controversial, so I beg forgiveness in advance. This table represents only my perception of the many dimensions of two competing theories of finance and investments. The demarcation between the two columns is far from crisp. For example, some who believe in a degree of market inefficiency also employ capital asset pricing model (CAPM) costs of capital, originally arising from the efficient markets literature. I hope this table will encourage additional productive debate within the profession.

Fabozzi, Focardi, and Jonas (2008) wrote an outstanding research piece for the CFA Institute on current issues facing the profession. Many of the quant models ("children of Fama/French," page vii) failed during the freeze-up of markets during 2007–2008 as quants headed for the exits all at once with very similar models, causing a reassessment of investment processes. One result from their extensive survey research was the conclusion that many investment organizations were seeking better ways to combine traditional fundamental security analysis with quantitative approaches. Linking their research with this *Valuation Handbook* resulted in my assessment summary in Exhibit 23.1.

For the other side of the debate of efficient versus inefficient markets, please see Fama (2009). Fama is very eloquent in how he articulates the case for efficient markets.

In the last row of Exhibit 23.1, I speculate that the profession may combine insights from both schools of thought in order to relax the assumption of Brownian motion and independent draws from distributions in order to create price formation models. These price formation models may incorporate Mandelbrot's research of fractional Brownian motion (Mandelbrot (2002) with memory, linked to DCF with ranges of bounded rationality around intrinsic value as the anchor and insights from multi-factor research of short term price effects (EPS surprises, etc.). Stay tuned.

Using the valuation perspectives from *The Valuation Handbook*, the next four sections outline several debates facing the profession. Certainly, other debates exist.

1. Does intrinsic value have any meaning?
2. "Mark to market" versus "mark to model."
3. Illiquidity crises and market meltdowns: effect on quantitative strategies.
4. Residual income versus cash flow return on investment models.

DOES INTRINSIC VALUE HAVE ANY MEANING?

Some say, "No one knows what the intrinsic value is, anyway." I suspect that the authors in this *Valuation Handbook*, who have spent their professional careers on the subject of valuation, would strongly disagree. As with any effective debate, trying to identify the underlying assumption (expressed, implied, or unstated) proves useful to understanding the beliefs of the participants. Why do valuation experts say that intrinsic value can be estimated with the techniques illustrated in this book? Why do some industry experts say that intrinsic value has no meaning? While I cannot definitively answer the questions, I can offer some possible reasons for this very fundamental disagreement.

From the mutual fund and other academic empirical evidence, let's say that I believe in perfectly instantaneously efficient markets. Almost by definition in this world of perfect market efficiency, price always precisely equals the intrinsic value derived from all information available to the market. As outlined in Exhibit 23.1, I may assume that the market consists of homogeneous investors with homogeneous expectations, who rapidly learn from their mistakes. Consequently, I may logically conclude that price always equals the intrinsic valuation of all the participants in the market. If price changes, that change represents the change in intrinsic valuation derived from those participants.

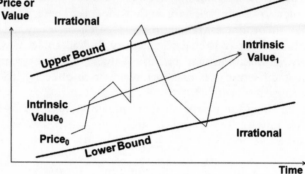

EXHIBIT 23.2 Prices Seldom Equal Intrinsic Valuations

While in this mode of thought, I know that small changes in assumptions cause large changes in intrinsic valuations. The sensitivity of intrinsic valuations to changes in assumptions provides another rationale for changes in prices. Price always equals the intrinsic value estimates of the market participants.

Switching modes, let's say that I now no longer believe in strong-form, perfectly efficient markets. I assume that investors with different intrinsic valuation models exist. I further assume that some market participants are not intrinsic value investors. They are traders who only use prices in their decision processes. If enough traders exist, deviation of price from intrinsic valuation becomes possible. Recall that developing intrinsic value models and applying those to specific companies require very significant time and cost on a continuing basis. Analyzing patterns from readily available prices becomes much less time-consuming with lower cost. Behavioral finance people and others call these people momentum traders, noise traders, technical traders, and other characterizations to distinguish these market participants from investors who rely on intrinsic valuations for their decisions.

Exhibit 23.2 illustrates the thought process and assumptions for investors who believe in the usefulness of intrinsic valuations. Prices seldom precisely equal intrinsic valuations. Sometimes they are higher. Sometimes they are lower. A strong but not perfect tendency exists for prices to migrate toward intrinsic value over time. However, since this is a probabilistic process, the migration path is not a perfectly straight line. The market price can overreact *away* from intrinsic value for significant periods of time, as illustrated in Exhibit 23.2.

Just to add richness to the process as illustrated in this *Valuation Handbook*, intrinsic valuations can be calculated purely from historical data or calculated from a cash flow forecast and a terminal value. They can be automated or hand calculated through a labor-intensive security analysis process one company at a time for the current year. I think that how one combines automated or expert-system DCF with analysts' input from history and forecast insights becomes a most critical aspect of the stock selection process. This probabilistic process flows from relaxing the assumptions of homogeneous investors and homogeneous expectations.

Exhibit 23.2 adds another behavioral finance/technical/sentiment dimension to the debate: upper and lower bounds of rationality. These bounds measure market overreaction. Models of these bounds of rationality may derive from standard errors around moving price averages or fundamental dispersion models around intrinsic valuations as the anchors (see Appendix B in Chapter 22). Since I assume markets are not perfectly efficient, prices can exceed the bounds periodically.

Which set of assumptions do you believe? What thought mode are you in? Logically, if you believe in highly efficient markets, you may decide to invest in passive index funds to avoid management fees and price impact costs. If you believe in inefficient markets, you may take a more active approach to your investment strategy. I recommend that you examine your beliefs, your assumptions, and the empirical evidence to decide your stock selection strategy—passive or active. This *Valuation Handbook* provides additional information for your assessment and decisions.

METHODOLOGIES: MARK TO MARKET, MARK TO MODEL

What methodologies apply? Randall Schostag's Chapter 15, "Portfolio Valuation: Challenges and Opportunities Using Automation," provides an extensive history of the field. Generally, the courts accept three methodologies:

1. Market price.
2. Comparables.
3. Earnings or discounted cash flow approach.

With current meltdowns and freeze-ups of several markets, the profession is exploring and debating new approaches. How can anyone establish a value if no one is trading the security? Or some trading is occurring, but not enough to provide confidence that the trades are representative of the true underlying intrinsic valuation. Or the trades occurred several days, weeks, or months ago.

"Mark to market" seems deceptively simple. However, I suggest that mark to market may rely on two assumptions—often unstated or implicit:

1. The market is perfectly, instantaneously, strong-form efficient at each moment in time.
2. The market can absorb any amount of volume on either the buy side or the sell side without changing the price.

Suppose we relax both these assumptions. Under these relaxed conditions, price does not equal intrinsic value at all times. Sometimes it is higher. Sometimes it is lower. And trading from noise traders can push the price further away from intrinsic value—at least temporarily.

Several theoretical reasons exist for prices to diverge from intrinsic values. We need to relax the assumption that the market consists of homogeneous investors. In addition to fundamental investors who rely on estimating intrinsic valuations from financial statements, other investor types exist. Momentum traders follow the trend in market prices, with no study of the fundamentals. Noise traders may employ concepts like Bollinger bands to determine likely inflection points in prices, again with no reference to financial statements. Vultures purchase stock from those needing immediate liquidity. Overlaps among investor types clearly exist. However, if every investor used the identical intrinsic valuation model and traded on only that information, *no trading would occur*. The fact that trading does occur and that ranges of bounded rationality around reasonable estimates of intrinsic valuations place limits on prices does suggest that various classes of market participants are active in the market.

With price no longer representing intrinsic value during every moment in time, our concrete foundation of efficient markets and the superiority of price as the primary determinant of intrinsic valuation cracks. Not using price exclusively creates a huge problem in valuation, because we have lost our anchor. We need to find a replacement.

For example, within the financial sector, many banks don't want mark to market, because the lower valuations of actual trades may wipe out their equity to make them insolvent. These banks argue, "Just wait a while; the market will come back. These nontraded securities are worth much more than stale market prices. *Their intrinsic valuations are much higher than their traded prices.*"

No one wants to see markets continue their freeze up, causing immense economic hardship throughout the world. To stimulate debate, permit me to offer one solution of many possible ones, arising from FMA PDDARI discussions at the CFA Society of Chicago. (See Appendix A of this chapter for a description of FMA PDDARI.)

- Disclose *both* mark to market and mark to model (DCF) so investors have the information they need for decisions.
- Solvency tests continue to rely on mark to market, *but*:
- While the markets continue to malfunction, regulators forbear some insolvent banks, depending on the degree of insolvency.

Consequently, this proposal suggests that GAAP still forces mark to market, but mark to model may be footnoted. (Disclosure could function the other way around: mark to model occurs on the financial statements, while mark to market occurs in a footnote.) During periods of extreme market distress, regulators may employ the footnote information on mark to model instead of the market information for regulatory compliance of equity capital requirements. By demanding empirical evidence to support the models consistent with measurements proposed in this *Valuation Handbook*, regulators may increase their confidence in the validity of mark to model for compliance purposes.

ILLIQUIDITY CRISES AND MARKET MELTDOWNS: EFFECT ON QUANTITATIVE STRATEGIES

After the 2007 meltdown, Fabozzi, Focardi, and Jonas (2008) extensively surveyed the profession to unearth how portfolio managers were reacting to the market freeze-ups and illiquidities, primarily during August 2007 when the "quants rushed for the exit to sell with largely similar models." In general, the "children of Fama/French" were attempting to identify the best ways to overlay traditional, labor-intensive DCF security analyst valuations over their multifactor models of price *change*. In contrast, no mention was made of the expert/automated approaches to DCF prevalent in this *Valuation Handbook*. Combining insights from the Fabozzi et al. research with this book raises some interesting and potentially useful possibilities. In my view, the two core questions are:

1. Should security analysts and portfolio managers start with discounted cash flow and then overlay multifactor quantitative strategies? *or*
2. Should they start with multifactor quantitative strategies and add intrinsic valuation as *one* additional factor?

With these questions, I am suggesting that DCF form the core of valuations. After all, DCF represents not just another factor, but a true long-term estimate of value—especially when markets fail to trade or are illiquid in the short term. However, reduced-form traditional Fama/French correlations of the factors driving price change may supplement the understanding of the price formation process through time.

What measurement criteria should researchers employ to measure the empirical results to these two alternative approaches? Chapter 4 (Tom Copeland: "Comparing Valuation Models"), Chapter 5 (Atra/Thomas: "Developing an Automated Discounted Cash Flow Model), and Chapter 22 (Thomas/Yang/Atra: "Lower Risk and Higher Returns: Linking Stable Paretian Distributions and Discounted Cash Flow") offer measurement methodologies to address the two core questions. These measurement criteria include robustness, accuracy, unbiasedness, predictive capability, and risk. Empirical results from Chapter 22 suggest that more accurate unbiased valuation models are more predictive, with lower risk at the tails.

Related to these two core questions is the debate between Fama and Mandelbrot—two giants in the field of finance and investments. Do returns follow lognormal distributions or stable Paretian ones? What are the best measures of risk? And, since this is *The Valuation Handbook*, how best to combine discounted cash flow valuation methodologies with the Fama/French/Grinold/Kahn multifactor approach or the Mandelbrot approach?

My own admittedly biased view is that DCF should form the core, while the multifactor approach should help model the price formation process around the core. Additionally, stable Paretian generating functions with memory should relax the traditional independent and identically distributed (IID) random draw assumptions found in traditional modeling. However, let the debates rage on.

DISCOUNTED CASH FLOW METHODOLOGIES

Once we agree that discounted cash flow should be an integral part of any investment process, the question arises: how? Traditionally, discounted cash flow has been a largely manual process to value one firm at a time for the current period. However, Chapters 3 to 5, 8, 11, 12, and 15 raise the potential of expert systems or automated approaches. Should the profession employ:

- The traditional largely manual process
- The automated approach?
- Some combination of both—if so, how?

Again, my admittedly biased view is to combine the best of both, as outlined in Chapter 22. However, these are central issues to the theory and practice of finance and investments. Consequently, they deserve much debate and empirically validating research.

Which discounted cash flow approach should analysts utilize? Two major schools of thought for valuation exist:

1. The residual income school.
2. The cash return school.

The Valuation Handbook covers both schools in much detail from the different perspectives of top practitioners. Both schools think that achieving returns above the cost of capital forms the most important strategic core of finance and investment. Meeting analysts' EPS expectations for the current quarter and Fama/French multifactor models fail to fulfill this most important strategic core. Exhibit 23.3 compares the residual income and cash return schools of thought. A review of the table reveals three primary differences:

Exhibit 23.3 Residual Income and Cash Return Schools of Thought

Similarities	Residual Income	Cash Return
Return on investment	More important to long-term shareholder wealth creation than quarterly EPS relative to market expectations	Same
Operating income	Exclude nonoperating income/expense	Same
Operating assets minus nondebt liabilities	Exclude nonoperating assets/nondebt liabilities	Same
Return on investment less cost of capital	Core operating metric	Same
Capitalize expenses with economic lives longer than one year (e.g., R&D, advertising, training, software, etc.)	Important to calculate returns comparable to cost of capital	Same
Capitalize operating leases	Yes	Yes

(Continued)

Exhibit 23.3   (*Continued*)

Differences	Residual Income	Cash Return
Treatment of depreciation, amortization, and accumulated depreciation	Subtracted to determine net operating income	Added back to after-tax operating income to produce gross cash flow
Treatment of inflation	Employs GAAP historical cost	Inflation adjusts gross plant with GDP deflator
Goodwill intangibles	Included in asset base	Some include in asset base; others exclude
Return measure	Net operating profit/net operating assets	IRR of gross cash flow over current dollar gross investment or gross cash flow – sinking fund depreciation/gross investment
Implicit assumption to make return measure comparable to cost of capital	Output declines with increase in accumulated depreciation	Output is constant over economic life of assets (one-horse shay)
Correction to make above assumption more realistic	Subtract economic depreciation instead of GAAP depreciation so RONA = IRR return on investment	Proprietary function to increase/decrease intrinsic value for asset life effects
Cost of capital or real investor discount rate	CAPM nominal weighted average cost of capital	Market derived discount rate using the valuation model to establish the rate that equates the present value of cash flows less debt to market value of equity; some adjust discount rate for leverage and size effects (CSFB HOLT, etc.); LCRT adjusts certainty equivalent cash flows in intrinsic value for size and leverage effects

Exhibit 23.3 (*Continued*)

Differences	Residual Income	Cash Return
Excess returns	Continue for T time period	Exponentially competed away
Valuation of start-ups	Requires analyst cash flow forecast	Same or option pricing function on gross capital and likely returns
Thought leaders	Tom Copeland, Joel Stern, Bennett Stewart, Jim Grant, Roy Johnson	Bart Madden, Chuck Callard, Rawley Thomas, Ricardo Bekin, Dennis Aust, Rafe Resendes, Dan O'Brycki

1. Residual income employs operating net income and operating investment net of accumulated depreciation. The cash return school uses gross cash flow and gross investment, by adding back depreciation and amortization and accumulated depreciation, respectively.
2. Residual income bases itself on historical cost, whereas cash return adjusts the data for inflation.
3. Residual income generally employs CAPM costs of capital, whereas cash return utilizes market derived discount rates.

Based on the chapters in this *Valuation Handbook*, the reader may decide which approach to follow.

Thank you for choosing *The Valuation Handbook*. We anticipate many views on what constitutes accurate valuations, and hope that our efforts produce more informed, in-depth discussions that result in more accurate decisions.

While discounted cash flow predates modern portfolio theory (MPT), MPT provided considerable insight into risk measurement and diversified portfolio construction. However, by focusing on price change, MPT strayed from the fundamental DCF roots of price level in finance. The *Valuation Handbook* authors suggest ways to integrate the fundamental soundness of DCF with evolving innovative thinking of twenty-first-century global finance. We intend that the integration promises to expand theory and modeling into a much more robust price formation process, using state-of-the-art methodologies and applications for decisions.

Based on studying *The Valuation Handbook*, what investment strategy do you choose—passive or active? To continue the dialogue, contact Rawley@LCRT.com.

APPENDIX A: FINANCIAL MANAGEMENT ASSOCIATION PRACTITIONER DEMAND DRIVEN ACADEMIC RESEARCH INITIATIVE (FMA PDDARI)

Because collaboration and effective communication have become critical to creativity in the information age, several paths exist for practitioners and researchers to join to improve practice, research, and teaching. These include facilitating communications among those who teach, who perform research, and who are in the finance business:

- Residence programs.
- Investment firms that hire academics.
- Conferences that mix academic and practitioner speakers.
- Special sessions at the Financial Management Association annual meetings that mix speakers.
- Firms that hire academics as consultants.

A recent effort that shows promise is the Financial Management Association Practitioner Demand Driven Academic Research Initiative (FMA PDDARI).

The PDDARI Platform

PDDARI facilitates a unique format for dialogue between academics and practitioners to debate pivotal finance challenges *articulated from practitioners' perspectives*. PDDARI engages "thought partners" in interactive discussions that seek genuinely new, even breakthrough ideas. Examples of the types of challenges that can be addressed include:

- A better theory than the capital asset pricing model for dealing with levels and changes in stock prices plus the associated measurement of risk.
- Improved valuation and communication tools to help management undertaking wealth-creating investments that may depress short-term quarterly earnings.
- Ideas for improving or replacing conventional discounted cash flow methodology derived from empirical findings in behavioral finance and advanced quantitative tools used by leading-edge quant portfolio managers.

An all-encompassing theme of PDDARI is to create avenues for practitioners to share with academic partners as well as fellow practitioners, the types of real-life problems encountered when making or implementing decisions. In other words, PDDARI strives to create a climate in which practitioners and academics can collaboratively address the current challenges in the field. The current and conventional practice reflects practitioners and academics functioning independently to address practical decision applications from their unique, individual perspectives. While the conventional practice produces results, it represents a silo: an isolated and uncoordinated system to understand and offer resolutions to practical day-to-day financial issues.

The immediate benefits of PDDARI provide a platform to increase planned, effective communication between practitioners and academics. It offers a centralized marketplace in which practitioners and academics may interact equally under established guidelines of full disclosure of commercial interests. Academics can discover which issues practitioners feel are central and can express their thoughts and knowledge in a proactive, efficient manner. Ultimately, PDDARI fervently desires that academics collaborate closely with practitioner thought partners on application topics to direct documented research in order to more effectively facilitate global practice.

In addition, PPDARI's long-term benefits offer:

- Thought partners to collaborate with academics on real-life practical problems.

    Strong incentives exist for practitioners to interchange with academics. Many practitioner thought partners perform advanced research themselves. Therefore, they are current on academic literature as well as practitioner research. Consequently, practitioners remain keenly aware of both theoretical and empirical issues involved in great research.

- Opportunities to engage practitioners and academics.

    The PDDARI has organized forums on the PDDARI web site (www .fma.org/PDDARI/PDDARI.htm), face-to-face meetings, and special sessions at the FMA annual meeting. PDDARI's coordinated effort provides for an interchange that is both planned and multifaceted. In addition, PDDARI plans to meet the needs of a continually evolving profession in the twenty-first century.

- Access to databases.

    Many practitioners may be willing to contribute access to proprietary databases to assist academics with relevant research projects, because meeting these challenges is most important to them.

- Publishing opportunities.

Because it addresses important issues in financial practice, PDDARI-initiated research should be attractive to leading research outlets. PDDARI's collaborative and respectful problem-solving climate also has the potential to change financial practice in meaningful and beneficial ways.

One example of how FMA PDDARI seems to be succeeding in bringing academics and practitioners together is the PDDARI working group supported jointly by FMA and the CFA Society of Chicago. This working group meets the third Thursday of each month to keep joint practitioner/academic research on track to solve problems relevant to the profession. Groups in other cities are in the formative stages.

Appendix B represents another FMA PDDARI example of a collaborative industry effort. It offers a list of the assumptions and theories deserving debate and empirical quantification. The new information age demands critical thinking to question these assumptions and theories in order to find creative solutions to the problems plaguing the profession.

In the new information age, students need to apply critical thinking to even the most classic articles. Often assumptions are *unstated or implicit*, instead of explicit. For instance, the articles by Nobel Prize-winning Miller and Modigliani assumed earnings are a good enough proxy for cash flow, without discussing the implicit assumption that capex equals historical dollar depreciation. Statisticians *assume, often implicitly*, that the upper moments of independent variables exist, so the central limit theorem applies. If Mandelbrot is correct that the upper moments do *not* exist, what should practitioners use instead?

Identifying the explicit assumptions and the implicit unstated assumptions in each of the chapters of this *Valuation Handbook* might prove to be a very useful exercise for students.

APPENDIX B: EXAMPLES OF ASSUMPTIONS AND THEORIES DESERVING DEBATE AND EMPIRICAL QUANTIFICATION

PDDARI seeks to bridge gaps in understanding by adopting two working assumptions to confirm mutual respect between the academic and practitioner silos:

1. Many practitioners perform theoretically sound and empirically valid research.

2. Many academics would like to publish research of value to practitioners that also meets accepted standards of scientific research.

Categories of Assumptions

There are six categories of assumptions:

1. Valuation (based on price *level*).
   - Miller, Modigliani.
2. Risk, risk measurement.
3. Utility theory.
4. Asset pricing (based on price *change*, such as CAPM).
5. Market efficiency and barriers to arbitrage.
6. International.

Examples of Assumptions and Theories

PDDARI applauds the relaxation of these assumptions and the challenge or the empirical validation of these theories.

1. Valuation (based on price *level*):
   a. Modeling accounting earnings without explicitly modeling the components of free cash flow creates adequate equity valuation models.
   b. Balance sheet items are irrelevant to valuation.
   c. Terminal value perpetuities provide accurate valuations.
   d. Output from assets declines proportionally to the increase in accumulated depreciation.
   e. Zero income and capital gains taxes exist for corporations and individuals.
   f. Zero estate taxes exist for individuals.
   g. The appropriate way to model risk is in the discount rate.
   h. The appropriate way to model risk is in the cash flows.
   i. Analysts' estimates lead intrinsic value and price changes.
   j. Business owners require a return on their equity investment.
   k. Market values are invariant to excess cash.
      - Miller, Modigliani:
        i. Market values are invariant to capital structure.
        ii. Market values are invariant to dividend policy.
2. Risk, risk measurement:
   a. Price changes follow a lognormal distribution.

     b. Upper moments in distributions exist.

     c. The mean in distributions exists.

     d. Distributions are symmetrical.

     e. Draws from distributions are independent from prior draws.

     f. The error terms in regression models follow normal distributions with finite variances.

     g. The conditions hold that are needed for the central limit theorem to apply.

3. Utility theory:

     a. Approximating expected utility by a function of expected return and standard deviation is adequate for making investment decisions.

     b. Expected utility theory is an adequate model for how investors make decisions under uncertainty.

4. Asset pricing (based on price *change*, such as CAPM):

     a. Investors possess homogeneous expectations for risk and return.

     b. The CAPM beta and standard deviation, which relate to price changes, are adequate measures of risk for both portfolio and corporate investment decision making.

5. Market efficiency and barriers to arbitrage:

     a. Markets are so efficient that no reliable ways exist to exploit any inefficiencies.

     b. In the aggregate, perfect arbitrage exists between the corporate returns on operating assets and the costs of capital available in the capital markets.

     c. Dispersions of prices around intrinsic valuations are zero.

     d. No noise or market sentiment exists.

     e. Markets do not overreact.

     f. Markets remain perfectly liquid with zero price impact costs.

6. International:

     a. Purchasing power parity holds.

     b. In the aggregate, cost of capital parity holds between countries.

As an illustration, some academics may simplify assumption 5 to say: "Is the market efficient?" In response, some practitioners may reframe the question: "How inefficient is the market?"

Both framings display bias of the authors. However, the practitioners' framing demands empirical quantification in order to *measure* the effect of the assumptions on practitioner high-stakes decisions with available information. It may also foster a most lively debate on the theories and best empirical research to address the applications.

REFERENCES

Fabozzi, Frank J., Sergio M. Focardi, and Caroline Jonas. 2008. *Challenges in quantitative equity management*. Charlottesville, VA: CFA Institute.

Fama, Eugene. 2009. Eugene Fama revisits efficient market hypothesis. 57th Annual Management Conference 2009, Friday May 29, 2009. http://chicagobooth.edu/mc/2009/2009coverage.aspx?video=special

Mandelbrot, Benoit B. 2002. *Gaussian Self-Affinity and Fractals*. New York: Springer-Verlag. 254-282 from Fractional Brownian motions, fractional noises and applications, *Siam Review*, 10, 1968, 422-437.

About the Editors

Benton E. Gup has a broad background in finance. His undergraduate and graduate degrees are from the University of Cincinnati. After receiving his PhD in economics, he served as a staff economist for the Federal Reserve Bank of Cleveland. He currently holds the Robert Hunt Cochrane/Alabama Bankers Association Chair of Banking at the University of Alabama, Tuscaloosa. He also held banking chairs at the University of Virginia and the University of Tulsa. He worked in bank research for the Office of the Comptroller of the Currency while on sabbatical.

Dr. Gup is the author or editor of 28 books. His articles on financial subjects have appeared in the *Journal of Finance*, the *Journal of Financial and Quantitative Analysis*, the *Journal of Money, Credit, and Banking*, *Financial Management*, the *Journal of Banking and Finance*, *Financial Analysts Journal*, and elsewhere. He is an internationally known lecturer in executive development and graduate programs in Australia (University of Melbourne; University of Technology, Sydney; Monash University, Melbourne); New Zealand (University of Auckland); Peru (University of Lima); and South Africa (Graduate School of Business Leadership). He has been a visiting researcher at the Bank of Japan and at Macquarie University, Sydney, Australia. He lectured in Austria, Brazil, Greece, Morocco, and Tunisia for the U.S. Department of State on current economic issues, and served as a consultant to the International Monetary Fund (IMF) in Uruguay.

Rawley Thomas is president of LifeCycle Returns, Inc. (LCRT) in St. Charles, Illinois. He served as assistant treasurer of SuperValu Stores, joined Callard, Madden in 1981, co-founded HOLT Planning in 1985, and directed value management research for the Boston Consulting Group for 11 years. Credit Suisse First Boston acquired the successor to HOLT Planning, HOLT Value, in early 2002. Mr. Thomas is vice president of practitioner services for the Financial Management Association International (FMA) and is chairman of the FMA Practitioner Demand Driven Academic Research Initiative (PDDARI) Advisory Committee. Currently, he serves on the Northern Illinois Accountancy Board and chairs the FMA PDDARI, supported by the CFA Society of Chicago. The objective of PDDARI is to facilitate the development of cutting-edge research useful to practitioners, their firms, and the profession. Through this research initiative the FMA hopes to encourage academic research that addresses practitioner needs and to encourage interaction between the practitioner and academic communities. LifeCycle Returns supports investment funds, consulting firms, and investment banks with process consulting and licensed platforms to create world-class capabilities in their use of value management principles.

EDITOR CONTACT INFORMATION

Benton Gup, Chair of Banking, University of Alabama
Box 870224, 200 Alston Hall
Tuscaloosa, AL 35487
bgup@cba.ua.edu

Rawley Thomas, President, LifeCycle Returns, Inc.
7N238 Barb Hill Drive
St. Charles, IL 60175-6804
rawley@lcrt.com

About the Contributors

Ashok Abbott received his MBA in finance from Virginia Polytechnic Institute and State University (VPI), Blacksburg, Virginia, in 1984, followed by a PhD in finance, also at VPI, in 1987. His PhD dissertation title was "The Valuation Effects of Tax Legislation in Corporate Sell-Offs."

His areas of focus are blockage discount, discount for lack of marketability/liquidity, control premiums, securities, active/passive appreciation in divorce, and event studies. He has also taught at the Graduate School of Credit and Financial Management held at Dartmouth College and Stanford University, and is now an associate professor of finance at West Virginia University.

Professor Abbott provides technical and econometric support for valuation firms with Business Valuation LLC. Recent clients include divisions of Standard & Poor's, Duff & Phelps, Willamette Management Associates, Houlihan Valuation Advisors, Anchin Block & Anchin, and members of national business valuation groups.

Professor Abbott has published extensively in scholarly research journals and made presentations at national and international conferences. He has also written a weekly column on small business issues. This pro bono service has been recognized by the Small Business Administration by designating Professor Abbott as the Small Business Advocate-Journalist for the year 2002. He has received frequent recognition and awards for his teaching.

Robert J. Atra is professor and chair of the department of finance at Lewis University in Romeoville, Illinois. Dr. Atra is also affiliated with LifeCycle Returns, Inc. of St. Charles, Illinois, where he researches automated discounted cash flow models. Prior to entering academia, he was a project finance officer for Mitsubishi Bank, where he valued numerous real estate and industrial projects. He has also held the position of senior business appraiser for a major accounting firm, responsible for valuing securities of privately held firms. His publications include articles in the *Journal of Financial Planning* and *International Review of Financial Analysis*.

Dr. Atra has consulted with businesses ranging from start-ups seeking private equity funding to Fortune 500 companies in the areas of valuation, financial modeling, performance analysis, managerial training, and critical thinking. He holds a PhD in finance from the University of Illinois–Chicago, an MS in finance from Northern Illinois University, and a BA in business from the College of the Ozarks. In addition, he holds the Chartered Financial Analyst designation from the CFA Institute.

Dennis N. Aust has spent nearly 30 years developing and implementing value creation strategies, frameworks, and tools for Fortune 500 and mid-cap firms in a variety of industries. His first major assignment was the successful turnaround/restructuring effort at FMC Corporation in the early 1980s, where he led the financial analysis effort for corporate development and developed the value creation framework that supported the turnaround effort throughout the firm. Following FMC, he joined Callard, Madden and Associates (CMA), where the CFROI valuation framework was originally developed in the 1970s. His focus at CMA was twofold: helping major industrial firms develop and implement strategies for value creation, and continuing to push the boundaries of the value creation discipline by developing approaches that were simultaneously more powerful yet significantly simpler to implement than first-generation approaches. During the 1990s he was an independent consultant, started and sold an online strategy journal, taught financial modeling (Purdue University North Central), and joined the strategy consulting practice at CSC. In 2001, he renewed his association with CMA to found CharterMast Partners LLC, which is dedicated to providing public and privately held companies guidance, support, and insights for developing and implementing best-in-class strategies for value creation.

Mr. Aust's articles covering strategic analysis, consulting, financial management, and innovation have appeared in the *Journal of Private Equity*, *Director's Monthly* (NACD),. "Managing Innovation in the New Millennium" (ICFAI, 2002) and "Stock Options—An Introduction" (ICFAI, 2005). He has spoken at conferences of the National Association of Accountants and the American Management Association. He holds an undergraduate degree in business and an MBA in management science from the University of Chicago Graduate Booth School of Business.

Arjan J. Brouwer is senior manager in the Accounting and Valuation Advisory Services group of PricewaterhouseCoopers in the Netherlands. He advises various listed and nonlisted companies on the application of International Financial Reporting Standards (IFRS), including the reporting of alternative performance measures. He teaches accounting at the University of Amsterdam and is working on a PhD on the use of alternative performance measures in the European Union.

Robert James Cimasi, MHA, ASA, CBA, AVA, CM&AA is president of Health Capital Consultants, a nationally recognized health care financial and economic consulting firm. With over 25 years of experience in serving clients in 49 states, his professional focus is on the financial and economic aspects of health care service sector entities, including valuation consulting; litigation support and expert testimony; business intermediary and capital formatting services; certificate-of-need and other regulatory and policy planning consulting; and health care industry transactions, including joint ventures, sales, mergers, acquisitions, and divestitures. Mr. Cimasi holds a Master's in Health Administration from the University of Maryland, the Accredited Senior Appraiser (ASA) designation in Business Valuation, as well as the Certified Business Appraiser (CBA), Accredited Valuation Analyst (AVA), and Certified Merger & Acquisition Advisor (CM&AA). He is a nationally known speaker on health care industry topics. He has been certified and has served as an expert witness on cases in numerous states, and has provided testimony before federal and state legislative committees. In 2006, Mr. Cimasi was honored with the prestigious Shannon Pratt Award in Business Valuation conferred by the Institute of Business Appraisers.

Thomas E. Copeland is the co-founder of Copeland Valuation Consultants. Measured by the number of citations over a 25 year period, he is among the top 100 (out of 12,000) authors in finance. His six books have been translated into 14 languages and sold around 1 million copies. *Financial Theory and Corporate Policy* has been continuously in print since 1979, and *Valuation: Measuring and Managing the Value of Companies* has sold over 350,000 copies. He has authored 60 articles in corporate finance, security market micro-structure, and experimental economics. Mr. Copeland earned his BS in economics from Johns Hopkins University, his MBA from Wharton where he graduated second in his class, and his PhD from the University of Pennsylvania. He taught at UCLA for 14 years where he was a tenured full professor, at NYU for 9 years, at Harvard Business School as visiting professor for 1 year, and as senior lecturer at MIT for 5 years. He won the best teacher award at UCLA and at NYU. For 11 years he was co-leader of McKinsey's worldwide corporate finance practice, and for 7 years he was managing director of Monitor's finance group. Recognized as a world-class authority on company valuation, he has twice testified before the World Court. He has consulted for roughly 200 companies in 40 countries.

Pat Dorsey is the director of equity research for Morningstar. He is the author of *The Five Rules for Successful Stock Investing: Morningstar's*

Guide to Building Wealth and Winning in the Market and *The Little Book That Builds Wealth: The Knockout Formula for Finding Great Investments*. He is responsible for the overall direction of Morningstar's equity research, as well as for communicating Morningstar's ideas to the media and to clients.

Mr. Dorsey holds a master's degree from Northwestern University and a bachelor's degree from Wesleyan University. He also holds the Chartered Financial Analyst (CFA) designation. He appears weekly on the *Bulls & Bears* show on the Fox News Channel, writes a monthly column on investing for *Money* magazine, and has been quoted in publications such as the *Wall Street Journal*, *Fortune*, the *New York Times*, and *BusinessWeek*.

James L. Grant is president of JLG Research and a finance professor at the University of Massachusetts Boston. He has served as advisory analyst at major Wall Street firms, including Credit Suisse Asset Management and Global Asset Management. Dr. Grant holds a PhD in business from the University of Chicago Booth School of Business and has been a featured speaker at industry conferences on value-based metrics. He serves on the editorial advisory boards of the *Journal of Portfolio Management* and *Journal of Investing*. Dr. Gant has published several articles in finance and investment journals and has contributed chapters to investment books. He is the author of *Foundations of Economic Value Added*, the co-author of *Focus on Value: A Corporate and Investor Guide to Wealth Creation*, and co-author and co-editor (with Frank J. Fabozzi) of *Equity Portfolio Management* and *Value-Based Metrics: Foundations and Practice*. His writings (with James Abate) on the value-based metrics approach to securities analysis have been adopted by the CFA Institute.

William J. Hass is CEO of TeamWork Technologies, Inc., a consulting practice in Northbrook, Illinois. Bill specializes in value-building strategy, performance improvement, board governance, and effectiveness and communication for boards and senior management teams. He has consulted with both large public companies and small private clients and reviewed hundreds of business plans. He is a co-author of *Building Value through Strategy, Risk Assessment and Renewal* (CCH, 2006) and of *The Private Equity Edge: How Private Equity Players and the World's Top Companies Build Wealth and Value* (McGraw-Hill 2009).

Mr. Hass was a partner at Ernst & Young, where he led the Midwest Strategy Practice and was involved in numerous restructurings. He is a Certified Turnaround Professional (CTP) and is a past national chairman of the 8,000-member Turnaround Management Association. Mr. Hass received his MBA in finance from the University of Chicago Booth School of

Business (1971) and has an undergraduate degree in engineering from the University of Illinois–Chicago. He has also served as a member and chairman of the Industrial Advisory Board of the UIC College of Engineering.

Roy E. Johnson has nearly 40 years of work experience encompassing corporate financial management, business consulting, entrepreneurship, education, and writing. His corporate accomplishments include implementing company-wide capital appropriation and financial planning systems along with shareholder value-based performance measurements at Pitney Bowes Inc. Prior to this company, he held financial positions at General Foods Corporation, W.R. Grace & Company, and The Hertz Corporation. He was a founding shareholder, board member, and financial adviser for a medical device company from 1988 through 2001.

Currently, he is an independent consultant and educator based in Ridgefield, Connecticut. From 1993 through 2008, he was a partner with Vanguard Partners, a management consulting firm that he co-founded. He co-founded another consulting firm, Corporate Strategy Inc., in the mid-1980s. His consulting work has been broad-based in strategy and finance, and includes linking value-based financial metrics to business strategy and operations. His work accomplishments and writings have been featured in *CFO* and *Shareholder Value* magazines plus other publications. Mr. Johnson has spoken on the subject of economic value-based financial performance at conferences and seminars across the United States during the past decade. He has taught economics and finance at the college and graduate school level at four institutions, and has facilitated corporate education workshops on business performance management and value-based finance. His book, *Shareholder Value—A Business Experience*, was published in October 2001 by Butterworth-Heinemann. Publicly owned consulting clients include Baldwin Technology Company, FMC Corporation, First Data Corporation, Hewitt Associates, Monsanto, Merrill Lynch, Penn Treaty American Corporation, Pitney Bowes, and Valmont Industries. Privately owned clients include DFB Pharmaceuticals, Pamida, Synchronoss Technologies, the Army & Air Force Exchange Service (AAFES), and several small owner/manager firms.

He holds a bachelor of arts degree from Upsala College and a master of business administration from Rutgers University School of Business.

Bartley J. Madden in the early 1970s at Callard, Madden & Associates was instrumental in developing the CFROI valuation model now used by institutional money managers worldwide. Since he retired as a managing director of Credit Suisse in 2003, his writings on public policy issues have been published as journal articles and monographs. This work has focused on freedom of choice for not-yet-approved therapeutic drugs, more effective corporate governance, and the valuation challenges posed by intangible assets. A selection of his work is available at his web site at www.LearningWhatWorks.com. Mr. Madden's current major project is a book, *Wealth Creation*, scheduled for publication in 2010 by John Wiley & Sons. It will focus on the role of business firms in creating wealth and a rising standard of living.

William F. Mahoney is a veteran investor relations practitioner, journalist, and author. He spent 20 years as a communications and investor relations professional with such companies as Motorola, Scott Paper, and Esmark, and 25 years as an editor of investor relations and corporate governance publications, including *Update*, which is the official publication of the National Investor Relations Institute; *Shareholder Value* magazine; and the newsletter *Valuation Issues*. He has written a half-dozen books on investor relations and corporate governance. He began his career as a reporter for the *Ft. Wayne News-Sentinel* after graduating from Marquette University.

Stanley L. Pollock earned his doctor of dental medicine (DMD) degree from the School of Dental Medicine of the University of Pittsburgh. After years of advanced specialty training, military service, and specialty board certification, he practiced oral and maxillofacial surgery in western Pennsylvania. He returned to academia and earned bachelor of science and PhD degrees in business and hospital science administration, and a juris doctor (JD) degree. He became interested in business appraisal and became a Certified Business Appraiser. The Institute of Business Appraisers raised Dr. Pollock to be a Master Certified Business Appraiser. He continued advanced studies and became a Business Valuator Accredited in Litigation Support (BVAL), Appraiser Accredited In Business Appraisal Review and a Certified Machinery & Equipment Appraiser. Specializing in professional practices, Dr. Pollock has valued professional practices and served as an expert witness across the country, and has presented seminars in his multiple fields of advanced expertise. He is the author of over 90 publications.

Shepherd G. Pryor IV is a managing director of Board Resources, a division of TeamWork Technologies, Inc. He focuses on board governance, finance, and director training. He serves on the board of Taylor Capital Group, a bank holding company, as chairman of the corporate governance committee, lead director, and member of the audit committee. In the past he has served on the boards of HCI Direct, a manufacturer and direct response retailer; Petrolane, Inc., a propane distribution company; and Archibald Candy Corporation, a manufacturer and retailer. He is a co-author of *Building Value through Strategy, Risk Assessment and Renewal* (CCH,

2006) and of *The Private Equity Edge: How Private Equity Players and the World's Top Companies Build Wealth and Value* (McGraw-Hill 2009).

Mr. Pryor is a member of the senior faculty at Keller Graduate School of Management, in Chicago, where he teaches finance courses, including mergers and acquisitions (M&A) and international finance. In addition, he serves as an expert witness, consultant, and member of nonprofit boards. He was formerly deputy group head for corporate banking at Wells Fargo Bank. Mr. Pryor received his MBA in finance from the University of Chicago Booth School of Business and his AB (cum laude) in economics from Princeton University.

Randall Schostag has conducted business analysis, valuations, and deal structuring for more than 35 years. He is the founder and president of Minnesota Business Valuation Group, LLC. He is a Chartered Financial Analyst (CFA) (Association for Investment Management and Research—AIMR), a Certified Business Appraiser (CBA) (Institute of Business Appraisers—IBA) further certified as a Master (MCBA), and an Accredited Senior Appraiser (ASA) (American Society of Appraisers—ASA). Randall has also earned the designation of Accredited Valuation Analyst (AVA) from the National Association of Certified Valuation Analysts (NACVA) and the designation of Business Valuator Accredited for Litigation (BVAL) from the IBA. He was a principal of a small, regional valuation firm (Hawthorne Company), and he has also been director of research and corporate finance for two regional investment banking firms. Mr. Schostag has published a weekly investment newsletter; provided analytical support for retail brokers, traders, and management; conducted underwriting due diligence; and prepared business valuations, fairness opinions, and solvency reviews. He has been a vice president and general manager of a commercial bank and a venture capital firm, and he was a co-founder of a national retail children's clothing manufacturing company. Mr. Schostag has provided litigation support on valuation matters, including working with court panels, bench report submissions, and expert testimony, and has also been a plaintiff in a valuation damages matter that required mediation, arbitration, federal district court proceedings, and appeals. He has completed valuation/consulting engagements for estate settlements and gift transactions, employee stock ownership plans, buy/sell agreements, merger/acquisition transactions, shareholder oppression, management buyouts, options, technology, goodwill impairment, purchase price allocation, intangible assets, and early-stage companies.

Andrew G. Sutherland is a vice president with Stern Stewart & Company in New York City. He has advised a wide range of public and private corporations on valuation, the cost of capital, mergers and acquisitions, capital

612

budgeting, financial policy, and performance measurement. He graduated with University Honors from the Tepper School of Business at Carnegie Mellon University with an MBA in finance, strategy, and quantitative analysis; and summa cum laude with a bachelor's degree in accounting from York University.

Gary K. Taylor graduated from Ohio University with a bachelor's degree in accounting. In 1996, he earned a PhD in accounting from Ohio State University. He is a certified public accountant (Ohio) and is currently an associate professor in the Culverhouse School of Accountancy at the University of Alabama. Dr. Taylor is a PricewaterhouseCoopers Faculty Fellow and director of the accounting PhD program for the Culverhouse School of Accountancy. He has also served as the director of the Garner Center Workshop Series. He has published in several academic journals, including the *Journal of Accounting Research*; *Journal of Accounting, Auditing and Finance*; *Issues in Accounting Education*; *Review of Accounting Studies*, and *International Journal of Auditing*. In 2003 Dr. Taylor was a winner of the University of Alabama Alumni Teaching Award.

David Trainer is CEO of New Constructs, LLC, an independent equity research firm, and managing partner at Novo Capital Management, LLC, an adviser to a hedge fund. A veteran investment strategist and corporate finance expert, Mr. Trainer specializes in divining the true economic profitability of businesses and its impact on valuation.

Institutional Investor magazine highlighted New Constructs for being ranked #1 for stock picking among all research firms. CNBC's *Squawk on the Street* and the Fox Business Network often cover the monthly release of the Most Attractive and Most Dangerous Stocks. *Forbes* magazine, the *Wall Street Journal*, the *New York Times*, *Fortune*, CBS *MarketWatch*, and *BusinessWeek* often reference New Construct's expertise on topics ranging from forensic accounting to options expense, valuation, quality of earnings, and interpretation of accounting rules and the notes to the financial statements.

Mr. Trainer has been a guest lecturer in the finance and investing classes at Columbia Business School, the Graduate School of Business at University of Chicago, and Vanderbilt's Owen Graduate School of Management. He is a member of the CFA Institute's Distinguished Speakers Lecture Series. Mr. Trainer also serves on the FASB and IASB special working group for reviewing changes to accounting rules regarding operating leases.

Mark C. Ubelhart's title at Hewitt Associates is "Architect, Human Capital Foresight, and Practice Leader, Value-Based Management." He consults in the fields of executive compensation and value-based management. This encompasses linking the principles of corporate finance and business valuation to a broad range of people management topics related to attracting, motivating, and retaining talent; employee engagement; business education; performance measurement; and goal setting. It also involves leading Hewitt's efforts to work with financial professionals, academics, and corporate management on human capital issues and research. Mr. Ubelhart is the architect of Hewitt's Human Capital Foresight™ methodology linking fact-based data and metrics, predictive analytics, and business results.

He has written several articles, including "Business Strategy, Performance Measurement, and Compensation," "Case Studies of Shareholder Value Incentives," and "Measuring the Immeasurable," which appeared in two summer 2001 issues of *Shareholder Value* magazine.

Before joining Hewitt Associates, Mr. Ubelhart was a vice president and division administrator of a money center bank's Corporate Financial Consulting Division. Under his leadership, this division conducted numerous consulting engagements for clients in areas of financial strategy, valuation of debt and equity securities, recapitalizations, mergers and acquisitions, and cost of capital-based target rates of return. He has 30 years of consulting experience in his fields.

Mr. Ubelhart has a BA in economics from Dartmouth College (Phi Beta Kappa) and an MBA in finance from the University of Chicago.

Jeffrey R. Williams is professor of business strategy at the Tepper School of Business at Carnegie Mellon University, and author of the award-winning method, "Sustainability Analysis," which guides managers through their most crucial challenge, "How do we best renew our competitive advantage?" His study of renewal centers on 50 markets ranging across manufacturing, service, high technology, and software industries, and is the focus of his critically acclaimed book, *Renewable Advantage: Crafting Strategy through Economic Time*. He is the author of 40 studies on business strategy, including works for the National Science Foundation, the Federal Trade Commission, the Sloan Foundation, and the *Journal of Law and Economics*, as well as the influential book, *Fundamental Issues in Strategy*.

He has served on the editorial board of the *Strategic Management Journal* and has received the California Management Review Pacific Telesis Award for best new thinking in management. His clients have included AT&T, IBM, McKinsey, Bristol-Myers Squibb, Southwestern Bell, Westinghouse, National Semiconductor, Mellon Bank, United Technologies, Goodyear, Bell Labs, and Seagate Technologies.

Dandan Yang is the LifeCycle Returns (LCRT) president's research associate. She performed the advanced SPSS/Excel research that formed the basis for Chapter 22, "Lower Risk and Higher Returns: Linking Stable Paretian Distributions and Discounted Cash Flow." This pathbreaking work on portfolio construction became the basis for her presentation to the FMA 2007 Annual Meeting in Dallas, Texas.

She has reviewed papers for the Financial Management Association (FMA) and actively participated in the FMA Practitioner Demand Driven Academic Research Initiative (PDDARI).

Prior to these activities, Ms. Yang earned a master of science in finance from the University of Texas at San Antonio and a bachelor's degree in mechanical engineering from Dalian University of Technology. She is a CFA Level III candidate.

Max Zavanelli founded Zavanelli Portfolio Research (ZPR) in 1979. Due to the success of his research for professional money managers, there was a demand for ZPR to manage discretionary accounts. In 1982, Mr. Zavanelli started managing discretionary accounts directly. In 1994, ZPR became three corporations and legal entities: ZPR Investment Management Inc., ZPR Investment Research Inc., and ZPR International Inc. ZPR Investment Management Inc. became the successor company for U.S. investment management.

Prior to founding ZPR, Mr. Zavanelli was an investment strategist at American National Bank in Chicago and a senior financial analyst at Mellon Bank. From 1990 to 1994 he held the position of Distinguished George Professor, chair of applied investments and research at Stetson University in DeLand, Florida. He was also a visiting professor of the Stetson University from 1983 to 1986 and was a board member of the School of Business from 1997 to 2006.

In 2000, Mr. Zavanelli founded the first mutual fund in Lithuania, the NSEL 30 Index Fund, which is a national index fund of the 30 largest float adjusted market cap Lithuanian stocks. Mr. Zavanelli is a chairman of the supervisory board of this fund. In April 2004, the ZPR U.S Small Cap Value Mutual Fund was started.

Todd A. Zigrang, MHA, MBA, CHE is a senior vice president at Health Capital Consultants (HCC). Mr. Zigrang has over 12 years' experience in providing valuation, financial analysis, and provider integration services to HCC's clients nationwide. He has developed and implemented hospital- and physician-driven MSOs and networks involving a wide range of specialties; developed a physician-owned ambulatory surgery center; participated in the evaluation and negotiation of managed care contracts; performed valuations of a wide array of health care entities; participated in numerous litigation support engagements; created pro forma financials; written business plans and feasibility analyses; conducted comprehensive industry research; completed due diligence analysis; and overseen the selection process for vendors, contractors, and architects. Mr. Zigrang holds a master's in business administration and a Master of Science in Health Administration from the University of Missouri at Columbia. He holds the Certified Healthcare Executive (CHE) designation from and is a diplomate of the American College of Healthcare Executives and is a member of the Healthcare Financial Management Association.

CONTRIBUTOR CONTACT INFORMATION

Ashok Abbott, Associate Professor of Finance, West Virginia University
217 College of Business & Economics
1601 University Avenue
Morgantown, WV 26506-6025
aabbott@wvu.edu

Robert J. Atra, Chair, Finance Department, Lewis University
One University Parkway
Romeoville, IL 60446-2200
atraro@lewisu.edu

Dennis N. Aust, Managing Director and Founder, CharterMast Partners
Ativo Capital Management LLC
11 South LaSalle Street, Suite 820
Chicago, IL 60603
Dennis.aust@chartermast.com

Arjan J. Brouwer, Senior Manager, PricewaterhouseCoopers Accountants N.V./University of Amsterdam
N.V. (KvK 34180285)
Thomas R. Malthusstraat 5
1066 JR, Postbus 90351
1006 BJ, Amsterdam, Netherlands
arjan.brouwer@nl.pwc.com

Robert James Cimasi, Health Capital Consultants, LLC
9666 Olive Boulevard
St. Louis, MO 63132
rcimasi@healthcapital.com

Thomas E. Copeland, Founder, Copeland Valuation Consultants, and Senior Lecturer, MIT
2541 Via Viesta
La Jolla, CA 92037
mtcopeland@yahoo.com, tcopeland@sandiego.edu

Pat Dorsey, Director of Equity Research, Morningstar
22 W Washington St
Chicago, IL 60602
Patrick.dorsey@morningstar.com

James L. Grant, JLG Research, and Professor of Finance, University of Massachusetts—Boston
jim@jlgresearch.com

William J. Hass, Managing Director, Hass Associates and TeamWork Technologies
4121 Rutgers Lane
Northbrook, IL 60062
wjhass@aol.com

Roy E. Johnson, Vanguard Partners
P.O. Box 1098
14 Hobby Drive
Ridgefield, CT 06877
r.e.johnson@sbcglobal.net

Bartley J. Madden, Independent Researcher
520 South Washington Street, Unit PH-2
Naperville, IL 60540
bartmadden@yahoo.com

William F. Mahoney, Editor, *Valuation Issues*
716 South Brandywine Street
West Chester, PA 19382
editor@valuationissues.com

Stanley L. Pollock, Professional Practice Planners, Inc.
332 Fifth Avenue, #213
McKeesport, PA 15132

Shepherd G. Pryor IV, Managing Director, Haas Associates and TeamWork Technologies
975 North Avenue
Highland Park, IL 60035

Randall Schostag, President, Minnesota Business Valuation Group, LLC, a subsidiary of Olsen Thielen & Co., Ltd
2675 Long Lake Road
St. Paul, MN 55113
rschostag@busvalgroup.com

Andrew G. Sutherland, Associate, Stern Stewart & Company
111 Broadway, Suite 1402
New York, NY 10006
asutherland@sternstewart.com

Gary K. Taylor, Associate Professor, University of Alabama
Box 870220, Room 326 Alston Hall
Tuscaloosa, AL 35487
gtaylor@cba.ua.edu

David Trainer, President, New Constructs, LLC
282 Spencer Creek Road
Franklin, TN 37065
David.trainer@newconstructs.com

Mark C. Ubelhart, Architect, Human Capital Foresight, and Practice Leader, Value-Based Management, Hewitt Associates
100 Half Day Road
Lincolnshire, IL 60069
Mark.ubelhart@hewitt.com
Markubelhart@global-analytics.com

Jeffrey R. Williams, Professor of Business Strategy, Tepper School of Business at Carnegie Mellon University
5000 Forbes Avenue
Pittsburgh, PA 15238
jrw@cmu.edu

Dandan Yang, LifeCycle Returns
7N238 Barb Hill Drive
St. Charles, IL 60175-6804

Max Zavanelli, President, ZPR Investment Research, Inc.
1642 North Volusia Avenue
Orange City, FL 32763
zprim@mpinet.net

Todd A. Zigrang, MBA, MHA, CHE. Health Capital Consultants, LLC
9666 Olive Boulevard, Suite 375
St. Louis, MO 63132
tzigrang@healthcapital.com

Index